The royal palace,
Westminster on 1

Archaeological excavations (1991–8) for the London Underground Limited Jubilee Line Extension Project

MoLAS Monograph Series

1 Excavations at the priory and hospital of St Mary Spital, London, Christopher Thomas, Barney Sloane and Christopher Phillpotts
ISBN 1 901992 00 4

2 The National Roman Fabric Reference Collection: a handbook, Roberta Tomber and John Dore
ISBN 1 901992 01 2

3 The Cross Bones burial ground, Redcross Way, Southwark, London: archaeological excavations (1991–8) for the London Underground Limited Jubilee Line Extension Project, Megan Brickley and Adrian Miles with Hilary Stainer
ISBN 1 901992 06 3

4 The eastern cemetery of Roman London: excavations 1983–90, Bruno Barber and David Bowsher
ISBN 1 901992 09 8

5 The Holocene evolution of the London Thames: archaeological excavations (1991–8) for the London Underground Limited Jubilee Line Extension Project, Jane Sidell, Keith Wilkinson, Robert Scaife and Nigel Cameron
ISBN 1 901992 10 1

6 The Limehouse porcelain manufactory: excavations at 108–116 Narrow Street, London, 1990, Kieron Tyler and Roy Stephenson, with J Victor Owen and Christopher Phillpotts
ISBN 1 901992 16 0

7 Roman defences and medieval industry: excavations at Baltic House, City of London, Elizabeth Howe
ISBN 1 901992 17 9

8 London bridge: 2000 years of a river crossing, Bruce Watson, Trevor Brigham and Tony Dyson
ISBN 1 901992 18 7

9 Roman and medieval townhouses on the London waterfront: excavations at Governor's House, City of London, Trevor Brigham with Aidan Woodger
ISBN 1 901992 21 7

10 The London Charterhouse, Bruno Barber and Christopher Thomas
ISBN 1 901992 23 3

11 Medieval 'Westminster' floor tiles, Ian M Betts
ISBN 1 901992 24 1

12 Settlement in Roman Southwark: archaeological excavations (1991–8) for the London Underground Limited Jubilee Line Extension Project, James Drummond-Murray and Peter Thompson with Carrie Cowan
ISBN 1 901992 28 4

13 Aspects of medieval and later Southwark: archaeological excavations (1991–8) for the London Underground Limited Jubilee Line Extension Project, Heather Knight
ISBN 1 901992 30 6

14 The prehistory and topography of Southwark and Lambeth, Jane Sidell, Jonathan Cotton, Louise Rayner and Lucy Wheeler
ISBN 1 901992 31 4

15 Middle Saxon London: excavations at the Royal Opera House 1989–99, Gordon Malcolm and David Bowsher with Robert Cowie
ISBN 1 901992 32 2

16 Urban development in north-west Roman Southwark: excavations 1974–90, Carrie Cowan
ISBN 1 901992 33 0

17 Industry in north-west Roman Southwark: excavations 1984–8, Friederike Hammer
ISBN 1 901992 34 9

18 The Cistercian abbey of St Mary Stratford Langthorne, Essex: archaeological excavations for the London Underground Limited Jubilee Line Extension Project, Bruno Barber, Steve Chew, Tony Dyson and Bill White
ISBN 1 901992 38 1

19 Material culture in London in an age of transition: Tudor and Stuart period finds *c* 1450–*c* 1700 from excavations at riverside sites in Southwark, Geoff Egan
ISBN 1 901992 39 X

20 Excavations at the priory of the Order of the Hospital of St John of Jerusalem, Clerkenwell, London, Barney Sloane and Gordon Malcolm
ISBN 1 901992 20 9

21 Roman and medieval Cripplegate, City of London: archaeological excavations 1992–8, Elizabeth Howe and David Lakin
ISBN 1 901992 42 X

22 The royal palace, abbey and town of Westminster on Thorney Island: archaeological excavations (1991–8) for the London Underground Limited Jubilee Line Extension Project, Christopher Thomas, Robert Cowie and Jane Sidell
ISBN 1 901992 50 0

The royal palace, abbey and town of Westminster on Thorney Island

Archaeological excavations (1991–8) for the London Underground Limited Jubilee Line Extension Project

Christopher Thomas, Robert Cowie and Jane Sidell

MoLAS Monograph 22

Museum of London Archaeology Service

Published by the Museum of London Archaeology Service

A CIP catalogue record for this book is available from the British Library

Production and series design by Tracy Wellman
Typesetting and design by Sue Cawood
Reprographics by Andy Chopping
Copy editing by Anne Marriott
Series editing by Sue Hirst/Susan M Wright
Post-excavation and series management by Peter Rowsome

Printed by the Lavenham Press

Front cover: the drain in one of the canon's houses (B15) on the station site (site F); a 16th-century ceramic watering can; the interior of Westminster Hall

Back cover: alluvial silt filling a ditch on the foreshore; a delftware bottle dating to 1627/8; the king's chamber in the early 19th century

CONTRIBUTORS

Principal authors	Christopher Thomas, Robert Cowie and Jane Sidell
Documentary	Patricia Croot and Christopher Thomas
Flint	Jonathan Cotton
Ceramic and non-ceramic building material	Terence Paul Smith
Prehistoric pottery	Louise Rayner
Medieval and post-medieval pottery	Roy Stephenson and Jacqui Pearce
Accessioned finds	Richenda Goffin with Jackie Keily
Plant remains	John Giorgi
Animal bone	Kevin Rielly
Photography	Edwin Baker, Andy Chopping, Maggie Cox
Graphics	Helen Jones, Kikar Singh, Gillie Newman and Peter Hart-Allison
Project managers	Al Green, Mike Hutchinson and Gordon Malcolm
Academic adviser	John Schofield
Editors	Anne Marriott, Richard Malt

CONTENTS

List of figures . . . xiv
List of tables . . . xvi
Summary . . . xvii
Acknowledgements . . . xviii

Introduction **1**

1.1 Current knowledge of the archaeology of Westminster . 1
1.2 Circumstances of excavation . . . 3
The study area . . . 3
Circumstances of excavation . . . 3
Post-excavation reports . . . 6
Previous excavations . . . 6
Antiquarian records . . . 6
1.3 Organisation of the report . . . 6
The integrated nature of the report . . . 6
The chronological narrative . . . 6
The review sections . . . 7
The specialist support sections . . . 7
The research archives . . . 7
Textual conventions . . . 7
Graphical conventions . . . 8
Dating conventions . . . 8

Geology and topography **2**

2.1 Introduction . . . 9
2.2 The River Tyburn . . . 9
2.3 Thorney Island . . . 9
2.4 The River Thames . . . 10

The Mesolithic to Early–Middle Bronze Age, *c* 6000 BC–*c* 1500 BC (period 1) **3**

3.1 Environmental and topographical background . . . 13
The River Thames . . . 13
Palaeoecology . . . 14
3.2 Archaeological background . . . 15
3.3 Archaeological evidence . . . 15
Structure 1: revetment . . . 15
Structure 2 . . . 15
Structure 3: revetment . . . 16
Open Area 1 . . . 16
3.4 Discussion . . . 23
The flint . . . 25
Lithics in the landscape . . . 27
Local and regional patterns . . . 28

The Late Bronze Age and Iron Age, *c* 1500 BC–AD 43 (period 2) **4**

4.1 Environmental and topographical background . . . 29
The River Thames . . . 29

Palaeoecology . . . 30
4.2 Archaeological background . . . 30
4.3 Archaeological evidence . . . 30
The River Thames foreshore . . . 30
4.4 Discussion . . . 31

The Roman period, AD 43–410 (period 3) **5**
5.1 Environmental and topographical background . . . 34
Palaeoecology . . . 34
5.2 Archaeological background . . . 35
5.3 Archaeological evidence . . . 35
Open Area 1 . . . 35
5.4 Discussion . . . 38

The Saxon period, AD 410–*c* 1040 (period 4) **6**
6.1 Environmental and topographical background . . . 40
The River Thames . . . 40
Palaeoecology . . . 40
6.2 Documentary and archaeological background . . . 41
6.3 Archaeological evidence . . . 41
Structure 4 . . . 41
Open Area 1: the foreshore to the north-east . . . 44
Open Area 2: the foreshore to the east . . . 45
6.4 Discussion . . . 45

The Saxo-Norman period, *c* 1040–*c* 1150 (period 5) **7**
7.1 Environmental and topographical background . . . 47
7.2 Documentary and archaeological background . . . 47
7.3 Archaeological evidence . . . 49
Building 1: the great hall . . . 49
Structure 4: revetment . . . 51
Open Area 1: the foreshore . . . 51
Open Area 2 . . . 54
Open Area 3 . . . 54
7.4 Discussion . . . 54

***c* 1150–*c* 1230 (period 6)** **8**
8.1 Environmental and topographical background . . . 56
8.2 Documentary and archaeological background . . . 56
8.3 Archaeological evidence . . . 58
Building 2 . . . 58
Building 3 . . . 58
Building 4 . . . 58
Structure 5: dock . . . 61
Structure 6: Westminster Abbey precinct wall . . . 63
Open Area 1: the foreshore . . . 64
Open Area 4: New Palace Yard . . . 65

		Open Area 5: Green Yard	67
		Open Area 6: Old Palace Yard	67
		Open Area 7	67
		Open Area 8: Westminster Abbey precinct (north)	67
		Open Area 9: Westminster Abbey precinct (south)	67
	8.4	Discussion	68
***c* 1230–*c* 1350 (period 7)**	**9**		
	9.1	Environmental and topographical background	70
		The River Thames	70
		Palaeoecology	70
	9.2	Documentary and archaeological background	71
		Westminster Abbey	71
		The precinct of the Palace of Westminster	73
	9.3	Archaeological evidence	75
		Building 2	75
		Building 4	75
		Building 5: gatehouse to New Palace Yard	75
		Building 6	75
		Building 7	80
		Building 8: gatehouse to the Green Yard	80
		Building 9	80
		Building 10: the Exchequer	81
		Building 11: St Stephen's chapel	82
		Building 12	85
		Building 13	85
		Building 14	87
		Structure 5	88
		Structure 7	88
		Structure 8	89
		Structure 9	89
		Structure 10: precinct wall between the Green Yard and New Palace Yard	89
		Road 1	89
		Open Area 1: the River Thames	90
		Open Area 4: New Palace Yard	91
		Open Area 6: Old Palace Yard	92
		Open Area 7	92
		Open Area 8: Westminster Abbey precinct (north)	92
		Open Area 9: Westminster Abbey precinct (south)	92
		Open Area 10	92
		Open Area 11	93
		Open Area 12	94
	9.4	Discussion	94

c 1350–c 1540 (period 8) **10**

10.1 Environmental and topographical background 96
The River Tyburn 96
The River Thames 96
Palaeoecology 96
10.2 Documentary and archaeological background 97
The Westminster Woolstaple 97
The king's ditch 97
Between King Street and the ditch 97
Canon Row 97
The earl of Kent's inn 99
The king's garden 99
Palace of Westminster 99
Westminster Abbey 99
10.3 Archaeological evidence 99
Building 1: the great hall 99
Building 4 101
Building 5: gatehouse to New Palace Yard 101
Building 6 101
Building 13 102
Building 14 102
Building 15: canon's house 103
Building 16 104
Building 17: the Jewel Tower 104
Building 18 105
Building 19: St Stephen's cloister 105
Structure 5: dock 106
Structure 7 106
Structure 9 106
Structure 11 106
Structure 12 106
Structure 13 106
Structure 14 106
Structure 15 107
Road 1 107
Road 2: St Stephen's Alley 107
Open Area 1: the River Thames 107
Open Area 4: New Palace Yard 107
Open Area 6: Old Palace Yard 108
Open Area 8: Westminster Abbey precinct (north) 108
Open Area 10 108
Open Area 11 108
Open Area 12 110
Open Area 13 110

Open Area 14 . . . 112
10.4 Discussion . . . 113

c 1540–c 1600 (period 9) **11**
11.1 Environmental and topographical background . . . 115
The River Thames . . . 115
Palaeoecology . . . 115
11.2 Documentary and archaeological background . . . 115
Westminster Palace . . . 115
Westminster Abbey . . . 116
Woolstaple Yard . . . 116
Canon Row . . . 116
Buildings on Canon Row (east side) . . . 116
11.3 Archaeological evidence . . . 118
Building 6 . . . 118
Building 13 . . . 118
Building 15 . . . 120
Structure 16 . . . 120
Structure 17 . . . 120
Structure 18 . . . 120
Structure 19 . . . 120
Structure 20 . . . 120
Open Area 1: the foreshore . . . 122
Open Area 6: Old Palace Yard . . . 122
Open Area 10 . . . 122
Open Area 11 . . . 123
Open Area 12 . . . 123
Open Area 14 . . . 123
11.4 Discussion . . . 125

c 1600–c 1740 (period 10) **12**
12.1 Environmental and topographical background . . . 126
12.2 Documentary and archaeological background . . . 126
Westminster Palace . . . 126
Westminster Abbey . . . 126
Buildings on Canon Row (east side) . . . 126
Woolstaple Yard . . . 128
12.3 Archaeological evidence . . . 129
Building 6 . . . 129
Building 8 . . . 129
Building 13 . . . 130
Building 15 . . . 130
Building 17: the Jewel Tower . . . 130
Building 20: dwelling house for the Jewel Tower . . . 130
Building 21 . . . 131

Building 22 . . . 131
Building 23 . . . 133
Building 24 . . . 133
Building 25 . . . 133
Structure 12 . . . 135
Structure 13 . . . 135
Structure 21 . . . 135
Structure 22 . . . 135
Open Area 4: New Palace Yard . . . 136
Open Area 6: Old Palace Yard . . . 136
Open Area 8 . . . 137
Open Area 11 . . . 137
Open Area 13 . . . 137
Open Area 14 . . . 137
Open Area 15 . . . 137
12.4 Discussion . . . 137

c 1740–1834 (period 11) **13**
13.1 Environmental and topographical background . . . 139
13.2 Documentary and archaeological background . . . 139
13.3 Archaeological evidence . . . 140
Building 8: gatehouse to the Green Yard . . . 140
Building 9 . . . 140
Building 20 . . . 140
Building 21 . . . 140
Building 22 . . . 140
Building 23 . . . 140
Building 24 . . . 140
Building 25 . . . 140
Building 26 . . . 140
Building 27 . . . 140
Building 28 . . . 140
Building 29 . . . 140
Building 30: 5 Old Palace Yard . . . 142
Building 31: 6–7 Old Palace Yard . . . 142
Building 32 . . . 143
Building 33 . . . 143
Structure 20 . . . 143
Structure 23 . . . 143
Structure 24 . . . 143
Road 2: Canon Row . . . 143
Road 3: Bridge Street . . . 143
Open Area 4: New Palace Yard . . . 143
Open Area 8 . . . 143

Open Area 14 144
13.4 Discussion 144

Westminster: a review of the data **14**
14.1 A review of the environment and topography of Westminster and the changing river levels 145
The Early Holocene template 145
The earliest environment 146
Clearance and cultivation 146
Transition to a tidal river 147
A Roman and Saxon satellite 148
Erosion, reclamation and urbanisation 149
Summary 150
14.2 The town of Westminster 151
Westminster in the medieval period 151
Westminster in the post-medieval period 152
14.3 Westminster Abbey 152
Origins and development 152
The abbey precincts 154
14.4 Westminster Palace 155
Origins and development 155
The layout of the palace 157

Conclusions **15**
15.1 Attainment of research aims 167
15.2 Further research questions 168

Specialist appendices **16**
16.1 Struck and burnt flint 170
Introduction 170
Struck flint 170
Burnt unworked flint 174
16.2 Ceramic and non-ceramic building material 174
Introduction 174
Roman ceramic building material 174
Medieval and post-medieval ceramic building material 175
Stone building material: post-medieval slates 178
Other non-ceramic building materials 179
16.3 The prehistoric pottery 179
Introduction 179
Summary of each assemblage 179
Fabrics 179
Forms and decoration 179
Contextual information 180
Other assemblages from the Westminster area 180

Comparison with other assemblages . . . 181
Conclusions . . . 181
16.4 The medieval and post-medieval pottery . . . 181
Methodology . . . 181
Palace group of sites . . . 181
Within the abbey . . . 182
Outside the abbey, to the north and west . . . 183
16.5 The accessioned finds . . . 184
Roman . . . 184
Medieval . . . 184
Post-medieval . . . 187
Discussion . . . 188
16.6 Plant remains . . . 188
Methods . . . 188
The sites . . . 189
Dating and feature types . . . 189
Sampling and processing methods . . . 189
Assessment and analysis . . . 189
Identification and recording methods . . . 189
General characteristics of the material . . . 202
16.7 Animal bone . . . 202
Methods . . . 202
Species representation: evidence for trends and status . 203
Exploitation and organisation of animal products . . 206
Animal size/type . . . 209
16.8 Radiocarbon dating . . . 210

French and German summaries . . . 211

Bibliography . . . 214

Index . . . 220

FIGURES

Fig 1 Map showing location of study area . . . 2
Fig 2 Map showing location of archaeological sites in the study area and the modern street plan . . . 4
Fig 3 Graphical conventions used in this report . . . 4
Fig 4 Contour survey . . . 10
Fig 5 Plan of the archaeological features and location of finds, period 1 . . . 16
Fig 6 Detailed plan of Structure 1 and Structure 3 . . . 18
Fig 7 Section through site P . . . 18
Fig 8 Detailed plan of Structure 2 and Open Area 1 . . . 19
Fig 9 Detailed plan of site B . . . 19
Fig 10 View of the partially excavated silts from site F . . . 20
Fig 11 View of the natural sand with accumulated silts above on site K . . . 21
Fig 12 Detailed plan of the archaeological features on site G . . . 22
Fig 13 Prehistoric pottery . . . 22
Fig 14 Detailed plan of the archaeological features on site S and Cromwell Green . . . 24
Fig 15 Detailed plan of the archaeological features on site C(i), period 1 . . . 25
Fig 16 Detailed plan of the archaeological features on site D . . . 25
Fig 17 The flint work from Cromwell Green . . . 26
Fig 18 The flint work from New Palace Yard . . . 26
Fig 19 The flint work from the southern and eastern edges of Thorney Island . . . 27
Fig 20 Plan of the archaeological features and location of finds, period 2 . . . 32
Fig 21 Iron Age material from Thorney Island . . . 32
Fig 22 Plan of the archaeological features and location of finds, period 3 . . . 36
Fig 23 Detailed plan of the archaeological features on site C(i), period 3 . . . 38
Fig 24 Plan of the archaeological features and location of finds, period 4 . . . 42
Fig 25 Interpretative plan of Structure 4 . . . 44
Fig 26 View of Structure 4 . . . 45
Fig 27 Plan of the archaeological features, period 5 . . . 48
Fig 28 Detailed plan of the great hall . . . 50
Fig 29 Detailed plan of the reclamation ditches on site C(ii) . . . 52
Fig 30 Wooden vessel . . . 52
Fig 31 Two ?11th-century ceramic crucibles . . . 53
Fig 32 Detailed plan of the boundary ditch on site D . . . 53
Fig 33 Detailed plan of the reclamation ditches on site K 54
Fig 34 Plan of the archaeological features, period 6 . . . 57
Fig 35 Detailed plan of Building 2 . . . 58
Fig 36 Detailed plan of sites C(i), D and J showing Building 3 59
Fig 37 Detailed plan of sites C(ii), K, L and U showing Building 4 . . . 60
Fig 38 View of Building 4 showing the hearths . . . 60
Fig 39 Detailed view of the east hearth in Building 4 . . . 61
Fig 40 Detailed plan of the dock . . . 62
Fig 41 View of the end of the dock wall . . . 62
Fig 42 Reconstructed section through Bridge Street . . . 63
Fig 43 View of the Westminster Abbey precinct boundary wall . . . 64
Fig 44 View of the interior of the great drain . . . 68
Fig 45 Plan of the archaeological features, period 7 . . . 72
Fig 46 Detailed plan of Buildings 5–9, 13 and Structure 10 76
Fig 47 View of Buildings 5 and 6 . . . 77
Fig 48 Pottery from the cesspit in Building 6 . . . 77
Fig 49 Five wooden vessels from the cesspit in Building 6 78
Fig 50 Histogram showing the breakdown of ceramic fabrics source by weight . . . 78
Fig 51 A wooden stirring stick from the cesspit in Building 6 79
Fig 52 Detailed plan of St Stephen's chapel . . . 82
Fig 53 View of the restored lower chapel of St Stephen: St Mary Undercroft . . . 83
Fig 54*a* View of the upper chapel of the Ste Chapelle, Paris . 84
Fig 54*b* View of the lower chapel of the Ste Chapelle, Paris . 84
Fig 55 The Ste Chapelle, Paris, from the north-west . . . 84
Fig 56 View of the north wall and stone base in Building 13 85
Fig 57 Section through Building 14 and the Jewel Tower moat, and plan . . . 87
Fig 58 Detailed plan of Structure 7, Structure 9 and Building 4 . . . 88
Fig 59 View of Structure 10 . . . 90
Fig 60 Detailed plan of Road 1 . . . 90
Fig 61 Iron spur . . . 93
Fig 62 Detailed plan of the ditch dividing Open Area 11 from Open Area 12 . . . 93
Fig 63 Ceramic vessel . . . 93
Fig 64 Copper-alloy mount . . . 94
Fig 65 Plan of the archaeological features, period 8 . . . 100
Fig 66 View of the interior of the great hall . . . 101
Fig 67 Iron key . . . 102
Fig 68 View of the drain in Building 15 with part of Road 1 in the foreground . . . 103
Fig 69 Fragments of a late medieval glass beaker . . . 103
Fig 70 Detailed plan of the Jewel Tower . . . 104
Fig 71 View of the Jewel Tower . . . 105
Fig 72 View of the ditch dividing Open Area 11 from Open Area 12 . . . 109
Fig 73 Copper-alloy bell . . . 109
Fig 74 Copper-alloy ?necklace . . . 110
Fig 75 Drawing and section of copper-alloy ?necklace . . . 110
Fig 76 Plan of Woolstaple Yard and surrounding buildings 111
Fig 77 View of Open Area 13 showing the chalk well . . . 112
Fig 78 Copper-alloy pilgrim badge . . . 112
Fig 79 Plan of the archaeological features, period 9 . . . 117
Fig 80 Detailed plan of the archaeological features in Building 6 and Building 13 . . . 119

Fig 81 Detailed plan of sites B, F and H showing Building 15, Open Area 14 and Structures 16–20 121
Fig 82 View of Structure 18 122
Fig 83 Detailed plan of the archaeological features on site E 123
Fig 84 Houses on the west side of King Street, behind which lay Open Areas 11 and 12 123
Fig 85 Copper-alloy buckle 123
Fig 86 Ceramic watering can <P14> 124
Fig 87 Ceramic watering can <P15> 124
Fig 88 Plan of the archaeological features, period 10 . . 127
Fig 89 Morgan's map of Westminster, 1682 128
Fig 90 Delftware bottle 129
Fig 91 Detail showing date stamp on delftware bottle . . 129
Fig 92 Detailed plan of the Parliament House 130
Fig 93 Section through the sequence of floors in the Parliament House 131
Fig 94 Detailed plan of Buildings 21–22 132
Fig 95 Ivory knife 132
Fig 96 Detailed plan of Buildings 24–25 134
Fig 97 View of Building 24 135
Fig 98 Tin-glazed wall tile 135
Fig 99 English tin-glazed ware plate 136
Fig 100 Rocque's map of 1746 139
Fig 101 Plan of the archaeological features, period 11 . . . 141
Fig 102 Detailed plan of sites C(i), D and J showing the kiln, Building 29 and Buildings 32–33. 142
Fig 103 Pollen diagram from Storey's Gate 148
Fig 104 Section of the Bayeux Tapestry 153
Fig 105 Reconstructed view of Westminster *c* 1200 156
Fig 106 Hollar's view of New Palace Yard 159
Fig 107 Vicars' houses in St Stephen's court 160
Fig 108 Windows at the south end of the lesser hall . . . 162
Fig 109 Coronation of Edward the Confessor 162
Fig 110 Interior of the king's chamber looking west . . . 163
Fig 111 North side of the king's chamber 164
Fig 112 East side of the queen's chamber and chapel . . . 164
Fig 113 Interior of the queen's chamber during demolition 165
Fig 114 West side of the queen's chamber and the cloister . 165

TABLES

Table 1 Details of Jubilee Line Project Extension sites . . . 5
Table 2 Details of Parliamentary Works Directorate sites . . 5
Table 3 Details of other sites 5
Table 4 Selected dating evidence, period 1 25
Table 5 Selected dating evidence, period 2 31
Table 6 Selected dating evidence, period 3 39
Table 7 Selected dating evidence, period 4 46
Table 8 Selected dating evidence, period 5 55
Table 9 Selected dating evidence, period 6 69
Table 10 Analysis of ceramic and wooden vessels from Building 6 79
Table 11 Selected dating evidence, period 7 95
Table 12 Selected dating evidence, period 8 114
Table 13 Selected dating evidence, period 9 125
Table 14 Selected dating evidence, period 10 138
Table 15 Selected dating evidence, period 11 144
Table 16 The documented palace buildings 161
Table 17 Struck flint work from all sites 171
Table 18 Struck flint work from Cromwell Green (WCG78) . 171
Table 19 Struck flint from all sites 172
Table 20 Details of the illustrated flints 174
Table 21 Burnt unworked flint 174
Table 22 Roman ceramic building materials 174
Table 23 Details of decorated floor tiles 175
Table 24 Prehistoric fabric types by site 179
Table 25 Medieval and post-medieval pottery fabric, form and decoration codes and date ranges 182
Table 26 Details of the illustrated medieval and post-medieval pottery 182
Table 27 Details of the pottery from site G 183
Table 28 Details of the pottery from site J 183
Table 29 Details of the pottery from site D 183
Table 30 Distribution of accessioned finds by site 184
Table 31 The excavated coins 184
Table 32 Details of bowls and platters from cesspit in Building 6 186
Table 33 Number of analysed soil samples by period and site 189
Table 34 Plant remains from sites H and B, periods 1 and 2 190
Table 35 Plant remains from site B, periods 7 and 8 191
Table 36 Plant remains from site B, Open Area 14, period 8 192
Table 37 Plant remains from site B, Open Area 14, periods 8 and 9 194
Table 38 Plant remains from site F 195
Table 39 Plant remains from site C, Building 13, period 7 . 196
Table 40 Plant remains from site D 196
Table 41 Plant remains from site E, Open Area 11, period 8 198
Table 42 Plant remains from site G 199
Table 43 Plant remains from site J 200
Table 44 Plant remains from site L 201
Table 45 Distribution of animal bone assemblages 202
Table 46 Percentage representation of the major mammalian domesticates from site B 203
Table 47 Species representation – hand collection 204
Table 48 Mammal and bird representation – sieved collection . 205
Table 49 Fish and amphibian representation – sieved collection 205
Table 50 Distribution of neonatal and infant bones 206
Table 51 Epiphysial fusion evidence 206
Table 52 Mandibular tooth eruption and wear data 206
Table 53 Chicken age and sex data 209
Table 54 Distribution of shoulder heights for cattle, sheep and dog 210
Table 55 Selected measurements of cattle, sheep, dog and chicken 210
Table 56 Radiocarbon dates obtained from the sites 210

SUMMARY

Archaeological excavations were carried out in advance of the Jubilee Line Extension Project at Westminster between 1992 and 1997. In addition, archaeological investigations were carried out for the Parliamentary Works Directorate within the Palace of Westminster between 1992 and 1995. Westminster is one of the UK's most important sites and was created one of England's original ten World Heritage sites as defined by UNESCO.

This report describes and discusses the archaeological investigations carried out by MoLAS during the 1990s. It also takes account of the investigations, both archaeological and antiquarian, that took place in the 18th, 19th and 20th centuries and attempts to put those investigations in context. The report is presented in an integrated fashion with all the strands of evidence brought together to enable a more complete understanding of the site. Survey work has accurately established the location of the standing buildings and more accurately located the works of previous archaeologists and antiquaries. The important work of the palaeoenvironmental project at Westminster, published fully elsewhere (Sidell et al 2000), is summarised. One of the principal objectives of the current research has been to provide a geological, topographical and environmental framework for Thorney Island, to define the island and its rivers and to understand their development. Whilst certain areas remain poorly covered (particularly to the south of the island) and certain periods remain less well covered, this has broadly been achieved and what remains is, for the most part, smaller detail. A high degree of confidence can now be placed in our understanding of the nature, shape and size of the island from the post-glacial period to the present, of the varying river levels and their effect upon the area available for habitation, and of the form and date of human attempts at reclamation. The major hiatus in foreshore deposits from the Iron Age to the 12th century, though, means that our knowledge of the environment and the changes to the river system over that period is less reliable.

The earliest activity dates to the Mesolithic and Neolithic periods. Flint assemblages from this period and two phases of revetment are described, as well as a variety of other features. There is also some evidence of activity in the Early Bronze Age.

Evidence for Roman activity remains slight although some features possibly of Roman date and some finds material continue to suggest a certain presence in the area. Traces of Saxon activity are similarly scanty but the finding of a timber structure, perhaps a bridge, and of an associated ditch and revetment dating to the late 10th or early 11th century is an important new indicator of activity in the area, suggesting an earlier date than has so far been accepted for occupation on the palace site.

Within the medieval period the sites fall into three categories: those within the royal Palace of Westminster, those within Westminster Abbey and those within the town.

Limited excavation has taken place within Westminster Hall and its foundations have been recorded. To the north lay a dock built in the 12th century adjacent to a stone building, perhaps a kitchen. The stone gates to New Palace Yard and the Green Yard have been found, with medieval stone buildings adjacent to each of them. That in the outer precinct may have been an inn. Within it was a cesspit containing important wooden and ceramic assemblages. That in the Green Yard was perhaps a government building. Excavations by the Jewel Tower uncovered the construction trench for the moat wall and found a surviving stretch of the Westminster Abbey great drain. The foundations of St Stephen's chapel have also been recorded and records from the 1940s show constructional evidence and floors from the associated cloister.

A large 13th-century building in the precincts of Westminster Abbey was associated with the October Fair. In its original form it had painted plaster walls and a central pathway. Later alterations included the insertion of timber partitions and hearths.

Reclamation on the foreshore indicates that the areas to the north of the palace were taken back from the river progressively and that almost all the area excavated had been reclaimed by the middle of the 14th century, although the eastern side was reclaimed only in the 16th century. One of the houses of the canons of St Stephen's chapel was found on the reclaimed land.

Post-medieval developments include alterations and the eventual rebuilding of the house in the Westminster Abbey precinct, the construction of a fine brick house on the site of the former Woolstaple and 18th-century houses built during the expansion of Westminster as a London suburb.

In the review sections at the end of Chapters 3–13 the recent findings are put into context and the many earlier investigations summarised to provide an overall picture of Westminster's development. Chapters 14–15 provide a description of the current state of our knowledge and list some of the most serious gaps.

ACKNOWLEDGEMENTS

The Jubilee Line excavations were funded by the Jubilee Line Extension Project (JLEP). Particular thanks should go to Paul Chapman and Marcus Karakashian of JLEP, who worked closely with MoLAS throughout the archaeological project, and to Natalie Beeson and Simon Kaye for their help during the publication phase. Mike Harvey, Mike Jenkins and Bill Clowes were of invaluable assistance during the site work. The contractor was Balfour Beatty Amec. Thanks are due to Mark Lewington, Chris Mansfield and Rob Weatherston. The excavation in Parliament Square (site J) was funded by Thames Water and the contractor was Brophy's.

The excavations in the Palace of Westminster were funded by the Parliamentary Works Services Directorate (PWSD). Thanks are due to Cecil Brown, Ralph Spence and Julian Nettle of the PWSD. The consulting engineers were Alan Baxter Associates. Thanks are due to Robert Bowles, Duncan Mercer and Clare Low. The contractor in the Jewel Tower Garden was Haymills.

The evaluation at 37–46 Parliament Street (site U) was funded by the Property Services Agency; the excavation was funded by English Heritage.

The plan drawings in this volume rely on a large number of works by other authors. These are too numerous to acknowledge in the captions and are therefore listed here: Smith 1807; Capon 1824; Capon 1923–4; Horsman and Davison 1989; RCHME 1924; Tanner and Clapham 1933; Green 1976; Colvin et al 1963; Colvin 1966; Schofield 1987; Poole 1870; Clarke 1883; Smirke 1836; Smirke 1837; Lethaby 1906.

Major thanks go to all those who worked on the various excavations, for without them this work would not have been possible. In particular, thanks are due to Ken Pitt, who supervised the excavations on site K, James Drummond-Murray, who carried out the watching brief on site A, and Chris Pickard, who carried out the watching brief on site N. The surveying was carried out by Duncan Lees, Kate Pollard, Steve Every and Marek Ziebart. The original digital drawings were produced by Josephine Brown and Sarah Jones and the final plans were prepared by Helen Jones. Lyn Blackmore drew our attention to the Westminster beaker sherds. Conservation was carried out by Kirsten Suenson-Taylor and Liz Goodman. The summary was translated into French by Elisabeth Lorans and into German by Simon Burnell, and the index was compiled by Auriol Griffith-Jones.

The environmental data discussed in this report have been collated both from individual site projects and from a wider geoarchaeological research project on the entire JLEP. Thanks, therefore, are extended to Keith Wilkinson, Rob Scaife and Nigel Cameron for their work on the geomorphology and palaeoecology of Westminster, to all the individuals on site who helped with the collection and treatment of the samples and to Peter Marshall and Alex Bayliss for their assistance with the radiocarbon dating.

1

Introduction

1.1 Current knowledge of the archaeology of Westminster

The historic core of Westminster is one of the best-known and most important landscapes in Britain and beyond (Fig 1). It includes some of Britain's finest standing medieval and post-medieval structures, ranging from the 11th- to 16th-century Westminster Abbey and the 11th- to 14th-century Westminster Hall (a Grade I listed building) to the 19th-century Victorian, Gothic revival, Palace of Westminster built by Charles Barry and Augustus Pugin after fire gutted its predecessor in 1834. It has been the permanent seat of parliament since its inception in the 13th century and was the site of one of the principal royal palaces from the 11th to the 16th century. It also contains two Scheduled Ancient Monuments: the Jewel Tower and the Westminster Abbey chapter house. Furthermore, whilst only partially surviving, the chapel of St Stephen (the lower chapel was, in fact, called St Mary Undercroft) in the Palace of Westminster was one of the most architecturally important medieval buildings in England and the undercroft is now a Grade 1 listed building.

Westminster is considered to be of such significance that it was one of the ten sites in England initially designated as deserving World Heritage site status and its landscape is a national archaeological priority.

Modern Westminster rests above a pivotal part of London's geology. Thorney Island itself is a relic of a larger system of prominent sand dunes or eyots laid down by the freshwater Thames at its confluence with the Tyburn, which bisected and sculpted the island into its later form. It is perhaps from this prominent position, raised up above the Thames and the Tyburn, that Westminster derives some of its importance both now and in the past. Geologically, its significance lies in the well-preserved sediments associated with the sand island itself; as noted below, these features are poorly researched yet fundamental to our understanding of the freshwater river of the Early/Middle Holocene and the evolution of the Thames, particularly the tidal river of later prehistory. Without the deposits preserved on and encircling Thorney Island, our current knowledge of the riverine history and palaeoecology of central London would be significantly impoverished.

Westminster is important not only for its associations and remains from the medieval period onwards but also for the evidence it provides, in the form of a Mesolithic flint axe from New Scotland Yard (Lacaille 1961, 134), of habitation stretching back more than 7000 years.

Indicators of later prehistoric activity include a Neolithic axe from Westminster Bridge, 30 struck flints from a silt layer above the sand at Westminster Hall (Whipp and Platts 1976, 353) and redeposited material at Treasury Green immediately to the north of Thorney Island (Cowie and Blackmore in prep). Ditches, gullies and other features found at Cromwell Green were interpreted as dating to the Iron Age (Mills 1980, 22–3) although this date has now been revised (Chapter 3.4). Further north, under Richmond Terrace, part of a timber revetment,

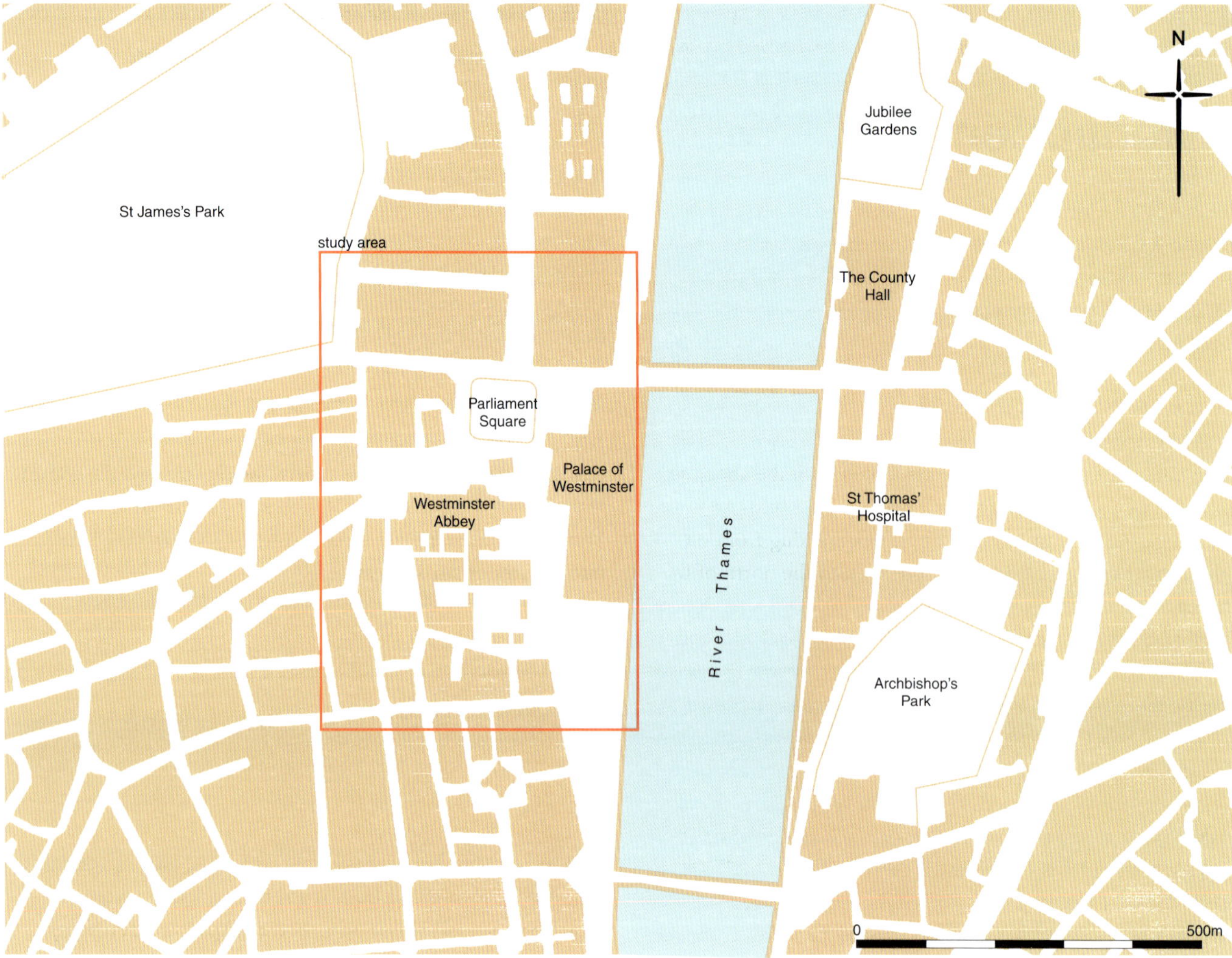

Fig 1 Map showing location of study area (scale 1:10,000)

with a single radiocarbon date of 2540±70 BP (HAR6393: 810–410 cal BC) uncalibrated, was located immediately to the north of one branch of the Tyburn (Andrews and Merriman 1986, 18).

No definite Roman features have been located on archaeological excavations, but most sites have produced finds, some of them possibly dating silts along the Thames foreshore. Antiquarian discoveries include a Roman coffin, found on the north side of Westminster Abbey and thought to have been reused during the Saxon period, stone walls and part of a hypocaust underneath the nave of Westminster Abbey (Westlake 1923, 2). It has also been suggested that the alignment of roads on both sides of the Thames indicates that Westminster was the site of a ford, although this should be treated with some caution (Sloane et al 1995, 369).

Little evidence of Saxon occupation has been found on Thorney Island. Westminster Abbey was founded by St Dunstan in *c* AD 959–75 and may have been founded on the site of an earlier minster church. Residual pottery and a coin of Ecgberht (*c* AD 835–9) from excavations in the undercroft suggest some activity in the area (Goffin 1995, 87). Immediately to the north of the island at least two phases of a substantial timber hall with associated pits dating from the late 8th and 9th centuries were found (Cowie and Blackmore in prep). This complex has been variously interpreted as a farm and a palace. A number of chance finds have also been made, including a sword from just to the south of the Victoria Tower and a group of finds from Westminster Bridge (Cowie 1988, 40).

Westminster Abbey was refounded by Edward the Confessor sometime in the middle of the 11th century and it has been assumed by the wider archaeological and historical community that he established a palace on the Thames side of Thorney Island at a similar time. The new abbey church was constructed in the Romanesque style. The dormitory was added in the 1070s and the refectory in the 1080s. The western range was probably of a similar date but this was swept away by Abbot Litlyngton in the 14th century to provide new apartments for himself. Fragments of the south arcade and apsidal eastern end of the church were found in the first half of the 20th century (Robinson 1910; Tanner and Clapham 1933).

Recent work has suggested that the western towers were rebuilt in the 12th century and that the nave may also have been rebuilt at this time (Tatton-Brown 1995). Major rebuilding works were subsequently carried out at the abbey between 1245 and 1269, during the reign of Henry III. These consisted not only of the rebuilding of the church but also of the construction of other buildings such as the misericord (Black 1976, 135). So much of the abbey was replaced at this time that little of the Romanesque building survives (excepting the undercroft to the east range of the cloister). There were many further additions, culminating in Henry VII's chapel at the east end of the church, completed in the early 16th century. A fire in 1298 seriously damaged the cloister and new buildings, including the infirmary cloister, new apartments for the abbot and a new cellarer's range, were constructed in the 14th century. At the Dissolution the abbey was made a cathedral. This lasted for only ten years (1540–50) before it was refounded by Queen Mary. Upon her death the abbey was reconstituted, retaining its name but having a dean and secular canons to run it.

Apart from the typical monastic buildings, there are known to be numerous other structures associated with the abbey. To the south of the precinct lay a mill reached by a bridge and the kitchen garden. The mill was fed by a channel dug from the Tyburn by the monks. Within the precinct, to the north of the church, lay the parish church of St Margaret, the belfry, the guildhall and many buildings associated with the October Fair, all within a precinct wall with gates to north, west and east. Outside the precinct to the west lay almshouses and the almonry.

The earliest surviving remnant of the palace is Westminster Hall (known in the medieval period simply as the 'great hall'), which was originally constructed by William Rufus in the late 11th century. To the south lay the 'lesser hall' which, it has been suggested, lay on the site of Edward the Confessor's hall. The lower storey of this structure dated to at least the reign of Henry I (1100–35) if not earlier. Between the two halls and projecting into the river lay the chapel of St Stephen, which was subsequently rebuilt in the late 13th and early 14th centuries with two storeys. To the north of the chapel lay its own cloister and a row of houses for its vicars. New Palace Yard lay further to the north and was brought within the palace as its outer court in the late 13th century, though major building works were not begun there until the second half of the 14th century (Horsman and Davison 1989, 283). The inner court lay to the south and consisted of the royal apartments and many other subsidiary structures. These included the lesser hall, the king's chamber (commonly known as the Painted Chamber), the queen's chamber and chapel and the prince's palace. All these structures were probably ranged around cloisters and had their principal apartments at first-floor level. The other standing building that survives from the royal palace is the Jewel Tower, constructed in the 1360s. Its moat and the southern waterfront of the palace were excavated in the 1960s (Green 1976).

In 1530 Henry VIII moved the royal court to Whitehall Palace. Westminster Palace became the permanent home of parliament with the lesser hall and the queen's chamber acting as the House of Lords at different times and St Stephen's chapel used as the House of Commons. The fire of 1834 destroyed much of the palace, with the exceptions of Westminster Hall, part of St Stephen's chapel and its cloister and the Jewel Tower. Most of the rest was demolished to make way for the new palace, designed by Barry.

By the end of the 13th century much of the highway from Westminster to the City of London, King Street (no longer existent), was lined with buildings (Rosser 1989, fig 4). Behind these lay vacant, marshy land that was progressively reclaimed throughout the medieval period. Westminster became a thriving settlement during the later medieval period with the principal domestic structures lying outside the abbey and palace precincts, along King Street and Tothill Street. The Woolstaple, one of the principal wool markets, lay immediately to the north of New Palace Yard.

Many of the King Street buildings were demolished to make way for Henry VIII's expanding Whitehall Palace. The palace lay on both sides of King Street/Whitehall, its principal domestic ranges being on the east side of the street whilst other elements, such as the tennis courts, the tiltyard and the cockpit, were on the west side. All this, however, lay off the historic Thorney Island although by that time the Tyburn was canalised into a series of small streams.

1.2 Circumstances of excavation

The study area

The study area comprises the whole of the geological area subsequently known as Thorney Island and the rivers that surrounded it. During the post-medieval period the landscape altered dramatically in that the rivers were either totally (in the case of the Tyburn) or partially (in the case of the Thames) reclaimed and built over. This volume, therefore, although it does consider the reclamation and encroachment to the east into the Thames, does not address the archaeological and historical findings from those areas to the south, north and west which, whilst they did indeed become part of Westminster from the 16th century onwards, did not lie on the original island. Thus it does not address the 17th- and 18th-century suburbs to the south of Westminster Abbey, nor the Westminster Abbey almonry to the west of Thorney Island, nor Whitehall Palace to the north, which is already well served in published form (Thurley 1999).

The study area measures 1.1km from north to south and 0.8km from east to west although, as stated above, by the end of the medieval period the area which actually formed Thorney Island was somewhat smaller at 560m from north to south and 330m from east to west). The Ordnance Survey grid reference for the approximate centre of this study area is TQ 30115 79560 (Fig 1).

Circumstances of excavation

The investigations discussed in this volume fall into two broad categories: those carried out in advance of the construction of the Jubilee Line Extension (JLE) and those carried out for the Parliamentary Works Directorate within the Palace of

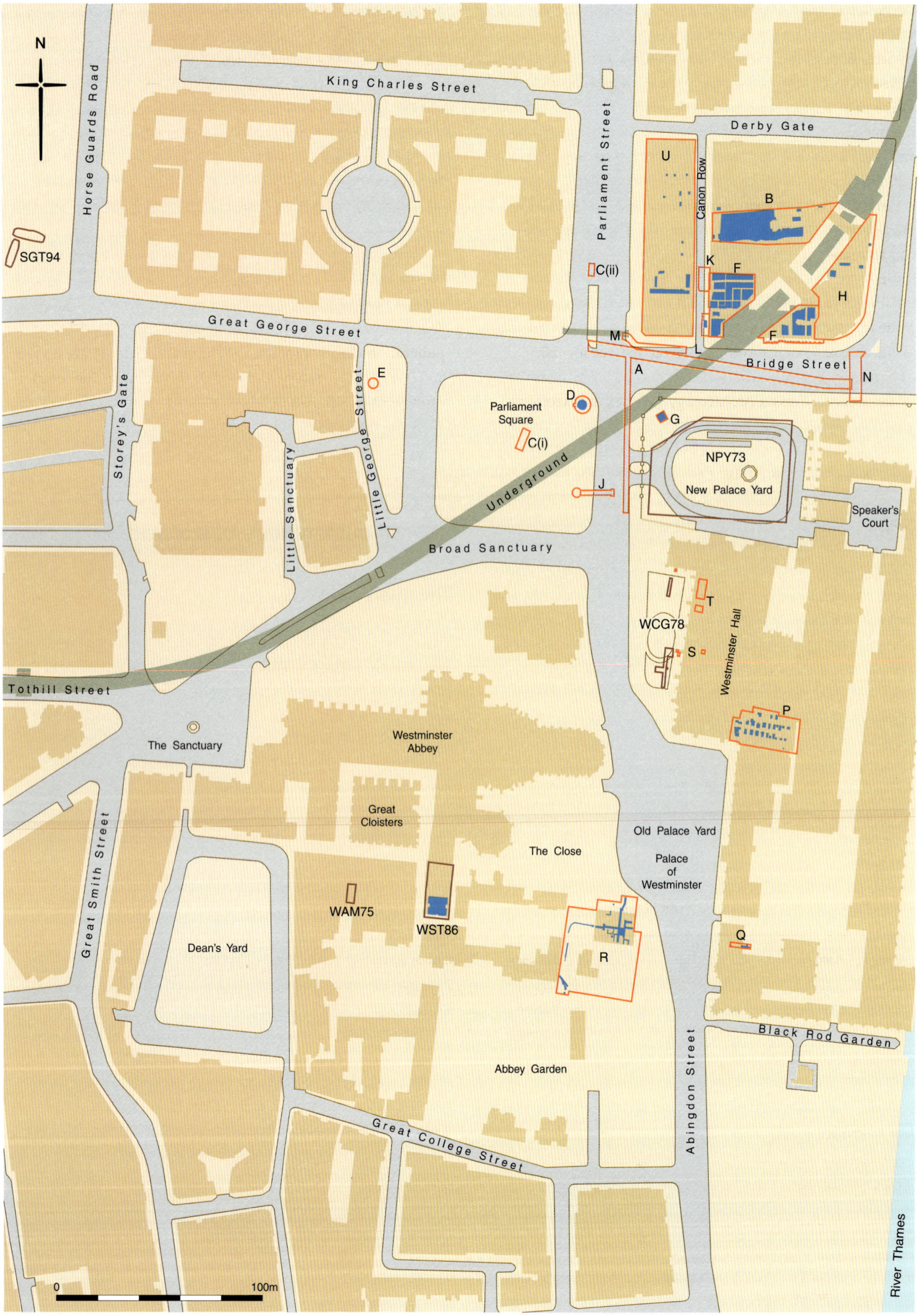

Fig 2 Map showing location of archaeological sites in the study area and the modern street plan (scale 1:2500). For key to site codes, see Tables 1–3

Westminster. The location of these sites is shown on Fig 2. The vast majority of the excavated material comes from the JLE projects which were carried out between 1992 and 1997. These varied in scope from large open area excavations within the site of the new underground station to small circular shafts dug for the purpose of pumping grout into the underlying geological substrata to prevent movement in the surrounding standing buildings.

In order for the reader to be able to locate the provenance of individual finds or archaeological strata quickly and accurately without the use of lengthy site codes to distinguish them, a series of prefix codes have been used in the form of a single letter. Table 1 lists the prefix codes, the addresses, the site codes and the type of investigation for each of the archaeological investigations carried out for JLEP.

One site, Storey's Gate (site code SGT94), was an evaluation by the Trust for Wessex Archaeology (Wessex Archaeology 1994). It is not described in this volume, as its findings did not warrant further excavation. Evidence from the site for the topography of the area and some flint artefacts which were recovered are, however, mentioned.

The second category of sites fully published in this report are those carried out within the Palace of Westminster for the Parliamentary Works Directorate. Table 2 lists the prefix codes, the addresses, the site codes and the type of archaeological investigation for each of those sites.

Several other sites receive mention in the report (Table 3) and two are partially described. One, 37–46 Parliament Street, funded by the Property Services Agency and English Heritage, has not been published and its stratigraphic sequence is described here. The other, Westminster Hall, has had an interim publication already produced (Whipp and Platts 1976, 351–5) and its sequence is also described in this volume. The location of these sites is shown on Fig 2.

Table 1 Jubilee Line Extension Project sites described in this volume, with prefix codes, addresses, site codes and type of investigation

Prefix	Address	Site code	Investigation type
A	Bridge Street and St Margaret St service diversions	BSM92	watching brief
B	Westminster Station site 5	WUS92	evaluation and excavation
C(i)	Parliament Square gas main diversion	PSW93	excavation
C(ii)	Parliament Street gas main diversion	PSW93	excavation
D	Parliament Square – Churchill Statue	PLS94	excavation
E	Parliament Square – Canning Green	PSQ94	excavation
F	Westminster Station sites 1, 2 and 6	WSS94	excavation
G	New Palace Yard	NPE94	excavation
H	Westminster Station site 4	SSE94	excavation
J	Parliament Square	PLQ95	excavation
K	Canon Row vent shaft	CNW97	excavation
L	Canon Row staircase S7	CWW97	excavation
M	Parliament Street stairs and subway	PMS97	watching brief
N	Bridge Street subway	BGS97	watching brief
-	Storey's Gate	SGT94	evaluation by Trust for Wessex Archaeology

Table 2 Parliamentary Works Directorate sites described in this volume, with prefix codes, addresses, site codes and type of investigation

Prefix	Address	Site code	Investigation type
P	St Stephen's chapel	PWC92	watching brief
Q	Chancellor's Court	PWV94	watching brief
R	6–7 Old Palace Yard and the Jewel Tower garden	OPY94	watching brief and excavation
S	Westminster Hall and Cromwell Green	WEH95	watching brief and excavation

Table 3 Other sites described in this volume, with prefix codes where applicable, addresses, site codes and type of investigation

Prefix	Address	Site code	Investigation type
T	Westminster Hall	WHL75	excavation
U	37–46 Parliament Street	PAR87	evaluation and excavation
-	New Palace Yard	NPY73	watching brief
-	Westminster Abbey misericord	WAM75	excavation
-	Cromwell Green	WCG78	excavation
-	Westminster Abbey undercroft	WST86	excavation
-	18 Great Peter Street	SAL94	evaluation and watching brief

Post-excavation reports

At the conclusion of each of the excavations on the JLEP, a post-excavation assessment was produced outlining the background to the site, the findings and the need for further work (analysis and publication). Reports for the Parliamentary Works Directorate sites and 37–46 Parliament Street were also produced although these are not, strictly speaking, assessment reports. Subsequently an assessment report on all the sites investigated for the Parliamentary Works Directorate was prepared (Thomas 1996). After all the investigations for the JLEP were completed an overall assessment was produced that summarised the findings and the need for further work on the whole project and stated the justification for including the other non-JLEP sites (Thomas and Cowie 1998).

Previous excavations

Many excavations have been carried out in the Westminster area since the early 1960s. The majority of these have been published in some form and are not described in detail here. Their locations are shown on Fig 2 and they are listed in Table 3. One section, however, from the Jewel Tower garden which was recorded in 1963 is reproduced and discussed here (see Fig 57) as it has a direct bearing on the excavations carried out there in 1994 and it is previously unpublished. The original can be located in the English Heritage archive.

Antiquarian records

Antiquaries have been recording both standing structures and their decoration, and buried archaeological material in Westminster since the 18th century. Much of this has been published in a disparate number of articles. This report's review sections aim to discuss these findings in the context of the more recently excavated material and efforts have been made to locate and illustrate this material with as much accuracy as possible. Clearly, the methods of surveying and location were less accurate than those employed today and thus these findings are located as a 'best fit'. For this reason, this material is illustrated differently from the more accurately recorded and surveyed material of the past few years.

Antiquarian records of four of the medieval standing buildings and one destroyed building are described in more detail in this volume. Westminster Hall, St Stephen's chapel, St Stephen's cloister and the Jewel Tower all retain some of their original fabric and elements have been recorded in the recent excavations within the Palace of Westminster. For this reason, previous records are incorporated with the excavated material to provide a more comprehensive account. The medieval Exchequer, which was sited to the west of the northern end of Westminster Hall, was recorded in some detail by Pearson in his report to a House of Commons Select Committee in 1884. This remains unpublished in any archaeological publication and it was therefore decided to include it here and to compare it to the published material from the site, which differs in a number of respects (Clarke 1883).

The location of finds from the prehistoric, Roman and Saxon periods listed in the Greater London Sites and Monuments Record (GLSMR) is also reproduced but, similarly, the location of some of these is uncertain. Where more accurate location of some of these data has been achieved, these have been relocated, for instance, the site where Roman hypocaust pilae were recorded as being found when the grave of Sir George Gilbert Scott was excavated in 1878. This is located to the nearest 10m in both a north–south and east–west direction in the SMR. The actual location of Scott's grave has been substituted and the SMR reference located in its centre.

One of the central aims of the project was to locate more accurately some of the existing standing buildings. This was considered desirable for two reasons: firstly because the buildings themselves are considered of vital importance to the understanding of the layout and topography of Westminster, and secondly because many of the antiquarian records (as well as some early archaeological records) were located with reference to these buildings. As a result a number of surveyed points were taken on the Palace of Westminster and Westminster Abbey. Digital copies were then made of the Parliamentary Works Directorate plans (at a scale of 1:100) and the Royal Commission of Historical Monuments plan of Westminster Abbey (RCHME 1924) and these were then related to the surveyed points.

1.3 Organisation of the report

The integrated nature of the report

The usual format of archaeological reports consists of a stratigraphic summary of findings, accompanied by plan and section data, followed by a series of chapters on, for example, pottery, accessioned finds, animal bone etc. These various strands are then drawn together into a short summary of conclusions and discussions.

The Museum of London Archaeology Service (MoLAS) produces an integrated format which represents a change from this traditional model. The first monograph in the MoLAS series outlines this approach (Thomas et al 1997, 6–8) and it is intended only to briefly summarise the strategy here. However, there are certain differences in this report, particularly in the case of the review sections, and the justifications for those are given below.

The chronological narrative

The presentation of the archaeological data is principally organised chronologically by means of a system of dated periods. These periods have been formed from the basic ceramic and stratigraphic phasing combined with evidence for clear changes to the layout or function of the study area. The environmental, palaeoenvironmental and topographical background and findings from this project are considered of fundamental importance to the study of Westminster and that background is outlined at the beginning of each period chapter. The detailed palaeoenvironmental findings for the JLEP have been published separately (Sidell et al 2000) but a summary of the findings at Westminster is presented here. A summary of the documentary and/or archaeological background follows in order to provide a background to the latest findings. Archaeological activity within each land-use zone is then detailed chronologically. Artefacts and environmental material that resulted from such activity are described as they relate to the particular feature, building etc. The narrative of each period concludes with a discussion and summary.

Each period is accompanied by a period plan showing major features and a table showing all relevant dating evidence. Because of the size of the study area and the fact that Westminster forms a landscape worthy of discussion in its own right, many plans showing greater detail are necessary to illustrate some archaeological activities. Illustrations of provenanced finds are presented alongside the description of the building, open area etc from which they came. Items that can be intrinsically dated to a particular period, but which were recovered from later features, are illustrated as part of a corpus of material within the period to which they originally belonged. The intention is to form a graphic catalogue of finds following the chronology of the site. This is fully cross-referenced (see below) to enable the reader to check at once the archaeological provenance of each object.

The review sections

Previous MoLAS publications following this format have produced thematic sections that allow detailed discussion of certain aspects of a site which are not defined chronologically and cannot, therefore, be discussed in the chronological narrative. This volume takes a slightly different approach. At present, there is a colossal amount of archaeological, antiquarian and historical data published on the Westminster area. Some of the antiquarian recording dates as far back as William Stukeley's recording of the Westminster Abbey belfry in *Archaeologia* 1 (Stukeley 1790, 43–8). This not only relates to the medieval period but to the prehistoric, Roman and, to some extent, Saxon periods too. It was felt that a review of this material, in the light of the substantial new findings published in the chronological narrative, would help to put these new findings into context and also begin to show new patterns of activity, and would provide the reader with a summary of much of the most important research and recording in the area without having to read many hundreds of articles and books, many of which are difficult to access.

The specialist support sections

In order to provide a more readable text, much of the necessary 'technical support' for conclusions and interpretations has been removed from the period and review sections. A separate report for each specialist discipline is presented in Chapter 16.

The research archives

All the major themes, along with much of the detailed data, that arise from each specialist research archive have been integrated into this volume. There remains a large corpus of material which is inappropriate for publication in this present format. This information includes detailed identification, quantification, measurement and description of the various assemblages, and is stored in a series of research archives, one for each specialist discipline. Researchers wishing to intensify the scope of their studies are directed to these archives, references to which are detailed in the bibliography. They are publicly accessible in the archive of the Museum of London, and can be inspected by arrangement with the Archive Manager at the London Archaeological Archive and Research Centre (LAARC) at Mortimer Wheeler House, 46 Eagle Wharf Road, London N1.

Textual conventions

The basic unit of cross-reference throughout the research archive for this project is the context number. This is a unique number given to each archaeological event on site (such as a layer, wall, pit fill etc.). Each context number (in square brackets) is prefixed by the site code (above, 1.2; Tables 1–3), for example:

C[100] representing context 100 from site PSW93;
C[+] representing unstratified and unrecorded material;
C[-] representing natural geological deposits.

There are several categories of finds which have been numbered within the research archive. Each catalogue covers material drawn from the total of sites excavated, so that there is no need for a site prefix. To indicate clearly to which catalogue reference is being made, a prefix appears inside a particular form of parenthesis:

<P1> refers to (P)ottery object no. 1;
<S1> refers to (S)mall find no. 1;
<T1> refers to (T)ile no. 1;
<F1> refers to (F)lint no. 1.

(Only illustrated pottery sherds and tiles have been catalogued.) The number of an accessioned find that has not been catalogued is given in angle brackets, prefixed by the site code, thus: D<5>. Environmental samples are numbered within curly brackets, prefixed by the site code, thus: B{3}.

The land-use units are described as B (Building), S (Structure), OA (Open Area) and R (Road).

Weights and measures are sometimes quoted in the text in the units used before metrication in the late 20th century. A foot (comprising 12 inches) is equivalent to 0.3m and a yard to 0.9m. An acre is 0.4 hectare, or alternatively a hectare is equivalent to about 2.5 acres. Sums of money are quoted in the text as cited in £ s d, where 12 pence (d) made one shilling (s) and 20 shillings (or 240d) a pound (£), and one mark equals 13s 4d, since modern equivalents would be misleading. An approximation to current values may be gained from, for example, the wages of: a skilled building worker who earned 2d per day in 1250, 4d per day in in 1400 and 6d in 1500, while a cow could be bought for between 6s and 11s in the Middle Ages, after *c* 1200 (Dyer 1989, xv; Dyer 2002, x). County names in the text refer to historic counties.

Graphical conventions

Because of the synthetic nature of this integrated report, precise details of truncation and horizontal stratigraphy (such as dumps and levelling material) have not been included on the site plans. The site and research archives hold the original site plans and a series of interpretative plans which developed into the present sequence. Fig 3 shows the drawing conventions. It was decided during the preparation of the overall assessment to produce the site plans digitally but using the standard MoLAS graphical conventions.

Dating conventions

Dating conventions used within the text and in Table 56 are as follows. Dates are given as years before Christ (cal BC). Where actual ^{14}C measurements are given, these are conventional ^{14}C ages (Stuiver and Polach 1977) and are quoted with the international standard known as the Trondheim convention (Stuiver and Reimer 1986). They have been calibrated with data from Stuiver et al (1998) using OxCal release 3.8 (Bronk Ramsay 2002). The date ranges have been calculated according to the maximum intercept method (Stuiver and Reimer 1986) and are cited in the text at two sigma (95% confidence), quoted in the form recommended by Mook (1986). This includes the recalibration of dates published previously including dates published in Sidell et al (2000).

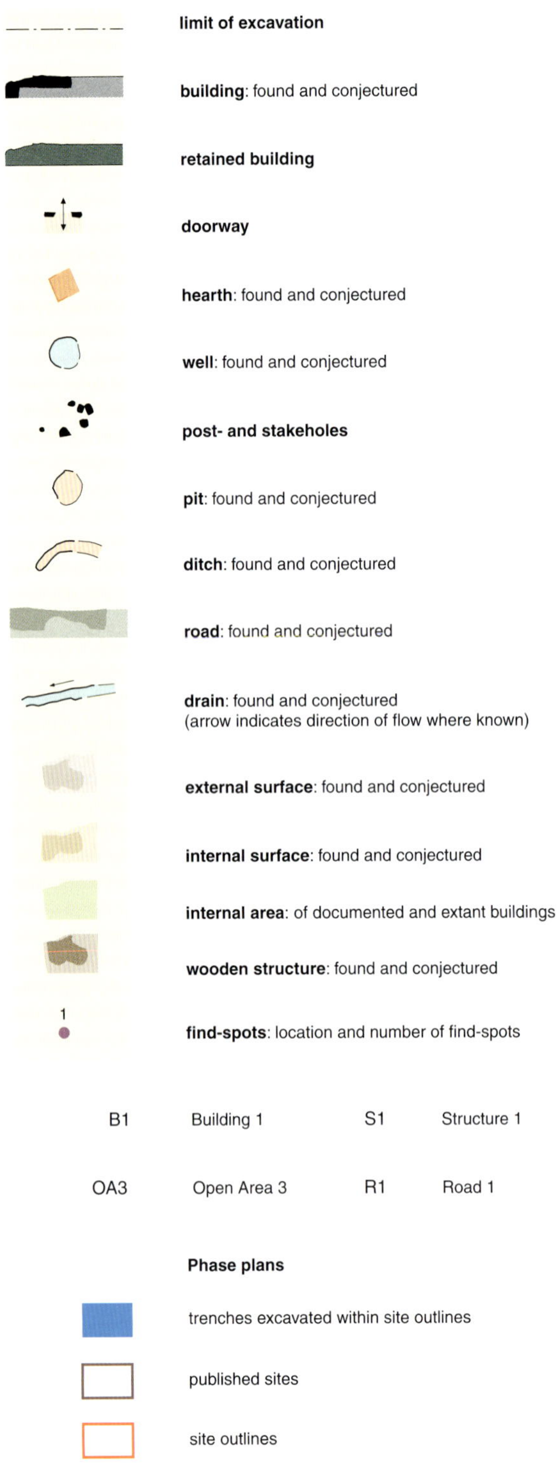

Fig 3 *Graphical conventions used in this report*

2

Geology and topography

2.1 Introduction

The historic core of the City of Westminster, around Westminster Abbey and the Palace of Westminster, lies on a gravel eyot or island on the western side of the Thames called Thorney Island. This sand and gravel island was formed by the bifurcation of the River Tyburn where it met the Thames. A contour survey (Fig 4) has been created using data from modern excavations, antiquarian observations and boreholes. The bias of data can be clearly seen and much more information is required, particularly to the south of Thorney Island where the main southern branch of the Tyburn does not currently appear clearly.

2.2 The River Tyburn

The River Tyburn, which rises in Regent's Park, flowed down present-day Marylebone Lane and crossed Oxford Street just to the east of Bond Street Underground Station, whence it continued to the site of Buckingham Palace. Its course from there has caused some debate but it was thought to have split into two streams, one southwards close to present-day Victoria, and one eastwards to Westminster. Much further work is required but it now appears that the area to the south and south-east of Buckingham Palace formed a large delta with numerous small islands surrounded by streams of varying size and depth. The islands that were formed varied considerably in height, the determining factor in their suitability for habitation. Those at a higher level were less likely to be inundated by the rising waters caused by relative sea-level increase and were thus more likely to be suited to habitation, whilst those at a lower level were more marginal and might have been subject to constant flooding. To the south-west the Westbourne stream entered the same delta area.

Whilst the Tyburn itself appears on the contour survey to have been a quite substantial river (at its mouth the northern channel is shown as being 160m wide between the contours at OD) it is important to remember that the actual channel was probably much smaller, having migrated within its flood plain, thus gradually cutting the feature observed on the contour survey. This migration will destroy that evidence, however, in the process of eroding the river's previous banks. It is therefore uncertain how wide at any time the river was.

2.3 Thorney Island

The largest, and probably the highest, of the islands within the Tyburn delta was what became known in the 8th century as Thorney Island. This had the added attraction of being adjacent to the River Thames and thus on a river more navigable than the Tyburn. The contour map (Fig 4) shows the natural topography of Thorney Island after both the gravel from the Devensian and the sand which overlies it had been laid down. The island consists primarily of sand and gravel overlying London Clay. In places, particularly along the Thames foreshore and in the lower lying areas at the north end of the island, yellow sand or sandy clay overlies the gravel. At the deepest points of the Tyburn channel, at the mouth of the northern channel, all the gravel has been eroded away and the river silts overlie London Clay.

The highest point of the island lies in the vicinity of Westminster Abbey at above 2.0m OD. To the south the ground slopes away to the southern stream of the Tyburn at about -2.0m OD with its mouth at about -3.0m to -4.0m OD. To the north of the abbey lies a plateau at above +1.0m OD under Parliament Square. The ground fell away to the west into the Tyburn to more than -2.0m OD. There is then a gradual fall into low-lying and probably marshy ground to the north of modern-day Parliament Square to the northern channel of the Tyburn. This channel has cut down to the Thames at -6.0m OD, presumably representing the Early Holocene river.

Evidence of other streams or inlets has been found along the Thames foreshore. One has been interpreted beneath New Palace Yard and another, perhaps 15m across and 2.0m–3.0m deep, under St Stephen's chapel (Chapters 3 and 4).

2.4 The River Thames

At the end of the Devensian, the Thames was a much wider and shallower channel than is now the case. The present width of the river at Westminster is approximately 240m. Boreholes indicate that the geological strata beneath the river lie at about -4.0m OD at the southern end of Thorney Island, rising to -3.0m OD to the north. Ascertaining the base of the post-glacial River Thames is, however, fraught with danger as the river has not only been cutting itself a new and potentially deeper channel over time as it has been artificially narrowed and the rate of water flow increased, but it has also been regularly dredged since the 19th century, which may have stripped away any remaining vestiges of the original river bed.

Although this study takes the Late Mesolithic as its starting point, a brief discussion of the Thames before this date is useful in placing the subsequent changes within a broader context. During the Devensian Late Glacial (Oxygen Isotope Stage 2 (OIS2)), specifically the Windermere Interstadial (*c* 12,000–11,000 cal BC), the Thames ran in a braided bedform cutting into the Shepperton Gravel (Bridgland 1994; Gibbard 1994, 12). At the close of this period, many of these channels appear to have been abandoned (Wilkinson et al 2000, 11), probably as a result of the decreasing flow competence through declining spring ice melts consequent on

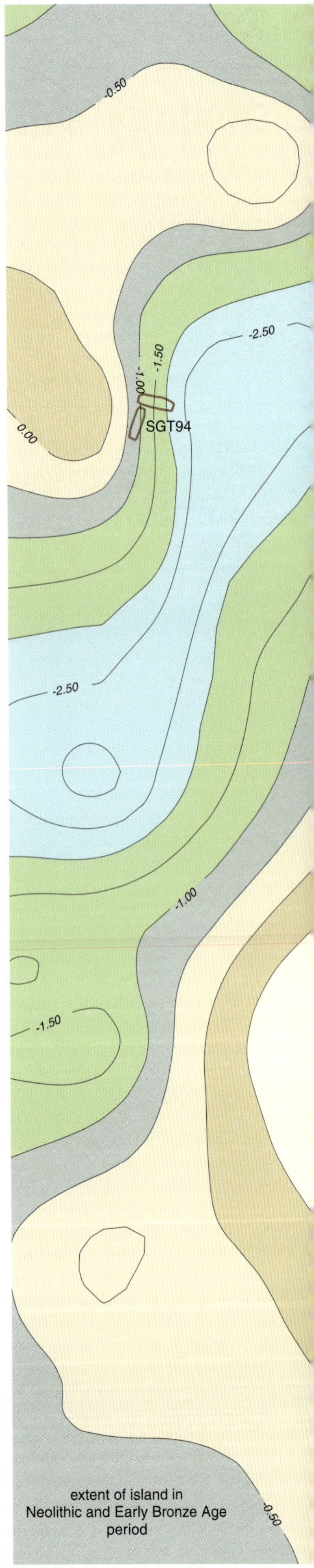

Fig 4 Contour survey with heights shown in metres above or below OD (scale 1:2500). For key to site codes, see Tables 1–3

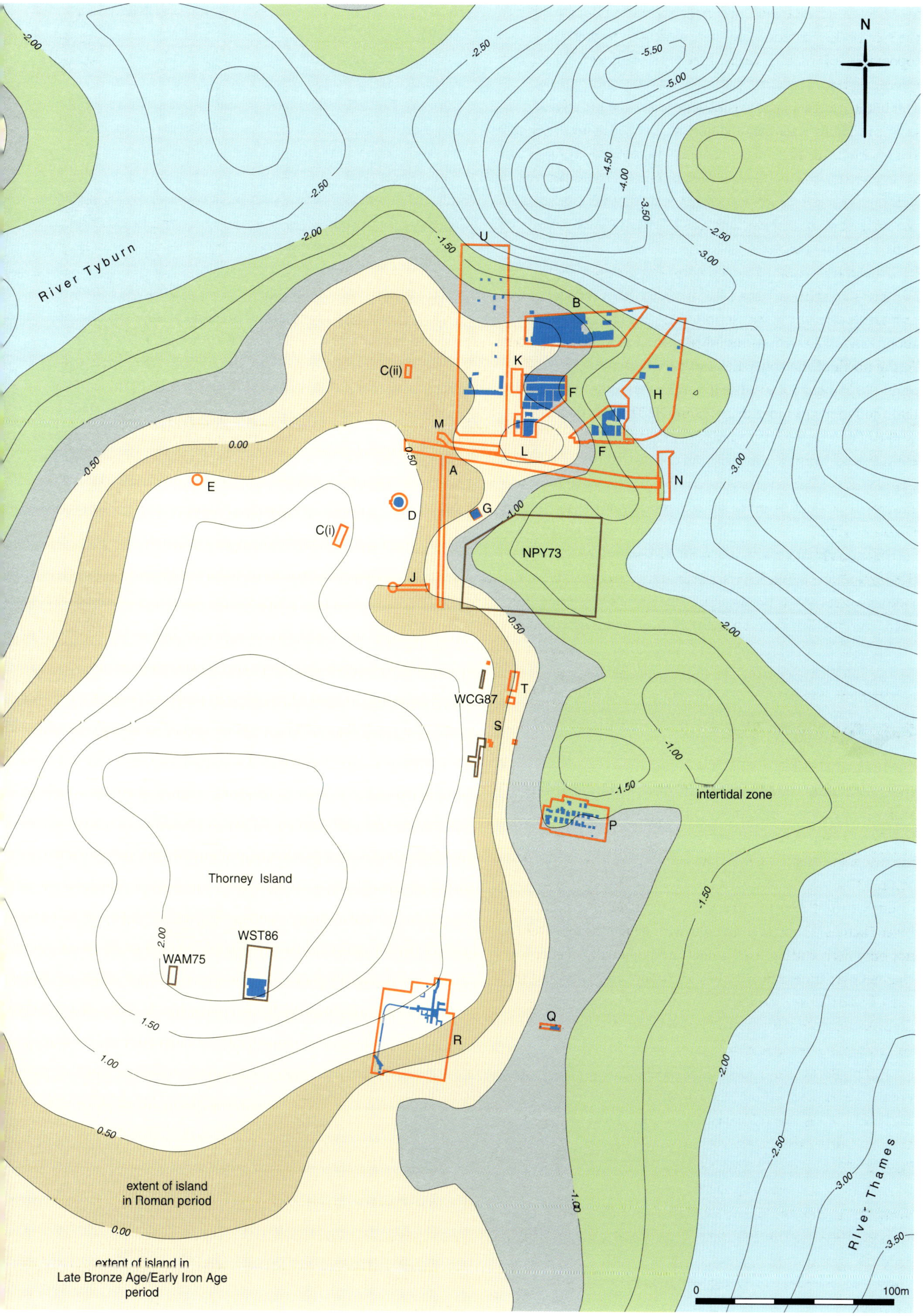
N
River Tyburn
River Thames
Thorney Island
intertidal zone
extent of island in Roman period
extent of island in Late Bronze Age/Early Iron Age period
NPY73
WCG87
WST86
WAM75
A
B
C(i)
C(ii)
D
E
F
G
H
J
K
L
M
N
P
Q
R
S
T
U
-5.50
-5.00
-4.50
-4.00
-3.50
-3.00
-2.50
-2.00
-1.50
-1.00
-0.50
0.00
0.50
1.00
1.50
2.00
0
100m

ice-sheet retreat. Biogenic sediment accumulated in several of the relict river courses at the end of the Windermere Interstadial, the Loch Lomond Stadial (*c* 11,000–9500 cal BC) and finally into the Early Holocene. The site at Silvertown Urban Village, Newham (Wilkinson et al 2000) is a good example of this with a peat-filled channel dating to the Loch Lomond Stadial. Some relict channels were relatively large and at Bramcote Grove (Thomas and Rackham 1996) distinctive sediments accumulated in a lake prior to 11,000 BC and into the Early Holocene before it finally silted up (Sidell 2003). Other than these channel fills, little sedimentation seems to have taken place in the Thames flood plain during OIS 2.

The sand eyots or dunes that have left relict features such as Thorney Island and the Bermondsey and Horsleydown islands are likely to have started forming in the Early Holocene under the freshwater regime. Because of the minerogenic nature of these features and the preponderance of radiocarbon dating in the earth sciences, none of these dunes have been well dated. A further reason for the difficulty in dating comes from the problems in reaching the contact to the underlying gravel that is often not tested archaeologically. A date was, however, obtained from the finely laminated sands of Thorney Island on site F, where a small piece of waterlogged wood was recovered. This dated to 4300 ± 60 BP (Beta 122929; 3100–2690 cal BC) and indicates that the sand islands were still being formed at this late date. The eyots form topographic highs upon which significant amounts of prehistoric activity are known, for example, the field systems on the Southwark islands (Sidell et al 2002). The importance, therefore, of establishing at what date they formed and would first have been available for occupation cannot be stressed enough. However, although the Pleistocene succession of the Thames has been extensively studied, the Holocene evolution has been relatively poorly researched in spite of its significance to the archaeology of the region. The landmark work of Devoy (1979) in relation to sea-level change in the mid and outer estuary is the major work on the subject, now supplemented by a geomorphological project funded by the JLEP (Sidell et al 2000).

Devoy's model, with a study area covering the Isle of Grain to Crossness, led to the construction of the now familiar 'Thames-Tilbury' model, using facies-based modelling and palaeoecological analysis. Intercalated peat and estuarine clay-silts were identified throughout the study area and classified as 'Tilbury' (organic) and 'Thames' (minerogenic) units. This has since been replaced with a simpler but wider ranging model. Three stages of relative sea-level change in the Thames are proposed, with an Early Holocene rapid rise in river levels from *c* 9500 cal BC, followed by a contraction in the estuary roughly contemporary with the Neolithic period (*c* 4000–2400 cal BC). This is shown by a filling of the flood plain with swathes of semi-terrestrial wetland, thought to represent a drop in the rate of rise comparable with the rate of land subsidence (an aspect continuing today). This is amply demonstrated in the London region by the many wetland sites that have been seen over the last decade (Meddens 1996; Sidell et al 2002). The final stage of the model shows the river rising more rapidly, submerging the wetlands with estuarine deposits, and progradation of the tidal head further and further upstream.

More detailed data exist for the development of the tidal river in the last two millennia, achieved through analysis of archaeological structures and horizons and their relationship to the height of the river (Milne and Milne 1982, 62; Milne 1985, 79; Brigham 1990). The Thames was tidal approximately to London Bridge in the 1st century AD, with highest astronomical tide at *c* 2.4m OD (Sidell 2003). Following this, there appears to have been a drop of approximately 1.3m until the beginning of the Saxon period when the river level began to rise again and the tidal head crept back upstream through and beyond the city. There was one final swing in the Late Saxon period, but evidence from sites such as Thames Court (slightly to the west of London Bridge) (Ayre et al 1996; Sidell 2003) indicates that the river levels began increasing once more from the 12th century, continuing to the present day.

3

The Mesolithic to Early–Middle Bronze Age, *c* 6000 BC–*c* 1500 BC (period 1)

3.1 Environmental and topographical background

The River Thames

The earliest information on the Thames from Westminster is actually very solidly founded in the shape of Thorney Island itself. As already mentioned the island is thought to have been formed as a result of the freshwater Thames depositing sands that in some places eventually became isolated islands, probably through a variety of processes including erosion and scouring and preferential sand deposition as in channel bars. The topographical situation is likely to have influenced this, namely, the major bend of the river combined with the proximity of the mouth of the River Tyburn. One radiocarbon date has been obtained from the sands of the eyot at site F (for location of sites, see Fig 5), from a twig preserved in the finely laminated sand and silt deposits at -2.09m to -2.12m OD dated to 3100–2690 cal BC (Beta 122929, 4300 ± 60 BP), suggesting that the sand was accreting in the mid to later Neolithic. Unfortunately, this does not come from the base of the sand islands – these persisted to at least -2.4m OD, but the underlying contact to the Thames gravel was not observed. A further date from site F of 2140–1730 cal BC (Beta 119790, 3570 ± 70 BP) from the contact at the top of the sands indicates that the end of the Neolithic/Early Bronze Age saw a change in sedimentation with sand replaced by finer grained material, probably indicating that the Thames course was migrating away from the sampled site. Although diatoms were not fully preserved in either the sand or overlying silts, one valve of the brackish water species *Nitzschia navicularis* was found, indicating that the silts may have been deposited by estuarine waters and that the site was periodically exposed, consistent with a suggestion that the swing in deposition from sands to clay-silts may be associated with a contemporary rise in relative river level.

The evidence from the samples collected at site H support the data, indicating that the initial Neolithic sand deposition in a medium energy channel was replaced by lower energy conditions at the end of the Neolithic as the main channel migrated away from this location. A radiocarbon date of 2560–2280 cal BC (Beta 127616, 3920 ± 40 BP) from the contact between the higher and lower energy deposits at site H (-1.23m to -1.27m OD) again suggests this change in the river took place at the end of the Neolithic. Subsequent to this change there is evidence both here and at site F for the formation of terrestrial surfaces in areas where the Thames had flowed previously and which could by then be considered the very margins of the flood plain.

Although Storey's Gate (SGT94) is not discussed in detail in this volume (Chapter 1.2), the site nevertheless provided important information on the relationship between the Tyburn and the Thames, reflected in the sedimentary sequence filling a large channel uncovered in the trenches. This channel cut into the sands of Thorney Island, but it is thought to be one of the branches of the Tyburn itself. The earliest deposits suggest that it was a relatively slowly flowing stream, or it may have been abandoned relatively quickly with the Tyburn migrating into another course. Unfortunately, it has not been possible to date this phase directly, but the subsequent phase of activity can be dated to the Early to Middle Bronze Age, at 1740–1430 cal BC (Beta 127617, 3300 ± 70 BP) demonstrating that the initial phase of Tyburn migration occurred before this date. The second phase here is dominated by the formation of organic muds, indicating *in situ* aquatic plant growth. However, the organic carbon content analysis shows that there was a constant input of flood silts, indicating that the channel was still flowing at this point. The diatom flora suggest that initially this water was entirely freshwater and was presumably derived entirely from the Tyburn, rather than the Thames backing up the channel. However, the upper levels of the organic mud show a change with the introduction of brackish water species, almost certainly associated with the Thames depositing estuarine mud. This may not have been constant, but certainly shows that either storm surges or the gradual migration of the tidal head reached Westminster by the Middle Bronze Age. It is extremely unfortunate that the reactivation and recutting of the channel from this point on led to major erosional events making it impossible to examine the phenomena in detail.

Palaeoecology

No evidence has been collected to date that provides information on the local environment before the Neolithic period. This is part of a wider problem in London arising from the scarcity of Mesolithic sediments and the difficulties of accessing them even when they are present. A site recorded slightly to the north of Thorney Island, at Richmond Terrace (RCH80; Andrews and Merriman 1986, 390), yielded a complex sedimentary sequence with a timber structure embedded within the upper levels of an organic-rich unit. Of most interest is the lower peat that gave a date of 8000–7350 cal BC (HAR 5741, 8580 ± 110 BP) as it is one of these rare Mesolithic accumulations. However, no analysis was undertaken on the sediments recorded here. The organic layer, recorded at -2.0m OD, is surprisingly high for a deposit of this date (see for instance the sample from site F, which dates to the mid Neolithic yet is recorded at -2.1m OD). Mesolithic sites are rare in London, and although there are some published accounts of Mesolithic environmental conditions (Wilkinson et al in prep; Thomas and Rackham 1996; Greig 1989), it remains a poorly understood period. This state of affairs is further compounded by there being a second undescribed peat horizon at Richmond Terrace, recorded at approximately -0.5m OD, dating to 2880–2470 cal BC (HAR 5742, 4110 ± 80 BP). Again, in comparison with other recorded dates from Thorney Island to the south, they are rather higher in altitude, but this may be a factor of contemporary sedimentation on higher ground toward the edge of the flood plain. Although it seems almost certain that these deposits represent freshwater marsh development (by comparison with other deposits locally), it is not possible to state this with certainty.

The investigations undertaken for the JLEP geomorphological project (Sidell et al 2000) at site H provide some of the most complete biological information for this period. From *c* 2300 cal BC, the litho- and biostratigraphical sequences here indicate that the opening of the Bronze Age saw a dominance of lime (*Tilia*) forest on the dry ground off the flood plain with oak (*Quercus*) and hazel (*Corylus avellana* type) as major components, growing to dominate the vegetation after the removal of lime. This corresponds with the picture of fen environment on the flood plain itself, with alder (*Alnus*) and sedge (*Carex* sp) fen. These aspects expand at the expense of the drier land, indicating a rise in water levels, although whether this is as a result of relative sea-level change, and/or local water-table fluctuation is uncertain. Cereal pollen with associated weeds of arable cultivation were recovered and indicate that by the Bronze Age, land had been cleared and taken into cultivation. It seems likely that the clearance reflected in the pollen spectra was to create pasture for raising livestock as well as setting aside land for growing cereals.

Storey's Gate (SGT94) provided clear information on the Bronze Age environment, where palaeoecological reconstruction characterises the vegetation cover on the margins of the Tyburn from the Early Bronze Age through to the late medieval period (see below) (Sidell et al 2000, 32–6). The basal sediments collected from the site indicated a dryland environment with local lime-dominated woodland, as well as oak and hazel. By approximately 1600 cal BC, the lime was no longer dominating the local area, leaving oak and hazel as major components. This lime decline, which has been noted from a number of other sites in London (see Rackham and Sidell 2000, 23) corresponds with an increase in waterlogged marshy conditions. Furthermore, the Storey's Gate sequence yielded cereal pollen, important evidence for the beginning of agriculture in the Westminster area during the Bronze Age, and confirms the reconstruction undertaken at site H. The pollen evidence from site E, which also shows the replacement of lime woodland by local oak woodland, supports this picture. In conjunction with the change from woodland to more open conditions in the Bronze Age, a marsh element developed, apparently as the Tyburn migrated away from the sampling site at Storey's Gate. This was part of a freshwater marsh forming in and adjacent to the relict channel, with fairly low levels of water and sediment input. The marsh was composed of species such as lesser reedmace (*Typha angustifolia*), sedges, water plantain (*Alisma* type), greater reedmace (*Typha latifolia*), alder and iris (*Iris*). This freshwater marsh element is also reflected in contemporary sediments from site E, with fen species such as greater reedmace, reedmace/bur reed (*Typha/Sparganium*), sedges and royal fern (*Osmunda regalis*).

The investigations at site F also contribute to this reconstruction. The sequence here dates from *c* 1600 cal BC when lime woodland also dominated to the east of Storey's Gate, indicating a relatively consistent vegetational pattern around Thorney Island. This rapidly changed to oak-/hazel-dominated woodland also supporting beech (*Fagus*) and ash (*Fraxinus*). Another corresponding point with the data from Storey's Gate is the introduction of cereal into the pollen spectra at this point in the Middle to Late Bronze Age. The data from site F indicate that the sample location may have been further away from the actual cultivated area, which may well have been on the other side of the Tyburn or atop Thorney Island itself. At site P, at a level of -0.15m OD, a series of cuts interpreted as possible ard marks were identified, in section only. These are thought to date from the later part of this period and may well confirm the hypothesis of localised cultivation on the island.

3.2 Archaeological background

Numerous prehistoric finds dating to the period before the Late Bronze Age have been recovered from the Westminster area in general and Thorney Island in particular. Thirty struck flints were found in a silt layer above the sand at Westminster Hall (Whipp and Platts 1976, 353) and discussion of this material appears in this volume (below, 3.4, and Chapters 16.1 and 16.3).

Immediately to the north of Thorney Island, a number of artefacts have been recovered. Redeposited material was recovered from the excavations at Treasury Green (immediately north of the study area, beneath 10 Downing Street and the old Treasury buildings), including a Neolithic axe head and a small group of struck flints thought most likely to date from the Mesolithic or Early Neolithic (Cowie and Blackmore in prep). There are also a number of less provenanced prehistoric finds from the area, including a Mesolithic flint axe from New Scotland Yard (Lacaille 1961, 134).

Previous excavations have also located prehistoric features, particularly the excavation at Cromwell Green (WCG78; Mills 1980). These features were regarded from the finds assemblage as being of Iron Age date but this report reassesses that material and concludes that the majority of it and the features themselves belong in this period (below, 3.4 and Chapters 16.1 and 16.3). Other finds that were identified at the time as being of Neolithic or Bronze Age date were also recovered from that site. Other, poorly provenanced material includes a Neolithic axe recovered from the area of Westminster Bridge.

There is already, therefore, clear evidence of activity on Thorney Island during the Late Neolithic and Early to Middle Bronze Age, with possible evidence of activity during the Mesolithic.

3.3 Archaeological evidence

The archaeological evidence is discussed in four parts. The structural evidence from each of the sites is addressed first; then follows discussion of the river regime, the foreshore areas and, finally, the activity on the higher ground of Thorney Island. The locations of the archaeological features excavated are shown on Fig 5.

Structure 1: revetment

Structure 1 on site P revetted the south side of the upper parts of a deep channel that was aligned approximately east–west (Fig 6). The channel fills are described below (Open Area 1) (Fig 7).

Five timbers or voids left by the timbers represent a revetment cut into the sides of the sloping bank of the channel. The majority of the timbers were so badly decayed that only voids were left although very decayed wood remained in two. The postholes appeared to be cut from between a level of -0.15m OD and -0.29m OD. They were pointed and ranged in diameter from 60mm to 0.21m although most were 0.15m to 0.21m across. The depths of many could not be established but in the case of those that could ranged from 0.60m to 0.86m deep. Because of the decayed nature of the wood it was impossible to ascertain whether there were horizontal timbers or wattle associated with them but this seems highly probable.

There was no dating evidence associated with Structure 1; its phasing is based purely upon the interpretation of the river levels at Westminster. This is explained in detail in Chapter 14.1. In summary the river level in the Thames would seem to have been at about -1.0m OD in 2000 BC. By about 1400 BC the river appears to have become tidal, with high tide at about -0.5m OD and low tide at -2.0m OD. This would suggest that decay was the principal reason for the probable replacement of Structure 1 by Structure 3 (see below) although the need for replacement may have arisen from abnormally high river levels caused by flooding. It seems highly unlikely that the two lines of posts would have been in use at the same time.

Structure 2

Structure 2 lay on the higher sands on the west side of site F (Fig 8). The structure was truncated both to the north-east and to the south-west. It consisted of a line of six postholes (possibly nine) aligned north-east–south-west. The line curved slightly but not enough survived to indicate whether it was a circular structure; if it were it would have had a very large diameter. One of these postholes was less clear than the others and may have been two postholes aligned north-west–south-east with the area in between them disturbed. About 0.7m to the south-west was a posthole which appeared to have originally been three postholes aligned north-west–south-east with the areas in between subsequently disturbed. It might also have been caused by animal or root disturbance. The postholes were roughly circular, about 0.15m–0.20m across and 0.16m–0.30m deep. They were all filled with a similar material to that sealing the area (layer F[7]; see below, Open Area 1). The postholes contained burnt flints and two contained later intrusive material including a possible fragment of ceramic building material and a modern fragment of copper. As discussed below it is possible that the postholes were originally cut from a higher level and that the sand layer F[7] which sealed them may have been a disturbed ground surface. There was evidence that two of the posts may have been pulled out but it seems more likely, on the whole, that they decayed *in situ*.

The function of Structure 2 is uncertain. It may have been a boundary fence, in which case the presence of the groups of postholes at right angles to it seems unusual, unless they formed a door or gap of some kind – it is more likely that they were disturbed by animal activity.

Structure 3: revetment

Structure 3 probably replaced Structure 1 and was placed slightly higher up the bank along the south edge of the channel (Fig 6). Many of the postholes lay partially beyond the limits of excavation and were revealed only in section. As recorded it consisted of seven timber posts, only two of which had any surviving wood at all. Although badly decayed the wood of one post, P[100], was tentatively identified as alder (*Alnus*) (Ian Tyers, pers comm). The post appeared to have had a branch left on it and a pointed base, indicating that it had been trimmed. The majority were cut from a level of -0.15m OD and were 0.18m in diameter and up to 0.64m deep. As with Structure 1 it was impossible to ascertain, owing to the decayed nature of the wood, whether there were associated horizontal timbers or wattle but this seems highly probable.

As in the case of Structure 1 there was no dating evidence associated with Structure 3; its phasing is based purely upon the interpretation of the river levels at Westminster. As discussed above, its line seemed to indicate that it was a structure separate from Structure 1. Stratigraphically, Structures 1 and 3 are unrelated so Structure 1 could in fact post-date Structure 3. In such a case Structure 1 would be seen as an attempt to reclaim land into the channel. This seems highly unlikely as no material was dumped behind either revetment, which seem to have been constructed purely as barriers against rising levels. In such a scenario it seems more likely that Structure 3 was constructed after Structure 1 once the latter had either become decayed or was damaged by the river. Structure 3 appears to have fallen out of use by the end of the Bronze Age, when the increasingly tidal river would have swamped it. Perhaps it and its predecessor were evidence of an attempt by the communities on Thorney Island to keep the flood waters back.

Open Area 1

Since there are no physical boundaries which can be used to divide Thorney Island at this time, the entire island has been defined as Open Area 1. However, since the investigations have taken place in certain discrete areas, Open Area 1 has been subdivided into the River Thames, the foreshore to the north-east, the foreshore to the east, and the higher ground.

Fig 5 Plan of the archaeological features and location of finds, period 1 (scale 1:2500). For key to site codes, see Tables 1–3

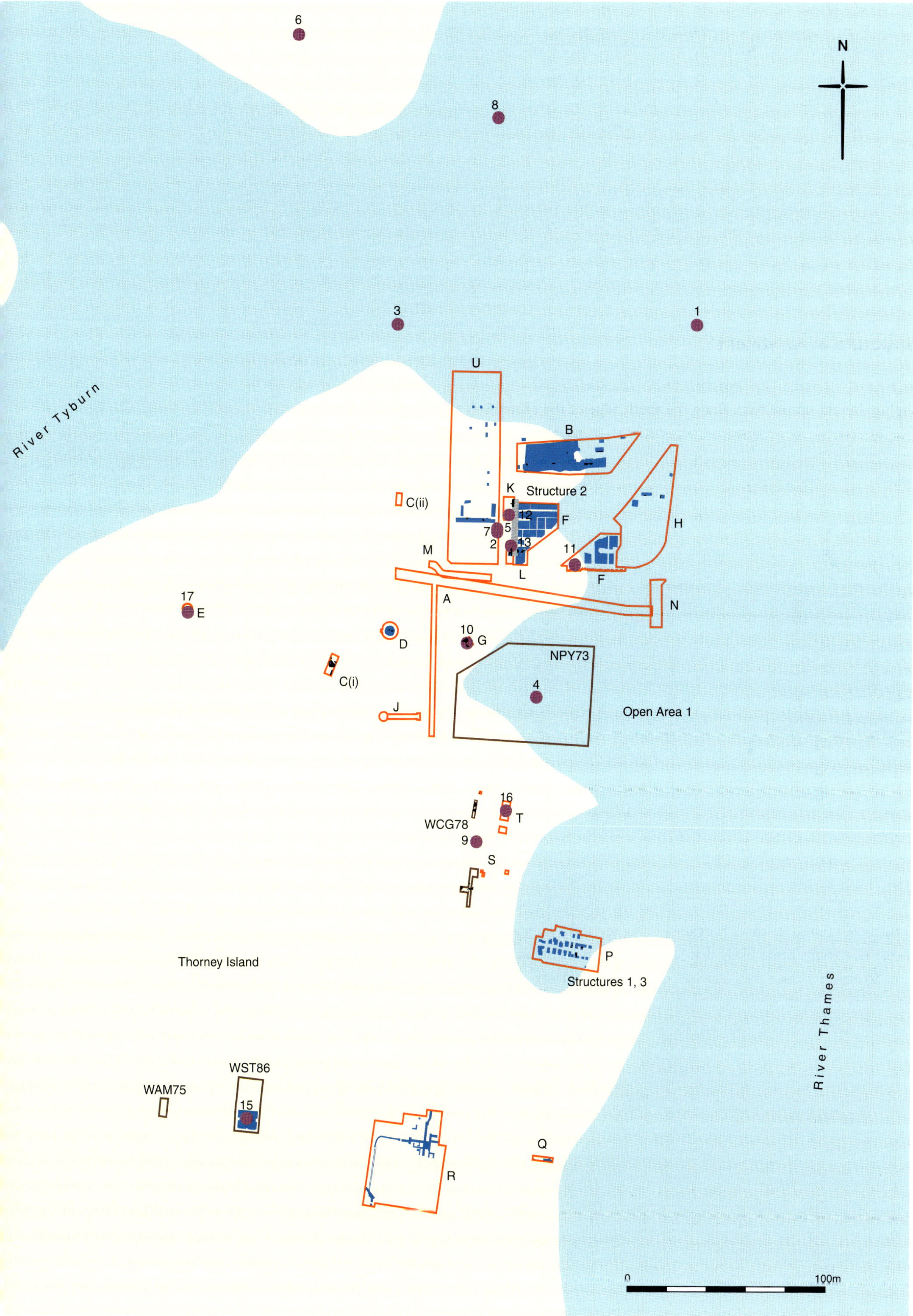
N
6
8
3
1
River Tyburn
U
B
Structure 2
K
C(ii)
12
F
H
7
5
2
13
11
M
L
F
A
N
17
E
D
10
G
NPY73
C(i)
4
J
Open Area 1
16
T
WCG78
9
S
P
Thorney Island
Structures 1, 3
River Thames
WST86
WAM75
15
Q
R
0
100m

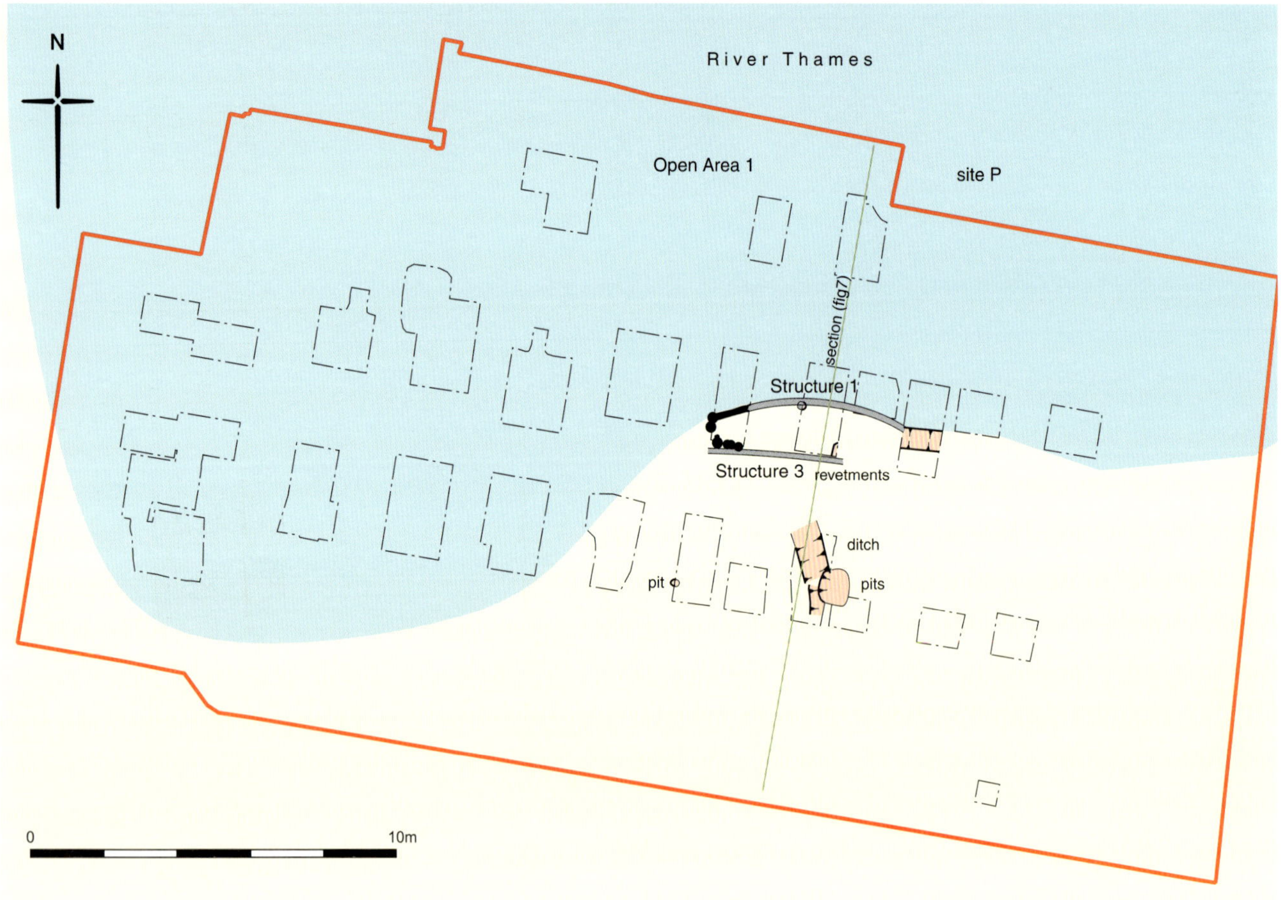

Fig 6 *Detailed plan of Structure 1 and Structure 3, period 1 (scale 1:200)*

The River Thames

On site B (Fig 9) the surface of the sand lay between 0.08m and -1.52m OD. It was highest on the west side of the site, and was generally lower towards the north and east. The sand was cut by two hollows and three small palaeochannels. Both hollows probably resulted from root action. One was 0.10m deep, filled with sand, and produced a flint blade and a small flint flake, both of which appeared to be not later than Early Bronze Age in date. The other hollow was 0.52m deep and filled with clayey sand. The palaeochannels, on a north–south alignment and filled with waterlaid deposits, may have been minor watercourses draining off the north side of Thorney Island. Their full dimensions were not established since they were only partially exposed in section, although channel B[125] was at least 3.0m wide and up to 0.49m deep and channel B[127] was at least 2.60m wide and 0.56m deep. Channel B[125] produced a flint core, which could not be

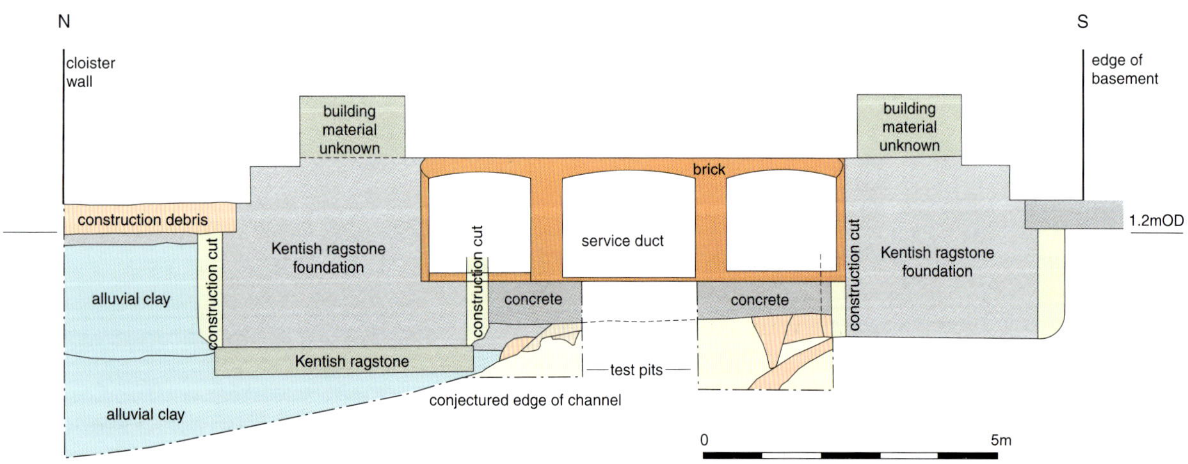

Fig 7 *East-facing section through site P showing the channel and the higher ground (scale 1:125)*

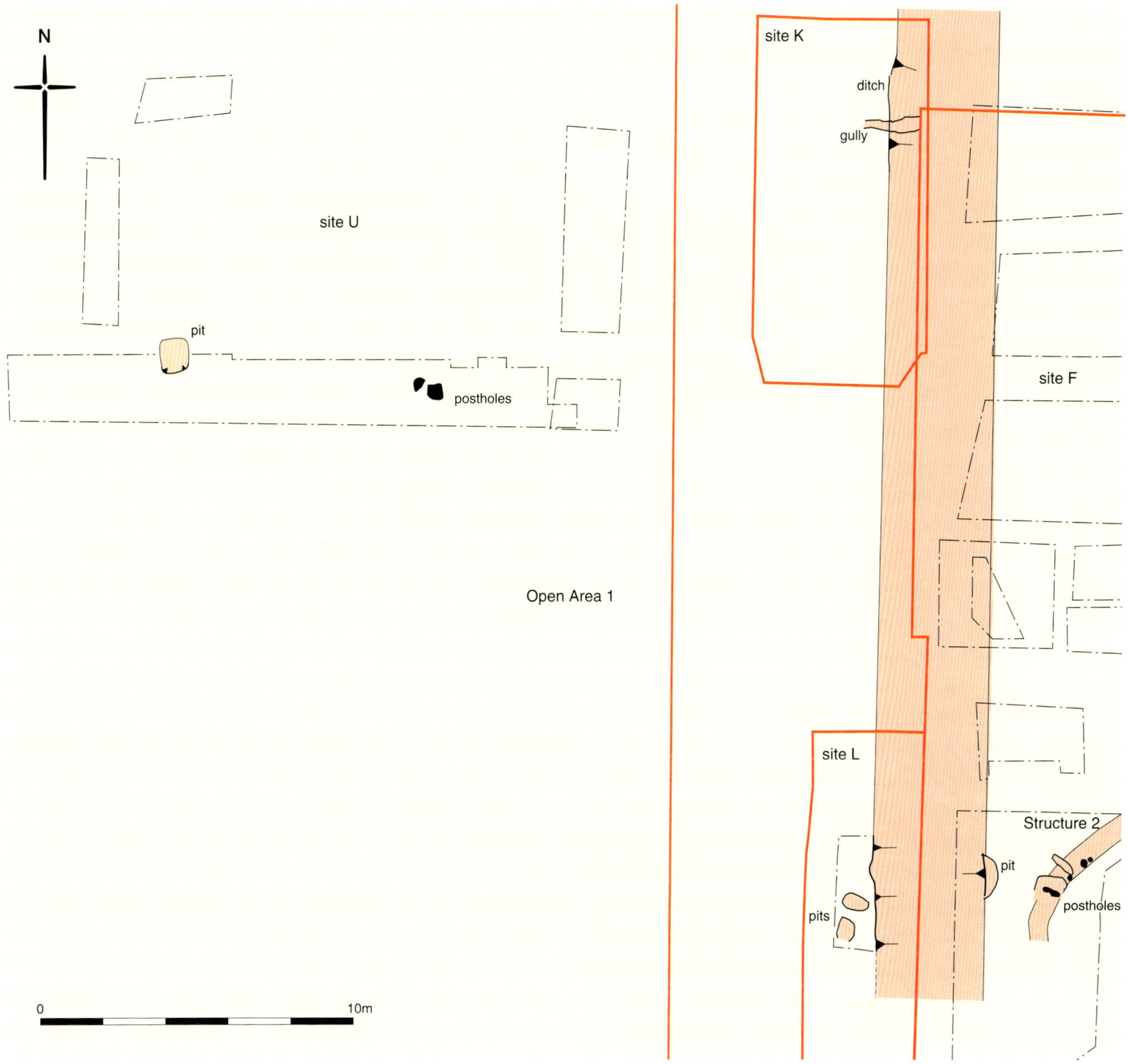

Fig 8 Detailed plan of Structure 2 and Open Area 1, period 1 (scale 1:200)

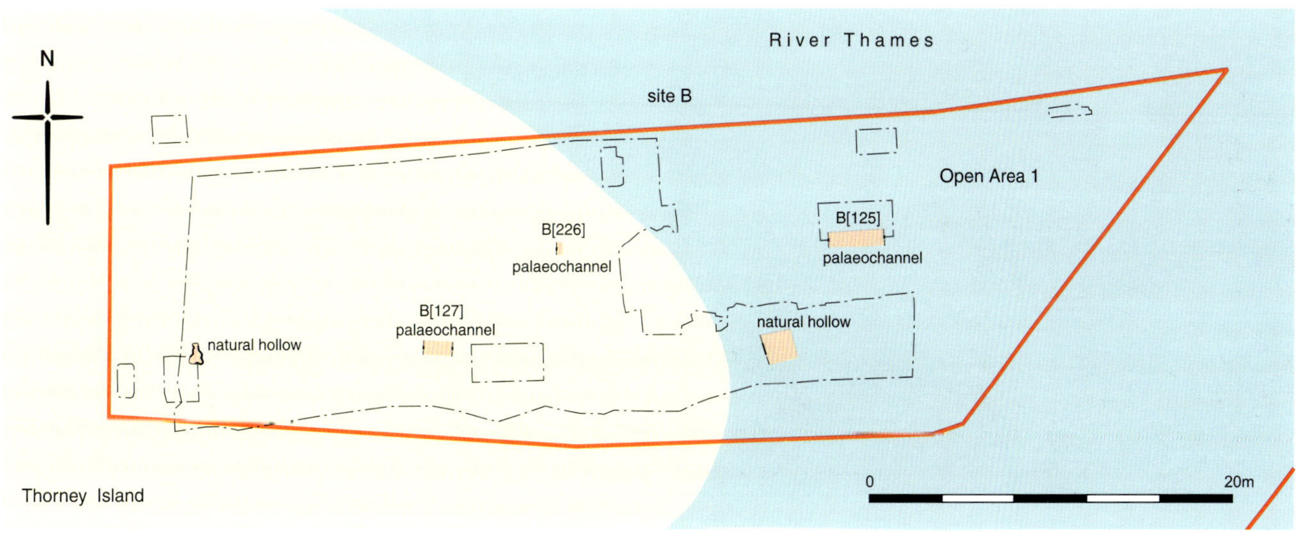

Fig 9 Detailed plan of site B showing the palaeochannels and the edge of the sand eyot, period 1 (scale 1:400)

closely dated but was probably struck before the Early/Middle Bronze Age. No datable artefacts were recovered from the other two channels. However, since the overlying fluvial deposits were covered by a layer of peat that produced a radiocarbon date of 1130–810 cal BC (Chapter 4.3), it would seem that all three channels are earlier than the Late Bronze Age.

The sand and the channels cutting it were covered by a thick blanket of grey or grey-brown waterlaid sediment, which generally became finer higher up the sequence. The earliest deposits consisted mainly of sandy silt-clay. These were overlain by finer material, mainly silty clay and clay. Since the change in texture was often gradual, the interfaces between strata were sometimes poorly defined. Within the sequence of waterlaid deposits there was a channel, 1.30m wide and 0.32m deep, seen only in section but apparently on a north–south alignment. The surface of the fluvial deposits was cut by another north–south channel, which was at least 0.58m deep. On the west side of site F untruncated sand was found at 0.16m OD on the west side sloping down to -0.02m OD in the north-east corner. Some 31m to the east (the other side of the existing underground line), sand was encountered at -1.96m OD. The slope of the sand in the western area had a gradient of approximately 1:18 and the difference in height between the two areas of the site suggests a gradient of 1:16. These suggest that there was a gradual slope in the sand forming the foreshore down to -2.2m OD some 6.2m further east before a sandbank raised the level by 0.4m. The sand then continued down into the river to the east.

Fig 10 *View of the partially excavated silts from site F with the sand containing the flints and pottery beneath, looking north-west*

Overlying the sand on the eastern part of the site was a series of waterlaid deposits. The earliest consisted of 0.5m–0.6m of black and yellow sand layers interleaved with occasional bands of grey silt. Over this were layers of blue-grey clay that averaged about 0.75m in thickness.

A section to the north-east revealed a different sequence of waterlaid deposits. Gravel lay at -1.65m to -1.51m OD and was overlain by blue-grey sandy clay and blue-grey clay F[189] to a depth of between 1.46m and 1.14m OD. A sample taken from F[189] at between -1.17m and -1.22m OD gave a radiocarbon date of 2140–1730 cal BC (Beta 119790, 3570±70 BP). The layer above, F[188], at -0.73m to -0.78m OD gave a radiocarbon date of 1520–1210 cal BC (Beta 119789, 3110±70 BP). No sands were present in this area although it lay only 3.0m to the north-east of the other section.

River sands and gravels on the west side of site H were covered by waterlaid deposits. The earliest of these deposits comprised grey-brown fine sands and sandy silt-clays, up to 0.24m thick. These were overlain by blue-grey silts and clays, up to 0.6m thick, the top of which lay at about -1.0m OD. The upper 0.5m of these fine sediments were bedded in wavy, parallel laminations. Their nature suggests periodic deposition from slow-moving water, possibly during flooding at the edge of a channel. It is not known how long these fluvial deposits took to accumulate. However, a sample taken from between -1.23m and -1.27m OD gave a radiocarbon date of 2560–2280 cal BC (Beta 127616, 3920±40 BP), suggesting that the deposits between these levels were laid down during the Late Neolithic. The pollen evidence suggests that at about this time the surrounding region was still quite wooded.

On site Q waterlaid silts were uncovered sealing the sand foreshore that sloped down from west to east from -0.86m to -0.96m OD on the east side and from north to south from -0.95m to -1.11m OD. The river-laid deposits consisted of sticky grey clay-silt under a similar, but browner and more friable, clay-silt that had frequent fragments of very decayed wood. The top of this was truncated by a concrete raft at OD.

The foreshore to the north-east

On site F, to the west of Structure 2 and sealed by F[7], was a truncated sub-circular pit about 1.35m in diameter and 0.25m deep (see Fig 8). It was filled with a light brown sand similar to layer F[7]. Layer F[7] itself overlay the terrace sand. It was a grey-brown silty sand, 0.20m thick, containing flint artefacts, burnt flints, waste flints and pottery (Fig 10). One sherd, <P1> (Fig 13), was probably derived from a Late Bronze Age fineware vessel. This layer apparently sealed and filled the postholes of Structure 2. It may have been either a fluvially deposited layer that filled the postholes after the posts had decayed or been pulled out, or the original ground surface that became mixed after flooding. The evidence from the distribution of the flints on site G (below, 3.4) suggests that the flints have not been disturbed at a later date. The surface of the sand, therefore, may approximate to a land surface.

Cutting layer F[7] was a north–south aligned ditch of which only the eastern edge was found on this site. It was filled with very similar material to F[7], also containing burnt and struck flints. What may have been the western edge of this feature was found on site L some 2.96m further west. It was filled with similar material and continued beyond both the northern and southern limits of the excavation. Here the fill L[57] contained a small plant assemblage of wetland plants including aquatic species (eg, crowfoots (*Ranunculus* subgen *Batrachium*), pondweeds (*Potamogeton* spp) and water plantain (*Alisma* spp)), bankside/marshland species (eg, celery-leaved crowfoot (*Ranunculus sceleratus*), spike-rushes (*Eleocharis palustris/uniglumis*) and sedges (*Carex* spp)) and a range of plants of disturbed ground and waste places (eg, chickweed (*Stellaria media*), goosefoots/oraches (*Chenopodium/Atriplex* spp), knotgrass (*Polygonum aviculare*) and stinging nettles (*Urtica dioica*)). One charred wheat (*Triticum* sp) grain and a small quantity of charcoal were also recovered from this assemblage.

This assemblage suggests that the ditch/gully contained water, although this may have been subject to periodic drying out, whilst the grain and charcoal point to the possibility of human activities nearby.

To the north lay the western edge of what may have been the same north–south aligned ditch on site K. Only the edges of this ditch were found as the centre had been disturbed by modern foundations and the new foundations for the underground station. This suggests the possibility that the ditch was in fact caused by slumping from the modern foundation works and was not a 'real' feature. If real it would have been more than 28m long and on site K was 1.08m deep. The ditch was sealed by a layer of pale grey sand that included worked flints and fragments of pottery dated to between the Late Neolithic and Early Bronze Age, similar to that found on sites F and L (Fig 11). Cutting the sand on site K was a shallow, east–west aligned gully, 0.45m wide at the east end and 0.22m wide at the west. It was a maximum of 0.13m deep and was filled with sandy silt containing charcoal and burnt flint (Fig 8).

To the west of the north–south ditch on site L were two shallow oval pits 0.11m and 0.12m deep. Both were filled with sand and charcoal and one contained a flint flake. These pits cut through the grey sand layer. They produced virtually no plant remains and consisted almost entirely of small wood fragments, a few charcoal flecks and, in pit fill L[61], a few pondweed (*Potamogeton*) and goosefoot (Chenopodiaceae) seeds.

On site U, cut into the sand, were a pit and two postholes, all filled by a pale grey sand with a dark brown clay overlying it. The pit in the north-western part of the area was truncated

Fig 11 View of the natural sand with accumulated silts above on site K, looking east

by a Victorian basement wall but measured 1.55m x 0.70m and was 0.22m deep. Both postholes were heavily truncated by later activity. One was approximately circular with a circular depression in the base, 0.45m across. Its depth was only 50mm but must originally have been more than 0.20m. The other, to the east, was of a similar size with a circular depression in the north-eastern corner.

The foreshore to the east

On site G river sand lay at about 0.5m OD. Its surface had been disturbed in places by roots, especially on the north-west side of the site (Fig 12), where there was a large irregular tree hollow, G[43], that was 0.65m deep. The primary fill of the hollow contained a partly decayed root, which gave a radiocarbon date of 1750–1510 cal BC (Beta 78165, 3350±50 BP). This indicates that the site was still dry enough in the Early Bronze Age for vegetation to grow. Its secondary fill, G[41], produced occasional fragments of burnt flint and a sherd of prehistoric pottery. The river sand and the tree hollow were covered by a thin layer of sand, disturbed by root action and containing occasional bone fragments, burnt flint fragments and flecks of charcoal and burnt clay. It also contained a fragment of pottery, <P2> (Fig 13), possibly from a Middle Bronze Age Deverel-Rimbury type urn – an identification which fits better with the chronology than the other possibility, namely, a Neolithic bowl.

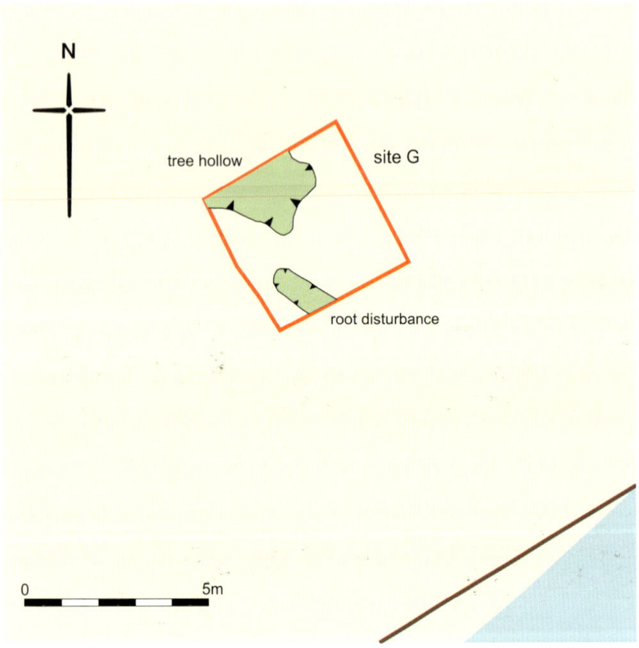

Fig 12 *Detailed plan of the archaeological features on site G, period 1 (scale 1:200)*

The site was then covered by a layer of sand, G[39], that lay at about 0.8m OD and was up to 0.2m thick. Waterlogged rush (*Juncus* spp) seeds suggest that the site was on or very near the water's edge. It also produced sherds of prehistoric pottery, struck flints and fragments of burnt flint. Most of the flints

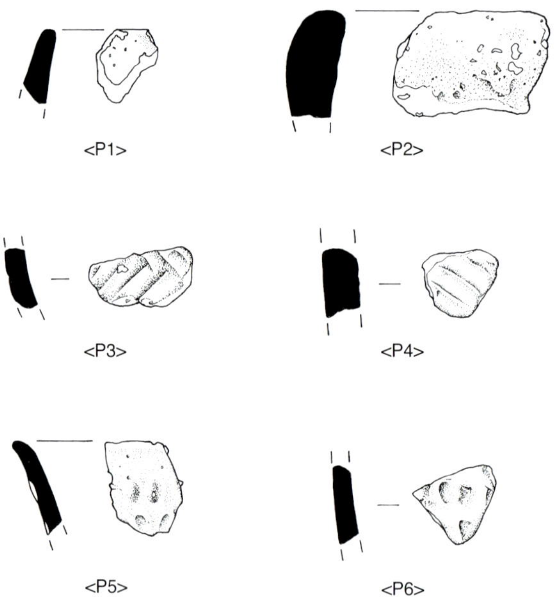

Fig 13 *Prehistoric pottery <P1>–<P6> (scale 1:2)*

were waste debitage but there were also 64 flakes, 13 blades and blade fragments and a core; two retouched tools were also recovered. On a technological basis the assemblage could date from the Mesolithic to the Late Bronze Age. It was thought that the retouched tools might have been leaf-shaped arrowheads characteristic of the Early Neolithic, although this identification is in question. Indeed, one may be a triangular arrowhead, a form which was still in use at the end of the Neolithic. This would agree more closely with the Early Bronze Age date for the underlying tree root. Most flints lay within the top 100mm of the deposit, indicating little vertical movement of artefacts. However, the area excavated was too small for any pattern to be discernible in their horizontal distribution. The flints were thinly scattered, possibly reflecting the site's peripheral position at the edge of Thorney Island, or perhaps suggesting that they had accumulated over a period of limited activity. The material probably came from temporary encampments on the river bank.

Flood layers were found on site P sealing the sand up to -0.15m OD. Although no dating evidence was found associated with these deposits their levels would seem to suggest that they were deposited during the Late Neolithic and Early Bronze Age, perhaps in part whilst Structures 1 and 3 were in use. They all lay to the east of the higher ground and consisted of an orange sandy clay sealed by a blue clay that was in turn sealed by an orange sandy clay. These deposits were filling a channel or inlet, the south side of which was revetted by Structures 1 and 3. One of them, P[118], contained a scapula and an almost complete mandible from a horse. The measurements of these bones indicate animals of comparable size. In all probability they are derived from the same animal, possibly from primary carcass processing and carcass disposal of a working animal, rather than waste disposal from domestic consumption.

To the south of Structure 1 on site P (see Fig 6), on the

higher ground, lay a number of features that have been ascribed to this period owing to their level and to the fact that they are overlain by river silts that elsewhere can be demonstrated to date to the Late Bronze Age or Iron Age. Part of a circular pit, 0.70m in diameter and 0.84m deep was found continuing beyond the edge of excavation. To the north lay a shallow gully aligned south-west–north-east, 0.52m across and 0.20m deep. To the east lay a north–south gully, at least 0.56m wide (probably originally 0.62m wide) and 0.22m deep. Just to the south of this gully lay two very narrow and shallow cuts in the sand. These were pointed, only 40mm–100mm across and at least 1.1m long. They may have been ard marks, indicating ploughing. They were aligned east–west, running parallel to the edge of Structure 1, and seem likely to pre-date Structure 3 as that was constructed higher up the slope, which was presumably then covered by water. Both these and the gully were filled with a waterlaid clay-silt-sand.

Probably post-dating the construction of Structure 3 were a number of other features that were overlain by the same river silts. A north-west–south-east aligned gully that sloped down to the north was 0.75m wide and 0.48m deep. It was filled with a clay-silt-sand waterlaid deposit that covered the natural sand, suggesting that it was filled when the whole area was inundated by rising river levels.

Fills of the channel to the north of Structure 3 consisted of brown sandy silt clays, and brown clays. Overlying the uppermost of these were two almost entirely decayed timbers laid end to end across the channel from north to south. In total these were 2.15m long and between 0.13m and 0.25m across. A further 0.22m to the east lay another decayed timber on a similar alignment and 1.15m east of this lay another aligned south-east–north-west. Because of the level of almost total decay of the timbers it was impossible to tell whether these were parts of a fallen tree or had been deliberately laid as some form of track across the infilled marshy channel.

On the east side of the island, on site S (Fig 14), a single posthole was found in a test pit. The posthole was 0.19m deep and was sealed by a layer of pale sand similar to that found on sites F and G. Here the layer was up to 0.32m thick and contained two pieces of burnt flint and a waste flake. Whilst only a single posthole was found this presumably relates to the similar postholes and gullies found on the previous site excavated in this area, Cromwell Green (WCG78). The relevant features from that site are shown on Fig 14. On that site five postholes, two gullies and two 'irregular depressions' were found containing worked flints and pottery. These were sealed by a grey sand layer containing pottery originally dated to the Late Iron Age (Mills 1980, 18–21). Revision of this dating (below, 3.4 and Chapters 16.1 and 16.3) has led to these finds being ascribed to the Late Neolithic to Early–Middle Bronze Age.

Immediately to the east stakeholes were found sealed by a pale brown sand containing about 30 struck flints and pottery (Whipp and Platts 1976, 353). This pottery has also been redated from the Iron Age to the Late Neolithic to Middle Bronze Age.

The higher ground

Sand and gravel lay at a higher level on site C(i) (Fig 15) and into it was cut a large east–west aligned feature, C[229], about 6.6m wide and at least 0.4m deep. It had a very shallow slope on the north side and a much steeper slope to the south. It was filled with yellow-brown sand containing one sherd of pottery. This feature may have been either a ditch or a quarry pit. Overlying the backfill was a compact gravel surface. To the north lay a shallow pit 0.97m in diameter and 0.20m deep, filled with brown sandy gravel, and the south-eastern end of what may have been a linear feature, 0.20m deep, filled with gravel and grey silty clay.

All these features on site C(i) cut into the natural ground surface and are interpreted as being of Late Neolithic or Early Bronze Age date. Only C[229] contained any datable material, one sherd of pottery, and that disintegrated during processing. It was identified, however, as being similar to that from site F which is dated to the Middle Bronze Age. The remaining pits have been assigned to this period on the basis of their fills, which were all largely sand- or gravel-derived whereas those from the subsequent periods were markedly different.

The attribution of these features to this period should be seen as tenuous without further dating evidence. However, if this attribution is correct then there was activity on the higher ground of Thorney Island in addition to the activity along the foreshore.

Two undated circular postholes were found cutting the sand on site D (Fig 16). They were filled with light grey sand, somewhat similar to that filling the postholes on sites F, S and U. Immediately to the east lay the south-western corner of a pit at least 1.10m east–west by 0.30m north–south and 0.16m deep. It was filled with brown sand and organic material.

Neither the postholes nor the pit on site D can be dated but their position in the sequence and their fills tentatively suggest they may date to the same period as the dated postholes on site F. The postholes suggest some form of structural activity with perhaps waste disposal in the pit.

Waterlaid sandy clays overlay the sand on the west side of the island, as the ground sloped down towards the Tyburn on site E. These deposits appeared to have been laid down by flooding of the island and contained flecks of charcoal and shell and two worked flints. A curving north-east–south-west aligned channel cut the waterlaid layers as they sloped down towards the Tyburn to the west. The channel was 0.30m deep and only its eastern side was located. It was filled with a dark green-grey clay that was similarly deposited by flooding.

3.4 Discussion

Previous work had suggested scattered finds from the Neolithic and Bronze Age and more intense activity from the Iron Age along the foreshore on Thorney Island. Revision of this dating

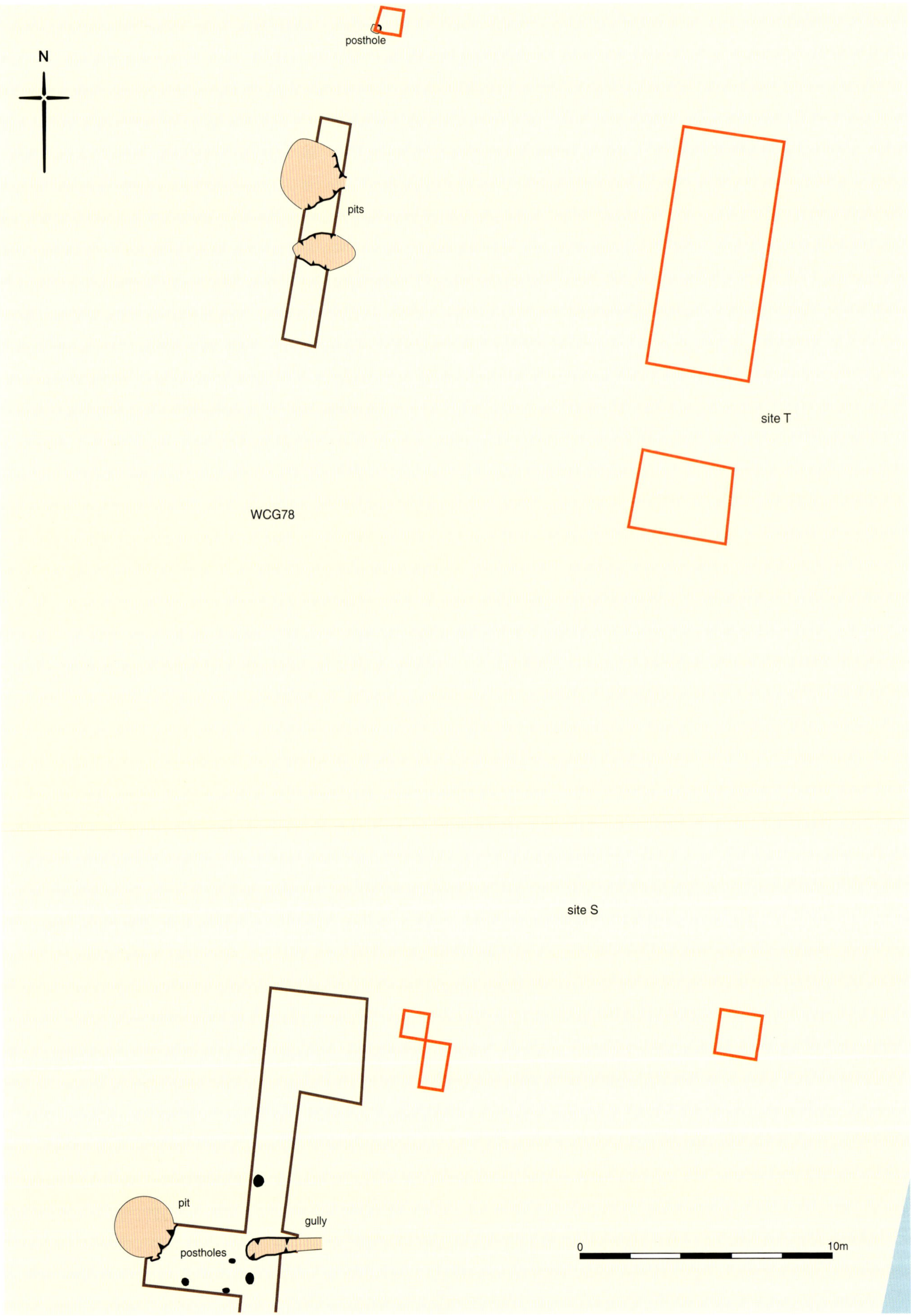

Fig 14 Detailed plan of the archaeological features on site S and the previously excavated features from Cromwell Green, period 1 (scale 1:200)

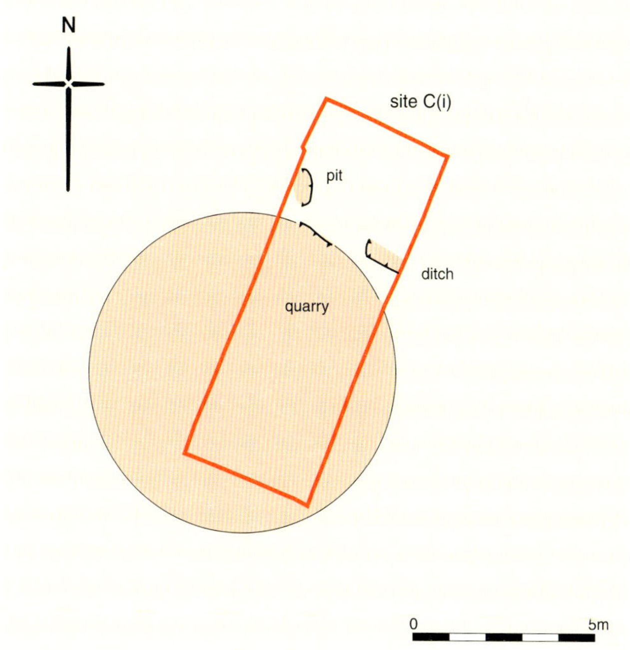

Fig 15 Detailed plan of the archaeological features on site C(i), period 1 (scale 1:200)

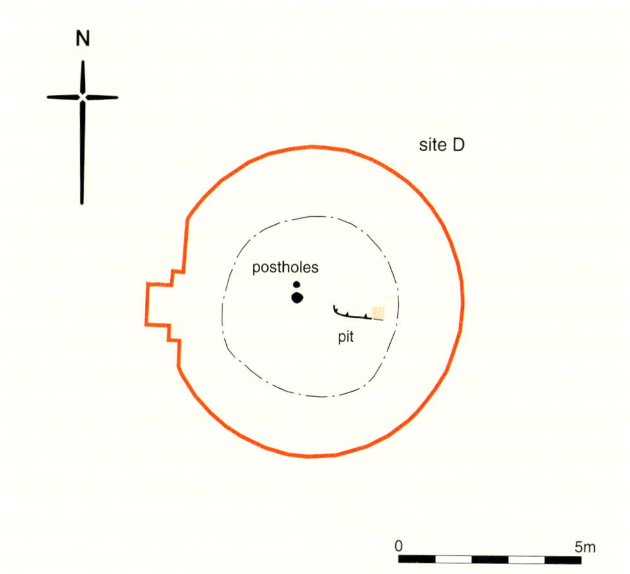

Fig 16 Detailed plan of the archaeological features on site D, period 1 (scale 1:200)

and the recent excavations indicate that this scheme should now be reversed, with the major evidence for activity now occurring in the Late Neolithic and Early Bronze Age and scattered find-spots pointing to some activity in the Late Bronze Age and Iron Age (Table 4).

The highest level of the Thames at Westminster during this period has been shown to have been at about -1.0m OD *c* 2000 BC and at about 0.5m OD *c* 1000 BC. It should be remembered that by this time the Thames was tidal and fluctuated between about -0.5m and -2.0m OD. These levels give the maximum areas of available land for occupation and can be compared on Figs 5 and 20.

The ceramic assemblages from the sand layer covering the foreshore from sites F, G, K, T and Cromwell Green date from the Neolithic to the Middle Bronze Age. The vertical distribution of flints within this sand suggests that this material has not been subject to redeposition and thus that it accumulated over a considerable period of time with the majority of the artefacts occurring in the top 100mm of the layer. The postholes and gullies also seem to be of a similar date.

Many of the features are undated, as indeed are Structures 1 and 2. These can only be positioned in the dating scheme by their levels and the suggested levels of the river at the time.

The flint

The most important assemblage of material from Thorney Island (Figs 17–19) is the flint, both in terms of the dating and in terms of the types of activity and comparison with other sites. The flint work was recovered from a wide area on the northern and eastern sides of Thorney Island, at points that would have overlooked the prehistoric courses of the Thames and the Tyburn. Over 60% of the material lay within a series of alluvial sands that mantle the natural contours of the island; smaller amounts were recovered from a handful of prehistoric

Table 4 Selected dating evidence, period 1 (see Chapter 16.3 for expansion of description codes)

Land use	Activity	Context	Evidence	Description	Date range
Structure 2	cut	F[7]	ceramic	FLIN; FLIN1	Late Neolithic/Early Bronze Age
Open Area 1	ditch	K[32]	ceramic	FLIN	Late Neolithic/Early Bronze Age
Open Area 1	cut	K[31]	ceramic	FLIN	Late Neolithic/Early Bronze Age
Open Area 1	cut	K[59]	ceramic	FLIN	Late Neolithic/Early Bronze Age
Open Area 1	foreshore deposit	G[39]	ceramic	CP; FLIN; FLIN1; FLIN2	Late Neolithic/Early Bronze Age
Open Area 1	foreshore deposit	G[47]	ceramic	CP; FLIN; FLIN1; FLIN2	Late Neolithic/Early Bronze Age
Open Area 1	foreshore deposit	G[47]	flint	arrowhead	Late Neolithic/Early Bronze Age
Open Area 1	foreshore deposit	G[48]	ceramic	FLIN	Late Neolithic/Early Bronze Age
Open Area 1	foreshore deposit	F[7]	flint	axe	Neolithic
Open Area 1	foreshore deposit	site F	radiocarbon date	Beta 119790; see Table 56	2140–1730 cal BC
Open Area 1	foreshore deposit	site F	radiocarbon date	Beta 122929; see Table 56	3100–2690 cal BC

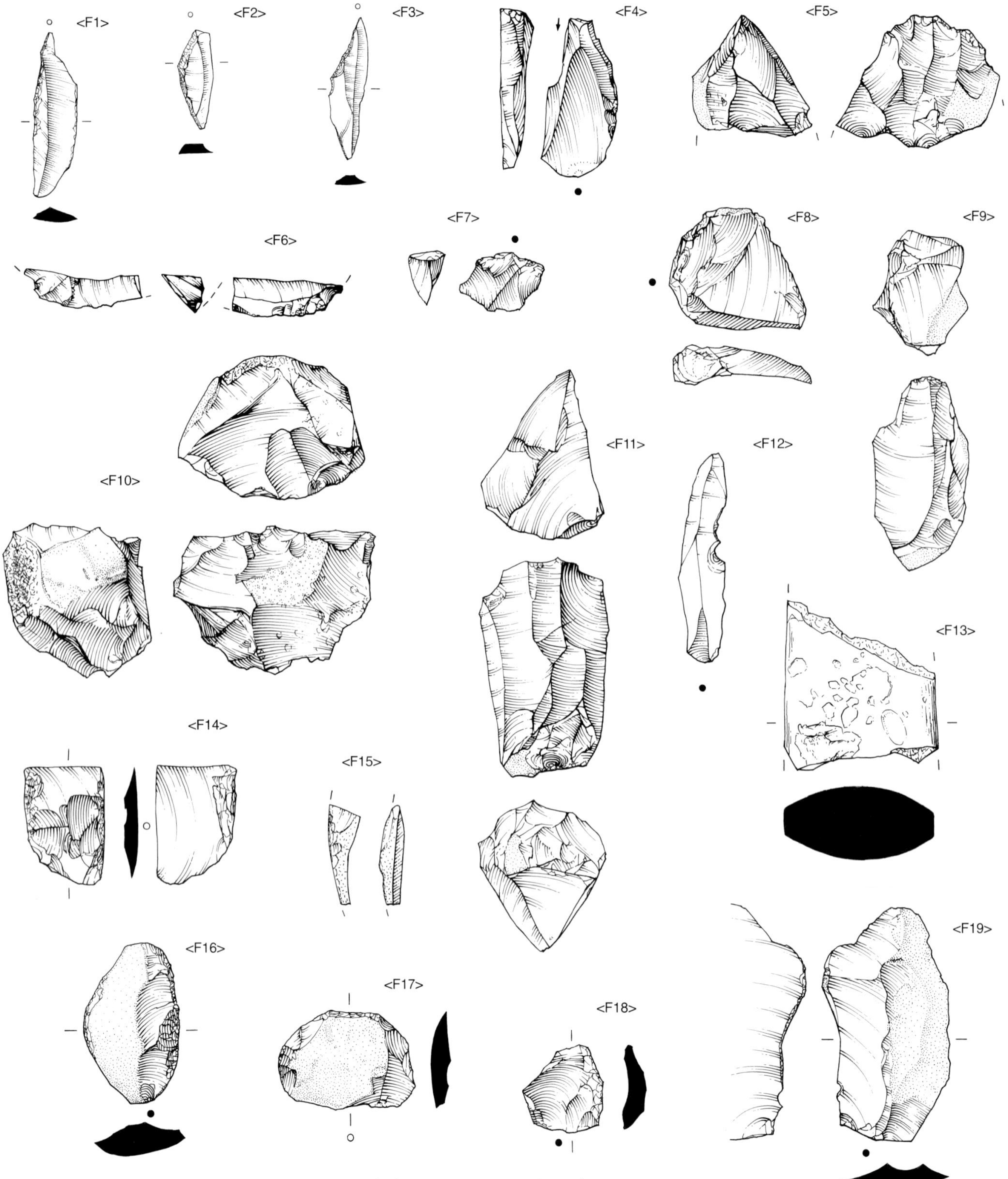

Fig 17 The flint work from Cromwell Green, <F1>–<F19> (scale 2:3 except <F1>–<F3> 1:1)

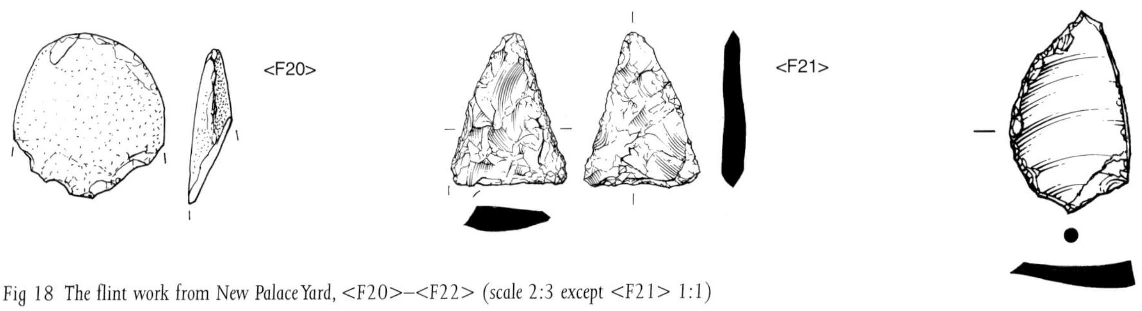

Fig 18 The flint work from New Palace Yard, <F20>–<F22> (scale 2:3 except <F21> 1:1)

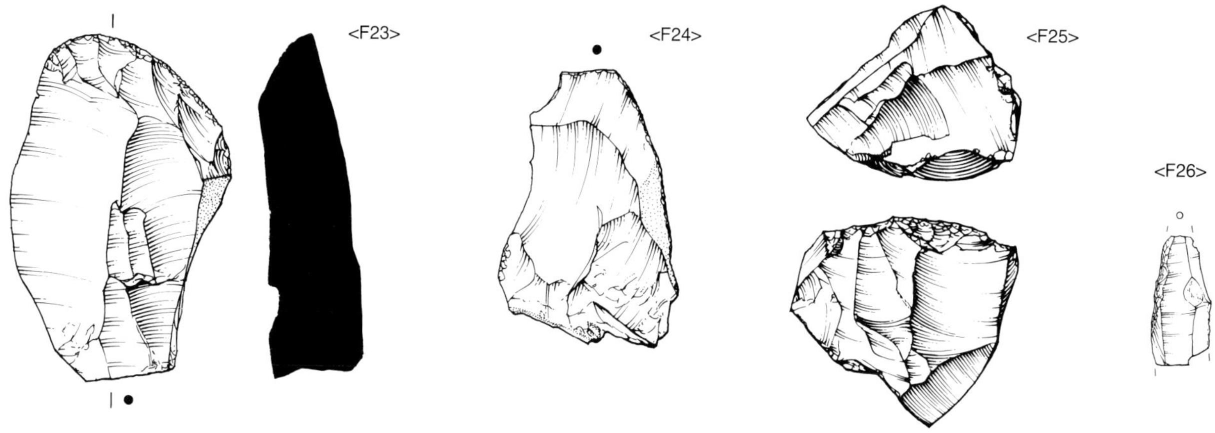

Fig 19 The flint work from the southern and eastern edges of Thorney Island, <F23>–<F26> (scale 1:1)

features sealed by these sands and from later contexts including the fills of several palaeochannels. Most of the burnt flint was recovered from the alluvial sands. Given the area's topographic advantages, it is no surprise that the material studied indicates a wide date range of activity that spans the period traditionally labelled later Mesolithic to later Neolithic/Early Bronze Age.

The dating and affinities of the flint work considered here rely on the recognition of diagnostic artefact types, for independent dating is limited to a few sherds of pottery of Neolithic/Early Bronze Age type recovered from several of the sites. These include two beaker sherds from Cromwell Green, and a possible collared urn sherd from site G (Chapter 16.3).

Traditional Mesolithic activity is attested by microliths, adze fragments, adze-sharpening flakes and a single burin. To these can be added a majority of the blades, blade cores and doubtless a number of the complete and fragmentary flakes and flakes/blades. The microliths appear to belong to narrow blade later Mesolithic forms, with the bi-truncated piece from site K perhaps related to basally retouched 'Horsham' points. No microburins were recognised amongst the limited assemblage and none of the scrapers need be this early either. The adze fragments and sharpening flakes complement the complete adzes recovered during building works adjacent to Westminster Bridge and from Thames dredging (Lacaille 1961, 131–2). The limited evidence currently available need not indicate anything more than small groups of people engaged in 'short-stay' activities, perhaps geared around the exploitation of adjacent foreshore resources such as animal game and flint cobbles. Further evidence of the presence of such groups in the locality is provided by the flint work recovered from the admiralty site to the north (Abbott 1919, 113–14; Lacaille 1961, 125–8) and by a red deer antler-base mattock from a former course of the Tyburn at New Scotland Yard (Lacaille 1961, 134).

Traditional Neolithic/Bronze Age activity is no better represented and comprises several fragments of ground flint axes and two arrowheads, together with a small beaker flint assemblage from a shallow gully at Cromwell Green (Fig 17). A number of the squat flakes and partially worked nodules (PWC) may be similarly dated. Both ground axes are of slender form: that from site F has marked side facets (as Field and Woolley 1984, 90 class Cii), which have been deliberately created, and it appears to have been broken before being burnt. Neither ground axe can be more closely dated within the Neolithic period and both fragments complement the complete axes recovered during Thames dredging works (Adkins and Jackson 1978). On balance, the two arrowheads are likely to belong within the traditional later Neolithic or Early Bronze Age. Though not closely dated, petit tranchet derivative types have turned up on later Neolithic henges (Green 1980, 113), whilst triangular/oblique arrowheads have reasonable early to mid second millennium cal BC associations (Green 1980, 114–15, 142–3). It is likely that the triangular arrowhead from site G was accidentally burnt, possibly during the cooking of an animal in whose carcass it had lodged; the quantity of burnt flint from this site is noted in Table 21 and is touched on further below. The small flint assemblage from shallow gully context [83] at Cromwell Green is associated with two sherds of beaker pottery, and includes a small thumbnail scraper of characteristic beaker type, together with a fragment of a second larger scraper. Associated pieces include a fragment of a flaked axe together with a number of squat flakes and small blades, many of which had been broken.

Lithics in the landscape

At site G analysis of the three-dimensional distribution of the flint work showed that a good proportion of it lay within the uppermost 100mm of the alluvial sands (here about 200mm thick), with apparently relatively little vertical dispersal down the profile. This suggests that much of the material is *in situ*, and has undergone little post-depositional disturbance. More significantly it rules out the possibility that the artefacts were redeposited with the alluvial sands, and also suggests that the top of the sands approximates to a palaeo-landsurface (or surfaces). Furthermore, the numbers of broken flake/blade fragments recovered from the alluvial sands here and elsewhere could also indicate that such surfaces had been subjected to a degree of weathering, reworking and trampling by people and animals. The wide date range of the struck flint recovered from the sands underlines the long availability of these surfaces.

Taken together, the likely overall density of struck flint work per square metre on Thorney Island appears to be low, especially when compared with the Mesolithic butchery and/or 'home-base' sites such as Three Ways Wharf, Uxbridge (Lewis in prep) and the B&Q site, Old Kent Road (Rogers 1990). This suggests either that the areas examined lay on the edges of more intensively utilised points in the local landscape, or that there was a genuinely low level of activity. In view of the likely topographical advantages that the locality offered (and the small-scale nature of the archaeological work), the former explanation is favoured here.

Though Thorney Island has produced only a small and restricted flint assemblage, the distribution of certain artefacts across the landscape hints at the presence of favoured locations and patterns of behaviour. Thus cores and core fragments are concentrated on a few sites (Cromwell Green, Storey's Gate and site K) that presumably lay close to areas of raw material available on the shingle foreshores and stream beds. Certainly, the odd ground axe apart, little in the way of non-local flint is present. Tool types typifying hunting activity are also present, for instance, the later Mesolithic microliths and Neolithic arrowheads, together with a few others such as scrapers (usually associated with the working of hide) and the single burin (usually associated with the working of bone/antler). However, the low numbers of scrapers and the total absence of microburins might be taken as evidence of short-stay opportunistic subsistence foraging rather than anything involving longer duration 'home-base' type activity, but again the small-scale nature of the archaeological work needs to be borne in mind. Furthermore, the quantity of burnt unworked flint recovered from a restricted area of the alluvial sands at site G is suggestive of localised cooking activity. It may be relevant that burnt mounds are often sited in low-lying streamside localities, as at Phoenix Wharf, Bermondsey (Merriman 1990).

Local and regional patterns

The Westminster material considered here can be compared with other lithic assemblages coming to light in the flood plain of the lower Thames valley (Warren 1977; Taylor 1996). Geographically, the closest are those appearing on the Surrey bank in north Southwark and Lambeth (Cotton 1992; Bishop 1996). Particular points of comparison include the restricted range of contexts from which the material is now regularly recovered in these low-lying areas, consisting for the most part of a few discrete features sealed by horizontal alluvial sands. The latter deposits routinely produce mixed assemblages of traditional later Mesolithic narrow blade microliths and adze-sharpening flakes alongside Neolithic arrowheads and ground axe fragments, with Early Bronze Age flint work and pottery sealed within the underlying features. This pattern of recovery is reasonably widespread and predictable and worthy of a further and more detailed examination than is possible here.

The major conclusion, however, is that whilst recent work has redated the activity and expanded our knowledge and the artefactual assemblage, much larger-scale excavation on what was then dry land is required to date the activity more accurately and to understand the settlement patterns.

4

The Late Bronze Age and Iron Age, *c* 1500 BC–AD 43 (period 2)

4.1 Environmental and topographical background

The River Thames

Much of this period, unfortunately, is not represented in the sedimentary record owing to a significant truncation that has removed any Late Iron Age, Roman and Saxon deposits. This hiatus is found on many sites in the Thorney Island area and the last sediments present appear to date from roughly 800 cal BC. Isolated later material is available enabling a few general statements to be made, but these should not be taken as representative of events around the whole of the Thorney Island area.

The palaeoecological evidence from the beginning of this period shows a transition from the dominance of freshwater conditions to the incursion of the tidal head into the study area. This is hard to date with any certainty. Freshwater conditions prevail at the upper reaches of a tidal river (for instance in the modern Thames at Teddington) and therefore the tidal head is likely to have moved upstream of Westminster by the time it is observed in the microfossil record. In all probability, it is towards the end of period 1 that the Westminster foreshore started being affected by tides, but it is not until the later Bronze Age that this can be proven. The best evidence is found in the diatom record from Storey's Gate, which indicates estuarine waters backing up the Tyburn at this date. The reasons for why this occurred at this particular date are unclear, but are associated with an increase in the rate of relative sea-level rise in southern England at this time (Long et al 2000). It seems possible that this fundamental change in fluvial conditions is at least partly the cause of Thorney Island eroding as it did.

The examination of site H indicates that by this period the channel observed from the Neolithic/Bronze Age transition had migrated away from the excavated area, leaving exposed mudflats, either at the edge of the palaeochannel or possibly the Thames foreshore. Towards the end of the Bronze Age, the diatom evidence indicates that marine influence had reached the site with the presence of outer-estuary species such as *Cymatosira belgica*. It also confirms the reconstruction at Storey's Gate of estuarine waters encroaching on Thorney Island as the tidal head migrated upstream at the rate of five metres per year (Sidell et al 2000). The diatom evidence for this initial phase shows the first non-freshwater assemblage to be outer-estuary flora, suggesting it was not a gradual but a rapid incursion of tidal waters. This will have had a dramatic effect upon the low-lying land surrounding Thorney Island, which appears to have become rapidly submerged.

During excavations for an underground car park at New Palace Yard, riverine deposits were encountered and sampled (Limbrey nd). These deposits dated from the Late Iron Age to the Saxon period. The mollusc fauna from the lowest horizons sampled (between OD and -0.3m OD) indicate a combination of local terrestrial (albeit marshy) environments subject to the forces of a large channel flooding the site and adjacent areas, bringing in terrestrial molluscs to this site. The sampled sediments at this horizon were intercalated sands and peats indicating a cycle of flooding and periods of marshy development.

Palaeoecology

Site B provides information on the development of the local vegetation in this period. As identified in the later years of period 1, the woodland element became denuded, with a very obvious reduction in lime (*Tilia*). Alder (*Alnus*) is certainly present, and indeed dominant in the sequence examined, but this appears to be derived from wetland conditions occurring close to the river side, rather than reflecting dryland forest cover. At *c* 1100 cal BC there are traces of some woodland species, including oak (*Quercus*) and hazel (*Corylus avellana*), and these should perhaps be envisaged as small stands surviving the major Bronze Age clearances on and around Thorney Island. The evidence for cereal cultivation previously noted remains consistent in this period again at site B, with cereal pollen and associated weed taxa in the pollen spectra. This is almost certainly derived from the dryland environment either beyond the Tyburn or possibly on Thorney Island itself. This picture of low-lying freshwater marsh fringing the higher ground, which was mainly open with sporadic woodland, is also supported further away from Thorney Island. At Great Peter Street (Malcolm 1994) two types of contemporary sub-environment are represented. First, there are pure aquatic species that could be associated with in-channel deposits; these include water plantain (*Alisma* spp) and crowfoots (*Ranunculus* subgen *Batrachium*). Second, there are marsh species, including rushes (*Juncus* spp) and sedges (*Carex* spp). Towards the end of the Bronze Age estuarine waters encroached upon Thorney Island, succeeding the alder carr freshwater marsh. Evidence for this comes from salt-marsh species such as thrift (*Armeria*) and goosefoots (*Chenopodium* spp).

The second phase of sedimentation observed at Storey's Gate can be dated to this period (Sidell et al 2000, 36). It is of minerogenic rather than organic sedimentation. The concurrent ecological change was a reduction of the reed swamp elements and a marked expansion of alder, with some willow (*Salix*) in addition. As seen at site B, the freshwater reed swamp here was also overtaken and destroyed through estuarine sedimentation as the area was flooded by brackish water and as the subsequent waterlogging caused a return to sedge/reed fen over extensive areas, removing the alder carr. Nevertheless, there is still a signal within the pollen profile of continuing cereal cultivation. This, presumably, was confined to the higher ground away from the encroaching Thames and Tyburn margins.

The Iron Age is poorly represented in all analyses undertaken in the Westminster area, owing in part to an apparent massive hiatus in the sedimentary sequence from approximately the mid Iron Age onwards, which removed any contemporary sediment deposited around the margins of Thorney Island. It is not possible to date the start of this erosion, but the encroachment of estuarine waters may have been the beginning of this the process. Although this did not affect the top of Thorney Island, excavations in this location have unfortunately not yielded appropriate sediment of this date either. Limited information is available from organic deposits at the base of a sequence from New Palace Yard (Greig 1992), indicating that in this location, at least, the mixed woodland environment of oak, lime and elm (*Ulmus*) was still present during the Late Iron Age. Some of the mollusc species (for instance, *Discus rotundatus* and *Carychium tridentatum*) also indicate the presence of some local woodland. Some wetland species were present but they formed only a small part of the assemblage, surprising from such a peaty deposit. A further peculiarity is present in the Early Iron Age deposits at Storey's Gate, namely, the presence of fir (*Abies*). Whilst it is possible that this was a component of the isolated treescape, the possibility of marine transport from some distance away should be borne in mind.

4.2 Archaeological background

It has previously been suggested that there was significant evidence of Iron Age activity on Thorney Island. Most of the pottery recovered from Cromwell Green had originally been dated to the Iron Age (Mills 1980, 29) but this has now been redated to the later Neolithic or Bronze Age (Chapter 3.4). Other Iron Age finds have been recovered from the area. A fired clay spindle whorl was recovered from riverlaid deposits at site T (below, 4.4; Whipp and Platts 1976, 353, fig 4 no. 12) and residual sherds dating to the Late Bronze Age to Early Iron Age were recovered from the Westminster Abbey undercroft (below, 4.4; Swain 1995, 80).

Other material from immediately to the north of the Tyburn has also been recovered. This includes redeposited material at Treasury Green and worked alder timbers at Richmond Terrace. These perhaps formed part of a timber revetment embanking the Thames, radiocarbon dated to 810–410 cal BC (Harwell 6393, 2540±120 BP) (Andrews and Merriman 1986). This consisted of a base plate with a vertical post and possible evidence of a second vertical post. The conditions under which this was recorded mean that its extent was not recovered with any degree of certainty. The location of the finds along with the new archaeological features is shown in Fig 20.

4.3 Archaeological evidence

The River Thames foreshore

The estuarine clay deposited in period 1 on site B was overlain by a distinct horizon of organic clays, silts and peat at about OD. Its surface was located between 0.48m and -0.61m OD. The organic peaty clay contained the fruits and seeds of a wide range of plants, especially wetland species, although plants of disturbed ground and waste places were also present, though less well represented. The plant assemblage suggests that the organic layers represent marshland or fen between the water's edge and drier land.

A sample from peat layer B[108] gave a radiocarbon date of 1130–810 cal BC (Beta 88701, 2800±70 BP) (Table 5), suggesting that the peat formed during the Late Bronze Age. Judging from the similarity of the stratigraphic sequence across site B it seems likely that the contexts in this group are broadly contemporary.

Similar layers of peat and organic clay at or just below OD lay on site F to the south and it is inferred that these date to the same period.

To the north-east on site H the surface of the estuarine silts deposited in period 1 was cut by three hollows or channels H[37], H[33] and H[35], which were about 0.25m deep and filled with peat. Hollow H[37] lay at -0.96m OD, whilst the others, further to the east, lay at -1.14m OD. They were all undated, but their peaty fills suggest that they may have been contemporaneous with the Late Bronze Age peat on site B. However, hollow H[37] contained occasional small fragments of chalk, which is an unusual material to find in a prehistoric context in central London.

4.4 Discussion

A number of problems of interpretation are associated with the Late Bronze Age and Iron Age periods at Westminster. The foreshore deposits seem to have been largely removed by a major erosional event occurring at some time between the Early Iron Age and the 12th century, although there is evidence for peat formation in the Late Bronze Age. A possible hypothesis is that the major flooding that occurred during the middle of the 11th century removed the foreshore deposits and deposited some silts on the higher ground, where the waters were shallower. It is therefore difficult to judge the pattern of deposition by the river although peat in the Late Bronze Age on sites B and F suggests a fall in the river level whilst peat recovered in New Palace Yard ata level of about OD, dated to the Late Iron Age through to the Early Saxon period, suggests another fall. There is certainly no evidence that the river was tidal at this point, though it had been in the Middle Bronze Age, which would certainly indicate a fall in the river level. Before this apparent fall in the Late Iron Age the river level may have risen to about OD, explaining the peat at this level. This is somewhat later than the radiocarbon dates for peat deposits at a nearby site in Richmond Terrace, which were recorded at -2.0m OD and -0.5m OD and gave respective radiocarbon dates of 8000–7350 cal BC (Harwell 5741, 8580±100 BP) and 2880–2470 cal BC (Harwell 5742, 4110±80 BP), but closer to the radiocarbon date of 810–410 cal BC from an alder 'base plate' resting on a peat layer at the same site (Andrews and Merriman 1986).

If the predicted river level during this period is correct, then the available area for occupation was greatly reduced, as can be seen from Fig 20. A slight increase of 0.5m or more decreases the amount of dry land even more dramatically. This might explain the reduced settlement and occupation evidence at Westminster. However, the progressive fall in the river level during the Iron Age as the tidal head moved back downstream would have increased the space available for occupation. As elsewhere (see Chapter 14.1) there does not seem to have been a reoccupation of settlements in the Iron Age after the fall in the river level. Clearly, however, Iron Age finds have been recovered, mostly beneath the abbey on the highest ground. This might suggest that the areas above 1.0m OD would be the most likely to have sustained settlement activity, with the marginal marshy land along the river being less favourable for habitation.

Certainly most finds have come from the higher ground although one artefact was recovered from the foreshore. This was a fired clay spindle whorl, T<1>, recovered from T[213], a blue-grey riverlaid clay (Fig 21). The spindle whorl has a running pattern of pinprick decoration and horizontal and vertical lines scratched to form irregular panels. A similar example, decorated with a pinprick pattern, was recovered from the General Post Office site in the City (GPO75) and other similar objects have been recovered from Iron Age settlement sites. The most comparable is from the hillfort at Danebury with a decoration of scratched lines interspersed with many fine dots (Poole 1991, 370–2, fig 7.42, no. 7.85). Other fired clay objects from Glastonbury and Meare lake village are decorated with similar patterns of incised vertical and diagonal lines and fine dots (Bulleid and St George Gray 1917, 557, pl 89, no. Y18; Coles 1987, 64–5, fig 3.9, no. D27).

Most of the remaining Iron Age finds came from the Westminster Abbey undercroft (WST86). This assemblage was

Table 5 Selected dating evidence, period 2

Land use	Activity	Context	Evidence	Description	Date range
Open Area 1	foreshore deposits	site B	radiocarbon date	Beta 88701; see Table 56	1130–810 cal BC

wholly residual but includes a rim with finger-tipping on the upper edge, <P7>, and a sherd from the shoulder of a carinated jar, <P8>, with fingernail decoration (Fig 21). The rim sherd also has part of a perforation or deep impression surviving. These feature sherds suggest a date in the Late Bronze Age/Early Iron Age transition period and parallels can be found in vessels from Heathrow, Petters Sports Field, Egham and Runnymede Bridge, Egham (Canham 1978, 21–2, figs 13.3, 14.35; O'Connell 1986, 65, fig 44, nos 34–9; Longley 1980, 165). The other sherds are all abraded flint-tempered body sherds with no diagnostic features. Surface treatments are confined to one sherd with burnished surfaces and one with external wipe marks. This does suggest that more evidence of occupation activity would be recovered from excavations on the highest ground.

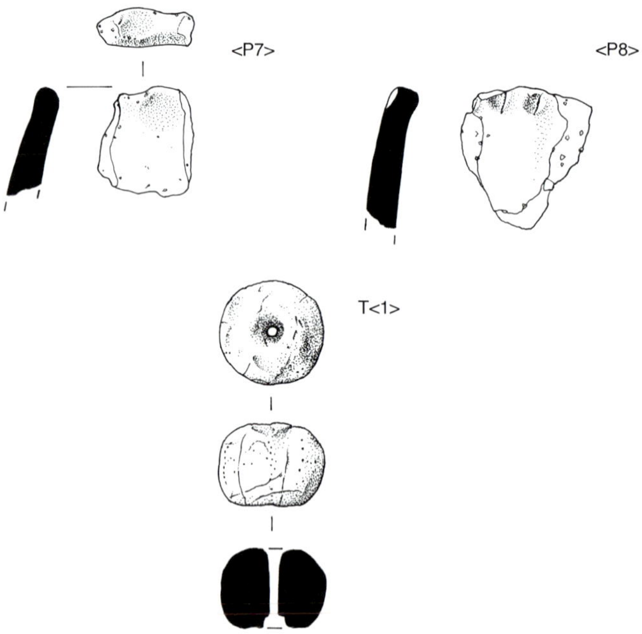

Fig 21 Iron Age material from Thorney Island: fired clay spindle whorl T<1> and pottery <P7>–<P8> (scale 1:2)

Fig 20 Plan of the archaeological features and location of finds, period 2 (scale 1:2500). For key to site codes, see Tables 1–3

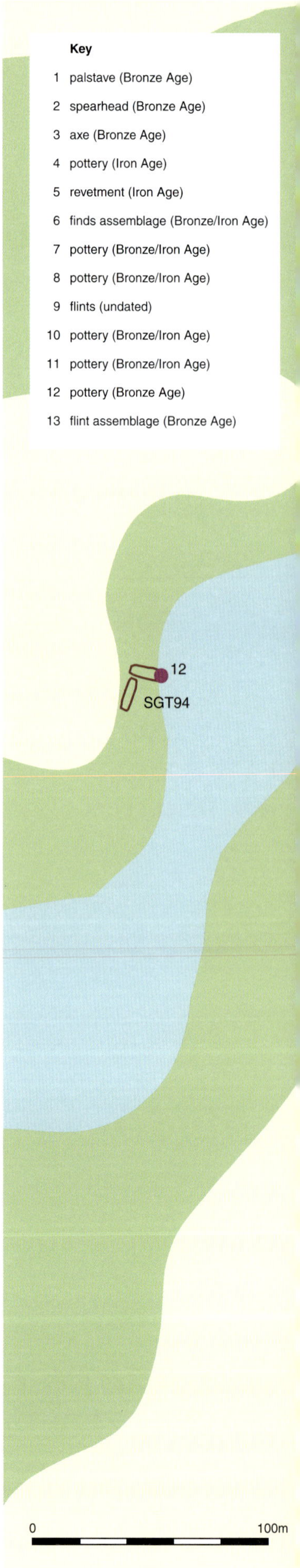

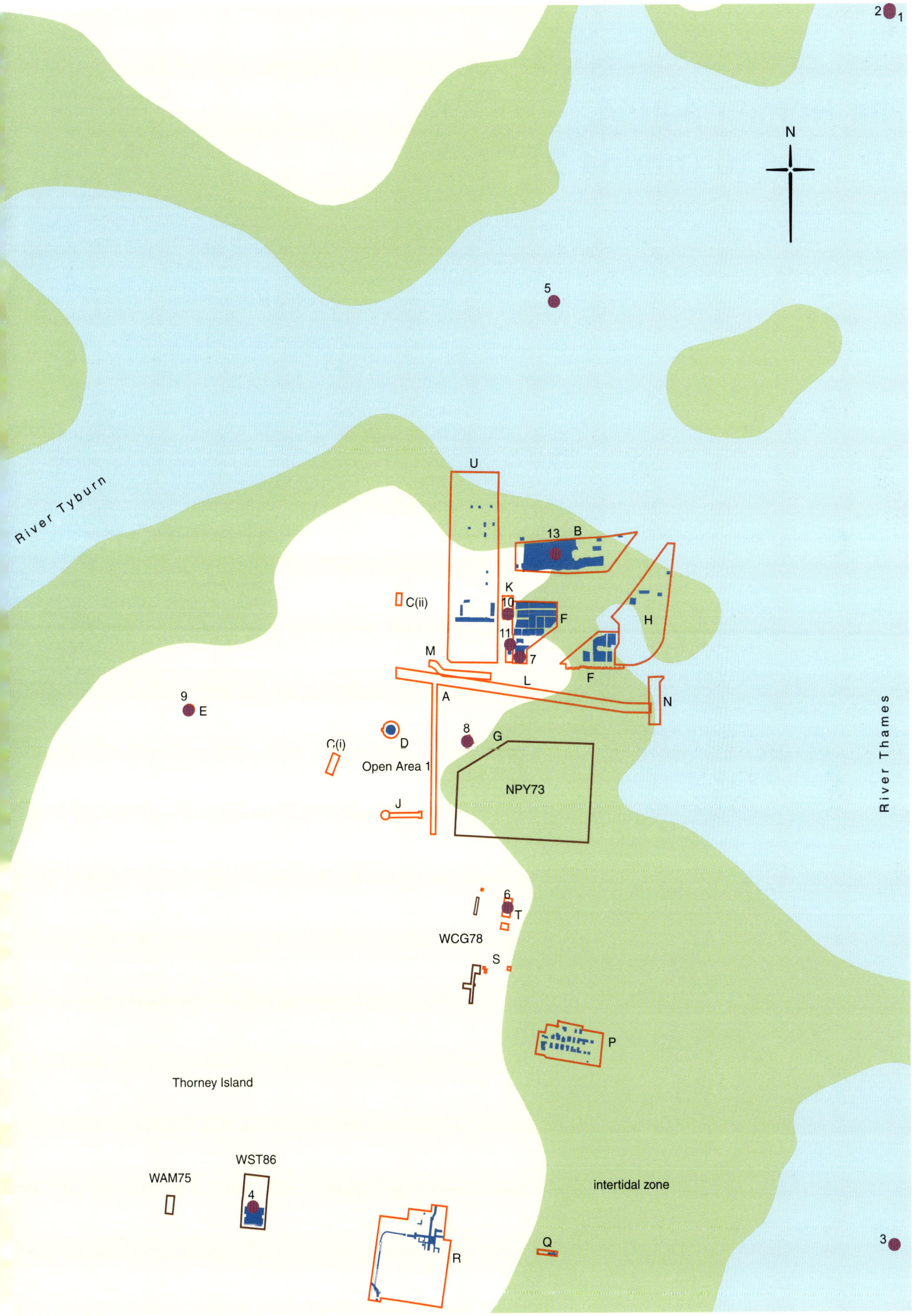

N
River Tyburn
River Thames
Thorney Island
intertidal zone
NPY73
WCG78
WST86
WAM75
Open Area 1
A
B
C(i)
C(ii)
D
E
F
G
H
J
K
L
M
N
P
Q
R
S
T
U
1
2
3
4
5
6
7
8
9
10
11
13

5

The Roman period, AD 43–410 (period 3)

5.1 Environmental and topographical background

Practically no evidence has survived from the Roman period. It is possible that very little sediment was being deposited at this date if conditions were similar to the Late Bronze Age and Iron Age, that is, scouring by the Thames removing sediment rather than depositing it. Certainly, there is no information about the Thames from the sites examined as part of the JLEP. In fact, the only evidence comes from several sites examined in the 1970s. At the site of Cromwell Green (Mills 1980, 21–2) flood silts containing abraded Roman pottery were identified but these may be Saxon in date; no detailed examination was undertaken, so it is not possible to establish whether this deposit was freshwater or estuarine. This is a particularly important question as other research in central London suggests that the mean tidal level of the Thames dropped relative to the land in the Roman period (Brigham 1990; Sidell 2003). This would have exposed more of the margins of Thorney Island and may have slowed the rate of erosion. Unfortunately, this must all remain speculation at present.

The excavation at New Palace Yard (Chapter 4.1) also yielded material of probable Roman date (Evans nd), although the date range extends into the Saxon period. The mollusc samples are thought on the whole to derive from freshwater conditions, but there are indications of serious floods. Evans suggests that by the Roman period, the influence of the Thames was less at this site then previously. This theory is based on reconstruction of a still-water environment in which reed swamp was able to take hold. He argues that this may have been due to a shift in the course of the river, but it may in fact have been due to a relative drop in river level, as identified at this date in other work (Brigham 1990, Sidell 2003). The final phase of sedimentation discussed with reference to the mollusc analysis indicates that once again the Thames was heavily influencing the site. Although this is thought in the original report to date to the late Roman period, the recalibration of the radiocarbon dates indicates that this phase could be dated to the Saxon period. It would seem that, as well as occasional floods, land that was previously exposed had by now been submerged for there is no evidence from the molluscs for terrestrial habitats. Evans discusses this in relation to a probable rise in relative sea level, and this suggestion is also supported by the other strands of research mentioned above.

Palaeoecology

Some limited information from New Palace Yard for this period has been published, but it should be borne in mind that the dating may not be wholly secure (Greig 1992). The pollen spectra indicate that the area was becoming increasingly waterlogged, with a constant presence of water pondweed (*Potamogeton* sp) and a concurrent reduction in the tree cover noted in the Late Iron Age levels at this site. Interestingly, there is an increase in herb species, particularly cereal, indicating that the area was being cultivated in this period. Whilst there does not appear to have been any evidence for cereal cultivation in the Iron Age from this specific area, it does seem that there was Iron Age cultivation in the area of Storey's Gate. The question is whether this represents a continuation of tradition from the earlier farming communities, or if this is a new agricultural system established under the Roman authority based in Londinium slightly to the east of Westminster. In the absence of additional information, this must be a question reserved for future investigations.

5.2 Archaeological background

No definite Roman features have been located on previous archaeological excavations carried out on Thorney Island. Roman artefacts have, however, occurred on most sites (Fig 22). Some of these may date silts along the Thames foreshore, such as an abraded sherd of Roman Oxfordshire red colour-coated ware found in the lowest silts of a stream channel at Cromwell Green (Mills 1978, 27), whilst others may reflect occupation sites, such as finds found beneath the abbey.

A number of antiquarian discoveries have been reported, mostly in the vicinity of Westminster Abbey. These include a Roman stone sarcophagus, found on the north side of the abbey, although it is described as being only 2ft below ground level (now at about 4.6m OD) (Poole 1870). Thought to have been reused during the Saxon period, it has an inscription indicating that it was originally for the remains of Valerius Armandinus. Roman walls and part of a hypocaust have been reported as coming from beneath the nave of Westminster Abbey (Westlake 1923, 2) and two pieces of Roman concrete floor from the southern side of the cloister and infirmary cloister (RCHME 1925, 148). The nave and choir of Edward the Confessor's church were also recorded as containing courses of Roman tile, and pieces of *opus signinum* were also recorded in dumped layers beneath the presbytery floor (Robinson 1910, 99–100; Tanner and Clapham 1933, 233). Whilst no features were found, during the excavation of the Westminster Abbey undercroft 27 sherds of pottery, stone (including marble) and large quantities of Roman brick and tile including a stamped flue tile were recovered (Waugh 1995, 80; Goffin and Crowley 1995, 97–9). Similarly, Roman residual finds were recovered from the excavation of the Westminster Abbey misericord in 1975 (WAM75). These consisted of nine sherds of pottery, two fragments of tile and one fragment of glass (Platts 1976, 159).

Other finds from the area listed in the Sites and Monuments Record include a vessel, a stylus, a bowl, a ring, a coin and a statue (Fig 22). A Roman boat recorded as having come from the Tyburn to the west of the island may, in fact, have been reused boat timbers in a revetment; there seems no good reason to ascribe them a Roman date.

It has been suggested that the alignment of the roads on either side of the Thames indicates Westminster to be the site of a ford. It is thought that this might have been the site of the original Roman river crossing during the invasion of AD 43. There is, however, no direct archaeological evidence for this (Sloane et al 1995, 369). The siting of Tothill Street (and indeed King Street) was clearly influenced by the natural topography, with Tothill Street crossing the shortest distance across the Tyburn. Continuing its line would take it underneath the abbey, across the highest ground, immediately south of the inlet into the Thames on site P and out on the sandbank into the Thames where the palace was later sited. This line certainly provides the maximum amount of dry ground and provides a persuasive route for a road but without any archaeological evidence it must remain speculation.

5.3 Archaeological evidence

Open Area 1

Aligned east–west across site C(i) (Fig 23), with its western terminus within the site but its eastern end outside it, was a ditch or robbed-out wall, 0.82m wide, with a possible posthole at the west end, though this may have been disturbance from a later posthole C[185] from period 6 (Chapter 8.3, Open Area 8). This disturbance also accounts for the single intrusive sherd of late 12th-century pottery. The possible robbed-out wall was 0.21m deep (with the possible posthole 0.35m deep) and was filled with blocks of unmortared Kentish ragstone, tile and gravel. The cut was sealed by the flood layer of the mid 11th century (Chapter 7.3, Open Area 3). The tile included fragments of imbrex and tegula and from fill C[184] in posthole C[185] (period 6) a fragment of combed box-flue tile that would have been used as part of a hypocaust. All are in fabric 2815 and date from the 1st to mid 2nd century (see Table 6). Materials in this fabric were manufactured at various kiln sites around Watling Street in the region between London and St Albans and perhaps also to the south-west of London. The overwhelming majority of the Roman ceramic building material found in the City belongs to this group, and the Westminster area was presumably drawing on the same sources of supply. One of the bricks shows two finger marks impressed into its top surface; just possibly these are an attempt at mortar keying, although this is not common on Roman bricks and is not likely to have been necessary anyway. It is no less plausible that the marks represent no more than a 'doodle', made by a worker in an idle moment at the yard. The flue tile, which is in the specific fabric 3006 (but close to fabric 2452), has mortar keying in the form of combing. It would have been used as part of a hypocaust heating system and therefore in a building of some social standing.

Between 3.05m and 3.25m to the south of and parallel to the robbed-out wall, overlying an undated gravel surface, were six unmortared blocks of Kentish ragstone C[199] in an area

0.67m wide and continuing off into the eastern limit of excavation. These formed a discrete feature but had no dating evidence associated with them; they were merely post-dated by the flood layers of the mid 11th century (Chapter 7.3, Open Area 3).

To the west of both walls lay a south-south-east–north-north-west aligned ditch whose relationship with the walls was not established, though it is likely to have been earlier than C[199]. It was up to 0.18m deep and 0.75m wide and its southern end was found. It was filled with grey clay with large quantities of charcoal and a few fragments of chalk and tile. One fragment of tile dates from the late 12th century but this is thought to be intrusive from linear cut C[194] in Open Area 8 (period 6); the remainder was dated to the 1st to mid 2nd century. This ditch does not seem likely to have belonged to the 12th century as it was definitely sealed by estuarine deposits, almost certainly of mid 11th-century date (Chapter 7.3, Open Area 3). Further to the south of the wall lay part of a shallow pit filled with orange silty clay. The function and date of this pit are uncertain but it was similarly post-dated by the alluvial deposits and itself post-dated the possible ditch/quarry pit from Open Area 1 in period 1 (Chapter 3.3).

The dating of the features from site C(i) is uncertain. Given that the flood layers sealing them probably date from the 11th century they must pre-date that. They are clearly of Roman date or later but the lack of associated finds means that they may date to the Saxon period and merely contain reused Roman material from a Roman building nearby. However, Saxon stone buildings are rare, although not necessarily so in relation to an abbey. The complete absence of any Saxon finds means that the features are provisionally dated to the Roman period. The function of the walls is also uncertain. The construction of the two would appear to have been different (one was laid in a cut, one on a pre-existing gravel surface), so they may not have been contemporary. They did, however, appear to be parallel and terminate on the same alignment though no wall was found to link the two. The lack of mortar associated with either wall suggests that these did not form major structures. The 13th-century north wall of Building 13 (Chapter 9.3, Fig 46), which cut through these levels, contained a fragment of Roman brick.

Whilst the other sites did not produce dated Roman deposits they did produce small quantities of residual or reused Roman artefacts, in particular tile, brick and *opus signinum*. Some fragments show signs of reuse in the form of mortar on broken edges, although this reuse could have taken place within the later Roman period itself. Some are associated with materials of later (medieval) date within the same context. The reused material demonstrates the availability of such materials in the medieval period, although it is not possible to be certain of its source. There are three obvious possibilities: (i) a building or buildings in the Westminster area itself; (ii) the Roman city of Londinium; and (iii) the Roman settlement at Southwark. The first would clearly be more convenient, though the latter two would offer more

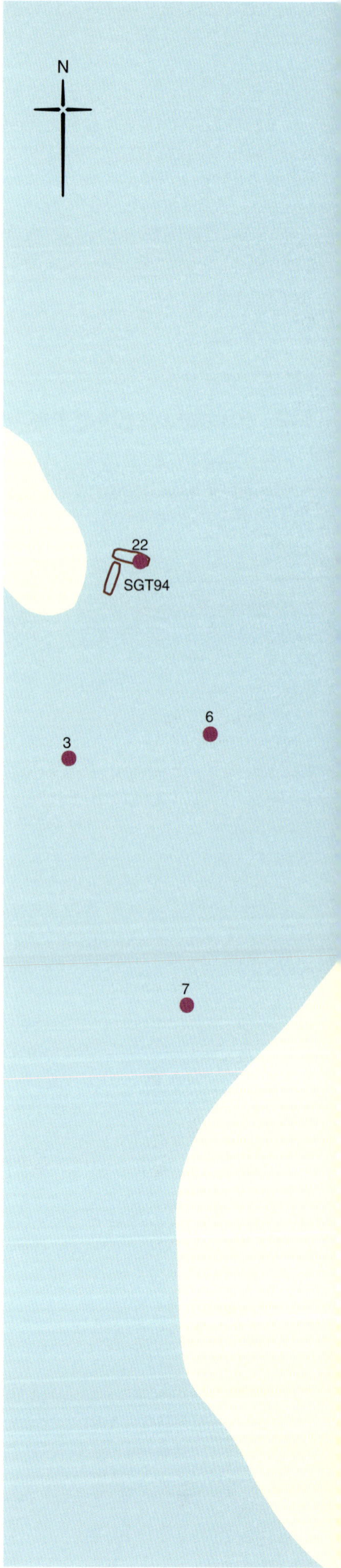

Fig 22 Plan of the archaeological features and location of finds, period 3 (scale 1:2500). For key to site codes, see Tables 1–3

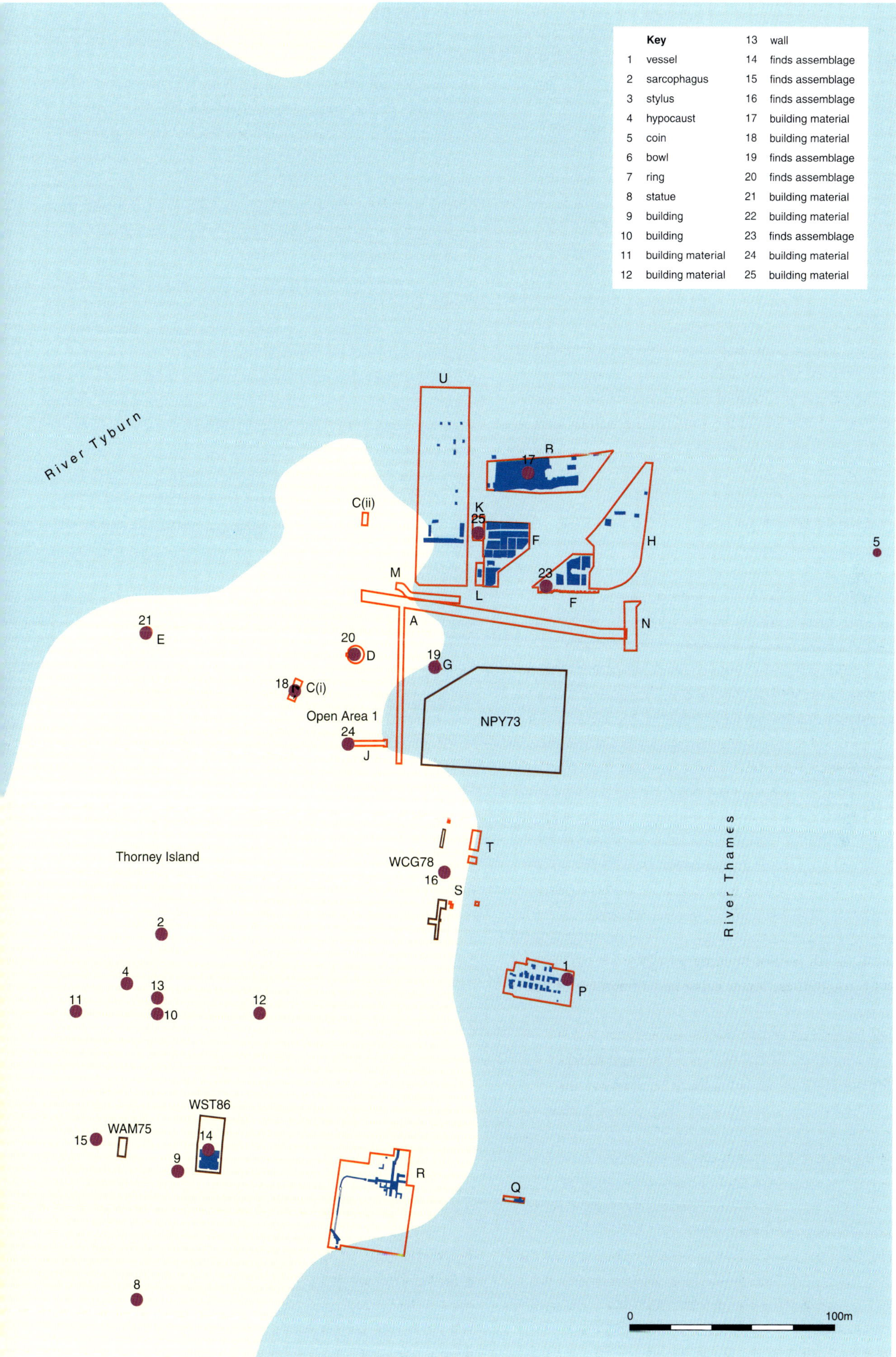
Key
1 vessel
2 sarcophagus
3 stylus
4 hypocaust
5 coin
6 bowl
7 ring
8 statue
9 building
10 building
11 building material
12 building material
13 wall
14 finds assemblage
15 finds assemblage
16 finds assemblage
17 building material
18 building material
19 finds assemblage
20 finds assemblage
21 building material
22 building material
23 finds assemblage
24 building material
25 building material
River Tyburn
River Thames
Thorney Island
Open Area 1
NPY73
WCG78
WST86
WAM75
C(ii)
C(i)
U
B
K
F
H
M
L
A
N
D
E
G
J
T
S
P
R
Q
0
100m

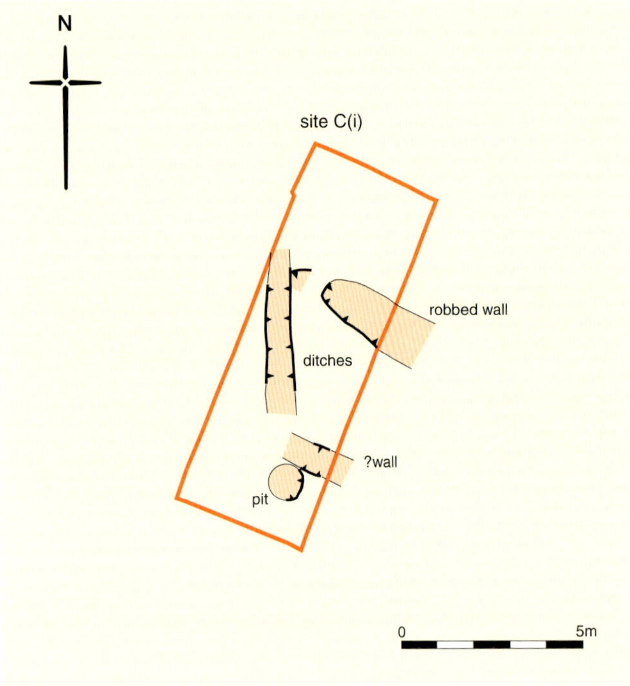

Fig 23 *Detailed plan of the archaeological features on site C(i), period 3 (scale 1:200)*

abundant supplies. The fact that the recovered material represents only a few different fabric types perhaps favours the first possibility since a greater variety was available in the city and Southwark. The reuse of *opus signinum* in the floor of Building 3 (subsequently robbed out) (Chapter 8.3, Fig 36) also suggests that the material came from a local origin as it seems unlikely that someone would go to the trouble of bringing in such a relatively fragile material for reuse. Fragments of Roman *opus signinum* flooring were recovered from G[15] and K[50]; the former were found in a dump with other Roman building materials, the latter with later building materials in make-up levelling. Two small pieces of daub were recovered from G[15]. Daub was used from prehistoric until recent times, but associated building materials from the context suggest that these pieces are of Roman date. One piece of Roman brick, <S1> from G[47] (period 1, OA1), presumably sank into the foreshore mud. The brick had mortar on one side with an impression of a possible goat or sheep hoof print.

Standing buildings in Westminster also retain Roman building material. The foundations to St Stephen's chapel, for instance, on site P appear to contain a fragment of Roman brick.

Other Roman artefacts recovered include three fragments of Mayen lava quernstone, <S2>, recovered from site G although residual in a later context (period 7, OA4). One of these fragments was part of the outer edge of a domestic hand-quern with diagonal tooling on the outside. It was part of the lower stone, the upper surface of which was abraded so that wear patterns were difficult to identify. The two other fragments were probably from another quern and were less diagnostic, with only three surviving worked surfaces.

5.4 Discussion

The extent and nature of occupation on Thorney Island during the Roman period continues to be uncertain. Most sites excavated uncover Roman building material and in greater quantities towards the high point of the island, in the area now covered by Westminster Abbey. Indeed, not only were the walls of Edward the Confessor's church partially built from Roman building material but there are reportedly *in situ* remains of Roman buildings beneath the abbey. A wall was supposedly found beneath the nave running at an 'oblique' angle to it (Westlake 1923, 2) and hypocaust pilae beneath the grave of the famous 19th-century architect Gilbert Scott, also in the nave. Neither of these two findings can be confirmed or disputed. It was also reported that two *opus signinum* floors were found beneath canons' houses on the south side of the cloister (RCHME 1925, 148). The depths at which these were found and the material beneath them strongly suggest that they are not Roman. The material beneath them sounds very similar to the 11th-century estuarine sediments excavated beneath the undercroft (Mills 1995). If so, these are further examples of medieval buildings reusing *opus signinum* floors as found in Building 3 (Chapter 8.3).

The possible Roman features on site C(i) should, like the antiquarian structures, be treated with caution There is no evidence to suggest that they are Saxon but they are in the same location as later boundary ditches and walls so may have formed an earlier boundary and been backfilled with Roman material.

The lack of Roman pottery and other artefacts should also be noted, for occupation in the area would normally produce such materials in some quantity. Some pottery has, however, been recovered from excavations at the Westminster Abbey undercroft (Waugh 1995, 80) where 27 sherds were found. Still, discussion above does lead to the conclusion that the likeliest source of the large quantities of Roman building material located on Thorney Island was *in situ* buildings on the crown of the island beneath what is now Westminster Abbey. There may also have been outlying structures beneath modern Parliament Square on relatively high ground in the region of site C(i). The lack of pottery and other domestic artefacts may reflect the lack of excavation within the heart of the activity and the reduced spread of domestic material relative to reusable building material. The sarcophagus found under the north green of the abbey in 1866 may have originated from elsewhere and been brought to Westminster but it seems unlikely that such a heavy tomb would have been moved far in order to be reused in a Saxon and/or medieval context, suggesting that it may have originated on Thorney Island.

The nature and dating of potential Roman structures on Thorney Island can only be highly speculative given the lack of *in situ* structural remains. In terms of dating, the building material recovered seems to date to the mid 1st to mid 2nd century (Table 6) and what little pottery has been found dates from the mid 1st to the early 4th century. It can therefore be

Table 6 Selected dating evidence, period 3

Land use	Activity	Context	Evidence	Description	Date range
Open Area 1	structural cut	C[202]	ceramic building material	tegula 2815; flue tile 3006	AD 50–150

suggested that any buildings on Thorney Island may have been constructed at a date of *c* AD 50–150 but that occupation could have continued until much later, perhaps even the 4th century.

Discussion of the nature of the Roman settlement on Thorney Island is equally speculative. The nature of the building material recovered is suggestive of high status, with fragments of box-flue tile from hypocausts and possible hypocaust pilae found *in situ* beneath the abbey. Large quantities of *opus signinum* from later contexts suggest that there were floors in this material, while fragments of stone, including marble, suggest high-quality architectural features (Goffin and Crowley 1995, 99). All in all, these indicate high-status buildings most probably situated on the highest ground beneath what is now Westminster Abbey. Perhaps the sarcophagus represents the tomb of one of the occupiers of the site.

6

The Saxon period, AD 410–*c* 1040 (period 4)

6.1 Environmental and topographical background

The River Thames

As with the Roman period, there is only limited evidence from the recent work at Westminster for the characteristics of the Thames at this time. Occasional references are made in the literature to flood silts, but these have not been examined in detail and are too vague to help with detailed reconstruction. The research from the Thames elsewhere in central London indicates that by the end of the Roman period mean tide levels were rising once more, relative to the land. This would have resulted in the tidal head migrating upstream again, the margins of Thorney Island becoming submerged and estuarine waters backing further up the Tyburn.

Palaeoecology

The evidence from New Palace Yard (Greig 1992) for the post-Roman period contrasts with that of the Roman levels; tree cover increases, with oak (*Quercus*), lime (*Tilia*) and alder (*Alnus*) once again dominating the tree spectra. Herbaceous species are still present, including Chenopodiaceae (possibly intrusive waterborne grains, but perhaps reflecting the incursion of brackish water). It appears that the forest cover regenerated to some extent after the Roman clearance and cultivation in the area, with a certain amount of alder carr recolonisation. This marshy component of the flora may well be associated with rising base levels. Nevertheless, there is still evidence for human activity and cultivation, though, if the woodland was able to regenerate, probably to a lesser degree than in the preceding period. Paradine and Arthur (Arthur and Paradine nd) identified locally that as well as semi-woodland, including elder (*Sambucus nigra*) and dogwood (*Cornus sanguineus*), some pasture could be found on the higher ground, whilst the site itself indicated waterlogged marshy areas (Armitage et al 1987). Interestingly, they identify watercress (*Nasturtium officinale*) and suggest that rather than a natural component of the boggy conditions, this was a cultivated species indicating that, in addition to the more usual cereal cultivation, the area was used for growing other food plants.

Cromwell Green nearby also provides some evidence (Greig 1992) for the vegetational succession in the Saxon period, indicating a situation similar to that found at New Palace Yard, with the addition of beech (*Fagus*) and hornbeam (*Carpinus*) throughout the sequence in the arboreal spectra. At the end of the sequence, presumed to be Late Saxon, walnut (*Juglans*) was also present. This species is also known from the medieval deposits at Broad Sanctuary (Mills 1982, 360) and may have been deliberately planted for the crop. Alternatively, walnut was a Roman introduction and the occurrence of it here may relate to unmanaged trees that had developed from earlier Roman planting. However, there is evidence for Saxon buildings in the Whitehall area which some have interpreted as a farm, so it is possible that the area was being systematically cultivated (Chaplin 1971).

6.2 Documentary and archaeological background

Little archaeological evidence of Saxon occupation has been found on Thorney Island. A number of chance finds have been made, including a sword from just to the south of the Victoria Tower and a group of finds from Westminster Bridge (Cowie 1988, 40) (Fig 24). According to legend Westminster Abbey was consecrated by St Peter after he appeared to Mellitus (first bishop of London) in AD 616. This legend first appeared in the late 11th century and has been exposed as a fabrication, but recent authorities have lent credence to the site as that of a Middle Saxon minster (Rosser 1989, 12–15; Harvey 1993, 2). Middle Saxon pottery has been recovered from the site of the Westminster Abbey misericord (Platts 1976, 159) and from the undercroft (Blackmore 1995, 80) and a coin of Ecgberht (*c* AD 835–9) was also recovered from the undercroft (Goffin 1995, 87). A charter of Offa, dated AD 785, granted the land for a monastic foundation. This charter is thought to be spurious but based on a real event, although some authors have suggested that this Offa may have been the 10th-century Offa rather than Offa the Great (Rosser 1989; Harvey 1993).

Immediately to the north of the island, on the Treasury Green site, at least two substantial timber halls, with associated pits, dating from the late 8th and 9th centuries were found. They have been variously interpreted as a royal palace and a farm (Cowie and Blackmore in prep). The initial hall was a sunken-floored building measuring approximately 7.2m x 5.4m whilst its replacement was built at ground level and measured 7.9m by at least 5.9m. It had an added porch and possibly a screened cross-passage. The area to the north appears to have been an associated yard bounded on the west side by a bank and ditch with a possible entrance. A variety of other pits and features were found within the yard. The dating of this complex farmstead is provisionally thought to be of the late 8th to mid 9th century with the first hall being of late 8th-century date and the second hall with its subsequent phases of 9th-century date.

Westminster Abbey was founded (or refounded) by St Dunstan during the reign of King Edgar (AD 959–75). This has variously been ascribed to AD 959 (Harvey 1993, 23), AD 960 (Rosser 1989, 13) and AD 971 (Sullivan 1994, 57). Of these, Sullivan's date is perhaps the most persuasive, placing the foundation after Edgar's meeting of the bishops and abbots in Easter AD 970 when Edgar is said to have decided to found 40 new monasteries. The actual foundation charter gives the date as AD 951, which is clearly erroneous. St Dunstan's church was described as a *monasteriolum*, or little monastery, and was inhabited by an abbot and 12 monks (Sullivan 1994, 56). This description was written some 20 years after the rebuilding by Edward the Confessor and whilst it may be open to some question it is likely to reflect the relatively modest nature of the establishment in the Late Saxon period.

Evidence of this Late Saxon foundation was thought to have been found in 1975 in the subvault of the misericord of the abbey (Black 1976, 141–2). On that site two phases of shallow slots (possibly beam slots), were found with associated postholes, possibly indicating timber buildings. The earliest phase was found in association with a sherd of Saxon pottery and the second phase with two sherds of 10th- or 11th-century pottery. Both phases were cut by a ditch dated to the mid 11th century by pottery and a coin, probably of Heinrich III, Holy Roman Emperor 1039–56 (Platts 1976, 159). However, these putative timber buildings post-dated silts that have been shown to date to the mid 11th century under the undercroft, suggesting that the buildings under the misericord date to the period of the Confessor's refoundation of the mid 11th century and might have formed temporary workshops or accommodation during the construction of the church. Regrettably, the deepest levels beneath the silts were not investigated and so any earlier evidence was not recovered.

6.3 Archaeological evidence

Structure 4

The sand on site J, located at between 0.99m and 0.95m OD, appeared to have been cut almost vertically in an east–west direction. It was uncertain whether this marked the edge of a natural stream or of a deliberately cut ditch, although the lack of silt at the base behind Structure 4 strongly suggests the latter. The cut was up to 0.22m deep. About 1.25m to the south lay another step in the sand, the base of which lay at between 0.69m and 0.61m OD. A borehole some 6.3m further south indicated the sand at a level of 0.37m OD, which suggests that the cut may have formed a ditch at least 0.62m deep with a series of steps cut into the sand.

Structure 4 formed a revetment against the upper bank (Figs 25–6). It consisted of badly decayed wooden planks attached to a series of wooden posts between 60mm and 100mm in diameter and up to 90mm in length. One posthole was also found behind the revetment, cut into the sand. The recorded length of the planking was 1.73m but it clearly continued to the west beyond the limit of excavation. At the point where the planking ceased, posts ran south from the bank into the ditch for a distance of at least 1.85m to the limits of the excavated area. Eleven posts were found to the south of the edge of the ditch and a further 11 were found cutting into the slope of the ditch itself. Another two were found cutting into the higher sand to the north. The posts along the eastern and western edges of the structure crossing the ditch were up to 140mm in diameter whilst those in the centre were smaller, ranging from 50mm to 130mm in diameter. The full width of this section of the structure is uncertain but was at least 2.13m and could have been as much as 4.21m. A further two posts were found between 5.37m and 5.67m east of the western edge of the structure but did not appear to be part of it as no further posts were found associated with them. This may have been due to truncation, however, by later wooden piles associated with Building 8 (period 7; Chapter 9.3).

Two posts were analysed for dendrochronological dating but although they were oak and contained 112 and 120 rings respectively, they could not be dated. Two further posts, J[80] and J[77], were sent for radiocarbon dating and produced results of AD 970–1220 (Beta 88696, 970±60 BP) and AD 770–1050 or 1080–1160 (Beta 88695, 1080±70 BP) respectively. Post J[77] produced two possible date ranges because of the nature of the calibration curve but the former has a 98% likelihood of being correct whilst the latter had a 2% likelihood. These dates are given to 2 standard deviations (ie, 95.4% confidence). At 1 standard deviation (68.2% confidence) the date ranges are 1000–1160 and AD 890–1020 respectively.

The structure forms a revetment against what was probably a ditch forming a boundary at least 0.62m deep and probably more than 8.0m wide. Contour projections on the sand further to the east suggest it may have been as much as 30m wide with a depth of more than 1.0m (Fig 4). Across it seems to have run a timber structure which lay on a line almost identical to the later entrance into the Palace of Westminster. It is therefore interpreted as forming a bridge crossing a wide ditch into the site of the palace. It clearly does not lead to the abbey site and suggests, therefore, that there was some activity on the palace site when it was constructed. It is also interesting to note that the ditch lies in the position of the later boundary between the Green Yard and New Palace Yard within the palace precincts. The presence of similarly sized large posts along either side may suggest that the full width of the structure was recorded at 2.13m but this remains speculative. River levels and the positioning of the high ground appear to have been such that the structure could not have operated as a landing stage into the river.

The dating of Structure 4 is more problematic. The radiocarbon dating at 2 standard deviations on the two posts would suggest that the structure was erected at some time between AD 970 and 1050; at 1 standard deviation the date range is tighter but less certain at 1000–1020. The date of AD 970–1050 just overlaps with both the Late Saxon period, when the abbey was refounded (*c* AD 959–71), and the beginning of the reign of Edward the Confessor (AD 1042–66). Whilst it is therefore possible that this structure dates to very early in the reign of Edward the Confessor, the balance of probability is that it was erected in the late 10th or early 11th century. This raises serious questions as to the origins of the palace. Whilst it is clear that the abbey had royal associations in the 10th and 11th centuries and that Edgar gave large areas of land in the vicinity to both the abbey and the Kings of Scotland (Schofield 1993, 40), the current interpretation has been that Edward the Confessor took the palace site for his residence in the middle of

Fig 24 Plan of the archaeological features and location of finds, period 4 (scale 1:2500). For key to site codes, see Tables 1–3

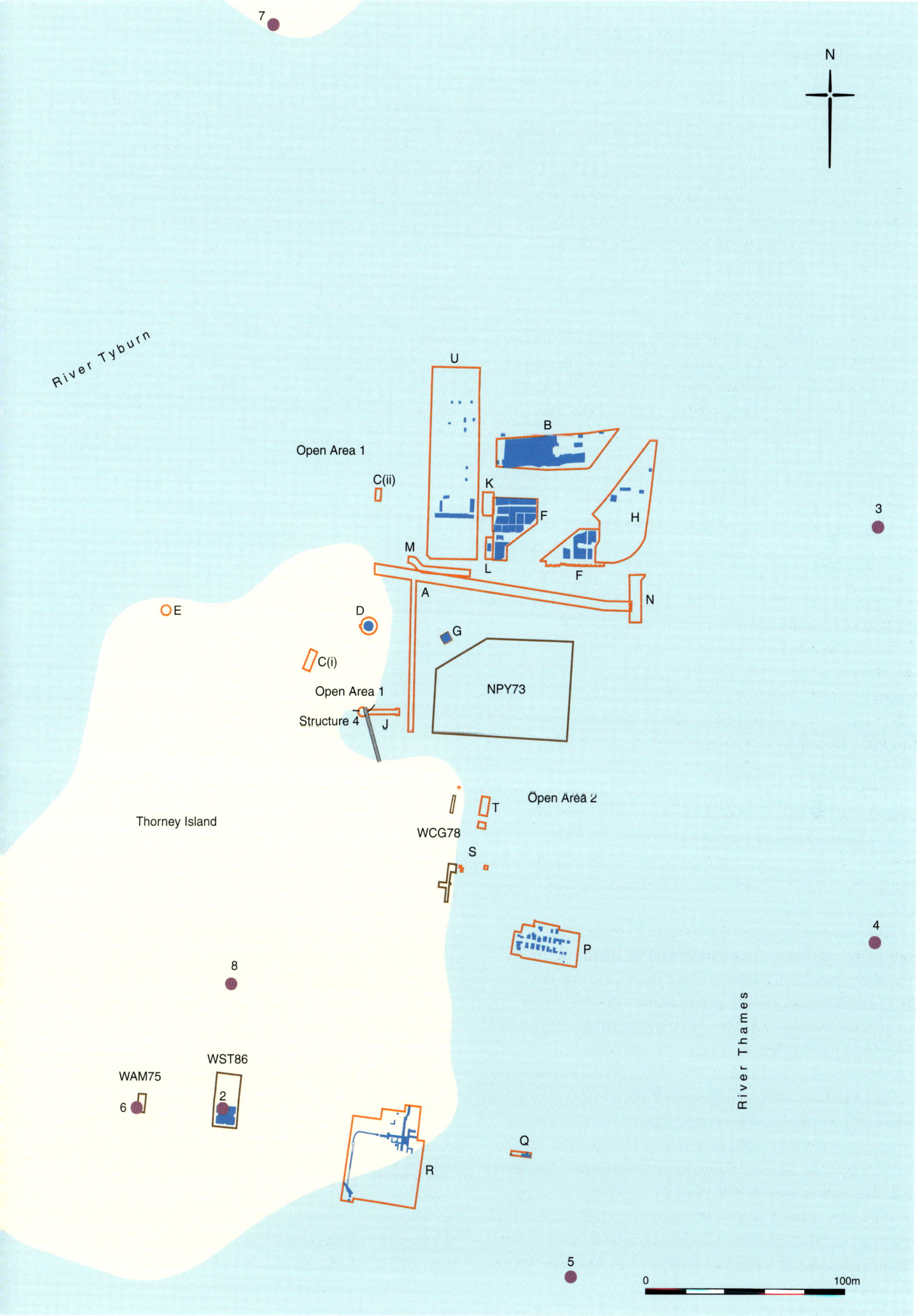
N
7
River Tyburn
U
B
Open Area 1
C(ii)
K
F
H
3
M
L
F
A
N
E
D
G
C(i)
NPY73
Open Area 1
Structure 4
J
Open Area 2
T
Thorney Island
WCG78
S
4
P
8
River Thames
WST86
WAM75
2
6
Q
R
5
0
100m

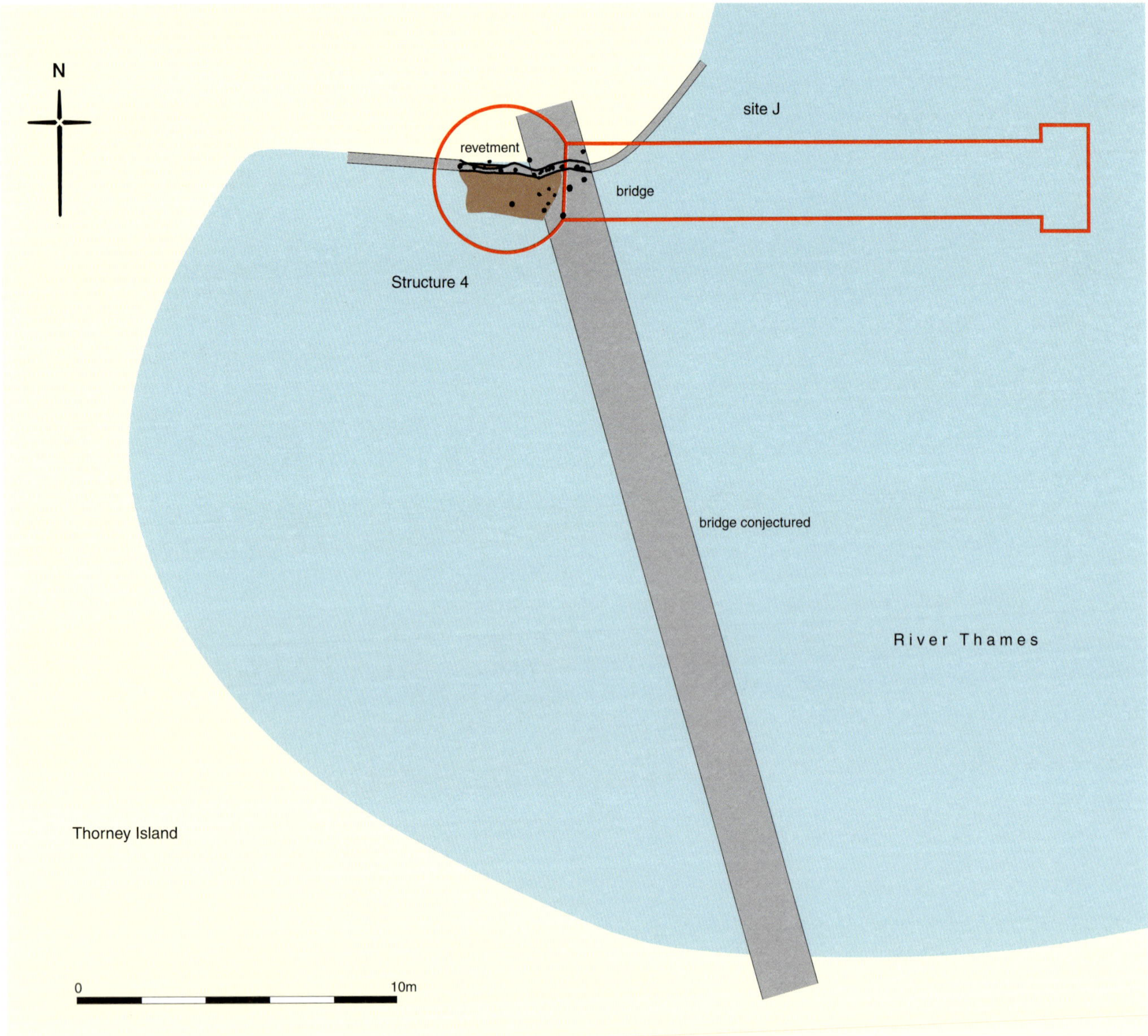

Fig 25 Interpretative plan of Structure 4 (scale 1:200)

the 11th century.

If the archaeological interpretation is correct then a bridge, on the same alignment and in the same position as the later medieval road, was erected over a revetted boundary ditch, leading into the site of the palace before the reign of Edward the Confessor. This might suggest that the palace was founded by a king before Edward the Confessor. Indeed it has been proposed that Cnut (1016–35) may have resided on the site, and the radiocarbon dates would be in keeping with such a date. If this were the case then the palace would presumably have lain to the south of Structure 4 in Open Area 2. However, the dating of Structure 4 would even allow for a construction date during the reign of King Edgar (AD 959–75), under whose aegis St Dunstan as Archbishop of Canterbury revived monasticism in England and founded (or refounded) Westminster Abbey some time after AD 960. The later western boundary of the palace lay less than 1.0m to the west of the excavated Structure 4. The site was not necessarily used by the monarch, however, and it need not have been a royal site. The ditch is shown terminating in Fig 25, but it is equally possible that both it and Structure 4 continued further west and formed the northern boundary of the abbey as well, which would lend more credence to a late 10th-century date.

Open Area 1: the foreshore to the north-east

On site C(ii) a grey waterlaid sandy clay, 0.30m thick, was deposited over the entire site. This was a flood layer deposited by the river and contained only residual Roman pottery. Its surface lay at 0.71m OD.

Elsewhere there appears to be evidence of widespread flooding of Thorney Island during the Late Saxon period towards the middle of the 11th century, and this waterlaid clay seems to be a similar deposit. It is, however, at a lower level here and was cut by a number of features dating to the mid to

Fig 26 *View of Structure 4, looking south, at the base of a grouting shaft (0.5m scale)*

late 11th century (Chapter 7.3, Open Area 1). It is therefore tentatively placed in this period.

On the west side of site F, a layer of grey-brown silty clay was deposited by the river to a level of about 0.8m OD. It contained no dating evidence but was sealed by late 12th-century fluvial deposits (period 6) and seems to have been deposited up to approximately the same level as similar deposits elsewhere. As with the deposits on site C(ii) this is tentatively placed here but could be dated slightly later.

Open Area 2: the foreshore to the east

Waterlaid clays and silts were found on site S up to a level of 1.42m OD; these were deposited before the construction of Building 1 (period 5; Chapter 7.3) although there was no dating evidence associated with them. They may in fact originate from the widespread flooding of Westminster in the mid 11th century as indicated in the Westminster Abbey undercroft (Mills 1995). Pressed into the top of the uppermost layer was chalk debris that may have originated from the construction of Building 1.

Similar material was found on site P. One layer, P[37], contained a goat skull fragment with an almost complete horn core attached. It probably derived from primary carcass processing and carcass disposal of a working animal, rather than waste disposal from domestic consumption.

6.4 Discussion

The Saxon period in this chapter covers the entire period from the Roman abandonment of Britain to the accession to the throne of Edward the Confessor in 1042. The evidence for activity on Thorney Island for much of this period is slight and until the mid 7th century is missing entirely. This, however, is not surprising given that archaeological evidence for this period across London is generally meagre.

At present, the only evidence for Middle Saxon activity comes from chance find-spots and from residual material found in later contexts beneath Westminster Abbey. As Fig 24 shows, the chance finds include two swords (both recovered from the Thames) and a binding strip (recovered from the Tyburn). These finds are therefore more likely to be residual and their provenances are poorly located.

The groups of finds recovered from under Westminster Abbey do, however, come from what was dry land at the time and are more indicative of occupation. They include 8th- to 9th-century pottery, copper-alloy pins and a silver coin of Ecgberht of Wessex dated to AD 835–9 (Blackmore 1995, 80; Goffin 1995, 87–90). A single Saxon sherd was recovered from excavations at the misericord in the abbey (Platts 1976, 159). The pottery, in particular, does not seem to include material of the same type as that found in the earliest phase of the nearby settlement of Lundenwic, which dates to the later 7th and early 8th century. The material from the abbey has a pattern similar to the finds from the Treasury Green excavation of the farmstead immediately to the north of Thorney Island, which also seems to date to the latter part of the 8th century.

The balance of evidence, therefore, for the Middle Saxon period suggests that there may have been a minster on the abbey site, which perhaps dated to the later 8th and 9th centuries and which may have been founded in response to the large settlement which grew up in the Covent Garden area with its cathedral sited to the east at St Paul's in the deserted Roman city. If such a minster did exist, its fate remains unknown: it could have remained in use until its refoundation between AD 959 and 971 or it may have been destroyed in Viking raids of the mid 9th century.

That an abbey was founded on Thorney Island between AD 959 and 971 is beyond doubt although there is no archaeological evidence for it. It was probably quite a modest establishment, certainly in comparison to its later incarnations, and was founded by St Dunstan on land in the bequest of King Edgar as a part of their monastic reforms. Finds from Westminster Abbey dating to the Late Saxon period include pottery, strap ends and a bone needle of the 10th and 11th centuries from the undercroft, and nine sherds of 10th- to 11th-century pottery from the misericord (Blackmore 1995, 80; Goffin 1995, 87–90; Platts 1976, 159).

At about the same time as the refoundation of the abbey or shortly afterwards, a wide boundary ditch was dug (possibly with a bridge built over it) to define the land that was subsequently to become the site of the royal Palace of Westminster and possibly to define the abbey as well (Table 7).

Table 7 Selected dating evidence, period 4

Land use	Activity	Context	Evidence	Description	Date range
Structure 4	timber	J[77]	radiocarbon date	Beta 88695; see Table 56	cal AD 770–1160

7

The Saxo-Norman period, *c* 1040–*c* 1150 (period 5)

7.1 Environmental and topographical background

No environmental material was recovered from this period but, as discussed below, there appears to have been a major episode of flooding on the island. Beneath the Westminster Abbey undercroft, over 1.0m of waterlaid silts up to a level of *c* 3.0m OD were found post-dating mid 11th-century features and cut by a ditch of a similar date (Mills 1995). Similar deposits were found during the excavation of the Westminster Abbey misericord although these were undated (Black 1976). Descriptions of *opus signinum* floors found under the abbey also record similar deposits to approximately the same level (RCHME 1925). This suggests that the *opus signinum* floors were in fact medieval and that the material had been reused (Chapter 5.4). Similar evidence from the excavations described below, on the higher parts of the island, also points to a period of flooding during the middle of the 11th century. It may have been this episode that caused the erosion on the foreshore leading to the hiatus between the Late Bronze Age and the 12th century.

7.2 Documentary and archaeological background

The Saxo-Norman period here begins with the accession to the throne of Edward the Confessor in 1042. It is generally accepted that under his influence Westminster increased markedly in importance, becoming one of the principal royal residences in the 1050s and the site of one of the foremost monastic establishments in the country (Fig 27).

The rebuilding of Westminster Abbey was carried out at Edward the Confessor's behest. The monk Sulcard states that it was motivated by Edward's veneration for St Peter and financed by the money that he had originally meant to spend on a pilgrimage to Rome. The church was intended to be a private royal church in the same vein as the German *Eigenkloster*, as were many French ducal monasteries and the royal French church of St Denis. Edward's time in France no doubt influenced him in this, as it did in his choice of the design of the church, constructed as it was in the Romanesque style and largely based upon the church at Jumièges. Much debate has focused upon the relative completion of the church by the time of Edward's death in 1066, a debate fuelled by the translation of the word *vestibulum*. The church was said to have been completed to the *vestibulum* by that date. The traditional translation of the word *vestibulum* has been 'porch' but evidence from St Riquier in Picardy indicates that it might have referred to the nave (Tanner and Clapham 1933, 229–30). The exact interpretation remains unclear although the Bayeux Tapestry does indicate a completed church by this date, though without the western towers. Many of the adjoining buildings surrounding the cloister were built

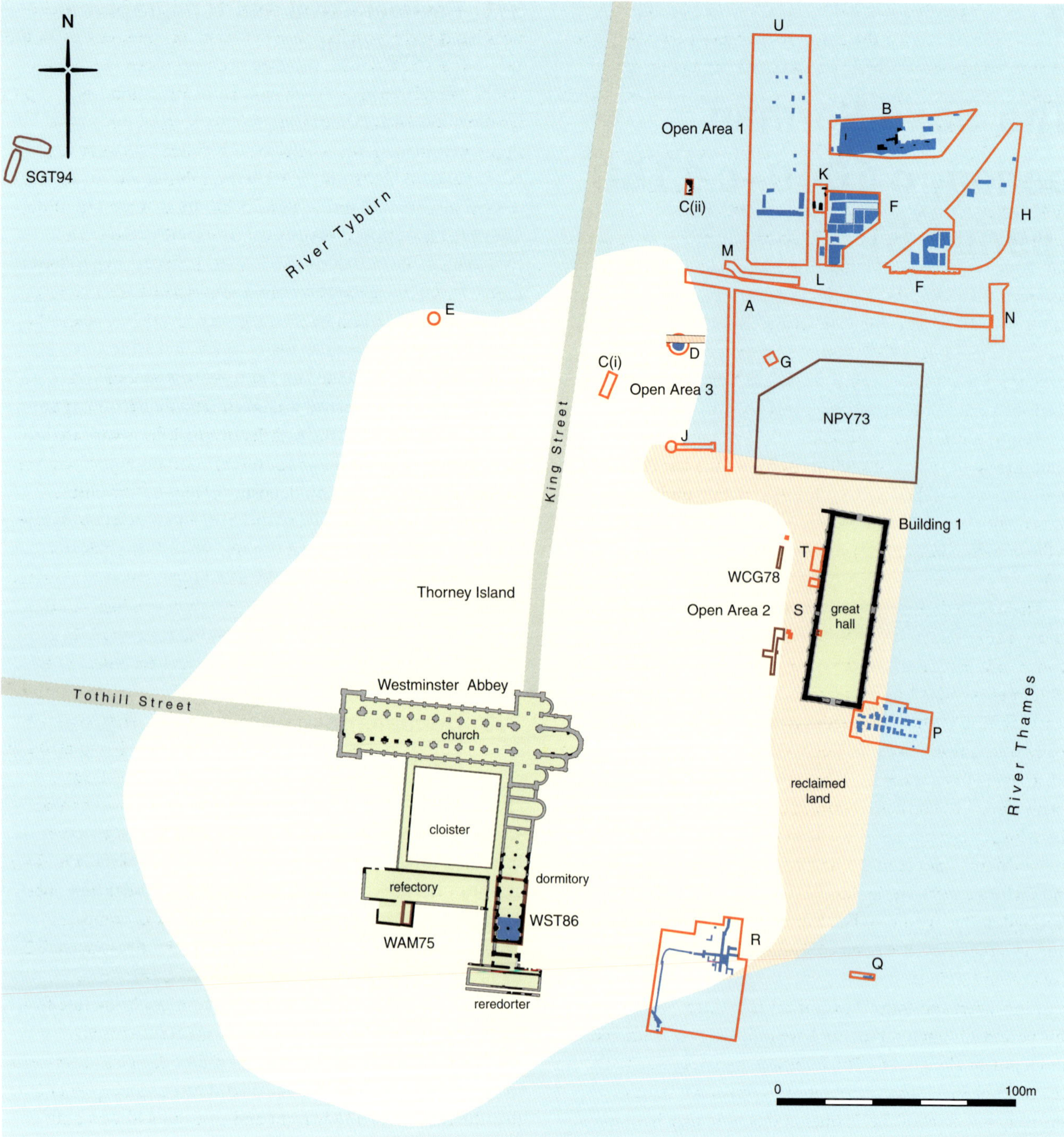

Fig 27 *Plan of the archaeological features, period 5 (scale 1:2500). For key to site codes, see Tables 1–3*

over the decades following the Confessor's death in 1066: the undercroft and dormitory in about 1070 and the reredorter and frater in about 1080 (Wilson et al 1986, 17). There are a few elements of 12th-century work on the west side of the cloister but it is uncertain whether these date to the first or second half of the 12th century and they are shown on the plan of features in period 6 (Fig 34). It is not known whether there was an earlier western range to the cloister but an earlier western cloister alley wall has been recorded. The new abbey was designed to house 80 monks rather than Dunstan's rather more modest 12 and indicates the far greater scale involved in Edward's conception of his new abbey.

Edward was too ill to attend the consecration of his church on 28 December 1065 and died a few days later. His funeral and burial took place in the abbey. Harold II and William the Conqueror were both subsequently crowned in the new abbey church in 1066, William on Christmas Day. Both were presumably trying to emphasise their personal choice by Edward the Confessor, and thus began the tradition of coronations at Westminster.

The structural history of the abbey church has been rewritten in part in recent years after work on the western towers suggested that the towers were rebuilt during the first half of the 12th century and that the nave was also rebuilt at this time (Tatton-Brown 1995). Quite how the junction of the 11th-century choir and the new 12th-century nave was made is unclear. It must have been most awkward and have given the church a peculiar look, with the nave rebuilt at a different angle to that of the choir.

That Edward the Confessor had a palace on the site of the later medieval palace is confirmed by the Bayeux Tapestry (Fig 104), where Edward is shown looking out on his nearly completed abbey to the west. The actual site of Edward's palace buildings is unknown although they are usually thought to have occupied the site of the later 'lesser hall'. It is possible that this hall had 11th-century foundations and may also have been the site of the main hall of William the Conqueror. There is some evidence that the lower storey contained Norman work (Lethaby 1906, 142–5) although this remains uncertain.

The new great hall (now known as 'Westminster Hall') was built during the reign of William Rufus, in the last decade of the 11th century (below, 7.3). It was certainly under construction in 1097 and was completed by 1099, when William held court in it for the first time (Colvin et al 1963, 45).

The town of Westminster was largely a creation of the mid to late 12th century. In the Domesday Survey of 1086 the manor of Westminster recorded only 19 villeins, 42 cottars and 25 houses inhabited by knights and by the abbot's men. The exact location of these properties is unknown but doubtless many were situated well outside the area of Thorney Island and what was later to become the town. The manor and the abbey's estate were more or less coterminous, stretching to the edge of the Tyburn valley in the west (modern-day Ebury Street), to Roman Watling Street in the north (modern-day High Holborn and Oxford Street), to the River Fleet in the east (modern-day Farringdon Road) and to the Thames in the south. Within this land was the convent garden of Westminster Abbey (modern-day Covent Garden).

King Street and Tothill Street must have already existed by this period although there may have only been very limited development along them. The foreshore lay some way to the east of King Street. Its exact location is unknown but the relatively low level of the Thames at this time may have meant that the riverbank was not revetted.

7.3 Archaeological evidence

Building 1: the great hall

A detailed plan of the great hall (now known as 'Westminster Hall') is shown on Fig 28. A step in the inside of the west wall was recorded at 1.90m OD protruding 0.75m from the face of the wall above. The wall was constructed from Kentish ragstone and chalk, bonded with yellow sandy mortar. A brick wall forming part of the early 19th-century floor supports sat on the footings at this level. It is probable that the top of the existing footings formed the original top of the footings but it is also possible that the wall has been cut away for the insertion of the brick wall. The foundations of the west wall were located on their external side in 1975, lying in a construction trench up to 0.60m wide. The footings were 1.20m deep, of which the upper 0.40m appeared to have been rendered (Whipp and Platts 1976, 353). An engineer's test pit dug in the angle of the front porch at the north end of the hall located the top of the foundations on the external face at 2.11m OD, protruding 0.67m from the face of the wall. A second step some 0.39m higher may have been an original feature or a later addition. The drawing shows this part of the wall in a different shading. The foundations here are 1.73m deep.

During the rebuilding works by Robert Smirke in the early 19th century, a number of architectural and archaeological records were made of the hall. Its original floor appeared to have been clay (0.10m–0.13m thick) overlaid by a black 'soil', presumably an occupation deposit, 0.18m–0.30m thick. Beneath the original floor lay about 0.9m of stone chippings, mortar, clay and sand (Smirke 1836, 416). It is unclear at what levels these deposits lay. Smirke suggests that the surface of the original floor lay at approximately 0.4m beneath the current floor level and therefore at about 2.92m OD. This would imply that the foundations were dug into the riverlaid clay beneath from a level of about 1.9m OD and that 0.9m of rubble then raised the level of the floor of the hall to about 2.8m OD with the floor laid on top, its surface being at about 2.9m OD. Smirke also states that there was 1.2m–1.5m of clay beneath the stone and mortar layer with gravel beneath. Gravel would thus lie at 0.4m–0.7m OD. A reconstruction drawing of the hall (Smirke 1836, pl xlvii) indicates the floor lying at the uppermost step in the footings, which have been recorded at 2.1m OD, implying that stone was dumped to level up the ground to this level and that the floor lay at 2.2m OD. This would suggest that the gravel lay at -0.4m to -0.7m OD. Given the variation in levels beneath the hall from the contour plot (Fig 4) neither theory seems entirely adequate. The levels on the surface of this clay elsewhere seem to vary from 1.0m to 1.2m OD and thus it is interpreted here that the reconstruction is right and that the hall was built from a level of c 1.2m OD and that its floor lay at c 2.1m OD. The dumped stone was presumably an attempt to raise the level of the ground above the footings before the first floor was laid. This would have both dried out the land and raised the floor level to protect it from flooding, although this did not always prove successful as was seen in 1236 when the Thames burst its banks and men had to row down the hall (Stow 1987, 413–14).

Much has been written about the great hall in the past but there is still much that is unknown. The actual layout of its interior is unclear. It has traditionally been assumed that the roof was supported on rows of posts, almost certainly two, which would have created a three-aisled building with the central aisle allowing a view of the king's throne at the southern end through to a possible door at the north end. The later rebuilding of the north end of the hall (period 8; Chapter

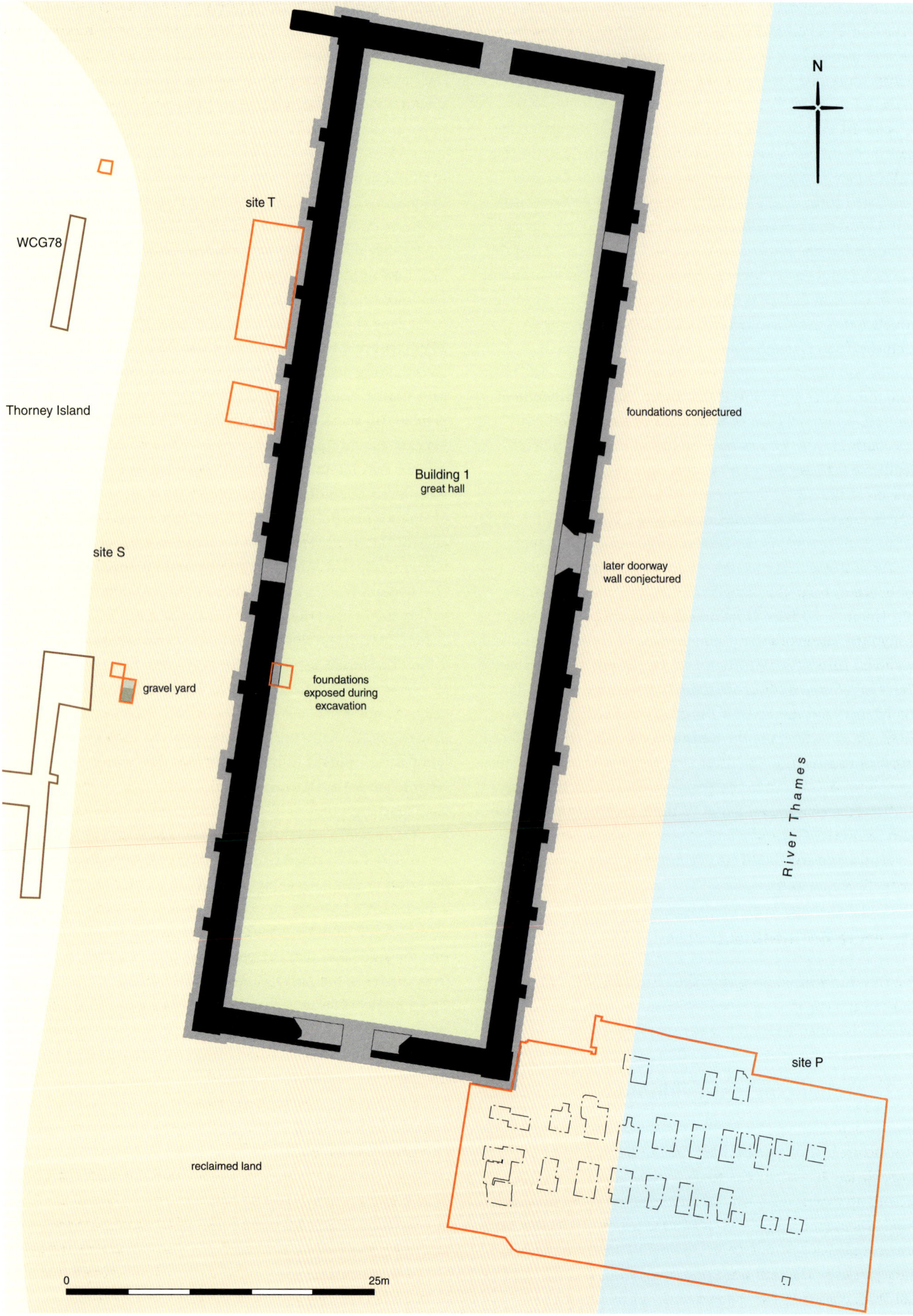

Fig 28 Detailed plan of the great hall (B1), period 5 (scale 1:400)

10.3) has removed any evidence for an original door at the north end. Doors recorded on either side of the hall towards the northern end suggest the presence of a 'screen's passage', perhaps indicating that there was not, in fact, a door in the north wall of the hall. During Smirke's refurbishment of the hall and the excavations that were carried out, attempts were made to find foundations for columns supporting the roof but with no success. Given that they would most probably have manifested themselves as nothing more than large postholes, this is hardly surprising. More recent suggestions that the roof was a single span without posts (Roland Harris, pers comm) cannot be discounted but seem unlikely. If the roof were of this construction, why would Richard II have gone to so much trouble to rebuild it in the same way unless it was in a parlous condition by this time?

The hall can be seen, when compared with the contour plan, to lie on a spit of gravel that lay at a slightly higher level, jutting out into the Thames with inlets or streams to both north and south. There is no evidence of an earlier building on the site of the hall, as proposed by other authors, and the suggested bowing of the east and west walls of the hall as in Saxon palaces (eg, Cheddar) has been shown by accurate surveying not to exist.

The hall was the largest hall of its kind in Europe when constructed, as far as is known, measuring some 72.81m x 20.71m. It was originally built with a triforium gallery running around the inside of the building linking with the first-floor windows, parts of which have been located (Smirke 1836). The form of the arcade is not entirely certain but Smirke's reconstruction seems unsatisfactory and Lethaby's much more likely (Smirke 1836, pl xlvii; Lethaby 1906, fig 1). This proposes large arches separated by two smaller arches around the triforium.

No archaeological evidence for the use of the structure has been recovered. Obviously large amounts were destroyed during the construction works of the 19th century but it is not known if any survives.

Structure 4: revetment

The silts that washed up against the revetment (S4) are undated and could be ascribed either to the Late Saxon or to the Saxo-Norman period. In either case they were cut by a robbed-out building (B3) during the latter part of the 12th century. These silts consisted of dark grey, blue and dark brown silty clays and sandy clays, some containing mollusc shells. Initially deposited up to a level of 1.04m OD in the region of Structure 4 and at least 0.75m OD further east, they were probably laid by rising river levels flooding the lower lying ground up to about the level of the top of Structure 4. Further flood layers up to 1.68m OD must have put the revetment out of use at some point during this period, probably towards the latter part of it. The relationship of the revetment to the great hall (B1), constructed at the end of the 11th century, is unclear but it had probably fallen out of use by the time the hall was built.

Open Area 1: the foreshore

The Late Bronze Age peat and peaty clay on site B was cut by two undated features, possibly natural channels. One, severely truncated, survived to a depth of 0.58m and was filled with silty clay. The other, aligned east–west, was 0.30m deep and filled with peat. Its south side was cut by a later channel on the same alignment which was 0.21m deep and filled with blue-grey clay. Both features were cut to the east by a further north–south aligned channel or ditch.

Another cut feature was 0.90m deep and filled with grey silty clay. Its full extent was not revealed, but two nearby features may have been part of the same feature. One, B[193], was at least 0.46m deep and filled with layers of silty clay. Its uppermost fill produced pottery dated to the mid 11th to mid 12th century. The other, B[212], was 0.49m deep and filled with similar material. It produced pottery dated to the late 13th to mid 14th century, which may have been intrusive, although a later medieval date for the feature cannot be ruled out.

The channels described above were overlain by fluvial silts and clays which had been truncated from above but survived to a maximum height of 0.95m OD on the west side of site B. The waterlaid deposits produced a few sherds of pottery dated to 1050–1150 and 1270–1400 (from contexts B[165] and B[189] respectively), suggesting that site B had not been reclaimed from the river until well into the medieval period. On the east side of the site an undated north–south aligned natural channel, B[241], was found within the fluvial deposits.

The truncated surface of the fluvial deposits on site B was cut by a number of channels, all of which were seen only in section. In one place the fluvial deposits and the underlying Late Bronze Age peat had apparently been completely eroded during the medieval period by three successive natural channels that were mainly filled with waterlaid clay. The earliest, channel B[76], ran approximately north–south, and was 1.22m deep. Its primary fill consisted of clay and peaty material. The watercourse was cut by an undated channel on a north-east–south-west alignment, and was over 0.74m deep. It was cut by a north–south channel, B[71], which was 0.87m deep and contained two fills. The channel cannot be closely dated from the finds, but probably dates to period 5 or 6 since it was cut by a mid 14th- to 15th-century rubbish pit, B[50]/[52]. On the west side of the site the fluvial deposits were cut by another undated (but probably medieval) channel. Aligned east–west, it was 2.40m wide and 0.51m deep.

Cutting the Late Saxon flood layer on site C(ii) was an irregular-shaped pit filled with and sealed by blue-grey organic mud. Also cutting the earlier flood layer was the south-eastern corner of a circular pit, probably 0.8m in diameter. Cutting this pit and the later flood layer were two pits, C[313] and C[310], that probably originally formed part of the same large pit measuring more than 3.6m x 2.2m. It was too shallow to have been a quarry pit since its base did not reach the underlying sand, nor was it used for the disposal of rubbish. To the south lay a linear cut approximately 0.6m wide that continued beyond the eastern limit of the site and may have acted as a drainage ditch. This ditch and the large pit were both filled with grey-brown waterlaid organic clays that covered the entire site. The clays contained very occasional mussel shell, oyster shell and molluscs and were presumably laid down by flooding of the Thames.

Cutting the flooding were two east–west aligned ditches draining down towards the Thames (Fig 29). The northern, C[304], was approximately 1.20m wide and 0.61m deep and extended beyond the limits of the site to east and west. It was filled with a light brown organic clay containing the horn core of a cow at its base and was sealed by a series of interleaved peats and clays containing small amounts of animal bone, oyster shell and mussel shell and one piece of leather offcut. Down the centre of the ditch were four squared stakes (40mm x 30mm) with a fifth lying to the south. Three of these, <S28>–<S30>, survived sufficiently to be analysed. All were oak and all had been trimmed or sharpened although <S29> was broken at both ends. The other two survived to 170mm and 160mm in length. They appeared to have been inserted into the ditch after it had partially silted up but were not revetting stakes. It is possible that this ditch was the same as C[282] (period 7; Chapter 9.3, Open Area 10), which would make this ditch much later. The lowest fill contained 14th-century pottery that would otherwise be intrusive. The latest fill contained part of a wooden plate or bowl, <S27>, made from ash (*Fraxinus* sp) (Fig 30).

The southern ditch C[320] also extended beyond the eastern and western limits of the site. It was aligned east–west but its southern edge was not found; it was at least 0.70m wide and 0.25m deep. At the base of the slope at the eastern end were a series of horizontally laid pieces of wattle, laid from east to west. Down the slope of the ditch at the western end was a wood and leather object, <S42>. It comprises three thin strips of willow/poplar (*Salicaceae* sp), *c* 3mm–5mm thick, partly overlapping and resting on a sheet of leather. At least one of the wooden strips appears to have been attached to the leather by means of iron nails or rivets. Between the wood and the leather are the remains of black and white deposits, possibly paint but more probably pitch and lime, which may have been painted

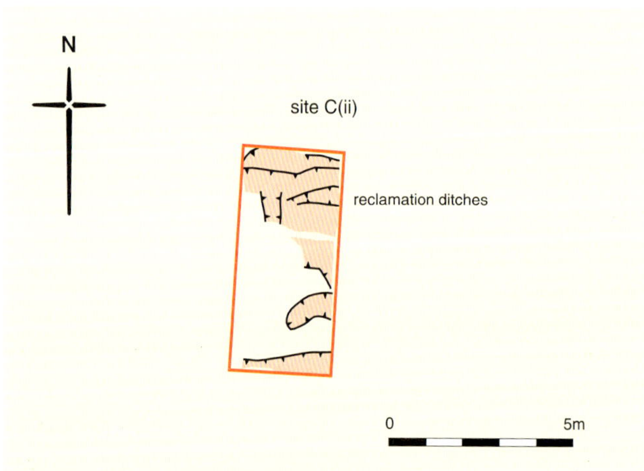

Fig 29 Detailed plan of the reclamation ditches on site C(ii), period 5 (scale 1:200)

Fig 30 *Wooden vessel* <S27> from Open Area 1 (*scale* 1:4)

on as a form of waterproofing. Since the object is incomplete it is uncertain whether it is part of a structural feature such as a drain lining, or a smaller artefact such as a bucket. The ditch was subsequently filled with a brown humic clay with large amounts of animal bone and wood and a fragment of leather or moss, <S26>. The animal bone comprised sheep/goat and pig as well as three bones identified as peacock. The latter species is a high-status food component. There was a notable absence of cattle, or even, with the exception of one rib, of cattle-sized fragments. These deposits are contemporary with those found at the Westminster Abbey undercroft (Pipe 1995) where a wide range of species, including, as here, high-status indicators, was found (Chapter 16.7).

Sealing this ditch was a layer of brown peaty clay with large amounts of wood and plant material and small amounts of animal bone and oyster shell. This suggests that the area was flooded at least periodically but that shallow waters allowed plants to grow on the marshy ground. Two ceramic crucibles, <S12> and <S13>, found in Open Area 13 in contexts dating to period 8 probably date to this period and may have been disturbed from here by the digging of a later pit (Fig 31). Both had been heated and had copper-alloy residues in their bases. It seems unlikely that they would have been used in this location but they may have been discarded here since the area was obviously dry enough on occasion for ditch- and pit-digging.

On site D flood layers consisting of grey and dark brown sand, probably dating to the early part of this period, were deposited up to a level of 1.11m OD. They were cut by a ditch aligned east–west (Fig 32). Its full profile was not quite seen but it was at least 1.3m and probably 1.45m wide. It was at least 0.85m deep, possibly with a flat base and a northern slope at 45° and a much steeper southern slope. Only 1.50m of its length was recorded but it was clearly a substantial boundary feature and it has been interpreted as the boundary between Open Area 1 to the north and Open Area 3 to the south. Its lower fill was a waterlaid grey silty clay with lenses of decayed wood and other organic material whilst its upper fill was a dark brown organic sandy silt with some fragments of chalk, oyster shell, molluscs, animal bone and wood. This appeared to overlie

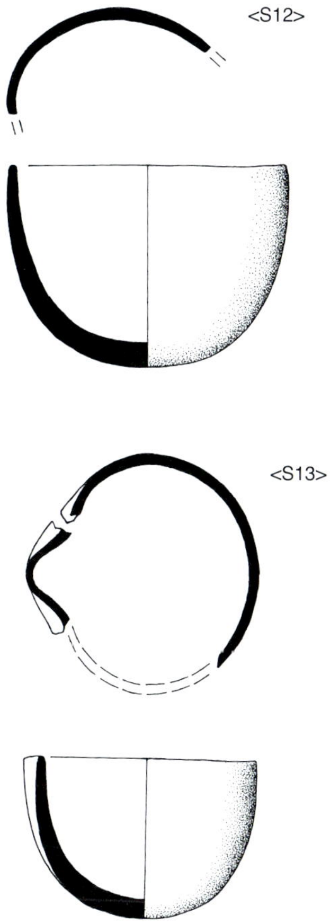

Fig 31 *Two ?11th-century ceramic crucibles, <S12>–<S13>, from site C(ii) (scale 1:2)*

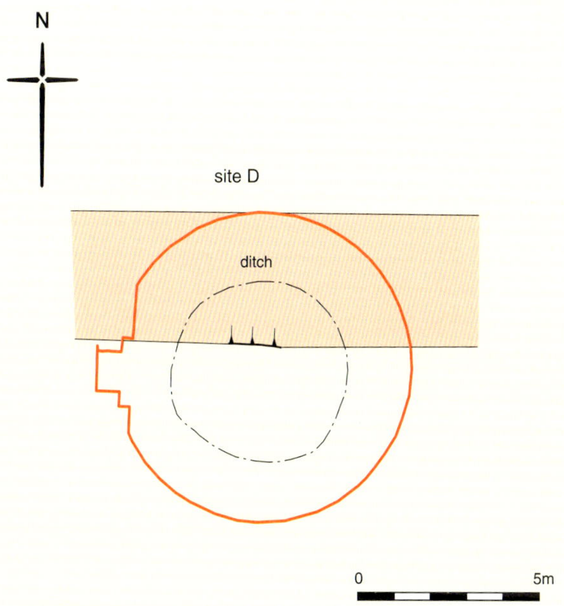

Fig 32 *Detailed plan of the boundary ditch on site D, period 5 (scale 1:200)*

the surrounding area as well as filling the ditch and contained pottery dated to this period. The botanical component of this ditch/gully fill sample consisted mainly of large and small wood fragments and shavings. Stem fragments and wood charcoal were also present in moderate quantities. The fruits and seeds were mainly from wild plants of wetland and disturbed habitats whilst there was also a little evidence for plant foods.

The wetland plants were mainly bankside/marshland species, for example, lesser spearwort (*Ranunculus flammula*), celery-leaved crowfoot (*R sceleratus*), hemlock (*Conium maculatum*), wild celery/fool's watercress (*Apium graveolens/nodiflorum*) and gipsy-wort (*Lycopus europaeus*). Plants of disturbed ground and waste places included large numbers of stinging nettle (*Urtica dioica*) seeds plus seeds of goosefoots/oraches (*Chenopodium/Atriplex* spp), knotgrass (*Polygonum aviculare*), red shank (*P persicaria*), pale persicaria (*P lapitholium*), spiny-milk thistle (*Sonchus asper*) and black nightshade (*Solanum nigrum*). Shrub/tree species were also represented, for instance, brambles (*Rubus fruticosus/idaeus*), elder (*Sambucus nigra*), sloe/blackthorn (*Prunus spinosa*) and hazel (*Corylus avellana*), the latter represented by large quantities of shell fragments; these plants may have been exploited as a food resource. Definite food residues included several charred rye (*Secale cereale*) grains and a few fig (*Ficus carica*) seeds.

A wetland environment is suggested not only by the plant macro-remains but also by the presence of Cladoceran *ephippia* 'water flea' eggs, which indicate standing bodies of water in the ditch though perhaps only periodically. The wild fruits suggest that the ditch may have been lined with a hedgerow in places. The plant food residues, other biological remains (large mammal bones, fish bones, eggshell) and artefactual debris (a few pottery sherds and ceramic building material fragments) suggest human activities nearby with the ditch possibly acting as a receptacle for the casual and occasional dumping of such material.

The extent of this ditch is uncertain but its large size and shape mean that it was probably more than a drainage ditch and its proximity to the later line of the northern boundary of New Palace Yard suggests that it may have been the earliest attempt at defining the boundaries of the palace, separating it from the foreshore. It would have acted as an obvious marker but was clearly too small to have formed a defensive boundary.

Deposits of silt and clay formed over site K to a level of 0.65m OD. The uppermost of these deposits was cut by a north–south aligned ditch more than 0.56m deep and 0.50m wide, the northern terminus of which was found. It is possible that this ditch originally cut the subsequent silty clay flood layers that covered the site to a level of about 1.0m OD. These flood deposits appear to be related to the widespread flooding of Thorney Island in the mid 11th century. Two further drainage ditches were subsequently cut into the flood silts during this period (Fig 33). One, up to 2.12m wide and 0.58m deep, appeared to be sloping down away from the river, suggesting that it was not simply feeding straight into the river but was either part of a more complex drainage system or, more probably, was a naturally formed channel. This channel was filled with alternate bands of orange sand, grey clay-silt, and brown humic peaty clays suggesting alternating periods of fast-moving water, slower moving water and shallow flood water on marginal ground respectively. The southern edge of the second

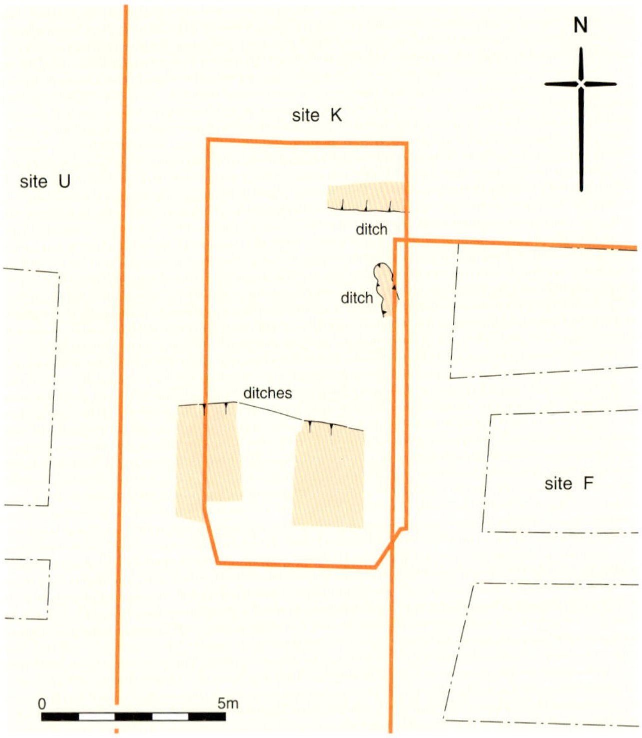

Fig 33 Detailed plan of the reclamation ditches on site K, period 5 (scale 1:200)

drainage ditch lay at the extreme north end of site K and was more than 0.80m wide and 1.75m long. It was 0.50m deep and was filled with alternate bands of dark grey and blue silty clays and orange sands, suggesting similar patterns of slow- and fast-moving water.

Similar silts and clays were deposited on site L up to a level of 1.16m OD. These were cut by an east–west aligned drainage ditch or natural channel of which only the northern side was found. It was at least 1.50m wide and, if its profile were matched on the southern side, would have been at least 3.0m wide. It was 0.62m deep, sloped down towards the river to the east and was filled with alternate bands of sand and silt containing charcoal at the base and dark grey clay with building material above. These fills suggest fairly fast-flowing water initially and slower moving water later with construction debris being dumped in it.

Open Area 2

Pressed into the top of the uppermost layer of the riverlaid clays and silts from the previous period was chalk debris that may have originated from the construction of Building 1. Overlying it was a gravel surface 0.20m thick. This was presumably a yard surface that would have been necessary with the increased use of this space after the construction of Building 1 and the unsuitability of the marshy ground beneath. Immediately to the west of Building 1 chalk debris appears to have formed a construction surface, although it could have been part of a temporary structure used during the work on Building 1 (Whipp and Platts 1976, 354). No dating evidence was associated with the gravel surface but it is most likely to date to this period as the earliest attempt to create a yard within the space to the west of Building 1.

Open Area 3

Covering the area of site C(i) was a light brown clay up to a level of 1.70m OD. It contained some flecks of charcoal and lenses of fine yellow sand. This layer represents flooding of the higher ground with the clay deposited under slow-moving conditions and the sand lenses under faster flowing conditions.

The flood layers are undated but were cut by features of mid to late 12th-century date and similar flooding can be seen on most sites in the area. Floodlaid clays in the vicinity of the great hall to the east clearly pre-date the construction of that building in 1097, and flooding to the south of Westminster Abbey seems to date to around 1050 (Mills 1995, 72).

7.4 Discussion

The abbey was rebuilt during the reign of Edward the Confessor and its claustral buildings completed during the latter part of the 11th century. Edward the Confessor's idea of Westminster Abbey as his own royal church was presumably adopted by William I as a means of gaining acceptance from English nobles, and his coronation there cemented Westminster's role. It was not until Henry III, though, that other monarchs returned to Edward's idea of Westminster functioning as a royal mausoleum.

By the end of the 11th century, William II had expanded his palace with what was the largest hall in Europe at that time. He had clearly seen Westminster as being his principal residence for otherwise he would have constructed his grand new hall at Winchester or Gloucester. Westminster remained, however, one of a number of residences, and royal 'progress' meant that the monarch was there only occasionally. The royal exchequer remained at Winchester.

Archaeological excavation in the other areas of the palace has been too limited to assess the extent of further building during this period.

Evidence from all sites suggests very substantial flooding on Thorney Island during this period. Much of this is, not surprisingly, undated but evidence from site C(ii) (Table 8) suggests it occurred around the middle of the 11th century and as it is clearly post-dated by the great hall it must have occurred before 1097. The floodlaid deposits found in the Westminster Abbey undercroft date to about 1050 and it would therefore seem probable that much of the island was subject to serious flooding at around that time.

The evidence from the areas to the north of the palace and those along the foreshore suggest that these areas were low lying and marshy after the period of flooding but were not directly within the river system. Indeed, evidence from

Table 8 Selected dating evidence, period 5 (see Table 25 for expansion of codes)

Land use	Activity	Context	Evidence	Description	Date range
Building 1: the great hall			documentary	see Table 16	1097–9
Open Area 1	ditch	B[191]	ceramic	EMSH; LOGR	1050–1150
Open Area 1	natural channel	B[201]	ceramic	EMSH	1050–1150
Open Area 1	foreshore deposit	B[165]	ceramic	ESUR; LOGR; ENPO	1050–1150
Open Area 1	ditch	D[69]	ceramic	EMSH	1050–1150
Open Area 1	cut	C[312]	ceramic	ESUR	1050–1150
Open Area 1	ditch	C[314]	ceramic	LOGR	1050–1150
Open Area 1	ditch	K[64]	ceramic	EMSH	1050–1150
Open Area 1	ditch	K[73]	ceramic	ESUR; LCOAR; SHER	1050–1150
Open Area 1	ditch	K[23]	ceramic	LCOAR	1080–1200
Open Area 1	ditch	K[24]	ceramic	LOGR	1050–1150

elsewhere (Ayre et al in prep) suggests that the river level may have been falling at this time. Most of the plant material represented at Westminster was of wetland plants reflecting the marginal nature of these areas. There was little evidence for economic activities except for a small number of charred cereal grains, fig (*Ficus carica*) seeds and possibly some of the wild fruits that may have been exploited from time to time. There was, however, more evidence for human activities alongside and in the boundary ditch closer to the main palace buildings on site D. The fact that ditches were dug to dry out and reclaim this land suggests that there were already ideas for expansion and that serious attempts were made to prepare the land.

8

c 1150–c 1230 (period 6)

8.1 Environmental and topographical background

It is at approximately 1200 that the hiatus recorded in the sedimentary sequence in many of the sites examined for the JLEP ends. As it has proved difficult to assign all the sequences to the periods discussed in this book, Chapter 9.1 (period 7) contains detail on the initial medieval sedimentation.

8.2 Documentary and archaeological background

It is likely that the nave of Westminster Abbey had been rebuilt by the middle of the 12th century, with new towers constructed at the western end (Tatton-Brown 1995, 174–5). The infirmary hall and chapel of St Katherine were also added in the 12th century. The ruins of the chapel still exist although the hall was replaced in the second half of the 14th century after the fire of 1298 (Chapter 10).

Evidence from the site of the later misericord suggests that, whilst the area was open at this time, and had a gravel yard, some construction was carried out, with a sleeper wall and a smaller partition wall built (Black 1976, 145–7). During the second half of the 12th century, there were more substantial changes in the undercroft beneath the dormitory on the west side of the cloister. The undercroft was subdivided into smaller bays with the creation of the Pyx chapel in the 12th century, St Dunstan's chapel in the early 13th century and other rooms also during the 12th century. The floor level in the southern three bays was reduced at this rime (Mills 1995, 76).

After the great hall, the earliest documentary references to buildings within the palace site occur during this period (Fig 34). The 'lesser hall' or 'white hall' was constructed before 1167 although this particular mention probably refers to the addition of a second storey to an existing building. The water gate and bridge which were situated at the north end of New Palace Yard are first mentioned in 1184 and may have been constructed at about the same time as the river wall and dock (below, 8.3, Structure 5: dock) in about 1179–80. The first documented reference to St Stephen's chapel is in 1184, also in this period. It may well be that the chapel already existed by this date but the traditional ascribing of its origins to the reign of King Stephen appears to rest upon the use of the name Stephen as a dedication, which seems highly tenuous. A chapel dedicated to St John was also in existence by 1186–7 and a building to house the Exchequer had been built, probably close to the royal apartments, by 1190. Other buildings documented as being constructed during the reign of Henry II include the king's wardrobe, the cloister, a kitchen and the king's chamber (later known as the Painted Chamber) (see Table 16).

The town of Westminster, certainly along King Street,

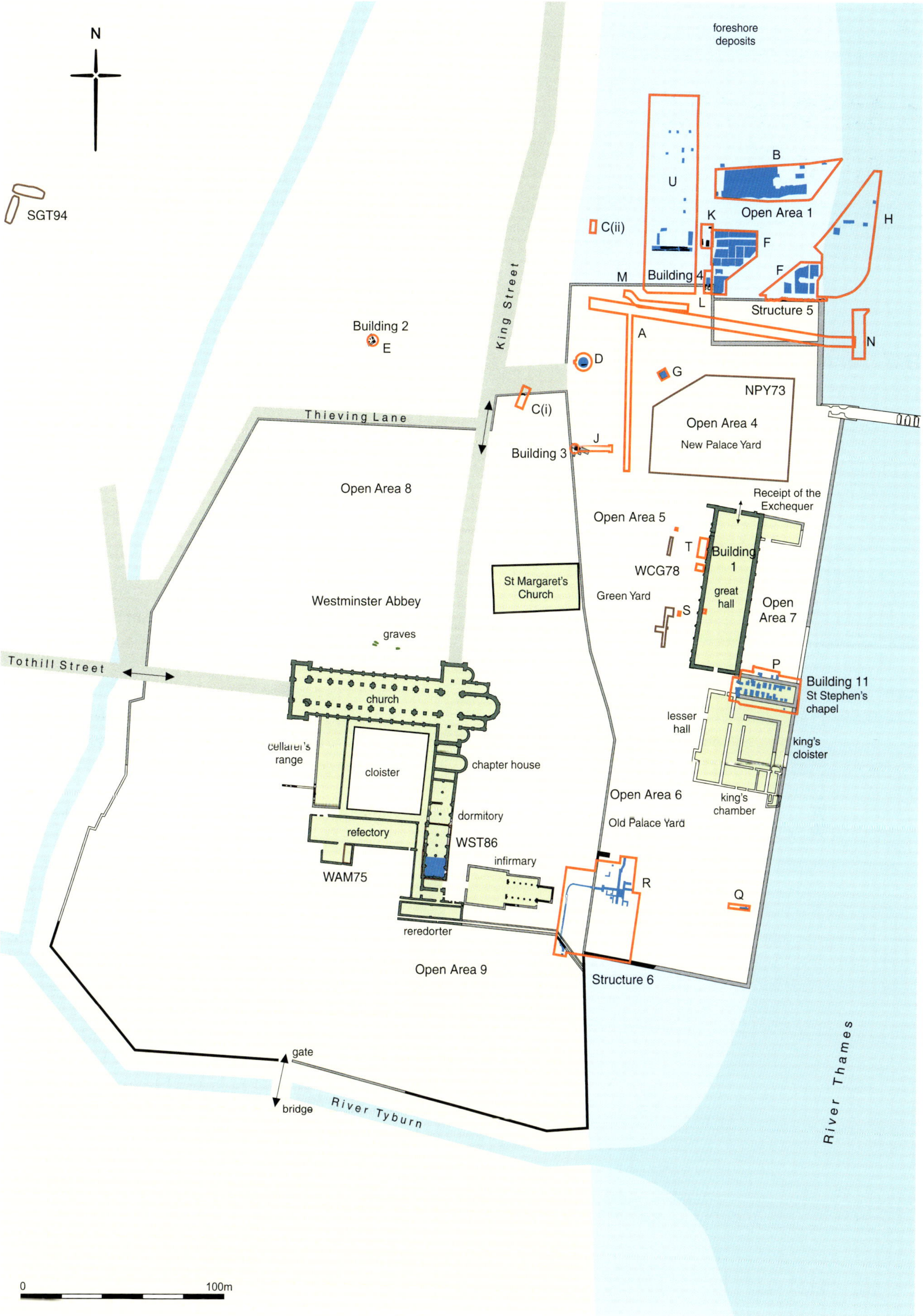

Fig 34 Plan of the archaeological features, period 6 (scale 1:2500). For key to site codes, see Tables 1–3

probably began to form in the second half of the 12th century and by the end of the 13th century King Street was in all likelihood lined with buildings along its entire frontage on both sides (Rosser 1989, fig 4). Evidence from the Treasury Green excavation indicated that from *c* 1160 the site was drained with large numbers of ditches laid out in a grid pattern. The rear of the structures and gardens fronting onto King Street to the east were found to date to the later 12th century onwards. These pieces of evidence suggest that there was progressive development along King Street during the later 12th and 13th centuries.

8.3 Archaeological evidence

Building 2

Overlying the ditch and external surface in Open Area 8 on site E lay the timber Building 2 (Fig 35). This was almost rectangular, measuring at least 1.7m east–west by 1.1m north–south with a large posthole in each corner and one smaller posthole on the south side. The posts would have ranged in size from 0.22m x 0.15m to 0.57m x 0.35m and were dug into the ground to a depth of 0.12m to 0.47m. The building had a floor of crushed Reigate stone.

The function of this building is uncertain but it may have been used for agricultural or domestic purposes; its size suggests it was little more than a shed. Though it was constructed before the definition of the gardens or back yards behind the properties of King Street (period 7; Chapter 9.3, Open Areas 11 and 12), it may still have been associated with early houses along that street. The original date for the construction of houses along King Street is uncertain but there is likely to have been some development by the end of the 12th century. Its position does not indicate whether it was associated with either the abbey or the palace, or whether it was outside both, although a relationship with the palace seems unlikely.

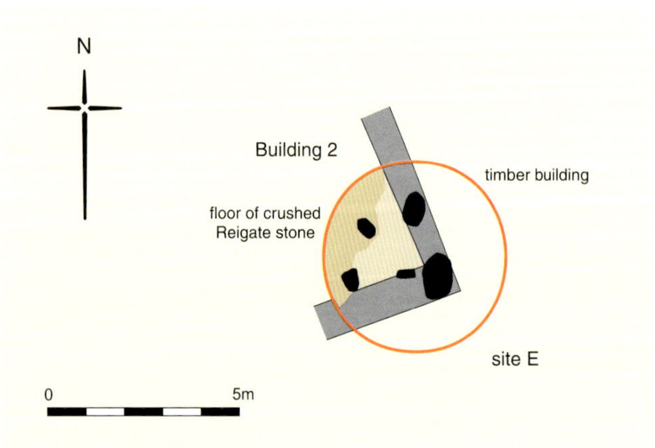

Fig 35 *Detailed plan of Building 2, period 6 (scale 1:200)*

Building 3

Building 3 on site J (Fig 36) was defined by a series of robber trenches that had removed the walls. Only the northern and western robber trenches lay within the area of excavation. The rounded corner at the north-western corner of the robber trenches suggests that the trenches were wider than the wall foundations, which would presumably have had a right-angled corner. The walls were therefore less than 0.8m wide. A similar rounded corner to the mortar bedding layer within the building suggests that it too was truncated when the walls were robbed out. The robber trenches were backfilled with similar alluvial material to that found around the building, along with large quantities of chalk and Kentish ragstone fragments as well as some Reigate stone fragments, Roman tile, Roman brick and pieces of *opus signinum*. There was clear evidence of reuse on the *opus signinum*, indicating that whilst it had originated as a floor in a Roman building it had been reused as a floor in a later one, presumably Building 3. A further cut to the north of the building, which may have robbed out the floor as well, also contained Kentish ragstone, chalk, Reigate stone, Roman brick, Roman tile and *opus signinum*. Within the area defined by the robber trenches was a mortar bedding layer, presumably for a floor.

The full extent of Building 3 is unknown but it measured at least 1.4m north–south by 0.7m east–west. Its walls were probably constructed from Kentish ragstone, chalk, Roman tile and brick, possibly with some dressed Reigate stone. The floor was probably of reused *opus signinum*. As is discussed elsewhere (see Chapters 5, 7, 16.2), the reuse of Roman building material on Thorney Island was extremely widespread. Building 3 appears to have been constructed and robbed out during this period. The top of the bedding layer for the floor lay at 0.84m OD; the floor surface, therefore, presumably lay at *c* 0.95m OD. Such a level was probably about 0.75m below the ground surface at the time, suggesting that Building 3 was a semi-basement. It is unclear whether there was a second storey above.

Building 4

Only the north wall to Building 4 was found on site L. It is shown in detail in Fig 37. It also formed the northern river wall on land reclaimed for the Palace of Westminster. To the north lay the Thames and its junction with the Tyburn. The wall, which was 0.96m wide, was constructed from roughly coursed Kentish ragstone blocks, with some Reigate stone, bonded with a cream mortar. The central section of the wall and the associated deposits were destroyed by a 19th-century brick sewer (Fig 38). Stone recorded in a borehole about 3.0m to the west was probably part of the same wall. The area immediately to the east in site F was truncated, but a narrow block of stratified deposits at the southern end of the site suggests that the wall did not return southwards through it. This means that the building either extended all the way across site F, returning southwards further east where the District and Circle Line now

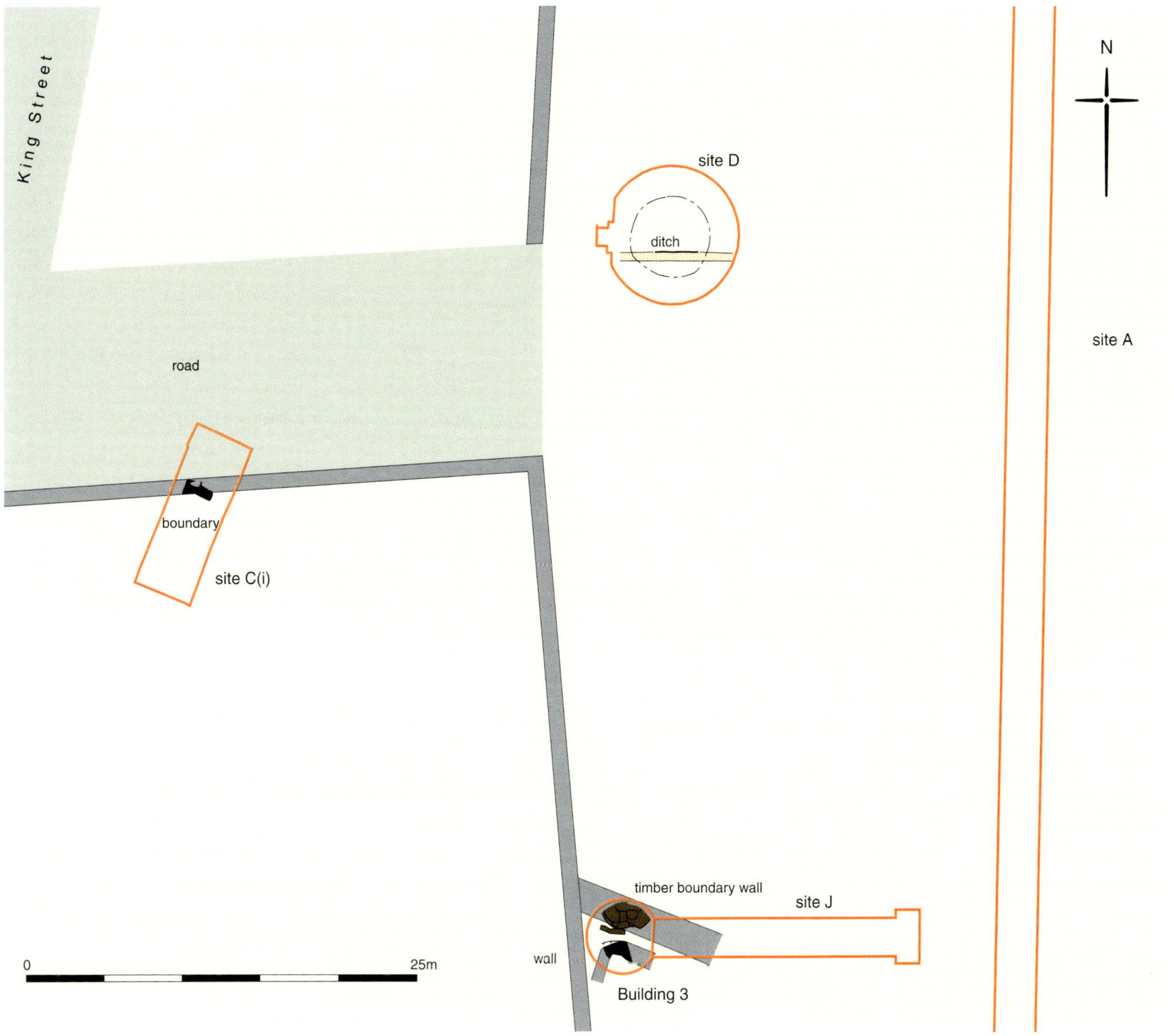

Fig 36 Detailed plan of sites C(i), D and J, showing Building 3 and other archaeological features, period 6 (scale 1:400)

lies (which would mean that the building was at least 14m across), or, more probably, returned along the line of the eastern edge of Canon Row, where Victorian foundations would have destroyed it. The building was at least 3.5m wide internally north–south, and if the southern wall aligned with the north edge of the dock to the west (Structure 5) would have been approximately 5.2m wide.

Overlying the footings of the wall on the west side was a dumped layer of blue-grey clay with building material and a layer of Kentish ragstone, yellow mortar and brown clay which formed a packing behind the wall. Over the blue-grey clay lay the remains of two stone ovens or hearths. Only a short section of the southern wall of L[51] was found, constructed from Reigate stone, chalk and sandstone. The wall was 0.14m wide and its curvature suggested that it did not coexist with the northern oven L[48]. However, the ash inside post-dated both ovens and may suggest from its limits that the two ovens formed an hour-glass shape and operated together. To the north, oven L[48] had walls 80mm wide on the east side and 0.20m on the north. Its walls were constructed from the same materials as L[51]. Sufficient evidence was found to suggest that the internal diameter of L[48] was about 1.50m. Inside the ovens was a layer of mixed ash, charcoal and silt. This was overlain by a stiff orange clay with patches of burnt clay and charcoal.

On the east side lay another stone oven (Fig 39), of which about one third was uncovered. Its diameter was about 1.12m and it was constructed from chalk, Kentish ragstone and Reigate stone blocks bonded with clay. It survived to a height of 0.25m and the wall on the east side was 0.28m wide. To the north the wall was 0.60m wide. Within the oven at the base was a mixed rubble layer consisting of chalk, Reigate stone, Kentish ragstone and tile with some animal bone and flint. This was overlain by a grey silt that lay under a yellow sandy clay that was in turn sealed by a compacted layer of tile, mortar and crushed chalk. This presumably formed the floor to the oven; over it was a burnt sandy clay with ash and charcoal.

It is suggested that this building was built at or around the

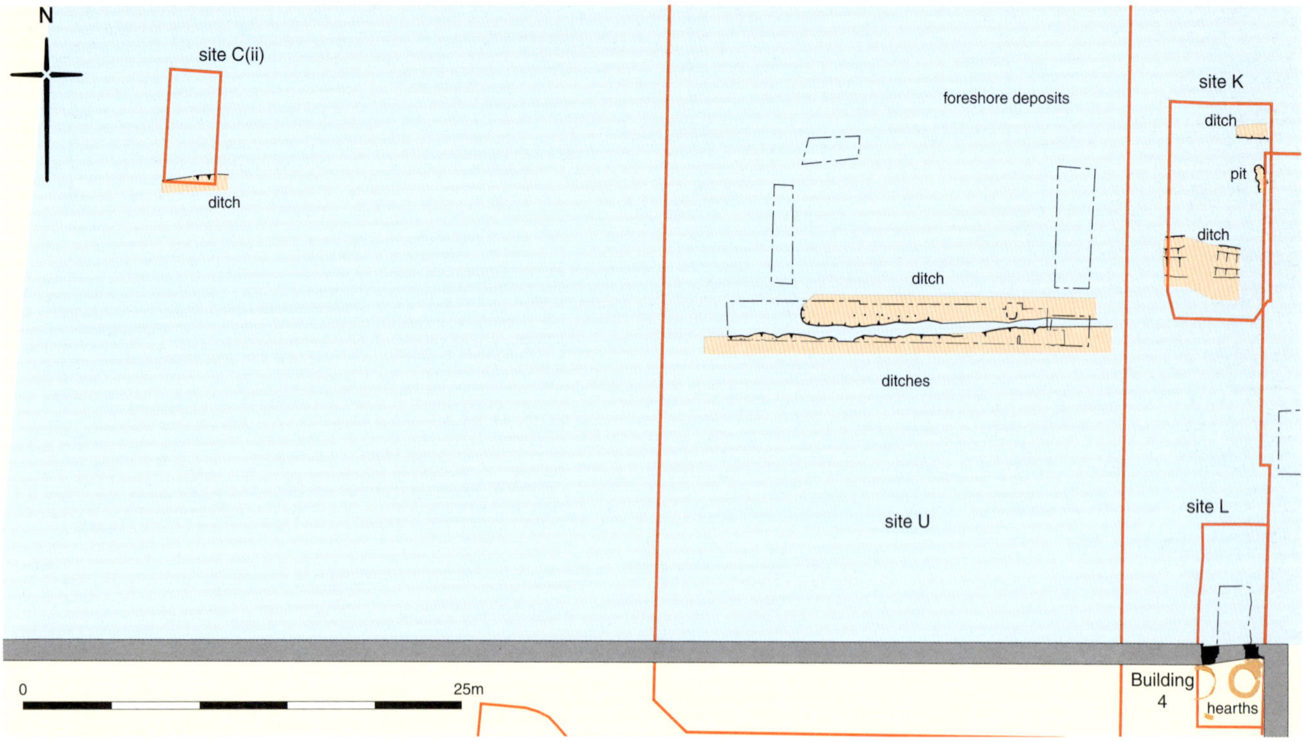

Fig 37 *Detailed plan of sites C(ii), K, L and U, showing Building 4 and other archaeological features, period 6 (scale 1:400)*

same time as the dock to the east and the major river defences in the late 12th century. Documentary evidence indicates that this work occurred in 1179–80 (Colvin et al 1963, 493) and this conforms well with evidence from Bull Wharf, in the City of London, where a timber revetment associated with a substantial rise in the river level can be dated to 1181 (below, Structure 5: dock) (Ayre et al in prep). It is uncertain whether the north wall of Building 4 was merely built as a river wall

Fig 38 *View of Building 4, period 6, showing the hearths truncated by the Victorian sewer, looking south (0.5m scale)*

Fig 39 *Detailed view of the east hearth in Building 4, looking south-west (0.5m scale)*

with a building added on to its southern side at a later date or whether the building was conceived as a single entity. Its less substantial nature compared with that of the river walls along the Thames frontage was no doubt the result of its more marginal position and might suggest that it was planned as a building from the start. The pottery from the ovens/hearths on the west side of the area investigated suggests a 12th-century date. A fragment of decorated 'Westminster' floor tile deposited in the eastern oven dating to the mid to late 13th century suggests that the oven pre-dates that period.

The function of Building 4 is uncertain. No assemblages of artefacts or ecofacts were found associated with the ovens, which makes their interpretation problematic. The eastern oven was clearly a very substantial structure and would appear to have continued in use during the 13th century (Chapter 9.3). The western hearths or ovens, though less substantial, were still large in size. A later sewer destroyed the junction between the two sides of the site but it may be that the oven on the east side of the site post-dated the western ones. No evidence of residues, slag or industrial processes was found, suggesting that the ovens may have been for cooking or baking. They were presumably cleared out regularly, so that the surviving burnt material may represent the last occasions on which they were used. The lack of animal bone in any sizeable quantities may not be of great significance but might suggest that the ovens were used for baking, especially as most meat would be cooked over open heaths and fires.

Structure 5: dock

Only just projecting into the southern edge of site F was a stone wall aligned north–south (Figs 40–2). It was partially truncated by two concrete posts but its full width was seen to be 2.64m. It was constructed from chalk and Reigate stone, bonded with buff-coloured sandy mortar. The base of the wall lay at OD and it survived to a height of 0.98m. Within the lowest course of stone was a timber base plate. On top of the lowest course was a layer of estuarine mud, 50mm thick, indicating that the area was flooded during construction. This wall formed the eastern river wall to the palace fronting on to the Thames.

Running westward from the wall and set back from its northern extent by about 0.35m was a timber structure that was recorded for a distance of 12.67m westwards and 0.40m southwards. It was truncated by the concrete piles for the new underground station along the south side of the site but timbers were removed from these holes when they were dug out and clearly the structure continued along the entire length. The surface of the structure lay at 0.50m OD and its base at about 0.25m OD. Where it was fully exposed towards the eastern end, it consisted of three horizontally laid oak planks, aligned east–west and 30mm–50mm thick, with a similar plank along the front hiding the construction behind. In some places were squared oak timbers underneath the lowest planks, up to

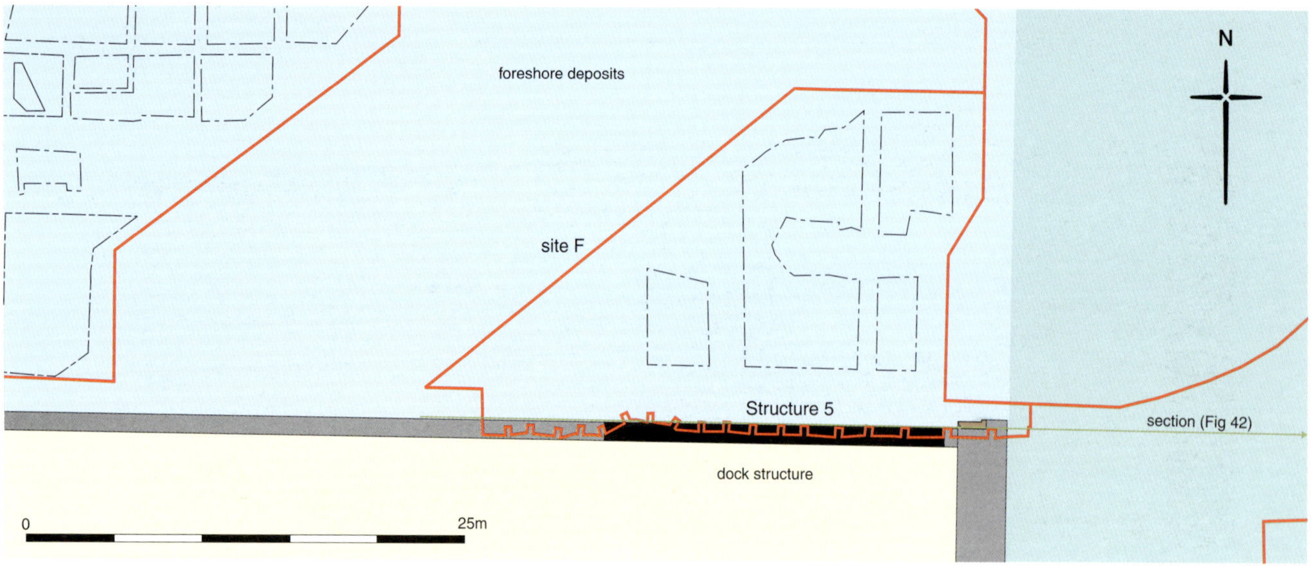

Fig 40 Detailed plan of dock (S5), period 6 (scale 1:400)

190mm x 160mm in section and aligned north–south. Similar timbers must have lain between the three planks to give the structure solidity and bind it together. Further west only single planks were recorded but truncation may have removed evidence of others. Between the timbers were dumped layers of sand and silt, while at the western end the structure lay over a 0.06m–0.12m thick layer of crushed Reigate stone. A similar layer was seen to the north of the quay. These layers may have been laid down at the same time but they were stratigraphically separated by the former Victorian walls to the buildings that lay on the site. An external dump adjacent to Structure 5 provided a single deer fragment amongst a small quantity of general food waste. This bone probably belongs to fallow deer, although there is also the possibility that it may represent a small red deer. In either eventuality, this bone would clearly have been derived from a high-status food item. The great majority of venison entering the town of Westminster during this period is likely to have derived from the series of enclosed deer parks which were set up, mainly, within the two centuries following the Norman conquest (O Rackham 1986, 123). It is possible, considering the proximity of this deposit to the palace, that this animal may have been captured within one of the royal parks.

Fig 41 View of the end of the dock wall (S5), looking south

Structure 5 seems to have formed a dock to the palace at its northern extent, on land reclaimed from the river. The river would have flooded the area to the north, forming an inlet from the Thames. The full extent of the dock has not been ascertained. Only its northern edge was seen and it was traced for a length of 12.67m from the inner edge of the river wall. When a shaft was dug without archaeological coverage to the south-west the contractors reported large numbers of timbers across the whole area, suggesting that the dock extended through that area and was therefore at least 19m long (east–west) and 5.0m wide (north–south). No areas have been excavated further west which might have uncovered it, but it clearly could not have continued behind site L as Building 4 lay to the north of the projected line of Structure 5. Whilst the east wall of Building 4 was not excavated, it was almost certainly along the line of the modern wall, immediately to the east of Canon Row (above, Building 4). This gives the dock a maximum length of 51m. The southern edge of the structure was likewise not located. An interesting reuse of boundaries

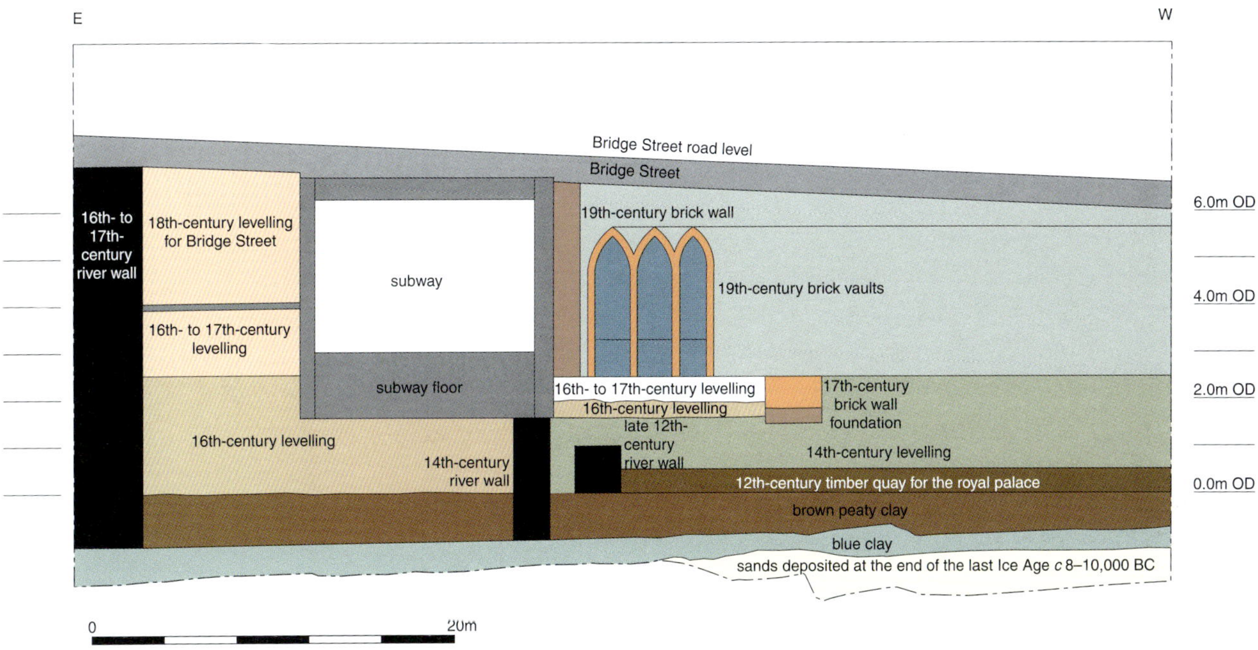

Fig 42 Reconstructed section through Bridge Street showing the natural edge of the island, dock and later deposits (scale 1:400)

might be suggested, however. The later boundary to the precinct which divided the palace from the Woolstaple, built in 1355 (Colvin et al 1963, 552), appears to lie exactly parallel to the dock and it is possible that it originally formed the southern wall of the dock before being extended upwards to form the northern precinct wall of the palace. This is speculation but, if it were the case, it would give the dock a width of 21.67m (Fig 40).

Five sources contribute to the dating of the dock. Pottery from the crushed Reigate stone layer covering the area to the north of the dock, which may have been the same as the layer upon which the dock rested at the western end, dates to 1150–1350. Tile in fabric 2271, found in a dumped layer between two of the planks, is thought to date to 1180 or later. Radiocarbon dating of one of the timbers produced a date of 800 ± 60 BP (Beta 88699, 1040–1300 cal AD) and a second produced a date of 890 ± 80 BP (Beta 88700, 1010–1280 cal AD). Documentary sources indicate that Ailnoth the engineer made (or remade) the stone river wall and quay at Westminster in 1179–80 (Colvin et al 1963, 493). Lastly, evidence from the City of London at Thames Court indicates that a new revetment was built there in 1181 as a response to a major rise in the tidal level, possibly as a result of the construction of London Bridge (Ayre et al in prep). A river wall would therefore have been essential at Westminster at this time. The documentary date of 1179–80 thus seems to fit well with the other dating evidence and this may indeed be the quay that Ailnoth built.

Suggested tide levels for this period from the excavations at Bull Wharf are a low tide of below -0.3m OD and a maximum high tide of approximately 2.0m OD (Ayre et al in prep). This indicates that the dock at Westminster would have been exposed at low tide and flooded at high tide. In that case it may have functioned in such a way that flat-bottomed barges were able to float on to the dock at high tides and then, as the tide went out, settle on the floor of the dock. They could then be unloaded before floating out again at the next high tide.

The large number of building works carried out and the expansion in the role of the palace during the later 12th century would have necessitated the construction of a dock for unloading the building materials, food and general provisions required.

Structure 6: Westminster Abbey precinct wall

The precinct wall of Westminster Abbey is thought to date from this period, although dating evidence is based purely upon documentary evidence. Green recorded that it appeared to form one build with the south waterfront of the palace thought to have been constructed during the minority of Henry III (1216–27) (Green 1976, 62). At Abingdon Street, three phases of wall were found (the third dating from after 1350: Chapter 10.3, Structure 11). The earliest exists only at the south-east corner, with the remains of a tower and the present standing wall abutting it. Structure 6 originally continued northwards across the line of the Jewel Tower to the immediate east of the abbey and a section in this area was observed in 1963 (Green 1976, 61–2, fig 1). The wall to the south of the Jewel Tower garden stands to its full height of about 8.5m (Fig 43).

During observations at Church House by Frank Cottrill in 1937, to the south-west of the abbey, a length of wall running east-south-east–west-north-west was discovered. Towards the north-west corner of the site this changed alignment to south-east–north-west. Although this wall's exact location is difficult to ascertain from Cottrill's notes, it has been plotted as closely as possible and was clearly the southern precinct wall. It appears to have extended right across the site, which was 77m long, to just short of the east side. At this point it turned to the south-east and formed the northern abutment to a bridge which crossed the mill ditch. Part of the southern abutment was also

Fig 43 *View of the Westminster Abbey precinct boundary wall (S6), with the later Jewel Tower (B17), to the right, looking west*

found under the southern edge of the site. A photograph of this bridge when it was earlier exposed appears in Westlake's *Westminster Abbey* (Westlake 1923, fig 11 ii). The main wall itself was 1.37m wide and had an offset of 0.25m on its south side and 0.18m on the north side. The wall survived to a maximum height of 2.23m and was constructed from Kentish ragstone bonded with yellow sandy mortar. The bridge abutments were similarly constructed.

As discussed under Structure 5, documentary dating, radiocarbon dating, finds dating and parallels from the City all suggest 1179–80 as a likely date for the construction of the river walls around the palace. Indeed, the evidence of the river levels indicates that such walls must have been in place to prevent widespread and serious flooding at high tide. Given that this was the case, it is inconceivable that Westminster Abbey should not have had walls to prevent flooding at the same time. It was also clear from the excavations at Abingdon Street that the precinct walls on the river side around Westminster Abbey and the Palace of Westminster were constructed as one build. The suggested date for the construction of Structure 6 is c 1180 and the same date is therefore proposed for the great drain of Westminster Abbey (below, Open Area 9).

Open Area 1: the foreshore

An east–west aligned linear feature, possibly a ditch, lay at the southern end of site C(ii) in a similar position to the earlier ditch C[320] (period 5; Chapter 7.3, Open Area 1). This ditch, C[305], was at least 0.59m wide and 0.25m deep (Fig 37). It was filled with a dark brown peat at the base, indicative of shallow slow-moving waters, with a few pieces of chalk in it, suggesting some building activity in the area. The fills of this ditch and of the alluvial layer F[4] (below) provided small quantities of bones, the latter (sieved assemblage) being composed mainly of pig and chicken bones. It was sealed by a layer of brown clay with lenses of sand and peat, suggesting repeated flooding with periods of shallower water. This ditch, and the entire site, was subsequently covered by a light brown ?estuarine clay, approximately 0.3m thick, probably deposited by flooding of the Thames. Elsewhere there is evidence of rising river levels in the late 12th century and this may date to that period.

On site F, in front of and pre-dating Structure 5, a series of deposits illustrated the environment of the foreshore. The lower deposits consisted partly of fluvial silts but mostly of humic peats and peaty clays, which presumably formed as marshland on the edge of the river over a long period. Structure 5 overlay these deposits. In front of it a series of blue and grey fluvial silts and clays were deposited up to a level of 0.26m OD with occasional patches of peaty material, indicating marsh forming up to a maximum level of 0.33m OD. These deposits were doubtless laid down by the Thames after the rise in river level from c 1180 onwards. Silt F[4] contained small quantities of animal bone, mainly pig and chicken. These deposits were within 5.0m of Building 4 and so were close to areas of occupation.

On site U a waterlaid layer of blue-grey organic clay containing decayed wooden stakes covered the area to a maximum thickness of 0.30m (Fig 37). Above this was a layer of light grey silty clay with frequent snail shells and wood. Cutting these layers was a series of east–west aligned ditches. On the north side lay one which was more than 8.15m long. At least 0.27m deep, it was probably 0.52m deep originally. It was filled with black silty clay U[23]. The edge of the cut was truncated further east but its fill appeared to continue for at least another 8.0m.

Within the fill was a stake line comprising eight stakes, between 30mm and 40mm in diameter. It is impossible to be certain whether they were associated with the ditch or whether they post-dated it but they are likely to have been some form of structure associated with the ditch, presumably designed to stop it silting up and blocking the passage of water.

Further waterlaid deposits sealed the ditch and were cut to the south by another ditch lying partially beyond the southern limit of excavation. Heavily disturbed by the roots of a tree in the centre, it was approximately 0.45m deep and more than 0.40m wide. Within it and associated with it was a stake line, 1.50m long, comprising nine stakes between 20mm and 70mm in diameter. The ditch was filled with a light grey sandy clay at the base, sealed by an organic blue clay with frequent snail shell, moderate charcoal flecks, part of a leather boot and two wooden stakes.

A third east–west aligned ditch also continued partially beyond the southern limit of excavation. It was at least 0.70m wide and 0.26m deep. It was filled with a waterlaid layer of blue silty clay with pebbles and sand. It was truncated by numerous later features but was at least 20m long. To the east it contained three fills and at the base a substantial timber that had probably washed in and wedged against the sides.

Both the ditches on the south side were partially truncated by a fourth east–west ditch that lay along the southern side of the trench. It was 3.2m long and at least 1.0m wide where it reached the southern limit of excavation, with a depth of 0.35m. It was truncated to the west and was filled with a layer of grey silty clay. At its western end it was filled with a deposit of blue clay, U[111], that sealed another stake line comprising 11 stakes, probably acting as a revetment. The stakes measured between 30mm and 60mm in diameter.

On the north side was a semicircular pit, 0.50m across and 0.14m deep. The area appears to have become flooded again with a deposit of red-brown clay containing a great deal of wood and a later layer of very sticky grey-green clay. This deposit appears to have been very swampy, full of tree roots, pieces of wood and leaves.

Further flood deposits were cut by a ditch and a pit. The earliest of these was a steep-sided ditch aligned north–south. It was more than 2.0m long and 0.64m deep. The base of the cut sloped downwards from north to south. It was filled with an organic grey clay with four distinct bands of decayed vegetation each 20mm thick. These bands of material appeared to be thick clumps of leaves that may have fallen into the ditch during the autumn, suggesting that it may have been open only for four years. To the west of the ditch lay an oval-shaped pit measuring 1.48m east–west, 1.0m north–south and 0.39m deep. To the east lay another pit, 0.50m wide and 0.14m deep.

There would appear to have been strenuous efforts made to drain the land along the foreshore to the east of King Street during the late 12th and early 13th centuries. Evidence of rising river levels takes the form of silts and clays deposited by the river over the foreshore. This confirms the evidence from the City that the Thames was rising from the late 1170s onwards and that this had a serious effect upon Westminster. River walls, jetties and docks were constructed around the palace but the peripheral land between the developing King Street and the river was not reclaimed during this period.

These drainage ditches should be seen both as attempts to drain the land before its full reclamation and as a way of disposing of waste material from the houses along King Street into the Thames. The stakes within the ditches would have acted as simple revetments, slowing the erosion of the sides, which would have silted up the ditches. The stakes were all chopped from alder (*Alnus*) tree branches (Ian Tyers, pers comm). The fact that a few pits were excavated towards the end of this period might suggest that the efforts to drain the land were successful.

The intervening riverlaid deposits indicate the continual rise in the river level but may also indicate sporadic flooding and periods of marsh formation, with leaves and tree branches falling into the marsh from wetland trees, such as alder, growing there. Indeed, evidence of alder tree roots was found. The north–south aligned ditch, which appeared to begin on the south side of the site, was presumably draining towards the Tyburn to the north but may have been open only for a few years.

Open Area 4: New Palace Yard

A waterlaid blue sandy silty clay with charcoal flooded site D to a level of 1.39m OD. This was cut by an east–west aligned ditch, 0.80m wide and 0.63m deep, that sloped down towards the river to the east (Fig 36). It was filled with brown-grey organic silt with lenses of plant remains and fragments of Kentish ragstone, mortar, animal bone, oyster shell, charcoal, pottery and leather. This was presumably a drainage ditch running into the Thames. It was overlain by a waterlaid black sandy silty clay with fragments of mortar, tile, wood, animal bone and pottery. Bones from this flood silt, D[57], represented a wide range of species, with chicken and pig as the dominant components (a notable comparison here to the Open Area 1 deposits, above), but also featuring common partridge and a variety of fish, including thornback ray, gadids (cod identified), herring, plaice/flounder, smelt and cyprinid. It is noticeable that the majority of the fish bones, in terms of either fragment or species count, represent marine and, probably, estuarine catches. This layer may have been deposited during a period of flooding, with the constructional and artefactual material in it representing continued activity in New Palace Yard.

The foreshore sand on site G was covered by undated waterlaid deposits, comprising a thin layer of sand, G[34], and a layer of brown-grey silty clay, G[33], containing partly decayed wood and fibrous plant matter. The latter was up to 0.25m thick, and its surface lay between 0.84m and 0.99m OD. The plants from this deposit were for the most part species commonly found in marshy environments, suggesting that at the time of deposition the site was very close to the edge of Thorney Island. The organic muds probably accumulated along the margins of the eyot during a period of rising river levels, perhaps in the years immediately before the construction of the river walls.

On the south side of Open Area 4, on site J, a waterlaid clay was overlain by a peaty clay whose surface lay at 1.09m OD. This deposit may suggest a fall in the water level, perhaps as a result of the construction of the river walls, leaving marshy unconsolidated ground. Further west, a series of waterlaid sands and silts were deposited. Sealing these and the disuse of Building 3 was a sandy soil horizon that built up over them.

As stated above, robber trenches were dug to remove the building material from Building 3 and two large pits were dug, containing discarded material from the building. The uppermost fill of these pits formed a gravel surface. Four further pits were dug but their fills gave no obvious clue as to their use.

Slightly to the north of the later 13th-century boundary wall between New Palace Yard and the Green Yard (Chapter 9.3, Structure 10), on site J, lay a complex area of intercutting pits and postholes, most of which continued beyond the area of excavation. The initial phase of activity saw the digging of a large pit at least 2.0m east–west by 1.0m north–south. This was later cut by another pit, at least 0.45m in diameter. In turn this was cut by a large pit that was more than 1.05m in diameter and 0.58m deep. None contained substantial quantities of refuse and their function remains unclear.

The pits were truncated by two large postholes, 0.40m apart. That on the west was 0.95m in diameter and 0.65m deep and its profile to the south suggested that the post had been deliberately removed on that side. The eastern posthole measured 0.84m x 0.70m and was 0.56m deep. A stakehole, 0.12m in diameter and 0.15m deep, lay to the east. These may have formed part of a timber palisade defining the boundary between New Palace Yard and the Green Yard before 1244. There was certainly a timber gatehouse in existence before the construction of the stone gatehouse of that date (Colvin et al 1963, 547) and a timber wall was presumably associated with it. If this interpretation were correct then the features to its south would have been in the Green Yard and not New Palace Yard; however, such an interpretation remains highly tentative and the other features have been described as belonging to Open Area 4 (New Palace Yard).

The posthole fills produced considerable information on the environment of the area. Two, J[22] and J[23], produced broadly similar plant assemblages in which the fruits and seeds represented a not particularly high species diversity, being mainly from wild plants of wetland habitats and disturbed/waste ground environments plus the residues of a few plant foods. Wood fragments, with some charcoal, were plentiful in both samples but particularly in J[22].

The wetland plants consisted of aquatics, for example, stoneworts (*Chara* spp), crowfoots (*Ranunculus* subgen *Batrachium*), water plantain (*Alisma* spp), and bankside/marshland species, for example ragged robin (*Lychnis flos-cuculi*), celery-leaved crowfoot (*Ranunculus sceleratus*), hemlock (*Conium maculatum*) (well represented), *Apium* spp, gipsy-wort (*Lycopus europaeus*), sedges (*Carex* spp) and rushes (*Juncus* spp). Green water cress/summer water cress (*Nasturtium officinale*) was recovered from J[22]; this grows at the edges of streams, ditches and springs and either just above or just below the level of the moving water. It is rarely in stagnant water, is intolerant of shade and usually found in calcareous water (Clapham et al 1987). This plant may have been collected and eaten. Plants of disturbed ground and waste places included large numbers of stinging nettle (*Urtica dioica*) seeds plus goosefoots/oraches (*Chenopodium/Atriplex* spp), chickweeds (*Stellaria media*), knotgrass (*Polygonum aviculare*), black nightshade (*Solanum nigrum*) and henbane (*Hyoscyamus niger*). A few trees and shrubs were also represented, for instance, brambles and elder; these may have been exploited as a food resource. Plant food residues included single charred barley (*Hordeum sativum*) grains and fig (*Ficus carica*) seeds in J[22] only.

These plant assemblages suggest wet conditions with some standing water, and this is supported by the presence of *ephippia* (in J[22]) and freshwater molluscs. Food residues suggesting human activities nearby were also represented by other biological remains (large mammal and fish bones).

Postholes J[25] and J[27] produced very similar results to the previous two postholes although with a smaller diversity of plant species. Thus the fruits and seeds represented mainly wild plants of wetland habitats (aquatic stoneworts and water plantain) and bankside/marshland species (for example hemlock and sedges), plants of disturbed ground and waste places (such as stinging nettle, goosefoots/oraches, knotgrass and henbane) and possible arable weeds (corn marigold (*Chrysanthemum segetum*), for example). A few trees and shrubs were also represented, for instance, brambles and elder; they may have been exploited as a food resource. An oat (*Avena* sp) and wheat (*Triticum* sp) grain in J[25] and [J27] respectively were the only definite food remains. Very fragmented wood and charcoal were also present.

These plant assemblages again suggest wet conditions with some standing water. The presence of freshwater molluscs and ostracods (the latter in J[27] only) supports this. The other weed seeds may have blown in from nearby and indicate disturbed habitats possibly associated with human activities, also indicated by a few large mammal bones in J[27] and charcoal fragments.

These plant remains provide a clear impression of the environment in New Palace Yard at that time. Largely undeveloped wasteland, subject to regular flooding, it would have been marshy and covered in numerous wetland plants.

To the south of the postholes lay a gully sloping down to the east, some 0.34m wide and 0.20m deep. Its eastern end was found, but to the west it continued beyond the limit of excavation. The fill appeared to have been waterlaid. It may even have been a drainage ditch dug in an attempt to drain the marshy land, possibly within the Green Yard rather than New Palace Yard.

Open Area 5: Green Yard

As stated above, the gully, Building 3 and its subsequent robbing, and the gravel surface that overlay it may have been activities occurring in Open Area 5 rather than Open Area 4 (New Palace Yard). In either case there is documentary evidence that a timber gate formed an entrance into the Green Yard and that this was taken down in 1244–5 when the stone gate (B8) was constructed.

Open Area 6: Old Palace Yard

No archaeological data were recovered from Open Area 6 in this period but it is thought that the residential part of the palace was defined at this time if not before. There is evidence to suggest that a wall ran west from the south end of the great hall, creating a residential area to the south (OA6) and an 'administrative' area to the north (OA5). A gate in this wall gave access.

Open Area 7

To the north of St Stephen's chapel, and dating from before its construction in the late 13th century, were found two layers of riverlaid deposits to a depth of 1.05m. The upper surface of these lay at 1.20m OD. They were presumably deposited by the river during the second half of the 12th century, when the river levels in the Thames rose significantly, and before the construction of the river walls. Some flooding over the river walls may still have occurred subsequently. This area does not appear to have been intensively occupied although only very small areas have been excavated.

Open Area 8: Westminster Abbey precinct (north)

Aligned east–west on site C(i) was a linear cut, possibly a ditch, 0.90m wide and 0.12m deep (Fig 36). Only a length of 1.20m was uncovered. Its fill contained tile and large amounts of shell. It was cut to the east by a large, approximately square, posthole. The socket for the post measured 0.53m x 0.40m x 0.24m deep and the shape of the posthole indicated that the post had been deliberately removed from the west side.

The ditch and the posthole lie in the area of the later precinct boundary to Westminster Abbey and may have been part of a 12th-century boundary, although without the investigation of larger areas this can only be speculation. The post was pulled out and the posthole backfilled at some time before the middle of the 13th century, presumably when Building 13 (Chapter 9.3) and the stone precinct wall were constructed.

On the west side of the island, on site E, a well-compacted layer of grey clay was laid with a possible gravel surface laid over it. This lay under a second gravel layer that may also have been a surface. A small posthole, 0.20m square and 80mm deep, cut the clay levelling layer, as did a pit measuring 0.80m x 0.75m x 0.48m deep. Overlying the gravel surface and the posthole was a dumped levelling layer of brown clay-silt. Cutting the pit on the north side of the site was an east–west aligned ditch about 1.0m wide and 0.45m deep. This was filled with a brown clay-silt with charcoal and some building material and shell. It was probably a boundary of some sort and not a drainage ditch for the fill did not appear to have been waterlaid. Overlying the ditch was Building 2 (above). Until the formation of the boundary dividing the properties along King Street (period 7; Chapter 9.2) it is difficult to be certain as to the status of this part of Thorney Island. It may simply have been waste ground to one side of King Street, it may have formed the back of much larger properties along King Street or it may have been part of general land in the ownership of the abbey prior to the formation of the precinct boundaries. In the absence of definitive evidence of boundaries around the precinct at this time it is included here.

Open Area 9: Westminster Abbey precinct (south)

Beneath the south-west corner of the later Jewel Tower garden was part of the Westminster Abbey great drain, which was found to survive almost intact (Fig 44). A manhole had, however, been cut through its roof (and subsequently covered over) and a part of the north-east wall was rebuilt. A section of the drain 6.50m long survived intact to be surveyed; the remaining length to the south-east probably survives in large part but could not be seen since modern disturbance to its roof had caused the drain to be infilled with debris. The walls consisted of Kentish ragstone, chalk and some yellow sandstone, with occasional medieval yellow brick presumably representing repairs. The drain was 0.92m wide at the level of the springing arch and 0.88m wide at the base. It was 1.58m high in total. There were either six or seven courses of masonry below the springing arch, which appeared to be rounded at its apex. The floor was laid in unmortared Kentish ragstone slabs. The level of the floor lay at 1.67m OD, while the exit to the drain some 18.7m to the south-east was at 1.33m OD (Green 1976, fig 5). This gives an incline of 1:42.5. Such a fall is consistent with that found at other monastic houses: the late 13th- to early 14th-century drain at St Mary Spital, for instance, fell 0.37m over a distance of 15m, a fall of 1:40.5 (Thomas et al 1997, 41). If the gradient of the Westminster Abbey drain was maintained then the floor level would lie at 2.93m OD where it exited the reredorter a further 51m to the west. Ground level in the undercroft to the north was at c 3.5m OD (Mills 1995, 75), leaving a gap of 0.5m–0.6m into the drains, similar to that recorded in the infirmary latrine at St Mary Spital (Thomas et al 1997, 71).

The walls of the drain were founded on timber piles although the timbers had rotted to leave voids. Seven were discovered, varying in diameter between 90mm and 0.17m and were up to 0.70m deep. They must have been required because

Fig 44 *View of the interior of the great drain, looking south-east (0.5m scale)*

of the marshy nature of the ground on which the drain was laid. The level from which the drain was cut is unclear but the arched vault began at 2.82m OD and the top of the vault must lie at about 3.10m OD.

There were four undated fills within the drain. The upper levels may well date to the period of disuse of the drain but without excavation it is impossible to be certain. The lowest fill was a brown sandy silt that was overlain by sand and gravel, then by a white sandy silt and finally by a dark grey silt.

Parts of the drain were recorded in the 1960s and published (Green 1976, 62, figs 4 and 5). It exited through a square opening in the precinct wall (S6) on to the foreshore, and was built as one with that wall. As discussed above, the dating of the construction of Structure 6 would now appear to be c 1180 so, given that the drain was built as one with it, it is now proposed that the drain was also built in c 1180.

The great drain exited the reredorter at the south end of the east range of the cloister and ran eastwards towards the river. A section of it survived in the basement beneath the kitchen of the buildings on the south side of the infirmary cloister (RCHME 1924, 91). From the infirmary cloister the drain probably diverted slightly to the south of an east–west alignment before turning to the south-east. This change in angle was to keep the drain within the precincts of the abbey and to ensure that it exited on to the foreshore south of the palace. By the middle of the 14th century, however, the palace had appropriated part of that land so that the drain actually ran beneath a part of the palace precinct.

8.4 Discussion

The rise in the river of c 1180 had a dramatic effect upon Westminster. The need for substantial river defences to protect the land from flooding became vital. There may have been a positive side to this rise in the river, however, as it would have allowed larger boats to get further up the river to Westminster and the construction of the dock (S5) would have enabled them to unload. With a high tide of c 2.0m OD, 1.5m of water would have covered the dock floor.

The process of definition of the various parts of Westminster also seems to have begun in earnest during the second half of the 12th century. Apart from the erection of river defences, there were timber walls and gates around parts of the palace precinct and it may be that similar boundaries were created around the abbey. Development along King Street certainly began with the reclamation of both sides of the street in the second half of the 12th century, closely followed by the building of houses. Some of those dwelling in King Street were wealthy courtiers and government officials who needed or wished to be close to the royal palace. Others were tradesmen who were required next to a royal palace and major Benedictine abbey.

Large-scale building in the palace was undertaken during the reign of Henry II (1154–89). There seems to be a distinct change in the character of the various areas of the precinct and in the building programmes carried out there. Documentary evidence indicates whole new ranges of structures built in the domestic area of the palace, including new apartments for the king. River walls and docks were built, with a gate through the river wall, and timber precinct walls and gates were built between the Green Yard and New Palace Yard. For dating evidence, see Table 9.

Evidence of habitation of these areas at this time appears to have been slight although it is more substantial than that from the foreshore. Human activity was, for instance, indicated by a similar range of cereals to that found in period 5 but with the addition of oats as well as cultivated fruits, fig and the earliest evidence for grape (*Vitis vinifera*) and cherry (*Prunus avium*), and wild fruits. Watercress (*Nasturtium officinale*) was found, but this may be a natural accumulation rather than a food residue. Wetland plants were again well represented; some of these plants in the structural cuts may have been collected incidentally along with sedges and rushes gathered as flooring materials. Possible residues of hay fodder were found in one sample although these may simply be indicative of the local habitat. The few samples from sites outside the palace to the north contained little evidence for human activities, whilst the wild plants suggested a marshy environment.

Table 9 Selected dating evidence, period 6 (see Table 25 for expansion of codes)

Land use	Activity	Context	Evidence	Description	Date range
Building 2	beam slot	E[40]	ceramic	LCOAR	1080–1200
	beam slot	E[55]	ceramic	LOND; SHER	1150–1300
Building 4	oven	L[49]	ceramic	LCOAR	1080–1200
Structure 5: dock	levelling	F[161]	ceramic building material	tile 2271; 2586; 2816	1200–1500
Structure 5: dock	levelling	F[161]	ceramic	LOND	1150–1350
Structure 5: dock	timber	F[185]	radiocarbon date	Beta 88700; see Table 56	1010–1280
Structure 5: dock			documentary	Colvin et al 1963, 493	1179–1180
Open Area 1: foreshore	yard surface	E[57]	ceramic	LOND; SHER; SSW	1150–1250
Open Area 1: foreshore	levelling	E[61]	ceramic	EMS; EMSH; SHER	1150–1200
Open Area 1: foreshore	pit	E[64]	ceramic	LCOAR; SHER	1150–1200
Open Area 1: foreshore	flood deposit	F[4]	ceramic	EMS; EMSS; SSW	1150–1250
Open Area 1: foreshore	flooding	C[299]	ceramic	?ANDE; EMSS; LOND	1150–1350
Open Area 1: foreshore	ditch fill	C[301]	ceramic	ANDE	1000–1200
Open Area 1: foreshore	ditch fill	U[23]	ceramic	LOND; SHER	1150–1350
Open Area 1: foreshore	ditch fill	U[159]	ceramic	LOND; SHER	1150–1350
Open Area 1: foreshore	foreshore deposit	U[169]	ceramic	LOND; SHER	1150–1350
Open Area 1: foreshore	foreshore deposit	U[116]	ceramic	LOND	1150–1250
Open Area 4: New Palace Yard	flood deposit	D[57]	ceramic	LCOAR; LOND; SHER; SSW	1200–1250
Open Area 4: New Palace Yard	ditch	D[60]	ceramic	LOND	1150–1350
Open Area 8	ditch	C[184]	ceramic	EMSH; EMSS; ?STAM	1150–1250

9

c 1230–*c* 1350 (period 7)

9.1 Environmental and topographical background

The River Thames

The medieval riverine deposits are highly complex in their derivation and contrast strongly with the sediments from the prehistoric period. It has not always been possible to ascribe the sequences to the exact periods used in this book and therefore it is possible that the theories outlined here may overlap across several periods. It is likely that increased occupation may have altered the mechanics of channel flow, leading to the transition from an erosional to an accreting regime that led to the redeposition of material after the period of hiatus noted above. The diatoms within the deposits indicate that the water body was certainly tidal. In fact, the sediments present at 0.46m OD exhibit the strongest marine influence within the entire sequence, indicating that, adjacent to Thorney Island, the Thames was strongly tidal, with the Tyburn channels also being affected by these processes. At a slightly higher altitude at Storey's Gate (0.52m OD) within these medieval sediments, the tidal influence decreased, with the brackish water diatoms assuming dominance over the marine species. This could be caused by several factors: it could be a pure reflection of events occurring in the main channel of the Thames, or the tidal head could have migrated slightly downstream, leading to a decrease in marine species relative to the brackish water species present in the sediments being deposited. However, the Tyburn channel is peripheral to the Thames, and the decrease in tidal influence at Storey's Gate, several hundred metres from the confluence of the two rivers, is more likely to be a result of local changes. Nevertheless, the medieval and later riverine deposits indicate a consistently tidal river with limited local fluctuations in the strength of the salinity signal. This could easily have been caused by seasonal events leading to increased flooding of sediment from upstream (ie, spring runoff with an increased freshwater signal) in contrast to sedimentation under conditions of highest astronomical tide bringing sediment from the outer estuary. Such fluctuation should not get in the way of the image of a gradually rising river (relative to dry land) becoming modified through embanking and reclamation, a tradition which continues today.

Palaeoecology

The pollen record from site F recommences in the late 12th century and includes a mixed assemblage with brackish water flora, for instance, sea plantain (*Plantago maritima*), goosefoots (*Chenopodium* spp), daisy (*Aster* type) and (non-cereal) grasses (Poaceae). The dryland taxa appear similar to those represented previously on Thorney Island in the Bronze and Iron Ages but, compared to the prehistoric period, there appears to be an increase in the strength of the signal reflecting nearby cultivation. This, together with the apparent planting of pine indicates significant modification of the natural landscape in this period.

Site E provides some limited environmental evidence from deposits thought to date from the 12th century. There appears to have been some woodland present at this date, with pine (*Pinus*), hazel (*Corylus avellana*) and alder (*Alnus*) reasonably prominent in the pollen record, and the resolution of the picture is increased by some records of lime (*Tilia*), ash (*Fraxinus*) and holly (*Ilex*). A further, rather unusual, aspect of the woodland species is the presence of spruce (*Picea*) and fir (*Abies*). These were probably deliberately planted to produce timber (softwoods tending to be fast-grown) rather than being a natural component of the local woodland, as with the pine also found here and at nearby site F. Alternatively, they may simply have been planted as ornamental trees. The herb pollen indicates that there were also scrubby areas, cultivated fields and marsh in addition to the woodland areas. The marsh will have been marginal to Thorney Island and leading down to the Tyburn/Thames confluence.

Additional information comes from site H. As with sites E and F, woodland cover nearby is indicated, with oak being the most dominant type represented. Nevertheless, the picture of a diverse woodland flora seen at sites E and F is maintained through the spectra identified at H. Rarer species were also identified here, including walnut (*Juglans*), spruce and sweet chestnut (*Fagopyrum esculentum*) (Roman and post-Roman introductions). The woodland element also included more common species: lime, ash and beech (*Fagus*). Evidence for cereal production was recovered, including the presence of rye (*Secale cereale*). It should be borne in mind that the pollen by this period may derive from local crop processing rather than actual field systems. Another economic plant recovered from this period was hemp (*Cannabis* type). A third ecological zone was identified from this site: marshland. Both fresh and estuarine sediments appear to have been present, leading to the development of a mixed ecological community including salt-marsh species such as thrift.

9.2 Documentary and archaeological background

By the end of the 13th century, Westminster had more or less gained the basic form that it was to retain for the next 500 years or so. The town of Westminster was centred around the streets of King Street, Tothill Street and Thieving Lane. As can be seen from Fig 45, King Street led from Fleet Street down to Westminster straight into the north gate of the abbey and then to its main north door. On its way the street crossed the Clowson stream (the remaining northern tributary of the Tyburn). It has been suggested that King Street was largely built up as far as Charing Cross, particularly on the east side, by 1300 (Rosser 1989, fig 4). At the gate to the abbey there was a turning to the east, which led into the palace gate, and one to the west, which led into Thieving Lane. This road followed the precinct wall of the abbey and continued round to meet the west gate. Here it joined with Tothill Street, the main road from the west to the abbey. Most of this street lay off the island, crossing the Tyburn only shortly before the abbey's west gate.

Westminster Abbey

Major rebuilding works were carried out at the abbey between 1245 and 1269, during the reign of Henry III (1216–72). This consisted not only of the rebuilding of the church, but also of the construction of other buildings, such as the misericord (Black 1976, 135). So much of the abbey was replaced at this time that little of the Romanesque building survives (excepting parts of the east range of the cloister and the ruined frater). The choir, transepts, a new lady chapel and the east end of the nave were completed. Continual additions were made to the abbey over the next three centuries, culminating in the completion of Henry VII's chapel at the east end of the church in the early 16th century. A fire originating in the palace in 1298 caused widespread damage to the claustral buildings and necessitated the rebuilding of many of them in the following period.

Apart from the typical monastic buildings, many other structures are known to have been associated with the abbey. To the south of the precinct lay a mill reached by a bridge and the kitchen garden. The mill was fed by a channel from the Tyburn dug by the monks. Outside the precinct to the west, on the other side of the Tyburn, lay almshouses and the almonry.

The northern precinct had presumably been enclosed by a wall by this date but there is no documentary evidence as to when it was constructed, although it was clearly in existence by 1280 since a building called the Long House is described before that date as abutting the sanctuary wall (Rosser 1989, 100). Numerous other structures lay within the northern precinct, which later became known as the Sanctuary, after the abbey's privilege of sanctuary. These included the parish church of St Margaret, the belfry, houses for the sanctuary men (Honeybourne 1932, 323) and buildings associated with and used by the merchants who attended the October Fair. There were gates out of the precinct to the north leading into King Street and to the west into Tothill Street.

The belfry was built in 1249–53 and survived as a structure until the mid 18th century. It was recorded by William Stukeley (Stukeley 1790, 43–8) during its demolition in 1750 and the foundations were again recorded early in the 20th century (Norman 1916, 14–17). The foundations were laid in chalk resting on timber piles, which must have been needed where the belfry overlay the earlier silts from the Tyburn, presumably below the 1.0m contour line. The main structure, measuring 23.92m x 22.91m, was built from Kentish ragstone and seems to have been of two storeys, 18.50m high, surmounted by a wooden spire. The lower floor contained two parallel passages running from east to west and two more from north to south across the centre of the building, one running from a door in the west wall. The upper floor was recorded by Stukeley as having an open cruciform shape, paved with stone and filled

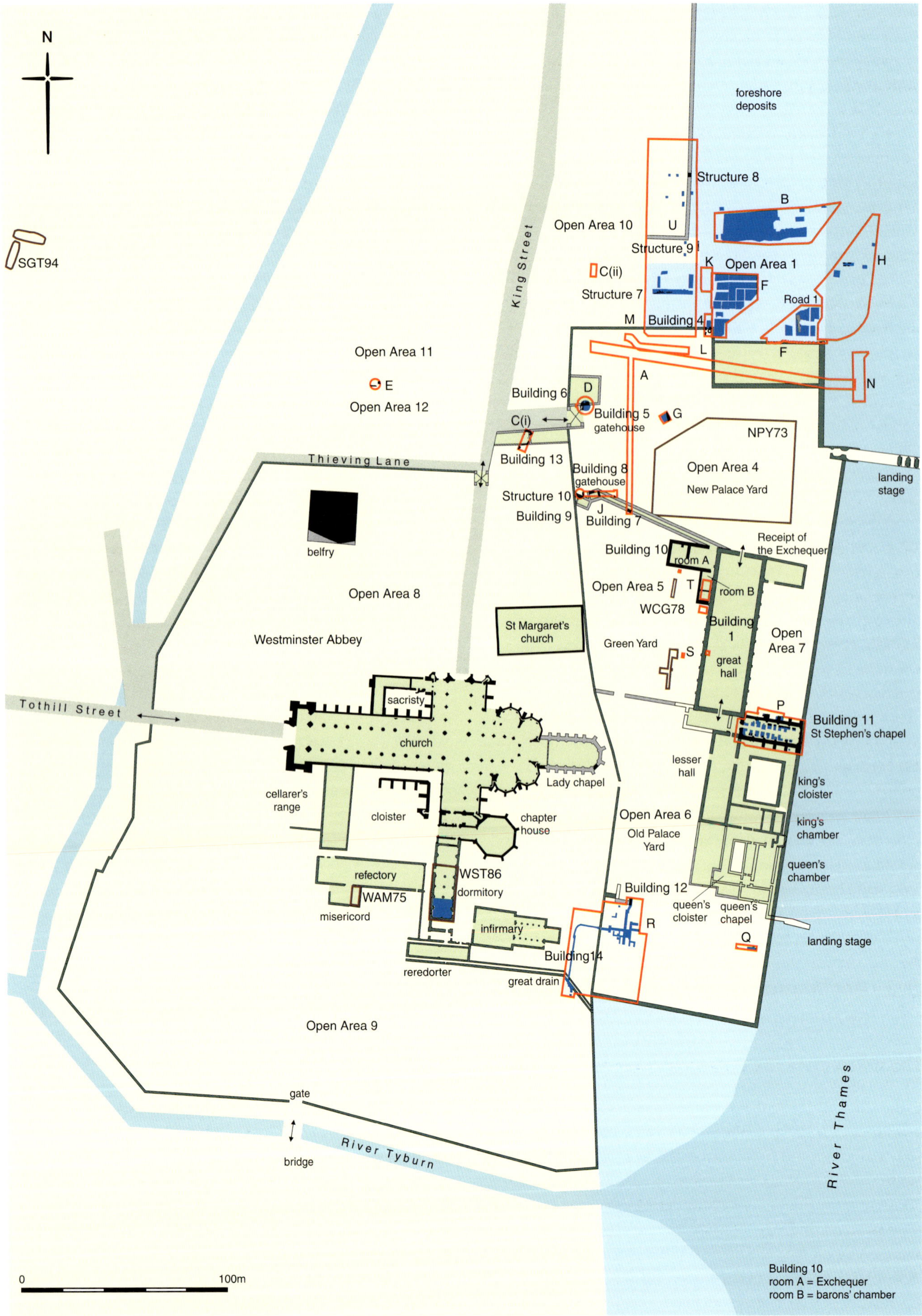

Fig 45 Plan of the archaeological features, period 7 (scale 1:2500). For key to site codes, see Tables 1–3

with tenements. Three of the four corners were entirely comprised of stone at the lower level with a staircase in the fourth up to the first floor. The other three corners were filled with rooms at the first-floor level. A second staircase on the outside was, according to Stukeley, added later.

Stukeley was clearly confused as to the date and function of this structure and it is now difficult to recover its exact form, but his records do at least present a picture of the building in 1750. Despite his contrary interpretation, there is no reason to suppose that this building was used for anything other than hanging bells and it was not a two-storey cruciform church. The parallel corridors on the ground floor presumably led to the ropes, the bells being in an open first floor, accessed by the internal staircase. There is no reason to doubt Stukeley's assertion that the external staircase was additional. It may be that it was added when the abbey was dissolved in 1540 and the belfry turned into tenements; perhaps the upper storey was floored at this time as well. The belfry was without doubt a highly imposing structure and a colossal building for its purpose. The reason behind such a substantial building design is unclear.

One of the main uses to which the northern precinct of the abbey was put was the holding of fairs, which happened each year (Rosser 1989, 97–101). Henry III granted the monks a charter in 1245 to hold two fairs in Westminster, each lasting three days, one in January and one in October. The October Fair was extended to two weeks in 1248 and to 32 days in 1298 when the January Fair was discontinued. From 1248, all other fairs were suspended and the London shops were closed for the duration of the fairs, a means of securing extra funds for the royal rebuilding of the abbey, which began at this time (Rosser 1989, 97–8). During the 13th century the Great Fair of St Edward, as the October Fair was known, was at its height. It was originally part of a progression of fairs that followed one another throughout the year. The traders would probably have moved from one to another, with cloth and wool being the most traded item. During the 14th century, however, the fair probably began to decline although it was still clearly a large affair throughout period 7. The other major difference during the 14th century was the dominance of London traders compared to fair-traders from all around the country (Rosser 1989, 106–9).

The precinct of the Palace of Westminster

In the 13th century, the precinct on the north side of the palace stretched at least as far as the northern end of the later Canon Row, and possibly as far as Enedehithe, approximately opposite modern-day Horse Guards. The estate on which Richard, earl of Cornwall, brother of Henry III, was building his inn in c 1234 (*Cal Close R Henry III*, 1231–4, 409) may have been granted to him by the king out of the precinct; it was granted to Westminster Abbey by Richard's son Henry and, known as Almayne, it remained part of the abbey's estate in Westminster. South of Almayne the precinct provided the king with land to reward royal servants, especially his clerks, and to give them accommodation near his palace. The area between Almayne and the great hall falls into four sections: (1) the area fronting King Street and extending eastward to a ditch running north–south that was called the 'ditch of the palace', or the 'king's ditch' (below), and southward to the palace gatehouse; (2) an area possibly partly west of this ditch but otherwise between the ditch and the Thames, granted to royal servants and eventually the site of the earl of Kent's inn; (3) the king's garden; (4) the courtyard later known as New Palace Yard.

The king's ditch

A ditch called the 'ditch of the palace', or the 'ditch of the king', ran roughly north–south between and parallel to King Street and the Thames, forming an eastern boundary to some of the properties in King Street. Its course is known only from documents, and not all the references can be minutely located. However, several instances are for the tenements on the east side of the Round Woolstaple, where the estate owned by Christ's Hospital was surveyed at the beginning of the 17th century (Chapter 10.2) (Schofield 1987, fig 57). The ditch ran down the eastern side of the tenements and then ran westward along the southern boundary, but thereafter its course is unknown. Most of the properties in the references below seem to be linked, but a firm descent of ownership, which positively locates the properties, has not yet been established.

The earliest reference found is from 1242, when Henry III ordered his clerk Edward, son of Odo the goldsmith, who succeeded his father as keeper of the king's works at Westminster, to give the ditch outside the gate of Westminster to Master David, the king's surgeon, to whom the king had granted it (*Cal Close R Henry III*, 1237–42, 422). Master David had a house near the palace in 1235, fronting the palace entry (Rosser 1989, 31).

In 1293 a tenement in the fee of the palace was bounded by the ditch of the palace on the south and east (WAM, 17491). In 1325 a messuage that adjoined the earl of Kent's inn on part of its northern side had the ditch of the king's palace on its eastern boundary (PRO, CP 40/261A, rot carte 1).

The property later acquired by Christ's Hospital is referred to several times, beginning in 1342 when a messuage had the ditch of the king on its eastern side and on the south side at the eastern end (GL, MS 12989). A deed of 1373 repeats this description (MS 12990), while in 1462 four tenements had recently been built between the Woolstaple Yard on the west and 'le kyngsditch' on the east and south (MS 12980).

Most properties on both sides of King Street and in Longditch and Tothill Street were bounded on at least one side by ditches, an integral part of the building process given the low-lying nature of the area. These were often included in grants of the adjoining land, but the fact that this particular ditch was referred to as the ditch of the palace, or of the king, indicates a long-lasting and significant boundary, possibly marking the palace precinct from an early date. It seems to have formed the boundary of the king's garden. It is unlikely to be simply a drainage ditch from the palace to the Thames, given its direction, and may be a natural feature of the river. Equally, since during the Middle Ages it was never referred to as a sewer or a stream (unlike the Clowson just to the north), it may have been a specially dug boundary ditch and bank, perhaps without running water in it. The grant in 1242 suggests that at that time part of it ran near the gate from King Street, perhaps even across the entry like a moat, and was granted to Master David in order for him to add its site to his property. If it had been a drainage ditch such an alienation would have been unlikely. The part at the eastern side of the Woolstaple must be very close to excavations in sites U or K.

Between King Street and the ditch

Land in this area, on the north side of the entry to the palace gate, was all held of the king as part of the fee of the palace. The keeper of the palace, a hereditary serjeanty belonging to the Levelond family and their descendants, had as part of his perquisites a messuage and garden that may have lain in this area, though the site has not yet been positively identified. A keeper in the 14th century acquired property in the Round Woolstaple, but this was not necessarily originally part of the keeper's fee. The house of Master David the king's surgeon lay by the gate in 1235, and presumably in 1242. Nearby outside the gate was the site of a house built by John of Upton, the marshal, who in 1240 was granted the messuage for 2d a year to the Exchequer (*Cal Chart R*, 1226–57, 251). The property stretched from the gate to the corner of King Street, and John divided it between his two sons Hugh and Robert (who were holding in 1280: PRO, CP 40/36, rot 123d) and daughter Joan, and had two or three tenants on the property. Its northward extent is not known: the house fronting the entry granted in marriage with his daughter was 14ft deep, with John's messuage north of that (WAM, 17365).

By 1308 there were also six shops fronting King Street with the entrance to the later Round Woolstaple on the north, again all held of the king for 2d a year to the Exchequer (PRO, C 143/72, no. 6).

The earl of Kent's inn

This site can be traced back to Master Odo the goldsmith, keeper of works to Henry III. Odo held land in Westminster by the beginning of the 13th century, including some in Longditch and at Enedehithe, the latter forming the nucleus of the inn of the archbishops of York at a later date, and he was reeve in the abbey's manor of Westminster in the second decade of the 13th century. By 1218 he was appointed keeper of works for the palace and began extensive repairs to the buildings, the riverside quay and precinct wall, followed by major rebuilding in the 1230s and 1240s (Colvin et al 1963, 494). He was presumably granted the property within the palace precinct during his keepership, and by 1236 it was his principal property, with a private chapel for his household for which he paid 4s a year to the sacrist of Westminster Abbey in lieu of oblations to St Margaret's, and he was granted the privilege of having a chantry in his chapel while it remained in his ownership and that of his heirs (WAM, 17333). Between October 1241 and Easter 1242 his office passed to his son Master Edward of Westminster, who inherited Odo's property soon afterwards as well.

The houses were described as being near the sluice, presumably the Clusebridge (the close bridge) where the Clowson passed under King Street, but probably lay back from the highway. In 1244 Edward, who was Henry III's clerk, keeper of works and general administrator at Westminster, was granted as a mark of favour the right to run a pipe for water to his house from the king's supply to Westminster. Edward died early in 1265, and his house was granted to Peter de Montfort, who was given freedom from livery there in March 1265 (*Cal Pat R*, 1258–66, 413), but Montfort was killed at the battle of Evesham later that year and the king granted the messuage to Sir Roger de Leyburn, Kt (*Cal Chart R*, 1257–1300, 55), to whom Edward of Westminster's son and heir Odo later quitclaimed (PRO, E 40/2508). The messuage was described as lying between the court of the king of England and the court of the king of Germany (Almayne) and between the house of John the cook and that of the archdeacon of York, stretching from the highway to the Thames. The houses of John and the archdeacon most likely fronted the highway, as the latter had been taken out of the estate: in 1272 Edward's younger son Thomas of Westminster quitclaimed to Robert Burnell, archdeacon of York, all right in the houses of his father which his brother Odo had sold to the archdeacon (*Cal Close R Henry III*, 1268–72, 566). The grant to Leyburn included also another messuage, probably on the south-west side. Despite the wording it is not clear whether these houses were completely alienated from the estate, and it is likely that all such grants were made at the behest of the king, who used the property near the palace to house his ministers and officials. Nor is it clear whether the grants above represented the whole of this property, or if Master Odo, who was king's remembrancer by 1273 until near his death in *c* 1291 (Crook 1980, 21–2), was still occupying part. A path 7ft wide at the southern end of the property for access to the highway was reserved to Odo and his heirs from the grant to Leyburn, but this may have been for the benefit of other tenants.

Sir Roger died in 1271 and the main property passed to his son William Leyburn, but by 1281 it seems to be the house of Otho de Grandison (*Cal Pat R*, 1272–81, 435), who had served Edward I overseas before his accession and returned to England in 1274, a trusted and confidential servant of the king; a royal council was held in his house outside the palace in 1292. He eventually left England in 1307 (Kingsford 1909). The house later passed to the king's brother, Edmund of Woodstock, earl of Kent, who also held for life a messuage formerly of Walter de Bedewynde, king's clerk, probably the houses at Clusebridge, which Edward II granted to his brother in 1321 after they were surrendered to the king by John of Ockham, wardrobe clerk and later baron of the Exchequer from 1317 (PRO, C 135/23 [fo 5]; *Cal Pat R*, 1317–21, 568; Tout 1920–33, ii, 270). After Edmund's execution for treason in 1330, Queen Isabella, widow of Edward II, obtained a grant of his Westminster property (*Cal Pat R*, 1327–30, 506), but after the fall of Roger Mortimer later that year the queen had to surrender her acquisitions (McKisack 1959, 101–2), which presumably included Kent's inn. An extent of Kent's property in Westminster taken at the beginning of 1331 described the messuage once of Otho de Grandison, of which part was held of the abbot of Westminster by the service of 2s a year (perhaps part of the 4s paid to the sacrist by Odo the goldsmith), as having no value beyond the outgoings because the house was ruinous and in need of repair. The other messuage was valued at 13s 4d a year (PRO, C 135/23 [fo 5]).

9.3 Archaeological evidence

Building 2

The posts to Building 2 on site E appear to have been pulled out of the ground by this period. The postholes for the eastern two posts were significantly larger than the actual post sockets, suggesting that the posts were pulled out of the ground from the north.

Building 4

The ovens of period 6 on the west side of Building 4 on site L went out of use during this period. A layer of silt was dumped into the hearth and a yellow clay floor was laid. Cutting the floor was a sub-rectangular hearth about 0.7m x 0.6m filled with a black ashy silt and a layer of tiles in off-white mortar on the southern and eastern sides, presumably forming a surround (Fig 58). The lack of burning suggests that this hearth was not intensively used before its disuse. Over it lay levelling dumps with small amounts of building material and some charcoal. Cutting them were two large postholes, approximately 0.6m across, with a possible third to the north. The southern two appeared to have a slot, possibly a beam slot, running part of the way between them. The northern was adjacent to the north wall of the building. These may have formed a substantial partition within the building or may even have been associated with the building's demolition. On the eastern side, the oven, L[48] (Chapter 8.3), appears to have continued in use up until the disuse of the building.

Building 5: gatehouse to New Palace Yard

Building 5 on site D abutted and therefore post-dated Building 6. It consisted of a rectangular area of chalk and Kentish ragstone, 2.0m north–south by 1.4m east–west, bonded with a brown coarse sandy mortar (Fig 46). The wall lay in a wide construction cut which clearly cut the construction cut to Building 6. The lack of material adhering to the south wall of Building 6 in this area suggested that only a short period of time elapsed between the construction of Buildings 5 and 6.

This wall was clearly far too substantial to have formed a buttress added to Building 6 and is interpreted as the north-eastern section of the gatehouse into New Palace Yard that was built in 1287–9 (Colvin et al 1963, 505). It lies on the projected site of the gatehouse immediately inside the precinct boundary. The southern wall to this gate passage has been found further west (site C(i): the north wall to Building 13) and a similar south-eastern section to the gatehouse would give the gate passage a width of *c* 7.0m.

Building 6

Only the southern wall to Building 6 was found on site D but its possible extent is conjectured on Fig 46. This gives a building over 11m x 14m internally, which seems rather large for this structure. It may have been divided up into more than one property or had a number of rooms or structures within the one property. The foundations to the wall were constructed from Kentish ragstone rubble whilst the above-ground wall was laid in rough courses and included occasional blocks of Reigate stone. The foundations were 0.45m–0.65m wider on the north side than the above-ground wall, which was 0.98m wide. They sat on a 100mm-thick bed of gravel. The footings were cut by an internal cesspit about 1.20m across and 1.67m deep, which extended beyond the northern limit of excavation (Fig 47). The fact that it cut through the foundations suggests that it was not planned as an original feature. The sides were formed by at least six planks of wood, four of which were recovered and consisted of three reused boat timbers and a plank that was apparently not reused. This plank contained some sapwood but no bark and gives a felling date for the tree of 1270–1310 (Tyers 1995). It was thought that the plank was almost complete to the outer surface, suggesting that the tree was felled closer to 1270 than 1310. Two of the reused boat timbers were datable but contained no sapwood and can therefore be assigned a date only of some time after 1217. This of course relates to their original use as part of a boat, indicating that the boat was broken up and the timbers reused within 80 years of its construction and probably much sooner.

The boat timbers are thought to have come from a type of clinker-built boat known as a 'cog', typically associated with the Hansa (Goodburn with Thomas 1997, 26–38).

The cesspit was filled with dark brown organic material, D[54], containing ceramic and wooden vessel assemblages (Figs 48–9). The amount of Kingston pottery in it is much higher than is found in similarly dated assemblages. For instance, the Kingston ware from a group at St Mary Spital amounts to only 4% by EVEs (Thomas et al 1997, table 8), the Trig Lane group 2 produced 31% dating to *c* 1270, and the fill of the city ditch at Ludgate produced 22% dating to the early 14th century (Vince 1985). Evidently the bulk of the ceramic material is derived from Kingston, which is understandable considering the site's proximity to the River Thames, the main route for the arrival of Kingston ware into central London (Table 10, Fig 50). This group of Kingston ware conical jugs was perhaps part of a batch of vessels such as those mentioned

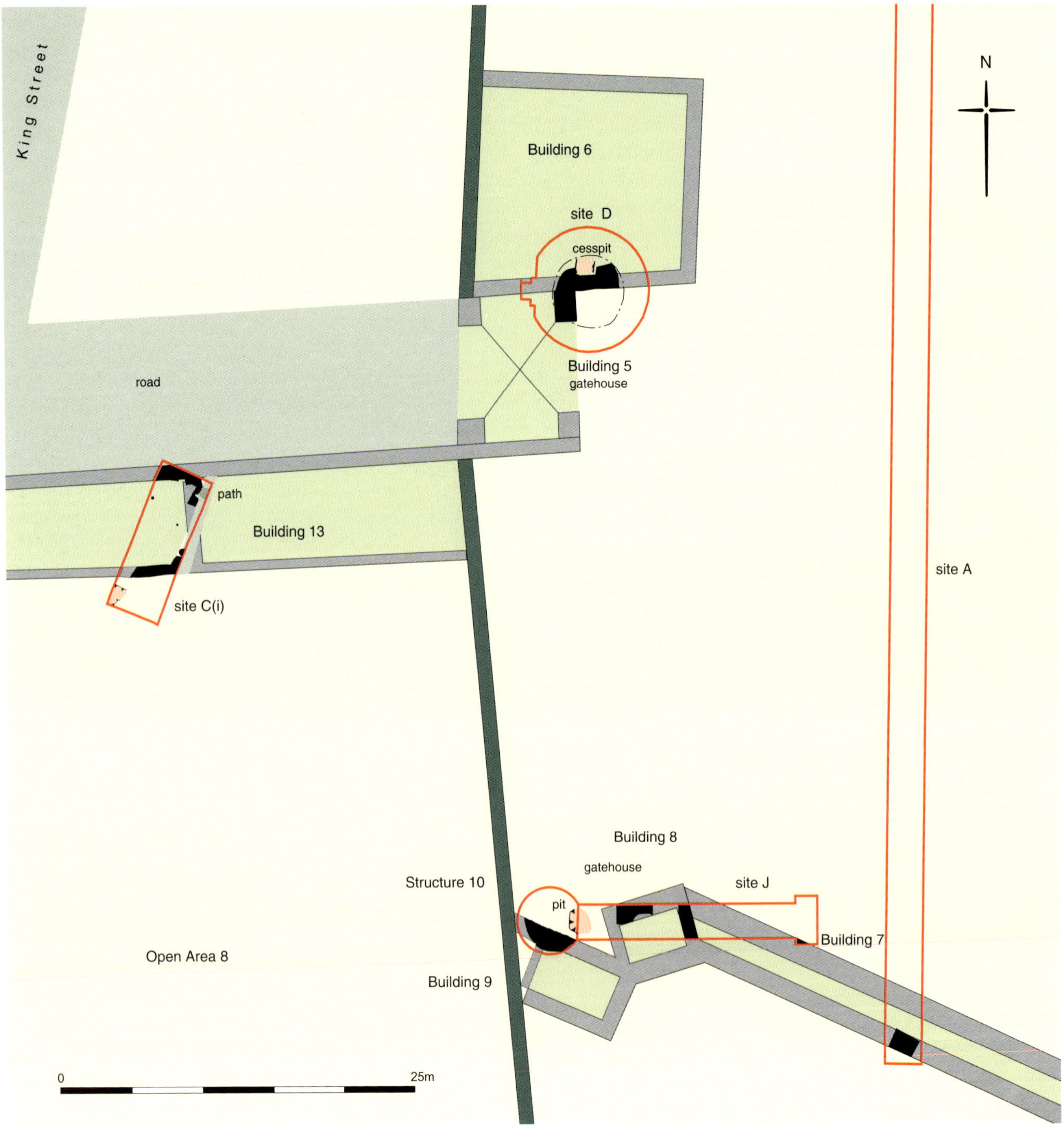

Fig 46 *Detailed plan of Buildings 5–9, 13 and Structure 10, period 7 (scale 1:400)*

in the calendars of Liberate and close rolls, which refer to royal orders for several batches of up to 1000 pitchers in 1264, 1265 and 1266. Some of the entries specifically mention delivery or carriage to Westminster. The records are transcribed here (Miller and Stephenson 1999):

Cal Lib R, 5 (1260–7)

p 145 3 November 1264

Allocate to the bailiffs of Kingston, in their farm of the town, 21s 5d spent in the purchase of 1000 wine pitchers against the feast of St Edward last past [5 January], and delivery thereof to Westminster.

p 162 8 February 1265

Allocate to the same 13s for 600 pitchers taken from them for the king and carriage thereof to Westminster.

p 210 13 April 1266

Allocate to the bailiffs of Kingston 14s for 700 pitchers taken for the king against Easter in the 49th year [1265].

p 252 26 December 1266

To the same: to have 1000 pitchers made in his bailiwick and sent to Westminster without delay for delivery to the king's butlers there.

Thus there are clearly records of more than 3000 vessels being sent to Westminster from Kingston over a relatively short period of time, although it cannot be said what size or shape

Fig 47 *View of Buildings 5 and 6, looking north (0.5m scale)*

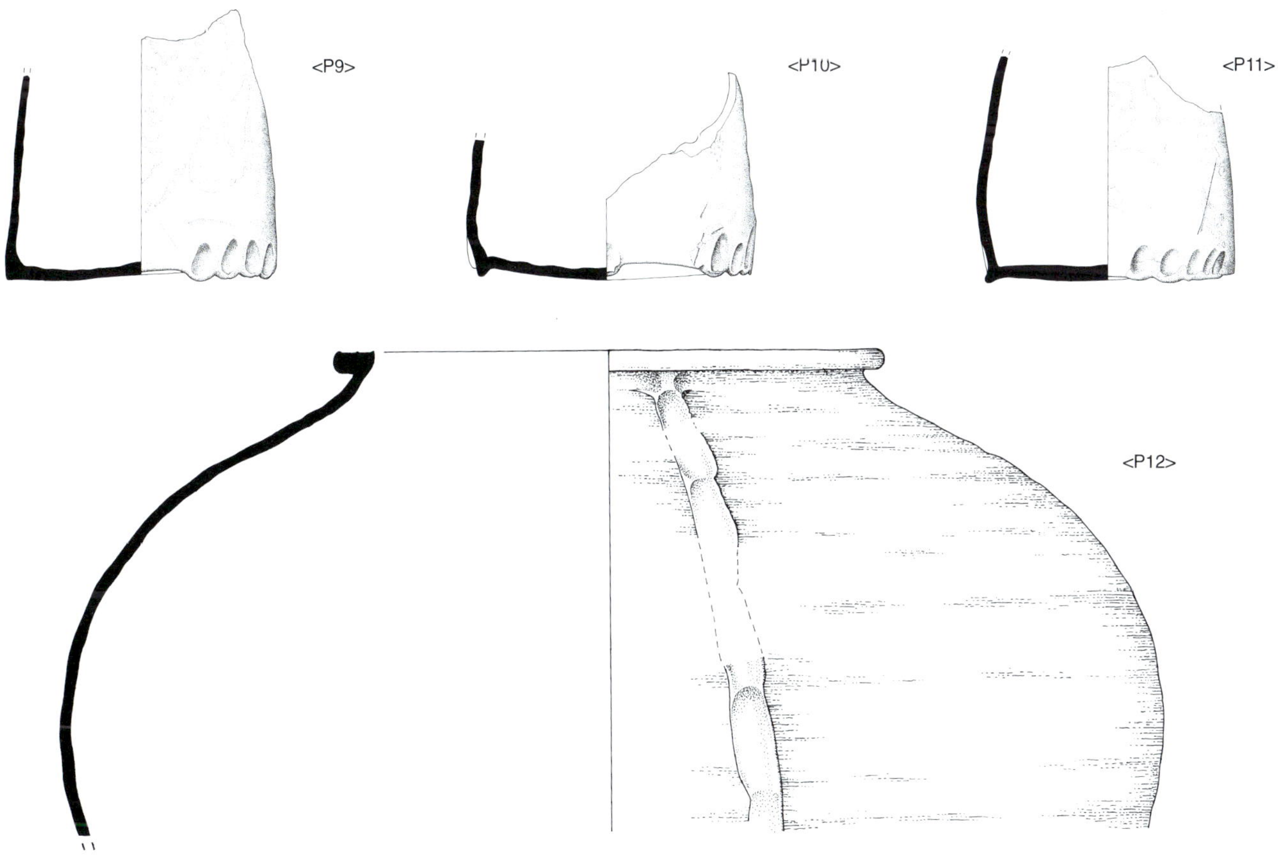

Fig 48 *Pottery <P9>–<P12> from the cesspit in Building 6 (scale 1:4)*

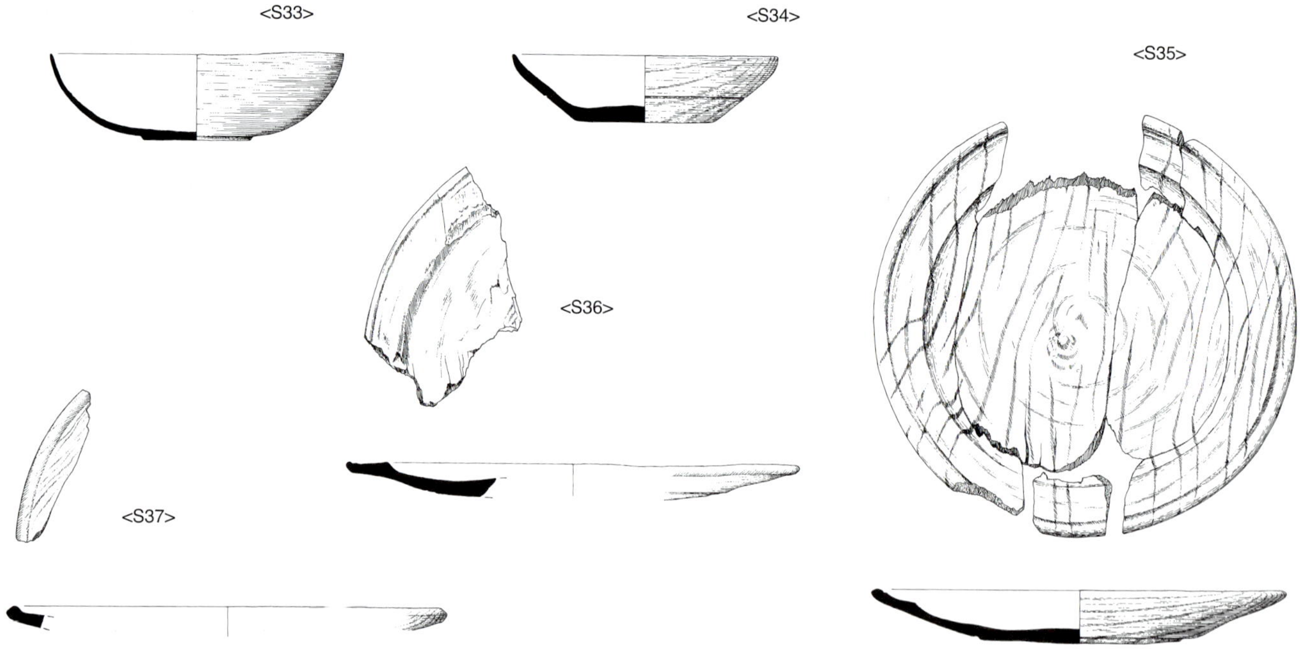

Fig 49 Five wooden vessels <S33>–<S37> from the cesspit in Building 6 (scale 1:4)

these were. Considering the uniform nature of the vessels from the cesspit it is possible that they came from one of these batches or a similar consignment. Conical jugs would have been in been in circulation from about the mid 13th century (Pearce and Vince 1988, 84).

This group is also important for its non-ceramic portion, which includes seven wooden vessels, <S31>–<S37>, and four fragments of potash vessel glass, <S9>. Here we have a better picture of vessels used on a medieval table. There are as many non-ceramic vessels as there are ceramic jugs, a clear indicator that the use of ceramic vessels was restricted to drinking, while food was served on wooden vessels (Table 10). The wooden objects recovered from this feature included four bowls, <S31>–<S34>, three platters, <S35>–<S37> (Fig 49), a possible stirring implement, <S38> (Fig 51), and two barrel fragments, <S39> and <S40>. All the bowls and platters are fragmentary and only one, <S35>, is almost complete.

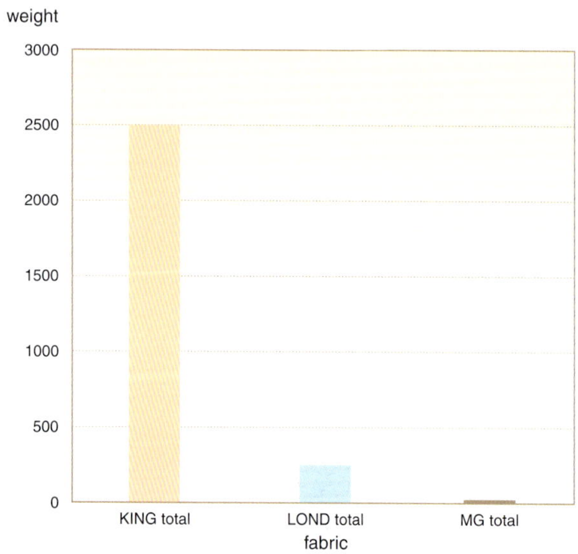

Fig 50 Histogram showing the breakdown of ceramic fabrics source by weight (in grams)

The bowls are all of a simple, plain design with a foot and a plain rim. Two of the fragments, <S32> and <S33>, have thin walls. The platters are larger, with either a beaded or a flat rim. None of the bowls or platters have any markings on them, thus differing from the group of 18 turned vessels recovered from a pit at St Mary Spital (Thomas et al 1997, 204, table 48), seven of which had branded or carved marks, thought to indicate ownership.

Groups of wooden vessels are rarely found; their survival here is due to the exceptional circumstances of the cesspit in which they were deposited. The present group of eight wooden vessels is substantial, although not as large as that from St Mary Spital, London (Thomas et al 1997, 204, table 48) (18 vessels) and The Austin Friars, Leicester (Clay 1981, 139–42) (10 vessels). The dating for the group is approximately the same as that from St Mary Spital (Thomas et al 1997, 59 and 204, table 48), that is, late 13th to mid 14th century, and there are similarities in the forms found in both groups, most notably between vessel <S34> and ash bowl <S55> from St Mary Spital.

Such wooden bowls were commonly used into the sixteenth century, in spite of the limitations of the material (Brears 1971, 13). This particular form of wooden vessel could be duplicated to some extent at this time by ceramic forms, examples of which come from production centres such as Kingston in Surrey and from the manufacturers of the local London-type wares, who were making both dishes and bowls. Although relatively unhygienic in comparison with ceramic vessels, wooden vessels were cheap to produce and were

Table 10 Analysis of ceramic and wooden vessels from the cesspit in Building 6 by estimated number of vessels (ENV) (see Table 25 for expansion of codes)

Fabric	Form	ENV	
wood	bowl	4	
wood	platter	4	
Total (wood)			8
KING	JUG CON	1	
KING	JUG CON	1	
KING	JUG CON	1	
KING	JUG CON	1	
KING	JUG RND	1	
Total (KING)			5
LOND	JUG TULBAL	1	
LOND	BAL	1	
LOND	JUG	1	
Total (LOND)			3
MG	JUG	1	
Total (MG)			1
Total (all)			17

durable, although prone to splitting and staining. They could be individually marked on the base to denote ownership, although in some cases this may indicate the initials of the maker. In 1559, the gentlemen of the Inner Temple ordered 'that from henceforth there shall not any ash cups be provided but the House be served in green cups, both of winter and summer' (Brears 1971, quoting Inderwick, F A (vol 1 1896) *A calendar of the Inner Temple records*).

One other find recovered from the cesspit was a mostly complete side-laced ankle shoe, <S41>.

The cesspit also produced a very rich botanical assemblage containing the residues from a large number of plant foods, while wild plants consisted mainly of wetland species and plants of disturbed ground and waste places. Plant foods included cereals, which were represented by a small number of both charred (free-threshing wheat (*Triticum* spp) and rye (*Secale cereale*)) and mineralised (barley (*Hordeum* spp) and oat (*Avena* spp)) grains, a large quantity of very fragmented cereal bran and a wide range of fruits. The latter included a large number of *Prunus* fruit stones, particularly cherry as well as sloe/blackthorn (*P spinosa*) and plum/bullace (*P domestica*). Fruit seeds were also prolific, particularly fig (*Ficus carica*), grape (*Vitis vinifera*), mulberry (*Morus* sp), apple (*Malus* spp) (represented by both seeds and endocarp fragments) and strawberry (*Fragaria vesca*). In addition, a small number of elder (*Sambucus nigra*) and blackberry/raspberry (*Rubus fruticosus/idaeus*) seeds and hazelnut (*Corylus avellana*) fragments were identified.

The weed seeds included a very large quantity of corncockle (*Agrostemma githago*) fragments. This is a common arable weed often found together with bran because it is a similar size to cereal grains and therefore difficult to separate, thus frequently becoming incorporated into bread or animal feed. There were relatively few other plants of disturbed ground and waste places but those that were recovered included nettle (*Urtica dioica*), goosefoots/oraches (*Chenopodium/Atriplex* spp), nipplewort (*Lapsana communis*), black nightshade (*Solanum nigrum*) and black bindweed (*Fallopia convolvulus*). Some of these are common arable weeds, for instance, hare's ear (*Bupleurum rotundifolium*), once common in cornfields in south and east England but now extinct (Stace 1991). The wetland plants included bankside/marshland and damp meadow species, for example, buttercups (*Ranunculus* spp), water dropwort (*Oenanthe aquatica/crocata*), hemlock (*Conium maculatum*), gipsy-wort (*Lycopus europaeus*), sedges (*Carex* spp) (represented by both achenes and utricles), spike-rush (*Eleocharis palustris/uniglumis*) and rushes.

The assemblage of botanical remains from the cesspit consists of the residues from food preparation (cereal grains, fruit stones) and consumption (cereal bran and fruit seeds). The mineralised grains may be evidence of grain consumption by animals or possibly humans in soups/pottages. The cereal bran is indicative of either human and/or animal faecal remains, with an exceptionally large number of mineralised and waterlogged puparia also suggesting the presence of cess. Some of the wetland plants (for example, the sedges and rushes), and the mineralised and waterlogged stems may include the residues of flooring materials, dumped in the cesspit to dampen the smell. The remaining weeds may be from crop-processing debris and/or from wild plants growing nearby. Other biological (charcoal, wood, large mammal and fish bones and marine molluscs) and artefactual (ceramic building material and pottery) debris suggests that the pit was also used for general rubbish. The small number of animal bones was approximately equally divided amongst food remains, a few birds (probably domestic) but mostly fish, and the remains of creatures that had probably fallen into the pit, including black rat and a few amphibians. One of the rats was immature, almost certainly suggesting the presence of a

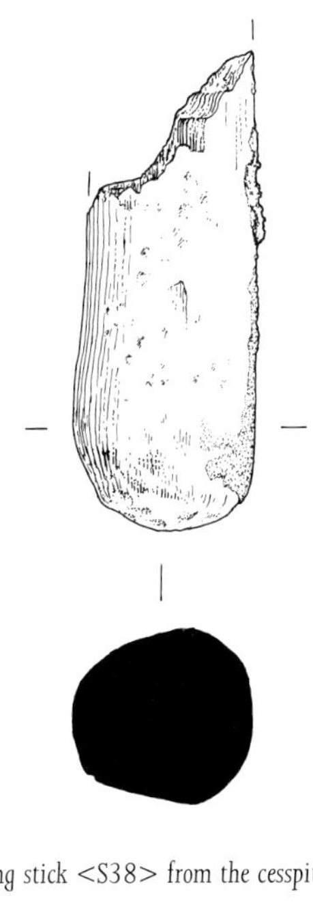

Fig 51 A wooden stirring stick <S38> from the cesspit in Building 6 (scale 1:2)

very local breeding population. The fish species recovered were small gadid, herring and cyprinid, possibly roach.

Before the end of this period the cesspit went out of use and was filled in with a clay layer containing Kentish ragstone, tile, mortar and charcoal. Further layers were dumped to level up the ground within the building.

The building clearly pre-dated the alterations in New Palace Yard caused by the latter's reduction in size to allow for the Woolstaple to the north. It may have formed part of a series of buildings surrounding the yard at this time or it may have been an isolated structure by the gate. The form of the buildings along the north side of the yard can be seen in Hollar's view of the 17th century (Colvin et al 1963, pl 36b). They seem to have been largely two-storey buildings with attics fronting on to the yard with single-storey additions to the front; many seem to have been half-timbered.

Building 6 has been conjectured as one large building from the excavated evidence and later property boundaries. It may, however, have consisted of more than one building within a single property. The presence of barrel bases in the cesspit and the relatively utilitarian nature of the finds and environmental assemblages suggest that it may have been a hostelry of some description. There were many such buildings in Westminster although there is less evidence for them at this date, only partly because of more meagre documentary evidence (Rosser 1989, 122–33). Such a site, immediately inside the gatehouse to the public part of the palace and on the route to the law courts, would have been ideal for an alehouse, tavern or inn or perhaps for soldiers guarding the gate, although this would seem more likely to have been constructed as one with the gate rather than before it.

Building 7

Only the base of the north wall of Building 7 was seen in tunnelling works. It was parallel to the southern precinct wall of New Palace Yard (OA4) and about 2.7m to the north-east of it (Fig 46). The entire width of the wall was not located but it was at least 0.43m wide. It was constructed from Kentish ragstone and some gravel and was bonded with orange sandy mortar. The phasing of this wall is uncertain but its base level and construction method was the same as that of Structure 10 and Building 8, which definitely belong to this period.

The status or nature of this building is also uncertain but it may have formed a range of structures along the south side of New Palace Yard possibly stretching from the gatehouse (B8) to the great hall (B1).

Building 8: gatehouse to the Green Yard

Only the base of this structure was seen as it was recorded in tunnelling works. Some of it was removed without record.

It consisted of Kentish ragstone bonded with a coarse sandy yellow mortar for a height of 0.25m (the remainder lay above the level of the tunnel). It was supported on timber piles, most of which were quite decayed. These ranged in diameter from 100mm to 240mm although most were between 120mm and 180mm. The longest recorded was 1.58m. The east wall was seen for its entire thickness (0.87m) and the timbers lay in a cut filled with blue clay. The west wall was not seen but its location can be estimated to within 0.2m. The south edge of the north wall was located but the northern edge lay beyond the limit of excavation. It was at least 1.24m thick. Part of the north wall was truncated by a brick well (period 10; Chapter 12.3, Building 8). When the well was removed, its loose backfill collapsed into the tunnel, indicating that the walls continued upwards for a considerable distance further.

This is interpreted as having been the west tower of the gatehouse that was built to replace a timber version in 1244–5 (Colvin et al 1963, 547). The internal measurements of the structure were *c* 4.2m south-west–north-east by at least 2.1m north-west–south-east. If the line of Structure 10 (the precinct wall, below) is continued, a conjectural reconstruction of the plan of the building can be produced (Fig 46). Such a reconstruction gives walls at the northern and southern end of the building *c* 1.4m thick and an internal measurement for the building of 4.2m x 2.6m.

Building 8 lies in the position previously attributed to the gatehouse and in the correct position for the later line of St Margaret Street. It does however lie on a very different alignment to that previously given to the building. This revised alignment is much more in keeping with the layout of the palace. It is parallel to the conjectured alignment of the precinct wall to the west and leads directly to the entrance into New Palace Yard to the north. The gatehouse has also been previously conjectured as lying inside the Green Yard rather than projecting into New Palace Yard. However, Hollar's view of New Palace Yard clearly indicates it projecting into New Palace Yard.

No evidence for the east side of the gatehouse was found but this was probably because the relevant portion was removed without record. Hollar's view suggests that there was no tower on the east side, merely a wall supporting the rooms above the tower and forming the east wall of the gate passage. By projecting the lines of the recorded sections of precinct walls a possible reconstruction of the gatehouse has been produced. The thickness of the east wall is unknown but it has been conjectured as being as wide as the north and south walls of the west tower which are, in themselves, partially conjectural. This gives a width of 4.85m for the gate passage.

Building 9

Adjoining the south side of the boundary wall (S10) between New Palace Yard and the Green Yard was Building 9 (Fig 46). Its other three walls were not found so that its size is unknown, but its probable internal measurements can be estimated at about 8.55m x 3.10m. The floor was formed from Reigate stone blocks, 80mm–120mm thick and up to 0.52m x 0.22m in size. They were laid in a construction cut backfilled with sand against the boundary wall (S10), suggesting that Building 9 post-dated Structure 10. If it were otherwise, the ground would surely have been prepared at the same time and there would have been no need for a cut in which to lay the floor slabs. It may, of course, be that it was the nature of the floor that was an afterthought rather than the building itself. Since the relationship of the walls of Building 9 to Structure 10 has not been found, it is uncertain whether the building formed a single structure with the wall.

In the centre of the excavated area lay a second layer of Reigate stone slabs on top of the first, 0.56m wide and 0.14m–0.16m high. Beyond it to the west lay a compacted levelling layer of sandy silt that partially overlay the lower layer of slabs and formed a level surface with the upper layer. This second layer of Reigate stone slabs could have been a wall of some sort but its level surface at the top, with no mortar adhering, suggests that it formed a raised platform or dais close to the west end of the building, with the lower layer of slabs forming the floor to the east as they did not continue westwards. It is not clear, however, why neither the lower nor the higher layer of slabs continued westwards but were replaced by a fairly compacted soil layer. Such a small part of the building has been recorded that this cannot be answered definitively at present. One possible reason might be that the west wall of the building was the boundary wall between the palace and abbey precincts, which ran at an acute angle compared to the building. If the raised layer of slabs formed some kind of dais at right angles to the other walls of the building then it might have started adjacent to the west wall but diverged from it by the time it met the north wall. Whilst the size of Building 9 is unknown, a gap of about 9.2m lay between the precinct wall to the west and the gatehouse (B8). If the building filled this space, which seems highly possible, allowing for the thickness of the wall at the east end, it might have been about 8.5m long internally.

Only a very small area of Building 9 was seen but it clearly formed a major building of some consequence. It lay within the Green Yard to the west of the gatehouse and may have been an accounts building related to the Exchequer, which lay to the east of the gatehouse.

Building 10: the Exchequer

The Exchequer lay to the west of the north end of the great hall. Elements of its foundations have been recorded, but are not entirely in agreement with each other (Clarke 1883; Select Committee 1885). An adjoining room (room B) that lay to the south was recorded in both reports and in 1975 on site T (Whipp and Platts 1976).

Room A

According to Clarke (Clarke 1883) the building measured 22.45m east–west by 9.40m north–south internally. The south wall was 1.73m thick; the full thickness of the western wall was not recorded and only a part of the north wall was recorded to its complete width, which was the same as that to the south. A door led from the south-east corner into room B and another door led into the great hall. This latter door was knocked through the remains of an earlier 11th-century door when Building 10 was constructed. The walls are all described as 'supposed Norman', except in the extreme north-west corner where a buttress on the corner of the great hall is described as being Norman. An internal north–south aligned foundation is also recorded towards the western end of the building.

A Select Committee report contains a plan prepared by Pearson, the architect of the replacement buildings (Select Committee 1885, fig 3). While this did not record the western extent of the building it does contain a significant amount of extra detail. The building is on a very slightly different alignment to that shown on Clarke's plan and a second doorway is shown leading out into the Green Yard (OA5) from the south side of the building immediately to the west of room B. Of greatest importance is Pearson's description of the dating of the walls. The south wall is partially obscured by a wall attributed to Soane. The internal wall is described as being 19th century in date and has therefore not been included on Fig 45. The north wall at the western end is described as being of William II's reign and therefore contemporary with the great hall (B1); this returns to the north, apparently defining a separate structure to the north-west of the hall. The remaining part of the north wall and the south wall are all described as dating to the reign of Henry III. Pearson also shows the original Norman and later Henry III doorways into the great hall.

The floor surfaces are not described nor the materials used to make the walls but these are likely to have been Kentish ragstone and chalk, with Reigate stone used for decorative features such as the windows and doors. A door jamb is described as existing on the east side of the door into the Green Yard (Select Committee 1885, 152).

Room B

Room B measured 13.40m north–south by 5.65m east–west and was subdivided by a thin east–west wall into two further rooms: that to the north measuring 8.25m long internally and that to the south 4.70m. The dividing partition was about 0.45m wide and had a door at the west end. The west wall was 1.10m thick and the south 1.73m thick, with a garderobe pit or cesspit at its east end where it abutted the west wall of the great hall. Both walls are described on Clarke's plan as being built during the reign of Richard II. Pearson, however, described them as dating to the reign of Henry III although he recorded only the ends of the south wall. Subsequent recording found the north face of the south wall on site T (Whipp and Platts 1976, 354). The thin chalk spread found on that site may have been the floor to this building or a construction layer associated with it.

The Exchequer was formed by room A and was a rectangular building of two storeys. It communicated via doors with room B to the south, with the Green Yard to the south and with the great hall to the east. There does not appear to have been any access to New Palace Yard. Such an arrangement would be logical given the public status of New Palace Yard as opposed to the administrative and financial status of the Green Yard and the need for security. The original door to the great hall was blocked up when the Exchequer was built. Building 10 was constructed by 1244; previously the Upper and Lower Exchequers had occupied another building of two storeys, possibly to the south of St Stephen's chapel (Colvin et al 1963, 539–40). The Lower Exchequer (or the Receipt) was where the money was received and the Upper Exchequer was where the accounts were drawn up. The Receipt of the Exchequer was subsequently rebuilt on the east side of the great hall, at the northern end, in the late 13th century (Colvin et al 1963, 541).

Room B was contemporary with room A and probably formed the inner chamber, or *thalamus secretorum*, for the barons to use as a conference room. It is uncertain how the two cells or rooms within it were divided. This was also a two-storey structure.

Building 11: St Stephen's chapel

The foundations to Building 11 have been recorded on both the inside and outside. It measures 22.0m x 8.5m internally, and was constructed from a level of 1.20m OD. Externally, it had three steps above that level before the main wall began some 1.0m higher. The wall and foundations were regularly coursed and constructed from Kentish ragstone with a chalk core bonded with an orange sandy mortar. Some fragments of Reigate stone were also noted as was one fragment of brick, which was probably Roman (Chapter 5.3). The courses varied in thickness from 0.12m to 0.23m. Internally, the foundations were seen only at a much lower level, beneath the 19th-century undercroft that was built beneath the lower chapel for heating ducts. Within this undercroft the walls (originally the foundations) are faced in brick. Beneath the floor of the undercroft the foundations protrude from the wall suggesting that they were cut back during the 19th-century construction. Fig 52 shows the surviving foundations and those areas where the foundations were rebuilt in brick, which was largely owing to the insertion of a number of brick tunnels through the walls.

The foundations, as recorded on the inside, lay in a construction cut. They were founded on a series of timber piles which had almost entirely rotted, leaving voids beneath the walls. An area of these can be seen on Fig 52 in the south-west corner. The later brick walls dating to the mid 19th century also overlay voids left by rotted timbers, suggesting that the timbers were probably still intact in the 19th century but had rotted subsequently, primarily because of the lowering of the water table after the construction of the embankment in the mid 19th century. The voids were mostly 0.15m in diameter and were at least 0.70m deep. These timber piles were driven in to form a solid base in the marshy ground with an 'engine' built by Thomas of Houghton (Colvin et al 1963, 511).

No surviving floor levels or stratigraphy associated with the chapel were found internally. However, in a disturbed layer consisting of concrete and soil at the top of the surviving

Fig 52 Detailed plan of St Stephen's chapel (B11), period 7 (scale 1:200)

sequence and cut into the fluvial sediments below were found the disarticulated remains of a number of human skeletons. These were not *in situ* and were probably disturbed by the construction of the undercroft in the mid 19th century. There were at least nine individuals present of, which three were possibly male and one possibly female. There was no evidence that any of the skeletons were immature (Conheeney 1995).

The current floor level of the undercroft chapel lies at 2.17m–2.19m OD, which is the same level as the top of the foundation steps. There is a raised platform at the east end at 2.55m OD, with the altar at 2.68m OD. The floor was apparently lowered by Barry by approximately 1.0m in the 19th century, which would suggest that it originally lay at *c* 3.2m OD, but it is unclear upon what this is based. Such a floor level would be consistent with the level of *c* 2.9m OD for the Norman floor of the great hall (Chapter 7.3, Building 1).

Documentary evidence makes it clear that there was an earlier chapel of St Stephen but there was no evidence of this despite the extensive excavations. There are a number of potential explanations:

1) the earlier chapel was on a different site;
2) the chapel had a similar ground plan and was completely removed when the later chapel was built;
3) the foundations as seen are the foundations of the earlier chapel and were reused;
4) the foundations of the earlier chapel were much shallower and so did not survive the insertion of the undercroft in the mid 19th century.

Of these, the third possibility seems highly improbable, given the documentary evidence concerning the timber piles, the digging of foundation trenches and the homogeneity of the foundations both internally and externally. The fourth interpretation also seems unlikely, while previous writers have suggested that the site of the earlier chapel was that of the later one (Colvin et al 1963, 511; Lethaby 1906, 142), which suggests that the first is similarly unlikely. The implication, therefore, is that the earlier chapel had similar dimensions to the late 13th-century chapel and that it was entirely demolished and its foundations robbed out before construction of the new chapel began in 1292.

Work started on 28 April 1292 and by June the foundation trenches were being dug (Colvin et al 1963, 510–11). Work lasted about 71 years and consisted of five campaigns. Colvin has summarised these as follows (Colvin et al 1963, 522):

1) 1292–7, construction of the lower chapel;
2) 1320–5, construction of the north and south walls of the upper chapel, gallery to Painted Chamber built;
3) 1331–4, construction of the east wall;
4) 1340–8, construction of the west wall, the roof and the vault;
5) 1348–63, glazing, painting and furnishing of the chapel.

Only the foundations and lower parts of the wall of St Stephen's chapel have been seen. The extent to which the walls above foundation level still consist of medieval stone is unknown. The eastern and western walls of the upper chapel have been demolished and there were many alterations to the building before the fire of 1834.

Barry carried out a reconstruction of the lower chapel which still exists (Fig 53). This and the upper chapel were heavily influenced by the royal chapel on the Ile de la Cité, La Sainte Chapelle (Figs 54–5), as is discussed in greater detail in Chapter 14.4.

Fig 53 View of the restored lower chapel of St Stephen: St Mary Undercroft © Crown copyright. NMR

Fig 54a *View of the upper chapel of the Ste Chapelle, Paris*

Fig 55 The Ste Chapelle, Paris, from the north-west

Fig 54b *View of the lower chapel of the Ste Chapelle, Paris*

Building 12

Part of wall R[35], constructed from Kentish ragstone and roof tile and bonded with orange, coarse, sandy mortar, was found running north–south in a sewer trench. It measured 3.0m in length, but its full width is not known to either east or west though it was at least 0.7m wide. Its top was at 2.96m OD, which is likely to have been at least 1.5m above construction level. It was at least 1.56m deep and continued beneath the base of the excavation. Its southern edge was found in alignment with the current northern property boundary of 6–7 Old Palace Yard. It is uncertain whether the wall turned to the east or west.

In his *Antiquities of Westminster* Smith recorded a north–south aligned wall, approximately 2.4m from the precinct wall to the west, about 6.35m long and about 1.1m thick (Smith 1807, fig p125). The inside of this wall lies about 8.55m from R[35]. If these two are related they presumably form a rectangular building about 8.0m–8.5m across internally and at least 10.8m long. This is highly speculative, however, as there is no definite evidence that wall R[35] turned to the west. It is also uncertain how this relates to the large masonry foundation recorded in a similar location (Green 1976, fig 3).

There is no dating evidence for Building 12 save for the pegtile in fabric 2271 incorporated in the wall. Such tile is dated to after c 1180. The form of the wall is very similar to that of 13th-century buildings elsewhere in Westminster (below, Building 13) but its phasing should be seen as highly tentative. It lies in the position usually attributed to the prince's palace, which lay on the west side of Old Palace Yard and was built at or before 1296 (Colvin et al 1963, 537).

Building 13

Only the southern and northern walls to Building 13, which extended to both east and west beyond the site boundaries, were excavated (Fig 46). The southern wall was 0.69m wide and was laid in a trench 1.45m wide. Constructed from chalk and Kentish ragstone blocks bonded with a light brown sandy mortar, it turned to the north at the east edge of the site for a distance of 0.7m before turning southwards again some 0.4m further east. This, along with the evidence for a path through the building (described below), may indicate an internal porch in the centre of the building. A fragment of Reigate stone that was removed by contractors from this area may have been a part of this internal porch. It was a fragment of a roll or bowtell, probably forming part of a round shaft although not enough survived to tell if it was engaged or free-standing (Samuel 1994). The construction trench had a 100mm-thick chalk scatter, presumably construction debris, at its base, which was overlain by a green-brown clay silt, a layer of orange mortar, chalk fragments and brown silt, and a brown sandy clay. To the south of the wall on the west side was a chalk wall bonded with a similar mortar. The function of this wall is unclear but it may have been defining a building to the south-west of Building 13. Its stratigraphic relationship to Building 13 is unclear.

The northern wall of Building 13 was constructed from Kentish ragstone and Reigate stone with some chalk, tile, Caen stone and a single Roman brick. It survived to 1.03m above foundation level. Mortared to the south side of the wall in the construction trench was a single block of Kentish ragstone measuring 0.50m x 0.40m with its surface at the same level as the top of the construction trench (Fig 56). Overlying the stone

Fig 56 *View of the north wall and stone base in Building 13, looking north (0.5m scale)*

was a brown organic deposit 10mm–20mm thick, possibly a wooden plank. Filling the remainder of the construction trench was a layer of chalk and mortar at the base sealed by a layer of grey sandy clay with gravel; the upper layer also contained animal bone, tile, oyster and mussel shell, and fragments of Kentish ragstone and Reigate stone, one of which formed part of a bead roll similar to, but more weathered than, that found in C[209], described below. These were presumably construction materials from the building and food waste used by those constructing it. The stone block was laid whilst the construction trench was empty but the possible wooden plank not until the construction trench had been backfilled.

Towards the southern end of the building was a circular pit, 0.50m in diameter and 0.26m deep, filled with chalk and mortar overlain by a layer of brown clay. Close to the north wall but not disturbing the stone attached to it were two rubbish pits. Pit C[220] was filled with brown silty clay with animal bone, tile and oyster shell at the base and mortar, Reigate stone and Kentish ragstone above, while the second pit contained a mixed sandy silt with Kentish ragstone, chalk, crushed Reigate stone, mortar, tile, charcoal and animal bone. These pits appear to have been dug to dispose of construction material and food waste, perhaps from the construction workers.

Over the pits was a series of floor layers. The earliest consisted of compact Reigate stone chippings with a plaster surface which was burnt. Pressed into pit fill C[209] below the floor but presumably deposited when the floor was laid was a fragment of Reigate stone from a much larger moulding. It formed part of a bead (small roll) with wave mould. It was highly ornamental and probably came from the interior of a building. The high finish and small scale of the moulding suggest a comparatively late date but its stratigraphic position indicates that it must be earlier. It seems unlikely that it came from this building unless it was waste material or damaged during construction; it may have came from another even earlier demolished building nearby. The Reigate stone floor was overlain by an orange clay floor which also had a plaster surface. This clay floor was in turn overlain by a sand floor that was worn away in a line directly to the south of the stone mortared to the wall, suggesting that it had been used as a path and that constant walking up to the stone had worn away the floor. This line runs directly to the possible site of a door in the south wall. Over the sand floor was occupation debris consisting of brown sandy silty clay with large quantities of oyster shell and animal bone and some painted plaster. The floor was then relaid in Reigate stone chippings which were sealed by another occupation deposit of dark silt with mussel and oyster shell, charcoal, animal bone and broken pottery. The floor was then relaid yet again in Reigate stone and Caen stone chippings with oyster shell, animal bone and charcoal and sealed by another occupation layer of dark silt with animal bone, oyster, mussel and cockle shell, pottery, and fragments of tile, chalk, Caen stone, Kentish ragstone and Reigate stone chippings. Up against the north wall was a deposit of white plaster that had clearly been adhering to the wall. Overlying the occupation layer was a levelling layer of orange clay with small quantities of Reigate stone chippings, tile, charcoal, pottery, Kentish ragstone and painted plaster. This lay under a layer of orange sand with mortar, chalk, Caen stone and Reigate stone chippings. These levelled the building up for another floor of Reigate stone chippings.

Two of the occupation deposits were broadly similar in their botanical composition and will thus be discussed together. Both contained very few fruits and seeds with mainly wetland plants, aquatics (stoneworts, crowfoots, water plantain (*Alisma* sp) in C[200]), bankside/marshland species (lesser spearwort (*Ranunculus flammula*), rushes (*Juncus* spp)), and a few disturbed ground species (for example, stinging nettle (*Urtica dioica*), chickweeds (*Stellaria media*) and parsley piert (*Aphanes arvensis*)). Charcoal was present in moderate quantities in both samples. The quantity and quality of the botanical remains offer little insight into these features. Some of the wetland plants may have been collected incidentally along with the sedges (*Carex* spp) and rushes, which may have been gathered as flooring materials. The main component of the two samples, however, was a large number of mammal bones, fish bones and oyster shells.

Cut into the Reigate stone floor were two stakeholes and a pit filled with discarded building material. A linear cut C[177] was also dug. This was 0.80m across and ran directly south from the stone attached to the north wall, apparently forming some sort of slightly sunken path through the building along the line of the worn area in the earlier sand floor. It was backfilled with a grey-brown silty clay and orange clay. The lower grey fill contained domestic refuse such as animal bone and pottery, and building material such as tile and painted plaster. A very large quantity of painted plaster was deposited adjacent to the north wall suggesting, along with the earlier deposit of painted plaster, that the building was originally covered in white plaster with red painted lines on it. When cut C[177] was backfilled the plaster would appear to have been stripped from the walls before a major refurbishment and rearrangement of the building.

The animal bone assemblage was composed almost entirely of pig, chicken and goose bones. The former species is largely represented by the partial remains of a very young piglet, while the majority of the chicken bones and a substantial proportion of those belonging to geese, were from young birds.

Building 13 lies in the northern part of the abbey precinct adjacent to the gates into the palace and abbey. The precinct had certainly been enclosed with a stone wall by 1280, and possibly during the early 13th century for the belfry was constructed inside the precinct in 1249–53 and it is probable that the precinct was already enclosed by that time. This would imply that larger-scale works than the rebuilding of the church alone were carried out during the reign of Henry III.

If Building 13 stretched across the entire width of the plot of land between the palace precinct to the east and King Street to the west it would have measured 34m–35m in length internally. This would seem an unusually large building and a more likely interpretation is that there were buildings to the east and west aligned north–south along the palace and King Street boundaries respectively, with Building 13 aligned east–west between them. Each building would then be about 11m across. Such a suggestion would place the west wall of Building 13 immediately to the west of the site, perhaps associated with the chalk wall that continued to the south. This would place the path and possible porch and doorway centrally along the south side of the building. The projected layout of the south door suggests that it may have had column shafts, which would point to quite a high-status building. The main route through the building was clearly aimed down the central path towards the stone against the north wall. This had a timber plank on it and must have been designed to support a substantial weight. It was obviously the central feature of the room. Quite what it supported is unclear but it may have been a statue, perhaps of St Edward, patron saint of the October Fair.

The plot of land outside the gatehouse was described as being vacant in c 1250 (Rosser 1989, 24), but there is conflicting evidence later for the buildings on this plot during the medieval period. In 1289 Abbot Walter de Wenlock bought three houses outside the north gate to be allocated to merchants of the October Fair, which was held in the abbey precincts every year (Rosser 1989, 101). Ralph Vineter had acquired two tenements outside the abbey gate by the end of the 13th century and by 1343 the plot was developed as the Holy Way Tavern (Rosser 1989, 24).

A possible interpretation for Building 13 is that it was one of the houses built in this area after 1250 and bought by Abbot de Wenlock in 1289. A fourth property was later added and all were leased at very high rates to merchants during the fairs: the four properties had a combined rental of £75 for the month of the fair and Henry Nazard paid £14 13s 4d each year for one property during the fair between 1311 and 1314 (Rosser 1989, 106). These houses were probably two-storey buildings with solars above; one had a cellar containing three shops (Rosser 1989, 101).

Building 14

Building 14 is conjectured from a section recorded by the Ministry of Works during landscaping and drainage works in the Jewel Tower garden during the late 1950s and early 1960s (Fig 57). The section and its information were not published in the report on the site (Green 1976) so have been included here. No further information was recovered during the recent works but the location of the drainage trench which produced the section was found.

No walls for the building were found but four phases of floor layers were recorded. They were all cut by the precinct wall and Jewel Tower, which was constructed in 1365–6. The floors must pre-date that, and in fact any of them (and therefore the building) could be earlier than this period.

The lowest floor was of mortar and tile ('humus and rubble') and was sealed by a layer of 'humus'. That was in turn sealed by a floor of mortar and tile ('humus and tile') which was sealed by another layer of 'humus' (these layers of 'humus' probably represent occupation debris on the floors). This was in turn sealed by a sand bedding layer for another mortar floor over which lay the fourth phase of floor, consisting of mortar and tile.

The extent of the building in which these floors were laid is unknown but it could not have stretched more than 6.12m to the east for that was the location of the precinct wall (Chapter 8.3). The floors stretched for a minimum of 1.42m to the west where they were cut by the mid 14th-century precinct wall (Chapter 10.3). The function of the building is unknown but it lay within the precincts of Westminster Abbey and to the south-east of the infirmary, with which it may have been associated. The east end of the infirmary chapel in fact lies some 3.75m to the north and 4.40m to the west.

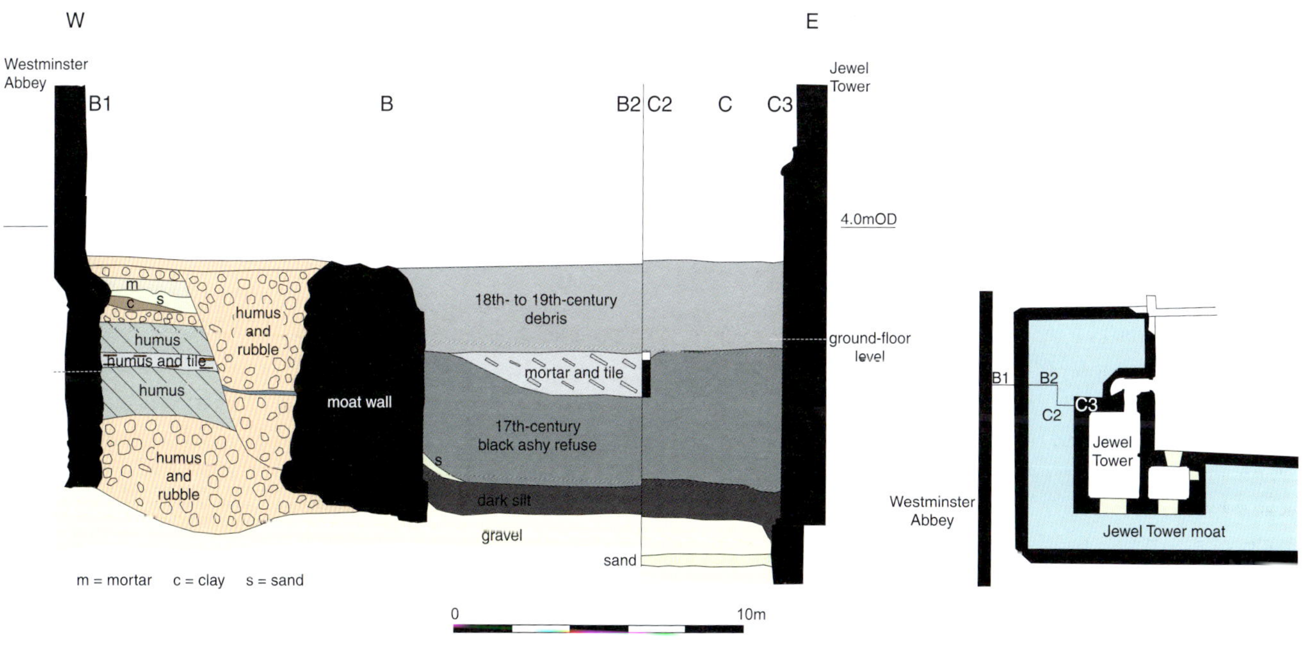

Fig 57 North-facing section through Building 14 and the Jewel Tower moat (B17) (reproduced courtesy of English Heritage), and plan (scale: section 1:250; plan 1:2000)

Structure 5

It is unclear whether Structure 5 (Fig 34) continued in use throughout this period. The putative revetment across Open Area 1 (below) would suggest that it fell into disuse.

Structure 7

Cutting through and sealing the period 6 flood deposits on site U were two substantial stake-and-wattle fences (Fig 58). The southern, U[16], ran from the south-western corner of the site for 10m and was made up of 36 stakes which, although they were not all directly in line, appeared to be part of one structure. Six stakes that were not directly in line with the rest may have been designed to strengthen the structure. All the stakes were quite heavily decayed at the top because the soil conditions were not particularly wet but were better preserved in the lower organic deposits.

Only two sections of wattle fencing survived but it must originally have stretched for the entire length of the line of stakes. At best the wattle survived to a height of 0.21m at the western end above the lower flood layer whereas the highest stake was 0.44m above the flood layer. At the west end the wattle survived for a stretch of 2.30m. It was heavily decayed but contained at least six strands of wattle. A further 1.10m east lay a shorter section of fencing 0.40m in length. This survived to a similar height but with fewer strands of wattle. These strands of wattle were approximately 10mm thick and were, in places, interwoven and entwined around the stakes. The stakes themselves varied in diameter from 20mm to 80mm (the majority were 40mm–60mm in diameter) and were roughly circular.

The wattle and the stakes in U[16] were sealed by layer U[13] that was dumped on top of and around the stakes when the fence went out of use. This must mean that the fence cannot have been used for revetting since the layer adjacent to it was sealing it. It must therefore have been a free-standing structure.

Running parallel to and broadly contemporary with the fence was a second stake-and-wattle fence, U[22], containing 26 wooden stakes and a small amount of wattle. Four of the stakes were not directly in line with the remainder and, as with the other fence, may have been added to strengthen it. However, there was also another set of stakes that seemed to form a parallel line running to the north of the main line but appearing to join on to it.

The northern fence U[22] began to the east of U[16] and ended at the same eastern point. It may be the case that it originally continued to the western end of the trench but was truncated by a later cut. However, the layer into which it was cut at the western end, U[55], curved around under U[16], as did layer U[87], which built up around the stakes, indicating that U[22] ended here and curved around to join up with U[16].

There was only one stretch of standing wattle *in situ* in U[22]. This was 1.10m long with the stakes being on the northern side of the wattle. It consisted of a number of strands 15mm–20mm thick, interwoven for strength. It did not stand to such a great height as U[16], for it was only 0.11m high, but what remained was better preserved. As with U[16] the wattle indicated that the stakes had been driven into the same flood deposit. On average the stakes in U[22] were slightly wider than those in U[16], varying between 30mm and 110mm although most were 40mm–50mm in diameter. Areas of collapsed wattle, presumably from its disuse, were also found.

Around U[22] were a number of trees, which may well have been used to anchor and strengthen the stakes.

Like U[16], fence U[22] was sealed by layer U[13], which surrounded it totally. This was dumped on the fence when it had gone out of use. Fence U[22] must thus also have been a free-standing structure and not used for revetment.

Possibly contemporary with U[16] and U[22] were eight stakes that appeared to have no pattern and not to be part of U[16] or U[22]. They all lay to the north of U[22] and were approximately 40mm in diameter except for one that was 60mm in diameter.

Around the base of the stake-and-wattle fences were two ridges running from their eastern end. The northernmost ridge, which was associated with U[22], curved around to the south at the western end and met the other where U[22] ended. These ridges were made up of a number of different layers that had been deposited by water. The highest point on the ridges was 0.88m OD, indicating that the river reached at least this level.

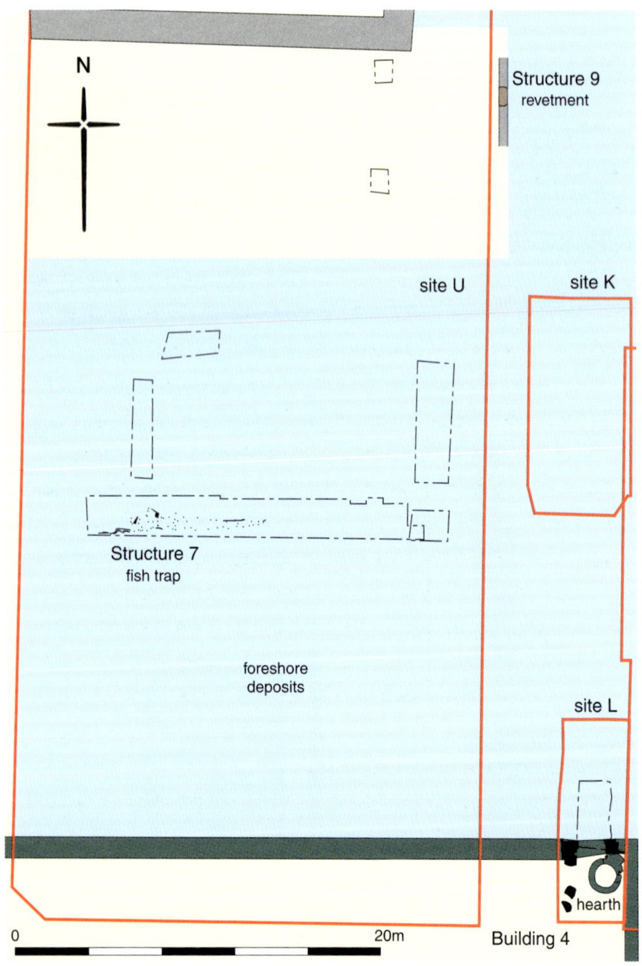

Fig 58 Detailed plan of Structure 7, Structure 9 and Building 4, period 7 (scale 1:400)

These two fences were apparently contemporary and, from the evidence of the silting around the base of the stakes, it seems that the northern stake line, U[22], joined on to the southern, U[16], at the western end and then curved around away from it before meeting it again 7.0m later where they both ended. The implications arising from this are various. First, water must have washed around the base of the stakes causing the silting and leaving a gap between them; second, they cannot just have been boundary fences since they were contemporary and so close together. Since it appears that the area was still very marshy and that water washed around the base of the fences, it is possible that they might have formed a fish trap with only a very narrow gap at the river end, a gap which then widened before being blocked off at the western end. It is clear that Structure 7 would have been under water at high-tide level (*c* 2.0m OD) but would have been exposed at low-tide level (*c* 0.3m OD). Fish would presumably have been trapped within the structure when the river fell to a level below *c* 1.0m OD. Evidence from Structure 6 and Open Area 1 suggests that progressive reclamation of other areas may have left the site of Structure 7 as an inlet from the river between land that had been reclaimed to north and south. Structure 7 continued westward as far as the properties behind King Street, later occupied by the Round Woolstaple (period 8; Chapter 10.2, 10.3).

Structure 8

Structure 8, on site U, consisted of a north–south aligned wall constructed from Kentish ragstone and reused green sandstone blocks bonded with yellow sandy mortar. It was bedded on a layer of yellow sand at least 0.7m thick (presumably in a construction cut). It survived to a height of 0.45m and was constructed from a level of 1.41m OD. Only a length of 1.0m was seen but the sand layer was recorded approximately 10m to the south, suggesting that the wall had originally continued at least that far. The exact function of this wall is unclear but the fact that there were no associated floor deposits suggests it may have been a property boundary.

Structure 9

Structure 9, also on site U, consisted of five wooden stakes, 40mm–80mm across, aligned north–south and surviving to a height of 0.34m (Fig 58). The southern two stakes were joined by wattle at the top and the central one was joined to the southern stakes by wattle at the base. Originally the stakes would probably have been more substantial with considerably more wattle between them, but this had decayed. The structure almost certainly continued to north and south but the circumstances of the watching brief precluded any further recording. The stakes were driven into blue organic clay at about 1.2m OD.

The function and dating of this structure is uncertain. It must pre-date the laying out of Canon Row, which occurred in the 14th century (Chapter 10.3, Road 2), and it is similar in construction to Structure 7, which did have dating evidence associated with it. Further, it was cut from a slightly higher level than Structure 7 and so is unlikely to pre-date it. It seems likely therefore to belong to this period and was perhaps some form of minor revetment at the back of marshy waste ground along the Thames.

Structure 10: precinct wall between the Green Yard and New Palace Yard

Defining the south side of Open Area 4 (New Palace Yard) and the north side of Open Area 5 (the Green Yard) was a wall (Figs 46, 59) constructed mostly from Kentish ragstone with some Reigate stone and chalk bonded with hard yellow sandy mortar. It was 1.10m wide and a length of 3.80m was recorded. It was founded on a bed of large unmortared blocks of Kentish ragstone and Reigate stone with smaller blocks filling the gaps. The upper part of the foundation lay in a construction cut whilst the unmortared part at the base had evidently been thrown into a construction trench the same width as the wall. Associated with the wall was a construction layer of grey silty sand with lumps of chalk and mortar.

The dating evidence for this wall suggests that it is contemporary with the gatehouse, which is known to have been constructed in 1244–5 (Colvin et al 1963, 547). East of the gatehouse (B8) lay a further stretch of what is probably the same wall on site A. It was at least 1.0m wide but here was constructed from chalk and flint.

Road 1

Road 1 on site F was a pathway aligned north–south in an area of Open Area 10 that had probably been reclaimed (Fig 60). Its earliest phase consisted of make-up layers of white mortar and gravel sealed by mixed brown sandy silt and sand for a path of gravel, Reigate stone chippings and chalk. The path was slightly cambered and was about 0.88m wide. Whilst truncated in places, it was seen over a total distance of 4.40m.

The second phase was laid after a riverlaid silty clay had been deposited, possibly during a flood. It consisted of more make-up layers for a path laid in Kentish ragstone, crushed Reigate stone and flint with some gravel and chalk. This phase varied in width from 0.85m to 0.68m and was seen over a total length of 6.17m. This, too, was sealed by a fluvial deposit, perhaps laid during a period of flooding. The third phase was laid over the fluvial clay in Kentish ragstone with some sandstone and Reigate stone in a single course. It was about 0.90m wide and was seen over a total distance of 8.0m. Immediately to the west of the path was a linear cut 1.74m long and up to 0.38m wide filled with gravel, stone and Reigate stone chippings. This was perhaps a pit dug to dispose of material not needed for the path.

The final phase consisted of crushed Reigate stone laid in between and over the Kentish ragstone paving. It is possible that this was part of the construction for the previous phase of pathway and did not represent a separate phase of activity.

Various component deposits within the path provided a moderate quantity of animal bone, largely composed of

Fig 59 *View of Structure 10, looking south (0.5m scale)*

cattle/cattle-sized fragments amongst a relatively wide range of species. As well as the ubiquitous mammalian and bird domesticates, there were single occurrences of both fallow and roe deer, clear indicators of a high-status diet. In contrast, a single worked antler fragment was found, denoting the possibility that one or more craft workshops may have been located in the vicinity.

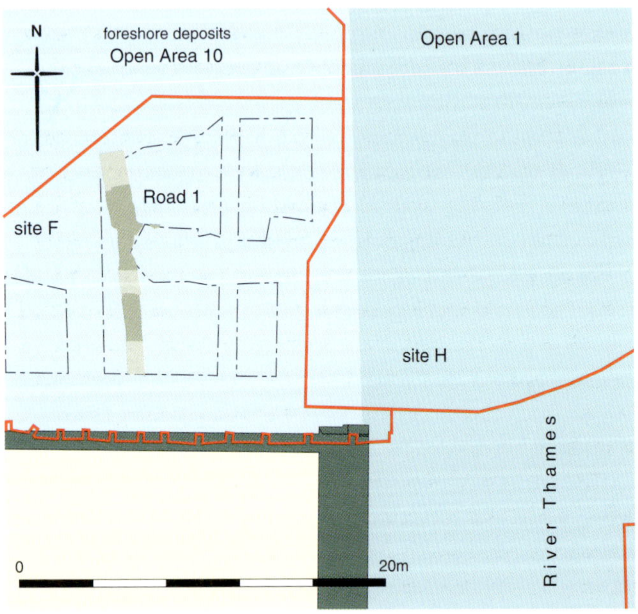

Fig 60 *Detailed plan of Road 1, period 7 (scale 1:400)*

Road 1 was a pathway leading from the edge of the palace along the reclaimed foreshore about 4.5m behind the putative river front. It is unlikely to have continued much further north as the area further to the west (site U) was still not reclaimed at this time and was open to the river.

Open Area 1: the River Thames

The difference between the deposits on the east side of site F (OA1) and those on the west side (OA10) suggests that some form of waterfront or revetment structure was built across the area. The boundary between the two must have lain along the site of a north–south aligned Victorian brick wall and been destroyed by it. Alluvial silty clays were deposited in Open Area 1 up to a level of approximately 0.83m OD. A hollow that formed immediately to the east of the putative revetment was filled with alluvial silty clays containing some cultural material, including building material and chalk. A second hollow or pit contained dumped material.

The prehistoric fluvial silts and clays on site H were overlain by layers of sand and cut by three features. One, only partially exposed, may have been a channel or pit. It was excavated to a depth of 0.4m, and was filled with clay. The other two were shallow and filled with silty clay. Other features, which on stratigraphic grounds appeared to be roughly contemporaneous with those described above, included two pits that were both about 0.4m deep. One was cut by two more very small pits. The mixed sand, clay and peat fills suggest they may have been filled by the river. All the features in this group were sealed by a deposit of fluvial clayey sand.

On site K alluvial deposits were found mixed with charcoal, mortar, gravel, roof tile, chalk and Reigate stone chippings suggesting that dumping was being carried out to reclaim areas still being flooded by the river. Large blocks of Kentish ragstone found in a small area on the west side were probably not a structure but were dumped to form an area of hardstanding. It is likely that this area was still open to the river at this time.

On site L grey silty clay was deposited by the river against Building 4 and to its north. Fragments of building material, animal bone and oyster shell in this deposit are evidence of occupation, construction and rubbish disposal nearby.

Open Area 4: New Palace Yard

Layers of clay were dumped in New Palace Yard on site D before the construction of Building 6. After its construction further material, consisting of grey silty clay with shell and animal bone and grey sand with Kentish ragstone fragments and mortar, was dumped in the yard. Dumped layer D[53] produced a very rich and species-diverse botanical assemblage broadly similar to cesspit assemblage D[54] in Building 6 but with the residues from economic plants (mainly food) and wild plants better represented, consisting mainly of wetland species and plants of disturbed ground and waste places.

Plant foods included cereals, represented by a moderate number of charred cereal grains, mainly of free-threshing wheat (*Triticum* sp) plus a few rye (*Secale cereale*) and oat (*Avena* sp) grains. A large quantity of very fragmented cereal bran was also present. Fruits included fig (*Ficus carica*), grape (*Vitis vinifera*), pear/apple (*Pyrus/Malus* spp), elder (*Sambucus nigra*) and blackberry/raspberry (*Rubus fruticosus/idaeus*) seeds and hazelnut (*Corylus avellana*), the latter represented by complete nuts and shell fragments. Other potential economic plants included ?hemp (cf *Cannabis sativa*), the stems of which were used for making rope, canvas and sacking, while the seeds could have been used for oil.

The plants of disturbed ground and waste places may have both been growing *in situ* and been imported as cereal weeds. The charred weed seeds, for example, stinking mayweed (*Anthemis cotula*) and scentless mayweed (*Tripleurospermum inodorum*), probably represent crop-processing waste. Other common arable weeds in the sample were corncockle (*Agrostemma githago*), corn marigold (*Chrysanthemum segetum*), knotgrass (*Polygonum aviculare*), red shank (*P persicaria*), black bindweed (*Fallopia convolvulus*), red dead nettle (*Lamium purpurem*), milk-/sow-thistle (*Sonchus oleraceus*), nettle-leaved goosefoot (*Chenopodium murale*) and hairy buttercup (*Ranunculus sardous*). Some of the weeds, for instance, fat hen (*Chenopodium album*) and stinging nettle (*Urtica dioica*), are good indicators of habitation, growing in nitrogen-rich soils such as rubbish tips. The wetland plants included occasional aquatics, for example, water plantain (*Alisma* spp), but mainly bankside/marshland and meadow species, for example, buttercups (*Ranunculus* spp), celery-leaved buttercup (*R sceleratus*), lesser spearwort (*R flammula*), hemlock (*Conium maculatum*), gipsy-wort (*Lycopus europaeus*), sedges (*Carex* spp) (achenes and articles), spike-rush (*Eleocharis palustris/uniglumis*), rushes (*Juncus* spp), lesser stitchwort (*Stellaria graminea*), grasses (Poaceae), docks (*Rumex* spp) and sheep's sorrel (*Rumex acetosella*). An interesting find was leaves of box (*Buxus sempervirens*), presumably cuttings from a garden.

Some of the weeds were particularly well represented, suggesting that they may have been collected for a specific purpose; for example, both hemlock and black nightshade (*Solanum nigrum*) were represented by very large numbers of seeds and both were used for medicinal purposes, as indeed were henbane (*Hyoscamus niger*) and poppies (*Papaver* spp); the last two, however, were not so frequent and thus may not have been used in this case.

The botanical assemblage in this sample suggests that the dump was being used for the disposal of the residues of food preparation (grain, fruits) and consumption, with the bran indicating faecal deposits (also suggested by puparia in the sample). Some of the weeds may have been growing on the dump itself although some could also be the by-products of cereal processing, particularly those preserved by charring. The wetland plants, for example, the sedges and rushes, and possibly the large amounts of stems, wood shavings and small wood fragments may be from the residues of disposed flooring materials, although again some of the wetland plants may have been growing on the dump itself. Other biological (charcoal, large mammal and fish bones and marine molluscs) and artefactual (ceramic building material, pottery and glass) debris suggests that the dump also contained the residues from other human activities.

The animal bone from D[53] provided a few domesticate bones, sheep/goat, chicken and duck, with a good proportion of fish. The building material may have been associated with the construction of Building 6. These levelling layers were covered by floodlaid deposits of grey silty clay with shell, daub, animal bone, charcoal and yellow sand indicating that New Palace Yard was still subject to occasional flooding. They were overlain by a compact yard surface of gravel, tile and mortar in a clay matrix. This was the earliest recognisable yard surface within New Palace Yard.

On site G fluvial deposits assigned to the previous period were cut by a north–south channel, up to 0.35m deep. The channel was filled successively with grey-brown sandy clay, brown peaty clay and blue-grey clay. The peaty clay contained occasional fragments of animal bone, oyster shell and Roman tile fragments, and gave a radiocarbon date of 740±50 BP (Beta

78164, cal 1190–1390 AD). The radiocarbon date is later than the latest pottery from the fluvial clay overlying the channel, which is dated to the second half of the 11th century, but is the reason for its attribution to this period, indicating that the pottery is residual.

The channel was overlain by fluvial clay, the surface of which lay at about 1.2m OD. It was cut by two small pits, one of which contained a large assemblage of charred cereal grains. These were covered by a layer of charcoal-flecked fluvial clay, G[19], containing fragments of Roman brick, tegula and imbrex roofing tile, stone rubble and residual pottery dated to the second half of the 11th century. This debris may have been washed out from the banks of Thorney Island or thrown in when the area was flooded.

On the south-western edge of site G the fluvial clay was overlain by a layer of buff mortar and cut by a small pit, G[27], which produced a large assemblage of charred cereal grains as well as mammal and fish bones. It also contained fragments of Roman tile and sherds of pottery dated to the second half of the 11th century. The mortar layer and the pit were overlain by mixed deposits consisting of clay and considerable quantities of occupation debris, including fragments of Roman tile, Kentish ragstone, chalk, mortar, animal bone, oyster shell and pottery dated to the second half of the 11th century. A sample from the deposits produced a small quantity of charred cereal grains and the seeds of wetland plants. These strata suggest that household and building refuse was being dumped in New Palace Yard at this time.

The waterlaid clay G[19] was also overlain by fluvial sand G[5] and G[14], which included a few charred grains of free-threshing wheat, rye and oats and charred arable weed seeds, as well as the remains of wetland species and disturbed ground plants. This was sealed by further fluvial deposits to a level of 1.66m OD.

Small quantities of bone from site G were found in channel fills and dumps within the flood layers. Amongst the small assemblages from these deposits there is a reasonable representation of small rodents, including mouse (probably house mouse, half the bones belonging to a partial skeleton recovered from pit G[27]) and black rat. It was noticeable that the food waste species included an abundance of fish, these belonging mainly to various gadids, cyprinids and smelt.

In the south-western corner of the yard on site J, sealing the postholes from the previous period, was a turf line that was later sealed by a compacted gravel yard surface and construction debris. One pit was dug to dispose of Reigate stone chippings, the debris from dressing stone mouldings. Otherwise little activity occurred in this corner of the yard.

Open Area 6: Old Palace Yard

Medieval levelling is represented by three dumped layers of grey sandy clay with mortar and charcoal to the south-east of the later Jewel Tower and Building 12.

This area of Old Palace Yard would seem to have been an open space, possibly a garden.

Open Area 7

Overlying the marsh deposits from period 6 was a layer of chalk and mortar, 0.46m thick, against the foundations of St Stephen's chapel (B11). It was overlain by modern rubble so there was no further evidence of the use of this area.

The chalk and mortar presumably reflects debris associated with the construction of the chapel and may have formed a surface for the yard created to the north. The function of this yard before the building of the cloisters in the last two decades of the 14th century is uncertain although there may have been a timber cloister there by 1361–2 (Colvin et al 1963, 526). After the construction of the cloisters in the late 14th century the yard became a very narrow space.

Open Area 8: Westminster Abbey precinct (north)

A compact brown silty clay was dumped to the south of Building 13 in order to level up the ground for a yard surface in chalk and Reigate stone chippings. This was covered with patches of occupation material.

This is the earliest evidence for surfaces in the northern precinct of the abbey and as such the earliest evidence for the use of the area. During the 13th and 14th centuries the northern precinct was used for the yearly October Fair. Buildings such as Building 13 were used during the duration of the fairs and yard surfaces would have been required, especially since the underlying ground consisted of marshy clays.

Open Area 9: Westminster Abbey precinct (south)

To the south of the Westminster Abbey great drain, and cut by the 14th-century precinct wall (Chapter 10.3, Structure 11), was a layer of mixed brickearth with building material that was cut by a rectangular pit. This was sealed by a grey-brown clay that was overlain by a mortar surface. It was unclear whether this surface was internal or external as no walls were found. Such a surface would, however, more often be internal because of its relative fragility.

Open Area 10

Dumping on site C(ii) raised the level of the ground and sealed the marshy deposits beneath. Overlying this at the north end was a wall consisting mainly of chalk blocks but with occasional Kentish ragstone bonded with yellow mortar. It was 0.50m wide and 1.15m long and extended into the eastern section. At its western end were three phases of external surfacing. The lowest comprised mixed clay, tile, chalk and gravel and was sealed by a compact gravel layer which was, in turn, sealed by a surface of mixed tile, gravel and chalk.

At the extreme north end of site C(ii), immediately to the north of the chalk wall and cutting the external surfaces, was an east–west aligned ditch. Only its vertical southern edge was located but it measured more than 1.1m across and was more than 0.4m deep. The ditch contained four fills, all of which appeared to be dumped. They contained some food waste (mussel shell) and building waste (tile and chalk) and one comprised a layer of chalk, suggesting construction activity in the area. The ditch was probably not filled in by the end of this period. One of the fills contained part of a 13th-century iron prick spur, <S16> (Fig 61). The ditch would appear to have lain behind and to the north of the properties erected around what became the Woolstaple Yard. The Woolstaple was not founded until 1353, which might suggest that the wall and ditch date to the mid 14th century. The pottery from the lowest two fills, however, although in small quantities, suggests a 13th-century date. The ditch may have formed a boundary and, perhaps, taken waste from the properties out into the Thames. If so it would seem to have been cleaned out regularly. This would not be uncommon; monastic drains, for instance were regularly cleaned out, leaving only the waste from their final uses (Thomas et al 1997, 54 and 75). It is also possible that this ditch was the same as C[304] (period 5; Chapter 7.3, Open Area 1) although the nature of the excavation made this impossible to ascertain. In either case it would seem to have been part of a long-lived boundary of some importance. It might even have denoted the boundary to the king's property (perhaps the king's ditch), a function it certainly seems to have performed in the next period.

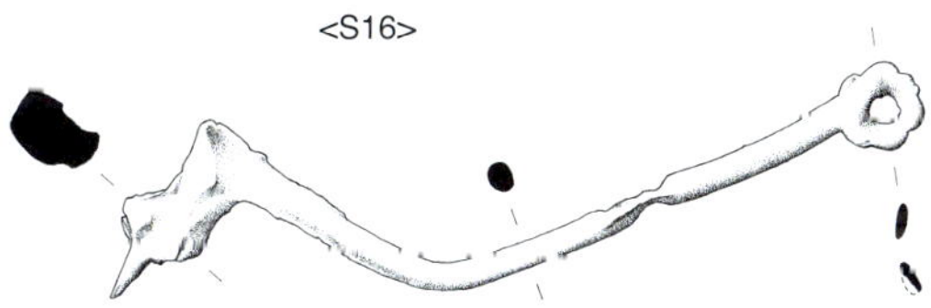

Fig 61 Iron spur <S16> from Open Area 10 (scale 1:2)

On the eastern part of Open Area 10, on site F immediately to the west of the putative revetment and river line, dumping raised the ground level and provided firmer, drier ground. This material was located to the east of Road 1. It included large amounts of mortar and building material, suggesting that construction activities were taking place nearby. There was some domestic refuse, including animal bone, but this was generally quite limited, indicating that occupation lay elsewhere. The upper layer contained a discarded Penn floor tile dating to the mid 14th century.

Small quantities of animal bone were found in a number of external dumps. Of interest amongst an otherwise commonplace overall assemblage was the recovery of the partial articulation of an infant sheep, perhaps indicative of local breeding. These deposits also provided single fragments of swan and haddock. The latter is somewhat unusual, as there were no other haddock bones found at these sites. It clearly represented a moderately sized fish, weighing about 2.2kg, which would appear, judging by the cut marks, to have had its head removed. The swan is an obvious high-status indicator, this bird often being referred to amongst the 'exotic' items served up at special occasions (Hammond 1995, 130).

Open Area 11

An east–west aligned ditch divided Open Area 11 from Open Area 12, which lay to the south (Fig 62). It sloped down to the west and presumably fed into the Tyburn. It was truncated to the east and north by a later ditch on a similar alignment (period 8; Chapter 10.3, Open Area 11) so its full width was not recoverable. It was more than 0.42m wide and was 0.16m deep. Two pits were dug in Open Area 11: one was a shallow scoop measuring 1.20m x 0.75m and 0.16m deep and containing small amounts of animal bone and Reigate stone chippings; the other measured 1.30m x 0.30m and 0.10m deep and contained small amounts of charcoal and shell and part of a ceramic vessel, <P13> (Fig 63). Across most of the area and sealing the ditch orange sandy clay was dumped containing oyster shell, tile, fragments of Kentish ragstone and pebbles with some charcoal and mortar. This deposit was seen in both Open Area 11 and Open Area 12 and was clearly intended to level up the ground before a new ditch was cut in the next period.

Open Area 11 was probably a back garden to one of the properties fronting on to King Street. It was divided from its next-door plot (Open Area 12) by a ditch that probably also acted as a drainage ditch flowing into the Tyburn.

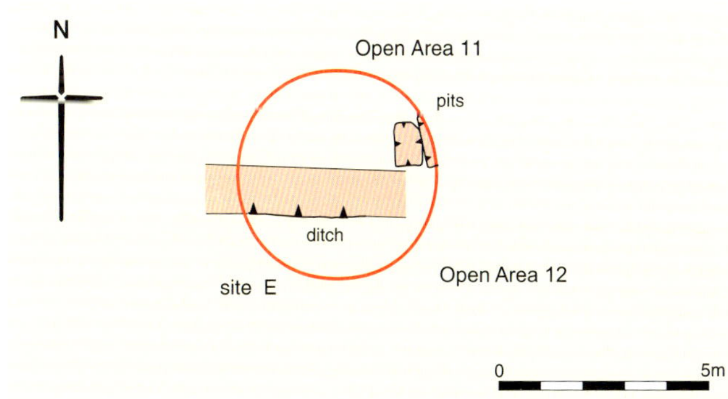

Fig 62 Detailed plan of ditch dividing Open Area 11 from Open Area 12, period 7 (scale 1:200)

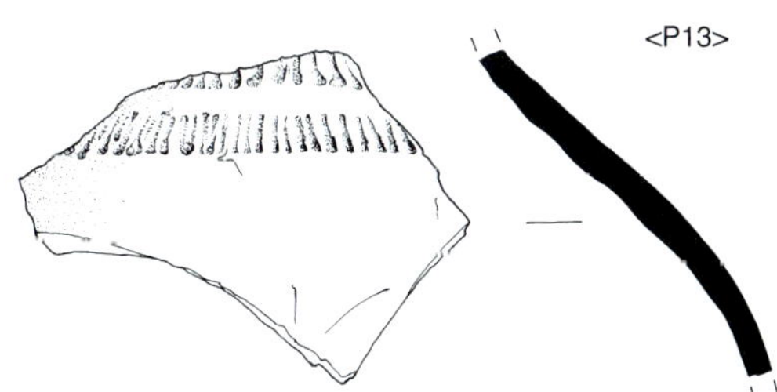

Fig 63 Ceramic vessel <P13> from a pit in Open Area 11 (scale 1:4)

Open Area 12

Only a small part of Open Area 12 lay within the confines of site E. The earliest levelling layer contained charcoal, oyster shell, mortar and part of a handled tool, <S17>. Its exact form and date are uncertain. Also recovered from here was a copper-alloy gilded shield-shaped mount, <S23> (Fig 64), decorated with the heraldic motif of *three lions passant gardant* signifying the arms of England. Such mounts may have been used to decorate horse harness, such as bridles, but they were often poorly made rather than being indicative of the highest ranks of society. This layer was sealed by the same deposit of orange sandy clay as was seen in Open Area 11 sealing the ditch dividing the two areas.

Open Area 12 was the back garden of another property fronting on to King Street. It may have been one of the most southerly of these properties as Thieving Lane lay only *c* 33m to the south of the ditch dividing Open Area 11 and Open Area 12 and properties there must have had their own back gardens or yards.

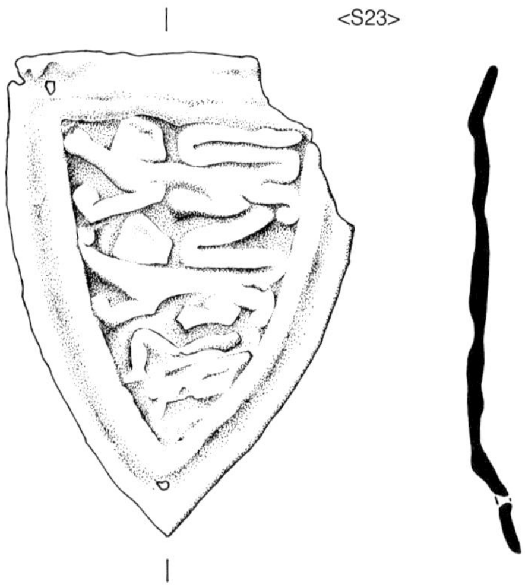

Fig 64 Copper-alloy mount <S23> from Open Area 12 (scale 1:1)

9.4 Discussion

The scale of activity at Westminster increased dramatically from the 13th century (Table 11). The expansion of the palace at a time of greatly increased expenditure by Henry III and the permanent siting of the Exchequer there created the need for large-scale building works. The animal bone and environmental assemblages make clear, however, that New Palace Yard was only just being formed and lay on the edge of habitation. The palace boundaries were either built or rebuilt in stone at this time and buildings within them such as the possible inn next to the great gate were constructed. It seems likely that there was a precursor to the stone gate to New Palace Yard, especially given the reference in 1235 to the house of Master David the king's surgeon lying by the gate (above, 9.2).

Similar rebuilding works at the abbey occurred during the same period and were not confined to the church alone. The northern boundary of the abbey seems to have been built in stone at this time and many of the structures which filled that area were also apparently built during the 13th century. Clearly, the October Fair was of major importance to Westminster's trade and provided an important source of wealth to the abbey at a time when it needed all the finances it could get.

There also seems to be some evidence that the town, too, was expanding at this time too. The documentary evidence makes clear that there was more evidence of activity on both sides of King Street during the 13th and early 14th centuries and the archaeological evidence confirms this. The properties on the west side were formed towards the south end of the street at this time and there was increased activity on the east side. In common with most urban reclamation works, the Thames at Westminster appears to have been embanked in piecemeal fashion by different property-owners, giving the river front an uneven look; clearly one property-owner wanted a fish trap on the river margins rather than dry land upon which to build whilst others expanded their properties eastwards into the river.

Table 11 Selected dating evidence, period 7 (see Table 25 for expansion of codes)

Land use	Activity	Context	Evidence	Description	Date range
Building 4	pit	L[25]	ceramic	TUDG	1320–1500
	levelling	L[42]	ceramic	KING	1230–1350
	hearth	L[35]	ceramic building material	tile 2271; 2537; 2586; 2587	1240–1450
Building 5: gatehouse to New Palace Yard			documentary	see Table 16	1287–1289
Building 6	cesspit fill	D[54]	ceramic	KING; LOND; MG	1270–1350
	make-up layer	D[41]	ceramic	KING; LOND; SHER	1240–1300
	cesspit timber	D[88]	dendrochronology		1270–1310
Building 8: gatehouse to the Green Yard			documentary	see Table 16	1244–1245
Building 9	make up deposit	J[50]	ceramic	LOND	1200–1350
Building 10: the Exchequer			documentary	see Table 16	–1244
Building 11: St Stephen's chapel			documentary	Colvin et al 1963, 522	1292–1363
Building 13	make-up layer	C[116]	ceramic	KING; LOND	1230–1350
Building 13	wall construction cut	C[191]	ceramic	?EMCH; EMSH; ESUR; KING; LOND; SHER	1230–1350
Building 13	rubbish pit	C[209]	ceramic	?EMCH; EMFL; LOND	1200–1250
Building 13	floor	C[179]	ceramic	LOND	1150–1350
Building 13	floor	C[181]	ceramic	LOND	1150–1350
Building 13	occupation layer	C[200]	ceramic	LOND; KING	1230–1350
Building 13	floor	C[201]	ceramic	LOND; LCALC	1150–1350
Building 13	occupation layer	C[196]	ceramic	LOND	1150–1350
Building 13	floor	C[197]	ceramic	LOND	1150–1350
Building 13	floor	C[165]	ceramic	LOND	1150–1350
Building 13	make-up layer	C[195]	ceramic	LOND	1150–1350
Structure 7	foreshore silt	U[92]	ceramic	CBW; LOND; SHER	1270–1500
Structure 9	wall	J[46]	ceramic	SHER	1150–1300
Road 1	road make-up	F[159]	ceramic	LOND; KING	1230–1350
Road 1	road surface	F[179]	ceramic building material	tile 2587	1240–1450
Road 1	road make-up	F[181]	ceramic	LOND; SHER; KING	1230–1300
Road 1	road make-up	F[144]	ceramic	LOND; SHER; KING	1230–1300
Road 1	flood deposit	F[157]	ceramic	LOND; SHER	1230–1350
Road 1	road surface	F[128]	ceramic building material	floor tile 2317	1300–1500
Road 1	road surface	F[153]	ceramic	KING	1230–1400
Open Area 1	levelling	K[53]	ceramic	EMSH; ESUR; KING; LCOAR; LOND; MG; SHER; SSW	1270–1300
Open Area 1	levelling	K[57]	ceramic	EMSH; KING; LCOAR; LOND; SHER	1230–1300
Open Area 1	foreshore deposit	L[21]	ceramic	LOND	1080–1350
Open Area 1	cut	H[44]	ceramic	KING	1230–1400
Open Area 1	levelling	F[137]	ceramic	LOND	1080–1350
Open Area 1	pit	F[134]	ceramic	LOND	1080–1350
Open Area 1	pit	F[135]	ceramic	LOND	1080–1350
Open Area 4: New Palace Yard	flood deposit	G[13]	ceramic	KING	1230–1350
Open Area 4: New Palace Yard	yard surface	J[10]	ceramic building material	tile 2271	1180–1500
Open Area 4: New Palace Yard	levelling	D[53]	ceramic	KING; LOND; SHER; SSW	1230–1300
Open Area 10	levelling	F[156]	ceramic	LOND; SHER	1230–1300
Open Area 10	levelling	F[160]	ceramic	LOND; SHER; KING	1230–1290
Open Area 10	levelling	F[168]	ceramic	KING	1230–1400
Open Area 10	pit	F[1]	ceramic	CBW; LOND	1270–1500
Open Area 10	pit	F[2]	ceramic	CBW	1270–1500
Open Area 10	levelling	C[272]	ceramic	KING; LOND; SHER	1250–1300
Open Area 10	ditch	C[281]	ceramic	KING; LOND; SAIN	1250–1350
Open Area 10	ditch	C[288]	ceramic	KING; LOND	1230–1300
Open Area 11	pit	E[49]	ceramic	EMSS; KING; LOND	1230–1350
Open Area 12	levelling	E[32]	ceramic	CBW; KING; LOND; SAIG; SHER	1280–1350
Open Area 12	levelling	E[32]	copper alloy	mount <S23>	1150–1340
Open Area 12	levelling	E[37]	ceramic	KING; SHER	1230–1300

10

c 1350–*c* 1540 (period 8)

10.1 Environmental and topographical background

The River Tyburn

At Storey's Gate (SGT94) the uppermost fills of the Tyburn channel suggest that salinity levels increased once more and that the tidal influence became stronger. This probably relates to a reversal of the factors that led to the previous decrease in salinity; either relative river levels had increased with the progression of the tidal head further upstream, and/or tidal water was dominating the Tyburn channel to a greater extent than before. However, the marine influence does not reach the levels encountered when the second phase of sedimentation began, at *c* +0.4m OD. Though this is doubtless confused by the mixing taking place within the Tyburn, it is certainly significant that the river was more weakly tidal at this location in the later medieval period than in the prehistoric periods.

The River Thames

Fluvial deposits from site H provide an image of rapidly changing conditions both adjacent to, and occasionally in, the main body of the tidal Thames. The likelihood is that deposits at this site were influenced by the changing configuration of the Thames/Tyburn confluence. The diatom data, although reflecting sedimentation from estuarine sources, point towards a less strong saline signal than observed here prior to the hiatus. This is an interesting point to note in comparison with the results from Storey's Gate but, again, unidentifiable seasonal fluctuations may be confusing the record. Nevertheless, by the late medieval/Tudor period, the diatom evidence suggests conditions that were predominantly freshwater. This corresponds with a possible revetment associated with water management, reflecting movement of fresh water into the river from Thorney Island.

A final piece of evidence on the Thames comes from a note in the report on the excavations at Abingdon Street (Green 1976, 74), which indicates that until the mid 16th century the excavated muds were below low-tide level and free of plant growth. Looking at the species list presented in this article, it is clear that brackish conditions prevailed here, with *Cyclotella striata* and *Cocconeis placentula* readily testifying to this. This confirms the complexity of depositional processes occurring around Thorney Island at this period.

Palaeoecology

Very limited information is available from this date in terms of ecological reconstruction. At Storey's Gate the channel appears to have finally dried out and become a terrestrial surface in the late medieval/early post-medieval period. Nevertheless, the pollen evidence suggests it remained damp and probably boggy for some time. A possible turf line at *c* +0.9m OD would suggest that the area had been formerly reclaimed but initially at least was not built over or used significantly at this period. At site H the pollen indicates that at this period cereals were continuing to be grown or processed locally (although probably not on the island itself). By the Tudor period deliberate dumping to raise the ground above flood levels had occurred and it was not possible to obtain a 'pure' ecological signal from such deposits.

10.2 Documentary and archaeological background

The Westminster Woolstaple

In 1353 a great council passed the Ordinance of the Staple, which established staples at several ports where aliens could export wool bought in England and the king could collect his customs. Each staple consisted of a corporation of mayor, constable and merchants, and a place to which goods were brought to be weighed and taxed: the staple for London was situated at Westminster (Power 1941, 97). Under the Ordinance, merchants and their goods coming to the staple were no longer subject to common law, but to law merchant, exercised by the mayor of the staple, whose jurisdiction at Westminster extended to Temple Bar and included not only debts but criminal cases as well. At Westminster the mayors were prominent and wealthy citizens of London, and the staple was dominated by city politics; occasionally a mayor of the staple was mayor of London at the same time. There was also a constable and a prison (Rich 1932–4, 124–6, 130; 192–3, list of mayors). The staple was frequently used for swearing bonds for debt before the mayor.

The king provided the site for the London staple in the precinct of Westminster palace, on part of the property he had just given to the canons of St Stephen, with access from King Street through property held by the keeper of the palace, an open area which became known as Woolstaple Yard or the Round Woolstaple. Presumably both holders were amenable since the value of their property was increased by the existence of the staple. The weigh-house was built on the south side of Woolstaple Yard, adjoining the north side of the palace gate from King Street. A house on the north side of the Round Woolstaple was known in 1462 as the 'old woolhouse', so may also have been connected with the staple. The staple was in operation by November 1353, when the carriage of merchandise and victuals had so chewed up the highway that the king ordered the owners of property around the staple to pave for 7ft outside their buildings, on the grounds that the value had increased with the establishment of the staple, and ordered the mayor of the staple to pave the remaining areas and to build a bridge or landing stage by the Thames for access; this, however, was superseded by a grant to John de Bedeford of customs for three years to carry out the paving and bridge, renewed in 1356 (*Cal Pat R*, 1350–4, 530, 538; 1354–8, 481). The increased value was evident in the valuation of a messuage held of the king by his surgeon Roger de Heyton: originally worth 20s a year, it was said to have doubled after 'the staples were erected' (PRO, C 135/126, no. 2).

The staple buildings were paid for out of the king's works: they included a water gate of stone, a hall and chamber for the mayor and constable, a kitchen and a weigh-house, all probably largely timber-framed. Building was complete in 1354 at a cost of £800. In 1355 a stone wall running east–west was built to separate the Woolstaple from New Palace Yard (Colvin et al 1963, 552). The roadway between the weigh-house and the landing stage, built across the canons' land, was eventually known as the Long Woolstaple. At the east end by the woolbridge there were six houses on the north side belonging to the king and initially connected with the staple.

The functioning of the Woolstaple is rather obscure. The economic importance of the domestic staples was soon superseded by the staple at Calais, but it is not clear how long the Woolstaple continued to be used. In 1437 the canons complained that the rents they received from the Woolstaple had dwindled from the 100 marks with which they were endowed, to 60s, and they received priory lands instead (*Cal Pat R*, 1436–41, 125).

The king's ditch

In 1383 a tenement in King Street granted to the dean and canons of St Stephen had the ditch of the king on the east (BL, Cotton MS Faustina B viii, fo 10v): this is probably one of the three isolated properties the college had acquired by *c* 1510 between Our Lady Alley and the Woolstaple gate (WAM, 18599). The ditch by the stone wall mentioned in the bounds of the canons' property in 1394 (below, Canon Row), is also likely to be the king's ditch.

Between King Street and the ditch

In 1342 a large holding, again held of the king, stretched from the highway to the king's ditch and may have covered most of the later Round Woolstaple (GL, MS 12989; PRO, C 143/217, no. 16). This holding was acquired by John Senche or Shenche, then keeper of the palace. In 1462, his successor, Elizabeth Venour, widow, granted a lease for 99 years of four adjoining tenements, recently built, with gardens and ditches on the east side of Woolstaple Yard (Round Woolstaple), bounded by the king's ditch on the east and south, and a garden on the north; the property measured 7 perches 2ft long, and 5 perches 12ft wide (at 6 ells to 1 perch, 128ft by 92ft) (GL, MS 12980). On the north side of Woolstaple Yard in 1462 was a tenement and garden, and a building called the 'old woolhouse' (GL, MS 12977). The property on the north and east sides of Woolstaple Yard was later acquired by Richard Casteler and given to Christ's Hospital.

Canon Row

In 1348 Edward III founded a college to serve the free chapel of St Mary and St Stephen within the Palace of Westminster, to include a dean and 12 secular canons as well as vicars, clerks and choristers. They were assured an income of £500 a year, with any shortfall from their revenues being made up by the Exchequer (*VCH* 1909, 566). In 1353 the king granted to the college sites near the chapel and the great hall, and land and houses lying within the fee of the palace north of the hall, which included buildings used for stabling the king's horses, the king's garden, which adjoined the stables, and the inn that had formerly belonged to the earl of Kent, which adjoined the north side of the garden. Also included were tenements that Roger de Heyton, the king's surgeon, had held of the king, and which may have lain near the later Woolstaple (*Cal Chart R*, 1347–1417, 133–7; PRO, C 135/126, no. 2).

The garden and Kent's inn later formed the site of the houses for the canons, but it is not clear whether this was intended from the start, or whether the king's grant was initially just to add to their revenues. Shortly afterwards in 1353, the Woolstaple was established at Westminster, and some of its buildings and the road to the woolbridge were on the college's property; the college received from the Exchequer the rent paid from the staple to the king (*Cal Close R Richard II*, 1369–74, 398).

The boundaries of the site used for the lodgings of the dean and canons were delineated in an agreement drawn up in 1394 between the college and the abbot and convent of Westminster over spiritual and temporal jurisdiction (BL, Cotton MS Faustina A iii, fos 293–314). Great trouble was taken to indicate the sites of these lodgings and to emphasise that the exemption from the abbey's jurisdiction applied only to this ground and the buildings on it, and only while inhabited by the members of the college. Though reference is made to the plots or places 'recently' allocated to each named canon, no mention is made of any buildings inhabited, though a couple of phrases suggest that the mansions of the canons were under construction at that time. As late as 1391 the king was granting individual canons accommodation within the palace, for example, in le Salcerie (possibly Building 9) within the second gate of the palace (*Cal Pat R*, 1388–92, 493; see also 391, 409), so building was presumably only recently started, as the document indicates.

There is similarly no mention in the document of 1394 of any road or way through the site (ie, a forerunner of Canon Row), but the reference to the 'gates or entrances' into the canons' plots shows that a way was planned, if not already laid out, in 1394. The existence of the 'new great gate of the canons' giving access into King Street, clearly the forerunner of St Stephen's Alley, may be tied in with the row, but is more likely to pre-date the canons' ownership, and be the entrance to Kent's inn.

There is no indication of the width of each plot, whether the ground was divided equally into 13 plots, or whether the dean had a larger plot; though the dean's plot is in the centre of the row of canons, the plot is described only as that of William de Sleford, canon, in the list of names. However, later evidence for the house sites indicates a width of 34 or 35 feet for each. It is not clear how wide the Woolstaple road was, and this and the six houses of the king (27ft deep) were included in the 575-feet length given for the site.

The dean's plot is presumably the one referred to in a grant in 1438, as being found unsuitable for building the dean's lodgings for want of good foundations; because of this, Sleford (dean 1369–96), had been given buildings on the south side of the Woolstaple road, by the palace wall and woolbridge, and his successor obtained the same buildings (*Cal Pat R*, 1436–41, 192). The problem with the foundations is a bit puzzling, since the site for the dean's house was presumably on a par with those of the canons either side, but may possibly indicate a natural or man-made ditch or something similar at that point. The grant of houses within and without the palace occupied by predecessors was a fairly standard part of the grant of the deanery, however, and may have been repeated long after a house was built for the dean in Canon Row. It may indeed have referred to a problem with the whole site, and account for the long gap after the grant before any building took place on the site. In any case, the problem seems to have been overcome by the early 16th century, when the last dean, John Chamber, was living in Canon Row.

In 1437 the college complained that the part of their endowment which came from staple rents had greatly reduced in value and the Exchequer only made up the difference with assignments; they asked for an alien priory (from which they could earn revenues) instead, and this was granted (*Cal Pat R*, 1436–41, 125). The college had surrendered to the king the six woolhouses in the staple on the north side of the road later called Long Woolstaple, lying between the woolbridge and the college's storehouse, possibly in return for the priory. These houses were then granted out by the king but surrendered in order that they could to be sold to the college for the chantry of William Prestwyk, canon (*Cal Pat R*, 1436–41, 123; 1441–6, 143–4).

In 1469 the dean and canons were granted licence to make a permanent grant to the vicars, clerks and choristers of the college of a rentcharge of 7 marks a year from their messuages, gardens, lands, tenements and shops in the New Rent in a lane running east–west with a gate at each end, later known as St Stephen's Alley, which still had the gates in 1547 (*Cal Pat R*, 1467–77, 150–1; PRO, E 315/105, fo 44v).

The college received licences in 1521 and 1529 to rebuild their property on the south side of the Long Woolstaple. In 1521 they were permitted to rebuild all the houses on the south side of the road between the stone wall bordering the Thames and the weigh-house, using the wall of the palace courtyard as a support and putting in windows and doors as necessary; they were also allowed to put pales with posts and gates within the palace 10ft from the wall to enclose and give access to their tenements (PRO, C 66/636, m 20), thus incorporating the palace wall into the houses. The licence was partially repeated in 1529, when they were permitted to rebuild their property between the weigh-house and the bell tower, with permission to enlarge the houses towards the tower upon the wall where necessary (PRO, C 66/654, m 7).

Since the college's foundation it had had to entertain visitors to the palace, and by the 16th century visiting churchmen and courtiers attending court were often housed by the canons: amongst those staying or living in Canon Row were Thomas Cranmer (1533), Thomas Howard, duke of Norfolk (1534, 1536), Thomas Lord Wriothesley, Lord Privy Seal (1544) and

William Paget, Secretary of State (1545). Some of the canons, who often had greater benefices elsewhere, seem to have leased out their houses in Canon Row.

The earl of Kent's Inn

Following its surrender by Queen Isabella (Chapter 9.2) the property may have remained in the king's hands until, in 1353, it formed part of the endowment of the college of St Stephen's chapel. It was bounded on the north by Almayne, near the northern end of the later Canon Row and, given that the canons also held the site of St Stephen's Alley, with tenements on either side extending to King Street, it is likely that the alley was the entrance to the inn. Its extent southwards is not known. The buildings were still standing in 1362 when the king paid for repairs to the roof (Colvin et al 1963, 525).

The king's garden

Little can be said about the remainder of the precinct forming the endowment. It consisted of the king's garden and stables, lying on the north side of the courtyard outside the great hall.

The house of Roger de Heyton, the king's surgeon, also given to the canons, was within the fee of the palace, but its location is uncertain. It probably lay near the palace gate and was later used for the Woolstaple, but it is also possible that it may have been a property carved out of the earl of Kent's inn, lying in King Street near St Stephen's Alley.

Palace of Westminster

The formation of the Woolstaple necessitated the construction of a new stone wall and gates in 1355 to separate it from the precinct and, in 1365–7, a bell tower along the wall (Horsman and Davison 1989, 283) (Fig 65). In the centre of New Palace Yard, between the north door of the great hall and the bell tower, stood an octagonal fountain, the remains of which were excavated in 1972–4 (Horsman and Davison 1989). The fountain uncovered was built at some time after the middle of the 14th century, but contained elements of an earlier structure, reused within it, suggesting that an earlier fountain may have lain on the same site. This fountain may have been incorporated into the timber halls constructed for the parliament of Richard II in 1397, which could not be held in the great hall because it was being rebuilt.

The rebuilding of the great hall, which involved the heightening of the walls and the construction of the magnificent hammerbeam roof by Master Hugh Herland, began in the 1390s and was completed in 1399. The sections were actually constructed at a place called the 'Frame' at Farnham in Surrey before being assembled in place at Westminster. New towers were built at the north end, flanking a large ceremonial doorway. A new window was built at the south end of the hall and flying buttresses on either side of the hall to take the thrust of the new roof. All these building works were carried out under the direction of Henry Yevele. He also built the new Jewel Tower for the king (B17) on land originally forming part of the abbey precinct. A number of other buildings are documented as having been built during this period (see Table 16) but few can be located. Parts of buildings found in the Jewel Tower garden may relate to works carried out by Edward IV from 1462 (Green 1976, 67).

Westminster Abbey

Work on the rebuilding of the remainder of the nave was not resumed until 1376 and was not completed until 1534, shortly before the Dissolution. The Lady chapel was replaced by the Henry VII chapel during the early years of the 16th century. This was used as a mausoleum for most of the Tudor and Stuart monarchs. Major rebuilding was carried out on the claustral buildings during the latter part of the 14th century. The new precinct wall (S11) was built around the Jewel Tower (B17), which was built on land appropriated from the abbey by Edward III. The fire of 1298, which had damaged the infirmary, led to the infirmary cloister being built, retaining the chapel of St Katherine on its eastern side. The cloister was surrounded by small houses for sick monks, following the common practice of increased segregation rather than communal living that became popular in the later medieval period. The prior also had a house built for him to the south of the frater.

One of the major works was the building of the abbot's house on the west side of the cloister, consisting of a range of buildings around a courtyard. The building of the abbot's house necessitated the removal of the cellarer's range to the south-west of the cloister forming a range on the east side of the outer court of the monastery known as Nine Elms (now known as Dean's Yard). A passage alongside the cellarer's range led to the gate leading out over the bridge to the mill. On the other side of the lane to the gate, opposite the cellarer's range, was the granary, built in 1376. This formed a long narrow building divided into bays with a line of central octagonal columns. Records of the southern end of this building were made by Frank Cottrill in 1935 and are held at the Museum of London.

A new almshouse dedicated to St Anne was built on the west side of the precinct in c 1509. There were lodgings for 12 men, with latrines which emptied into the Tyburn stream. The houses fronted on to a cloister with various other buildings arranged around it.

The October Fair declined in the 14th century and no mention is made of it after 1487 (Rosser 1989, 113). The function of the buildings in the northern precinct of the abbey must have changed to take account of this.

10.3 Archaeological evidence

Building 1: the great hall

In 1393 it was decided to 'repair' the great hall although repair seems hardly an adequate description (Colvin et al 1963, 528–9). The walls were heightened by 2ft (0.61m) and a new

Fig 65 Plan of the archaeological features, period 8 (scale 1:2500). For key to site codes, see Tables 1–3

hammerbeam timber roof was constructed by Hugh Herland (Fig 66), the main effect of which was to dispense with the need for columns within the hall and create a single open space (assuming that there were columns in the original build: Chapter 7.3, Building 1). The Romanesque windows were removed or blocked in and larger Perpendicular windows inserted, particularly the great south window which took up much of the south wall (this window was reset by Barry in the new Palace of Westminster in the 1840s in his new south wall). A grand northern entrance to the hall was created, with two flanking towers built around a large ceremonial door. Niches around the towers and inside the hall were constructed to show the 13 statues of the kings of England from Edward the Confessor to Richard II as well as two larger statues of those two kings. In order to support the hammerbeam roof flying buttresses were constructed along the west side of the hall. Examination of these buttresses on site S indicates that either they were rebuilt totally in the 1880s when the buildings which had conglomerated around the hall were demolished and the new buildings constructed or they were refaced and underpinned in brick and concrete.

The floor in the hall associated with the rebuild was laid in Purbeck marble; it was apparently at the same level as the current floor, which was laid in the 1830s (Smirke 1836, 416).

Building 4

Building 4 (Fig 45) was demolished at some time around the middle of the 14th century to make way for the new street of Canon Row (R2). No material from its demolition was recovered.

Building 5: gatehouse to New Palace Yard

After the construction of a pier base and some levelling in Open Area 5, gravel surfaces overlay the wall of Building 5 (Fig 45), indicating that it had been demolished. If its identification with the gatehouse into New Palace Yard is correct then this must have occurred at around the time that the new gate was constructed in 1397 (Colvin et al 1963, 548). This gate probably lay to the west of the earlier gate (B5), outside the palace precinct, thus allowing the old gate to remain standing until the new one had been constructed.

Building 6

An east–west aligned cut, more than 1.62m long, 0.66m wide and 0.25m deep, was filled with a layer of brickearth and cut by a north–south aligned beam slot for an internal partition, which ran northwards from the south wall. Whilst this beam slot clearly pre-dated the levelling to the west, the edges of those layers appeared to respect the line of the beam slot suggesting that the partition remained in use. The levelling consisted of mortar and brickearth sealed by a sand bedding layer for a brick and cobbled floor surrounding a burnt cobbled hearth. The brick types were made from the 15th century to the

Fig 66 *View of the interior of the great hall, looking south*

late 17th century. The levelling deposits included an iron key, <S14> (Fig 67). Over the hearth lay a deposit of fire debris comprising charcoal and grey silt. To the east of the cobbled floor lay a second beam slot along the same line as the earlier one, suggesting that the partition was replaced. Within the beam slot was a posthole, presumably forming an upright within the partition. An 18th-century drain had destroyed all deposits contemporary with the hearth to the east of the partition (Chapter 12.3).

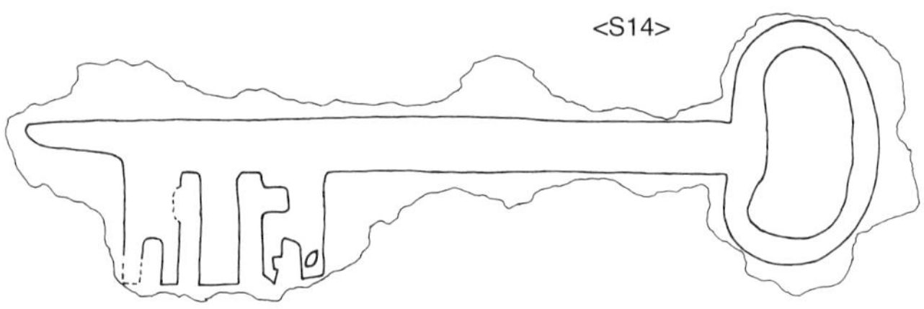

Fig 67 *Iron key <S14> from Building 6 (scale 1:2)*

Clearly, some change in function occurred during this period when the cesspit had gone out of use. Partitions were inserted and hearths laid. Hollar's view of New Palace Yard from the 17th century (Colvin et al 1963, pl 36b) shows the range of buildings along the north side of the yard. Many had single-storey extensions on the front, which may be reflected archaeologically by the pier base excavated to the south in Open Area 4 (below). These buildings along the yard may have been a variety of inns and shops for use in what was a public space in front of the main law courts sited in the great hall.

Building 13

Building 13 underwent substantial alterations during the middle of the 14th century. The plaster appears to have been stripped from the walls (Chapter 9.3) and a new floor laid in clay with a patch of intense burning, suggesting a hearth. To the north of the hearth lay a posthole that originally contained a post about 100mm in diameter. The post may have been associated with the hearth, perhaps being one side of the support for a spit. Levelling layers of sand and gravel were dumped in the building for a new floor of Reigate stone chippings, gravel and mortar. Overlying the floor was a dark occupation layer with small quantities of charcoal and animal bone. Levelling layers with building material fragments and charcoal were then dumped into the building and sealed by a dumped layer of small Caen stone, Reigate stone chippings and chalk fragments, suggesting that there may have been alterations to the building's fabric at this time. Further levelling was cut by a square stakehole 80mm across. To the west two rectangular pits were dug, one up against the north wall. Both contained Reigate stone chippings, tile, Kentish ragstone and chalk fragments, again suggesting that buildings works were being carried out.

An orange clay floor was subsequently laid in the building, sealed by a floor of Reigate stone chippings that was overlain by a thin black layer of occupation debris. Cutting the Reigate stone floor were eight postholes in a north–south line from the north wall up to the edge of the site. One of these contained two sockets for posts, indicating that there were in fact nine posts. The posts were mostly circular and varied from 80mm to 190mm in diameter: six were 150mm in diameter or more, three much smaller. They lay on the east side of the former path (Chapter 9.3) and would originally have formed a partition on the east side of the door into the building. A gap between the most southerly posthole and the next in line of 0.65m may have been the site of a narrow doorway in the partition. One of the postholes contained an iron staple, <S51>.

A single posthole *c* 0.1m across was found some 1.8m to the south-west. This was close to the edge of excavation and it is therefore uncertain whether it formed part of a more complex structure. To the west of the partition, against the north wall, a large oval pit, 1.15m across, was filled with building material and glazed tile.

Building 13 had clearly changed function by this time. The walls were stripped of their plaster, rebuilding works were carried out (as shown by the deposition of substantial quantities of waste building material), domestic activities were occurring (such as the hearth burning) and partitions were erected to subdivide the room. The stone against the north wall and the path through the building also appear to have gone out of use or at least to have lost their significance.

By the middle of the 14th century, with the decline of the October Fair, the houses in this area (now five in number) were rented out without reference to the fair for less than half the rate of the late 13th century (Rosser 1989, 110–11). This may be the period when the painted plaster was stripped from the walls and new floors laid. By the end of the 14th century there were seven houses rented out for a combined total of £21 6s 8d (Rosser 1989, 111). Perhaps it was during this time that partitions were constructed in the building. Building 13, or one of these seven houses, may now have become the Holy Way Tavern, which was developed in 1343 (Rosser 1989, 37). If Building 13 was not a tavern it must have fulfilled a very different function from that in the previous period, such as a shop or a domestic dwelling. In 1486–7 (the time of the demise of the fair) Westminster Abbey paid £230 to rebuild four houses and the Saracen's Head (Rosser 1989, 79). This may equate with the removal of the partitions and the deposition of layers of building material. From this time on there were hearths in the structure, suggesting a domestic function, although it is unknown whether there were other hearths elsewhere in the building during the earlier periods. A copper-alloy octofoil mount, <S22>, recovered in period 10 from Building 22 may have originated from this period and this building.

Building 14

A layer of topsoil overlay the floors in Building 14 (Fig 45) and no further evidence of its destruction has so far been recorded. It was, however, cut by Building 17 and by Structure 11, which were constructed in this period. The topsoil overlay the construction trench to Building 17, suggesting that Building 14 was demolished at the same time as the construction of Building 17, although it is possible that horizontal truncation had removed any later deposits that might have indicated a gap in time between the demolition of the one and the construction of the other.

Building 15: canon's house

Within site F and Open Area 14 was Building 15 (Fig 68). Only the southern and western walls were found, the northern and eastern walls having been destroyed by the London Underground District and Circle Lines and a Victorian basement respectively. The eastern wall can, however, be projected from the riverfront wall (S13), giving the building a total length of 13m east–west.

The south wall included a large vaulted drain that probably returned northwards at the west end of the building and formed part of the west wall. This had been badly truncated by a 19th-century brick wall so that only the outside of the west wall survived. The walls were built from chalk bonded with soft yellow mortar. The drain was 0.77m wide internally and about 1.05m high from the floor to the underside of the vault. The floor itself was laid in Kentish ragstone on a bed of crushed chalk and was cambered. It was covered in a very hard, concreted mortar. The vault was constructed from chalk

Fig 68 View of the drain in Building 15 with part of Road 1 in the foreground, looking east

although two of the keystones were of Reigate stone. The drain sloped down towards the east and presumably exited into the Thames. On the south-west corner of the building was a chalk buttress with some reused dressed Reigate stone blocks. The 19th-century wall had destroyed the relationship of the buttress to the wall but that was clearly its function. It measured approximately 0.95m x 0.60m and was 0.48m deep. It rested on a layer of mortar overlying a layer of sand. The cut in which it was laid sloped down towards the west and to the west of the buttress was a layer of Kentish ragstone under planks of wood forming part of the construction of the buttress. A similar plank of wood was inserted into the south wall of the building.

Within the building, a series of dumped levelling layers was found, immediately to the north of the drain. The relationship of these to the drain was not certain but they appeared to be abutting it, which suggests that a large area had been dug out, possibly removing earlier alluvial deposits, after the construction of the drain had been backfilled. The drain fills contained 13th- to 14th century pottery and 13th- to 15th-century tile. This dumping contained little in the way of domestic occupation debris but large quantities of building material fragments, indicating that they were dumped contemporaneously with the construction of the building. No floors or evidence of the occupiers or use of the building survived. Four fragments of a late medieval glass prunted beaker, <S8> (Fig 69), were found in the backfills of the drain from the next period, suggesting it may have been in use in this building during this period. This style of beaker would usually be found in a fairly wealthy household.

Building 15 was probably one of the canons' houses that were built after 1394 when an agreement was drawn up delineating the boundaries of the site. The property was for the dean and 12 canons of St Stephen's chapel, although the site of the dean's house was apparently too marshy and he was for a while allocated a site by the clock tower. The entire plot shown on Smith's plan (Smith 1807, fig p 125) was 575ft (175m) long, but this included the king's houses along the Woolstaple street and the street itself. The site for the canons' houses probably measured about 455ft–470ft (138m–143m) as each

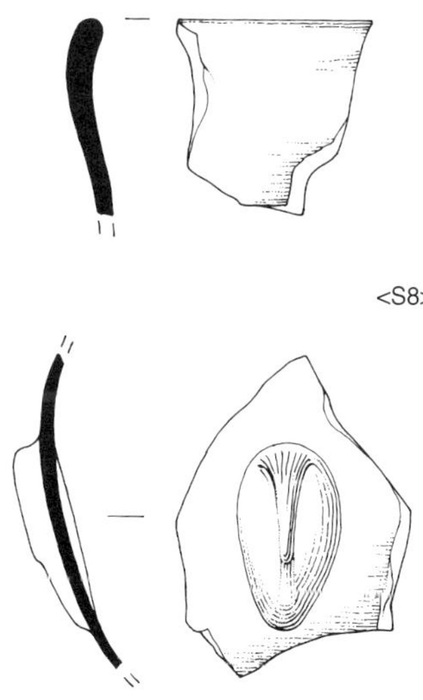

<S8>

Fig 69 Fragments of a late medieval glass beaker, <S8>, from Building 15 (scale 1:1)

house was said to be 35ft–36ft wide. It is possible that the first plot was indeed never built upon since a later wall appeared to be defining the properties along Long Woolstaple on the southern side of site F. The distance between it and Building 15 was 10.75m (35ft 3in), apparently forming a vacant property before the first of the canons' houses.

The drain beneath Building 15 may have continued underneath all the houses, acting as their sewer, for it seemed to be too large for a single house. The thickness of the walls and the buttressing suggest that the houses were of two storeys.

Building 16

Building 16 contains Building 10 room B (Chapter 9.3), which was probably the *thalamus secretorum* or barons' conference room adjoining the Exchequer. It was formed by the construction of a wall between the flying buttresses to Building 1, south from Building 10 room B, which it incorporated. The whole structure, including the former Building 10 room B measured 62.5m x 5.5m internally. There is no reason to suppose that the *thalamus secretorum* did not continue in use during this period. The remainder of the building may also have been divided into a number of rooms, but no archaeological evidence of this was recovered during the building works in 1884.

Building 17: the Jewel Tower

The Jewel Tower still stands largely complete although alterations and repairs, particularly to its parapet, have been carried out. The structure is 'L'-shaped, measuring 11.45m north–south and 12.25m east–west on its longest sides. On the ground floor is an entrance passage with a spiral staircase leading to the upper floors. The building has three storeys with two rooms on each floor (Figs 70–1).

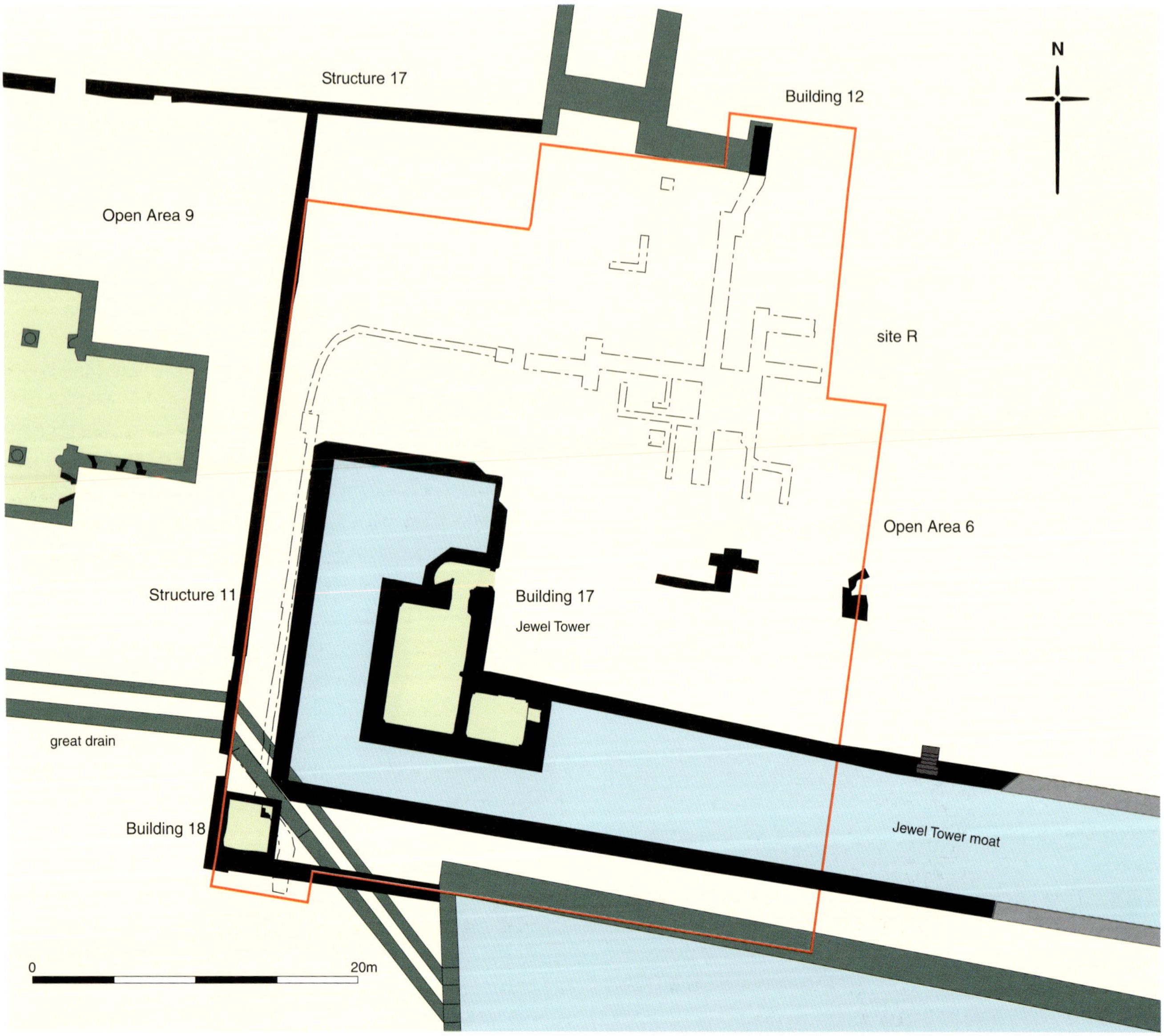

Fig 70 Detailed plan of the Jewel Tower (B17), also showing Building 12, Building 18, the great drain and structures found in the Jewel Tower garden in the 1960s, period 8 (scale 1:400)

Fig 71 View of the Jewel Tower, looking west

The Jewel Tower is surrounded on three sides by a moat, which fed into the Thames. About 4.0m wide on the west side and 7.35m wide to the south, it is 2.60m deep from the top of the surviving walls to the gravel at the base. The moat walls are constructed from Kentish ragstone and laid on elm wall plates over elm piles. Previous excavations have located the moat wall's construction trench, which was 1.54m wide and 2.05m deep. Its upper fills were rediscovered on site R and consisted of a layer of cream mortar with Kentish ragstone and chalk fragments and some flint, and a layer of brown sandy silt with chalk fragments and charcoal with some fragments of tile and Kentish ragstone.

The Jewel Tower was built in 1365–6 for the king's personal jewels and valuables on land that was previously part of the precinct of Westminster Abbey. The tower was appropriated by Edward III, to the annoyance of the monks of Westminster Abbey. It was designed by Henry Yevele and built by Thomas Hardgrey and Maurice Young. The moat was used as a fishpond by William de Husseborne, keeper of the Privy Palace, who died shortly afterwards, much to the glee of the monks, from a pike caught from the moat (Colvin et al 1963, 535). A set of steps led down to a landing stage on the north side of the moat and there was evidence that a bridge crossed it just to the east of the landing stage (Green 1976, 64).

Building 18

In the extreme south-west corner of the Jewel Tower garden lay Building 18, which measured 2.70m east–west by 2.90m north–south. Its western and southern walls can still be seen at ground level. Part of its eastern wall has been reset and can be seen but excavation showed that it had been reset in the wrong location. It abuts the precinct wall of *c* 1374–6 and overlies the construction trench of the Jewel Tower, thus clearly post-dating both.

The walls, which were 0.46m thick, were built out of Kentish ragstone with some chalk, bonded with a cream chalky mortar. The floor consisted of Kentish ragstone and Reigate stone slabs laid on a compact bedding layer of brown sand. An entrance lay in the south-east corner, which was floored in a compact layer of Reigate stone chippings and tile bonded with cream mortar.

Building 18 appeared to be medieval in construction and was definitely built after 1376, though it cannot be dated exactly. It cut off the access around the Jewel Tower moat and was probably a single-storey structure. It may have been used for storage or perhaps formed a porch to an entrance into the abbey. A later doorway lies in this corner of the Jewel Tower garden but it is unclear whether this replaced an earlier one.

Building 19: St Stephen's cloister

St Stephen's cloister lies to the north of the chapel (B11) and to the east of the great hall (B1). It had a belfry, a range of buildings (almost certainly the vicars' hall, buttery, kitchen and pantry) to the north and a further range to the east, including some of the vicars' houses, which stretched further to the north as far as the north end of the great hall. Originally constructed by William Hanney between 1384 and 1395, it was rebuilt by Dean Chambers in 1535 although some 14th-century walls and three doorways to the vicars' houses were seen in 1834 (Colvin et al 1963, 526–7). The cloister has been heavily restored on two further occasions since, once after the fire of 1834 and once after the Second World War, when a bomb hit the House of Commons.

During rebuilding and underpinning works in the 1940s trial holes were dug, exposing some of the foundations and stratigraphy associated with the cloisters. The inner wall of the cloister on the east side was found to be 1.37m wide and 1.63m deep below floor level and was built from stone rubble in a construction cut filled with sandy gravel. The same wall on the south side was of a similar construction but only 0.91m wide although its base was laid at a similar level. The southern, northern and eastern outer walls of the cloister were also exposed. That on the east side was approximately 0.65m wide above ground with a foundation 1.10m wide, while that on the north had a foundation 0.85m wide. This wall was constructed on shallow foundation arches. Both the northern and eastern walls were described as being constructed from stone rubble in lime mortar and were 2.20m deep below floor level.

The stratigraphy in the eastern cloister alley consisted of

blue clay sealed by brown clay 0.91m thick, both pre-dating the construction of the walls and both presumably alluvial deposits. The brown clay was sealed by a layer of sand, lime and charcoal 0.71m thick. which must represent levelling for the floor above. This layer was cut by a rubbish pit and then sealed by the paving that formed the floor of the cloister alley.

The existing two-storeyed cloister indicates that the buildings around it were also of two storeys. This allowed access between the upper storey of the chapel on the south side and the belfry and buildings to the north. The vicars' hall seems to have been sited at first-floor level on the north side of the cloister next to the belfry with the pantry, buttery and kitchen beneath. Later drawings of the vicars' houses in New Palace Yard indicate that they too were of two storeys. The cloister contains a small two-storey oratory on the west side.

Structure 5: dock

The dock wall on the east side (Fig 34) was demolished at some point around the middle of the 14th century and a new river wall (S13) built further to the east. The dating of the disuse of Structure 5 and the building of Structure 13 is uncertain. However, a river wall further east must have been constructed by the time that the canons' houses were built (above, Building 15) at the end of the 14th century. The dock may have remained partially in use during the 13th century but the interpreted revetment dividing Open Area 1 from Open Area 10 in period 7 would probably have meant that it went out of use then.

Structure 7

Layer U[13] was dumped over Structure 7 (Fig 45) and signalled its disuse. By the late 14th century a new river wall (below, Structure 13) had been constructed, the canons' houses built and Canon Row laid out. The area containing Structure 7 was no longer in the river system by that period and lay in the back gardens to the properties around Woolstaple Yard (OA10).

Structure 9

Around Structure 9 (Fig 45) a waterlaid brown clay, 0.35m thick, was deposited, sealing the structure. By the 14th century, new river walls had been built much further east and this area now became gardens of buildings on the east side of Canon Row.

Structure 11

Structure 11 consists of the largely complete Westminster Abbey precinct wall of *c* 1374–6. It stands to a height of about 8.5m and is constructed from Kentish ragstone bonded with cream mortar. A hole was drilled through this wall during works in the Jewel Tower garden, which revealed that the wall above the footing level (3.56m OD) is 0.92m thick. The footings step out approximately 80mm on the inside but do not appear to step out on the outside. In a section recorded by the Ministry of Works in the late 1950s and reproduced here (Fig 57), the footings can be seen to be 2.28m deep and are founded on sand and gravel.

The wall branched east and west to the north of the Jewel Tower: the eastern portion met the original precinct wall (Structure 10), which has now been demolished although it was found during earlier works (Green 1976, 67), while the western section continues to the north-east corner of the infirmary cloister.

Structure 12

To the south of the wall surrounding Open Area 13 on site C(ii) lay a circular chalk and brick well (Fig 77) in a wide square construction cut. Its base lay at -0.12m OD (presumably a little below the level of the water table) and its first 1.47m were constructed only from chalk. Above that level the inside was constructed from chalk but the outside from brick, presumably for visual effect. At the base the well lay on four heavily decayed timbers, 0.12m thick and 0.20m wide. It had an internal diameter of 0.73m. The well seems to have been constructed after 1380 and was subsequently either raised or rebuilt at the top in brick (period 10; Chapter 12.3, Open Area 13).

Structure 13

In a service trench (site A) a north–south aligned Kentish ragstone wall bonded with soft cream mortar survived to a height of 2.60m. It contained some Reigate stone and probably had a worked Reigate stone face to the east. It was more than 1.0m wide and rested on timber base plates at -1.0m OD.

No dating evidence was found associated with this wall but its founding level, construction and size suggest it was not the same wall as that in Structure 5 and its position was about 4.3m to the east. It is therefore conjectured to be a river wall built to replace the late 12th-century river wall. It must have been in place by the late 14th century, when the canons' houses were built (above, Building 15). The evidence from Open Area 1 (Chapter 9.3) indicates that the river was depositing silts to the west of this line during the 13th century, implying that this wall could not have been built until the 14th century.

The river wall probably continued northwards to the point where the Clowson stream (the canalised branch of the northern arm of the Tyburn) exited into the Thames.

Structure 14

In a service trench (site A) an east–west aligned wall constructed from chalk, Reigate stone and some flint was found at 2.0m OD. It survived to a height of 0.40m and was more than 0.50m wide. The wall was 3.0m long and extended to both east and west. The stone was bonded with a soft cream mortar.

The wall may have formed the north wall of a range of buildings on the south side of Woolstaple Yard. The southern edge of the wall was not found so there was no evidence for floor surfaces. There was no dating evidence associated with the wall but its level and form suggest a late medieval date and the Woolstaple itself was not founded until 1353 (Colvin et al 1963, 552).

Structure 15

During the excavation of a test pit at the east end of site B workmen revealed the remains of at least one timber structure. The remains included three stakes, which projected out of river silt at the bottom of the test pit. The clay to the east was higher, suggesting that alluvium had accumulated against the riverside face of the structure. The workmen also recovered a number of other pieces of wood. Although these were not recorded *in situ* it seems likely that they were associated with the stakes. Two of the largest pieces were identified as oak (Ian Tyers, pers comm) and had been worked. One, which was lying flat at -0.32m OD, appeared to be part of a plank, aligned approximately east–west, while the other was a stake that was roughly square in cross section, and had been trimmed to a point at one end. Two other pieces were identified as beech.

The timber remains probably represent at least one waterfront structure, possibly a revetment. The fragments were not suitable for dendrochronological dating. However, the presence of beech (*Fagus*), a species absent from Roman and Saxon waterfront sites in central London but present in later contexts, suggests that the structure was not built before the medieval period. It may have been a continuation of the waterfront as defined by Structure 13 to the south or possibly a jetty protruding into the river from it.

Road 1

Dumping in Open Area 14 sealed Road 1 (Fig 45) and signalled its disuse.

Road 2: St Stephen's Alley

A layer of sand was dumped over Building 4 to provide a bedding for the earliest road surface in sand and gravel on site L at 1.98m OD. To the east, over the former oven L[48], more substantial levelling was required as the internal ground level was lower. Dumped layers with charcoal, building material and animal bone were deposited before the gravel road surface was laid. Over the gravel surface was laid a second surface comprising cream mortar, chalk, Reigate stone chippings and sand. More rubble, including chalk, mortar and Reigate stone chippings, was dumped over the road surface as the bedding layer for further road surfaces. Some evidence of later road layers was noted in section but these had been almost entirely destroyed by the insertion of services such as sewers, water mains, electricity cables and gas pipes and no dating evidence was recovered from them.

Road 2 formed the access to the newly created houses for the canons of St Stephen's chapel, which were built after 1394 and lay between the road and the river (Colvin et al 1963, 525). A gate led from the south end of the street into New Palace Yard (OA4). To the west of the street lay properties surrounding Woolstaple Yard. Road 2 lay on a different alignment from that of the modern road (south-south-west–north-north-east as opposed to north–south as it currently lies), probably until the mid 18th century, when the current street pattern was formed.

Open Area 1: the River Thames

On site H the fluvial deposits dated to the mid 13th or 14th century (Chapter 9.3) were covered by further waterlaid deposits comprising laminated sands, silts and clays. The top of this sequence was located at about -0.3m OD.

The earliest of these layers, H[29], may correspond to a layer previously recorded in a test pit that produced 15th-century pottery. One layer, H[10], produced a substantial portion of a 15th-century coarse border ware cooking pot, and the uppermost layers contained fragments of brick and tile that probably date to the Tudor period. Further east a layer of waterlaid clay produced 16th-century pottery. The presence of these finds in riverine deposits indicates that while site H had still not been reclaimed from the Thames in the late medieval and Tudor periods it was close to the site of habitation.

Open Area 4: New Palace Yard

A pier base was constructed on site D approximately 1.1m to the south of Building 6. This was subsequently largely robbed out but enough remained to show that it was constructed from Reigate stone and probably measured 0.6m square. This may have formed part of a single-storey extension to the front of Building 6 (above).

A levelling layer was dumped on site D as bedding for a gravel yard surface. A similar gravel surface was found overlying Building 5 at a higher level, suggesting that the surface to the east had slumped. Over it another dumped layer of grey sandy silt was sealed by a compacted surface of grey sandy silt and gravel with charcoal, oyster shell and tile.

On site G the fluvial clay dating to the early to mid 13th century (Chapter 9.3, Open Area 4) was covered by a dumped layer of dark grey silty sand, up to 0.15m thick and containing occasional fragments of medieval tile, chalk, mortar, oyster shell and bone. This may have been put down as part of a land reclamation project, probably at about the time that New Palace Yard was created, which would date it to the 1280s. It was cut by a small pit, G[11], 0.18m deep, and two small pits or postholes, G[23] and G[46]. Feature G[11] was cut by a small pit or posthole and sealed by a layer of moderately compact sandy gravel, 100mm thick, which may have been the remnants of a metalled surface. The putative surface was covered by a layer of sandy clay containing fragments of medieval tile.

The pit or posthole G[46] was 0.40m deep and filled with sand. It was covered by a layer of sand, G[18], which apparently served as the base for a metalled surface of loose sandy gravel, G[17]. The gravel surface was cut by a pit, G[25], which was up to 0.72m deep and filled with sand and silty clay.

The gravel layers G[7] and G[17] may have formed part of the same metalled surface. They were respectively located at 1.66m and 1.72m OD, and were therefore at a similar level to the series of 14th-century chalk and gravel surfaces found about 40m east-south-east of the site during the 1972–4 excavations in New Palace Yard, which were located between about 1.2m and 2.3m OD (see Horsman and Davison 1989, fig 5).

The cut features in this group probably represent temporary timber structures, such as the halls erected in the Yard for Richard II's parliament in 1397.

Open Area 6: Old Palace Yard

To the east of Building 18 lay a garden soil layer comprising brown clay with charcoal flecks. It post-dated the construction of Structure 11 and pre-dated Building 18. To the north of Building 18 was a rubbish pit filled with brown clay mortar, chalk, tile and charcoal, post-dating the construction of the Jewel Tower moat.

None of this can be dated but it was all stratigraphically later than the construction of the Jewel Tower in 1365–6 and contained no post-medieval material, indicating that this part of Open Area 6 remained as garden or open land. To the north of the Jewel Tower moat, building foundations, possibly dating to the 15th century, have been located (Green 1976, 67).

Open Area 8: Westminster Abbey precinct (north)

Dumping on the west side of site C(i) raised the ground level in Open Area 8. These layers all sloped down towards the south. Towards the west a number of pits were dug. Pit C[20] was filled with green sandy clay with small quantities of tile and mortar and larger amounts of burnt wood. It may have been dug to discard building material, perhaps after repairs resulting from a fire. Three more pits were dug, one containing a very high proportion of charcoal, presumably fire debris, possibly from a hearth. Another, C[146], was a cesspit at least 1.1m across and 0.4m deep. Its lowest fill comprised cess with large quantities of charcoal, while the upper fill was a green sandy clay with lenses of black silt with large quantities of oyster shell and animal bone and some mussel shell. This pit lay only 1.25m south of Building 13 and was perhaps dug to dispose of waste from that building. Cutting the cesspit was a rubbish pit, 2.12m across and 0.41m deep, filled with grey sandy silt and large amounts of tile, mortar, ash and charcoal and some Reigate stone fragments. To its west was a stakehole, 100mm in diameter and 0.25m deep, which still contained some very decayed wood.

Open Area 8 continued to be used as the public part of the precincts of the abbey and to house the October Fair up until the late 15th century, although at a much reduced scale. This part of Open Area 8 was used for digging pits, largely to dispose of waste materials, probably from the inhabitants and users of Building 13.

Open Area 10

A robbed-out wall on the east side of site K probably formed the eastern back wall of the gardens to the properties around Woolstaple Yard. The minimum width of the robber cut was 0.32m, indicating that the wall was no wider than that. The trench itself was filled with white and yellow mortar with fragments of chalk and Kentish ragstone. Its width suggests it was no more than a boundary wall. To its west lay a series of make-up layers and external surfaces consisting of yellow mortar with gravel and fragments of Kentish ragstone and tile. These presumably formed yard surfaces in the back gardens of the houses surrounding Woolstaple Yard. On the west side of site K were three pits containing redeposited alluvial material similar to that found in the layers below and small amounts of refuse such as oyster shell, charcoal, animal bone and tile. None of the pits lay fully within the site but they were fairly large, one being 2.05m across and more than 0.85m deep, a second more than 1.0m across and 0.3m deep, and the third more than 1.8m across and 0.9m deep.

Cutting the levelling deposit from period 7 on site U were two shallow oval pits filled with brown clay with charcoal and mortar. Over these was dumped a levelling layer, U[12], 0.30m deep, of light brown-grey silty clay with fragments of tile. This was cut by a large rectangular pit.

Further dumping of grey, silty clay U[1] with animal bone suggests occupation material being deposited in gardens. Into this were cut a row of three stakeholes and two rubbish pits. Pit U[3] was filled with brown silty clay with oyster shell, animal bone, tile fragments and charcoal flecks. Pit U[20] was filled with brown silty clay with shell and pebbles sealed by a grey clay containing pebbles, chalk flecks, Kentish ragstone lumps, charcoal and oyster shell. Pit U[3] was cut by an east–west aligned trench, 0.30m wide and filled with rubble, possibly indicating a wall that had been robbed.

This area had clearly been reclaimed from the river and formed one of the back gardens to the properties around the Woolstaple market. Both the levelling deposits and the pits indicate that occupation material from the houses was being discarded. The robbed-out wall may have formed one of the property boundaries between the gardens.

Some 27m south-south-west of site U was a mortar surface on site M at a level of about 2.0m OD. This appeared to be an internal floor. It was undated but its form and level suggested that it might be medieval. If so, it is likely to have been the floor to one of the buildings on the east side of Woolstaple Yard.

The buildings around this market were surveyed by Ralph Treswell between 1603 and 1609 (Schofield 1987, fig 57). Site U would appear to be in the garden of George Thursby during the early 17th century. The back wall of the garden seems to align with the 19th-century front (west) wall of 37 Parliament Street.

Open Area 11

A new ditch was dug to replace the period 7 ditch on site E (Fig 72). It was about 0.80m wide at the west end and 0.95m wide to the east and had a large rectangular pit measuring 1.80m x 1.65m in the centre. The fills of this pit were so similar to those of the ditch that it seems likely to have been part of the same feature. The ditch was a maximum of 0.56m deep. Both the pit and ditch were filled at the base with a dark grey waterlaid sandy silty clay with pebbles and some shell and Reigate stone fragments. The ditch presumably acted as a drainage ditch as well as a boundary between Open Area 11 and Open Area 12. It was subsequently backfilled with a grey-brown sandy silty clay with oyster shell, tile fragments and small quantities of bone, Reigate stone chippings, mortar, charcoal, Kentish ragstone and chalk. The fill also contained a copper-alloy bell, <S18> (Fig 73), which could have been discarded by inhabitants of the house associated with Open Area 11 or Open Area 12. Such bells had a wide variety of uses, as fashion accessories ornamenting clothes, for example, or as insignia of religious activities such as those used by pilgrims (Spencer 1998, 123) or as an object to ward off evil, like a talisman. The ditch fill did not produce a great deal of botanical material and consisted mainly of charred cereal grains with free-threshing wheat (*Triticum* sp) and oats (*Avena* spp) although most of the grains could not be identified. Two charred seeds of stinking mayweed (*Anthemis cotula*), a characteristic arable weed, were also identified. Several wild plants were also present: buttercups (*Ranunculus* spp), celery-leaved crowfoot (*R sceleratus*) and elder (*Sambucus nigra*).

Little interpretation of environmental conditions may be made on the basis of the botanical material, with most of the material being from food-processing residues; other debris from human activities appears to have been thrown into this ditch with a few large mammal and fish bones and marine shell being recovered from the sample residue. The only indication of the local habitat was the presence of Cladoceran *ephippia*, which suggests standing bodies of water.

The animal bones were recovered from both the primary fills and the backfills of the ditch. The primary fill produced a near complete horse femur, a few cattle and chicken bones, and then, from the sample, a loose tooth of a neonate/infant calf

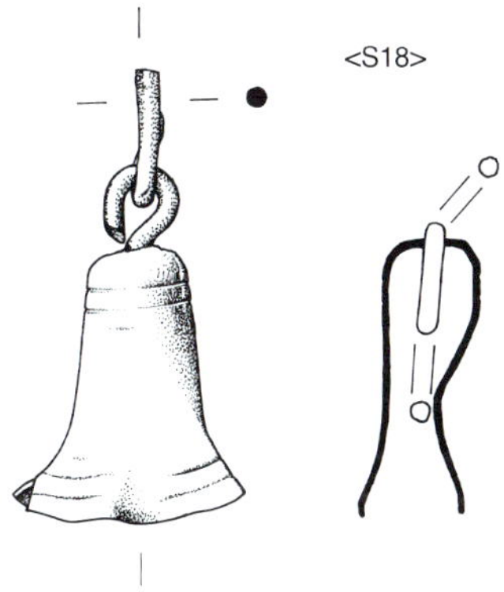

Fig 73 Copper-alloy bell <S18> from Open Area 11 (scale 1:1)

Fig 72 View of the ditch dividing Open Area 11 from Open Area 12, looking south (0.5m scale)

and a small collection of fish bone. The former may either demonstrate the use of veal in the vicinity, or perhaps represent an infant mortality. This evidence would therefore suggest local affluence or the local breeding/stalling of cattle respectively.

Within Open Area 11 were three rubbish pits. Pit E[18] measured 0.6m x 0.7m and was 0.2m deep. It contained oyster shell and small quantities of charcoal, animal bone and tile. Pit E[20] measured at least 1.8m x 0.8m and was 0.3m deep, containing charcoal, bone, tile, oyster and cockle shell and mortar with small quantities of chalk. It was slightly stained green towards the base, suggesting that some cess may have been deposited in it. Pit E[31] was 1.2m across and at least 0.3m deep and contained charcoal, oyster shell, animal bone and small quantities of tile. Grey silt containing some domestic waste such as charcoal and oyster shell was dumped over the pits to level up the ground.

Part of a possible necklace, <S47> (Figs 74–5), recovered from this area in period 10, dates to the first half of the 16th century and may originally have been used and deposited during this period (or possibly period 9). It is made up of wound and coiled copper-alloy wirework chain attached to a central strand that consisted of more coiled wirework, bone beads and a degraded glass bead. These decorative elements may have been repeated intermittently in between the plainer segments of twisted wires, or may perhaps have formed the focal point of the jewellery.

During the 15th century precious metal chained necklaces became popular with the upper classes (Egan and Pritchard 1991, 318). Archaeological evidence indicates that they were also made of less valuable metals such as copper alloy. Beads were not popular for necklaces during the medieval period apart from when they were used in rosaries (Margeson 1993, 5). However, glass and bone beads were used with wirework jewellery in the late 15th and early 16th centuries (Margeson 1993, 5). A more elaborate example, having some of the same basic elements as this example, was found at Pottergate, Norwich (Margeson 1993, 8).

Open Area 11 remained in use as the back garden of a property fronting on to King Street. The rubbish pits presumably contain the domestic material discarded by the occupants of the property.

Open Area 12

Two pits lay in the small area of Open Area 12 which was excavated on site E. Pit E[23], which was 1.0m across and 0.31m deep, was a rubbish pit filled with large quantities of oyster shells and charcoal, animal bone and tile. To its south lay a large probably rectangular pit more than 1.8m across and 0.6m deep, filled with oyster shell and small quantities of charcoal and chalk. This may have been a rubbish pit although the quantity of waste discarded was not high. The pits were sealed by dumping, which was similar to that found in Open Area 11 and also contained domestic waste such as charcoal, tile, animal bone and oyster shell.

Open Area 12, like Open Area 11 remained in use as the back garden of a property fronting on to King Street. The rubbish pits presumably contain the domestic material discarded by the occupants of the property.

Open Area 13

Open Area 13 is more clearly defined as an individual property around Woolstaple Yard, which was founded in 1353, than is Open Area 10 (Fig 76). Indeed, the chalk wall and ditch forming the north side of the property (Chapter 9.3, Open Area 10) remained in use during the first part of this period and may indeed have dated from this period.

To the south of the wall lay the circular chalk and brick well

Fig 74 Copper-alloy ?necklace <S47> from Open Area 11 (scale c 1:1)

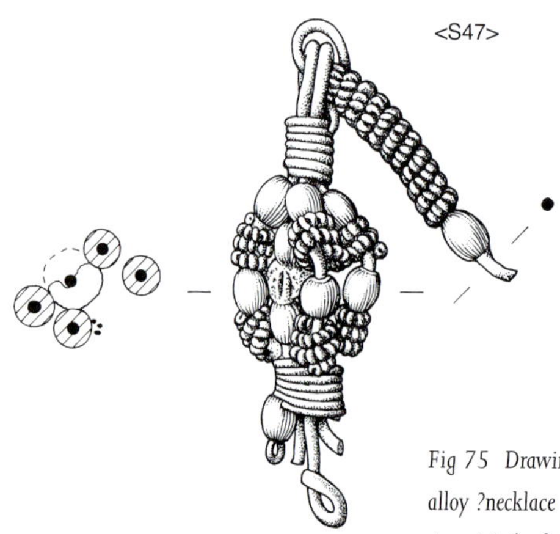

Fig 75 Drawing and section of copper-alloy ?necklace <S47> from Open Area 11 (scale 1:2)

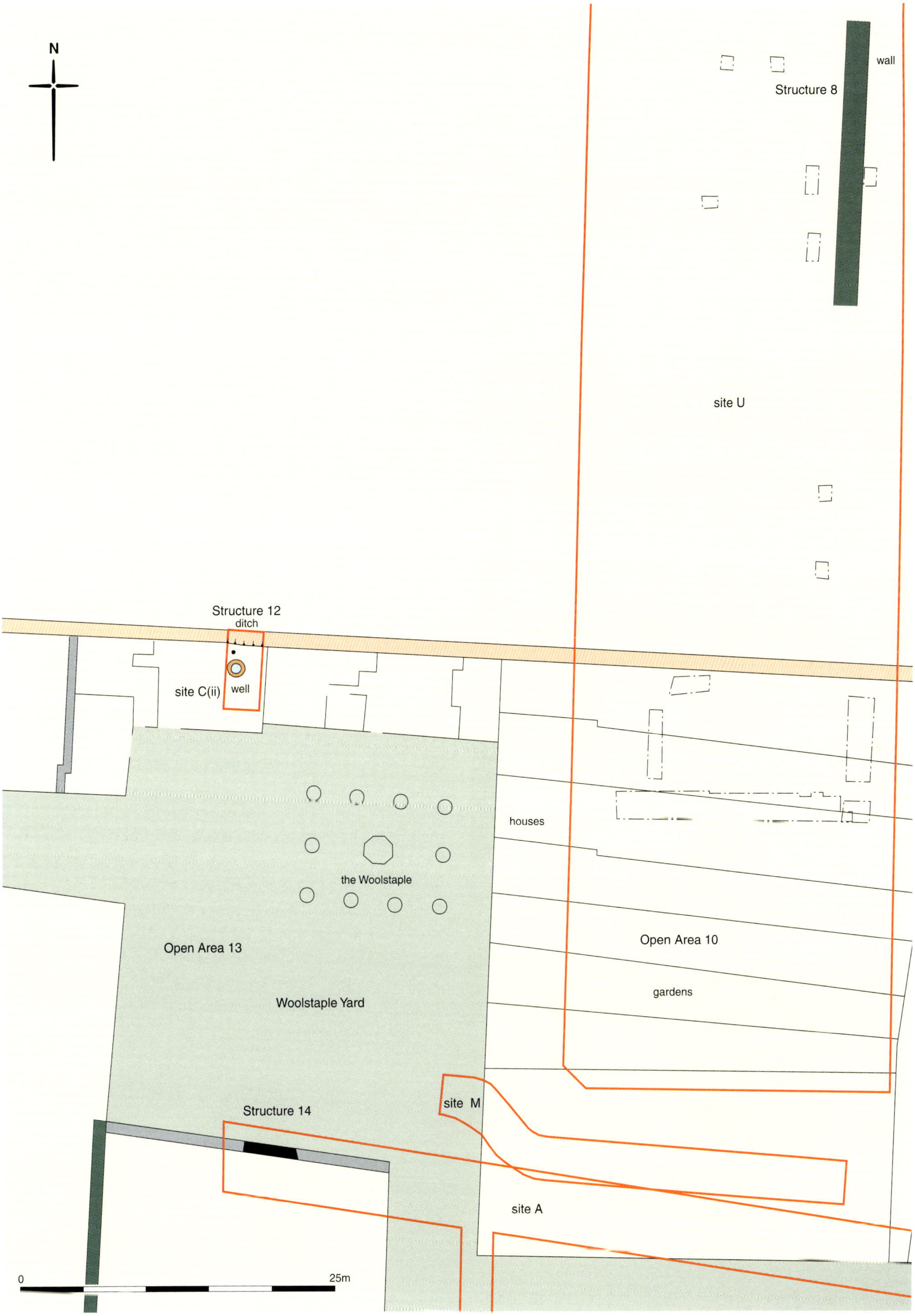

Fig 76 Plan of Woolstaple Yard and surrounding buildings, including Open Area 10, Open Area 13, Structure 8, Structure 12 and Structure 14, period 8 (scale 1:400)

Structure 12 (Fig 77). Over the remainder of the area, dumping raised the ground level. This dumping contained large quantities of food waste (animal bone, whelk, cockle and oyster shell), charcoal and building waste (tile, mortar, chalk, Kentish ragstone and Reigate stone). Sand layers were also dumped, probably to act as surfaces, and a rubbish pit was dug in the south-west corner of the area excavated. This contained two residual ceramic crucibles, <S12> and <S13>, which are 11th-century in date and are described in Chapter 7.3, Open Area 1. At some point, dumping at the north end sealed the ditch and part of the wall, indicating that they had fallen into disuse. What replaced them as boundaries, if anything, is unknown.

Fig 77 View of Open Area 13 showing the chalk well, looking south

Open Area 13 was probably one of the back yards to the buildings surrounding Woolstaple Yard, of which a plan exists from the early 17th century (Schofield 1987, fig 57). The hall and chambers for the mayor and constable of the staple, the weigh-house and the kitchen (Colvin et al 1963, 552) may have been included among these buildings, but may equally have been sited along the north side of the street that ran towards the Thames and a landing stage under the current Bridge Street. The waste discarded does not appear to be indicative of high status for this period. The building waste suggests construction activity in the area, presumably associated with the houses themselves, which are likely to have been half-timbered on stone foundations as, apparently, were many of the houses along King Street. Medieval window glass, <S11> (Chapter 12.3, Building 23), may have originated from these buildings and a fragment of vessel glass, <S10>, from the same building could conceivably have been used in one of these buildings.

Open Area 14

The Saxo-Norman and medieval fluvial silts and clays on site B (Chapter 7) were cut by a number of late medieval and Tudor features, including eleven rubbish pits, a posthole and an irregular slot. These were located in the western (landward) two thirds of the site, which had probably been reclaimed from the river.

Possibly the earliest feature in this group was the irregular slot, B[223], which was 100mm deep. The posthole was 0.47m deep, filled with the remains of a badly decayed wooden post. It was dated to this period because it was cut by one of the pits, B[218].

The rubbish pits survived to depths of between 0.17m and 0.90m. Most contained considerable quantities of household refuse, including pottery, animal bones and shells of oysters and mussels and occasionally winkles and whelks. Most also contained building debris, especially fragments of peg tile, some of which had a brown splash glaze, characteristic of tile made before the late 15th century. A particularly notable find was a copper-alloy horseshoe pilgrim badge, <S21>, from fill B[143] in pit B[268] (Fig 78). This is similar to a badge from Nieuwland in the Netherlands, which is dated to c 1375–1425. One other find from the rubbish pits was a late medieval copper-alloy buckle pin, <S19>. One pit, B[218], may have been later in date, since its primary fill produced a large fragment of pantile of type commonly dated to the 17th century although most of the finds assemblage indicated a late medieval date.

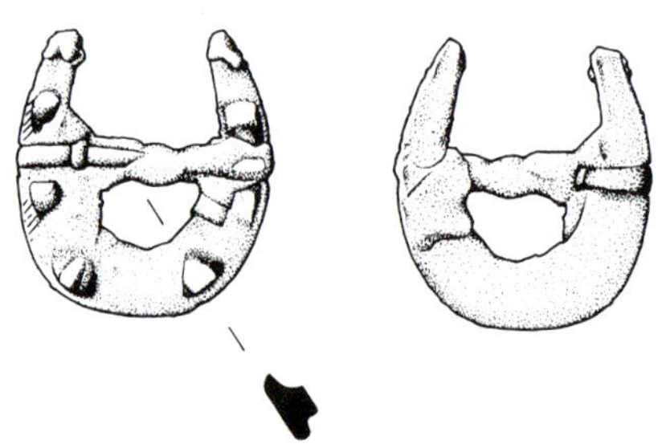

Fig 78 Copper-alloy pilgrim badge <S21> from Open Area 14 (scale 1:1)

On site F two phases of east–west aligned stone wall were aligned with the south wall of Building 15. Both were heavily truncated but are assumed to have gone as far as Building 15 and defined its back garden. No trace of the walls was found further west beyond the truncation limits so their form is very uncertain. The earlier merely comprised crushed mortar and Reigate stone chippings in the base of a cut that was 0.3m deep, 0.9m long and survived only to a width of 90mm. It was sealed by a demolition layer of mortar, Kentish ragstone, Reigate stone and chalk, which itself underlay a dumped layer. That was cut by the second phase of chalk wall. It survived to a height of 0.4m and was 0.3m wide. Only a 0.6m-length of wall survived.

To the north of these walls lay a rubbish pit containing large quantities of building material and small quantities of domestic refuse such as shell and charcoal. It was cut by an east–west aligned linear trench 0.32m wide. That was in turn cut by another linear trench aligned north–south, parallel to the west wall of Building 15. These were sealed by dumping, which was cut by two wooden stakes.

Over the area to the west and south, a layer of grey silty clay with large amounts of chalk and charcoal was dumped, presumably representing initial early activity in the area. On the west side there was further dumping containing building material and some domestic waste. This was cut by two postholes: one oval, measuring 0.60m x 0.52m and 0.17m deep, and the other sub-rectangular measuring 0.50m x 0.34m and 0.12m deep. After the posts had been removed or had decayed, a chalk surface was laid. This was covered by a sand and gravel surface at 2.0m OD.

Most of the animal bones recovered from this area were taken from the site B pit fills and, in particular, from pits B[268], B[123] and B[218]. The pits from this site provided copious quantities of heavily butchered cattle fragments, with lesser amounts of sheep/goat and pig. It is noticeable that the range of species is fairly large, including domestic birds, especially chicken, as well as high-status markers such as fallow deer, rabbit and pike. Various other game and fish species were also well represented (from the sieved deposits), clearly showing the exploitation of a wide variety of resources. The fisheries used would appear to be concentrated within riverine and estuarine waters (Chapter 16.7). Of some interest amongst these pit assemblages was the presence of two examples of hornless sheep skulls, one each from B[123] and B[268], perhaps indicative of a variety where horns were absent in either one or both sexes. A severe case of osteoarthritis was noticed on a cattle pelvis from B[268], the acetabulum (hip joint) displaying marked eburnation (that is, polishing) and peripheral bony growth. This could conceivably be indicative of an age- and/or work-related modification. There is also a slight indication of local craft activities, with the presence of a goat's horn core (from B[268]) that had clearly been separated from its hornsheaf prior to disposal (the butchery is described in Chapter 16.7). Such an action is likely to have taken place at the horn worker's shop.

10.4 Discussion

That the settlement continued to expand during period 8 is clear from both the documentary sources and the archaeological evidence (Table 12). The river front east of King Street was extended and there was further reclamation. This appears to have occurred at about the time that the site was granted by Edward III to the staff of his newly created college of St Stephen's chapel. It is characterised by one of the canon's buildings (Building 15) and by several rubbish pits dated to the mid 14th or 15th century which were scattered across the western two thirds of site B, indicating that, by this time, the area had been reclaimed from the river and was occupied. Plant remains recovered from the pits were similar to those coming from previous periods, with a mix of economic plants (cereal grains, fruits, flax, hemp, hop, dyer's rocket) and wild plants indicative of wetland and disturbed/waste ground environments. The only definite evidence for cultivated pulses was also found in this period.

Activity in the palace precincts was also intense during this period. The main building works were associated with the completion of St Stephen's chapel (B11) and the construction of the cloister (B19) and vicars' houses, the alterations to the great hall (B1), the construction of the Jewel Tower (B17), the new gatehouse, belfry and precinct wall in New Palace Yard, and various other documented structures. Equally importantly, there was increased activity in New Palace Yard associated with its full inclusion in the palace layout and complete reclamation. The palace had by this time reached the greatest definition of its courtyard layout with each area assigned its own status and function.

Disaster struck the palace in 1512, when fire destroyed large areas of the precinct, particularly, it is thought, those areas on the west side closest to the abbey. As a result of this conflagration, Henry VIII decided to abandon the Palace of Westminster as his residence and began to look around for new houses. The principal site for his new palace was at Whitehall, immediately to the north of the Tyburn, although he increased the royal use of other sites near London with his acquisition of Hampton Court, Greenwich and Nonsuch and the building of Bridewell Palace (1515–23). For the purposes of phasing, the end of period 8 within the palace is taken to be 1512.

The abbey also had major building works carried out during this period with the building of the infirmary cloister, the prior's house, the abbot's house and the cellarer's range. The nave and Lady chapel were also rebuilt during this period. The affairs of the abbey were clearly not all satisfactory, however. As with all landowners their property values fell, one of the catastrophic consequences of the Black Death; their numbers were also much reduced in its aftermath and the value of one of their major sources of income, the October Fair, declined to nothing by 1487. Ultimately, however, these were 'blips' in the otherwise upward curve in the fortunes of the abbey, which came to an abrupt end at the Dissolution in 1540.

Table 12 Selected dating evidence, period 8 (see Table 25 for expansion of codes)

Land use	Activity	Context	Evidence	Description	Date range
Building 1: the great hall			documentary	Colvin et al 1963, 528–9	1393–9
Building 6	hearth	D[29]	ceramic building material	brick 3046	1450–1700
Building 6	beam slot	D[21]	ceramic building material	floor tile 2894	1350–90
Building 13	floor	C[172]	ceramic	LOND; TUDG	1380–1550
Building 13	occupation layer	C[169]	ceramic	SIEG	1300–1550
Building 15: canon's house	drain	F[88]	ceramic building material	tile 2271; 2586; 2816; 3046	1450–1700
Building 15: canon's house	drain	F[106]	ceramic building material	brick 3033; 3046	1450–1700
Building 15: canon's house	drain	F[106]	ceramic	KING	1230–1400
Building 17: the Jewel Tower			documentary	see Table 16	1365–6
Building 19: St Stephen's cloister			documentary	see Table 16	1394–6
Structure 11			documentary	Green 1976, 67	1374–6
Structure 12	cut for well	C[270]	ceramics	EMCH; KING; LOND; MISC; TUDG	1380–1550
Open Area 1	foreshore deposit	H[2]	ceramic	CBW; PMSR; PMRE; RAER	1480–1550
Open Area 1	foreshore deposit	B[44]	ceramic	CBW	1400–1500
Open Area 8: Westminster Abbey precinct (north)	cesspit	C[147]	ceramic	TUDG	1380–1550
Open Area 10	structural cut	K[21]	ceramic building material	tile 2587	1450–1500
Open Area 10	yard surface	K[19]	ceramic building material	tile 2588	1240–1450
Open Area 10	pit fill	K[51]	ceramic	KING	1230–1400
Open Area 10	pit fill	U[19]	ceramic	CBW	1350–1500
Open Area 10	pit fill	U[4]	ceramic	CBW; LOND	1270–1500
Open Area 10	dumping	U[4]	ceramic	CBW; LOND	1270–1350
Open Area 11	ditch	E[70]		CBW; KING; LOND; SIEG	1200–1500
Open Area 11	rubbish pit	E[19]		CBW; KING; LOND; SHER	1270–1500
Open Area 12	levelling	E[8]	ceramic	CBW; TUDG; MART; PMRE	1500–1600
Open Area 13	levelling	C[261]	ceramic	CBW	1350–1500
Open Area 14	pit	B[29]	ceramic	CBW	1350–1500
Open Area 14	pit	B[30]	ceramic	CBW; PMRE	1400–1500
Open Area 14	pit	B[110]	ceramic	CBW; CHEA; LCGR; SIEG	1380–1500
Open Area 14	pit	B[116]	ceramic	CBW	1350–1500
Open Area 14	pit	B[118]	ceramic	CBW; KING	1350–1500
Open Area 14	pit	B[121]	ceramic	CBW	1350–1500
Open Area 14	pit	B[143]	copper alloy	pilgrim badge <S21>	1350–1500
Open Area 14	pit	B[146]	ceramic	CBW; CHEA; LLON; LOND	1400–1500
Open Area 14	pit	B[147]	ceramic	CBW; KING; LOND	1350–1500
Open Area 14	pit	B[148]	ceramic	CBW; KING	1350–1500
Open Area 14	pit	B[154]	ceramic	CBW; LOND	1350–1500
Open Area 14	rubbish pit	B[128]	ceramic	CBW; CHEA; DUTR; LMHG; LOND; MGCOAR; SHER; TUDG	1380–1500
Open Area 14	rubbish pit	B[49]	ceramic	CBW; KING; LOND; SAIN	1400–1500
Open Area 14	pit	B[56]	ceramic	CBW	1350–1500
Open Area 14	pit	B[185]	ceramic	KING; TUDG	1380–1500
Open Area 14	rubbish pit	B[142]	ceramic	CBW; CHEA; KING; LLON; TPW; LOND	1430–1500
Open Area 14	pit	B[179]	ceramic	CBW	1350–1500
Open Area 14	rubbish pit	B[186]	ceramic	ANDA; CBW; CHEA; KING; LMHG; LOND; MG; MGCOAR; SHER; TUDG	1380–1500
Open Area 14	rubbish pit	B[160]	ceramic	CBW; LLON; SHER	1400–1500
Open Area 14	rubbish pit	B[206]	ceramic	CBW; LLON; SIEG; SPAM	1450–1550
Open Area 14	pit	B[214]	ceramic	CBW; DUTR; LMHG	1380–1500
Open Area 14	levelling	F[111]	ceramic	KING; SHER	1300–1400
Open Area 14	levelling	F[27]	ceramic building material	tile 2271; 2586; 3090	1450–1800
Open Area 14	levelling	F[90]	ceramic building material	tile 2271; 2586; 2587; 3073	1400–50

11

c 1540–*c* 1600 (period 9)

11.1 Environmental and topographical background

The River Thames

No new data were collected from this period; indeed, much of the area that was previously wetland had been reclaimed by this date.

Palaeoecology

Limited information on the natural ecology of the area is provided by a pollen sequence recorded through a ditch at Broad Sanctuary in 1979 (Mills 1982). The ecological signal was confused by an apparent mixture of cess and economic products, including flax (*Linum*), hemp (*Cannabis*) and buckwheat (*Fagopyrum*), in the ditch, but some useful information can be gleaned from this sequence. A limited arboreal spectrum was recorded, including oak (*Quercus*), birch (*Betula*), lime (*Tilia*), pine (*Pinus*), walnut (*Juglans*), beech (*Fagus*) and ash (*Fraxinus*). The group did not dominate the assemblage and it is possible, therefore, that these species do not represent substantial local woodland, but may reflect small stands, having been blown in or brought on to site through aquatic transport. It does seem likely that willow (*Salix*) and yew (*Taxus*), constant throughout the profile, were growing locally as these species are generally heavily under-represented in pollen profiles. A further element of the assemblage characterises the aquatic group, probably forming part of the ecozone marginal to the stream, and includes greater and lesser reedmace (*Typha angustifolia*) and water plantain (*Alisma* sp), marsh-marigold (*Caltha* type) and meadowsweet (*Filipendula*). A further aspect of the area is represented by a group of ruderals, species tending to live in the sort of open/waste ground found in urban areas between buildings. Species include buttercup (*Ranunculus* type), stitchwort (*Stellaria* spp), mouse-ears (*Cerastium* sp), nettle (*Urtica* type), bittersweet (*Solanum dulcamara*) and plantain (*Plantago* sp). Grasses and sedge species were also present, but these may be derived from human use of the species for things such as animal feed, bedding/thatch and so on, rather than being part of the local ecological conditions in and around Broad Sanctuary.

11.2 Documentary and archaeological background

Westminster Palace

The serious fire of 1512 in the palace persuaded Henry VIII to abandon the site as his principal residence. In 1530 he acquired the site of Whitehall, where he began the process of building himself a new residence. In 1547 St Stephen's chapel was dissolved and the upper chapel became the home of the House of Commons for the next 287 years. The House of Lords continued to use the lesser hall in the palace before moving to the former queen's chamber. The law courts remained in the great hall and the other buildings were progressively given over to parliamentary uses. Many of the trappings of government moved with Henry to Whitehall although the Exchequer and all the buildings that went with it remained at Westminster. These buildings saw one of the major construction schemes at Westminster at this time (Fig 79). The Exchequer itself was widened by one bay to the north and a large new range was built to stretch from the Exchequer up to the gate into the Green Yard to the west. These additions can be seen clearly on Hollar's view of New Palace Yard.

Westminster Abbey

The deed of surrender was signed by the abbot and monks on 16 January 1540. The abbey was valued at £3470 0s 2¼ d (Wragge 1909, 450) although it has also been variously quoted by Dugdale as being £3471 0s ½d and Speed as £3997 6s 4¾ d (Dugdale 1817, 280). Whatever the true figure it was the second highest in the country after Glastonbury Abbey. After the Dissolution, since Henry VIII would not sanction the destruction of the royal coronation and burial church where his father had been interred only 31 years earlier, the abbey was made a cathedral on 17 December 1540, the consecration taking place two days later. Thomas Thirleby was created its one and only bishop.

During the 1540s the infirmary chapel of St Katherine was dismantled, as was the refectory and the kitchen.

In 1550 it was decided that the see of Westminster was unnecessary and it was abolished on 30 March. The church remained a cathedral church, but within the see of London and not Westminster. Soon after the accession of Mary in 1553 the dean and many of the prebendaries were replaced. The charter restoring the abbey as a monastic house is dated 10 November 1556 and the first monks arrived ten days later. There were 16 monks under the new abbot, Abbot Feckenham, who repaired and restored the shrine to Edward the Confessor. Upon the death of Mary the abbey was dissolved again, this time on 10 July 1559. On 21 May 1560 it was reconstituted as the College of St Peter, Westminster and was run by a dean and canons.

Woolstaple Yard

The property on the north and east sides of the Woolstaple Yard was acquired by Richard Casteler and given to Christ's Hospital. The individual tenements on the east side shown in Treswell's plan were standing in 1579, when the northernmost one was let to Winifred, dowager marchioness of Winchester (GL, MS 13029); the lease soon passed to the Trevor family, who held it well into the 17th century.

Canon Row

After the dissolution of the college of St Stephen in 1547, most of the canons' houses were sold by the Crown (one had already been granted away by Henry VIII in 1536). Records of the grants are known for most of the houses, but only three can be firmly identified with later sites. Present information on the houses on the east side has been gathered together below.

Buildings on Canon Row (east side)

It is presumed here that there were 13 sites of roughly equal frontage to Canon Row (34ft–35ft), starting behind the buildings fronting Long Woolstaple. The property at the corner of Long Woolstaple and Canon Row was called the 'storehouse belonging to the canons' in 1437 (*Cal Pat R*, 1436–41, 123), and in 1739 was the White Horse alehouse, belonging to the Revd Dennison Cumberland and tenanted by Richard Lawrence, with three other houses adjoining (PRO, WORK 6/62). East of these were the six houses belonging to the king, which were 27ft deep and adjoined the woolbridge. The accounts below start from the south and go northwards.

No. 1
Measured 35ft in front and 195ft from street to river.

No. 2
Comprised a brick house, yard and garden in the possession of Ann Nelthorpe, with a wharf, toft and warehouse behind it between the garden and the Thames measuring 130ft long, 7ft against the Thames and 33ft against the garden of Nelthorpe. The measurements would suggest that this property equates to Building 15.

No. 3
Measured 34ft in front, 183ft from street to Thames, and 34ft 8in along the river. In 1535/6 it was in the possession of Dr William Knight, archdeacon of Richmond and canon of St Stephen, for life, and was granted by Henry VIII to William, bishop of Norwich, to form part of the bishopric's lands, to take effect after the death of Knight, and confirmed by parliament (PRO, C 65/144, no. 17). In 1540 the bishop granted the property to Richard Southwell for his good service, to hold for 40 years from Knight's death (which was in 1547) without rent, and in May 1548 the bishop granted the reversion to Thomas Smythe, Esq., one of the king's principal secretaries, for 200 years, again without rent but to keep in repair (Thynne Papers, Longleat, vol 2, fo 12; IHR, m/f X71/1). At the same time, Sir Ralph Sadler, Kt, then master of the king's wardrobe, made an agreement to sell to Smythe the lease for years he had of the house for 200 marks (£133 6s 8d). The sale was to be completed at Michaelmas 1550, when Smythe could take possession, unless Sadler's tenant, William Watson, merchant of London, who actually dwelt there, was willing to leave the house before then (Thynne Papers, Longleat, vol 2, fo 15). However, by March 1550 Smythe had sold his interest to Sir John Thynne, Kt, and the other interests had also been surrendered, as Thynne was apparently occupying the house (Thynne Papers, Longleat, vol 2, fo 201, an inventory of clothes

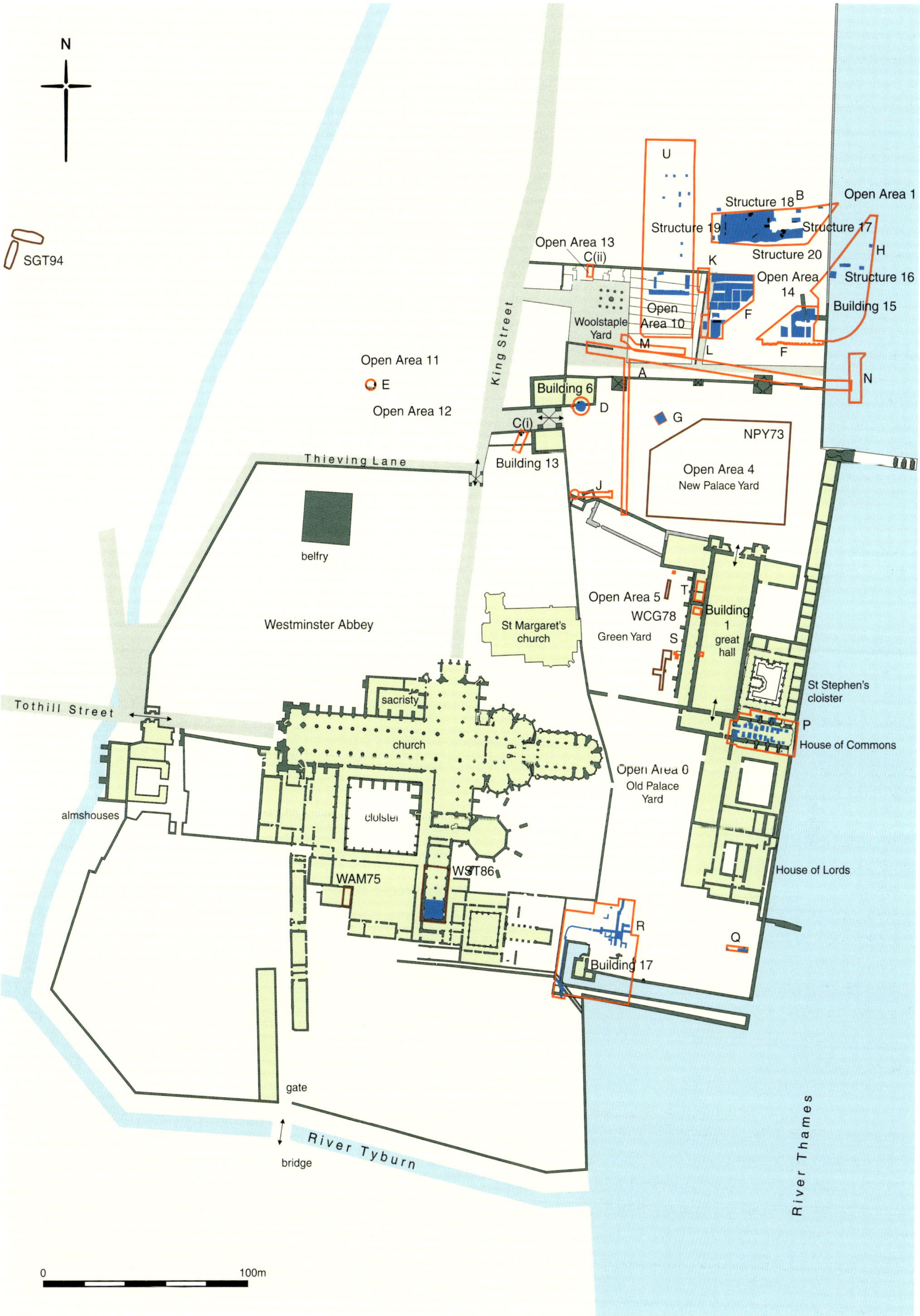

Fig 79 Plan of the archaeological features, period 9 (scale 1:2500). For key to site codes, see Tables 1–3

kept at Canon Row). In 1562 Sir John undertook extensive building work on his house in Canon Row, involving bricklayers, carpenters, smiths and plumbers. Items mentioned include nails for the locks on the street doors, riveting nails for the door in the lower gallery, iron bars for the new windows upstairs in the tower, joists for the hall, boards of oak and elm, the strengthening of the door for the new cellar, tiles for paving and for the roof, a door at the foot of the stairs and a girder over the great chamber, lattice for the cellar, mending of the waterstairs, a glass lanthorne and a lock on the watergate. One carpenter was paid for making a coop for capons in the kitchen and for setting up five bedsteads; another for 177yd of wainscot with ceilings; and another for wainscot and ceilings for the hall and great chamber. A gutter was laid in the tower, and the gutter over Lord Hertford's garderobe (his property adjoined on the north side) was repaired. Timber and coals were brought to the house by river and unloaded on the waterside. Some additional work was done in 1568, including tiling, and liming and mending the walls of the gallery (Thynne Papers, Longleat, vol 49, fos 15–21v; IHR m/f XR 71/25).

No. 4, no. 5, no. 6
Based on the width of 34ft–35ft per canon, this was the site of Manchester Buildings, which in 1696 measured 103ft to the street, 108ft to the river, and 222ft 5in from street to river, and would take three houses.

This was originally Hertford House, and is presumably the house of Edward Seymour, Lord Hertford, third son of Edward, duke of Somerset, where he secretly married Katharine Grey at the end of 1560. He was still occupying the house in 1601.

No. 7, no. 8, no. 9
The site of Wharton House, later Dorset House, later Dorset Court. Wharton House was the residence of Philip Wharton, Lord Wharton, in 1589; it was later occupied by Lady Dorothy Hastings.

No. 10
There is little information regarding this property in period 9. The numbering of this and the next two items is somewhat tentative.

No. 11, no. 12
The site of Derby House. John Thorpe's drawing of c 1600 is of the plan of a house thought to be Lord Derby's house in Canon Row, measuring approximately 70ft to the street. In 1552 Edward earl of Derby purchased from the Crown two messuages and two adjoining gardens with all appurtenances including wharves, in the occupation of two of the canons, Allen Cooke and John Vaughan, which he may have rebuilt (*Cal Pat R*, 1550–3, 410.). In 1570 he built some additional accommodation there (Coward 1983, 25). His grandson William, earl of Derby, was building 'a stately house' in Canon Row in the late 1590s, according to John Stow (Stow 1987, 403).

No. 13
Possibly the site of the house of Anne, duchess of Somerset, widow of Edward Seymour, duke of Somerset. She married Francis Newdigate, who bought a house in Canon Row from Lord Hunsdon. He bequeathed it to the duchess in 1582 (HMC, MSS of the Marquess of Bath at Longleat, iv, 190), and at her death in 1587 she left it to her eldest surviving son, Edward, Lord Hertford. There is some uncertainty about whether Hertford occupied this property, as he had a house in Canon Row long before her death. It is likely that her house was near the northern end of the Row, for there was some dispute with Lord Burghley about whether Queen Elizabeth was happy about the raised terrace walk the duchess had made in her garden, which gave a view into the privy garden at Whitehall. The queen was said to have been well contented to allow it, as it was for the duchess, and although the duchess offered to give the key to the Lord Chamberlain when the queen was at Westminster, the queen was said to have trusted the duchess with it and promised to walk there when at Westminster. As other houses with raised walks also looked into the orchard and garden of Whitehall, many others had to be trusted to move or lock up their walks and windows, though it was asserted that the view into the garden was no greater than that from across the river (HMC, Salisbury MSS, xiii, 327).

11.3 Archaeological evidence

Building 6

A brickearth floor was laid in Building 6 (Fig 80) that was overlaid by a disturbed layer of grey sandy silt, sand, oyster shell and tile, including broken 'Flemish' tile fragments. This may have represented a disturbed floor surface with an occupation deposit over it. It was cut by a small north–south aligned brick drain, which sloped down to the south. This was sealed by a light brown clay floor.

Building 6 continued in use during this period. There was little evidence as to its function although with the replacement of the hearth by a brick drain its layout clearly differed from that of the previous period.

Building 13

At some point, the timber partitions in Building 13 (Fig 80) were stripped out and the posts removed. Layers of sandy clay and mortar were dumped over the backfilled postholes and a clay floor laid over them. Inserted into it was a single stake, which was burnt *in situ*. Overlying the floor was a crushed Reigate stone floor surface sealed by a layer of occupation debris, including oyster shell, charcoal and small quantities of animal bone. It is possible that a compacted layer of mixed grey clay, sand and silt with bricks, mortar, flint, Reigate stone

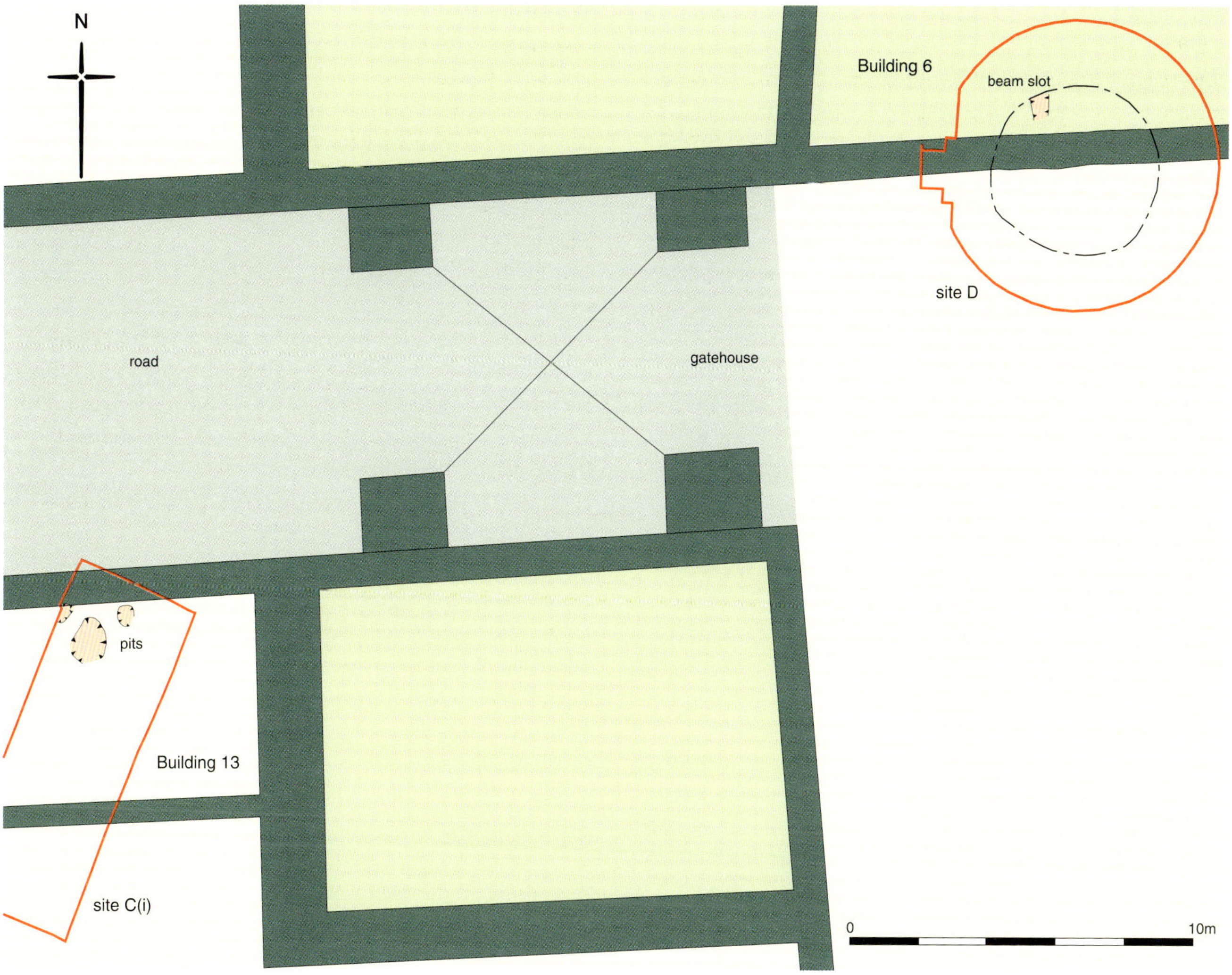

Fig 80 Detailed plan of the archaeological features in Building 6 and Building 13, period 9 (scale 1:200)

chippings and chalk to the west may have been a disturbed hearth, contemporary with the floor. To the south-west lay two pits, neither of which had any obvious function nor, because of later truncation, could they be stratigraphically linked to the floor surfaces in this period. Sealing the floor was a sand floor sealed by a thin black occupation layer. Probably contemporary with this floor was a hearth consisting of roof tiles set upright in clay and surrounded by one large and two smaller pieces of Kentish ragstone. Associated with this hearth were two layers of brown sandy clay with charcoal, ash and lumps of burnt clay, presumably rake-out deposits from the hearth. A pit, slightly to the west of the hearth, about 0.5m across and 0.51m deep was filled with charcoal and clay with some animal bone and building material. This must also have been debris from the hearth, which seems to have continued in use throughout the relaying of the floor surfaces described below.

The floor was relaid in sand and was covered by a black layer of occupation debris containing charcoal, oyster shell and mussel shell. The three floor layers and occupation layers described in this and the previous paragraph were recorded as six individual layers, although at least 14 such deposits could be seen in section, all extremely thin, illustrating the constant relaying of floors in this building.

The floor was relaid in sand and into it was cut a small pit containing large amounts of charcoal, possibly rake-out material from the continued use of the hearth. The pit and the floor were overlaid by yet another layer of occupation debris containing a high percentage of charcoal. The hearth was partially robbed out by a cut containing mixed material including large amounts of oyster shell, charcoal, brick and mortar.

Building 13 clearly underwent a further change of use during this period when the timber partitions were removed. The dating of this is uncertain; it may equate with the rebuilding of four houses and the Saracen's Head in 1486–7 (the time of the demise of the October Fair) by Westminster Abbey, which cost £230 (Rosser 1989, 79). The Saracen's Head was certainly in existence by 1398 (Rosser 1989, 37). The floors were clearly relaid on a regular basis and much domestic food refuse was discarded. The building continued in use with little change until the south wall was rebuilt and the western wall constructed during the 17th century (Chapter 12.3, Buildings 13 and 22).

Building 15

This building is perhaps no. 2 Canon Row (Fig 81). There was no activity surviving from this period within the building, although a number of alterations were made to the drain. A masonry wall was inserted across the west end of the drain at approximately the point where the drain turned to the north. It consisted of chalk, Reigate stone, Kentish ragstone, brick and tile in a series of builds. Cut into the top of the drain was a brick opening which had removed part of the original stone springing arch. This may have been inserted to provide a chute into the drain after the masonry wall to the west, which presumably blocked off the original access, had been built. Abutting this wall on the east side was a drain fill consisting of grey silty clay with lenses of yellow sand containing large quantities of animal bone and small amounts of oyster and mussel shell. The remaining depth of the drain was filled with up to 0.98m of mixed material, consisting of gravel and mortar at the base, sealed by layers of sand, silt and clay. These might have been deposited both as waste in the drain and by the river to the east entering the drain. These fills contained the fragments of a medieval glass prunted beaker, <S8>, described in Chapter 10.3. The masonry wall may have been inserted either because alternative arrangements had been made in other properties using this exit or because of modifications to Building 15.

The animal bone assemblage recovered from the lower fill was relatively large and rather unusual. It featured only a small proportion of bones belonging to the major mammalian domesticates (most of the bones representing these species and species size in Tables 46–8 are from the disuse fill), and was instead largely composed of bird, small mammal and small rodent fragments. The majority of the bird bones belonged to dove, probably domestic, this species represented by at least three relatively compete adult skeletons, with a few bones representing juveniles and pullets. It can perhaps be assumed from the wide age range that these represent a supply from a local dovecote. Amongst the other food species present there are a number of small passerines and some fish. Of interest in the latter case is the concentration of relatively small species, including eel, herring and smelt. A possible explanation for this bias may be that these bones represent the remains of faecal material. Indeed, a proportion of the smelt vertebrae do show signs of erosion typical of the damage done to bones that have travelled through the digestive tract. Amongst the non-food species was a large number of small rodent bones, probably all belonging to rat and mouse, and, appropriately, a few cat bones. The species of rat could not be identified, although it is likely to be black rat (the earliest incidence of the brown rat in this country appears to date to the 18th century, see Lawrence and Brown 1973, 101), while a few of the mouse-sized bones could be identified as house mouse. Additional finds from this deposit included a single fragment belonging to a foetal/ neonate sheep plus one belonging to a heron. As suggested for similar finds elsewhere on this project, the recovery of such a young animal strongly suggests the keeping/breeding of farm animals in the vicinity. The heron is another clear indicator of high status.

Structure 16

On site H, four wooden posts, between 0.14m and 0.20m in diameter, had been driven deep into the medieval and Tudor alluvium. Immediately to the east were three stakeholes, which were between 80mm and 90mm in diameter and did not penetrate the alluvium as deeply as the posts. Two contained fragments of badly decayed wood. The posts probably represent the remains of an openwork structure built on the early Tudor foreshore. Indeed, they may have been the supports for a jetty extending out into the river. Smaller posts or stakes, represented by the stakeholes, may have been associated with this structure. The structure is probably early Tudor in date, since land reclamation appears to have taken place on site H during the second half of the 16th century.

Structure 17

Stone foundations, apparently representing the south-eastern corner of a structure, cut through two Tudor pits on the east side of site B (Fig 81). The foundations were mainly of rough hewn blocks of Kentish ragstone and chalk bonded with sandy mortar, although they also incorporated pieces of Reigate stone and flint, and occasional fragments of brick.

Structure 18

Towards the north side of site B a foundation of stone rubble and sand lay in a construction trench that survived to a depth of 0.40m (Figs 81–2). The foundations also contained frequent fragments of brick and peg tile. The bricks were generally dated from the mid/late 15th century to *c* 1700. The remaining space in the construction trench had been backfilled with silty clay containing frequent fragments of mortar and chalk and moderate fragments of peg tile and brick (the latter of similar date to those in the foundation).

Structure 19

On the west side of site B wall foundations of chalk bonded with a creamy sandy mortar lay in a construction trench that survived to a depth of 0.70m (Fig 81). It is thought that the foundations may have been of 16th-century date. They also incorporated apparently later masonry, consisting of red bricks bonded with yellow sandy mortar. The bricks were 2 inches in thickness, suggesting they were of Tudor date.

The function of the structure is uncertain but it lay in an area behind one of the former canons' houses, close to the back of the property where it met Canon Row.

Structure 20

On site B a row of four narrow slots, aligned north-east–south-west, appeared to mark the position of a fence or wall made of vertically set planks or staves that had been driven into the ground (Fig 81). The slots varied from 0.5m to over 0.6m in

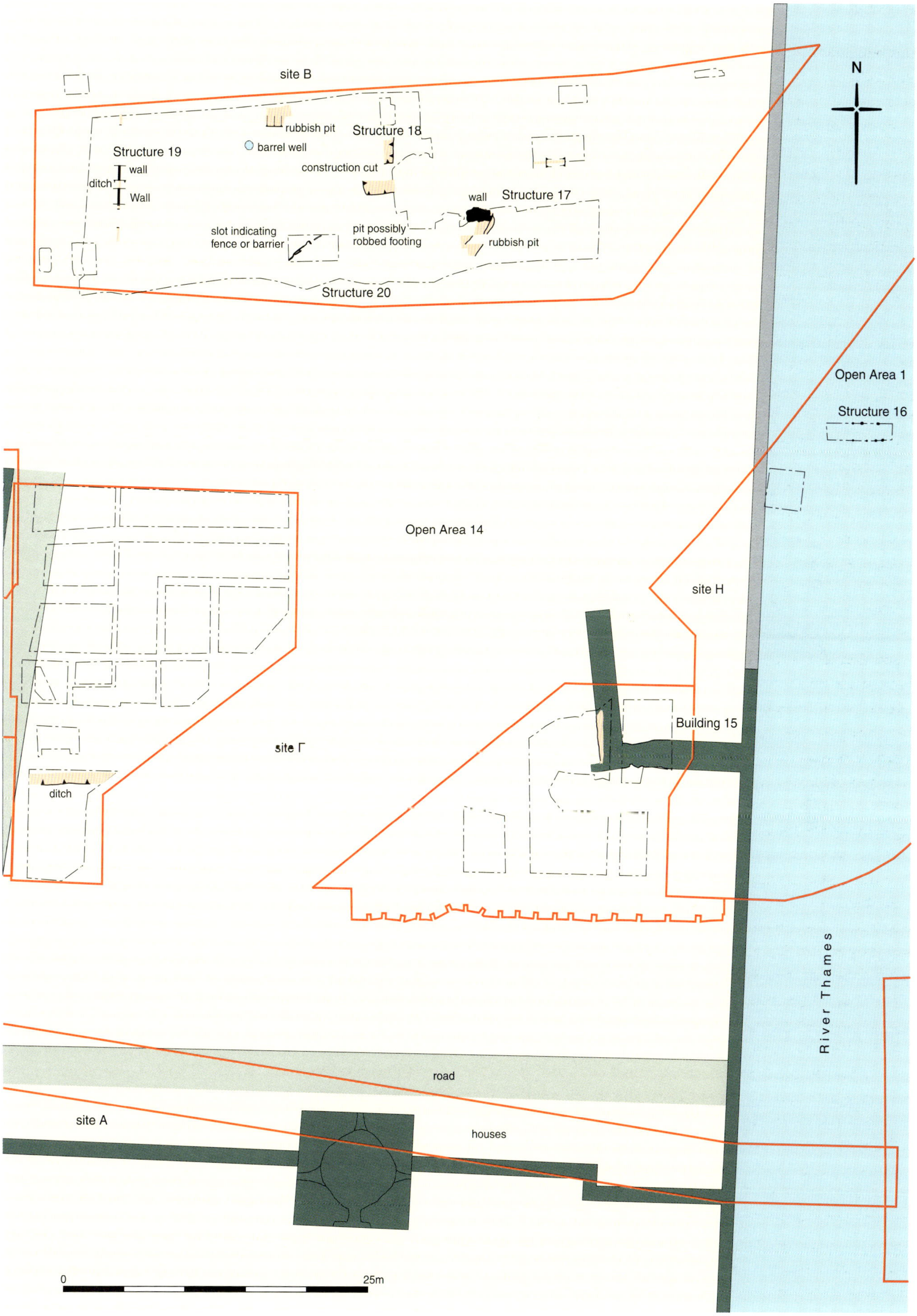

Fig 81 Detailed plan of sites B, F and H showing Building 15, Open Area 14 and Structures 16–20, period 9 (scale 1:400)

Fig 82 *View of Structure 18, looking south-west (0.5m scale)*

length, and were up to 80mm wide. One survived to a depth of 0.98m. The date of the structure is unclear since the slots were empty apart from debris that had fallen in from overlying 19th-century make-up for the basement floor of St Stephen's House. However, the nature and alignment of the structure suggests that it pre-dates 18th- or 19th-century developments in the area. Nor can it be earlier than late medieval in date, since it was cut through the fill of a pit dated to the 14th or 15th century. It therefore seems most likely that the structure dates to the Tudor period.

Open Area 1: the foreshore

Three successive channels in the eastern half of site B appeared to be of early post-medieval date. They were filled mainly with river silts. The earliest, B[80], which was over 2.0m wide and 0.8m deep, was filled with alluvial clays. The former watercourse was cut by a second channel, B[62], which was 0.54m deep. The third channel, B[16], was about 0.3m deep. It contained a residual medieval mount, <S24>.

The channels would have formed when this part of the site was still foreshore. This must have been before the late Tudor period, since reclamation dumps on site H, to the east, suggest that the area had been reclaimed from the Thames by the beginning of the 17th century.

Open Area 6: Old Palace Yard

Two undated levelling layers were found in the region of Building 18. Both signify its disuse and the return of the entire area to an open area. Overlying the former floor of Building 18, this layer comprised demolition material, probably from the building itself, including Kentish ragstone, chalk and mortar.

Open Area 10

At some point during this period or early in the next period, the wall defining the back of the properties around Woolstaple Yard on site K was robbed out. Large-scale dumping was carried out in the area, levelling up the ground to about 1.9m OD. There was some evidence for external surfaces being laid during this phase of activity. The deposits consisted of layers of sand and silty clay containing fragments of tile, brick, chalk, mortar, Kentish ragstone and Reigate stone. This suggests widespread demolition and/or building activity during the 16th century. There is no evidence as to whether a new back wall to the properties was built elsewhere. It is likely, however, that this area remained as part of the properties until their demolition in the early 18th century, when Canon Row was resited on its current alignment.

Open Area 11

A third phase of the east–west aligned ditch on site E (Fig 83) divided Open Areas 11 and 12, gardens behind properties that fronted on to King Street (Fig 84). Only a 1.0m length survived later truncation but it is interpreted as having originally crossed the whole area. It was 0.46m wide and contained evidence for the dumping of domestic waste, such as small quantities of chalk, oyster shell and charcoal.

Two rubbish pits lay in Open Area 11. Both lay partially beyond the limits of excavation: one appeared to be circular, measuring 0.60m in diameter and 0.23m in depth, and was filled with grey silty clay with oyster shell, animal bone, tile and charcoal; the second was much larger, measuring more than 1.8m across and 0.22m deep, and was filled with grey-brown sandy silt with large quantities of charcoal and oyster shell, as well as mortar, tile and animal bone. Both the ditch and the pits were sealed by levelling layers containing domestic refuse and building material. One, E[5], contained a rim fragment of a copper-alloy clapper bell, <S43>, and a copper-alloy buckle, <S44> (Fig 85). The domestic refuse included animal bone, which consisted of a few bones including cow, sheep and pig plus a single roe deer fragment. The latter species, as suggested for the other deer remains found within these sites, is a clear indicator of high status.

Open Area 11 continued in use as the back garden of a property fronting on to King Street with domestic waste being disposed of in rubbish pits.

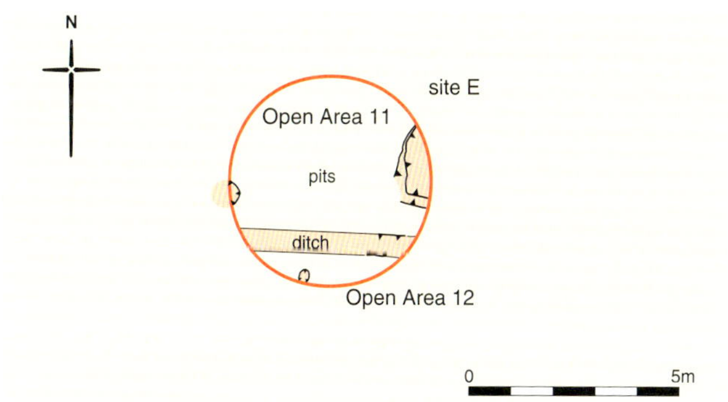

Fig 83 Detailed plan of the archaeological features on site E, period 9 (scale 1:200)

Open Area 12

A single posthole lay to the south of the ditch dividing Open Area 11 and Open Area 12 on site E (Fig 83). It was 0.23m in diameter and 0.36m deep.

Open Area 14

The Tudor foreshore on site H (Fig 81) was covered with dumps of sand, up to 0.6m thick, which contained fragments of brick (probably of Tudor date) and tile, and pottery dated to between 1550 and 1600.

Three pits and a well dated to the 16th century were found further inland on site B (Fig 81). All had been severely truncated by later activity. Two were domestic rubbish pits (B[224] and B[252]) containing considerable quantities of animal bones, oyster shells and other household refuse. Pit B[224] survived to a depth of 0.47m and may have been part of adjacent pit B[218], which had been dated to the mid 14th to mid 15th century. However, its primary fill, B[221], produced artefacts suggesting that it was probably later in date.

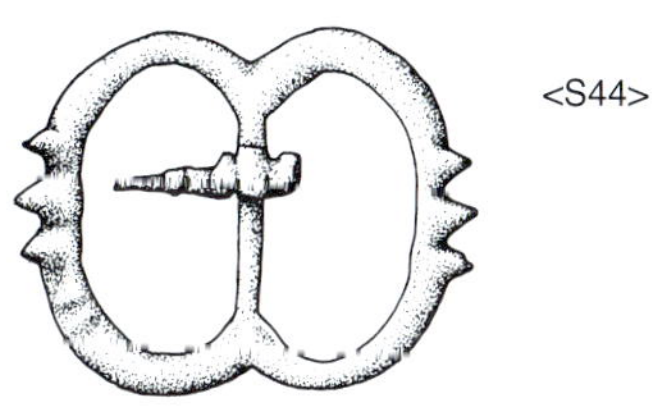

Fig 85 Copper-alloy buckle <S44> from Open Area 11 (scale 1:1)

Fig 84 Houses on the west side of King Street, behind which lay Open Areas 11 and 12 (watercolour, c 1820, by an anonymous artist; Guildhall Library (Print Room), Pr.W2/KIN/whi)

The finds included part of a bowl in London-area early post-medieval redware (PMRE), which could have been made as late as 1600, and a fragment of Dutch brick, which was either late medieval or early Tudor in date. In addition, one of the upper fills, B[150], contained a late medieval or Tudor 'Flemish' floor tile and a fragmentary whittle tang medieval knife, <S15>. Pit B[252], which survived to a depth of 1.35m, produced PMRE, fragments of peg tile, a small piece of leather (probably from the sole of a shoe) and pieces of a copper-alloy buckle. Both pits contained a considerable number of residual artefacts, mostly pottery dated to the mid 14th to 15th century, but fill B[151] in pit B[224] also produced a 15th-century jetton and a copper-alloy finger ring, <S20>. The third pit, B[250], survived to a depth of 0.85m. It had been partly dug through pit B[252], and was filled with sand, gravel and building debris comprising fragments of chalk, Reigate stone, Kentish ragstone and tile. It also produced a few sherds of residual mid 14th- to 15th-century pottery.

The well B[170], which had been dug down to the top of the terrace sand, survived to a depth of 0.76m. It was lined with a wooden barrel, which was very badly decayed. The pottery from its fills B[166] and B[168] consisted mainly of PMRE and London-area post-medieval slipped redware (PMSR): jugs, cauldrons or pipkins, and a bowl. However, context B[168] also included two complete watering cans, one with green glaze (PMSRG), <P14> (Fig 86), and one in PMRE, <P15> (Fig 87). They are closely similar in form, with thumbed handles, a rim guard and rose sprinkler, connected to the rim by a strut, now missing. There were also 26 sherds from a third watering can in PMSR. The context is dated to the second half of the 16th century, when PMSRG appears to have been more common. The only other pottery in these 16th-century contexts is early border ware (EBORD), part of a cup and a drinking jug, made probably at Farnborough Hill until c 1480–1550.

The watering cans from the well fill were deposited over a short period of time, presumably dropped into the well when being filled with water. The presence of watering cans indicates that horticultural activity was being carried out in the immediate vicinity of the well, although it is not possible to ascertain if this was a pleasure garden or a market garden.

After the well had fallen out of use it was backfilled with B[166], which contained frequent fragments of peg tile (including medieval tile with brown splash glaze), oyster shell, moderate animal bone and sherds of late 15th- to 16th-century pottery, mainly in PMRE and PMSR.

In general, the animal bone assemblages from these fills are similar to those from period 8, with cattle dominating the collections, but also with a wide range of domestic and wild food species, including birds as well as a number of fish species. Rabbit is particularly well represented, principally within pit B[224], this collection belonging to a minimum of five individuals. The fish species follow the general pattern towards the exploitation of riverine and, especially, estuarine fisheries (Chapter 16.7). Food waste deposited within the well fills included the partial articulation of a foetal/neonate calf, again demonstrating the presence of local husbandry. The relatively large number of rat-sized bones from this period/area (Table 47) represent mainly the remains of a single partial skeleton from pit B[252].

Fig 86 Ceramic watering can <P14> from Open Area 14 (height 350mm)

Fig 87 Ceramic watering can <P15> from Open Area 14 (height 319mm)

On the western side of site F lay an east–west aligned ditch, F[9], of which only the southern edge survived. The part that was excavated was 0.90m wide so the complete feature would presumably have been at least 1.80m wide. It was at least 1.0m deep and was filled with grey-brown silty clay with large quantities of chalk, tile, mortar and charcoal, moderate amounts of wood, oyster and mussel shells and Reigate stone chippings, and a few fragments of Kentish ragstone and chalk. It also contained a very corroded, possibly copper-alloy button, <S45>. This ditch presumably formed a substantial property boundary and was on a similar alignment to Building 15 to the east, although no trace of the ditch was found on the eastern part of the site. No occupation material was found on site F as truncation had removed all evidence of it.

11.4 Discussion

Little evidence on the sites excavated was found to demonstrate either the Dissolution of Westminster Abbey or the fire in the Palace of Westminster (Table 13). The lack of material within the palace areas excavated may not be significant but is interesting, given the decline in the palace's importance and fortunes during the 16th century. The alterations to Building 15 may have been associated with the Dissolution whilst those in Building 13 may reflect the cessation of the October Fair. Documentary and cartographic evidence along with numerous engravings do, however, indicate that the Exchequer on the west side of the great hall was rebuilt in the second half of the 16th century. The range was extended by a bay northwards and this north-facing elevation can be clearly seen in engravings by Hollar and Smith.

The most significant evidence for activity was in Open Area 11, the area behind the houses on the west side of King St, and Open Area 14, the areas behind the other former canons' houses. The activity in Open Area 14 consisted not only of rubbish pits and a barrel-lined well but also of constructional work, including three stone foundations (S17, S18 and S19). There was also evidence for further reclamation into the Thames. It would seem, therefore, that the Dissolution and the abandonment of Westminster as a royal residence did not affect the continued lives of the inhabitants of the town, who seem to have prospered and extended their properties. How much of this could be attributed to the new money brought in by owners to former monastic properties and how much to the continued prosperity of the northern part of Westminster, which lay equally close to Whitehall Palace, is difficult to assess. Although there is evidence of reuse of materials and existing structures at many dissolved monastic houses, for instance St Mary Spital (Thomas et al 1997), there were also wealthy members of the establishment living in some of these properties who were prepared to lavish money on them, for instance St John's, Clerkenwell (Sloane and Malcolm in prep), Pope's house on the former site of Bermondsey Abbey (Steele in prep) and the mansion at Charterhouse (Knowles and Grimes 1954; Barber and Thomas 2002).

Table 13 Selected dating evidence, period 9 (see Table 25 for expansion of codes)

Land use	Activity	Context	Evidence	Description	Date range
Building 6	occupation deposit	D[18]	ceramic building material	floor tile 3080	1450–1550
Building 13	occupation layer	C[80]	ceramic	FREC; PMR	1600–1800
Building 13	rubbish pit	C[66]	ceramic	MG; FREC; PMR	1550–1800
Building 13	make-up layer	C[70]	ceramic	FREC	1550–1700
Building 15	drain disuse	F[104]	ceramic building material		1450–1700
Building 15	drain disuse	F[97]	ceramic	BORDY; DTGW; PMSR; PMRE	1550–1600
Structure 18	wall	B[200]	ceramic building material	tile 2271	1450–1700
Open Area 1: foreshore	foreshore deposit	N[26]	ceramic building material	brick 3033	1480–1700
Open Area 1: foreshore	dumping	H[1]	ceramic building material	brick 3033	1450–1700
Open Area 1: foreshore	natural channel	B[16]	ceramic	PMSR; PMRE	1550–1650
Open Area 1: foreshore	levelling	B[6]	ceramic	PMSR	1550–1650
Open Area 10	levelling	K[40]	ceramic	CBW; MG; BORDY; PMR; PMRE; RAER	1550–1600
Open Area 11	levelling	E[5]	ceramic	CBW; BORDG; BORDY; FREC; PMSR; PMRE	1550–1600
Open Area 14	rubbish pit	B[221]	ceramic	CBW; CHEA; KING; LCGR; LOND; MG; SAIM; SHER; PMRE; RAER	1480–1600
Open Area 14	rubbish pit	B[251]	ceramic	CBW; CHEA; KING; LOND; SHER; PMRE; DUTR; LANG; SIEG	1480–1600
Open Area 14	well	B[166]	ceramic	CHEA; EBORD; PMSRG; PMRE	1480–1550
Open Area 14	well	B[168]	ceramic	PMSRG; PMRE	1550–1650

12

c 1600–*c* 1740 (period 10)

12.1 Environmental and topographical background

By the 17th century all the sites excavated fell within areas reclaimed from the river, so there were no new data recovered concerning the environmental background or the river regime.

12.2 Documentary and archaeological background

Westminster Palace

The declining fortunes of the Palace of Westminster were turned around during the 17th century. This was no doubt as a result of the rise in the influence of parliament during the middle years of the 17th century and the abandonment of Whitehall as a royal residence by William III. Certainly, there were major new building schemes undertaken there. The east side of New Palace Yard was rebuilt during the early years of the 17th century, and a new Star Chamber was built. By the end of the century the bell tower had been given to the parish of St Margaret and had been demolished. In 1706 the great gatehouse to New Palace Yard was also demolished, in order to widen the road. New buildings were constructed along the west side of the great hall, in particular around the Fish Yard.

Among the many new buildings constructed in Old Palace Yard were the Parliament House (B20) (Fig 88) and ranges of buildings on the eastern side of the Yard, in front of the House of Lords and the old queen's chapel, as can be seen in Morgan's map (Fig 89).

Maps of the time also show that the river front had been extended eastwards, thus creating space for buildings and gardens.

Westminster Abbey

The break-up of the precincts of Westminster Abbey can be identified clearly from the 17th-century maps. Whilst the outline of its shape is still visible, the northern precinct had become covered with housing around the street called Sanctuary. Bow Street still used the old boundary to the precinct as its southern side although houses and shops would, no doubt, have had their doors punched through it. The belfry is still clear on Morgan's map and it survived throughout this period.

Buildings on Canon Row (east side)

As with period 9, the accounts below start from the south and go northwards.

No. 1

In c 1740 consisted of two houses, occupied by Benjamin

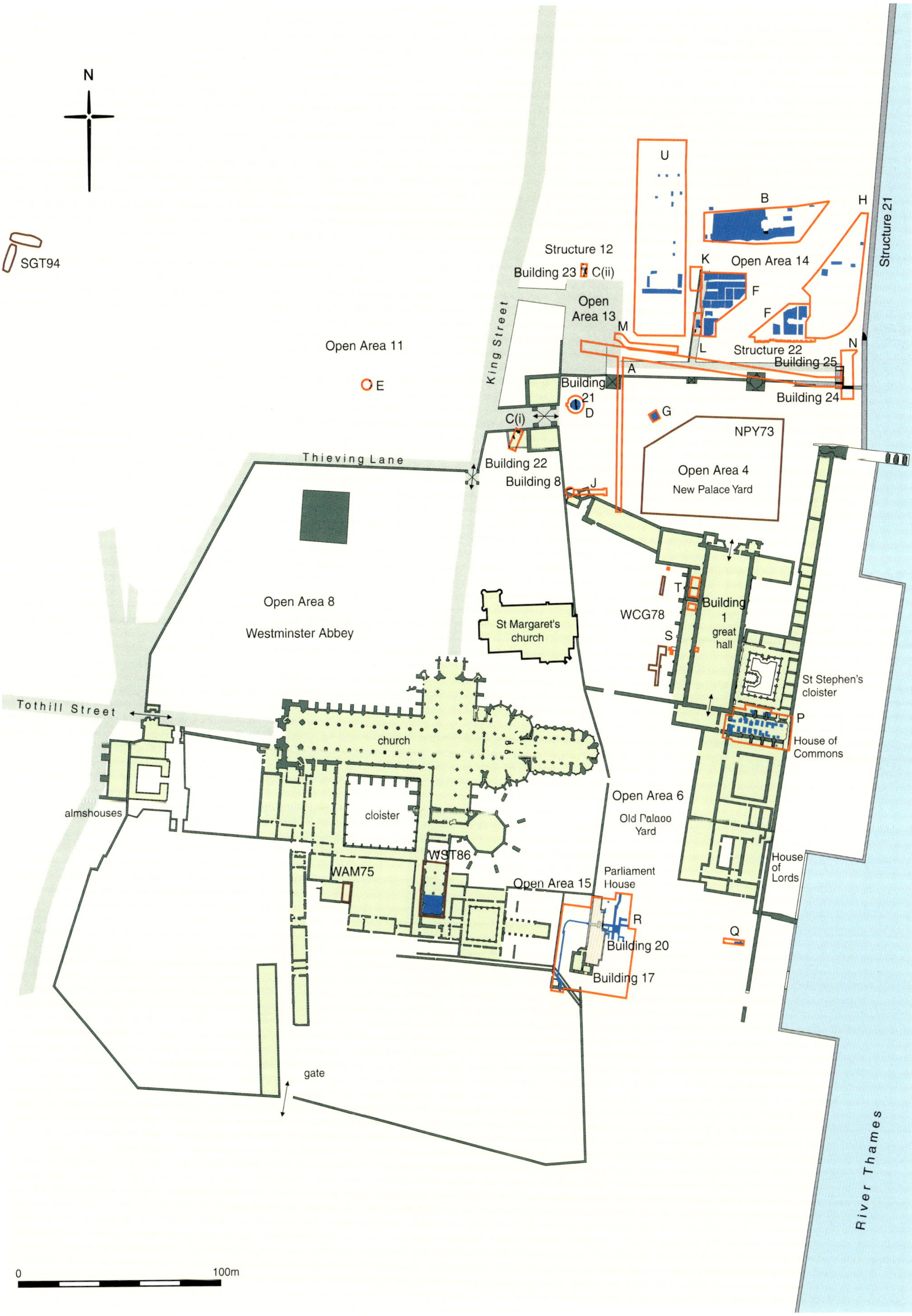

Fig 88 Plan of the archaeological features, period 10 (scale 1:2500). For key to site codes, see Tables 1–3

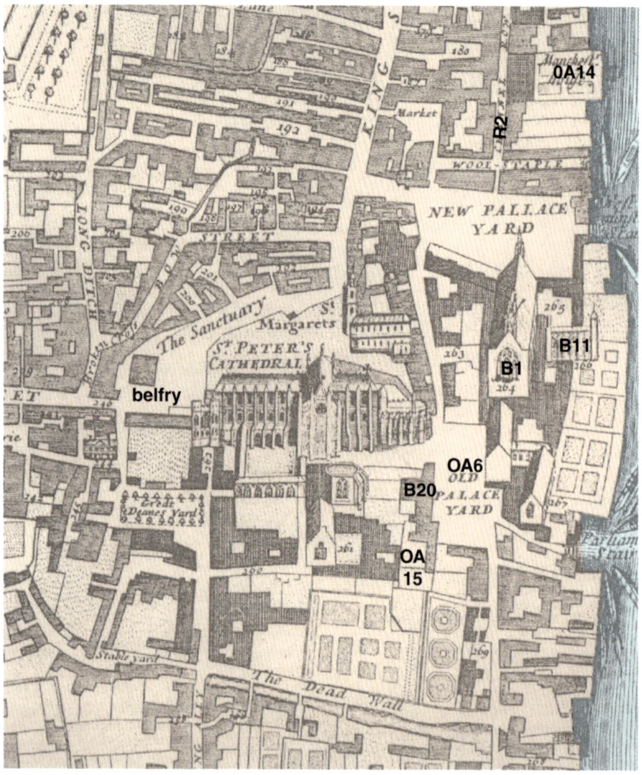

Fig 89 *Morgan's map of Westminster, 1682*

Holmes and John Wallinger, with a piece of garden ground behind towards the Thames, late in the tenure of Susanna Higgins and then John Wallinger.

No. 2
There is no information regarding this property in this period.

No. 3
Still occupied by the Thynne family in the 17th century: Sir Thomas Thynne, Kt, had plate and goods there at his death in 1639 (Thynne Papers, Longleat, vol 79, fo 24). His grandson Sir Thomas, 2nd Bt, created Viscount Weymouth in 1682, had stables on the slip of land on the opposite side of Canon Row in 1696. This also was the freehold of the bishops of Norwich in the 18th century, so may have been acquired with Dr. Knight's house. The plot ran north–south along Canon Row, its north end level with the house site, leaving the 12-foot width of Canon Row between them, and measuring 14.5ft at the north end, 11.5ft at the south end, and 133ft long. It was formed by covering over (or filling) the king's ditch, which formed the eastern boundary of the Round Woolstaple houses. Weymouth died in 1714, and was succeeded in the title and property by his great-nephew, also Thomas. Soon after coming of age the latter sold both sites in 1733 for £850, the slip having formerly had 'tenements lately pulled down', to Thomas Funge, citizen and carpenter, who immediately sold them to John Wallinger of London, merchant. However, the bishop of Norwich brought a suit to recover possession as part of the bishopric, and in 1737, when Weymouth refunded the purchase money, the property was conveyed back to the bishop (LMA, BRA 437/09). Wallinger then presumably took a lease from the bishop, as he was the occupier when the Commissioners for Building Westminster Bridge bought the property soon afterwards.

No. 4, no. 5, no. 6
Based on the width of 34ft–35ft per canon, this was the site of Manchester Buildings, which in 1696 measured 103ft to the street, 108ft to the river, and 222ft 5in from street to river, and would take three houses.

Hertford house was bought by Sir Henry Montague, earl of Manchester, after 1628; he stated he spent a great deal on it to make it a fit habitation for a nobleman, and in 1641 bequeathed it to his wife for life, and then to his eldest son Edward (PRO, PROB 11/192, fo 373, PCC 47 Rivers). By 1696 the mansion had been demolished and replaced by Manchester Buildings, about 22 houses north and south of a central east–west alley, in the ownership of James Le Quien of London (CWA, acc 10/272).

No. 7, no. 8, no. 9
The site of Wharton House, later Dorset House, later Dorset Court. The freehold belonged to Henry, earl of Lincoln, in 1616.

No. 10
This was the site of 3 Manchester Terrace in 1620, lying between Wharton House and Derby House. These are presumably the messuages adjoining Wharton House, which belonged to the earl of Lincoln. The numbering of this and the next two items is tentative.

No. 11, no. 12
The site of Derby House. This seems to be the house drawn by John Thorpe in about 1600, showing a rectangular house on Canon Row, arranged around a formal internal court with a terrace and garden behind towards the river. The house was the meeting place for the parliamentary Committee for Both Kingdoms during the Interregnum; it was also used as lodgings for state officials, and for the Dutch ambassador in 1658 (de Beer 1955, 222). It was still in the possession of the earls of Derby in 1675, when it had 17 hearths (PRO, E 179/253, fo 25), but was used by the Lords Commissioners of the Admiralty as their office by 1674, and Samuel Pepys the secretary had lodgings there. (*Cal S P Dom*, 1673–5, 267; 1676–7, 11) By 1697 Derby Court had been built beside the house, perhaps the area on the south side shown on Morgan's map of 1682, but the house still stood in 1720.

No. 13
There is no information regarding this property in this period.

Woolstaple Yard

The main outlines of the individual tenements around the yard remained the same into the 18th century, but by then their use had changed: the gardens of the houses on the east side had been infilled with slaughterhouses, and a passage through to Canon Row created through the Trevors' former house (Chapter 11.2; GL, MS 22635/21).

12.3 Archaeological evidence

Building 6

Building 6 on site D was demolished in this period. It was overlain by Building 21 on the west side and cut by a large brick culvert on the east side. These changes may have been associated with the demolition of the great gate to the palace in 1706 (Colvin et al 1963, 548).

Building 8

Cutting through the southern edge of the north wall of the gatehouse tower on site J was a brick well. Only the base of this was seen in tunnelling works, for the remainder lay above the tunnel. The well was oval in shape, measuring 1.00m east–west x 0.90m north–south internally, with walls constructed from red brick 0.22m thick and bonded with grey mortar. The internal face was also rendered with grey mortar. A timber plank, 30mm thick, lay across the base of the well. The primary fill of the well, deposited during its use, was a black ashy silt 0.25m thick with charcoal and an intact tin-glazed bottle, <P16> (Figs 90–1). This vessel was found in association with a number of later sherds, which indicate a deposition some time in the mid 18th century. The handled bottle is decorated with a bird-on-rock scheme, which consists of a central panel depicting, in blue and white, birds sitting on rocks surrounded by flowers and sprays of foliage. There are panels of an overlapping lattice pattern above and below the central panel. The outside of the handle is covered in solid blue, and underneath its lower terminal is a painted date of 1627(/8?). There is a solid band of blue above the base. The bottle is intact apart from some minor damage around the rim. The decorative scheme, inspired by blue-and-white Ming *kraak* porcelain, was a popular motif among pot decorators in the first half of the 17th century. The pattern is often associated with Christian Wilhelm (Tait 1960, 36–42), who was an immigrant from the Low Countries and settled at Pickleherring quay in Southwark. He was originally involved with the manufacture of vinegar and smalt, a blue glass containing cobalt oxide, which is finely ground for use as a blue pigment. Wilhelm was in dispute with an Abraham Baker over infringement of an agreement about smalt production (Edwards 1974), which led to Wilhelm diversifying into pottery production in about 1618. In 1627 or 1628 Wilhelm petitioned the king for a grant of privilege for the manufacture of smalt. A total of six bottles dated and decorated with similar bird-on-rock schemes are known in museums and private collections. They may have been produced at Pickleherring pottery as a special edition to demonstrate the

Fig 90 Delftware bottle <P16> from Building 8 (height 192mm)

Fig 91 Detail showing date stamp on delftware bottle <P16> from Building 8

ability of Wilhelm's factory to produce high-quality wares, perhaps in support of his petition to the Crown. This may explain the presence of this vessel within the precinct of the Palace of Westminster.

It is probable that the building remained in use when this well was dug, which suggests that the wall through which it was cut was part of the foundation and not the above-ground wall. It is unlikely that the well-diggers would have realised this until they had taken out substantial deposits and they may have been unconcerned about cutting through the foundations. The building almost certainly went out of use when the new St Margaret Street was laid out in about 1740 and at this time the well was probably backfilled.

Building 13

The south wall of Building 13 on site C(i) was demolished during this period and rebuilt about 1.5m further to the south, creating Building 22. The floors of the latter were then laid over the former south wall of Building 13.

Building 15

No archaeological evidence for the demolition and disuse of Building 15 was found. No written documentary evidence (above, Buildings on Canon Row, no. 2) exists either.

Building 17: the Jewel Tower

Previous excavations have shown that the Jewel Tower moat was infilled during the 17th century (Green 1976, 59). Archive photographs show the construction of numerous brick structures in the moat, many of which appear to date to the 17th century.

Building 20: dwelling house for the Jewel Tower

Building 20 lay to the north-east of the Jewel Tower on site R (Fig 92). A 2.60m-length of wall, aligned north–south and 0.44m wide, was constructed from red brick bonded with orange sandy mortar. This formed the east wall of the building

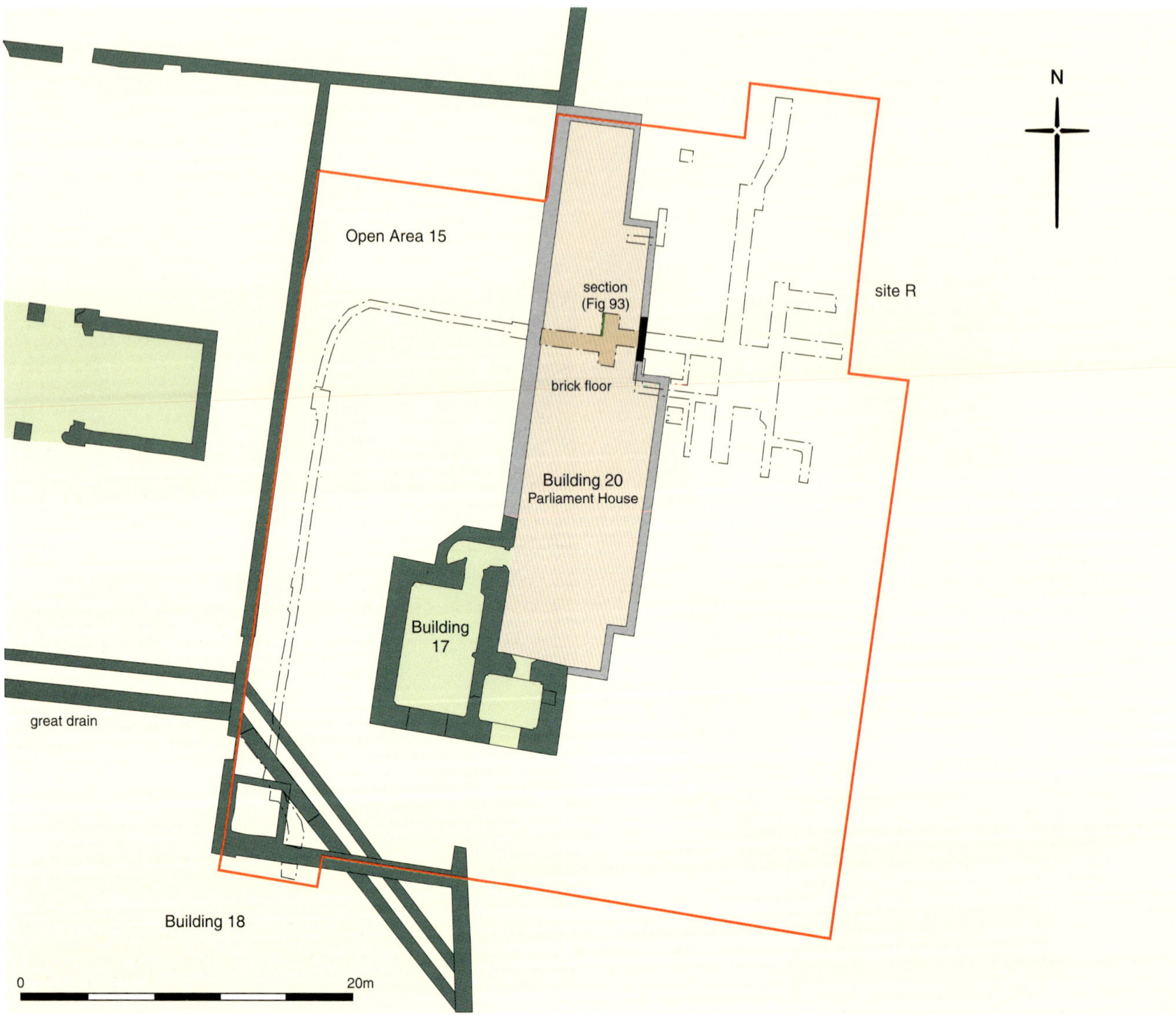

Fig 92 Detailed plan of the Parliament House (B20), period 10 (scale 1:400)

and continued both to the north and south of the area excavated. A section through the deposits within Building 20 (Fig 93) shows that there was a series of dumped levelling layers beneath a red brick floor bedded on a layer of white mortar. Overlying the floor was a black occupation deposit. The building was refloored in mortar, which was also overlain by a black occupation deposit. The building was then levelled before layers of tile and mortar formed another floor, again overlain by an occupation deposit. The final layer in the sequence was a brown clay floor. This was cut by a curving red brick wall bonded with white mortar, 0.20m thick. This may have formed part of an internal drain or sump.

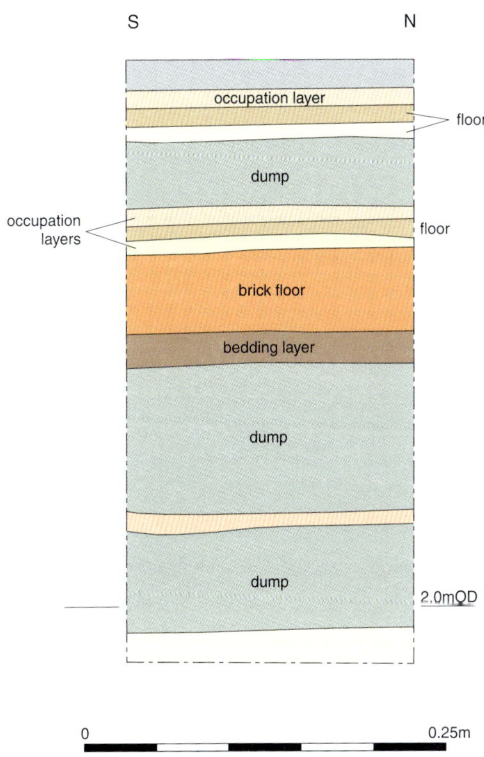

Fig 93 West-facing section through the sequence of floors in the Parliament House (B20) (scale 1:5)

Building 20 was probably a building that adjoined the Jewel Tower and was used as the dwelling house for the officers of the Parliament House (the Jewel Tower). It is described as being half-timbered but no evidence was found for this, although it is possible that the lower parts of the walls were constructed in brick supporting a timber superstructure. The bricks from the east wall suggested a 17th-century date, although the dwelling house to the north of the Jewel Tower was in the tenure of Sir Richard Shelley in the 16th century (Taylor 1965, 16). Structures in this position are shown on maps of the 17th and 18th centuries. The sequence of floors within the structure show that it was in constant use and was regularly refloored. The brick floor was presumably its original floor but occupation material built up on top of this and rather than clear this material, the floor was relaid in mortar and clay several times. The limited nature of the works and the nature of the recording have not allowed any interpretation of the internal layout of this building. However, the insertion, probably in the 18th century, of another brick wall, possibly a drain, does suggest that the function of rooms within the building may have changed.

Building 21

Overlying a dumped sand layer in Open Area 4 on site D was a brick and Reigate stone wall aligned north–south. It was bonded with grey mortar with the Reigate stone blocks overlying the bricks. Only the eastern side of the east wall was found and this continued to both north and south (Fig 94). The construction of this wall was very similar to that of the drain to the east in Open Area 4 (see below), the bricks of which probably date to the late 17th or early 18th century. Building 21 may well have been constructed at the time of the demolition of the great gate in 1706. It is not certain that it formed a building rather than just a boundary wall but analysis of maps of the period might suggest that this wall formed the east wall of a building fronting southwards on to Union Street, which lay along the line of the former entrance into New Palace Yard.

Building 22

The south wall of Building 13 on site C(i) was demolished and rebuilt about 1.5m further to the south (Fig 94) in chalk blocks bonded with an off-white mortar. The foundation was of a similar construction but was 0.10m–0.32m wider on the north side. The main wall above the foundation was 0.50m wide and survived to a height of 1.40m. Running north from the foundation was a burnt silty clay deposit with large quantities of charcoal. It overlay the demolished south wall of Building13 and was itself cut by a north–south aligned gully filled with gravel.

At the north end of the building lay a clay floor overlain by a grey sand layer. Associated with these was a rectangular brick hearth, measuring 1.77m x 1.06m, laid against the north wall of the building. It was overlain by a layer of charcoal and silt. Immediately to its west was a stakehole, 0.25m in diameter, presumably for one side of a spit. Another stakehole, 0.20m in diameter, lay to the south of the hearth. Two pits of uncertain usage were dug inside the building, one filled with orange clay and the other with green clay. A third pit was lined with a barrel, <S49>, containing copper-alloy mount <S22>, which was perhaps originally deposited in Building 13. To the south lay a brick drain, including one block of Kentish ragstone, bonded with grey mortar. It was aligned west–east before it turned southwards and sloped down to the south. The base was laid in bricks and was 0.42m wide, the walls being the thickness of a single brick (70mm). The drain was subsequently demolished and backfilled with demolition debris and ash. Dumped to its north were levelling layers comprising sand overlain by mortar, then charcoal and sand under more mortar.

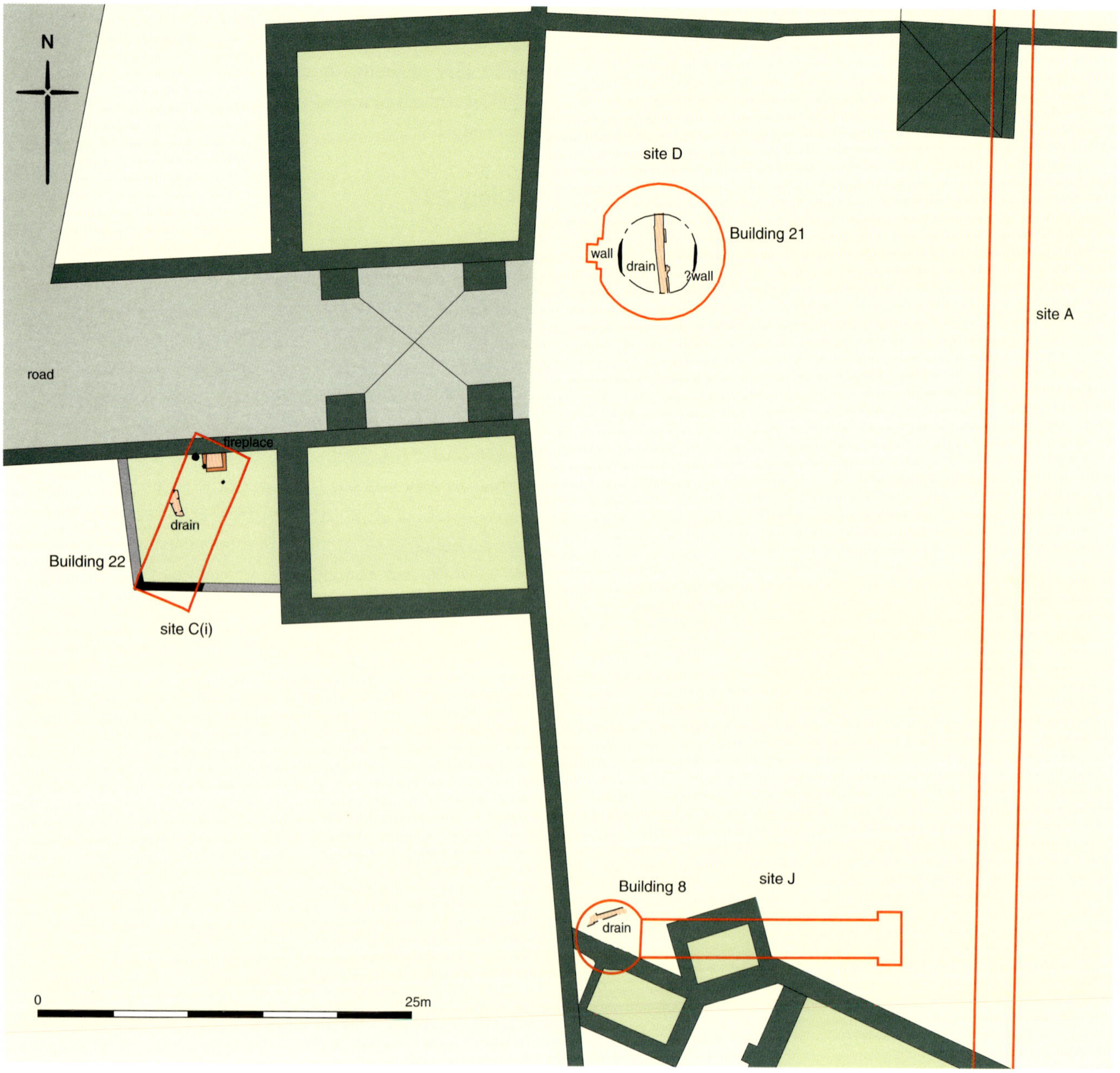

Fig 94 Detailed plan of Buildings 21–22, period 10 (scale 1:400)

The brick hearth was relaid in brick, this time measuring 1.20m east–west (possibly 2.0m) by 0.86m north–south. It was bedded on a layer of sand that overlay a yellow clay layer.

An unstratified ivory knife, <S52> (Fig 95), possibly dating to the end of the lifetime of this building, came from site C(i) and may have originated there. It is complete, including blade and handle. Such an integrated knife with a blunt blade may have been used for feather curling. This specialist activity was undertaken as part of the production of clothes, headdresses, hats and costumes. The maintenance of such items would involve sprucing up limp and straight feathers by curling them around a blunt blade. An example of a bone knife possibly used for this purpose was found in Building IV at the excavations at Aldgate, and was dated to the 18th century (Grew 1984, 98). A fragment of an ivory knife was found in a pit fill at St Mary Spital with ceramics dating to the late 17th to early 18th

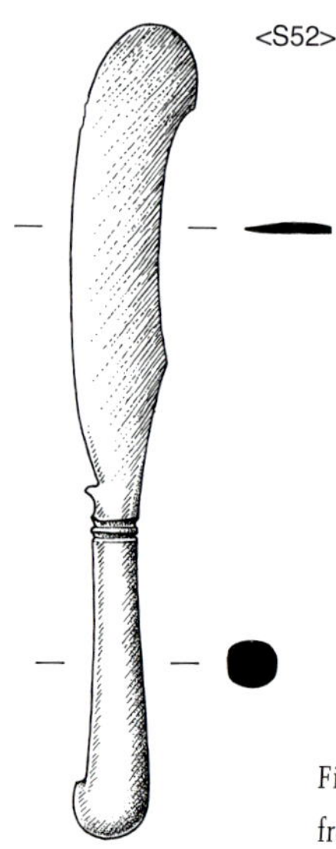

Fig 95 Ivory knife <S52> from site C(i) (scale 1:2)

century, once again perhaps made for feather curling (Thomas et al 1997, 172).

The building was reconstructed during the 17th century but seems to have continued in use with a similar function. The hearths were built against the main wall of the building and were laid in a manner more common in the 17th and 18th centuries. The reason for the rebuilding of the south wall is unclear; it was evidently not to give the building the appearance of a more fashionable structure for chalk rather than brick was used. It may have been that the earlier south wall of Building 13 needed replacing. The dumped layer in Open Area 8 upon which the new wall was built contained pieces of burnt wood and charcoal, perhaps suggesting that fire had damaged part of Building 13. Whatever the reason, the building was enlarged but retained its domestic status.

Building 23

Building 23 was erected over the former Open Area 13 on site C(ii), probably in the early to mid 17th century. It was a brick-built structure extending beyond the limits of the excavation in all areas.

Room A

Room A measured more than 3.2m north–south by more than 1.5m east–west. It was bounded by red brick walls bonded with very pale yellow or white mortar. The north wall (which may have been external) was 0.90m wide while the east wall was 0.45m wide where it divided room A from room B but much wider where it bounded the cesspit to the north of room B. The room was floored in mortar bedded on a layer of sand which lay on dark green clay that had been deposited to raise the level for the floor.

Room B

Room B measured more than 1.2m north–south by more than 1.1m east–west. It shared its west wall with room A and its north wall with the cesspit. The cesspit itself had a brick floor and was surrounded by brick walls on three sides (its east wall was not found). It had planks laid east–west in the centre running up to the west wall. It was filled with two deposits of light brown cess with a layer of clinker and white material sandwiched in between. At some point it appears to have gone out of use, for a stone slab, 80mm thick, was laid over it. It is possible, however, that this did not cover the entire cesspit and was therefore contemporary with it. The cesspit contained fragments of a residual medieval glass vessel, <S10>, and medieval window glass, <S11>, which may have originated from the earlier buildings on the site.

Room C

To the north of room A and the cesspit was an area with a red brick wall aligned north-west–south-east across it. It was not clear whether this area was internal or external but as no floors were seen it may have been external, perhaps a garden. It is also not certain whether this area was associated with Building 23 or another building nearby.

Building 24

The full plan of Building 24 has not been recovered. Its southern and western walls on site N have been excavated and the eastern can be conjectured from the parts of the river wall (S21) found to the north-east (Fig 96). The form of the building at its northern end is unclear. The west wall turned westwards, defining Building 25, whilst the east wall continued as the river wall (S21). There does not appear to have been a north wall to the building yet the deposits clearly show that the area to the south was internal.

The building was 9.06m wide and if it ended to the north where the west wall returned westwards it measured 9.36m north–south.

The south wall was constructed from chalk and Kentish ragstone bonded with creamy white mortar and was 1.50m wide (Fig 97). The west wall survived to a total height of 3.0m and was constructed from chalk and Kentish ragstone blocks bonded with creamy white mortar. The construction technique was very similar to that of the south wall. It appeared to be 0.8m wide but this was hard to establish as, for much of its length, the western edge of the wall lay beyond the limit of excavation and, at the extreme north end, much of the stonework was replaced by the brick cellar in Building 25.

A series of make-up layers for the floors, primarily consisting of layers of sand, were dumped within the building. These were sealed by two compact cream mortar floors separated by a sand and gravel floor. These continued from the south wall northwards beyond the northern end of the west wall, indicating that the building continued north of that point. The lowest floor was at 4.60m OD and the highest at 4.79m OD. A blue-on-white tin-glazed tile from the demolition deposits N[5] in period 11 (Fig 98) may indicate the decorative scheme on the walls.

Building 25

To the west of Building 24 lay Building 25, also on site N (Fig 96). Although little has been excavated the four walls of the building have been recovered, giving its extent as 8.80m north–south by 3.30m east–west. The western wall was formed from similar materials to that of the walls in Building 24: chalk and Kentish ragstone. At the north end was a brick room, 3.30m x 1.40m, which was only seen at its extreme eastern end where it joined Building 24. The red bricks were laid in English bond and were 100mm thick, suggesting a date not later than the late 17th century. The wall survived to a height of 2.50m and the beginnings of a brick barrel vault could be seen. It is unclear whether the remaining area of Building 25 was also vaulted but there appeared to be a similarly sized brick room to the south of the northern one.

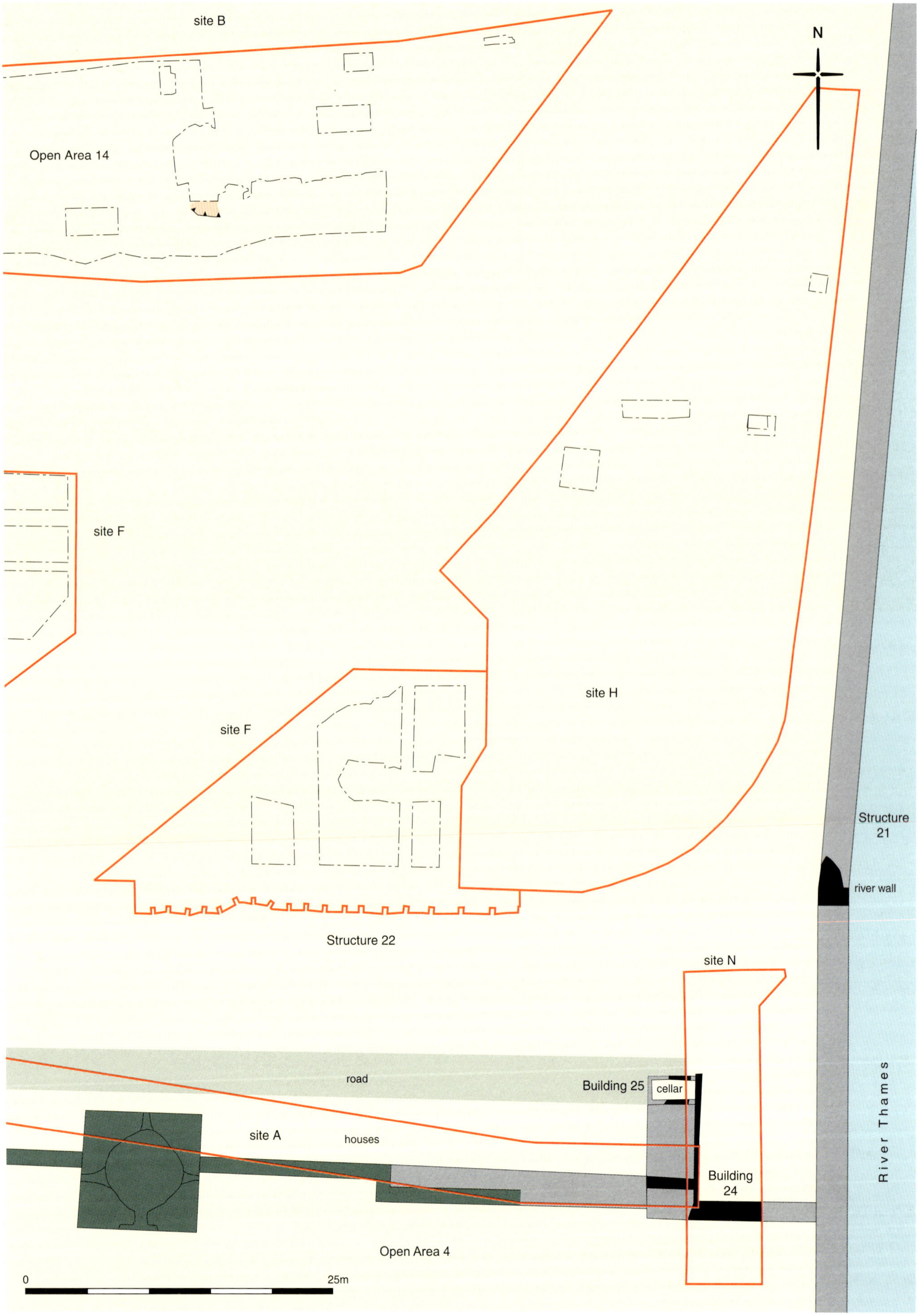

Fig 96 Detailed plan of Buildings 24–25, period 10 (scale 1:400)

Fig 97 View of Building 24, looking south (0.5m scale)

Structure 12

The well, Structure 12 on site C(ii), in Open Area 13 (Chapter 10.3) was either rebuilt or raised in brick by a height of 0.47m, retaining its internal diameter of 0.73m. The bricks were bonded with orange mortar and no chalk was used as it had been in the previous construction. It seems to have been constructed in the very early 17th century as the pottery is thought to post-date 1600 while the pottery and glass in its backfill suggest a date of 1590–1620. It went out of use when Building 23 was constructed over it. An iron hinge, <S50>, and part of a large plain inverted baluster stem from a wine glass, <S54>, were in the well backfill.

Structure 13

No evidence for the destruction of Structure 13 was found but it presumably went out of use in this period when the new river wall (S21) was constructed.

Structure 21

Structure 21 was a roughly coursed Kentish ragstone and flint wall bonded with hard white chalky mortar. It was at least 2.1m wide. It was found to the east of site F and on site N and formed the east wall of Building 24. Its original function was probably as the river wall.

N<5>

Fig 98 Tin-glazed wall tile N<5> from Building 24 (scale 2: 1)

Structure 22

Structure 22 appeared in the southern section of site F. It was truncated in the centre by concrete piles inserted for the new underground station but appeared to have measured at least 1.96m east–west, although the two halves of the structure had different constructions, which may indicate that they formed two structures. On the east side, Structure 22 consisted of a chalk foundation 0.50m high, above which was a red brick wall a further 0.50m high bonded with cream mortar. The bricks and mortar were consistent with a 17th-century date. The wall appeared to be aligned north–south. To the west was found the lower part of the wall, which was of red brick (55mm in thickness) bonded with cream mortar. Behind, the wall appeared to consist largely of chalk as the eastern part had. The upper part did not survive. The areas to the east and west of the exposed part of Structure 22 were not seen and so it is not entirely clear on what alignment it was constructed or how extensive it was. It lay directly over the northern edge of the former dock (S5), which would appear from map evidence to have been a property boundary with properties lying to the south. It may therefore be tentatively suggested that Structure 22 formed, in part, an east–west aligned boundary wall or wall to a building with a north–south dividing wall running south from it. The brick may have been the external face of the east–west wall with the chalk forming the core of the wall. This might explain the difference in construction and the fact that the wall was not noted further north and seems to be too wide for a single wall.

This boundary appears to be consistent with the northern edge of the king's houses fronting on to Woolstaple Yard.

Open Area 4: New Palace Yard

On site D, a cobbled yard surface consisting of Kentish ragstone and Reigate stone chippings was laid over a dumped layer of sand. The sand pre-dated the construction of Building 21 and post-dated the demolition of Building 6. The cobbled yard appeared to have subsided and a mixed layer of crushed mortar and sandy silt was dumped as a base for a light brown clay surface.

To the east, the pier base to the south of Building 6 was mostly robbed of its stone, and a brick, Reigate stone and Kentish ragstone drain was constructed, aligned north–south and sloping down to the south. The bricks are thought to date from the late 17th or early 18th century. The floor of the drain was laid in brick and a bedding of grey sand and mortar although most of it was robbed out before the backfilling of the drain. The west wall of the drain was constructed before the east wall. The east wall consisted of a course of bricks laid on edge, under a course of bricks laid on bed, under a course of Reigate stone and Kentish ragstone sealed by further courses of bricks. The bricks were bonded with grey chalky mortar. The east wall was reused as the foundation for Building 29 (period 11; Chapter 13.3). An English tin-glazed ware plate dating to this period was recovered from site G (Fig 99).

In the south-west corner of Open Area 4 on site J lay a drain constructed from red brick and floor tile. It was aligned east-north-east–west-south-west and sloped down from east to west (Fig 94). An inlet entered the drain on the north side. The brick formed the walls whilst the tile formed the floor. The entire drain was 0.44m wide but internally it was 0.17m. It is not

Fig 99 English tin-glazed ware plate <P17> from site G, Open Area 4 (Diam c 195mm)

clear to what it related. The fill produced very little botanical material, with fruits and seeds representing a small range of wild and cultivated plants. The wild plants included wetland species with aquatics, for example, stoneworts, water plantain (*Alisma* spp), and bankside/marshland plants, for example celery-leaved crowfoot (*Ranunculus sceleratus*), gipsy-wort (*Lycopus europaeus*), and disturbed ground weeds, for example, goosefoots (*Chenopodium* spp) and stinging nettle (*Urtica dioica*). Hedgerow plants included two possible food plants: blackberry/raspberry (*Rubus fruticosus/idaeus*) and elder (*Sambucus nigra*), while cultivated fruits were represented by fig (*Ficus carica*) and grape (*Vitis vinifera*) seeds. There was also a very large amount of fragmented wood and charcoal.

The botanical assemblage reflects conditions within the drain. The presence of aquatic plants suggests bodies of water, although these may not have been permanent. Cladoceran *ephippia* ('water flea' eggs) and freshwater molluscs in the same sample also indicate the presence of water. The remaining plant material would have been from wild plants growing close by; elder and brambles may have been part of a hedgerow. The fig and grape seeds may have blown into the feature or may possibly make up part of a backfill together with the other remains from the sample, which consisted of a few large mammal bones and brick/tile fragments and large amounts of mortar and clinker/coal fragments.

Open Area 6: Old Palace Yard

Open Area 6 is defined as the area to the east and north of Buildings 17 and 20. Levelling layers dumped here consisted of dark grey silty clay, yellow sand R[4] and R[7], black silty clay and a layer of crushed Reigate stone that probably represents demolition material. Layers R[4] and R[7] both contained redeposited human bone, suggesting that the sand had been dug from elsewhere (possibly from the cemetery of Westminster Abbey or St Margaret) and dumped here.

The area to the east of the Parliament House seems to have remained as open land. Sand and Reigate stone chippings were dumped as levelling material, the latter suggesting either chippings from the dressing of Reigate stone blocks for new buildings or the demolition of Reigate stone structures nearby.

A drawing by Leonard Knuyff (1650–1722) shows the

Jewel Tower on the extreme left with the buildings adjoining it being Building 20. To the east lies a formal garden that appears to have had its northern end at the current north end to 6–7 Old Palace Yard and its south end by the Jewel Tower (period 11; Chapter 13.3, Building 31).

Open Area 8

A levelling layer of mottled clay with building material fragments was cut by two pits, one containing chalk fragments and the other a brown mortar layer sealed by a brown organic deposit. All this activity occurred between the demolition of the old south wall of Building 13 and the construction of the new south wall of Building 22.

The new south wall of Building 22 was laid over a dumped layer of green sandy clay with charcoal and pieces of burnt wood. After the construction of Building 22 a green clay layer was dumped as a base for a mortar surface.

Open Area 8 was much reduced in scale during the 17th and early 18th centuries by the encroachment on it for housing. However, its shape as the former northern precinct to Westminster Abbey can still be partly seen on maps of the late 17th century (Fig 89).

Open Area 11

A fourth phase of ditch on the same alignment as that in period 9 may have divided Open Area 11 and Open Area 12 on site E. Only a short length of it survived on the east side, where it was 0.48m wide and 0.17m deep. It was filled with grey sandy clay with oyster shell, animal bone and small quantities of charcoal. A second east–west aligned ditch to the north was 0.60m wide and 0.23m deep. It sloped down to the west as the previous ditches had done and was filled with grey silt with charcoal, oyster shell, brick, tile and mortar. A partially articulated small dog, consisting of three foreleg elements, was recovered from this ditch, E[4/7].

Within Open Area 11 lay a cesspit measuring more than 0.28m x 0.20m and 0.10m deep, containing small quantities of animal bone, ceramic building material, oyster shell and ash. To its east lay a rubbish pit filled with mortar and tile with small quantities of animal bone and brick. A possible necklace, <S47>, dating to the first half of the 16th century and described in Chapter 10.3, was found in a layer dating to this period.

Open Area 11 continued in use as the back garden to a property fronting King Street during the 17th century. These properties were not demolished until the late 18th century.

Open Area 13

An east–west aligned Kentish ragstone wall was built, some 0.75m to the south of the earlier boundary (Chapter 9.3, Open Area 10) but on the west side of site C(ii) rather than the east. It was 0.33m wide and 0.90m long where it entered the western section. Immediately to the south lay well Structure 12, which was either rebuilt or raised in brick during this period.

The houses around Woolstaple Yard were still in use during the early part of the 17th century. By the end of this period, though, there was a large-scale change, with the construction of a new brick building (B23) over the former Open Area 13.

Open Area 14

The primary fill B[159] of pit B[184] comprised grey sandy clay with large quantities of Reigate stone, some roof tile and some copper-alloy objects, including fragments of slag or waste, a piece of sheet and a rim fragment of a residual medieval copper-alloy vessel, <S25>. Subsequent fills also contained large quantities of building material. Most bricks from the pit were dated from the 15th century to *c* 1700, but some from fill B[157] had been reused, and fill B[111] also produced brick dating from after *c* 1670.

Cut into Open Area 14, on site F, was a roughly circular brick well between 1.64m and 1.78m in diameter. The sides of the well were a single brick wide and they were bonded with a cream/white mortar. The bricks and mortar were typical of the 17th century.

Open Area 15

Open Area 15 lay to the west of the Jewel Tower and was probably cut off from the remainder of Open Area 6 by the construction of Building 20.

Levelling to the west of the Jewel Tower moat was cut by a brick wall that may have formed part of a drain at least 0.40m deep. This was, in turn, cut by a rubbish pit containing mortar, ash and charcoal. To the south lay a large rubbish pit dug up against the Jewel Tower moat wall, at least 3.8m long, containing 17th-century brick, tile, mortar and chalk.

Open Area 15 was created by the construction of Building 20 but remained in use as external land, either as a garden or as waste land, much as Open Area 6 had done previously. It seems to have been quite actively used for the digging of pits to dump either construction or demolition material.

12.4 Discussion

The increasing urbanisation of Westminster and the blurring of the boundaries between it and London are evident both in the documentary and the archaeological record although they are clearer in period 11. The encroachment of housing into the northern precincts of the palace and abbey reflects the increasing needs of the general population and the desire for more housing.

The greater activity in terms of building, general archaeological evidence and the reclamation into the Thames within the palace area probably reflects the growing importance of parliament, which, of course, reached its apex during the 1640s. It seems very likely that its increasing role and status directed attention away from Whitehall and back to Westminster.

As can be seen on other sites, reuse of former monastic or monastic-owned buildings is commonplace in the 16th century and rebuilding becomes more common in the 17th century (Thomas et al 1997). The same can be seen to be true of Woolstaple Yard, the houses around which continued in much the same usage after the Woolstaple lost its importance and after Westminster Palace was abandoned as a royal residence. However, by the mid 17th century the houses seem to have been demolished to make way for new brick houses, no doubt more up to date and in the prevailing fashion. For dating evidence, see Table 14.

Table 14 Selected dating evidence, period 10 (see Table 25 for expansion of codes)

Land use	Activity	Context	Evidence	Description	Date range
Building 8	well	J[121]	ceramic	TGW	1630–1700
Building 21	wall	D[47]	ceramic building material	tile 2271; 2276; 2586	1480–1800
Building 22	occupation layer	C[40]	ceramic	FREC	1550–1750
Building 22	make-up layer	C[84]	ceramic	PMR	1600–1800
Building 22	hearth	C[1]	ceramic building material	brick 3046	1450–1700
Building 22	rubbish pit	C[13]	ceramic	PMR; EMFL	1600–1800
Building 23	construction cut	C[251]	ceramic building material	brick 3036; tile 2276; 3115	1600–1800
Building 23	construction cut	C[251]	ceramic	CBW; BEAG; BORD; DUTR; DUTSL; FREC; PMBL	1600–1700
Building 23	cesspit	C[255]	ceramic	TGW	1600–1800
Building 24	floor	N[37]	ceramic	CHPO; PMBL; PMR; RBOR; TGW	1720–1800
Structure 12	construction cut for well	C[250]	ceramic	CHEA; LOND; MG; TUDG; BORD; DUTR; PMBL; RBOR; MPUR	1600–1700
Structure 12	well	C[253]	ceramic building material	brick 3046	1450–1700
Open Area 4: New Palace Yard	drain fill	J[2]	ceramic	TGW	1630–1800
Open Area 4: New Palace Yard	drain	J[3]	ceramic building material	floor tile 8370; brick 5230	1450–1700
Open Area 4: New Palace Yard	surface	D[5]	ceramic building material	brick 2150; 2250	1666–1900
Open Area 8	levelling	C[23]	ceramic	PMR	1600–1800
Open Area 14	pit	B[111]	ceramic building material	brick 3032; 3033	1666–1700

13

c 1740–1834 (period 11)

13.1 Environmental and topographical background

No data were recovered from this period concerning the environmental background or the river regime.

13.2 Documentary and archaeological background

In common with other suburban areas, Westminster expanded dramatically during the 17th and 18th centuries and much of the marshland on the fringes of the settlement was drained and built upon. The Tyburn had, by this period, become known as the Long Ditch along the west side of the former island and was probably little more than a stream. Many streams are shown on late 17th-century maps crossing the northern part of the area and probably entering the Thames a little to the north of modern-day Derby Gate. By the time of Rocque's map of 1746 (Fig 100) the Tyburn had all but disappeared.

The major change in Westminster was the construction of Westminster Bridge in 1750. Designed by Charles Labelye, it cost £400,000 to build. Between 1750 and 1754 Parliament Street and Bridge Street (R3) were laid out to provide better access to it. Horwood's map of *c* 1800 shows Parliament Square, which was created in the latter part of the 18th century (Horwood 1813). Parliament Street remained only half its current width until the 19th century, when King Street was

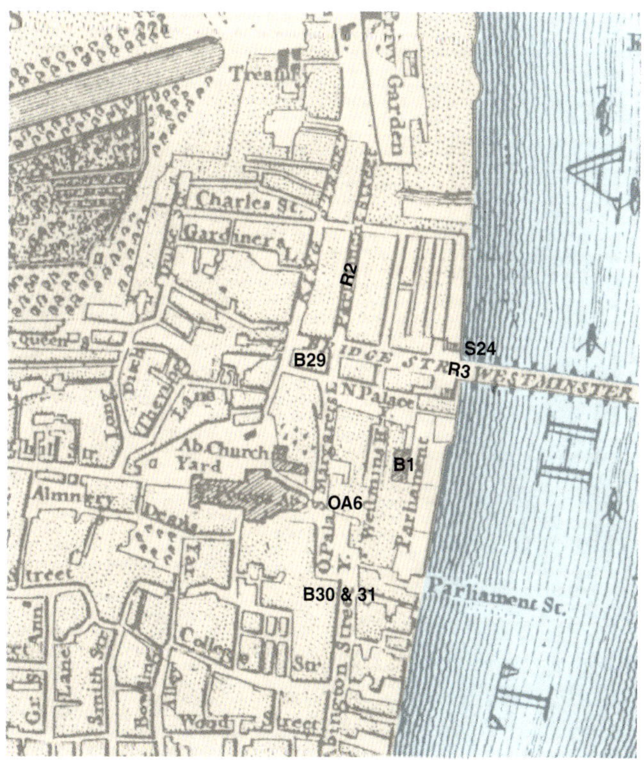

Fig 100 Rocque's map of 1746

demolished to make way for the new government offices and Parliament Street was widened. The original street was defined by houses on its western side (B26 and B27) (Fig 101).

Like Manchester House and Derby House, which became courts of tenements, Dorset House similarly became Dorset Court. In 1764 Dorset Court consisted of 12 tenements lying each side of an internal court running north–south, measuring 99ft 6in along Canon Row. Two other tenements lay in Canon Row adjoining Dorset Court (CWA, acc 1039).

The demolition of the gatehouses allowed wider streets to be created into the palace area. New buildings were constructed on the south and west sides of Old Palace Yard (below, Buildings 30 and 31).

13.3 Archaeological evidence

Building 8: gatehouse to the Green Yard

The gatehouse was clearly still in use at the end of the 17th century as it can be seen on maps of the period (eg, Morgan's map of 1682; Fig 89). However, by the 1740s the new street pattern was laid out in Westminster and the gatehouses were demolished so that the streets could be widened. The well from the previous period was backfilled, probably at this time, with grey mortar.

Building 9

Building 9 was demolished to make way for Buildings 32 and 33.

Building 20

The Parliament House was condemned by parliament in 1754 because of the parlous state of its buildings. It was demolished to make way for 6–7 Old Palace Yard (B31) (Taylor 1965, 16).

Building 21

Building 21 was demolished, probably at some time around the middle of the 18th century when the street pattern was altered and Building 29 was constructed. About 0.5m of material was dumped over the demolished building to level up the ground for Building 29.

Building 22

Two pits were dug within the building: one, which measured 2.55m x 0.90m and was 0.29m deep, contained a mixed grey-brown sandy silty clay with some fragments of building material; the other was a circular rubbish pit, 0.38m in diameter and 0.36m deep, containing a bucket filled with organic sandy clay. Two of the iron hoops from the bucket survived. It contained clay pipe dating to the late 18th or early 19th century.

Building 22 continued in use during the 18th century, probably with a similar function as that in periods 9 and 10. Demolition probably took place in about 1800.

Building 23

Building 23 was demolished when the new Parliament Street was laid out in the 1740s. A layer of demolition debris lay over the cesspit and dumped layers including brick, tile, chalk and mortar lay over room A. Cutting these was a pit filled with gravel.

Building 24

The main deposit overlying the floor in Building 24 was a layer of brick rubble with some chalk and mortar, up to 0.55m thick. This was presumably the remains of the demolished building. Building 24 was demolished to make way for Road 3 in the 1740s.

Building 25

Building 25 was presumably demolished at the same time as Building 24 to make way for Road 3 in the 1740s.

Building 26

Building 26 formed the basement of one of the houses on the west side of Parliament Street before it was widened. The east wall of the house lay along the eastern edge of site C(ii). The southern wall was found dividing it from Building 27. The walls were constructed from red brick and bonded with hard white mortar.

Building 27

Building 27 formed the basement of one of the houses on the west side of Parliament Street before it was widened. The east wall of the house lay along the eastern edge of site C(ii). The northern wall that divided it from Building 26 was found. The walls were constructed from red brick and bonded with hard white mortar.

Building 28

The rendered brick wall of a cellar aligned north–south was found at the southern end of site C(i). To its east lay a tile floor. It was presumably one of the buildings shown on Horwood's map of 1799 on the east side of King Street, south of Union Street, which were demolished in the 19th century when the Square was created (Horwood 1813).

Building 29

Building 29 on site D fronted on to St Margaret Street to the east (Fig 102). The east wall of the building was constructed from

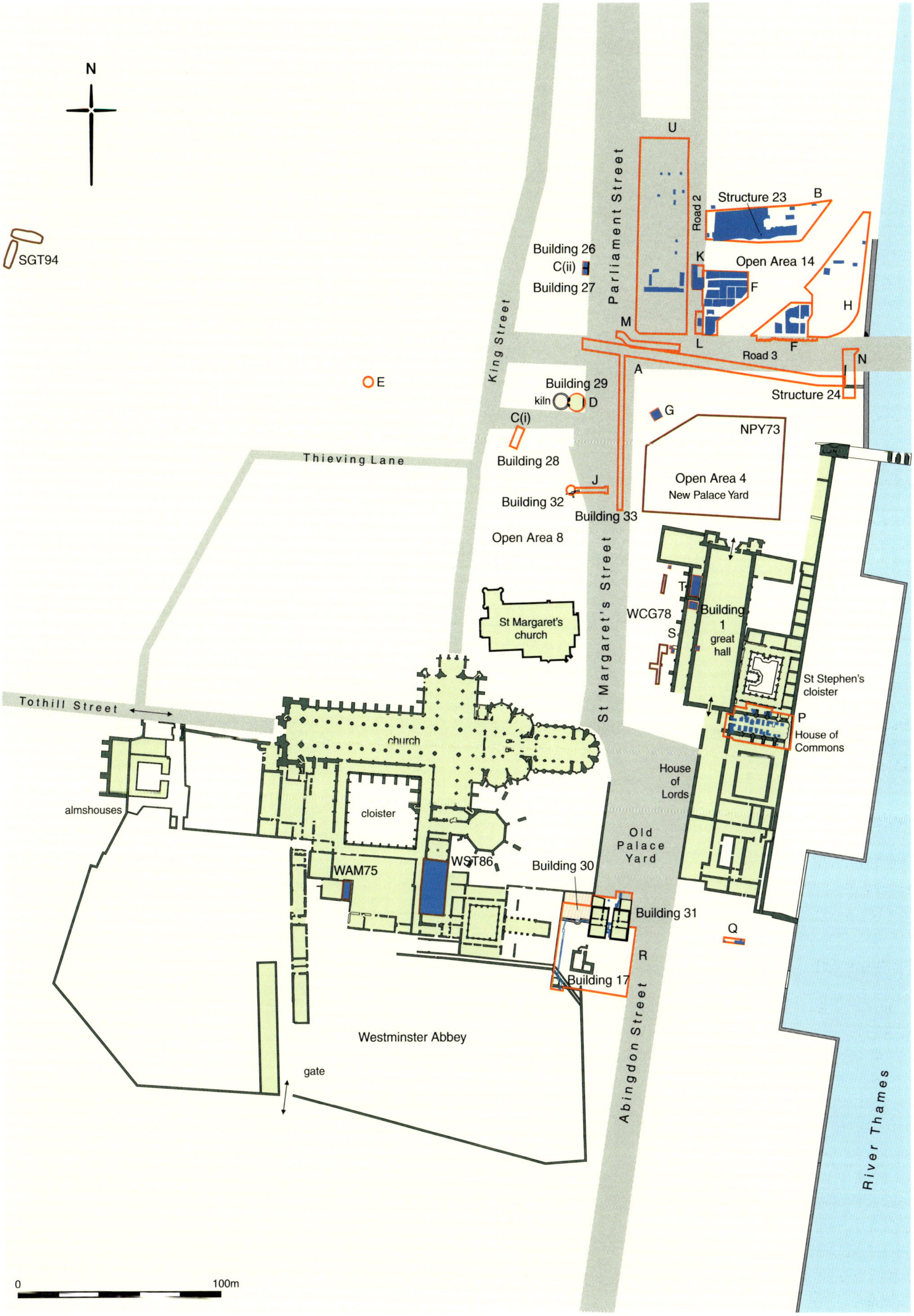

Fig 101 Plan of the archaeological features, period 11 (scale 1:2500). For key to site codes, see Tables 1–3

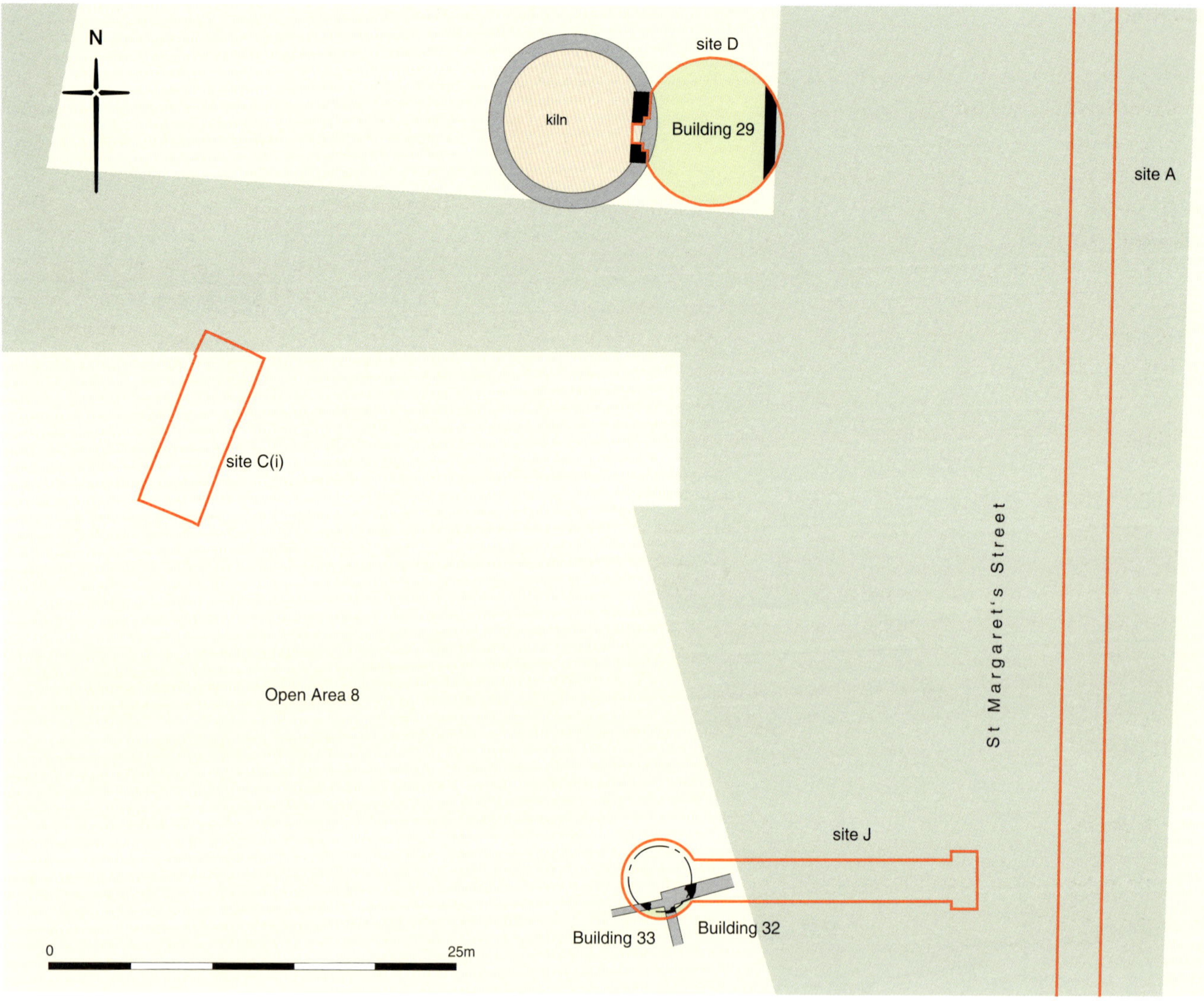

Fig 102 Detailed plan of sites C(i), D and J showing the kiln, Building 29, and Buildings 32–33, period 11 (scale 1:400)

post-1670 red brick bonded with hard white mortar, with a step about 0.15m wide in the foundations. It overlay and reused the east wall of the drain in Open Area 4 (below) as its foundation. The west wall was constructed from red and purple brick 2$^{1}/_{2}$ in (65mm) thick, bonded with hard white mortar and plastered on the inside. The width of the building was about 5.25m.

In the west wall was a recess 1.80m wide and 0.30m deep, leading to an arched opening 1.20m wide and more than 0.60m high. The top of the arch was 0.85m down from ground level. The arch continued westwards for 0.67m before opening out into what was apparently a circular, domed, kiln structure. In the north wall of the opening leading into the kiln was a flue, 0.26m wide, which fed upwards.

Most of the kiln structure lay beyond the limits of the site, so its exact function remains unclear. Its diameter is unknown but it must have been at least 3.0m. There is no evidence as to what was fired in the kiln (assuming that it was not a very large oven).

Building 30: 5 Old Palace Yard

Only parts of the south wall to Building 30 were found on site R. It was constructed from red, purple and yellow brick bonded with hard white mortar. The wall was 0.38m wide. Parts of the remains uncovered indicate a bay on the south side of the building overlooking the Jewel Tower.

Building 31: 6–7 Old Palace Yard

Building 31 survives as a standing building. It is clear, however, that it was originally two structures, separated by a corridor extending the length of the building from north to south. The east wall of this corridor was 0.62m wide and was constructed in red brick and bonded with white mortar. The corridor extended out to the front of the present light wells at the front of the property.

Building 31 was built to replace Building 20 in 1754–6 as the latter had fallen into ruin (Smith 1994, 2). The building originally continued southwards but these parts have now been demolished. The two buildings were intended for the Clerk and Assistant Clerk of the Parliaments with the Clerk probably residing in the eastern house and the Assistant Clerk in the western (Smith 1994, 2).

Building 32

A basement on site J was found with its base lying on the remains of Structure 10 (Fig 102). To its south-west lay Building 33. The two buildings shared a south-east–north-west aligned wall, which was constructed from reused Reigate stone blocks bonded with grey mortar. The wall was 0.56m wide. The north wall of the basement was constructed from red brick and reused Reigate stone blocks bonded with a pale grey mortar and was plastered on its internal face.

Only a small area was found but this appeared to form a building that largely lay to the south-east of the area excavated.

Building 33

Building 33, also on site J, was a basement that lay immediately to the south-west of Building 32 and shared its dividing wall, which was aligned south-east–north-west (Fig 102). The north wall of Building 33 was built from red brick with some reused Reigate stone and sandstone blocks and bonded with pale grey mortar. Some of the bricks had traces of other mortar on them, suggesting they had been reused.

Only a small area was found but this appeared to form a building that largely lay to the south of the area excavated.

Structure 20

Whilst no archaeological evidence for the disuse of Structure 20 was found, cartographic evidence makes it clear that it must have disappeared by this period, if not during the last period.

Structure 23

One feature on site B appeared to be of 18th-century date. This was a severely truncated brick wall on a north–south alignment, which incorporated reused brick dated from the mid to late 15th century to the mid to late 17th century.

Structure 24

On site A, some distance to the east of any other archaeologically recognised features, was a Kentish ragstone wall, bonded with cream mortar, 2.0m across (east–west) with its surface at 6.51m OD. The extent of the wall from north to south is unknown. The western face was 3.10m east of Structure 21.

This is so far east, the masonry is so massive, and the level so high that it is interpreted as being one of the piers of Labelye's Westminster Bridge of 1750.

Road 2: Canon Row

It is likely that at some time during this period an arched brick sewer was laid in Canon Row. A pit and a narrow slot probably date to this period too.

The road may have been realigned at this time, in conformity with its current alignment, although it was probably widened in the 19th century on the east side.

Road 3: Bridge Street

Over the demolition layer in Building 24 a series of levelling layers was dumped. These consisted of a mixed deposit of sand, silt and clay at the base sealed by a layer of brick and tile and a layer of brown silty clay. These were cut by a heavily disturbed 18th-century brick wall. That was in turn sealed by layers of mortar, ash, rubble and gravel, which seemed to be levelling and bedding layers for the road of Bridge Street. Constant relaying and resurfacing of that road had removed any evidence of its original surface.

Open Area 4: New Palace Yard

The brick drain on site D went out of use. The west wall was partly demolished and the floor of the drain robbed out. The drain was backfilled but the east wall was retained as the foundation to the east wall of Building 29. The ground was then levelled up. Site D was, by this time, no longer a part of New Palace Yard. The demolition debris produced a very small and mixed botanical assemblage, with fruits and seeds representing a few wetland plants, for example celery-leaved crowfoot (*Ranunculus sceleratus*), rush (*Juncus* spp) and weeds of disturbed ground, for example, goosefoots (*Chenopodium* spp), stinging nettle (*Urtica dioica*) and black nightshade (*Solanum nigrum*), plus a single charred ?oat (*Avena* sp) grain. Wood and charcoal flecks were also found. Little interpretation may be made on the basis of such a small botanical assemblage: the wild plants may either have been growing in the destruction debris or have been deposited with other rubbish from elsewhere. There was a range of other biological and artefactual debris in the sample, including large and small mammal bone and fish bone, marine molluscs, Cladoceran *ephippia*, brick/tile, mortar, chalk and metal fragments.

On site G evidence was found for 18th-century development on the north side of New Palace Yard. The earliest feature in this phase was a truncated trench on a north-west–south-east alignment. It was 0.30m deep and had been backfilled with loose silt, mortar/plaster and fragments of ceramic building material and Reigate stone. Brick walls were then constructed on the site. These were undoubtedly the cellar walls of houses built along the north side of the Yard when Bridge Street was laid out in the 1740s. These basements were later backfilled with clay and brick and mortar rubble, presumably during the demolition of the buildings in 1854.

Open Area 8

Sealing the mortar surface of period 10 on site C(i) was a mixed levelling layer of orange, brown and green clay with fragments of building material. This was cut by a pit with a clay lining filled with organic material in many very thin layers, suggesting that the pit had filled up over a long period of time. Overlying this was a very thick (more than 0.55m) dumped layer of mottled clay/sand with fragments of building material. This was presumably dumped after the building had gone out of use, although the south wall remained standing. Within the former building a layer more than 0.45m thick of dark brown sandy silty clay with brick fragments was dumped, signalling the disuse of the building. It was cut by two large pits containing brick and mortar rubble.

Open Area 8 continued in use during the later 18th century, although much changed in scale after the laying out of the new streets of St Margaret Street, Parliament Street and Bridge Street. It changed even further during the 19th century when Victorian buildings were constructed, the foundations to two of which were seen on site C(i).

Open Area 14

Two 19th-century glass artefacts were recovered from site B. These were the base of a pale blue rectangular medicinal bottle, <S53>, and a fragment of bright blue vessel glass, <S55>.

13.4 Discussion

The 17th century and particularly the 18th century saw the change in Westminster from being a recognisable settlement in its own right with clearly defined boundaries to becoming engulfed by the suburban sprawl of London. The modern street pattern was to a large extent formed by the end of this period.

The character of Westminster also changed during the 18th century. The abandonment of Whitehall led to parliament staying at Westminster and government being mostly based along Whitehall. The construction of Westminster Bridge, the second crossing of the Thames within central London after London Bridge, also had a major impact not only on Westminster and Lambeth but on London as a whole as communications between the two sides of the river became easier.

The two events that most dramatically changed the appearance of Westminster occur at the end of archaeological activity described in this book. First, the fire at the Palace of Westminster in 1834 destroyed or severely damaged much of the medieval palace, and these buildings (except the great hall, the lower storey of St Stephen's chapel, the cloister and the Jewel Tower) were swept away to make room for Barry's neo-Gothic palace. Second, the embankment, which houses the London Underground District and Circle lines, was constructed. This reclaimed about 35m of the river, creating a uniform river front to the north and south of Barry's new palace.

Table 15 Selected dating evidence, period 11 (see Table 25 for expansion of codes)

Land use	Activity	Context	Evidence	Description	Date range
Building 23	make-up layer	C[245]	ceramic	PMR	1600–1800
Building 31: 6–7 Old Palace Yard			documentary	Smith 1994, 2	1754–6
Road 3: Bridge Street	levelling	N[5]	ceramic	BORDY; LONS; PMR; TGW	1670–1750
Open Area 4: New Palace Yard	destruction debris	J[4]	ceramic	SWSG; TGW	1730–70
Open Area 14	levelling	B[3]	ceramic	TPW; TWG; SWSG; PMR; PMSL; STSL	1720–1800

14

Westminster: a review of the data

14.1 A review of the environment and topography of Westminster and the changing river levels

This section attempts to draw together and summarise the information collected for this project and available in the literature that has been presented in the narrative sections above. In many ways, ecological and topographical data are sometimes difficult to match exactly with an archaeological narrative; significant developments in the fluvial or vegetational history do not always occur within periods based on human activity defined by archaeologists. Often, ecological change and, more frequently, fluvial change are governed by factors such as climate change and tectonic shift rather than by anthropogenic causes. Nevertheless, the human story is intertwined with landscape history as both recipient and often partial instigator of the effects of fluvial and ecological change. It is for this reason that the geomorphology of Thorney Island during the Holocene has been included within this archaeological study and, more widely, within the research along the route of the Jubilee Line Extension (Sidell et al 2000).

The Early Holocene template

Very little direct evidence is available for the appearance of the area in the Early Holocene. However, the dataset for central London has grown significantly during the last few years, with evidence gathered mainly from deposits deeply buried in the tributary valleys of the Thames (Lewis 1991; Scaife et al in prep; Wilkinson et al in prep) and from palaeochannels cut during the Late Devensian, which were subsequently abandoned and gradually filled with organic detritus (Thomas and Rackham 1996; Wilkinson et al 2000). Ecological data from these sites suggest that the advent of the Holocene saw a cold open landscape cut through the centre by a relatively high-energy, shallow, freshwater river, with several channels traversing a wide flood plain probably interspersed with sand and gravel bars. The Tyburn would have been cutting down to the level of the Thames, probably also following a braided course, with the level of the river in the order of -6.0m OD. A further significant point to note about the Early Holocene landscape is that, based on the available evidence, there was no Thorney Island. The river curved in the general area it does now, although somewhat to the south, but the island is not thought to have been present as perhaps anything other than a slightly raised gravel bar.

Vegetation would have been limited; it is unlikely that much, if anything, grew on the flood plain and gravel bars. A scrubby tundra-like cover should be envisaged on the higher ground away from the flood plain, perhaps on the gravel terrace to the north and west of Westminster. Initially, the species in question would have included pine (*Pinus*), juniper (*Juniperus*) and willow (*Salix*), with alder (*Alnus*) and reedmace (*Typha*) as constituent parts of the wetland group (MoLAS 2000, 20). The climate warmed relatively rapidly and tree cover would have developed on the gravel terrace away from the flood plain, with an increase in species such as pine and birch (*Betula*); inhabitants such as reindeer and horse would have given way to red deer and aurochsen.

There is similarly no direct evidence from the Westminster area for a human presence at this date. Nevertheless, from some of the tributary valleys, such as the River Colne in west London (MoLAS 2000, 49), there is evidence for Late Upper Palaeolithic/Early Mesolithic activity. Furthermore, recent work in north Southwark and Lambeth (Sidell et al 2002), just across the river from Westminster, has shown that there was a contemporary human presence here in what was a very different landscape 10,000 years ago.

The earliest environment

Unfortunately, no evidence has yet been recovered from Westminster relating to contemporary Mesolithic ecology. A great opportunity was missed when the site at Richmond Terrace was examined in 1983 (Andrews and Merriman 1986), and deposits thought to date to the Mesolithic period were found. At the time, environmental archaeology was less of a standard tool than it is today, which may account, in part at least, for this oversight. It is the sites excavated along the Jubilee Line that have contributed the most to the biological and geomorphological reconstruction of the area. The earliest evidence, however, dates to the Neolithic/Bronze Age transition, leaving roughly five thousand years unaccounted for since the end of the Devensian cold stage. During this period, data from elsewhere indicate that the progression from the tundra-like cover to a more wooded landscape had resulted in a temperate mixed woodland consisting of oak (*Quercus*), hazel (*Corylus*), elm (*Ulmus*), lime (*Tilia*) and alder (*Alnus*). This situation continued unchanged until roughly 4500 cal BC when a widely recognised decline in elm occurred across southern England (Scaife 1988). Though this was not synchronous everywhere, it does appear in London relatively contemporaneously in most pollen profiles of the appropriate date. It is unfortunate that the pollen record from the Westminster sites indicates that it has been just missed on all sites. This may be as a result of Early Holocene truncation, although another possibility is that sediment simply was not accreting here at this date. The elm decline is thought to have occurred as a mixture of human and parasitic factors, notably that initial opening up of this woodland cover enabled the elm bark beetle, *Scolytus scolytus*, to transfer with greater facility a parasite that attacked elm trees (Girling 1988). This led to a significant change in the appearance of the woodland cover, with a different composition and generally less woodland presence. By this time, too, the flood plain would have appeared less bare, with the river margins vegetated, soils over the previously exposed gravel and relict channels filling with organic debris.

During this period, Thorney Island was forming and would have developed from one of many bars into a fixed focal raised position in the flood plain by the end of the Neolithic. It seems unlikely that the island was densely vegetated; the pollen record collected from Neolithic/Bronze Age transitional deposits indicates local oak woodland, but this could be on the gravel terrace located to the north and west. The eyot at this time would have been surrounded by a freshwater river at approximately -2.5m OD, flowing more deeply and slowly than in the Mesolithic. The Tyburn stream would also have flowed up to and around Thorney Island, which would have formed part of a deltaic complex at the confluence of the two rivers. Although this was a period of rising sea levels, the Thames and Tyburn here were both freshwater at this date. Nevertheless, as the gradient to the sea gradually became shallower, there is likely to have been a small effect upon river levels relative to the land.

The margins of the rivers were fringed with marshy deposits, including alder carr and sedge fen. Although this marshy element persisted and the rivers were less easily fordable than in the Palaeolithic and Mesolithic, the Thorney Island area would have held attractions for the human population, particularly from the end of the Neolithic when it stabilised, which may in fact have happened slightly earlier (but after 3000 cal BC). Islands are well known as 'ritually charged' places (Brown 1997, 288), with river valleys having exerted strong spiritual significance on prehistoric human populations (Bradley 2000, 8). In addition to a good defensible territory with a substantial water supply, the biological evidence indicates that many raw materials such as timber for building and fuel were close by, along with the marshlands supplying reeds and rushes for thatch and fodder, as well as the animals living wild, in the woods, marshes and indeed the rivers. Finally, the river itself, which was navigable to communities with boats, would have been a further incentive. Although no Neolithic boat has yet been identified in London, the technology is known from other parts of Britain and Europe. Moreover, river valleys provide clearly focused routeways, and in the Early Holocene the Thames valley would have led far out into the North Sea basin and down to the confluence with the Rhine, thus opening additional paths into Continental Europe.

Clearance and cultivation

Central London was sparsely populated in the Early Neolithic, and the new information from Thorney Island makes a strong case for suggesting that in part this may be because of the instability of the flood plain and the eyots that were still forming. Nevertheless, there do appear to have been cultural factors that led the contemporary human groups to prefer the gravel plains of west London and the terrace/flood plain margins of east London. This could have been as a result of tradition, or from a desire to use an area previously inhabited (the monuments of west London, for example, may have provided a spiritual link to ancestral groups) or simply because the land and available resources made for an easier life. Whatever the reasons were (and almost certainly they were a combination of environmental and behavioural), the area around Westminster and Southwark suddenly became much more important at the end of the Neolithic, and reasons for this must be sought.

A likely consequence of the establishment of sedentary existence and the production of food surpluses is an increase in population; starvation and death through malnutrition are less likely, as is death through the accidents associated with a mobile hunter-gatherer community. Furthermore, with an organised society, there may be more time available for purposes other than simply seeking food, water and shelter, time which can then be used for artistic, spiritual and also war-like pursuits.

As a population grows, a requirement for additional land to grow more crops and raise more stock is created, as is a need for additional living space. If this is assumed for the Late Neolithic communities in both east and west London (where evidence for farming societies has been found), then it is logical to see the increase in population in central London as an incursion arising from this chain of events. Furthermore, by this point the sand eyots had stabilised and soils developed on them. Although it is not possible to be entirely sure, the islands appear to have covered several hectares at the beginning of the Bronze Age, shortly after which the western end of the large Southwark Island at Hopton Street (Ridgeway 1999) was taken into cultivation.

As has been mentioned elsewhere, the direct evidence for cultivation on Thorney Island is not conclusive. Possible ard marks were observed in section at site P and are considered by stratigraphic association to date to the Bronze Age. The ecological record is of assistance here. The second major denudation in the vegetational succession occurs in the mid Bronze Age when the native lime, *Tilia cordata*, decreases drastically in pollen spectra across London (MoLAS 2000, 23). This is considered to be the period when large-scale forest clearance takes place to allow more land to be acquired for farming and settlement. It has been observed in all the contemporary pollen spectra collected across Thorney Island and at Storey's Gate (Fig 103), indicating that the area formed part of the central London farming concern and supporting the inference from the putative ard marks that the island itself was cultivated. In addition to the evidence for large-scale clearance of the remaining woodland (although it was only partial clearance: stands of oak forest should be envisaged as relict traces of the earlier woodland cover) the pollen spectra also include cereal and associated weeds. It is not possible to identify which cereals were being cultivated, although it seems likely that wheat (*Triticum* sp) was being grown, with (albeit limited) evidence from site L for this.

It is in fact surprising, in view of the way other prominent places were treated at this date, such as the Fennings Wharf barrow, the Nine Elms foreshore and the Phoenix Wharf burnt mound (Sidell et al 2002), that no evidence of Bronze Age ritual has yet been found on Thorney Island. As discussed throughout this volume, Thorney Island would have been a prominent point within the flood plain at this date, yet it does not appear, on the current evidence, to have played any part in ritual tradition. Still, the small-scale nature of the investigations, particularly on the higher ground, does not preclude the possibility that the island was in fact a special place in the broader landscape at this date.

Transition to a tidal river

It is in the mid Bronze Age that the ritual activity mentioned above might occur; this is the date when the biological record indicates that the tidal head migrated upstream beyond Thorney Island. There is a school of thought that holds that the timber structure on the Vauxhall foreshore, just across the Thames, was used in ritual practices, possibly as a result of the rising waters (Sidell et al 2002). The evidence from Thorney Island suggests that the tidal head migrated upstream relatively rapidly, at approximately 5.0m per year. For a community accustomed to a river that flowed in one direction only, getting used to seeing it begin to flow first one way and then the other, as well as watching its level rise, must have been an unsettling process, especially as the size of the island would consequently shrink. The added complication of the tidal range would contribute to a feeling of instability. Early on, the tidal range is likely to have been quite small, possibly less than a metre or so, but on a gently sloping foreshore this would have still have meant that large areas of previously stable land would have been submerged at high tide.

The diatom evidence shows that the initial tidal signal was strong, with assemblages of outer estuary diatoms. It is not possible to be sure exactly when the tidal head reached Westminster: it was by *c* 1200 cal BC at least, but may have been a few hundred years earlier. Owing to the very ephemeral evidence for human occupation of Thorney Island, it is not possible to gauge accurately the human response to the encroachment by the Thames, and indeed by the Tyburn as well. However, the data from Lambeth and Southwark suggest that the area was abandoned when the low-lying fields were inundated. If the community that farmed the south bank of the river was the same as that which apparently cultivated Thorney Island then it seems likely that environmental pressure in the form of rising waters drove the occupants of this area away as well. And yet continued examination of the diatom record indicates that subsequent to this, the tidal head actually migrated downstream, resulting in less encroachment on Late Bronze Age/Early Iron Age Thorney Island. It is not possible to establish exactly what the conditions would have been like. There may have been a slight tidal effect, like there is at modern Teddington even though the water is fresh rather than brackish, as is the case in the sedimentary record at Westminster for this date. Quite why this happened is unknown, and in fact is one of the biggest enigmas in the Holocene history of the Thames. It could be associated with crustal movement or with actual sea-level change. This seems less likely since an actual drop in sea level is not postulated elsewhere around southern England at this date. It is certainly a case for further analysis. The irony of course is that the area need not have been consistently abandoned, for in the Iron Age the effect of the river on Thorney Island would have been negligible.

It seems likely that cultural factors played a major part in the

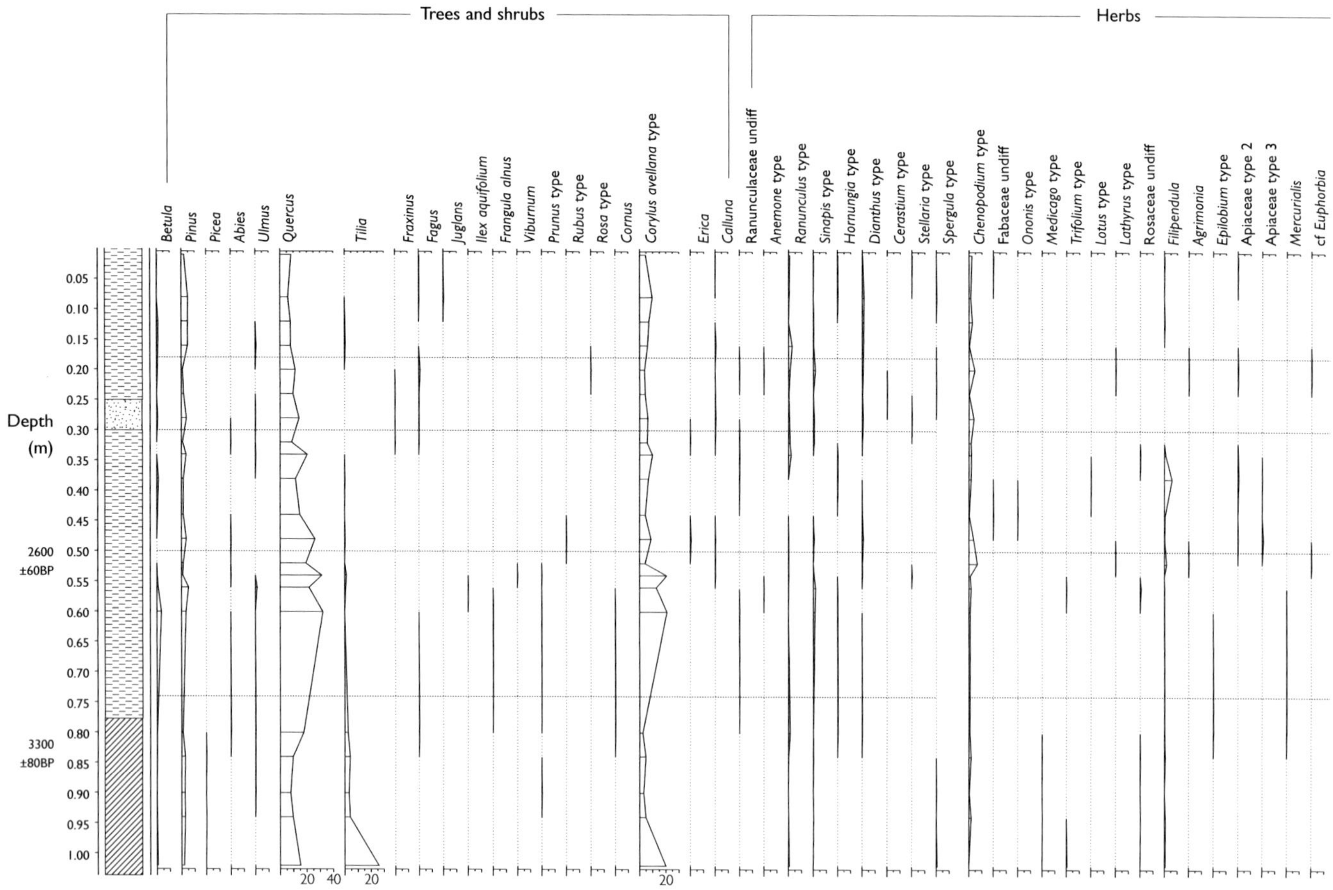

Fig 103 Pollen diagram from Storey's Gate

choice of Iron Age communities to eschew the central London flood plain – it was not simply environmentally derived. A likely consequence of the depopulation, however, is the regeneration of woodland. Without a substantial community requiring land for fields, pasture and homes, cleared areas would not have been maintained, and oak forest, still present in pockets in the Bronze Age, is likely to have expanded. The very limited evidence from Thorney Island, at New Palace Yard (Greig 1992), indicates an Iron Age woodland with limited arable cultivation in the region of Storey's Gate, but it is uncertain how extensive these fragments of the landscape were.

Another factor that makes this part of the story difficult to unravel is the break in sedimentation at this date. Most of the Iron Age, Roman, Saxon and early medieval deposits are 'missing' from sites on the margins of the island. The nature of the hiatus is such that it has proved impossible to establish whether this occurred in one event, or many. Nevertheless, there must have been a major event or significant change in riverine patterns in the early medieval period that led, in whole or in part, to massive removal of sediment.

A Roman and Saxon satellite

The history of the river at this date cannot yet be established from evidence collected from Thorney Island; the erosion mentioned above destroyed all contemporary sediments from the excavated sites. The deposits on the top of the eyot are terrestrial and therefore uninformative about the fluvial history of the Thames and Tyburn. From elsewhere in London it is known that, during the Roman period, the tidal head continued its downstream migration, passing through the Roman city of Londinium (Brigham 1990), and coming upstream once again in the late Roman period. The downstream progression is a continuation of the trend noted at the end of the Bronze Age. Again, what leads to the reversal is unknown, but is almost certainly linked to wider issues such as relative sea-level rise or complex estuarine processes. It is not considered to be associated with Roman encroachment on the flood plain margins. There would have been tidal processes acting here, at least from the mid Saxon period, but perhaps not in the Roman and Early Saxon period. This possible lack of tidal processes, and thus of the benefits to be derived from being within the tidal range, is perhaps a reason why the area may be only thinly occupied in the Roman period, at least.

Although only limited activity has been noted for the Roman period, Thorney Island, which was peripheral to Londinium, was taken into cultivation once again. Doubtless the period of abandonment would have meant an initial phase of clearance once the establishment of the settlement had occurred. This has been noted in the pollen record from New Palace Yard (Greig 1992), although it has not been tightly dated and is described only as 'Roman'. Nevertheless, the imposition

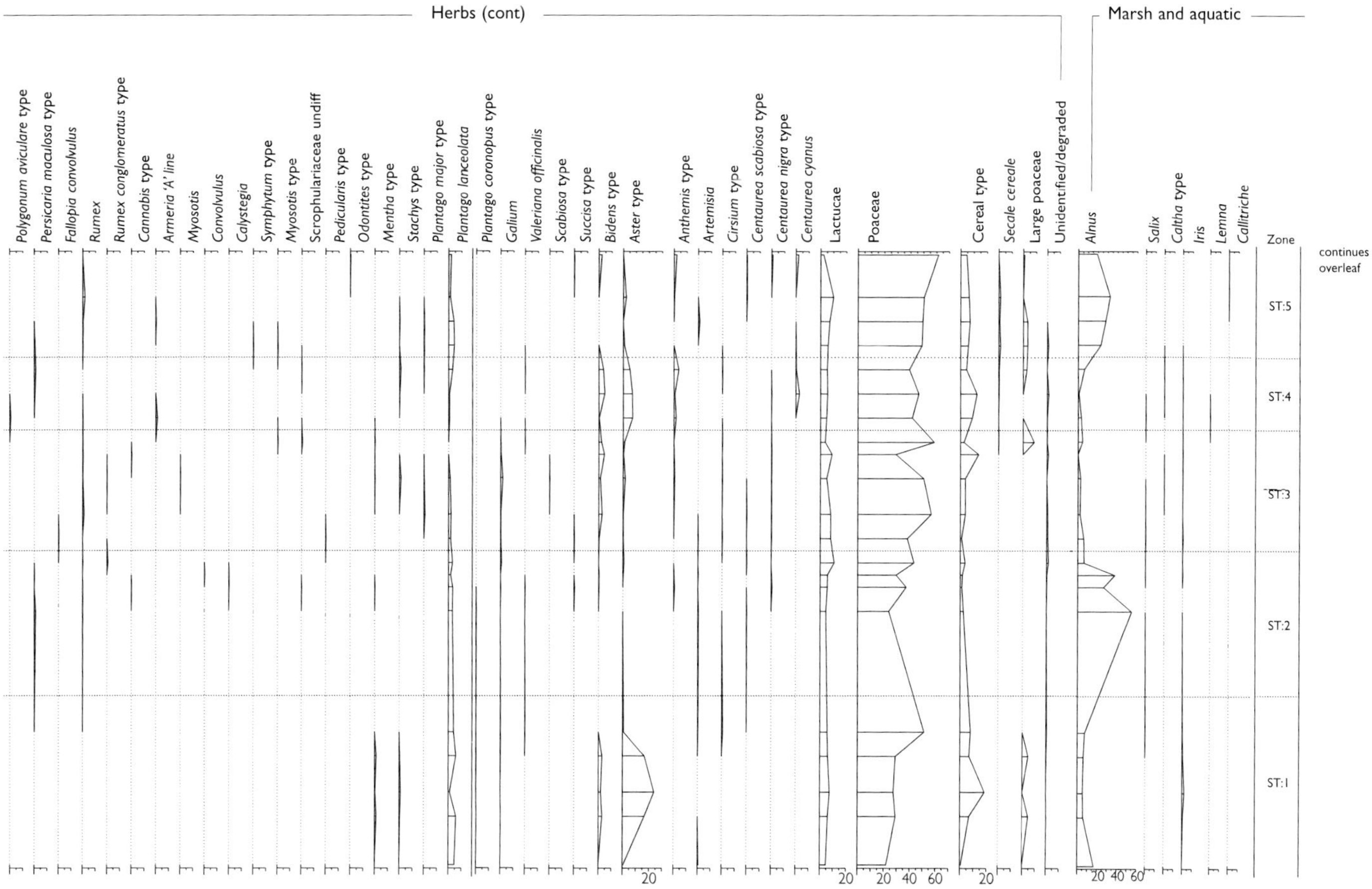

Fig 103 (cont)

of a substantial town in an area previously only sparsely populated would have required major changes to supply the new population adequately with sufficient food and it would have been common sense to cultivate the land peripheral to the town. Thorney Island would have been a relatively large, well-defined block of land with a good supply of fresh water, this making perfect sense for arable cultivation or stock raising. Woodland clearance would have been required, timber from which would consequently have provided material for the construction of the new town, as well as fuel to provide warmth for the population and heat for industrial processes. Indeed, it may have arisen the other way around: following woodland removal to build the town, the area was taken into cultivation to feed it.

The change from the Roman to the Saxon way of life impinged noticeably on the landscape. Initially, there was an hiatus; at some point, probably fairly late in the Roman period, when the emphasis was laid upon rural rather than urban situations, the field systems around Thorney Island were abandoned. As happened after the Bronze Age withdrawal from the area, the open landscape was once more gradually encroached upon by woodland. One change that is not associated with human intervention is the increase in alder carr fringing the island as a result of the rising waters noted above, dating to the end of the Roman/Early Saxon period. Interestingly, one part of the tree cover was lime (*Tilia*), which until this date had not been seen in quantity since the clearance of lime in the mid Bronze Age. This, when taken in conjunction with the rise in marshy conditions, shows that the Early Saxon environment was directly comparable with the pre-agricultural situation found in the Early Bronze Age: an interesting perspective on the regenerative powers of natural ecology versus the impact of the human species on its environment.

Nevertheless, some evidence for Early Saxon cultivation is apparent, though obviously on a much smaller scale than under the Roman administration, doubtless linked to a smaller population locally and a more self-sufficient society in comparison with the great consumer centre of Londinium. Pasture has been identified, as has the possible cultivation of watercress in conjunction with the more conventional cereal cultivation. As well as this broadening of food types in the historic period, additional species were added to the indigenous spectra, notably walnut (*Juglans*), probably grown both for the nuts and the wood itself, or as an ornamental species.

Erosion, reclamation and urbanisation

It is with the advent of the medieval period that Westminster comes into its own as a dominant political centre. The river had, by this time, become fully tidal at Westminster, with a tidal range probably in the order of *c* 3.0m in the 12th century (Milne and Milne 1982, 61, for work at Trig Lane). The massive

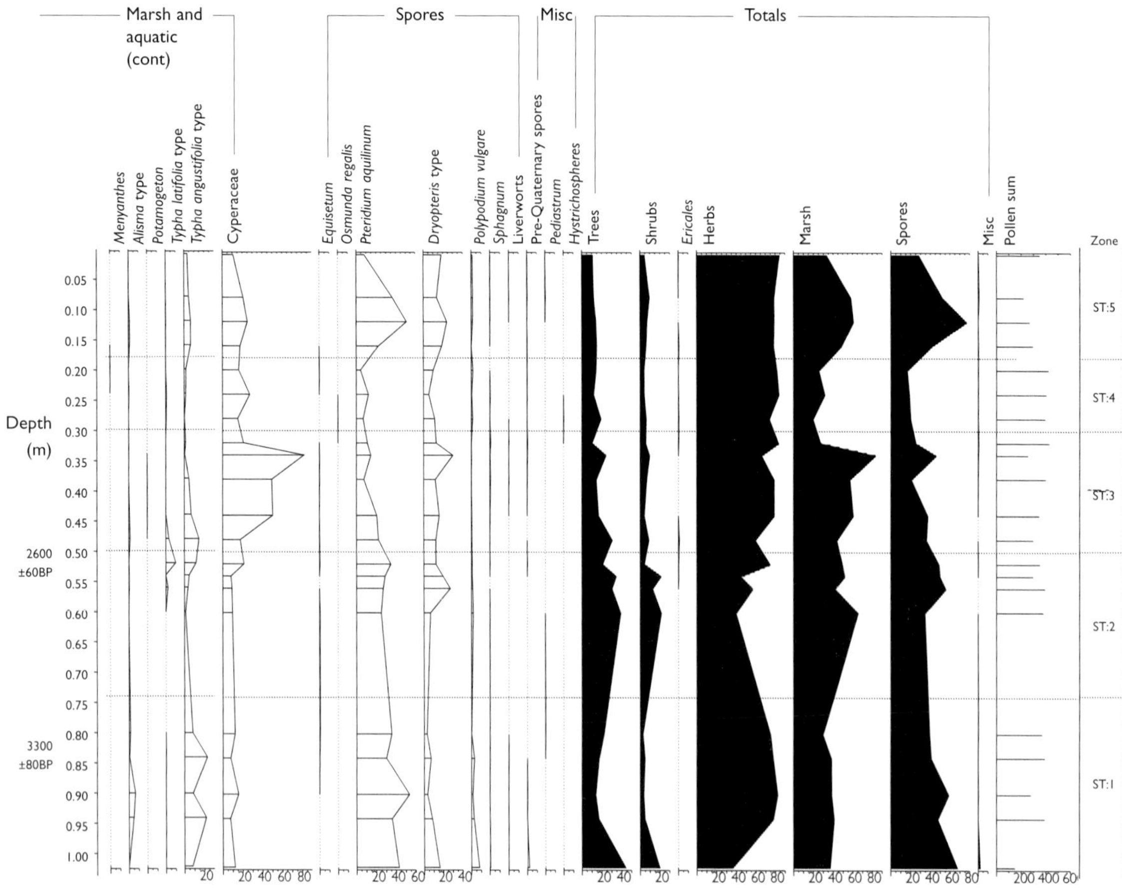

Fig 103 (cont)

hiatus, either wholly or in part dating to the early medieval period, indicates that the river was undergoing substantial change. This may be partly associated with the construction of London Bridge, the massive piers of which practically halved the width of the river, leading to a weir effect, backing up waters behind it (Watson et al 2001). A knock-on effect would be to change previously established patterns of scouring. Further aspects such as land reclamation and increased revetting are likely to have altered the Thames/Tyburn regime yet more by constricting the channels and changing their courses. In combination with this, relative sea level is known to have followed a steadily rising trend from the end of the Late Saxon period, perhaps contributing to the erosion and flooding identified across Thorney Island from the early medieval period onward. The evidence from this project (sites C(i), D and J) and from under Westminster Abbey (eg, Mills 1995 and Black 1976) of substantial deposition of silt in the mid 11th century on the higher ground of Thorney Island indicates that there was a period of major flooding, which may have been responsible for the erosion along the foreshore.

The process of urbanisation makes detailed ecological reconstruction difficult as anthropogenic activity means that it is not always possible to differentiate between managed and wild ecology. However, there are certain clear points. Initially, woodland was retained to a degree, and, in fact, some softwood plantations seem to have been established, perhaps to supply the rebuilding of the town. The data are ambiguous with reference to the presence of actual field systems: crops were certainly processed on the island, but the fields may have been further away, perhaps nearer Storey's Gate, where some evidence was recovered. This seems more likely than local cultivation considering that the area was more important than it had ever been before, so that land would have been at a premium, particularly as fairly unproductive salt marsh was taking up some areas close to the waterfront.

By the later medieval period and into the post-medieval, the ecological signal is hopelessly confused. What seems likely is that deforestation was total, so as to provide as much land as possible for new buildings, roads, yards and so on. There were probably some ornamental and garden trees/plants remaining, such as box (*Buxus*) and fruit trees, but certainly no relict stands of the wildwood. Marshy areas would have remained present on any unrevetted river margins, and vegetation would have fringed open areas and ditches, but these would have been scrubby weeds. It seems very unlikely that anything other than fruit was cultivated locally by the end of the medieval period.

Summary

The ecological history of Thorney Island has developed in a fairly cyclical pattern, directly associated with the needs of the human societies occupying the area throughout the late prehistoric and historic periods. Land was required on several occasions in order to create settlements and produce food, and woodland was therefore removed. In the hiatus between occupation from the Iron Age to Roman, Roman to Saxon and then finally into the medieval period, the natural woodland was tenacious enough to regenerate, providing timber and other resources to assist the development of the urban centre. The history of the river owes less to the impact of the human population; it was the reverse rather, in that it was people who were affected by the river. The first progression of the tidal head up to and beyond Westminster may well have led to the abandonment of the area in the Late Bronze Age. The subsequent retreat of the waters and emergence of land do not appear to have been exploited by the local population. The changes in the medieval period, probably a combination of marine/estuarine processes, river defences and bridging, led to drastic alterations in the fluvial regime, causing flooding and scouring on an unprecedented scale. The story of human occupation of Thorney Island is one where the development of human society has been intricately interwoven with topographical change.

14.2 The town of Westminster

Westminster in the medieval period

In the Saxo-Norman period Westminster was very much isolated from the City of London and existed as an outlying settlement. Indeed it may have been partly for this reason that Edward the Confessor found the site so attractive (Brooke and Keir 1975, 26), although the new archaeological evidence from Structure 4 (Chapter 6.3) casts some doubt upon the theory that Edward first settled the site as a residence.

By the 14th century, the road from London to Westminster was built up from end to end. It had almost certainly existed in the Saxon and possibly in the Roman period. This road, King Street, led northwards from Westminster to join the Strand and Fleet Street. By the later medieval period it was lined with both tenements and more major houses. The major houses were invariably on the river side, presumably as this granted them many benefits, particularly access. North of Thorney Island against the river lay York House (the London residence of the bishops of York), to the north of which lay Scotland Yard (given to the kings of Scotland, although it is unclear whether or not it was ever used). At the junction of King Street and the Strand was the Hospital of St Mary Rounceval. Along the Strand lay the London residences of the bishops of Durham, Lincoln and Norwich, followed by the Savoy, the home of Edward the Black Prince and later the site of the Savoy Hospital, which was founded by Henry VII.

The town of Westminster ended at the bars, which were situated where King Street crossed the Tyburn, by this time called the Clowson stream (a little to the south of where modern-day Downing Street now lies). Much of the town was owned by either the abbey or the palace and it may be that all of it was originally in their possession. A succession of fine houses was constructed along the eastern side of the street, mirroring the wealthy residences along the Thames to the north. The northernmost was Almayne, built in c 1234 by Richard, earl of Cornwall, brother of Henry III. Further south, houses were built for royal servants, especially clerks. This land eventually became the residence of the earls of Kent. By the later medieval period, properties facing directly on to the street included inns, alehouses, shops and houses used by a wide variety of tradesmen.

To the north-west of Westminster lay the open fields now covered by St James's Park. In the approximate location now covered by St James's Palace lay St James's Hospital, a leper hospital founded in about 1100. Another hospital, somewhere in the vicinity of St Martin in the Fields, catered for the insane. This was closed in 1403 on the orders of Henry IV, allegedly because the noise of the insane irritated him (Knowles and Hadcock 1971, 369). It may have been at around this time that St Mary Bethlehem began to cater for the insane (Thomas et al 1997, 126).

To the west of Westminster lay Tothill Street, all of which lay off Thorney Island. The Tyburn stream lay to its south and the road must have crossed it some way further to the west, beyond which lay open countryside. Tothill Street itself was reached from Thorney Island by a bridge that led to the abbey gate and to Thieving Lane, which followed the line of the abbey precinct. Tothill Street contained houses and inns on the north side, one being the Sun Inn at the beginning of the 17th century (Schofield 1987). On the south side of the street lay the Westminster Abbey almonry, bounded by the Tyburn stream on both its western and southern sides. It was run by the abbey almoner and had buildings in which pilgrims and travellers could stay. It may have had shops and other tenements fronting the street which were leased out.

The area to the south of Westminster was marshland created by the Tyburn and its neighbour, the Westbourne. The occasional gravel eyot may have had some form of occupation but most of this land was open fields throughout the medieval period. The area was known as Tothill Fields. The name Tothill is thought to be derived from 'toot hill', a Saxon phrase meaning an area of high ground that could be used for a beacon. The fields were used for tournaments, pasture for cattle and for growing vegetables. The land would have been particularly suitable for cultivation as it was likely to have been regularly flooded. This might also have meant that the area would have regularly been marshy and unsuitable for occupation until the land was drained. According to Stow, in 1256 John Mansell, the king's councillor, invited the kings and queens of England and Scotland, numerous barons and citizens, and the bishop of London to a feast at his house in Tothill Street but there were so many guests that he had to erect tents and pavilions in the fields to accommodate them all (Stow 1987, 421). A horse burial ground was sited near to the horse ferry, which crossed the river to Lambeth (Cowie and Pipe 1999).

Westminster in the post-medieval period

The principal change in the 16th and 17th centuries was the amalgamation of the distinct properties to the north of Thorney Island into Whitehall Palace. Most of this lay to the north of the island and stretched up on both sides of the street to the former kings of Scotland's house. This general layout remained until the 18th century.

The area to the west along Tothill Street was already relatively well built up during the medieval period. The main change to this area occurred in the 17th century, by which time the Tyburn streams had been canalised and had almost disappeared. The marshy fields to the south of Westminster were drained and used for housing. This was very extensive by the end of the 17th century, as shown on Morgan's map, whilst the area to the north-west of Westminster remained as open land as, in the form of St James's Park, it still does today.

During the 18th century, as common to many districts of London, widespread changes were made involving the laying out of new wide streets and squares and the formation of distinct parks. Examples of these streets are Parliament Street, Bridge Street and Birdcage Walk; squares such as Smith Square were built and St James's Park was created by the early 19th century between Westminster, Birdcage Walk, the Mall and Buckingham Palace.

The only other area into which Westminster could be extended was the Thames and, as with all other riverside areas of central London, extensive reclamation was carried out to gain more land. The main alteration to Westminster's relationship to its surroundings was the building in 1750 of Westminster Bridge, which linked Westminster to Lambeth. This was the first bridge after London Bridge to cross the Thames in central London and was vehemently opposed by the lightermen and boatmen of the Thames. Once built, it opened up many other opportunities for the Thames to be crossed, and linked communities in a way previously not possible.

14.3 Westminster Abbey

Origins and development

A Saxon abbey?

Chapter 6 summarises the evidence for a Saxon church on the site. In short, there is no archaeological evidence for such a building and the documentary evidence must be treated with caution; Westminster Abbey was notorious as a centre of forgery in the late 11th and 12th centuries (Brooke and Keir 1975, 369). However, in some cases these documents were merely forged by the abbey when they were attempting to provide written documentation for their lands for which no written documentation existed. The lack of archaeological evidence for a Saxon minster should also be treated with caution as this may reflect rather the lack of modern archaeological excavation under the abbey, where a Saxon minster would be sited. Saxon finds have been made, including pottery, coins and a stone sarcophagus. This sarcophagus was Roman but into its lid is carved a cross, which is thought to have been made during the Saxon period (Poole 1870, 123). The level of the sarcophagus suggests that it must have been laid in its final position after the rebuilding of the abbey in the 13th century. It seems highly unlikely that it was reused twice, suggesting that either the cross is medieval or that the lid comes from a Saxon coffin, and was reused with a Roman sarcophagus to inter a 13th- to 15th-century man.

The generally accepted interpretation now is that there may have been a Saxon minster (a church with parochial duties) on Thorney Island dating to the mid or later 8th century, possibly founded in AD 785 by Offa. Its location would presumably have been a response to the growth of the nearby settlement of Lundenwic.

From minster to monastery: Dunstan's refoundation

Westminster Abbey was founded or refounded by St Dunstan, archbishop of Canterbury, on land made available by King Edgar. Traditionally a date of AD 959 has been ascribed to this (Chapter 6.2) but the foundation charter says AD 951, although it refers to Dunstan as archbishop rather than bishop, which makes a date after AD 960 preferable (Rosser 1989, 13). One author has set a date of *c* AD 971, after the meeting at Easter AD 970 when Edgar was said to have ordered the foundation of 40 new monasteries (Sullivan 1994, 57). In any case, the founding or refounding of the abbey is clearly to be associated with the monastic reforms of Dunstan and the land it was on was in the grant of King Edgar. The abbey was described (after its rebuilding by Edward the Confessor) as having been small (*monasteriolum*) and inhabited by 12 monks.

The site of this church is, like any previous minster, likely to have been under the site of the present church. Its form is unknown. As discussed in Chapter 6, the timber building found beneath the abbey misericord, previously attributed to this foundation, now seems much more likely to have been a temporary building built during Edward the Confessor's rebuilding of the abbey.

Royal patronage: Edward the Confessor's new abbey

Building work on the new abbey at Westminster began in the 1050s and was probably more or less complete by the consecration in 1065 (Fig 104). The claustral ranges are thought to have been completed by Abbot Gilbert Crispin in about 1100, when the west range was finished (Robinson 1910). The style is considered to be based largely upon that at Jumièges in Normandy, an abbey with which Edward the Confessor was well acquainted. The effect of the construction of this new church upon the architectural style in England must have been enormous.

A major piece of research in recent years has resulted in the

Fig 104 Section of the Bayeux Tapestry, showing Edward the Confessor surveying the completed abbey from his palace (© Reading Museum Services, Reading Borough Council)

discovery that the western towers and the walls of the nave were rebuilt in the early 12th century and that Edward the Confessor's nave did not survive until the late 14th century (Tatton-Brown 1995). This must have led to a most peculiar juxtaposition of nave and choir between *c* 1150 and *c* 1250, when the choir was rebuilt, since the Confessor's church was on a markedly different alignment. A more significant problem would lie on the north side of the church. The south-east corners of the earlier and later naves finish in identical places; this is because of the positioning of the cloister, which takes up one bay of the south transept in the later church because the east range of the cloister was retained. The north-east corners of the earlier and later naves were in completely different positions. If the new nave was built a century or so before the new choir, how was the junction between the new nave and the old choir made?

Two chalk-lined cists found during the 19th century appear to be aligned with this phase of the abbey and were at a lower level than the sarcophagus (Poole 1870). It is therefore suggested that they belong to either period 5 or period 6.

Henry III's rebuilding and the later additions

The rebuilding of the abbey under Henry III was a conscious attempt at display and a desire to illustrate the importance of kingship. It sought to place at the focus of the abbey the recently sanctified Edward the Confessor, whom Henry greatly admired and with whom he wished to be identified.

Stylistically the rebuilding of the abbey once more took on strong French connotations and influences with the chevet and radiating chapels. Much has been written about the Lady chapel, which seems to have been constructed in the early 1220s before Henry embarked on his rebuilding of the abbey. Given that it was constructed some way east of the old church, the implication must be that there was already the intention to rebuild the abbey although there seems no reason to doubt Henry III's influence over its design and Colvin makes clear that cost of the rebuilding was borne by the royal exchequer. Given the evidence that the nave had already been laid out on a new alignment, perhaps around the middle of the 12th century (Tatton-Brown 1995), it might even be suggested that the rebuilding of the choir was under discussion at a similar time, especially given the problems mentioned above in joining the new nave to the old choir.

That there were considerably larger numbers of buildings constructed during the 13th century has become clear from the archaeological excavations. It would appear that the precinct was enclosed by a stone wall during this period and that the belfry was constructed then. It would also seem that the rise in the importance of the October Fair meant that buildings, both temporary and permanent, were required to house its merchants and at least one excavated by the gate dates to this period; documentary evidence suggests there were at least three at this time (Rosser 1989, 101).

The burial ground remains to be excavated in large part, but the reused Roman sarcophagus may have had a third phase of use as it was at a higher level than the two chalk cists from the earlier period and appears to have been on the same alignment as Henry III's abbey, although the earlier rebuilding of the nave could mean that this dated to the later 12th century.

The 14th-century works at the abbey were chiefly concerned with the monastic areas and focused little on the church. The serious fire of 1298 led to Abbot Litlyngton rebuilding the infirmary with a new infirmary cloister and parts of the main cloister itself. He also provided himself with a range of new monastic apartments on the west side of the cloister. The former cellarer's buildings of the west range were rebuilt to the south.

The nave was not fully rebuilt until the early 16th century and its reconstruction during the 15th and 16th centuries was beset by financial difficulties though it does not seem to have been one of the most pressing priorities. No doubt the constant effects of plague and disease depleting the monastic numbers took its toll on the community (Harvey 1993). The western towers of the abbey were not completed until the work of Nicholas Hawksmoor in the early 18th century. One of the most important additions to the abbey fabric was the Henry VII chapel, which replaced the Lady chapel in the early years of the 16th century. This building is rightly considered one of the finest pieces of late medieval architecture in England, with one of the most beautiful fan-vaulted ceilings anywhere. It formed the repository for most of the Tudor and Stuart monarchs' tombs.

The abbey precincts

The total area covered by the abbey precincts (before the appropriation of a small area to the east for the Jewel Tower in 1365) was approximately 56,850m^2 (14 acres). This can be compared to the precincts of other monastic houses in London: St Mary Spital covered approximately 51,500m^2 (12.7 acres); St Mary Graces 19,300m^2 (4.75 acres) (Thomas et al 1997, fig 72, 116); St Mary Clerkenwell 37,400m^2 (9.25 acres) (Sloane, in prep); the London Charterhouse 85,700m^2 (21.2 acres) (Barratt and Thomas 1991, fig 2); St John's Clerkenwell 71,000m^2 (17.5 acres). The inner precinct alone of a similar Benedictine house such as Peterborough Abbey measured 68,000m^2 (16.8 acres) (Thomas et al 1997, 116). Thus it can be seen that the precincts of Westminster Abbey were large but by no means the largest, even for urban or suburban houses of London and would have been dwarfed in size by some of the rural monastic houses: Fountains Abbey, for instance, had a precinct of some 283,500m^2 (70 acres). Monastic precincts in the urban or suburban environment were constrained by the property available and clearly the Westminster Abbey precincts were constrained by the limits of Thorney Island. The limits of the Saxon abbey are unknown but it is possible that any abbey on the site would not have been required formally to define its boundaries until either the Late Saxon or early medieval periods. By this time it shared the island with the palace and the ever-expanding town.

The abbey owned many other properties both close to Westminster and at some distance: many of the houses along King Street and Tothill Street were owned by the abbey, the almonry lay on the south side of Tothill Street with the Tyburn streams on its south and west sides, and the convent garden lay to the north of the Strand on the site now occupied by Covent Garden.

The abbey proper can be divided into two precincts. That to the south included the cloister and should be seen as the private part of the abbey. The northern precinct was the public space and included the belfry and the site of the October Fair.

The southern precinct

The southern precinct was entered by at least three gates. The principal entrance was through a gatehouse which lay to the south-east of the main gate from Tothill Street. The east wall of this gate survived into the 19th century and was drawn by William Capon in August 1808 (Capon 1824, views 6 and 7). Attached to it on the east side was the bishop of London's prison. A second gate exited the precinct on the south side and led to a bridge over the mill ditch on to an island with the abbey mill at its eastern end next to the Thames. The mill was in existence by 1281–2 (Westlake 1923, 368) and it is likely that the bridge was already in existence by this date. Indeed, records made by Frank Cottrill during the rebuilding of Church House in 1937 suggest that the bridge formed a single build with the precinct wall of the abbey which, it is suggested above (Chapter 8.3, Structure 6), was constructed in *c* 1180. It is, of course, uncertain whether this stretch of wall was of the same phase but it is probable. The third gate entered the precinct from the residential, inner ward, of the palace and was a private entrance. It entered the abbey to the south of the Lady chapel.

The boundary walls themselves were probably built in *c* 1180 although there was evidence of earlier builds (Green 1976) and it is possible that the precinct boundary was already well established.

This southern precinct was mainly made up of the private monastic areas, to which the general public was largely excluded. The south-western area, entered through the gatehouse in front of the west door of the abbey, was known as Nine Elms and was the outer court. It contained the granary and other such buildings with the 14th-century cellarer's range to the west. A gate through the cellarer's range led to the abbey gardens, which lay to the south of the monastic cloister.

The cloister itself was originally surrounded in usual Benedictine manner by the monks' dormitory, over storerooms on the east side, the frater on the south side and the cellarer's range on the west side. The east side also contained the Pyx chamber, where the nation's coinage was weighed and tested, a treasury and the vestibule to the chapter house. To the south of the frater lay the kitchen and the misericord, where meat was prepared for monks in the infirmary. In the second half of the 14th century the cellarer's range was moved to the south-west of the cloister to make way for the new abbot's lodgings. Accommodation was built for the prior to the south-east of the frater.

Running south from the south-east corner of the cloister was a passage (known as the Dark Cloister) which led to the reredorter at the southern end of the dormitory. To the east lay the infirmary, which originally comprised an open hall with a chapel dedicated to St Katherine at the eastern end. The hall was replaced with a cloister after the fire of 1298. By this time there was an increasing move towards providing individual space within both the monastic infirmary and the dormitory, as opposed to the earlier communal arrangements, and the cloister provided separate rooms for sick monks. The infirmarer's hall lay in the south-east angle of the cloister. There may have been other buildings associated with the infirmary, such as an infirmary kitchen, and one building would seem to have been on the site later taken by Edward III for his personal Jewel Tower.

The northern precinct

The northern precinct of the abbey was entered by two gates: the gate from Tothill Street, which led to the west door of the abbey, and the gate from King Street, which led to the north door. These were the two main processional entrances and the street layout and siting of the entrances are clearly linked. Both roads crossed the shortest routes across the Tyburn and both led to the main entrances into the abbey. The siting of one of the principal entrances in the north transept is unusual and may reflect the fact that the road was already in existence or at least had to be sited where it was, and a north porch in the nave, directly in line with the road, would have left no space for the choir on the high ground. It is remarkable that, when compared to the contour map of the highest ground, the abbey church occupies exactly the full extent of that contour to east and west.

The northern precinct was the public part of the abbey precincts and included the parish church of St Margaret. It is thought that this may originally have been sited inside the abbey but that at an unknown date a new church was built. Originally the parish of St Margaret covered a wide area up to Holborn and across to St Bride's but was later subdivided, the parish of St Martin in the Fields, for instance, being cut out of it.

The boundary walls were certainly in existence before the late 13th century and, like the walls around the southern part of the precinct, may well have originated earlier. It seems quite likely, for instance, that walls around the northern part of the precinct would have been built when the southern was enclosed and defended against the river in *c* 1180, and it is equally possible that the precinct boundary had already been established. There was evidence in period 6 from site C(i) of a ditch containing a posthole. Such a short length was found that little can be said of it but it was close to the line of existing and later boundaries and may have formed a foundation for a timber wall. Further excavation would be required to demonstrate any earlier boundaries and their origin. An even earlier boundary may have been the ditch from the late 10th or early 11th century which seems to have formed a boundary to the palace site and, if it continued, may well have formed a boundary to the 10th-century abbey too.

In the angle of the north transept and the nave was a two-storey building forming the sacristy. The eastern room had a cellar entered by a staircase, with a second staircase and a thin (?Tudor) brickwork fireplace added at a later date.

The belfry was built in 1249–53 and it is likely that the precinct was enclosed with a wall and gates on the northern side during the 13th century. The northern precinct was used as the site of the October Fair from the early 13th century until about 1400 although it was in decline during most of the 14th century. Numerous buildings were constructed there for merchants, some permanent, of high status, such as Building 13, others probably temporary.

14.4 Westminster Palace

Origins and development

The earliest contemporary reference to the palace at Westminster is its depiction on the Bayeux Tapestry showing Edward the Confessor looking out westwards towards his newly completed abbey (Fig 104). William of Malmesbury, writing in the 12th century, also describes Edward the Confessor in his palace at Westminster (Lethaby 1906, 131–2). Gaimar, another 12th-century writer, provides an even earlier origin to the palace, describing the dispute between Cnut and his nobles over the tide as happening at Westminster but there is no contemporary evidence for this.

The first archaeological evidence for a pre-Saxo-Norman palace is provided by Structure 4, which may have consisted of a timber bridge crossing a wide revetted ditch, constructed in the mid 10th–mid 11th century. This does not necessarily imply a palace but it does suggest occupation of the palace site and the need for a substantial boundary or defence and permanent access across it. Whilst it is possible that this structure dates to the first years of the reign of Edward the Confessor (1042–66), the balance of probability is that it dates to the early 11th century, possibly during the reign of Cnut, although it could be even earlier than that, perhaps as early as the reign of Edgar (959–75). Until more of this structure is found, however, its interpretation as a bridge must remain tentative, although strongly favoured over a jetty.

Further archaeological work is essential if the origins of the palace are to be understood; there seems no reason why the palace might not have been founded at a similar period to the refoundation of the abbey, some time between AD 960 and 971. Apart from chance finds such as an 8th-century sword found in Victoria Tower Gardens (to the south of the Victorian Palace of Westminster) (Dunning and Evison 1961), an 8th- to 9th-century binding strip made of gilded silver and a possible 9th-century coin hoard from the Thames at Westminster Bridge (Cowie 1988, 41), there is no evidence of earlier Saxon occupation. Three pieces of wood were found towards the southern end of Cromwell Green, to the west of the great hall, in a stream channel. One of these was a plank dating to cal AD 660–980 (Harwell 3423, 1220±80) and the others, although heartwood, gave similar dates. These may have been washed down the channel and their origin is uncertain. Other finds of Middle Saxon date come from the site of the abbey.

The choice of Westminster as a royal house, whether by Edward the Confessor or earlier, must surely have been influenced by the rise in the importance of the city of London only 2.25km downstream. The decision to reoccupy the city as 'Lundenburgh' and to abandon the Saxon emporium 'Lundenwic' may have moved the settlement further away from Westminster but its rise as a trading settlement was meteoric.

Development as a royal palace

William I clearly saw the need to continue using Westminster as one of his royal palaces. With Winchester and Gloucester, it remained one of the three principal royal palaces for the next century or so. During this period the king was, most of the time, peripatetic, that is to say, on progress around his kingdom (which also included parts of France). The idea of being based at a single venue began to appear only during the reign of Henry II, becoming firmly established during the reign of

Henry III. This was a result of the formalisation of government and the need to site the offices of state in one central location. The royal treasury had previously been sited at Winchester, but a building for the Exchequer was based in Westminster by 1190 and two new buildings were constructed in the 13th century.

Other royal houses remained in use but Westminster became the principal seat of the monarch until the early 16th century as it combined a residence with the seat of government and the seat of the law courts. As such it attracted many nobles and members of the court in general. These were housed either in residences within the palace or on palace or abbey property along King Street to the north. Many of the royal favourites found accommodation within the inner court of the palace. Edward II's favourite, Piers Gaveston, for instance, had chambers beneath the king's own chamber (the Painted Chamber). This expansion of the palace's activities lies behind its need to reclaim more land in the 12th and 13th centuries, in particular the outer court or New Palace Yard (Fig 105).

The increasing importance and use of Westminster as a royal palace no doubt influenced the decision to build separate chambers for the queen in the 13th century, including chapels and perhaps ranges of structures arranged around a cloister. Henry III also saw Westminster Palace and Abbey as centres for design, architecture and art. His son Edward I and his later descendant Edward III followed in his footsteps with St Stephen's chapel, which had a major influence upon design and architecture in 14th-century England, and the magnificent paintings in the king's chamber (or Painted Chamber), very influential on medieval design and art.

That the palace was becoming overcrowded with buildings in its residential quarter can be seen from the need of Edward III to appropriate part of the abbey precincts for his new Jewel Tower. Just before this was built he had separated part of the outer court off for use as the king's Woolstaple. This and the new houses for the canons of the collegiate foundation of St Stephen were built on reclaimed land on the north side of the palace. Expansion of the palace buildings also took in the eastern side of the precincts: the vicars' building and cloister were constructed here as was a range including the Star Chamber on the east side of New Palace Yard.

From palace to parliament

The barons had frequently been consulted by the monarch but parliament, involving both the House of Commons and the House of Lords was, ironically enough, the work of a Frenchman, Simon de Montfort, and had its earliest meetings in the 1240s. The Lords would generally meet after being in

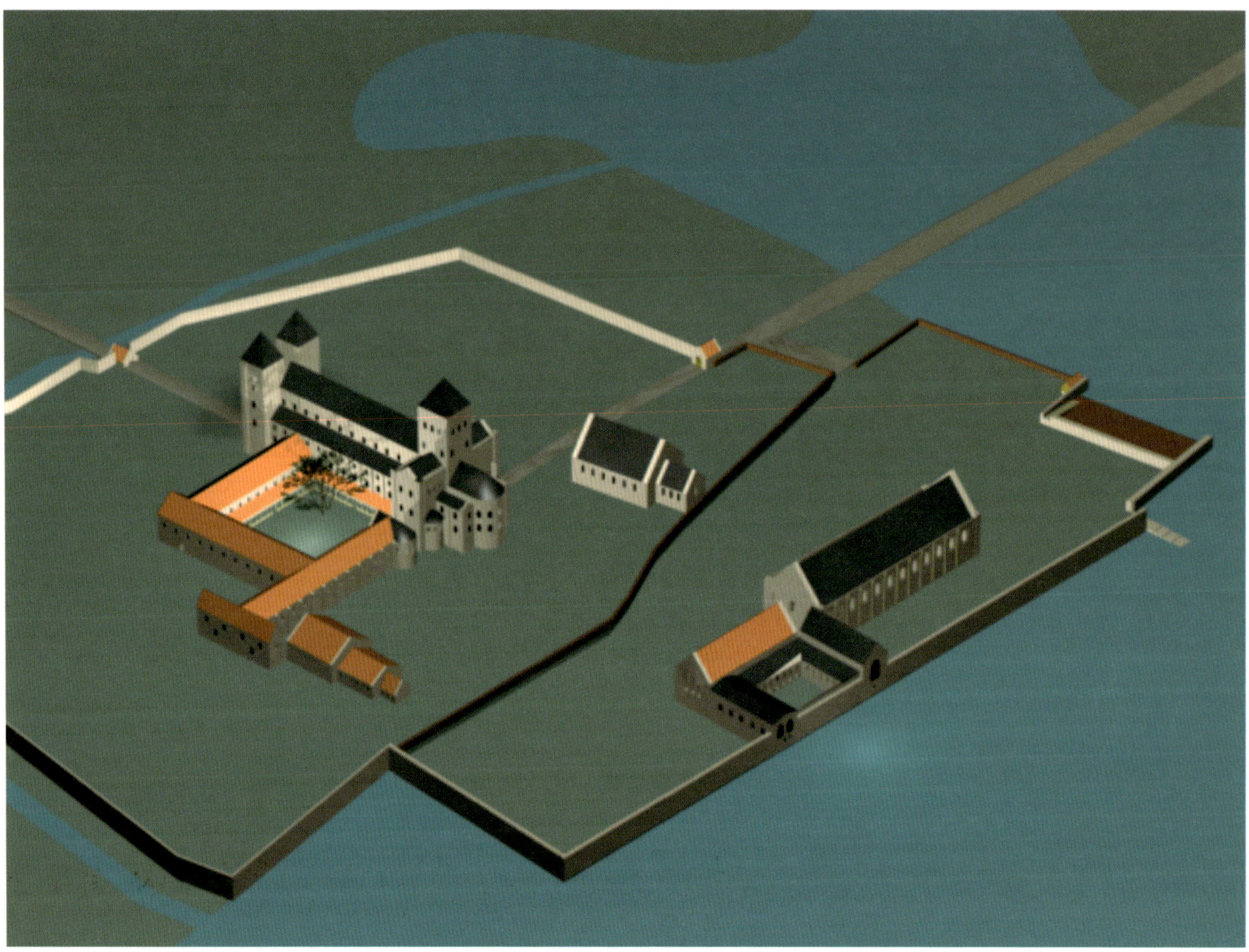

Fig 105 *Reconstructed view of Westminster c 1200*

attendance on the king in his lesser hall. After the king retired to his personal chamber (the Painted Chamber) the Lords would continue their discussions in the lesser hall. This was the principal site of the Lords' meetings until the 16th century, when they moved to the former queen's chamber.

The Commons met in a variety of places, sometimes in the refectory and sometimes in the chapter house of Westminster Abbey. In 1547, when St Stephen's chapel was dissolved, the upper chamber was granted to the Commons as their meeting chamber whilst the lower chamber was used by the Speaker as his dining room. The site of the Commons' deliberations between 1540 (the Dissolution of the abbey) and 1547 (the Dissolution of St Stephen's) remains unknown (Thomas Cocke, pers comm 1999).

The siting of the Commons in the narrow medieval chapel forced the laying of the benches against the opposing walls and was a major factor in the development of the English, and later British, parliament. Numerous alterations were made to St Stephen's to accommodate the members of parliament, among them works by Wren and major modifications in 1801 to allow for the new Irish members.

The archaeological record so far recovered seems to suggest a decline in the 16th century accompanying the royal abandonment of the site as a residence after the fire of 1512. It is interesting to note that a considerable upsurge in activity appears in the 17th and 18th centuries, possibly reflecting the rise in the importance of parliament. In the years immediately following the abandonment of Westminster by Henry VIII, much of the government followed him to Whitehall, which was designed not only as a residence but also as a seat of government (Simon Thurley, pers comm). The Exchequer and the law courts remained at Westminster along with parliament but little else, although the Exchequer was rebuilt on a large scale in the 16th century. In the middle of the 17th century, parliament reigned supreme and the seat of power returned to Westminster. It is still the case that parliamentary buildings lie in Westminster and most governmental buildings lie in Whitehall.

The layout of the palace

The overall palace layout and site

The layout of the Palace of Westminster can be seen to have developed by the late 13th century into a form similar to that of many English castles, particularly those of Norman and Angevin origin, such as Windsor or Chepstow. The palace was sited in a defensible position on an island adjacent to the Thames and surrounded by high stone walls and gates. The need for a defensible site might never have actually been necessary but could be viewed as an element of royal caution.

In its final form as a royal seat the palace consisted of three courtyards or wards: the outer court or New Palace Yard (OA4), the middle court or the Green Yard (OA5) and the inner court or Old Palace Yard (OA6). Progression through the first two was essential to gain access into the inner court and the status of each court rose from the outer to inner courts. Such an arrangement was typical of 11th- to 13th-century castle or palace layout although on a somewhat grander scale. In this form the palace occupied an area of approximately 33,680m^2 (13.63 acres) by the end of the 13th century. By the end of the 14th century it had been reduced slightly in size to approximately 31,115m^2 (12.60 acres) because of the loss of the Woolstaple, although this was partly redressed by the appropriation of part of Westminster Abbey for Edward III's new Jewel Tower. By the end of the 13th century, the outer court represented 36.1% of the total palace area, the middle court 26.8% and the inner court 37.1%. By the end of the 14th century the outer court had diminished in size and represented only 28.7% of the total palace area, the middle court 29% and the inner court 42.3%.

The positioning of the three precincts was largely influenced by the natural contours of the island. The buildings to the south of St Stephen's chapel lie on a higher bank of sand which juts out into the Thames. The southern river wall closely reflects the sweep westwards of the higher sand towards the abbey. St Stephen's chapel lies over a reclaimed stream channel. A second sandbank then juts back out into the Thames forming the site of the great hall and the Green Yard to the west. New Palace Yard lies in an area of marshy, boggy, ground, possibly an inlet, to the north and this probably represents the reason for its enclosure and use at a later date.

Some parallels must also be drawn with the site of the early medieval royal palace in Paris on the Ile de la Cité. Here the palace shared its island with one of France's premier cathedrals, Nôtre Dame, although for historical reasons that church did not act as the coronation or burial church, as at Westminster; for the French kings these were sited at Rheims and St Denis respectively. As discussed above (Chapter 9.3, Building 11) the form of the royal chapel in the Parisian palace, the Sainte Chapelle, was explicitly copied for the refounded chapel at Westminster, St Stephen's, and a college of secular canons was similarly attached. However, the influence of the Sainte Chapelle on French architecture was limited whilst St Stephen's was fundamental to the development of 14th-century architecture in England (Wilson 1990, 192).

Although geographically situated more at the heart of Paris, the Ile de la Cité was, like Westminster, an island and had been occupied during the late prehistoric and Roman periods and, as well as being the site of the great Merovingian cathedral, was the precursor to the medieval Nôtre Dame.

The palace defences

The earliest boundary so far uncovered has been the wide ditch on site J, dating to the late 10th or early 11th century. It is possible that this boundary defined the northern extent of both the abbey and the palace, sometime after the refoundation of the abbey between AD 959 and 971. It had clearly gone out of use by the later 11th century and there is evidence, during this period, of a possible boundary ditch towards the northern end of New Palace Yard on site D. This was evidently somewhat more than a drainage ditch and may have been defining the northern edge of the palace at the time, but it was clearly not defensive and there was no evidence of any other defence such as a wall or timber palisade.

Other defensive walls, banks and ditches from the 10th to 12th centuries should not be ruled out. Only small areas of the palace precincts have been uncovered and it is quite conceivable that such defences have yet to be recovered archaeologically. In particular, the area to the west of the south end of the great hall seems to have been the principal entrance into the inner part of the palace from the outset and may hold evidence as to the nature of the early boundaries of the palace precinct, particularly before the construction of the great hall in 1097.

Essentially, the evidence at present suggests that the palace precincts were defined from the outset but that no large-scale boundary walls were constructed until the late 12th century.

Documentary evidence indicates that there was a timber gateway leading into the Green Yard before the construction of the stone gate in 1244–5 (Colvin et al 1963, 547). Three large postholes immediately to the north of the wall and gateway of the 1240s may have been the sockets for an earlier timber palisade. These posts were removed after 1230 (presumably when the stone wall was built in 1240) but the dating for their insertion is less well defined, although they appear to have been erected after 1150. This might imply that the Green Yard, at least, was enclosed by a defensible timber palisade during the reign of Henry II, which would equate with the evidence of a timber boundary wall on site C(i) possibly defining the abbey precincts at a similar time. In addition, during the same period, the river walls were being constructed in stone to provide a defence against the rapidly rising river, partly caused by the dam created by the construction of London Bridge in *c* 1176–1209.

A possible interpretation might therefore be that stone walls were built around the river side of the palace and abbey on their southern and eastern sides in *c* 1180 as a defence against the rising river. At a similar time the internal boundaries between the palace precincts, the boundary between the palace and the abbey, and the northern and western boundaries of the abbey were constructed in timber with timber gates. Whether there was any boundary on the north-west side between King Street and New Palace Yard is uncertain but it must be viewed as likely; there was certainly a precursor to the stone gate of 1287.

The definition of the precincts in a more formal way during the 12th century might be explained by historical and/or design reasons. The increasing importance of Westminster over the other royal houses in the reign of Henry II and the increasing need for a single main residence and seat of government may have led to a need to create separate yards for residential, administrative and public purposes. Such an arrangement would have been familiar in the larger castles of royal or baronial ownership.

Throughout the 13th century there appears to have been a desire to replace any wooden boundaries in stone: the stone gate and boundary wall to the Green Yard were built in the 1240s and a new gate and, presumably, a boundary wall were built around New Palace Yard in the 1280s. The abbey's northern precinct wall was also built in stone, probably in the 1230s. Other rebuilding works in stone during the reign of Henry III and Edward I can be seen at Dover Castle and the Tower of London. Whilst this may have been caused partly by the need to replace decaying timber structures and the desire for a more imposing appearance, a further reason may have been political. The turbulent period towards the end of John's reign, owing to the baronial revolt, the offer of the throne to Louis of France and the siege of Dover Castle, followed by the uncertainty of the early years of Henry III's reign as a result of his minority and consequent lack of authority, may have made the increased strength and security of the Palace of Westminster an important consideration. The construction of high stone walls and gatehouses would at least have formed an imposing barrier even if they did not have the strength or solidity of Dover Castle or the Tower of London.

New Palace Yard

New Palace Yard, like the outer ward of a castle or the outer court of a monastic establishment (for instance, the northern precinct of Westminster Abbey immediately to its west), was, for most of the time, a public space. Up until the end of the 12th century it was probably little more than marshy waste ground forming a none too spectacular forecourt to the great hall. A fairly substantial ditch on the same alignment and just to the south of the 14th-century northern boundary wall to New Palace Yard may have formed the northern boundary to the yard in the late 11th and 12th centuries. Rapidly rising river levels from the late 12th century necessitated the construction of a river wall to the east, and the need for the unloading of building materials and provisions for the expanding palace meant that a quay was built as well (S5). The river gate was presumably constructed as part of the river wall and jetty, which was built (or rebuilt) from 1179–80 by Ailnoth (Colvin et al 1963, 493). Evidence from Bull Wharf in the City of London suggests that river levels began to rise substantially between 1170 and 1181, which would explain the need for a river wall (Ayre et al in prep). Buildings to the west of the quay (eg, B4) to some extent enclosed the yard. It is uncertain if these buildings formed part of the yard at this time but there seems to have been no other access to them; the foreshore lay to the north and the quay to the east. It is not until the late 13th century that documentary evidence indicates that the yard was surrounded by a wall and provided with a gatehouse (B5) built in 1287–9, but there was clearly a gate to the yard by 1235. At this time it was also paved with gravel and stone surfaces that were frequently replaced. Even by the late 13th century the development of the yard was piecemeal, but there were clearly a number of structures around its perimeter. It may even have had a fountain at this time, for fragments of 12th-century stone from an earlier fountain were reused in the 14th-century fountain (Horsman and Davison 1989, 287). The jetty on the east side of the yard, providing passenger access to the palace via the river, consisted of at least three sub-rectangular stone bases, 4.92m long and 1.83m wide, upon which lay timber planks (Vulliamy 1849, 71).

Major alterations and development of the yard were carried out from the mid 14th century onwards. When Edward III founded the Woolstaple in 1353, some of it was on land that had formerly been part of the yard. A new northern boundary wall was built to divide the two and a bell tower constructed in 1365–7. Hollar's view of the Yard in 1647 shows a range of buildings along this wall; it is unknown whether these were medieval or later in date, but at least one of them must represent the inn (B6). Two new gates were built: one leading to Canon Row and one to Woolstaple Yard. The great gate was also rebuilt in 1397–9 by Richard II. Hollar's view suggests that it had either two or more probably four large polygonal towers (Fig 106).

A range of buildings along the east side of the yard included the Star Chamber. In the centre of New Palace Yard lay the great octagonal fountain between the great hall and the bell tower. It was 8.14m across and was founded on relieving arches built from brick and Kentish ragstone. It lay over an earlier culvert, which continued to feed it. The fountain was built after the middle of the 14th century and before 1399 when it was painted for Henry IV's coronation. Rebuilt in 1441–4, it was demolished in 1658–60 (Horsman and Davison 1989, 288–90).

From the late 13th century, the yard was used for feasting halls at coronation banquets for the many guests who could not be accommodated in the great hall. These were temporary structures built in timber; at least one hall and a kitchen were constructed for the coronation of Edward I in 1272 and 15 halls, a scullery and a salsary for the coronation of Edward II in 1307. In 1397 an open-ended temporary timber hall was constructed for the parliament, which could not be held in the great hall because it was being rebuilt at the time (Stow 1987, 415).

The Green Yard

The Green Yard lay between the outer and inner courts and may have been a part of the palace from its inception. It would certainly seem to have been defined by the ditch revetted by Structure 4, which may date from the late 10th or early 11th century, and by the boundary with the abbey on the west and the great hall on the east. It definitely had a timber gate (and archaeological evidence of a timber boundary wall dating to after 1150) at its northern end before the construction of the stone gate (B8) and the stone boundary wall (S10) in 1244–5. The yard probably also had a boundary wall and gate leading into Old Palace Yard at the south end. It is uncertain when that wall was constructed. It may have been that the Green Yard and Old Palace Yard were originally a single entity and that the two areas were divided at a later date. A gate is thought to have given access to St Margaret's church to the west (Smith 1807, 31).

Building 3 is the earliest known building within the Green Yard but too little has been excavated to interpret its function. By 1244 the Exchequer (B10 room A) had been moved from its former site to the west side of the great hall. Attached to it was the barons' meeting room or *thalamus secretorum* (B10 room B). Also adjacent to the great hall was the knights' chamber, built in 1244. All these buildings were of two storeys but were constructed with low-pitched roofs so as not to block the windows of the great hall (Colvin et al 1963, 540).

Colvin has previously stated that there was no evidence of conscious design in the layout of the royal houses of the 12th and 13th centuries (Colvin et al 1963, 121) but there does seem to have been an attempt to make the Green Yard the administrative centre. The buildings were somewhat disconnected in that the Receipt of the Exchequer, for instance, was moved after the fire of 1263 but still lay on the east side of the great hall and not on the west. It was, however, in the space

Fig 106 Hollar's view of New Palace Yard, 1647 (copyright Museum of London)

between Old and New Palace Yards. The Exchequer was the first department of state to become fixed and its siting at Westminster can be seen as a defining moment in the journey that led to Westminster becoming the pre-eminent royal, and governmental, site.

By 1326 the Auditors of Foreign Accounts were housed in a new building (later to become the Augmentation Office) adjacent to the Exchequer, and the building known as 'Hell', which may have originated as a treasury in the 14th century, also lay in the Green Yard (Colvin et al 1963, 542). Whilst the function of Building 9 to the east of the gatehouse in the Green Yard is unknown it was obviously of some importance, given its thick Reigate stone slab floor, and it too may have been associated with the financial departments of state. A building known as the 'salsary' was built in the Green Yard in 1307 but there is no more detailed evidence as to its location.

St Stephen's court

The foundation of a college of canons with a dean and 12 vicars for St Stephen's chapel led to the formation of a court to the north of the chapel. The cloister lay directly to the north of the chapel with a courtyard to the north of that. A range of two-storey houses was built in 1361–6 along the east side of both cloister and yard for the 12 vicars (Fig 107). These stretched from the chapel to the gate to New Palace Yard. The cloisters themselves (B19) were built in 1394–6, rebuilt in the early 16th century, and restored after both the fire of 1834 and bomb damage during the Second World War. The northern side of these was formed by St Stephen's belfry, constructed in 1353–96, and a series of other buildings. These were almost certainly the vicars' hall with the buttery, kitchen and pantry beneath, all built in 1389–94. The cloisters and buildings were on two floors. The building forming the northern side of the court was the Receipt of the Exchequer, adjacent to which was a gate giving access to the court from New Palace Yard. The Receipt of the Exchequer, built in or before 1272, formed an east–west building to the east of the north end of the great hall. The earlier Receipt of the Exchequer building may have lain elsewhere and it has been speculated that it lay in the angle formed by the great hall and St Stephen's chapel, where the later cloisters lay (Lethaby 1906, 147), although Colvin disputes this and suggests that it may have lain to the south of the chapel (Colvin et al 1963, 540).

Fig 107 Vicars' houses in St Stephen's court (Smith 1807, fig p 28)

Old Palace Yard

Old Palace Yard (OA6) was the inner court of the palace and is likely to have formed its earliest enclosure, although the original palace site may have included the site of the later Green Yard. No archaeological or antiquarian evidence exists for any of the pre-Conquest buildings. That there was a palace at this time is beyond doubt; the Bayeux Tapestry (Fig 104) clearly shows Edward the Confessor's palace to the east of the abbey. Archaeological evidence (Chapter 6.3, Structure 4) suggests there may have been even earlier occupation (perhaps even royal) on the site dating to the late 10th or early 11th century. There has been much speculation that the 12th-century lesser hall lay on the site of the hall of Edward the Confessor and William I.

The layout of much of Old Palace Yard is unknown. Many of the buildings were destroyed by fire in 1512. The principal buildings on the east side of the court, however, are well documented and described and their layout is known. A gate to the west of the south end of the great hall led into the court, at which point the residential part of the palace was reached. The date at which this became defined is, however, uncertain. Another gate gave direct access to the abbey and a set of stairs led to another jetty into the Thames towards the southern end of the precinct.

From what is known of this area it seems likely that the palace developed along 'claustral' lines. The buildings seem to have been arranged around a series of small courtyards; as the buildings were of two storeys, so the walkways around the courtyards were also of two storeys. It is possible that much of the palace was laid out in this fashion, although piecemeal construction in the later periods when the available space was becoming short may have been less formally arranged. Such a layout should not be seen as confined to the principal cloister of a monastic house. Monastic houses often developed into a series of closes or courtyards, separated by function, sometimes surrounded by walkways or alleys and sometimes not (Thomas et al 1997, 101). Indeed many manor houses, Elizabethan and Jacobean mansions, and university colleges were laid out in a similar format. At Westminster, St Stephen's cloister lay to the north of St Stephen's chapel, a cloister (the king's cloister) lay to the south with the king's chamber (the Painted Chamber) on the south, the lesser hall on the west and St Stephen's chapel on the north. Foundations and recorded buildings to the south of the king's chamber suggest another cloister (the queen's cloister) bounded on the north by the king's chamber, on the east by the queen's chamber, on the south by the queen's chapel and another unidentified building, and on the west by an unidentified building. The layout of the other buildings is not known (except for the Jewel Tower) although the general location of some is known.

The principal storey for the royal apartments was the first floor. The lower storeys may have been used for wardrobes, storage and for the chambers of royal favourites. This arrangement included St Stephen's chapel and was the reason for the construction of two-storey cloisters. It is likely that the prince's palace also had its principal buildings at first-floor level. The earliest evidence for this arrangement is the addition of a second storey to the lesser hall, probably during the reign of Henry II.

A brief summary of the principal known buildings within Old Palace Yard is given below (Table 16).

Table 16 The documented palace buildings, with locations and dates

Building	Location	Earliest documented date	Building no.
Edward the Confessor's hall	?Old Palace Yard	?	
great hall (Westminster Hall)	Green Yard	1097–9	B1
lesser hall (White Hall)	Old Palace Yard	–1167	
water gate and bridge	New Palace Yard	–1184	
St Stephen's chapel	Old Palace Yard	–1184	B11
St John's chapel	?Old Palace Yard	–1186/7	
Exchequer		–1190	
king's wardrobe	?Old Palace Yard	Henry II	
cloister	?Old Palace Yard	Henry II	
kitchen	?Old Palace Yard	Henry II	
king's chamber (Painted Chamber)	Old Palace Yard	Henry II	
queen's chamber	Old Palace Yard	–1236	
king's almonry	?	–1240	
timber gate	Green Yard	–1244	
barons' chamber	?	–1244	
Exchequer	Green Yard	–1244	B10
kitchen	?	–1244	
knights' chamber	?	1244	
gate to Green Yard	Green Yard	1244–5	B8
king's lavatorium	Old Palace Yard	–1259/60	
prince's chamber	Old Palace Yard	?Henry III	
Receipt of the Exchequer	east of Great Hall	–1272	
timber hall	New Palace Yard	1272	
kitchen	New Palace Yard	1272	
new queen's chamber	Old Palace Yard	1272–1307	
new queen's buttery	Old Palace Yard	1272–1307	
new queen's bathroom	Old Palace Yard	1272–1307	
new queen's aviary	Old Palace Yard	1272–1307	
kitchens	?	1283–4	
great gate	New Palace Yard	1287–9	B5
house of Otho de Grandison	?	–1288/9	
green chamber	?	1288–9	
prince's palace	Old Palace Yard	–1296	?B12
royal nursery	?	–1297	
almshouse	?	–1307	
timber hall (x 15)	New Palace Yard	1307	
salsary	?Green Yard	1307	?B9
scullery	?	1307	
white chamber	?	1307–11	
king's bridge	Old Palace Yard	–1308	
St Stephen's by the Receipt	?	c 1311	
auditors of foreign accounts	?	1326	
gate to Westminster Abbey	Old Palace Yard	–1327	
Piers Gaveston's chamber	?Old Palace Yard	–1327	
Roger Mortimer's chamber	?Old Palace Yard	–1327	
Keeper of the Privy Seal's chamber	?	–1340	
chapel	?	1342	
chamber	?	1343	
chapel of Our Lady of the Pew	?	–1348	
Star Chamber	New Palace Yard	1349	
palace prison	?	–1351	
St Stephen's bell tower	east of great hall	1353–96	
hospice	?	–1354	
gate to Canon Row	New Palace Yard	–1354	
vicar's house (x 13)	New Palace Yard	1361–6	
Jewel Tower	Old Palace Yard	1365–6	B17
clock tower	New Palace Yard	1365–7	
earl of Northampton's chamber	?	–1373	
'hell'	?	–1373	
vicars' hall	?east of great hall	1389–94	
vicars' buttery	?east of great hall	1389–94	
vicars' kitchen	?east of great hall	1389–94	
vicars' pantry	?east of great hall	1389–94	
St Stephen's cloister	east of great hall	1394–6	B19
timber hall	New Palace Yard	1397	
great gate	New Palace Yard	1397–9	
timber-framed chamber	Old Palace Yard	1442–3	
timber-framed chamber	Old Palace Yard	1451–3	
king's poultery	?	–1458	
king's valet's chamber	?	–1458	
earl of Salisbury's chamber	?	–1461	
building in Jewel Tower garden	Old Palace Yard	1463	
queen's withdrawing chamber	?Old Palace Yard	1466	
queen's wardrobe	?Old Palace Yard	1466	
queen's chamber	?Old Palace Yard	1482	
kitchen	?	1482	
'paradise'	?	–1483	
new chambers	?	1496	
stable	east of B1?	1504	
'purgatory'	Old Palace Yard	–1509	
tennis court	?	1509	
Court of Wards	Old Palace Yard	?	
dean's house	New Palace Yard	?	
gate to Old Palace Yard	Old Palace Yard	?	
king's squire's chamber	?Old Palace Yard	?	
chamber of queen's ladies-in-waiting	?Old Palace Yard	?	
Woolstaple gate	New Palace Yard	?	
'heaven'	Old Palace Yard	?	

THE LESSER HALL

The lesser hall or White Hall, as it was known, is thought to have been sited on the original site of Edward the Confessor's hall. There is no archaeological evidence for this but it seems the logical site. It consisted of a north–south hall of two storeys, the upper being added by Henry II. The lower storey had a screens passage at the north end, which must have been designed for when the building had only a single storey. Thus the northern end would have been used for preparing food prior to bringing it into the main dining area. It is unclear whether this arrangement was maintained after the addition of the upper storey. During the later medieval period the upper storey was the principal room and formed the king's dining hall as well as a reception room and the site of deliberations by the Lords. The southern end contained lancet windows with 'dog-tooth' mouldings characteristic of the second half of the 12th century, presumably original windows added during the construction of the upper storey (Fig 108). The lesser hall was bounded on the east by a two-storey cloister that gave access to the king's chamber and St Stephen's chapel. Somewhere to the west must have lain the main kitchen and immediately in front of the building lay a small fountain or washing area fed by the palace water supply.

Fig 108 Windows at the south end of the lesser hall (Lethaby 1906, 145 fig 8)

It is uncertain whether the fireplace, indicated on a plan of 1807 (Smith 1807, fig p 125), was original or an addition. The building was known by a number of other names, principally the White Hall.

THE KING'S CHAMBER

The king's chamber (or Painted Chamber) formed the king's personal apartments and appears to have been constructed during the reign of Henry II, when it may have formed a chamber for both king and queen. It was certainly separate from the queen's chamber by the 13th century. This room was famous throughout Europe for the paintings on its walls (Fig 109). The first phase of work on them dates to *c* 1230–63, before a fire led to their replacement from 1263 to *c* 1280. These works were all carried out at the behest of Henry III although they were not completed until the reign of his son Edward I. Indeed the earlier phase of painting included the queen's chamber, which was newly built. Two further phases of painting were carried out: the first during the reign of Edward I, from 1288 to 1307 and the second in the reign of Edward II, from 1307 to 1308 (Binski 1986, 16–24).

On the north side at the eastern end was a small private oratory for the king adjacent to where the king's bed lay (Binski 1986, fig 3). This was viewable from the royal bed, which lay against the east wall. The room was used as both a personal bedchamber and a reception room (Fig 110).

The ground floor appears to have been divided by wide stone walls (Smith 1807, fig p 125) and was used during the reign of Edward II for chambers for his favourite, Piers Gaveston. Both storeys were linked to the lesser hall and St

Fig 109 The coronation of Edward the Confessor, copy by Charles Stothard (copyright Society of Antiquaries of London)

Fig 110 Interior of the king's chamber, looking west (watercolour, 1817, by William Capon: Guildhall Library (Print Room), Pr.W2/HAL/int)

Stephen's chapel by a two-storey cloister, the roofline of which could still be seen after the cloister's demolition (Fig 111).

THE QUEEN'S CHAMBER

The earliest documented reference to the queen's chamber comes from 1236 and there is reason to believe that it was constructed at around that time by Henry III for his queen. It was rectangular and, like the other buildings, had its main chamber at first-floor level. A series of lancet windows looked out over the Thames (Figs 112–13). The function of the ground-floor room is uncertain but it may have served as lodgings for courtiers like the ground floor of the king's chamber. The first-floor chamber communicated via a hall at the north end with the king's chamber, a staircase and what is interpreted as a cloister to the west. A door in the south-west corner of the room also led into the putative cloister (Fig 114). This cloister is suggested from the likely layout of the buildings and the presence of stone walls shown on 19th-century plans by Smith and Capon. A door adjacent to the one into the cloister led into the queen's chapel. A building called the 'new queen's chamber' was built during the reign of Edward I (1272–1307). It is unclear whether this replaced or was additional to the queen's chamber of Henry III and, if it replaced it, to what purpose the original queen's chamber was put.

In the 17th century the queen's chamber was used as the meeting place for the House of Lords and it was in the lower storey of this building that Guy Fawkes and his co-conspirators laid their barrels of gunpowder.

THE QUEEN'S CHAPEL

The date of construction for the queen's chapel is not documented but it may have been built at the same time as the queen's chamber. The slightly odd disparity in the roof levels between the two might suggest, however, that they were not contemporary (Fig 112). The chapel was aligned east–west and was at first-floor level. It is unclear what lay at ground level; it is not impossible that it too was a two-storey chapel as St Stephen's was. It was reached from a vestibule, which appears to have led into both the putative cloister and the southern end of the queen's chamber (Fig 114). It had two rows of three lancet windows in the east wall at each level but in overall scale

Fig 111 North side of the king's chamber (watercolour, c 1805, by Frederick Nash: Guildhall Library (Print Room), W.W2/PARL)

the chapel seems to have been significantly smaller than that of St Stephen. It was later known as the prince's chamber.

BUILDINGS TO THE SOUTH AND WEST OF THE QUEEN'S CHAMBER

These buildings are highly speculative and should be seen as a suggested layout for the palace based on the claustral pattern. Capon indicates stone walls to the west of the queen's chamber, which might suggest a cloister with a building to the west, and Smith shows 'old stone walls' in these locations. The model of development of medieval palace and grand house architecture makes the courtyard or claustral design a distinct possibility for the likely layout and the walls found do conform to such a pattern, but excavation would be required to understand the layout and development of this area. The building to the west of the chapel is hypothetical.

There were clearly many other buildings within the inner palace courtyard for which the location remains unknown. It is also known that the palace was so congested with buildings that

Fig 112 East side of the queen's chamber and chapel (engraving, 1807, by John Thomas Smith, artist and engraver: Guildhall Library (Print Room), Pr.W2/PARL)

Fig 113 Interior of the queen's chamber during demolition in 1823 (Colvin 1966, 171 fig 126 bottom)

Fig 114 West side of the queen's chamber and the cloister in 1823 (Colvin 1966, 173 fig 128)

the king had no space for his Jewel Tower in 1365 other than his garden. Not wishing to relinquish this he purloined a part of the abbey precinct.

THE PRINCE'S PALACE

Little is known of the prince's palace. Its site is thought to have been on the west side of Old Palace Yard adjacent to the precinct wall to Westminster Abbey. It was probably the palace of Edmund, son of Henry III, and was damaged by the fire of 1298. It was repaired during the reign of Edward II and included halls, chambers, chapels and kitchens. It became the residence of Edward, the Black Prince. Two walls, one recorded by Smith (1807) and one from site R, suggest a rectangular building in the right area for the prince's palace. The prince's palace was presumably added to and altered after its original inception. If it developed similarly to other areas of the palace it may have started as a small group of buildings that were then extended and complemented with other structures, eventually forming ranges of buildings around courts or yards. It is also likely that the main apartments would have been sited at first-floor level.

THE RIVER FRONT

The river front was probably embanked in *c* 1180 to protect the palace from substantial rises in the river level. Whilst many rebuilding, restoring or refacing works were later carried out, it is likely that the main river defences were constructed at this time and remained largely unaltered until the 16th or 17th centuries. A stone wall was built east from the abbey wall along the promontory of sand and gravel that jutted out into the river. The abbey wall and the palace wall were built as one, suggesting a degree of co-operation between the two. The wall then turned north, passing beyond the eastern end of the king's chamber and St Stephen's chapel. Documentary evidence makes it clear that the river washed right up to these buildings; there were timber posts beyond the chapel, perhaps to prevent boats banging into the wall.

The river wall continued north to the edge of the palace. Jutting out from the wall were two jetties (known as bridges), providing river access into the palace. One lay at the south end and gave access to the residential part of the palace, whilst the other led through a gateway into New Palace Yard. When the new Palace of Westminster was built, the stone foundations covered with timber planks of this latter jetty were found near where Big Ben now stands (Vulliamy 1849, 71).

The river front originally turned west to the north of the palace and some of the area to the north remained in the river system until the 14th century. This provided the site for the dock (S5), which was built in about 1180.

In the mid 14th century, large areas of land were reclaimed to the north of the palace and the river front was pushed slightly eastwards to the east of the dock. This new land was required as the site for the new canons' houses for St Stephen's chapel (Chapter 10.3, Building 15).

15

Conclusions

15.1 Attainment of research aims

Many archaeological investigations have been carried out in Westminster. This book attempts to summarise them and to provide a context for them. The importance of Westminster both historically and archaeologically cannot be overstated. The area of Thorney Island and the surrounding and adjacent rivers of the Thames and Tyburn should be considered as a single archaeological site. Westminster has been at the centre of English history for the last 1000 years and clearly has much earlier origins whose status, importance and nature remain unclear.

The archaeological investigations at Westminster should be considered as a moderately comprehensive evaluation; in other words, the date, type and potential of the deposits can be defined and, to some extent, the broad framework and form of the site can be described. However, much of the detail remains to be recovered, the development is poorly understood in many cases and, crucially, the origins remain tantalisingly enigmatic. In order to provide a research framework for future investigations it is important, firstly, to define what is known.

One of the principal objectives of the current research has been to provide a geological, topographical and environmental framework for Thorney Island, to define the island and its rivers and to understand their development. Whilst certain areas remain poorly covered (particularly to the south of the island), and certain periods remain less well covered, this has broadly been achieved and what remains is, for the most part, smaller detail. A good degree of confidence can be had in the form, shape and size of the island from the post-glacial period to the present, in the varying river levels and their effect upon the area available for habitation, and the form and date of human attempts at reclamation. The major hiatus in foreshore deposits from the Iron Age to the 12th century, though, means that our knowledge of the environment and the changes to the river system over that period is less reliable. The overall form, distribution and layout of the abbey precincts, palace precincts and town can be described with some degree of confidence. This book has also postulated a chronology for these developments and interpretations as to how and why they developed. In particular the definition of space, public, private and administrative, within the palace and abbey precincts are of central import.

The work of many other archaeologists, historians and antiquaries has made Westminster one of the best-researched sites in Britain. The standing buildings have been subject to detailed scrutiny, the documentary sources to exhaustive interrogation and many now-lost buildings have been recorded to a high standard. As a result, the large number of small-scale investigations carried out by MoLAS can be put into a much wider context and some of the details of the development of the palace and abbey buildings can be described and located. The accurate location of the existing buildings was therefore seen as a fundamental starting point for the understanding of Westminster's development.

Before discussing the future research questions that might be directed at the archaeology of Westminster, one important point should be made. Despite the destruction of archaeological deposits with limited or no archaeological recording through construction works such as Barry's Victorian palace, the 19th-century Underground, the New Palace Yard car park and the governmental offices along Whitehall, large areas remain relatively undisturbed and the archaeological survival in these areas is likely to be excellent.

15.2 Further research questions

Superficially it would appear that Westminster is one of the most thoroughly researched and published sites in Britain and might therefore warrant less investigation in the future than many other sites. Such an impression, whilst understandable, should be strenuously contradicted.

Although this project has provided significant new data on key issues, for instance, the development of the tidal river, sedimentary models and the vegetational succession on and around Thorney Island, it has also highlighted areas where questions still cannot be answered. These are noted here as requiring both primary data collection and synthetic analytical research. One example has come to light through the palynology. Data from a number of the pollen spectra examined from the area, together with the possible ard marks viewed in section at site P, can be seen as providing possible evidence for Bronze Age agriculture. These data cannot yet, however, be regarded as conclusive proof of a prehistoric agricultural community on the island. More work is needed to prove it conclusively and then to research further the detail: for instance, exactly when was the putative community established, how much land was used, was there a mixed farming economy and which species of crops and animals formed the core of the concern?

With reference to general palaeoecological reconstruction, this project has gone a long way towards outlining a picture of the changing vegetation occurring on and around Thorney Island within the study period. However, a perennial problem in London is the difficulty of reconstruction of the ecology of the urban centre. This is the case here, where only very sketchy detail can be described. In order to refine this, more data collection is needed before it will be possible to define the ecology of historic Westminster with some confidence.

Several questions relating to the history of the Thames itself also require analysis. One of the most obvious gaps revealed by this project relates to the history of the river between the Iron Age and the Saxon period. This time period is generally 'missing' in the stratigraphy because of erosion and scouring, probably in the 11th century when significant flooding has been recorded as well as changes to river defences and bridging structures. Some contemporary deposits are preserved in isolated pockets, for example on top of Thorney Island, but those in the crucial locations around the island have been lost. Yet this period is of great significance, not only for constructing theories of how Thorney Island became settled and urbanised, but for the contemporary central London flood plain generally. This is in sharp contrast to our information regarding the Bronze Age, where the tidal status of the river is relatively clearly understood. Furthermore, although the Roman Thames in the city of London is also comparatively well understood, the lack of information from Westminster makes it extremely difficult to track the migration of the tidal head with the accuracy required not only to tell the history of the river adequately, but to understand issues such as why the Roman and Saxon cities were located in the topographical positions finally fixed upon and why Thorney Island was peripheral to these *foci* until the Late Saxon period. The history of the river is central to the understanding of the archaeology of central London and is therefore a research topic of prime significance. Furthermore, its past is the key to its future in the current period of sea-level rise, a subject of no little concern to the contemporary occupants of Thorney Island.

It is clear that there has been occupation of some kind in the area from at least the later Neolithic. The extent, type and nature of the occupation in the Neolithic, Bronze Age and Iron Age periods remain elusive. Most investigations have been confined to the foreshore, where the material appears to suggest habitation. So little investigation of deposits of these periods has been carried out on the higher ground that a proper analysis of the settlement is currently out of the question. That occupation occurred next to the rivers is not surprising. The distribution of features and artefacts demonstrate this and similarities can be seen elsewhere (particularly in Southwark). The area investigated is much smaller and therefore the quantity of material recovered is concomitantly reduced. Larger flint assemblages might warrant detailed analysis of the spread of material by its contour to analyse whether the patterns alter by type or by date depending upon their level. The contour map (Fig 4) is far too crude to allow such an investigation of the flint but could easily be refined; at the moment the number of artefacts simply does not warrant it. Investigation of the palace and, in particular, abbey sites would help to understand how the areas of higher ground were utilised. The small-scale nature of the investigations has hampered attempts to understand the prehistoric settlement.

The nature of Roman activity in Westminster is equally, if not more, tantalisingly elusive. As discussed in Chapter 5, the Roman building material, which is regularly recovered from archaeological investigations and found reused in medieval buildings from the 11th century onwards, the antiquarian records of buildings from beneath the abbey church, the stone sarcophagus and the continuing speculation concerning the Roman road and river crossing all suggest Roman settlement of some kind on the island. It would seem to be substantial and possibly of high status. Is it religious, military or secular? What date range does it encompass? The answers are most likely to lie on the highest ground, beneath the abbey or in its direct vicinity, and any opportunities to investigate should be taken.

The origin and development of the abbey remain shrouded in legend and speculation. The highly tentative hypothesis that it originated as a minster dedicated to St Peter in the 8th century just to the south of the Middle Saxon settlement of Lundenwic (with the cathedral of St Paul just to the east of the settlement) should be investigated. A 9th-century decline, associated with that of the settlement, might also be postulated but remains speculation. That there was a 10th-century refoundation as a result of the monastic reforms of St Dunstan and King Edgar is certain. Its form, scale, layout and importance are unknown.

The origins of the palace have generally been accepted as being associated with Edward the Confessor. There has been some speculation that Cnut might have resided there but such a view has been in the minority. The highly significant discovery of a revetted ditch bordering the palace and abbey precincts with what seems to have been a bridge entering the site of the palace, almost certainly pre-dating the reign of Edward the Confessor, brings a new focus to research into the palace. The possibility that there was a palace during the reign of Cnut or even Edgar should be investigated if at all possible.

The broad scheme of the layout and development of the palace can be described. The early layout and development of Old Palace Yard is, as yet, unknown. The later use and layout of the yard is also unclear, particularly on the west side. The prince's palace, the kitchens, numerous ancillary buildings, the lesser hall and the gate all require investigation. The archaeological evidence for the diet and status of the inhabitants remains a major research aim. Whilst there is much documentary evidence it should remain a cause for concern that other archaeological assemblages are interpreted in relation to one of the highest status sites by documentary evidence alone.

The decline in the importance of the palace during the 16th and early 17th centuries and its subsequent recovery of its position as the premier political site in England and Britain should also be further investigated archaeologically. The historical basis for this is well known but how does it manifest itself in the archaeological record?

Many aspects of the abbey during the medieval period also warrant serious investigation. In particular, the northern precinct has received little attention. Further work is also required on the origins, dating and development of the boundaries and gates to the precinct; the drains, water supply and sanitary arrangements; the development of the infirmary; the buildings in the southern precinct; the form of the nave in the 12th century; and the abbey mill.

The documentary records of the town have received much-needed attention recently (Rosser 1989). Its development, layout and the status of its inhabitants require further archaeological research, as does the canalisation of the Tyburn streams and the bridges over them.

Some of the research aims are of crucial importance at a national and international level as befits the status of the monument as a World Heritage site. Clearly, any disturbance to either the below-ground deposits or the above-ground structures should be archaeologically recorded to the highest standards possible. However, a wider question arises as to the use of research-driven archaeological investigation to answer a number of specific research aims and to provide a more informed basis for the future conservation of the monument.

The recent excavations and their integration with previous investigations have thus allowed us to define what we know and what we would like to know about the Westminster area of Thorney Island. The pressing research agenda and the most critical research questions for future works in the area might be defined thus:

- What is the nature of prehistoric settlement on Thorney Island?
- Is there any 'ritual' aspect to the prehistoric settlement?
- What is the nature and date of Roman occupation on Thorney Island?
- Is the Roman settlement religious, military, political or domestic?
- Was there a river crossing at Westminster and can this be associated with the Roman invasion of AD 43?
- Was Westminster Abbey founded as a minster during the Middle Saxon period?
- Did Westminster Abbey decline in the 9th century along with the settlement of Lundenwic?
- Is there archaeological evidence for the 10th-century refoundation of Westminster Abbey?
- At what date did Thorney Island become used as the site of a royal palace and can this be associated with the 10th-century refoundation of Westminster Abbey?
- How does the artefactual and ecofactual material compare with the documentary evidence of 'high status'?
- What was the form and layout of the residential area of the palace (Old Palace Yard) and how did it develop?
- Can the hypothesis that the middle ward of the palace developed as an administrative and governmental area from the 12th and 13th centuries be further substantiated archaeologically?
- How was the northern precinct of the abbey used and what is the archaeological evidence for the October Fair?
- Can the decline in the palace's fortunes of the 16th century and the rise in the importance of parliament from the 17th century be recognised archaeologically?

16

Specialist appendices

16.1 Struck and burnt flint

Jon Cotton

Introduction

The purpose of this report is to provide an overview of the nature and significance of the prehistoric struck and burnt flint recovered from eight sites examined as part of the Jubilee Line Extension Project (Westminster) between 1992 and 1997 (sites B, C, E, F, G, K, L and Storey's Gate (SGT94)).

Between them, the eight sites produced a total of 255 struck flints and over 400 fragments of burnt unworked flint, although the material was unevenly distributed and ranged from a single piece of worked flint at site C(ii) to 84 pieces at site G. While burnt unworked flint was recorded on six sites, the bulk of it came from sites F, G, K and SGT94.

In addition to these JLEP sites, the opportunity has been taken here to incorporate the flint work recovered from a further five non-JLEP sites – NPY73, WHL75 (site T), WCG78, WST86 and SAL94 – examined in the Westminster area between 1973 and 1994. A majority of these lay to the south and south-east of Parliament Square, and were dealt with by MoLAS, its predecessor bodies and others.

Between them, these five sites produced 269 pieces of struck flint, ranging from two pieces recovered during a watching brief at NPY73 to 169 pieces at WCG78. (No data relating to the presence of burnt unworked flint were collected.) Incorporation of this material here has the twin benefits of extending the geographical range and size of the lithics dataset from the Westminster locality, and of allowing a reassessment of the potentially important but hitherto largely unremarked lithic assemblage from WCG78 (Collins 1980, 27–8) (Table 18).

This report therefore provides an overview of 524 pieces of struck flint from 13 separate sites distributed across the area of ancient Thorney Island (Tables 17–19). Burnt unworked flint data from six JLEP sites are also presented (Table 21). The report utilises data contained in the various site assessment reports prepared for individual JLEP sites and in earlier published accounts (Whipp and Platts 1976; Mills 1980; Mills 1995), augmented where appropriate by recent re-examination of the flint work held in the archive; detailed reports on the material by site are held in the relevant site archives. The archive is lodged with the Museum of London under the individual site codes and may be consulted by prior arrangement with the Archive Manager at the London Archaeological Archive and Research Centre (LAARC) at Mortimer Wheeler House, 46 Eagle Wharf Road, London N1.

Struck flint

Contextual considerations

Broadly speaking, the struck flint assemblage was recovered from four main groups of contexts:

1) from the fills of discrete features cut directly into the natural

sands and gravels of Thorney Island (57 pieces or 11% of the total assemblage);
2) from a series of horizontal sandy alluvial deposits laid immediately over these natural sands and gravels by a relatively fast-flowing freshwater stream (332 pieces or 63% of the total assemblage);
3) from later features usually but not exclusively cut into these alluvial sands (101 pieces or 19.6% of the total assemblage);
4) from the upper fills of natural palaeochannels (34 pieces or 6.4% of the total assemblage).

Despite the presence of small groups of material from discrete features sealed beneath the alluvial sands at WCG78 and from the fills of palaeochannels at SGT94 and site B, it is convenient to deal with the flint work as one (albeit mixed) assemblage in the first part of this overview. However, the various context types are identified in Table 17 (for all sites) and Table 18 (for WCG78) and in the concluding discussion.

Furthermore, in view of the small size of the areas actually excavated it was not usually feasible to attempt to record artefacts within the alluvial deposits three-dimensionally. This inevitably restricts comment on such matters as their vertical and horizontal distributions within the profile. Limited three-dimensional recording of an area of *c* 6.5m^2 at site G, however, showed that a reasonable proportion of the flint work (*c* 47%) lay within the uppermost 100mm of the deposits. Interpretation of the horizontal distribution of the lithics here

Table 17 Struck flint work from all sites, by context type

Site	Prehistoric features	Alluvial sands	Palaeochannel	Unphased/residual
NPY73				2
T		48		21
WCG78	57	71		41
WST86				7
B		1	1	5
C				1
SAL94		21		1
SGT94			33	5
F		37		2
G		77		7
E		2		
K		66		?8
L		9		1
Totals	57	332	34	101

Table 18 Struck flint work from Cromwell Green (WCG78), by context

Context / Type	[22]	[81]	[83]	[85]	[92]	[95]	[102]	[109]	[111]	[214]	[220]	[227]	Total
Flakes		6	9	1	2		8	5	1	7			39
Blades	1	9	6		2	1	4			15	1	1	40
Flake/blade fragments		13	14	1	2		3	2		10	1	6	52
Cores		1			1		1	3		1		1	8
Core fragments							3		1			1	5
Core-tablet							1						1
Rejuvenating flake		1											1
Partially worked nodules			2	1			1	1	1			3	9
Microlith										3			3
Adze fragment							1						1
Scraper		1	2						1				4
Arrowhead		1											1
Miscellaneous retouch							1						1
Flake axe fragment			1										1
Flake knife		1											1
Total	1	33	31	3	7	1	23	11	4	38	2	12	169

Key
Context numbers: [83], [227], ?[109]: phase 1, fills of features cutting natural sands and gravels; [81], [214]: phase 2, alluvial sands; [85], [92], [95], [102], [111]: phase 3, fills of features cutting alluvial sands; [22], [220]: unphased

was, unfortunately, hampered by the size of the area examined and by the low numbers of artefacts recovered. The possible significance of these points is returned to below.

Raw material

The bulk of the raw material (estimated at >95%) comprises cobbles of rolled gravel flint with heavily worn and pitted cortex, with colours ranging from orange through to grey-brown (often on a single piece). Occasional use is also made of nodules of Bullhead Bed flint, which has a characteristic green cortex, orange sub-cortical banding and smoky grey-brown interior. In addition, a handful of pieces appear to utilise chalk flint, which is here typified by a fresher and thicker white cortex and grey-black interior; one of the two ground axe fragments is also likely to have been of chalk flint (the other is too heavily burnt for certainty).

Ground axes apart, all the raw material used was readily obtainable from the local terrace gravels exposed along the courses of the Thames and the Tyburn. This includes the few pieces of non-axe chalk flint, which probably represent the incorporation of stray nodules of such flint within the terrace gravels rather than direct exploitation of flint-bearing chalk deposits, the latter some kilometres distant from the Westminster area.

Condition

The assemblage is in fresh condition, with little evidence for post-depositional wear and tear, though in view of the relatively fine-grained nature of the sediments in which the bulk of it lay this is not altogether surprising. A small percentage of worked pieces (<4%) have been burnt, presumably accidentally, including one of the two ground axe fragments, one of the two arrowheads and one of the five microliths. A somewhat larger percentage has been patinated to varying degrees ranging from marginal to total, as at WCG78, though it is unlikely that this latter observation bears any chronological implications dependent as it is on variables such as ground water conditions, soil mineral composition and flint type (eg, Lewis in prep). Breakage, particularly of the flake/blade component, was evident at several sites, notably WCG78, site G and site F.

Typology and technology: waste material

The assemblage can be divided into waste and retouched pieces, the former making up 93.8% of the total assemblage (96% if miscellaneously worked pieces are incorporated). Waste pieces comprise flakes and spalls, blades, cores, core-tablets, crested pieces and rejuvenating flakes, partially worked nodules (PWC), nodular shatter and various broken fragments (Table 19).

FLAKES, SPALLS AND BLADES

Flakes and spalls (small flakes <10mm in length) form the largest single category, representing 41% of the total assemblage, followed by flake/blade fragments (22.5% of the total assemblage) and blades (12.5%). These figures vary between individual sites: for example, flakes/spalls comprise only 23% of the assemblage at WCG78, but 78.5% at site G. Despite such differences, primary, secondary and tertiary flakes

Table 19 Struck flint from all sites, by artefact type

Site	NPY73	T	WCG78	WST86	B	C(ii)	SAL94	SGT94	F	G	E	K	L	
Type														Total
Flakes	1	30	39		2		12	9	16	66	2	34	4	215
Blades		9	40		1	1		2	7			6		66
Flake/blade fragments		12	52	2			2	9	13	13		11	4	118
Cores		1	8	1	1			4	1			5		21
Core fragments			5	1				3		1		5		15
Core-tablet			1									1		2
Rejuvenating flake		4	1		2		2	1				5		15
Partially worked nodules		9	9		1		3	3				5	1	31
Microlith			3					1				1		5
Adze fragment			1									1		2
Adze-sharpening flake									1				1	2
Scraper			4				1							5
Polished axe fragment	1								1					2
Arrowhead			1							1				2
Crested piece		1	2	1			1							5
Miscellaneous retouch		2	1				2	5		1				11
Burin		1												1
Flake axe fragment			1											1
Flake knife			1											1
Not seen				2						2				4
Total	2	69	169	7	7	1	22	38	39	84	2	74	10	524

are all present, representing the full notional cycle of core reduction. Where examined, most of the flakes have plain butts, as at site G, with some showing signs of platform abrasion, as at site F. Flakes with faceted butts are in the minority.

While both soft and hard hammer techniques appear to have been used to detach flakes, soft hammer techniques were preferred for the production of blades. Apart, however, from several robust crested examples longer than 70mm (from site T and a residual piece from WST86) few of the blades were of any size. Those from site F are typical, and range from 66mm to 19mm in length and from 18mm to 6mm in width. A single blade from WCG78 has been notched.

Broken flakes/blades are much in evidence, particularly at WCG78 and site F, where they form nearly 31% and 33% of the total site assemblages, respectively.

CORES, TABLETS, REJUVENATING FLAKES AND PARTIALLY WORKED NODULES

In all 21 cores are present, representing 4% of the total assemblage. Of these, 17 come from three sites, WCG78, SGT94 and site K. The same three sites produced 13 of the 15 core fragments, 17 of the 31 partially worked nodules and nodular shatter, seven of the 15 core-rejuvenating flakes and both the core-tablets.

The majority of the cores and fragments derive from the production of blades as opposed to flakes, though none were of large size. Of the 21 complete examples, 11 were single-platform, usually pyramidal types, five were two-platform types, of which one, from WCG78, was a small opposed platform core some 57mm in overall length, four were multi-platform globular or irregular types, and one was keeled. The single multi-platform core from site T had been reused as a hammerstone. In addition to the 21 cores, two others, one each from WCG78 and site K, appear to have reutilised fragments of flaked adzes.

Core preparation pieces include crested pieces (all of blade-like form), often employed to prepare cores for the production of blades, core-tablets, used to completely rejuvenate a striking platform, and rejuvenation flakes, the latter usually employed to renew an abraded or step-fractured platform edge.

Partially worked nodules and nodular shatter indicate the testing of nodules for knapping suitability, and represent a perhaps less formal, more opportunistic approach to (usually) flake production.

Typology and technology: retouched tools

Discounting opportunistic miscellaneously retouched pieces, the formal retouched tool element makes up 4% of the total assemblage and is composed of core tools, consisting of fragments of adzes and axes, and of implements fashioned on flakes/blades, including scrapers, microliths, arrowheads, a burin and a knife.

CORE TOOLS

In all seven fragments belonging to core tools are present and make up 1.3% of the total assemblage. These can be divided into flaked and ground types. The flaked pieces include two adze fragments reused as cores from WCG78 and site K, two adze-sharpening flakes from sites F and L and part of a possible axe butt from WCG78. The ground pieces comprise the butt of a slender axe of pearl grey flint from NPY73, and a fragment of heavily burnt mid section belonging to a second slender artefact with markedly faceted sides from site F.

Of these pieces, only the ground axe butt from NPY73 is likely to have utilised chalk flint brought in from a distance (the second ground piece is too heavily burnt to tell); the remainder of the pieces appear to make use of locally available gravel flint.

FLAKE/BLADE TOOLS

These can be divided into formal retouched pieces, of which there are 14 (2.6% of the total assemblage), and informal, miscellaneously retouched pieces, of which there are 11 (>2% of the total assemblage).

Formal retouched pieces comprise scrapers, microliths, arrowheads, a burin and a flake knife.

There are five convex end and end/side scrapers (0.9% of the total assemblage) worked on broad flakes, four of which are complete. Of these, three complete and one fragmentary piece were recovered from WCG78 (Table 18), with the fifth complete piece, an end scraper, from SAL94. Two of the four from WCG78, a small 'thumbnail' example and a patinated fragment of a larger piece, lay within a small gully sealed by alluvial sands.

Five microliths were recovered (0.9% of the total assemblage), three from WCG78 and one each from SGT94 and site K. As far as can be judged, these belong to narrow-bladed forms, and comprise one small scalene piece from WCG78, three small obliquely backed pieces, two from WCG78 and one incomplete burnt piece from SGT94, and one bi-truncated piece from site K.

Two arrowheads are present (0.4% of the total assemblage). These comprise one petit tranchet derivative form steeply worked on a snapped flake/blade mesial piece from WCG78, and a small burnt triangular piece from site G with neat bifacial retouch covering both faces. The latter is almost symmetrical with a squared-off butt. Close inspection of the butt, however, suggests that the present form is the result of the reworking of a leaf-shaped or asymmetrically barbed arrowhead, the latter possibility the more likely option, though its heavily burnt surface makes certainty difficult.

The two remaining formal tools comprise a single burin worked on a robust core fragment of blade-like form from site T, and a broad flake knife with marginal retouch along one long side from WCG78.

Eleven further pieces fall within a miscellaneously retouched category. The five pieces from SGT94 are typical, in that the retouch is usually confined to the margins of small flakes or blades. The single piece from site G, comprising a small asymmetric flake with bifacial retouch along one margin and cortex along the other, was initially identified as a rough variant of a leaf-shaped arrowhead, though this is not an interpretation favoured here. The illustrated flints are listed in Table 20 and are illustrated in Figs 17–19.

Burnt unworked flint

Data are available for only six JLEP sites and are presented in Table 21. This confirms that the bulk of the burnt flint by number of pieces and/or weight was recovered from sites G, F, K and SGT94. The pattern established by the struck flint is repeated, in that most of the material came from the alluvial sand layers, although that from SGT94 was recovered from the fills of a palaeochannel.

Table 21 Burnt unworked flint, by number of pieces, weight and average weights

Site	No. of pieces	Weight (g)	Mean weight (g)
B	6	54.0	9.0
G	319	2374.0	7.5
F	104	986.0	9.5
SGT94	31	594.0	19.1
L	11	85.0	7.7
K	54	712.0	13.1

Table 20 Details of the illustrated flints (Figs 17–19)

Number	Context	Accession no.	Fig no.	Type
<F1>	WCG78 [214]	<254>	17	microlith
<F2>	WCG78 [214]	<251>	17	microlith
<F3>	WCG78 [214]	<213>	17	microlith
<F4>	T[3026]		17	burin
<F5>	WCG78 [102]	<54>	17	adze fragment
<F6>	WCG78 [7]	<2a>	17	adze sharp flake
<F7>	WCG78 [83]	<24>	17	axe/adze fragment
<F8>	WCG78 [102]	<64>	17	core-tablet
<F9>	WCG78 [109]	<128>	17	core
<F10>	T[305]		17	flake core
<F11>	WCG78 [109]	<125>	17	blade core
<F12>	WCG78 [81]	<34>	17	notched blade
<F13>	WCG78 [7]	<2>	17	ground axe fragment
<F14>	WCG78 [81]	<114>	17	arrowhead (petit tranchet derivative type)
<F15>	WCG78 [83]	<32>	17	scraper fragment
<F16>	WCG78 [81]	<112>	17	scraper
<F17>	WCG78 [111]	<37>	17	scraper
<F18>	WCG78 [83]	<93>	17	scraper
<F19>	WCG78 [81]	<4>	17	flake knife
<F20>	NPY93 [74]	<59>	18	ground axe
<F21>	G[47]	G<49>	18	arrowhead
<F22>	G[39]	G<48>	18	arrowhead
<F23>	SAL94 [201]	<343>	19	convex scraper
<F24>	SGT94 [1563]		19	utilised secondary flake
<F25>	SGT94 [1034]		19	single-platform pyramidal core
<F26>	SGT94 [1565]		19	microlith

16.2 Ceramic and non-ceramic building material

Terence Paul Smith

Introduction

Ceramic building materials were recovered from most sites, the majority more or less fragmentary and most of medieval or post-medieval date; a little Roman material was also recovered. All the material has been examined and fabric types have been ascertained by binocular microscopic examination (x10); the fabric type numbers are those in use at the Museum of London; samples are also retained at the Museum of London. Except where it was too fragmentary for certainty, the material has also been classified by form. A little non-ceramic building material was also recovered, including some unusually shaped slates.

Roman ceramic building material

A little Roman ceramic building material, all of it fragmentary, was present on most sites. That from C[184], the fill of a robbed-out wall, may have been deposited within the Roman period itself and may therefore represent a building at or close to the site, even if the material does not come from the robbed-out wall itself (Chapter 5.3, Open Area 1). It is a meagre amount, consisting of two fragments of brick and one of box-flue tile. All belong to the familiar London area fabric group 2815, which was in use between the mid 1st and the mid 2nd century. It was manufactured at various kiln sites around Watling Street in the region between London and St Albans and perhaps also to the south-west of London.

Otherwise, the Roman material must be regarded either as residual or as reused at a later date. The material suggests that particular types were selected for reuse, bricks being more useful in this respect than other types; tegulae were probably the next most suitable type, whilst the awkwardly shaped imbrices and the hollow flue tiles were least satisfactory. The percentages by weight and by number of fragments of each type from this group of sites are given in Table 22.

Most of the fabrics belong to the 2815 group; others present, neither in large quantities, are fabrics 2454, from the Eccles area of Kent (made *c* AD 50–80), and 3060, from the Radlett area of Hertfordshire (made *c* AD 50–120). A possible brick fragment from D[17] may be in the Roman

Table 22 Percentages by weight and number of fragments of Roman ceramic building materials

	Weight %	No. of fragments %
Brick	70·1	66·3
Tegulae	23·2	23·3
Imbrices	2·5	3·5
Flue tiles	0·7	1·2
Uncertain	3·6	5·8

fabric 3028, perhaps from the Hartfield area of Sussex, although it is possible that this amorphous fragment is from a much later Netherlands floor tile. Most of the fragments are of bricks, although roofing tiles (tegulae and imbrices) are also present.

Medieval and post-medieval ceramic building material

Quite large amounts of medieval and post-medieval ceramic building materials were recovered, the great preponderance being in the form of roofing tile fragments. A small amount of material is from buildings or structures but the vast majority exists as dumped material, pit fills and the like.

Floor tiles

Few floor tiles were recovered from the sites. The medieval tiles fall into four groups: decorated and plain-glazed 'Westminster' tiles, decorated and plain-glazed Penn tiles, other tiles of English manufacture, and plain-glazed 'Flemish' tiles. Some post-medieval plain-glazed 'Flemish' tiles were also recovered. 'Westminster' tile designs are referred to by the numbers given them in Betts (2002); Penn tile designs are referred to by the numbers given them in Eames (1980), preceded by the letter E.

DECORATED AND PLAIN-GLAZED 'WESTMINSTER' TILES

Fabric types: 2195, 2199, 2892
These are tiles of rather poor quality, often with bumpy surfaces and with their designs ill defined. They are named from their first recognition in the Muniment Room and in St Faith's chapel at Westminster Abbey (Degnan and Seeley 1988, 11–18), but the name does not indicate the place of manufacture. The distribution of known examples does, however, suggest production somewhere in the London area (Betts 2002, 3). There is some reason to believe that one (not necessarily the only) tile yard was near Farringdon Road, Clerkenwell, where a kiln found in the 19th century produced tiles, the descriptions of which suggest that they were of 'Westminster' type (Price 1870, 31–6; Betts 2002, 10–11). The date range of these tiles, although not entirely unproblematic, seems to run from the mid to the late 13th century. Both decorated and plain tiles were made, and both types are represented here. None were *in situ*, most coming from dumps or pit fills.

A decorated tile from C[65] (C<31>) is in brown and yellow and shows design W99; it measures ?mm x 116mm x 27–28mm. That from B[143] shows part of a circular border in yellow on a brown background, but is too incomplete for identification; it preserves none of its dimensions. All other examples have a plain glaze. Those from F[65] and L[55] are triangular in shape, the former 27mm thick and with a yellow glaze over white slip, the latter 22–24mm thick and with a dark green glaze. Fragments of square tiles from F[2] and F[48] are 26mm and 27mm thick respectively, and both have dark green glaze; that from B[220] is 23mm thick and has a greenish brown glaze.

PENN TILES

Fabric types: 1810, 1811, 2894
The tile yard at Penn in Buckinghamshire was important in the period from the 1330s to the 1380s and produced roofing tiles as well as floor tiles. The latter were traded over a wide region, including the Chilterns and the middle Thames valley and as far east as London (Eames 1980, 221–6). Their quality is superior to that of the earlier 'Westminster' tiles. The yard produced both decorated and plain-glazed tiles, though the latter were not greatly used within the London area. A few pieces, four decorated and the others plain, were found at this group of sites, none of them *in situ*; one was unstratified. The decorated examples are listed in Table 23.

Table 23 Details of decorated floor tiles

Context	Fabric	Dimensions (mm)	Design no.
B[0]	2894	110 x 109 x 21	E2070
B[145]	1811	? x 113 x 20–23	E2835
B[186]	1810	? x 113 x 20	E2535
D[21]	2894	? x 110 x 17–20	[previously unpublished]

A plain-glazed example from B[157] measures 127mm x 126mm x 26mm and has a dark green (almost black) glaze; another, from B[222], measures ?mm x 114mm x 20–21mm and has a mottled green glaze; a small fragment from a dump, F[156], preserves no dimensions but has traces of green glaze.

OTHER TILES OF ENGLISH MANUFACTURE

Fabric types: 2194, 2324
Floor tiles were made at various other places in England in the 14th and 15th centuries. It is not always possible to identify the place of manufacture, and occasionally it is not possible to be certain whether particular tiles are of English manufacture or imports from the Netherlands (see below). Just a few fragments were recovered, two from F[40], three from F[97], and one from F[160], none of them *in situ*. Those from F[40] have green glaze, in one case almost black; the other fragments appear to be unglazed, although it is more likely that their glaze has worn off. Dimensions are not preserved. A tile from F[8] may possibly be an English product, but is more probably of 'Flemish' manufacture, and is therefore considered in the following section.

PLAIN-GLAZED 'FLEMISH' TILES

Fabric types: 1813(?), 1977, 2191, 2317, 2318, 2323, 2850, 3063(?), 3076, 3080
Imported plain-glazed tiles from the Greater Netherlands, often referred to as 'Flemish' (Smith 2002, 272–7), usually show particular fabric types, containing calcium carbonate and/or silty inclusions. Unlike tiles of English manufacture, they were fired before the application of glaze (and its underlying slip where used) and then fired again. After demoulding they were trimmed using a wooden template as a guide. To prevent this

from slipping, small nails were knocked into it and these pressed into the soft clay. No attempt was made to plug these holes and they remain in one or more corners, and occasionally in the centre, as clues to Netherlands manufacture, although sometimes they may be obscured by the slip.

Three fragments, possibly from a single tile, formed part of the occupation debris of Building 6: D[18]; other pieces were recovered from ditches, pits or dumps: B[150], C[65] and C[66], E[5] and E[13], F[97] and J[1]. Where dimensions are preserved, the tiles are between *c* 133mm and *c* 155mm square; thicknesses vary between 23mm and 31mm. The glazes are brown, buff, green and yellow, one being mottled green and buff; that from E[13] shows possible remains of slip, suggesting original glaze which has been lost; that from F[128] is unglazed. The piece from J[1] is in an uncertain fabric, possibly 3063. A fragment from F[8] is in fabric 1813, which is normally an English fabric; the tile, however, has an oval nail-hole, suggesting 'Flemish' manufacture from raw material lacking the usual fabric inclusions. The tile is 22mm thick and has a green-brown mottled glaze. There is a knife cut across its diagonal, made before firing so that the tile could be snapped into two triangular tiles. In this case, however, the tile may not have been snapped, in which case the cut would serve as a bastard joint, giving the impression of two similarly coloured triangular tiles.

Both the documentary evidence (Keen 1971, 148) and the archaeological evidence (Betts 1997, 65–6) indicate that the plain-glazed tiles were imported into London from the 14th to the 16th centuries; unglazed examples, like that from F[128], are probably post-medieval in date. It would be incautious to draw conclusions of too firm a nature from this small amount of material derived from non-primary contexts, yet the greater preponderance of 'Flemish' over English (including Penn) products does reflect the general situation in the London area, including the City. It is likely that, despite the sea voyage involved, the 'Flemish' products were economically competitive with their English rivals, probably because the marine transport charges were only a small percentage of the f.o.b. (free on board) costs of the material. There is firm documentary evidence for the use of the 'Flemish' tiles in Westminster: amongst others, the architect Henry Yevele supplied 'tiles of Flanders for the paving of floors (*arearum*) and other work' at 6s 8d per thousand for use at Westminster Palace in 1365 (Salzman 1967, 145, which gives the figure 8000 tiles; Harvey 1984, 359, which gives the figure 7000 tiles).

UNGLAZED NETHERLANDS TILE

A tile fragment from the external surface F[128] is unglazed; no dimensions are preserved, although these tiles are typically larger than the plain-glazed tiles. The unglazed examples were imported from the Netherlands, probably beginning some time in the 17th century. By this time, the northern Netherlands was far more economically important than the southern Netherlands (present-day Belgium); the tiles therefore probably come from the new Dutch Republic, though this included that part of the erstwhile Flanders now lying within the province of Zeeland.

Wall tiles

TIN-GLAZED WALL TILE

Fabric type: 3067

A small fragment of tin-glazed wall tile was recovered from an external dump, N[5], N<5> (Fig 98). It is too fragmentary for the design to be identified, but it is in blue-on-white and includes two swans; it is 7mm thick. It is of mid to late 18th-century date and probably of English manufacture.

Roofing tiles

Large quantities of fragmentary roofing tiles were recovered from the various sites. Most are peg tiles, although there are a few fragments of early roofing tile types and one fragment of pantile; ridge tiles were recovered from some of the sites.

SHOULDERED TILES AND OTHER EARLY TYPES

Fabric type: 2273

Just a few fragments of early tile forms were recovered, all of them from ditches or pits and none, therefore, relating to specific primary contexts; they come from B[128], B[151], B[179] and C[205], the last having pitch or bitumen on it. Some show brown glaze. One piece is 18mm–19mm thick, but no other dimensions are preserved. The fragment from B[151] may be either from a shouldered tile or a flanged tile; the other pieces are probably from shouldered tiles. Both types were in use within the London area between the mid 12th century and the late 12th or early 13th century (Betts 1990, 221–5). The shouldered tiles are characterised by the constriction in their upper third, forming a kind of neck in which there is normally a single hole, probably for a nail rather than for a peg. The tiles are usually well glazed on their lower third, that is, on the portion which would show in a completed roof. The flanged tiles show a distinct taper, allowing them to overlap one another down the roof slope; they have flanges down the sides, somewhat like Roman tegulae, and the central strip is normally glazed. The tiles were used in conjunction with curved tiles although none of these were recovered from these sites. The flanged and curved tiles used together formed the least heavy of medieval ceramic roof coverings, but they would have been expensive to manufacture and unwieldy to lay. The thick shouldered tiles would have been expensive, awkward to handle both at the yard and on the roof, and formed by far the heaviest of medieval ceramic roof coverings: they were probably the least satisfactory roof covering ever to be used in the London area (Smith 1998–9, 66–71).

These early roofing types are often associated with monastic buildings in London and elsewhere, although they were also used on secular houses belonging to the well-to-do, for example in Cheapside in the City (Betts 1990, 221–5). It is perhaps a little surprising, therefore, that they are so poorly represented at Westminster, although caution is needed in assessing such dumped material. It is possible, however, that the tiles were used less in Westminster than in the City.

PEG TILES

Fabric types: 2271, 2276, 2586, 2587, 2816, 3062, 3090

Most of the peg tile recovered was in the form of small fragments from non-primary contexts such as ditches and dumps. It does not warrant detailed consideration. Peg tiles from the floor of Building 13 included glazed forms, suggesting a date of not later than *c* 1500, whilst the material also includes fabric 2587, not normally found before *c* 1240 or after *c* 1450. A hearth in the same building, C[96], and one in Building 4, L[35], were both constructed from roofing tiles. Right from their inception roofing tiles were used for purposes other than their primary one of roofing and the construction of hearths was a common enough feature (Moorhouse 1980, 41–3).

These and other tile fragments from the sites are in fabrics familiar from the London area. Almost certainly, they were made within the London area itself. Peg tiles in the same fabrics as the shouldered and other early tiles probably began in the mid 12th century; other fabrics were introduced in the later 12th century and subsequently, although fabric 2276, with its distinctive fine moulding sand, did not begin until *c* 1480. Peg tiles might be fixed to the roof battens using either pegs or nails (Keily 1998, 32). The typical London-area tile has two peg/nail holes towards the top, often asymmetrically disposed. Most are circular, and indeed circular holes were the only ones used in the London area down to about the end of the 15th century; thereafter, different shapes – square, diamond-shaped, hexagonal – were sometimes introduced, although circular holes remained predominant. A few of the tiles from these sites show holes other than circular in shape. Down to about the end of the 15th century too it was common (though not universal) for the tiles to be glazed on their lower third, which was the portion that would show in the finished roof. Sometimes, this glaze took the form of a smooth coating ('cover-glaze'), but more often it was applied in tiny droplets in a kind of spatter technique ('splash-glaze'). A few tiles from these sites show cover-glaze; many more show splash-glaze. The majority of the fragments, however, are unglazed. In some cases these unglazed fragments may well be the upper portions of glazed tiles.

Amongst all this shattered material, only two tiles preserve their full dimensions: one from D[54], in fabric 2587 and dating to *c* 1240–1450, measures 272mm x 158mm x 13mm; one from C[251], in fabric 2276 and dating to later than *c* 1480, measures 270mm x 147mm x 13mm–15mm. A larger number preserve their widths and these show a greater than normal consistency, with only a few departing from the range 154mm–160mm. Just possibly, this indicates purchase from a limited number of yards, even when the tiles are of different dates. Even so, most fall below the minimum dimensions laid down by Edward IV in 1477, which stipulated that roofing tiles should be 'in Length Ten Inches and [a] Half and in Breadth Six Inches and a Quarter of an Inch, and in Thickness Half an Inch and Half a Quarter [of an inch]' (this equates to 267mm x 159mm x 16 mm) (Lloyd 1925, 45; Salzman 1967, 230). Some of the tiles (in fabric 2276) certainly post-date this legislation and show that it was not always followed. One very narrow tile from B[150] measures only 120mm across; this was probably a verge tile, used at the edge of the roof to maintain the stagger of the other tiles.

A tile from B[222] is only 8mm–9 mm thick, an unsatisfactory product when most fall within the range 11mm–15mm. Concern about insufficient thickness was expressed not only in the legislation of 1477 but also in a series of proclamations, slightly differently worded, from the end of the 13th century, one of which insisted that roofing tiles should be *bien quyte et bien plumbe, et de veil escauntilounn* ('well fired and well glazed, and of the old scantling') (Riley 1859, 288; cf 278 and Latin version at 279), 'scantling' probably referring to thickness rather than to overall dimensions.

PANTILE

Fabric type: 3094

Just one fragment of pantile was recovered, from a pit, B[220]. It is 15mm thick; other dimensions are not preserved. Pantiles dating from the late 16th century have been found at the Rose Theatre in Southwark (Bowsher and Miller in prep), but were first imported on a large scale from the Netherlands into the London area in the early 17th century (Betts 1992, 76). English versions were being made before the end of the century (Moxon 1700, 4). Their social status was never high and they were used principally for sheds, outbuildings and the like, or, on higher status houses, for the shallower upper pitches of mansard roofs, for which peg tiles were not suitable and where, significantly, they were not visible from street level. They were probably never highly regarded in an area such as Westminster.

Bricks

A number of bricks were recovered, mainly from pits, dumps, or other non-structural contexts. A few are from walls, floors or wells. The majority date to before 1700.

FLEMISH-TYPE BRICKS

Fabric type: 3031

A few examples of these distinctive off-white to yellow or light brown bricks were recovered, though none from structural contexts: they come from B[221], F[76] and F[130], and K[21]. Their date range appears to run from some time in the 14th to some time in the 15th century. Paul Drury coined the useful term 'Flemish-type' for these bricks (Drury 1993, 8–9), which are found in London and Essex (Ryan 1996, 31–6). The cognomen reflects the fact that it is not entirely certain whether these bricks are imports from the Netherlands (including Flanders) or English products, although the distribution of Essex examples (Ryan 1996, 33, map 4) and their similarity to Netherlands bricks (Hollestelle 1976, 95–9) strongly suggest that they are imports. Their occurrence along the Thames, both in the City and at Westminster, is hardly surprising. There are some documentary references to the import of bricks in the medieval period, sometimes under the specific designation 'Flanders tiles' (and variant forms), and indeed importation (as proper cargoes, not as ballast) seems to have been part of regular trade (Smith 1985, 23–6); such trade was, however, on a small scale: the majority of bricks used in England in medieval times were home-produced. Assuming that the bricks from Westminster are indeed imports, then their small number reflects this general situation.

LATE MEDIEVAL AND EARLY POST-MEDIEVAL RED BRICKS

Fabric types: 3033, 3046, 3065

These bricks, all in variants of a basically similar fabric, were in use in the London area from some time in the medieval period down to *c* 1700; examples as early as *c* 1380–1400 have been found in walls excavated in Lower Thames Street in the City (Keily 1998, 37), but more often they appear to date from the mid 15th century onwards. They are a common find in the London area and were almost certainly manufactured in the area. They were used in the walls of Structure 18 (B[200]) and Structure 23 (B[164]), for a floor in Building 24 (N[19]), hearths in Building 6 (D[29]) and Building 22 (C[1]), and for the well C[253]. Others are from non-structural contexts, some of them associated with Buildings 13, 15, 22 and 24. A few are overfired, but most are well-made products. Some show the sunken margins, slightly depressed borders along one or more edges of one (usually the upper) bedface, which are characteristic of these bricks. They result from the bricks being carried individually, and still in the mould, to the drying ground, where they were placed flat for (at least initial) drying; during demoulding, small 'lips' were sometimes pulled up on the edges and these were simply pushed down using the bottom edges of the mould itself; the sunken margins were an incidental effect of this procedure (Betts 1996, 6–10).

LATE MEDIEVAL OR POST-MEDIEVAL YELLOW BRICK

Fabric type: 3073

A brick in fabric 3073 was recovered from the external dump F[90]. Such bricks are not especially common in the London area, and it is likely that they were brought in from elsewhere in south-east England. They are often large in size, as is this example at 250mm x 126mm–127mm and with an irregular thickness of 23mm–60mm. At present it is not possible to refine their date range: they may be of late medieval or post-medieval date.

LATER POST-MEDIEVAL RED BRICKS

Fabric types: 3032, 3034

Bricks in these closely related fabrics are harder and darker than the earlier bricks, being dark red to purplish. They not infrequently show organic inclusions and/or voids where these have burned away. They represent domestic ashes and other material (known as 'Spanish' at the time), added to the raw material to aid firing and save on fuel (Lloyd 1925, 48–50). The material was also stiffer than that of the earlier bricks, so that they could be demoulded at the maker's bench and carried in batches, separated by small boards known as 'pallets', to the drying ground, where they were able to be set on edge for initial drying. A few have been overfired and have vitrified faces. The bricks date from just after the Great Fire of London of 1666 down to the 19th century. They were used for the wall in Structure 23 (B[164]), where they were combined with bricks, perhaps reused, of the earlier type. They were used for the floor or yard D[5], and were also recovered from the non-structural contexts B[111], B[167] and B[168].

POST-MEDIEVAL DUTCH PAVING BRICKS

Fabric type: 3036

These were recovered from B[221] and C[251]. They were imported from the Netherlands, where they had been made since the 15th century, although their export to England did not begin until the early to mid 17th century, probably for reasons internal to the Dutch economy. Those same reasons probably lie behind the beginning of importation of pantiles and unglazed floor/paving tiles at about the same time (see above). In brief, the Dutch ceramic building materials industry had developed to serve a growing population (and hence a building boom) which was not sustained. Dangers of over-production thus led to the seeking of new markets abroad for materials which, unlike the glazed tiles, were of relatively low value but of high bulk and therefore not intrinsically suited to long-distance trade.

The small bricks were normally proper cargoes, not ballast. They continued to be imported down to the early 19th century. They are of small format, dense texture and yellow-buff colour, these characteristics resulting from the use of dredged-up river mud, mostly from the River IJssel in the province of Holland, for their manufacture: this contained few inclusions but had a high lime content – sometimes larger shell fragments may be seen in the bricks – and this determined the colour; the mud was so soft that larger bricks would have slumped under their own weight and so the bricks were made to the smaller format. Their principal use in England, where their social status was not high, was for paving, although they were also used for cisterns and for soap boilers' vats and very occasionally for walling; an especially favourite use was for stable yards, where their dense, hard surfaces facilitated washing down (Hollestelle 1976, 121–4; Smith 1997, 12–15, Smith 2001, 31–42)

Stone building material: post-medieval slates

The slates from E[251] are of some interest. Five of them were recovered, mostly complete. They are cut to a bag shape with a straight top; towards the top are two round or square holes for nails; one has an oval hole towards the bottom (that is, within the bulbous part of the bag shape), but this is probably accidental. Lengths vary between 122mm and 148mm, widths between 65mm and 98mm, and thicknesses between 3mm and 8mm. The nail holes are between 3mm and 6mm across. It is possible that the slates were used to create a decorative roof, but their unusual shape and their small size make it more likely that they were hung vertically as wall-cladding, offering protection from penetrating rain but probably used more for their decorative effect. Slate-hanging was most popular from the Stuart through to the Regency period (Clifton-Taylor 1987, 173–5); the Dutch paving brick (fabric 3036) found in the same context is consistent with such a date.

Other non-ceramic building materials

Two small pieces of daub were recovered from G[15]. Daub was used from prehistoric down to recent times, but associated building materials from the context suggest that these pieces are of Roman date.

Several very small fragments of painted wall plaster were recovered from C[172] and C[176]. Some are plain white and some show a red stripe, the one complete stripe being 4mm wide. These were used to cover the walls of Building 13.

Fragments of Roman *opus signinum* flooring were recovered from G[15] and K[50]; the former were found in a dump with other Roman building materials, while the latter were found with later building materials in make-up levelling and must be regarded as residual. They presumably came from a Roman building somewhere in the area.

16.3 The prehistoric pottery

Louise Rayner

Introduction

This report considers the prehistoric pottery from sites F, G and K. Although each site produced only a small amount of pottery the material has been examined and recorded in order to refine the dating and enable comparison with other prehistoric assemblages from the London region.

The pottery was recorded using the standard MoLAS/SS system, based on the guidelines set out by the PCRG (Prehistoric Ceramics Research Group 1995). Each sherd was examined with a x20 binocular microscope and defined by the dominant inclusions visible in the fabric. The fabric definitions for this assemblage are very broad owing to the small size and poor condition of the sherds, but where possible fabrics have been distinguished by the size and frequency of the main inclusion. Form and decoration codes were also recorded where identifiable. The sherds are quantified by count and weight (Table 24).

Summary of each assemblage

A combined total of 55 sherds (172g) were recorded from the three sites. The majority were recovered from site G, which accounted for 36 sherds (142g). Of the remaining sherds 15 (21g) were from site K and four from site F (9g).

The condition of the sherds from all three assemblages is poor and all showed signs of surface abrasion. Few feature sherds are present, with only two rim sherds and two decorated sherds identified. Consequently few forms could be attributed and close dating is problematic; all sherds are considered to be of prehistoric date on the basis of fabric.

Table 24 Prehistoric fabric types by site, quantified by sherd count and weight (see below for expansion of description codes)

Site	Fabric	Sherd count	Weight (g)
G	CP	2	9
G	FLIN	15	39
G	FLIN1	6	15
G	FLIN2	11	74
G	QU	1	4
G	VOIDS	1	1
F	FLIN	3	7
F	FLIN1	1	2
K	FLIN	15	21
Total		55	172

Fabrics

The majority of the sherds are flint-tempered, with only three other fabric types identified: clay pellet inclusions (CP), quartz-rich (QU) and unidentified voids (VOIDS). The flint temper is all burnt, crushed white flint and ranges in size from 0.5mm to 5mm. The better preserved sherds were defined on the basis of the flint temper size and surface treatment, and broadly fall into two types, which are not chronologically exclusive:

FLIN1
A hard fabric with medium (0.25mm–1.00mm) flint, fairly well sorted. These sherds tend to be thin-walled (4.00mm–6.00mm) with smoothed surfaces.

FLIN2
A hard fabric with coarse to very coarse flint (1.00mm–3.00mm or greater), poorly sorted. These sherds are thicker walled (8.00mm–10.00mm) with untreated surfaces.

The quartz-rich and unidentified void fabrics are represented only by single sherds; the fabric defined by clay pellets has two sherds recorded.

Forms and decoration

None of the sherds are large or complete enough to be confidently assigned to a particular form. Two rim sherds and two decorated sherds are the only feature sherds present.

<P1> F[7] (Fig 13)
Small, upright, rounded rim in fabric FLIN1. The sherd is very small in size and probably derives from a Late Bronze Age fineware vessel.

<P2> G[48/41] (Fig 13)
Sherd of thickened rim in fabric FLIN2. The wall thickness is 10.00mm. The form and date of this rim sherd can be only tentatively suggested but may derive from a Neolithic bowl or possibly from a Middle Bronze Age Deverel-Rimbury type urn. However, it must be noted that the fabric is somewhat different

from that normally used for Deverel-Rimbury urns in the London region.

<P3> G[39] (Fig 13)
Sherd decorated with a row of impressed lines forming a herringbone pattern. The sherd is thin-walled (4.00mm) with a sandy matrix and very rare coarse flint. Dating a single decorated body sherd is problematic but a Neolithic to Early Bronze Age date seems most probable.

<P4> G[47/49] (Fig 13)
Decorated sherd with a single row of incised oblique lines, probably from a collared urn. The soft, buff fabric has clay pellet inclusions and the sherd is relatively thick-walled, although severely abraded.

Contextual information

All the sherds from site G were recovered from the natural foreshore sands of the island, G[39], G[41], G[47], and G[48]. The sherds from site F came from a similar foreshore sand deposit, F[7]. Some of the sherds from site K were recovered from alluvial sands, K[31] and K[59], but twelve sherds were in the fill of a ditch/gully, K[32].

Other assemblages from the Westminster area

A number of other sites in the Westminster area have produced prehistoric pottery and three of these assemblages were re-examined.

Cromwell Green

The ceramic assemblage from Cromwell Green (WCG78) included a total of seven prehistoric sherds. The published pottery report assigns two decorated sherds, <P5> and <P6> (Fig 13) (5g), to the fill of a gully, F[82], which also contained worked flint (Platts 1980, 26). Although initially dated to the Iron Age, the identification of these sherds as Beaker pottery is now widely accepted (Needham 1987, 101; Merriman 1987, 324). One of these sherds is a rim, which is slightly everted and tapers to a rounded profile. Both sherds are in very poor condition with the surfaces badly abraded and damaged from over-vigorous cleaning. The decoration on the external surface of both sherds consists of sub-triangular-shaped impressions, possibly executed with a fingernail. Despite the apparent variation in surface colour, which appears to be a result of the abraded condition, it seems likely that the two sherds derive from one vessel.

The fabric is sparsely flint-tempered in a hard, dense matrix (flint up to 4.00mm), which is somewhat atypical in comparison to other Beaker pottery from London. The other known London examples are both from Southwark: a group of 55 sherds from Calvert's Buildings, 15–23 Southwark Street, and a single decorated sherd from 106 Borough High Street. The fabric of the Southwark Street sherds is fine with quartz and sand inclusions (Swain 1992, 67); the Borough High Street sherd is soft with some sand and sparse finely crushed flint (Barrett 1978, 197–9).

The other five sherds (20g) from this site are all flint-tempered body sherds. There are no diagnostic features but the size and density of the flint inclusions and the wall thickness would suggest a Middle Bronze Age date or earlier for these sherds.

The great hall

The great hall (site T) assemblage is comparable to that recovered from Cromwell Green. A total of 15 sherds (85g) are present, all in flint-tempered fabrics probably of Middle Bronze Age or earlier date. The sherds were recovered from T[211], a layer of dark brown silty sand (Whipp and Platts 1976, 353). There is one rim sherd with a simple rounded profile and one sherd with an applied lug or small boss, which may be part of a bossed cup. Bossed cups (or knobbed cups) form part of the Deverel-Rimbury assemblage and other examples have been recovered from the Thames at 'London', at Tagg's Island near Hampton and Stoneyfield cemetery, Farnham and a 'degenerate' example from Kingston Hill (Needham 1987, 111). The cups are also known from Essex at Mucking, Ardleigh and North Shoebury (Brown 1985, 78–81, figs 62.15, 63.29).

A fired clay spindle whorl, T<1> (Fig 21), was recovered from T[213], a blue-grey clay deposit (Whipp and Platts 1976, 353, fig 4 no. 12). The spindle whorl has a running pattern of pinprick decoration and horizontal and vertical lines scratched to form irregular panels. A similar example, decorated with a pinprick pattern, was recovered from a site in the City (GPO75) and other similar objects have been recovered from Iron Age settlement sites. The most comparable is from the hillfort at Danebury, with a decoration of scratched lines with numerous fine dots between them (Poole 1991, 370–2, fig 7.42 no. 7.85). Other fired clay objects from Glastonbury and Meare lake village are decorated with similar patterns of incised vertical and diagonal lines and fine dots (Bulleid and St George Gray 1917, 557, pl 89 no. Y18; Coles 1987, 64–5, fig 3.9 no. D27).

Westminster Abbey dorter undercroft

The final assemblage reconsidered during this study was from the dorter undercroft (WST86). This assemblage was recovered wholly residual but includes a sherd from the shoulder of a carinated jar with fingernail decoration, <P7>, from context [344], and a rim with finger-tipping on the upper edge, <P8>, from context [411] (Fig 21). The rim sherd also has part of a perforation or deep impression surviving. These feature sherds suggest a date in the Late Bronze Age–Early Iron Age transition period and parallels can be found in vessels from Heathrow, Petters Sports Field, Egham and Runnymede Bridge, Egham (Canham 1978, 21–2, figs 13.3, 14.35; O'Connell 1986, 65, fig 44 nos 34–39; Longley 1980, 165). The other sherds are all abraded flint-tempered body sherds with no diagnostic features. Surface treatments are confined to one sherd with burnished surfaces and one with external wipe marks.

Comparison with other assemblages

The assemblages from the three JLEP Westminster sites are also comparable to material recovered from Royal Docks Community School, Newham (PRG97), a site which is also located on gravel islands surrounded by inlets of the River Thames. The range of fabrics is similar with both a variety of flint-tempered and clay pellet fabrics (Rayner 1997).

A comparable clay pellet fabric also occurs in assemblages from 29 Addington Street, Southwark (WSB90) and 4–10 Lower Marsh, Lambeth (WBR88), both of which are just across the river in north Southwark and Lambeth. All these sherds appear to be from Bronze Age collared urns, which seems probable for <P4> (Fig 13).

Conclusions

The feature sherds from these JLEP Westminster sites are tentatively placed in the Neolithic to Early Bronze Age date range, although clearly much of the assemblage cannot be closely dated and some of the flint-tempered sherds are possibly of later date. Other assemblages from Cromwell Green and the great hall include pieces diagnostic of the Early and Middle Bronze Age, whilst the undercroft assemblage includes sherds with characteristics indicative of a Late Bronze Age–Early Iron Age date.

Clearly the recovery of prehistoric pottery from these sites is further evidence for activity on Thorney Island in the prehistoric period. This would appear to be one of several locations along the River Thames where gravel islands were intermittently occupied, possibly as seasonal settlements or camps. The dating of these assemblages, although not well defined, does suggest activity over a considerable period of time.

16.4 The medieval and post-medieval pottery

Roy Stephenson and Jacqui Pearce

Methodology

The pottery assemblages from these sites have been dealt with using standard Museum of London methodologies. All material was originally dated in order to provide a chronology to support the stratigraphic sequence. Paper and computer spotdate records form part of the project archive. Fabric codes used both in archive and in the main text are standard to the Museum of London; a summary of the main fabrics is given below. These are based on the system of Common Names which identify a range of fabrics and associated forms that derive from a common source.

Where pottery comes from sealed groups of a size where analysis is deemed worthwhile (Orton and Pearce 1984, 34) quantification by EVE (Orton 1975, 21–34) has taken place and is presented by form and fabric in the appropriate section. Form types are again based on standardised types.

An attempt has also been made in each period to characterise the pottery assemblages in terms of other 'typical' contemporary assemblages and to relate the material to previously published corpora of pottery from Westminster. Illustrations are limited to unusual vessels and those which appear in interesting associations.

Principal fabrics and forms, giving date ranges, are listed in Table 25; this list also serves as a check of medieval fabrics present on the sites.

Palace group of sites

Medieval pottery from site G

The earliest medieval pottery, dated to the 11th and 12th centuries, was represented by the presence of such fabrics as early Surrey ware (ESUR), London-area greyware (LOGR), early medieval shell-tempered ware (EMSH) and early medieval sand- and shell-tempered ware (EMSS). G[19] produced a medium-sized group of these types of sherds; it included a possible sherd of Winchester ware. G[14] produced a small amount of red-painted ware (REDP) imported from the Rhineland.

Later medieval pottery was represented by solitary sherds of London-type ware (LOND) and Kingston-type ware (KING) from contexts G[13] and G[22].

Post-medieval pottery from site G

This site produced an unstratified tin-glazed ware (TGW) plate decorated with 'Chinaman among Grasses' (Fig 99), a pattern clearly inspired by the Chinese ceramics and artefacts so in vogue in the late 17th and 18th centuries. The vessel undoubtedly belonged to a household which aspired to own Chinese goods but had to be content with copies.

Medieval pottery from site D

The early medieval pottery is limited to small amounts of London-area greyware (LOGR) and a solitary sherd of Stamford ware (STAM), which is a very hard durable glazed whiteware. The later medieval pottery consists of sherds of mundane locally produced wares such as London-type ware (LOND), Kingston-type ware (KING) and south Hertfordshire-type greyware (SHER).

The earliest pottery, apart from residual Roman sherds, is an EMSH cooking pot from Open Area 1. Period 6 produced from Open Area 4 a medium-sized group of wares typical of the first half of the 13th century. This group includes sherds from two shelly-sandy ware (SSW) cooking pots, fragments from LOND and coarse London type (LCOAR) jugs and a SHER cooking pot.

The later medieval pottery is entirely derived from local traditions that occur in the city, these being LOND, KING, SHER and, to a much lesser extent, Mill Green ware (MG). This can be demonstrated using the ceramic group from the fill of the cesspit D[54] (B6, period 7).

Table 25 Medieval and post-medieval pottery fabric, form and decoration codes and date ranges

Code	Expansion	Earliest date	Latest date
Fabrics			
ANDA	Andalusian lusterware	1250	1450
ANDE	Andenne-type ware	1050	1200
BEAG	Beauvais green-glazed ware	1500	1600
BORDY	Surrey-Hampshire border whiteware with clear (yellow) glaze	1550	1700
CBW	coarse Surrey-Hampshire border ware (rare pre-1300, common after 1350)	1270	1500
CHEA	Cheam whiteware	1350	1500
CHPO	Chinese porcelain	1580	1900
COLS	Colchester-type slipware	1480	1550
DTGW	Dutch tin-glazed ware	1512	1800
DUTR	Dutch red earthenware	1300	1650
DUTSG	Dutch red earthenware with sgraffito decoration	1480	1550
DUTSL	Dutch slipped red earthenware	1500	1650
EBORD	early Surrey-Hampshire border whiteware	1480	1550
EMCH	early medieval chalk-tempered ware	1050	1150
EMFL	early medieval flint-tempered ware	970	1100
EMS	early medieval sandy ware	970	1100
EMSH	early medieval shell-tempered ware	1050	1150
EMSS	early medieval sand- and shell-tempered ware	1000	1150
ENGS	English stoneware	1700	1900
ENPO	English porcelain	1745	1900
ESUR	early Surrey ware	1050	1150
FREC	Frechen stoneware	1550	1700
KING	Kingston-type ware (possibly from 1200)	1230	1400
LANG	Langerwehe stoneware	1480	1550
LCALC	calcareous London-type ware	1080	1200
LCGR	Low Countries greyware	1350	1500
LCOAR	coarse London-type ware	1080	1200
LLON	late London-type ware	1400	1500
LMHG	late medieval Hertfordshire glazed ware	1340	1450
LOGR	London-area greyware	1050	1150
LOND	London-type ware	1080	1350
LONS	London stoneware	1670	1900
MART	Martincamp-type ware	1480	1650
MG	Mill Green ware	1270	1350
MG COAR	Mill Green coarseware	1270	1400
MPUR	Midlands purple ware	1400	1500
PMBL	post-medieval black-glazed redware	1600	1900
PMR	London-area post-medieval redware	1580	1900
PMRE	London-area early post-medieval redware	1480	1600
RAER	Raeren stoneware	1480	1610
PMSR	London-area post-medieval slipped redware	1480	1650
PMSRG	London-area post-medieval slipped redware with green glaze	1480	1650
RBOR	Surrey-Hampshire border redware	1550	1900
REDP	red-painted ware (mostly found after AD 970)	900	1250
SAIG	Saintonge ware with even green glaze	1280	1350
SAIM	Saintonge ware with mottled green glaze	1250	1650
SAIN	Saintonge ware	1250	1650
SHER	south Hertfordshire-type greyware	1250	1500
SIEG	Siegburg stoneware	1170	1350
SPAM	Iberian red micaceous ware	1480	1650
SSW	shelly-sandy ware	1140	1220
STAM	Stamford-type ware	1050	1150
SWSG	white salt-glazed stoneware	1720	1780
TGW	unsourced English tin-glazed ware	1570	1800
TGW C	tin-glazed ware with 'Orton type C' decoration	1630	1800
TPW	transfer-printed whiteware	1780	1900
TUDG	'Tudor green' ware	1350	1500
WINC	Winchester ware	970	1100
Forms			
BOT	bottle		
BOWL CONC	concave-sided bowl		
CHP	chamber pot		
JAR	jar		
JAR SM	small jar		
JUG	jug		
JUG BAL	baluster jug		
JUG CON	conical jug		
JUG RND	rounded jug		
JUG TULBAL	tulip-shaped baluster jug		
PIP	pipkin		
PLATE	plate		
TUL	tulip-necked baluster jug		
WAT	watering pot		
Decoration			
HD	highly decorated style		
WSD	white slip decoration		

Table 26 Details of the illustrated medieval and post-medieval pottery (see Table 25 for expansion of codes)

Catalogue no.	Context	Date range of pot (period)	Date range of context (period)	Land use	Fig no.	Fabric	Form
<P9>	D[54]	7	7	B6	48	KING	JUG BAL
<P10>	D[54]	7	7	B6	48	KING	JUG BAL
<P11>	D[54]	7	7	B6	48	KING	JUG BAL
<P12>	D[54]	7	7	B6	48	KING	JAR
<P13>	E[49]	7	7	OA11	63	LOND	JUG
<P14>	B[168]	9	9	OA14	86	PMSRG	WAT
<P15>	B[168]	9	9	OA14	87	PMRE	WAT
<P16>	J[121]	10	10	B8	90, 91	TGW	BOT
<P17>	G[+]	7/8/9	–	OA4	99	TGW	PLATE

Within the abbey

The earliest medieval pottery dates from the mid 11th century and was characterised by the presence of ESUR and LOGR.

Groups from the mid 12th century contain a small amount of non-local wares, including STAM. After this date the most predominant ware present is LOND, together with small quantities of KING and MG. There are small quantities of

Table 27 Details of the pottery from site G (see Table 25 for expansion of codes)

Period	Land use/activity	Fabric	Date range
7	Open Area 4, alluvium	ESUR JAR; LOGR JAR; WINC; EMSH JAR; EMSS JAR	1050–1150
7	Open Area 4, dump	ESUR JAR; LOGR JAR; EMSH	1050–1100
7	Open Area 4, alluvium	LOND	1080–1350
7	Open Area 4, alluvium	REDP	900–1250
7	Open Area 4, alluvium group 7	LOGR; KING	1230–1350

Table 28 Details of the pottery from site J (see Table 25 for expansion of codes)

Period	Land use/activity	Fabric	Date range
6	Open Area 4, groups 7 and 8	LOGR JAR; STAM	1050–1150
6	Open Area 6, group 8	KING BOWL; KING (burnt)	1230–1400
7	Building 9, group 12	LOND JUG BAL	1200–1350
7	Structure 9	SHER JAR; SHER	1150–1300
10	Building 8, well	TGW BOT (bird-on-rock)	1730–70
10	Open Area 4	RAER	1480–1550
10	Open Area 4	TGW C JAR SM	1630–1800
11	Building 32	LOND JUG	1150–1350
11	Open Area 4	TGW C CHP; SWSG; ENGS	1730–70

imported Saintonge ware (SAIN). The later medieval pottery includes locally produced wares such as coarse border ware (CBW). There is a significant number of Siegburg (SIEG) sherds (B13, period 9) derived from jugs and a drinking bowl. There were also significant quantities of Siegburg in the group recovered from the Deanery (Hurst 1960). The material from the Deanery appears to be a clearance group dating to the first quarter of the 16th century, plus a quantity of later pottery dating to the late 16th or early 17th century.

The post-medieval pottery present from this site cannot be regarded in the same light as the post-medieval pottery from the Deanery group, which produced a range of TGW vessels as well as fragments from an imported Iberian majolica plate. The imported pottery is limited to small quantities of Frechen stoneware, and an insignificant quantity of other imported sherds such as Dutch redware (DUTR). The bulk of the pottery consists of mundane, locally produced earthenwares, such as post-medieval redware (PMR).

Outside the abbey, to the north and west

The bulk of the pottery from site B (WUS92) consists of everyday domestic wares, common throughout the London area during the second half of the 14th and the 15th century. Cooking and tablewares predominate, and there is little evidence of any industrial activity, although there are KING crucible fragments, which are indicative of metalworking on

Table 29 Details of the pottery from site D (see Table 25 for expansion of codes)

Period	Land use/activity	Fabric	Date range
5	Open Area 1	EMSH JAR	1050–1150
6	Open Area 4	SSW JAR (x2); LOND JUG; LCOAR JUG; SHER JAR; LOND WSD JUG; LOND JUG (x2)	1200–50
6	Open Area 4	LOND JUG	1150–1350
7	Building 6	KING BOWL CONC (x4); KING; KING JUG RND; KING JUG; LOND JUG BAL; KING; LOND; LOND JUG BAL; LOND TUL; MG	1270–1350
7	Building 6	SHER JAR; LOND JUG BAL (x2); KING TUL; KING JUG BAL; LOND HD JUG; KING JUG; LOND JUG	1250–1300
7	Open Area 4	SSW; LCOAR	1150–1250
7	Open Area 4	SHER JAR; SSW; KING; LOND JUG	1230–1350
8	Building 6	KING; LOND JUG	1230–1300
8	Building 6	LOND	1080–1350
8	Building 6	KING; LOND	1230–1350
8	Open Area 4	LOND	1080–1350
9	Building 6	KING; LOND	1230–1350
10	Open Area 4	LOND	1080–1350
10	Open Area 4	KING; KING PIP	1230–1350
11	Open Area 4	KING; KING JUG	1230–1350

or near the site at C(ii). The high level of fragmentation, with very few complete profiles or joining sherds, as well as the sherd-links recognised between contexts, and the chronological mixing of many contexts, are all consistent with the process of land reclamation in the late medieval period. Most of the pottery derived from the series of period 8 pit fills from Open Area 14.

Imported pottery of the period (*c* 1350–1500) is represented by sherds from four different vessels in Saintonge ware from south-west France. Three of these are jugs with mottled or plain green glaze (SAIM; SAIG), but there are also two sherds in contexts B[151] and B[271] from a single vessel of unusual form, which may have been a handled bowl. The only other contemporaneous imported pottery is part of a cooking pot in Low Countries greyware (LCGR) from B[221], which is never very common in London, and the base of a frying pan in Dutch red earthenware (DUTR) from B[126].

Later medieval imports during the 15th century consist of DUTR, including parts of two frying pans from B[128] and B[251]; LCGR, part of a cooking pot in B[110]; Siegburg stoneware (SIEG), mostly small sherds from drinking jugs of uncertain form, but also the rim of a *Jakobakanne*, a 15th-century form, from B[251], and a jug base, sooted externally from the same context; Langerwehe stoneware (LANG), part of a jug from B[251]; and Andalusian lusterware (ANDA), the handle from a vase or jug from B[186].

The post-medieval pottery from site C(ii) included Beauvais green-glazed ware (BEAG) and Dutch sgraffito-decorated ware (DUTSG).

16.5 The accessioned finds

Richenda Goffin and Jackie Keily

A total of 205 accessioned finds were recovered from 10 sites (Table 30). For each entry the catalogue number (in angled brackets) is given, then a brief identifier of object type and the figure number where appropriate; this is followed by the accessioned find number (in angled brackets), context number (in square brackets), date of object, date of context from which object was recovered, land use.

Roman

Ceramic

<S1>
G[47], Roman, period 1, OA1
A fragment of Roman brick, mortared on one side. This surface had an impression of the hoof of a possible goat or sheep.

Stone

<S2>
G[27], Roman, period 7, OA4
Three fragments of Mayen lava quernstone. One of these fragments was part of the outer edge of a domestic hand-quern with diagonal tooling on the outside. It was part of the lower stone, the upper surface of which was abraded so that wear patterns were difficult to identify. The two other fragments were probably from another quern and were less diagnostic, with only three surviving worked surfaces. Such residual finds confirm the presence of Roman activity in the vicinity of Thorney Island. These have been noted on other sites such as Westminster Abbey (Goffin 1995, 87).

Medieval

Coins and jettons

<S3>–<S7>
As can be seen from Table 31, only three coins and two jettons were recovered from the sites in this project. Only the two medieval coins could be fully identified.

Glass

<S8> Beaker (Fig 69)
F<11>, F[130], period 8, period 9, B15
Incomplete; diameter of rim 120mm. Four fragments of soda glass beaker with large applied prunts or *Krautstrunk* decoration. Such drinking vessels are likely to have been used by wealthy households.

<S9> Vessel
D<24>, D[54], medieval, period 7, B6
Four fragments of potash vessel glass were recovered from the medieval cesspit D[54].

<S10> Vessel
C<14>, C[255], ?medieval, period 10, B23.
Small fragment of green vessel glass, unassignable to a particular form.

<S11> Window
C<26>, C[251], medieval, period 10, B23
A few fragments of undecorated medieval potash window glass in very poor condition.

Ceramic

<S12>–<S13> Crucible (Fig 31)
C<5> and C<6>, C[273], period 4–5, period 8, OA13
Fragments of two small ceramic crucibles *c* 50mm–60mm in diameter. The fabric consists of a hard whiteware now turned grey, identified by the broad category of early medieval coarse whiteware (EMCW). This is characterised by an ill-sorted clay with rounded and sub-angular

Table 30 Distribution of accessioned finds by site

Site	Iron	Copper alloy	Lead	Ceramic	Organic	Glass	Stone	Flint	Other	Total
B	7	26		3		3		6		45
C	5	5	1	5	6	3	5	1	1 silver	32
D	2	1	2	1	14	1	1		1 silver	23
E	6	7						1		14
F	1	4	1	3		1	1	5		16
G				1			1	45		47
J	1			1				5		7
K		2						9		11
L								4		4
N		1 (comp)		5						6
Total	22	46	4	19	20	8	8	76	2	205

Table 31 The excavated coins

Site	Catalogue no.	Accession no.	Context	Material	Type	Ruler	Earliest date	Latest date	Comment
B	<S6>	B<1>	B[151]	copper alloy	jetton		?1400	?1500	
B	<S7>	B<2>	B[158]	copper alloy	jetton		?1300	?1400	
C(i)	<S4>	C<2>	C[80]	copper alloy	coin		1695	1775	
C(i)	<S5>	C<4>	C[81]	silver	coin	Edward I	1280	1281	long cross penny
D	<S3>	D<15>	D[+]	silver	coin	Henry II	1158	1180	penny; London

inclusions. When unused the inclusions still maintain their original colour and it is possible to identify pink and rosy quartz, which is typical of clay from the Reading Beds of the Surrey whiteware tradition. The crucibles are hemispherical in shape, and both show evidence of being used. Their appearance has been altered because of the heat, there are signs of partial vitrification and both vessels have copper-alloy residues in their bases.

Such crucibles made in this fabric are often associated with the Saxon and Norman period in London (Bayley et al 1991, 392). Find-spots are usually concentrated within the City itself, often in the area around Cheapside and the Guildhall (Allen and Vince 1991, 11).

Iron

<S14> Key (Fig 67)
D<17>, D[32], period 8, period 8, B6
Complete; length 160mm, bow 45mm x 28mm, bit 22mm x 38mm (for terminology of keys, see Egan 1998, 111). A rotary key with kidney-shaped bow. The key has a slightly narrowed tip, and may originally have had a slightly thicker shank at the handle end. The bit has symmetrical clefts of a similar pattern to a better preserved example from Baynard House, Queen Victoria Street of late 14th-century date (Egan 1998, 118, fig 91 no. 328). The latter was found in a dumped layer that contained both high-quality as well as more utilitarian objects (Egan 1998, 14).

<S15> Knife
B<31>, B[150], medieval, period 9, OA14
Incomplete; existing length 88mm, width 13mm. Fragment of blade and part of whittle tang.

<S16> Spur (Fig 61)
C<17>, C[281], period 7, period 7, OA10
Incomplete; overall length 128mm, length of point 26mm. Iron prick spur, one arm missing, the other curved with a Type B terminal (Ward Perkins 1940, 95). The point is cup-shaped, the actual goad part measuring 10.5mm in length. No exact parallel has been found, but a rowel spur with similar side-pieces has been dated by Blanche Ellis to *c* 1250–1300 (J Clark, pers comm), which also fits in with the ceramic dating of *c* 1250–1350 for the deposit. During the 13th and 14th centuries there were many variants of the prick spur form. In addition, throughout this period the shape of the terminals on one spur was not always the same, as one of them could be slotted, and the other one bolted or hooked into the strap (Ward Perkins 1940, 99). This may be the case with the spur from site C(ii), but since only one arm survives, it is only a possibility. By the second quarter of the 14th century prick spurs had generally been superseded by rowel spurs, although they are still found after this period in this country (Ellis 1995, 128). A fragment of a rowel spur of silvered iron of probable medieval date was recovered from the excavations at Broad Sanctuary, Westminster to the north-west of Westminster Abbey (McIsaac 1982, 355).

<S17> Tool
E<12>, E[32], nd, period 7, OA12
Incomplete; surviving length 135mm, width 10mm widening to 23mm, width of arm 7mm. A possible tool with a hole for suspension at the top of the handle. This handle widens before dividing into two arms, one of which is missing. The other arm is incomplete.

Copper alloy

<S18> Bell (Fig 73)
E<2>, E[24], period 7/8, period 8, OA11
Incomplete; height of bell 25mm. Part of a decorated copper-alloy bell, flattened. The clapper and suspension loop are formed from the same piece of metal, twisted at either end. The upper part of the bell is decorated with two parallel incised bands, with similar decoration also present on the lower part. The bell is not dissimilar to one found from Billingsgate Lorry Park watching brief (BWB83), City of London, which was recovered from a deposit dating to between the late 13th century and the first half of the 14th century (Egan and Pritchard 1991, 341). That bell has an integral suspension loop, whilst the loop on the present example is separate and consists of a twisted piece of wire which also forms the clapper. Such bells had a wide variety of uses, from purely secular fashion accessories ornamenting clothes to insignia of religious activities such as those used by pilgrims (Spencer 1998, 123). Another possible circumstance in which they were known to have been used was as an object to ward off evil, like a talisman. A late 16th-century example can be seen in the painting of the infant Philip, by Juan Pantocha de la Cruz (1594). The child is shown wearing a reliquary on his chest, and around his girdle are suspended different types of amulet, one of which is a clapper bell suspended from a chain (Bedaux 1995, 34). Organic remains, possibly straw or grass, were found inside the bell, and may have been around the loop for the clapper. It is not possible to know whether this represents a post-depositional occurrence or whether it was there before burial.

<S19> Buckle pin
B<19>, B[160], medieval, period 8, OA14
Incomplete; length 46mm. Copper-alloy buckle pin. Such a large pin is likely to have been attached to a large or medium-sized buckle frame.

<S20> Finger ring
B<16>, B[151], medieval, period 9, OA14
Complete; external diameter 22mm. Copper-alloy finger ring.

<S21> Pilgrim badge (Fig 78)
B<7>, B[143], period 8, period 8, OA14
Incomplete; height 25mm, width 22mm. Copper-alloy horseshoe pilgrim badge with pin attachment; the horseshoe is decorated with further additions made of another material, representing the nails in the shoe. The method of attachment is a pin positioned horizontally midway down the badge. It is very similar to a lead-alloy badge from Nieuwland, Holland, from the van Beuningen Collection, which has glass decorations representing nails and is dated *c* 1375–1425 (van Beuningen and Koldeweij 1993, 303, no. 921).

<S22> Mount
C<1>, C[13], medieval, period 10, B22
Incomplete; diameter 25mm. A copper-alloy mount of octofoil form with missing rivet. Such mounts, made from sheet copper alloy, appear in London deposits in the early 13th century but become much more common in the late 14th to early 15th centuries (Egan and Pritchard 1991, 162). Many similar mounts have been recovered from City waterfront sites such as Swan Lane and Billingsgate Lorry Park (Egan and Pritchard 1991, 194–5). The present example is probably medieval, by comparison with other similar types, but residual, found in C[13], associated with the 17th-century rebuild of Building 13.

<S23> Mount (Fig 64)
E<11>, E[32], period 7, period 7, OA12
Incomplete; length 52mm, surviving width 38mm. Copper-alloy gilded shield-shaped mount, with perforations on two edges for rivet attachment, one edge broken. Decorated with heraldic motif of three lions, signifying the arms of England. A smaller shield with the same decoration, found at Billingsgate in the City of London, has a stud projecting from the rear (Griffiths 1995, 70–1, fig 53). The arms can be identified as those of England before 1340, *three lions passant gardant*. After this date the arms of France were added to those of England, although it is thought that small objects continued to be decorated with the old heraldic arms (Griffiths 1995, 65). Such mounts may have been used to decorate horse harness,

such as bridles, but they were often poorly made rather than being indicative of the highest ranks of society. The shield appears to have been a very common design, representing *c* 33% of the known examples of pendant mounts (Griffiths 1995, 63). This type of decoration, using copper-alloy pendants, appears to have been used from the 12th century onwards and the use of heraldic motifs on pendants was particularly popular in the second half of the 13th century (Griffiths 1995, 62). Heraldic devices such as shields were also used to decorate ceramics during this period, both inlaid floor tiles and pottery. Stamped bosses of shields, and fleurs-de-lis were used on Kingston-type wares spanning the period from the mid 13th to the mid 14th century (Pearce and Vince 1988, 43; Goffin 1991, 317, fig 2). This coincides with the period of the Welsh and Scottish wars of Edward I (1272–1307) (Griffiths 1995, 62). The gilding is detectable only on the lion part of the decoration, now surviving just as small flecks, with no gold present on any other part of the mount such as the edges of the shield.

<S24> Mount
B<39>, B[16], medieval, period 9, OA1
Incomplete; dimensions 13mm x 13mm. Square-shaped mount with two rivet holes, one rivet *in situ*; surface has diagonal scratches, possibly randomly incised. Rivets positioned inside two of the corners.

<S25> Vessel
B<13>, B[159], medieval, period 10, OA14
Incomplete; rim diameter *c* 240mm. Fragment of copper-alloy vessel.

Organic material

<S26>
C<30>, C[314], nd, period 5, OA1
Originally thought to be a piece of fine thread, now thought more likely to be a fragment of leather or a piece of moss.

Wood

<S27> Plate or bowl (Fig 30)
C<28>, C[298], nd, period 5, OA1
Incomplete; diameter *c* 260mm. Approximately half a plate or bowl, now flattened. There is a groove around the inner edge of the rim and an S-shaped mark has been burnt on to the outer surface near the base. Similar S-shaped marks have been found on the bases of two wooden bowls excavated at Milk Street in the City of London (Keys 1998, 201–2, fig 162 no. 554, and 203, fig 163 no. 563) and other marks have also been noted (Keys 1998, 197). Such marks are thought to have been made for identification, possibly indicating an owner or user. Marks are also present on some of the wooden vessels excavated from a pit at St Mary Spital (Egan 1997, 204). Made from ash (*Fraxinus* sp).

<S28>–<S30> Stakes
C<27>, C[296], nd, period 5, OA1
Three incomplete stakes with sharpened points; all three are oak (*Quercus* sp).
Surviving length 160mm, width at widest end 44mm. Tapering to a trimmed point at one end.
Surviving length 95mm, width 40mm. Both ends broken, one just beginning to come to a point.
Surviving length 170mm, width 40mm. Broken at both ends, one end cut diagonally, forming a flat point.

<S31>–<S37> (Fig 49)
A range of artefacts including ceramics and organics was recovered from a wood-lined cesspit within Building 6. The accompanying pottery is of late 13th- to early 14th-century date. The wooden objects recovered from this feature included four bowls and three platters (Table 32) a possible stirring im ement and a number of barrel fragments. All of the bowls and platters are fragmentary and only one, <S35> is almost complete. One further fragment of wooden platter D<6>, D[54], could not be located for inclusion in this discussion.

<S38> Stirring stick (Fig 51)
D<21>, D[54], nd, period 7, B6
Incomplete; surviving length 101mm, diameter at rounded base 35mm x 47mm tapering to 33mm x 36mm at broken end. An incomplete stirring stick or other implement. It is roughly oval in section and is at its widest at the rounded base, which is slightly roughened, tapering along its length. The top of the implement is broken off and missing. The object is slightly flattened along one side.

<S39> Barrel
D<1>, D[54], nd, period 7, B6
Incomplete; diameter at top 275mm, diameter at base 245mm, thickness 20mm. Approximately half of a barrel end with a bevelled outer edge. There are the remains of an 'X' mark knife cut in the top surface.

<S40> Barrel
D<2>, D[54], nd, period 7, B6
Incomplete; diameter at top 255mm x 235mm, diameter at base 225mm x 225mm, thickness 19mm. A complete barrel end with a bevelled outer edge; there is some damage to the edges.

Leather

Identification and dating by Alison Nailer.

<S41> Shoe
D<10>, D[54], period 7, period 7, B6
A near complete side-laced ankle

Table 32 Details of bowls and platters from cesspit in Building 6

Catalogue no.	Form	Accession no.	Context	Survival	Diameter at top (mm)	Diameter at base (mm)	Height (mm)	Species of wood	Graining	Comment
<S31>	?bowl	D<7>	D[54]	fragmentary				cf *Alnus*		small base fragment; external turning lines
<S32>	plain bowl	D<5>	D[54]	profile	*c* 150	*c* 77	*c* 45	*Alnus*		internal and external turning lines; thin walls
<S33>	plain bowl	D<18>	D[54]	profile	*c* 165	74		cf *Alnus*		internal and external turning lines; thin walls
<S34>	plain bowl	D<19>	D[54]	profile	145	85	*c* 35	*Alnus*		internal and external turning lines; groove on external side
<S35>	platter	D<4>	D[54]	near complete	230	120	*c* 15	*Alnus*	knot near centre	internal and external turning lines; part of internal rim blackened
<S36>	platter	D<9>	D[54]	profile	*c* 250		*c* 23+	cf *Alnus*		internal turning lines; rough base with no obvious foot; blackened
<S37>	platter	D<8>	D[56]	rim fragment	*c* 260			*Alnus*		external turning lines

shoe. Both the sole and upper survive in quite good condition, showing no signs of heavy wear.

Composite organic object

This object was the subject of a conservation treatment project by Emily Williams (1994) and the results are summarised here.

<S42>
C<29>, C<32>, C[316], nd, period 5, OA1
Two fragments from the same incomplete object. Accession C<32> is the larger and is of wood and leather, comprising three thin strips of willow/poplar (*Salix* sp), *c* 3mm–5mm thick, partly overlapping and resting on a sheet of leather. At least one of the wooden strips appears to have been attached to the leather by means of iron nails or rivets. Between the wood and the leather are the remains of black and white deposits. The white layer has been identified as calcium carbonate but it has not been possible to identify the black deposit. The black layer is, however, definitely associated with the white layer and both are definitely intentional. It has been suggested that the white layer may be a gesso ground for the black layer. Gesso consists of calcium carbonate with an added size (gelatin) to produce a hard, waterproof surface and is often used to prepare a porous surface for a layer of pigment. Since the object is incomplete it is uncertain whether it is part of a structural feature such as a drain lining, or a smaller artefact such as a bucket.

Accession C<29> is much smaller and is also made up of wooden strips on leather with traces of a white pigment, possibly calcium carbonate, and possibly pitch. This object is in a very poor condition and is very fragmentary, but is similar to the object described above. The white deposit and the possible pitch may have been for waterproofing. Because of its fragmentary nature it is impossible to identify the original form or function of the object.

Post-medieval

Copper alloy

<S43> Bell
E<9>, E[5], nd, period 9, OA11
Incomplete; rim diameter 100mm. A small rim fragment of a cast copper-alloy clapper bell.

<S44> Buckle (Fig 85)
E<7>, E[5], period 9, period 9, OA11
Complete; length 31mm, width 24mm. The buckle has a double oval frame with intact pin. The outside edge of each loop of the frame is decorated with three central spines.

<S45> ?Button
F<7>, F[8], nd, period 9, OA14
Incomplete; diameter 15mm. A possible copper-alloy button; very corroded.

<S46> Mount
F<1>, F[23], period 10/11, period 1, OA1
Incomplete; length 26mm, width 16mm. Part of an oval copper-alloy mount attached to leather; probably part of a clasp for a purse or bag.

<S47> ?Necklace (Figs 74–5)
E<3>, E[3], period 8/9, period 10, OA11
The object is made up of several fragments of copper-alloy wirework chain, forming a highly decorative dress accessory such as a necklace. Each section measures *c* 23mm in length and consists of separate lengths of coiled twisted wire wound round a thicker central wire. One end of the twisted wire segments is trimmed with a bone bead, while the other end terminates in a loop that forms the link for the next section. Another fragment comes from a more elaborate part of the ornament. It consists of four parallel strands of wound wires, alternating with bone beads attached to a central hook. Running through the centre of the ornament and fixed to the other strands with horizontal twisted wires is a central strand consisting of bone beads and one degraded glass bead. These decorative elements may have been repeated intermittently in between the plainer segments of twisted wires, or may perhaps have formed the focal point of the jewellery. Probably dates to 1500–50 (G Egan, pers comm).

During the 15th century precious metal chained necklaces became popular with the upper classes (Egan and Pritchard 1991, 318). Archaeological evidence indicates that they were also made of less valuable metals such as copper alloy. Beads were not popular for necklaces during the medieval period apart from when they were used in rosaries (Margeson 1993, 5). However, glass and bone beads were used with wirework jewellery in the late 15th and early 16th centuries (Margeson 1993, 5). A more elaborate example, with some of the same basic elements as the one found here, was found at Pottergate, Norwich (Margeson 1993, 8). The copper-alloy wirework on this occasion had been used as a frame around two bracteate pilgrim badges, and further embellished with glass beads. It is thought to be late 15th/early 16th century in date. Later examples have been excavated in London, dating to the 16th and first half of the 17th centuries. A copper-alloy headdress from Butlers Wharf shows an elaborate combination of decorative wirework with glass and bone beads, thought to have been in use *c* 1600 (Murdoch 1991, 212–13).

<S48> Vessel
B<4>, B[+], post-medieval, –,–
Incomplete; diameter 280mm. Part of a copper-alloy cauldron with an everted rim.

Iron

<S49> Barrel hoop
C<9>, C[13], nd, period 10, B22
Incomplete; surviving length of longest fragment 360mm, width 30mm. Part of an iron barrel hoop, in a number of fragments. Some small fragments of the wooden barrel also remain.

<S50> Hinge
C<16>, C[251], nd, period 10, OA13
Incomplete; surviving length 125mm, width 23mm. Hinge fragment; very corroded and fragmentary.

<S51> Staple
C<15>, C[136], nd, period 8, B13
Incomplete; a small fragment of a staple; corroded.

Ivory

<S52> Knife (Fig 95)
C<7>, C[+], period 10/11, –, –
Complete; length 140mm, maximum width of blade 18mm. A complete ivory knife, including blade and handle. The bulbous tip of the blade, the pronounced hump or angle on the back edge of the knife and the pistol-grip is typical of the style which was popular in the second quarter of the 18th century (Singleton 1973, pl 3 (a)); possibly used for feather curling.

Glass

<S53> Bottle
B<24>, B[145], period 11, period 11, OA14
The base of a 19th-century pale blue rectangular medicinal bottle.

<S54> Wine glass
C<13>, C[251], period 9/10, period 10, OA13
Incomplete; surviving length 69mm, diameter at widest point 24mm. Part of a large plain

inverted baluster stem from a wine glass, dated *c* 1590–1620. Probably from a funnel-shaped goblet of Broad Street-type production.

<S55> Vessel
B<23>, B[220], period 11, period 11, OA14
A fragment of bright blue glass dating to the 19th century.

Discussion

The precinct of Westminster Abbey

Medieval accessions from the one site, C(i), within the abbey were scarce but included a silver coin, a long cross penny of Edward I (1272–1307) and structural elements, presumably from Building 13, such as the fragments of worked stone and an iron staple. An octofoil mount made from sheet copper alloy was found in period 10 but probably dates to the late 14th to early 15th centuries. No objects with any obviously religious associations were found.

Outside the abbey and palace precincts

Fourteen accessions were recovered from a series of dumps, ditches and pits at site E. These features dated mainly to the medieval period, but such activity also occurred during the 16th century. Several copper-alloy items of dress or horse accessories survived, none of particularly high status but nevertheless of interest since they may reflect the symbolism and ritual of the medieval period. The shield-shaped gilded copper-alloy mount, for example, possibly used on horse harness, is decorated with the heraldic motif of *three lions passant gardant*, the arms of England before 1340. Heraldic designs were very popular, particularly in the second half of the 13th century (Griffiths 1995, 62) and were often used on cheap, mass-produced items, perhaps for use by retainers and servants rather than by the nobility themselves (ibid). Although such mounts are therefore, not uncommon and not indicative of particular wealth, the occurrence of this example, decorated with the arms of England, in the vicinity of the Palace of Westminster makes it of particular interest. The small decorated copper-alloy bell, possibly used for a secular or religious purpose, is also of interest since the ceramic dating of the deposit in which it was found confirms the dating of a similar bell from the Billingsgate Lorry Park in the City of London (Egan and Pritchard 1991, 341).

A small assemblage of medieval accessioned finds was recovered from medieval deposits at C(ii) or residually in later deposits. Some of these objects are structural in nature, such as the window glass, but most are domestic or utilitarian, such as the 13th-century iron spur and the wooden plate or bowl. The fragments of two crucibles containing copper-alloy metalworking deposits were recovered from a late medieval rebuild of a medieval chalk well and are probably residual, as such fabric types and forms are more typical of an early medieval date. Features cutting the alluvial clay provided good preservation of organic material, including the fragment of a wooden plate or bowl made from ash, and the wood and leather object with possible pitch/paint remains. An unusual copper-alloy pilgrim badge or brooch in the shape of a horseshoe found with ceramics dating to the mid 14th to 15th century in a rubbish pit in Open Area 14 on site B is paralleled by a lead-alloy badge from the Netherlands dating to *c* 1375–1425 (van Beuningen and Koldeweij 1993, 303, no. 921). This site also produced a range of utilitarian and personal objects: a fragmentary knife, part of a copper-alloy vessel, a plain copper-alloy finger ring, a mount and a buckle pin.

The prunted beaker from site F is one of the few objects that may have come from a wealthy household; it was imported from northern Europe and probably dates to the later medieval period.

Sites associated with the Palace of Westminster

The largest group of finds of medieval date was recovered from a timber-lined cesspit of late 13th- to early 14th-century date from Building 6 in site D. The waterlogged pit provided good preservation conditions and it produced a variety of wooden, glass and ceramic vessels of apparently utilitarian quality. The leather recovered from this feature also reflects this lack of status. The wooden vessels consisted of eight bowls and platters and barrel fragments. Wooden vessels were very common throughout the medieval period but do not usually survive outside waterlogged conditions. Groups of bowls and other vessels have been recovered from St Mary Spital, London and the Austin Friars, Leicester (Clay 1981, 139–42); there are many individual finds, too, for example, from York and London (Keys 1998, 196–217). It is suggested that Building 6 may have been used as a hostelry and that the contents of the cesspit were items used there. An iron key, found in period 8, may also have been used in Building 6.

Post-medieval

Few post-medieval accessions were recovered apart from clay pipe fragments and some vessel glass. The highest quality artefact is the possible necklace of copper-alloy wire, bone and glass beads, which probably dates to the first half of the 16th century. Although not made from the most expensive of metals, it would have formed part of a relatively elaborate dress accessory, such as a necklace or headdress. Rather later in date is the unstratified ivory knife from site C(i), which may have been used as a feather curler and dates to the 18th century. This may have come from Building 22 prior to its demolition.

16.6 Plant remains

John Giorgi

Methods

During the excavations of the JLEP Westminster sites, environmental soil samples were collected from a range of potentially well-dated features for the recovery of biological data. This included the retrieval of archaeobotanical remains for information on the nature of economic and/or human activities and the character of the local environment, both on a spatial and temporal basis. Individual assessment reports have been prepared for each of the nine sampled sites and a summary document also prepared for an overview of the potential of the archaeobotanical material (Giorgi 1997). These reports are available for consultation in the Museum of London archive.

The sites

A total of 76 bulk samples were collected from nine sites. These were divided into two groups according to area: those situated on Thorney Island and those lying off the island on the foreshore or in the river.

The sampled sites off Thorney Island were sites B (which included site H) (BOT/ASS/05/95; BOT/ASS/06/96) and F (BOT/ASS/04/95; BOT/ASS/11/96). Forty-six bulk samples were collected from these sites.

A total of 30 environmental soil samples were collected from six sites on Thorney Island. These were sites C, E (BOT/ASS/01/95), D (BOT/ASS/02/95), G (BOT/ASS/03/95), J (BOT/ASS/13/96) and L (BOT/ASS/34/97).

Dating and feature types

Table 33 shows the number of samples from each period by site that were selected for analysis. It shows that samples were taken from the Neolithic through to the post-medieval period (periods 1 to 11) although most of the samples (44 or 61%) were from medieval deposits (periods 5 to 8). The remainder (17 or 24%) were from prehistoric deposits (periods 1 to 2), and post-medieval deposits (10 or 14%) (periods 9 to 11). No samples were assessed or analysed from Roman and Saxon deposits (periods 3 and 4).

The samples were taken mainly from natural deposits associated with alluvial and marsh deposition which made up almost half (32) of the analysed samples with the remaining ones coming from the fills of pits (18), ditches (7) and various cut features (14).

Sampling and processing methods

The samples were processed according to the potential level of preservation of biological remains in the samples. Thus, samples that appeared to contain well-preserved organic remains by survival in an anoxic environment, were sub-sampled (500g) and the sub-samples wet-sieved to 0.25mm with the resultant material being stored in Industrial Methylated Spirits (IMS). The remaining parts of these and all other samples were processed in a flotation machine using sieve sizes of 0.25mm and 1.00mm for the recovery of the flot and residue respectively. The flots and residues were dried, with the residues being sorted for biological and artefactual material.

Assessment and analysis

The samples were initially assessed to establish the range, frequency and diversity of the various forms of biological remains present within the samples. On the basis of the assessment results, 71 samples from the nine sites were selected for further analysis of the plant remains, with the majority of these samples coming from sites B, F and H.

Identification and recording methods

The plant remains were separated into different size fractions for ease of sorting and scanning and identified using a binocular microscope, the seed reference collection housed in the Environmental Section, MoLSS and seed reference manuals (Berggren 1981; Beijerinck 1947). The rich organic samples were sorted and scanned wet while the other samples were examined dry. Charred plant remains (with the exception of charcoal) were extracted and quantified in absolute numbers while waterlogged and mineralised material was only scanned and abundance of individual

Table 33 Number of analysed soil samples by period and site

Period	1	2	5	6	7	7/8	8	9	10	11	
Site											Total
Foreshore or river											
B		1					16	6			23
H	3	4			2	1					10
F		5		2				2			9
On Thorney Island											
C					2						2
D			1	1	2					1	5
E							1				1
G	1			1	6						8
J			4	4					1		9
L		3		1							4
Total	4	13	5	9	12	1	17	8	1	1	71

species recorded using the following system:
+: 1–10 plant items
++: 11–50 plant items
+++: 51–250 plant items
++++: 251+ plant items.

Identifications were entered on to the MoLAS ORACLE database system and tables of results generated by site and edited in Excel. Ecological information is based mainly on Clapham et al (1987) and Stace (1991). The results are shown in Tables 34–44 and were ordered by period and land use.

Table 34 The plant remains from sites H and B, periods 1 and 2

			Site		H	H	H	H	H	H	H	B
			Period		1	1	1,2	2	2	2	2	2
			Land use		OA1	OA1	OA1	OA1	OA1	OA1	OA1	OA1
			Context		H[36]	H[36]	H[33],H[36]	H[33]	H[33]	H[33]	H[33]	B[23]
			Sample		H{20}	H{19}	H{18}	H{15}	H{16}	H{17}	H{4}	B{3}
Latin name	English name	Plant part	Habitat/use	P								
Indeterminate		WD		C	+++	+	+	++	+	+	+	++
Characeae			E	W	+		+					++
Ranunculus acris/ repens/bulbosus	buttercups		ABCDEG	W	++	+	+	+	+	+	+	++++
R flammula L	lesser spearwort		EG	W								+
R sceleratus L	celery-leaved crowfoot		E	W								++
R subgen *Batrachium* (DC) A	crowfoots		E	W	+	++	+++	++	+	++	++	+
Ranunculus spp			ABCDEG	W	+		+	+		+		++++
Brassica/Sinapis spp			ABFGHI	W				+			+	
Reseda luteola L			ABGHI	W		+						
Viola sp	violet		ABCDG	W				+				
Hypericum sp	cat's ear		BD	W								++++
Chenopodium spp	goosefoot etc		ABCDFH	W	+		++					+
Atriplex spp	orache		ABFGH	W								++
Rubus fruticosus/idaeus	blackberry/raspberry		CFGH	W	+		++	++	+	+	++	++
Prunus spinosa	sloe/blackthorn		CFG	W	+							
Conium maculatum L	hemlock		CEG	W								+
Apium sp			EFI	W								+
Apiaceae indet				W			+					+
Polygonum sp			ABCDEFG	W								+
Rumex spp	dock		ABCDEFG	W				+			+	+
Urtica dioica L	stinging nettle		BCDEFGH	W	++		+			+		++
Humulus lupulus	hop					+						
Ficus carica L	fig		FI	W		+		+				
Alnus glutinosa (L) Gaertner	alder		CE	W	++	+	+		+	+		
A glutinosa (L) Gaertner	alder	CK	CE	W	+	+	+	+		+	+	
Corylus avellana L	hazel		CF	W	++		+	++		I	+	
Solanum nigrum L	black nightshade		BF		+		+					
Mentha spp	mint		ABCEFGI	W	+	+	+	+		+		+
Lycopus europaeus L	gipsy-wort		EH	W		+					+	++
Stachys palustris L	marsh woundwort		AE	W								+
cf *Lamium purpureum*	red dead nettle		AB	W								+
Labiatae indet			ABCDEFI	W								+
Sambucus nigra L	elder		BCFGH	W	+	++	+	++	+	++	++	+
Carduus/Cirsium sp	thistles		ABDEG	W			+				+	
Lapsana communis L	nipplewort		BCF	W								+
Alisma spp	water plantain		E	W	++		++	+				+
Potamogeton sp	pondweed		E	W				+				
Zannichellia palustris L	horned pondweed		E	W				+				
Juncus spp	rush		ADEH	W	++	+++	+++	++		++	+	++++
Sparganium erectum L	branched bur-reed		E	W								++
Eleocharis palustris/ uniglumis	spike-rush		E	W	++							+++
Schoenoplectus (L) Palla	bulrush		E	W								+
Carex spp	sedge		CDEH	W	++	+++	+++	+	+	+++		++++
Cyperaceae indet			ABCDEFI	W								++
Poaceae indet	grass		ABCDEFHI	W								++
Indeterminate				W	+	+	+	+	+	+	+	+
Indeterminate		ST		W	+++	++	++	++		+	++	++

Table 34 (cont)

Latin name	English name	Plant part	Habitat/use	P	H	H	H	H	H	H	H	B
			Site		H	H	H	H	H	H	H	B
			Period		1	1	1,2	2	2	2	2	2
			Land use		OA1	OA1	OA1	OA1	OA1	OA1	OA1	OA1
			Context		H[36]	H[36]	H[33],H[36]	H[33]	H[33]	H[33]	H[33]	B[23]
			Sample		H{20}	H{19}	H{18}	H{15}	H{16}	H{17}	H{4}	B{3}
Indeterminate		WD		W	++++	++++	++++	++++	+++	++++	++++	+
Indeterminate		PT		W		++++					+++	
Bryophyta indet	moss			W	++	+++	++	+			++	++

Key

Plant part codes: BN = bran; CK = catkin; EC = endocarp; FL = floret; LF = leaf; PT = plant tissue; R = rachis; ST = stem; TH = thorns; UT = utricle; WD = wood

Habitat/use codes: A = weeds of cultivated land; B = weeds of disturbed ground and waste places; C = plants of wood, scrub and hedgerows; D = grassland plants; E = plants of damp or marshy land; F = edible wild plants; G = medicinal plants; H = wild plants with other economic uses; I = cultivated plants

Preservation (P): C = carbonised; W = waterlogged

Frequency: + = 1–10; ++ = 11–50; +++ = 51–250; ++++ = >251 plant items

Table 35 The plant remains from site B, periods 7 and 8

Latin name	English name	Plant part	Habitat/use	P	7	7	7,8	8	8	8	8
			Period		7	7	7,8	8	8	8	8
			Land use		OA1	OA1	OA1	OA1	OA1	OA1	OA1
			Context		B[31]	B[31]	B[30/31]	B[30]	B[30]	B[29]	B[29]
			Sample		B{14}	B{13}	B{12}	B{11}	B{10}	B{9}	B{8}
Triticum cf *aestivum* type	bread/club wheat		FI	C		1	3				
Triticum sp	wheat		FI	C		1					1
cf *Avena* sp	oat		AFI	C							1
Cerealia	indet cereal		FI	C		1					
Indeterminate		WD		C	+	+++	+++	+++	+++	+++	+++
Characeae			E	W	++++	++++	++++	++	+	++	++
Ranunculus acris/repens/bulbosus	buttercups		ABCDEG	W	+	+	++	+	+		++
R arvensis L	corn crowfoot		A	W							+
R sardous Crantz	hairy buttercup		ABE	W	+			+			
R flammula L	lesser spearwort		EG	W							+
R sceleratus L	celery-leaved crowfoot		E	W				+			
R subgen *Batrachium* (DC) A	crowfoots		E	W	++	++	++	+			+
Ceratophyllum demersum L	rigid hornwort		E	W				+	++	++	++
Brassica/Sinapis spp			ABFGHI	W				+			+
Reseda luteola L	weld/dyer's rocket		ABGHI	W	+	+	+	+	+	+	++
Hypericum sp	cat's ear		BD	W				+			
Silene sp	campion/catchfly		ABCDF	W			+	+			
Stellaria media gp	chickweeds		ABCDE	W				+			+
S graminea type	lesser stitchwort		CD	W							+
Stellaria spp	chickweed/stitchwort		ABCDEG	W							+
Chenopodium sp	goosefoot etc		ABCDFH	W	+		+		+		+
Atriplex spp	orache		ABFGH	W	++	+	+	+	+		+
Vitis vinifera L	grape		FI	W			+	+		+	+++
Rubus fruticosus/idaeus	blackberry/raspberry		CFGH	W	+	+	+			+	+
Potentilla spp	cinquefoil/tormentil		BCDEFGH	W		+	+				++
Potentilla/Fragaria sp			BCDEFGH	W							+
Prunus spinosa L	sloe/blackthorn		CFG	W		+					+
P avium type	cherry		CFGI	W							+
Prunus sp			CFGI	W		+					+
cf *Malus* sp	apple/crab apple		CFHI	W							+
Conium maculatum L	hemlock		CEG	W				+			
Polygonum aviculare agg	knotgrass		ABG	W			+				+
P persicaria L	red shank		ABEH	W	+		+				
P hydropiper/mite	water pepper		E	W			+				
Rumex acetosella agg	sheep's sorrel		AD	W					+		+
Rumex spp	dock		ABCDEFG	W	+		+	+	++		+
Urtica dioica L	stinging nettle		BCDEFGH	W	+	+	++	+	++		+++
Humulus lupulus L	hop		CGHI	W			+	+	+	+	++

Table 35 (cont)

			Period		7	7	7,8	8	8	8	8
			Land use		OA1	OA1	OA1	OA1	OA1	OA1	OA1
			Context		B[31]	B[31]	B[30/31]	B[30]	B[30]	B[29]	B[29]
			Sample		B{14}	B{13}	B{12}	B{11}	B{10}	B{9}	B{8}
Latin name	English name	Plant part	Habitat/use	P							
Ficus carica L	fig		FI	W	+	+	+	+	+	+	++++
Alnus glutinosa (L) Gaertner	alder		CE	W							+
A glutinosa (L) Gaertner	alder	CK	CE	W	+						
Corylus avellana L	hazel		CF	W		+	+				
Solanum nigrum L	black nightshade		BF	W		+	+			+	+
Verbena officinalis L	vervain		BG	W							+
Mentha sp	mint		ABCEFGI	W				+			
Lycopus europaeus L	gipsy-wort		EH	W	+		+				
Prunella vulgaris L	self-heal		BCDG				+				
Lamium purpurem L	red dead nettle		AB	W			+				+
Marrubium vulgare L	white horehound		BG				+				
Labiatae indet			ABCDEFI	W		+	+	+			
Sambucus nigra L	elder		BCFGH	W	+	+	++		+	+	++
Chrysanthemum segetum L	corn marigold		AHI	W				+			
Carduus/Cirsium sp	thistles		ABDEG	W			+				
Centaurea sp	knapweed/thistle		ABDGH	W							+
Lapsana communis L	nipplewort		BCF	W			+				
Picris echioides L	bristly ox-tongue		BC	W					+		
Sonchus asper (L) Hill	spiny milk- /sow-thistle		AB					+			
Alisma sp	water plantain		E	W	+	+	+				
Potamogeton spp	pondweed		E	W	+	+	++				
Zannichellia palustris L	horned pondweed		E	W	++	++	++	+	+		++
Juncus spp	rush		ADEH	W	+	++	+++	+++	+++	++	++
Eleocharis palustris/ uniglumis	spike-rush		E	W					+		
Schoenoplectus lacustris (L)Palla	bulrush		E	W	+						
Carex spp	sedge		CDEH	W	++	+	+	+	+		++
Cyperaceae indet			ABCDEFI	W				+	+		
Poaceae indet	grass		ABCDEFHI	W				+	+		
Indeterminate				W	+		+	+	+	+	+
Indeterminate		ST		W						+	
Indeterminate		WD		W	++++	++++	+++	+++	+++	+++	+++
Indeterminate		PT		W		++++	+++				++++
Bryophyta indet	moss			W		+++	++	++	++	++	+++

Table 36 The plant remains from site B, Open Area 14, period 8

		Context			B[116]	B[146]	B[121]	B[147]	B[154]	B[126]	B[128]	B[49]	B[142]
		Sample			B{29}	B{30}	B{35}	B{36}	B{37}	B{32}	B{34}	B{5}	B{31}
Latin name	English name	Plant part	Habitat/use	P									
Triticum aestivum type	bread/club wheat		FI	C		3	1	1	2				
T cf *aestivum* type	bread/club wheat		FI	C			1	3		1	1	1	
Triticum sp(p)	wheat		FI	C	1	3		3	1	2		1	
Triticum sp	wheat	R	FI	C				1	1				
Secale cereale L	rye		FI	C			1			1			
Triticum/Secale sp	wheat/rye		FI	C						1			
Hordeum sativum L	barley		FI	C		2			1		2	1	
Hordeum/Triticum sp	barley/wheat		FI	C								1	
cf *Avena* sp	oat		AFI	C				1					
Cerealia	indet cereal		FI	C	2	2	7	4	2	1	1	7	
Silene alba/vulgaris	white/bladder campion		ABDF	C								4	
Silene spp	campion/catchfly		ABCDF	C								12	
Lychnis flos-cuculi L	ragged robin		CDE	C								4	
Agrostemma githago L	corn cockle		AB	C				1					
Silene/Stellaria spp	campion/stitchwort		ABCDEG	C								2	
Pisum sativum L	pea		FI	C	1								
Anthemis cotula L	stinking mayweed		ABGH	C					1				

Table 36 (cont)

Latin name	English name	Plant part	Habitat/use	P	B[116] B{29}	B[146] B{30}	B[121] B{35}	B[147] B{36}	B[154] B{37}	B[126] B{32}	B[128] B{34}	B[49] B{5}	B[142] B{31}
Poaceae indet	grass		ABCDEFHI	C				I				I	
Indeterminate		WD		C	++++	++++	++++	++++	++++	++++	++++	+++	+++
Characeae			E	W			+				+		+
Ranunculus acris/repens/bulbosus	buttercups		ABCDEG	W				+	+		+	+	
R sardous Crantz	hairy buttercup		ABE	W				+					
R flammula L	lesser spearwort		EG	W					+				
R sceleratus L	celery-leaved crowfoot		E	W									+
Ranunculus spp			ABCDEG	W				+	+	+	+		
Papaver cf *rhoeas*	field poppy		ABGH	W		+							
P somniferum L	opium poppy		BGHI	W	++	+					+		+
Papaver spp	poppy		ABGHI	W	+	++	+	+					+
Chelidonium majus L	greater celandine		BC	W					+				
Brassica spp	wild cabbage/turnip/mustard		ABFI	W						+	+		
Brassica/Sinapis spp			ABFGHI	W	++	+	+++	++	++	+++		++	+
Raphanus raphanistrum L	wild radish/charlock		A	W							+		
Thlaspi arvense L	field penny-cress		AB	W						+		+	
Reseda luteola L	weld/dyer's rocket		ABGHI	W	+		++	++		++	++	++	+
R lutea L	wild mignonette		AB	W	+				+				
Viola sp	violet		ABCDG	W		+							
Silene spp	campion/catchfly		ABCDF	W	++	+	++	++	++	+++	++		
Lychnis flos-cuculi L	ragged robin		CDE	W	++		+++	+	+				++
Agrostemma githago L	corn cockle		AB	W						+			+
Stellaria graminea type	lesser stitchwort		CD	W	+	+	+	+	+	+	+		
Stellaria spp	chickweed/stitchwort		ABCDEG	W			+						
Caryophyllaceae indet				W							+		
Montia fontana ssp *chondrosperma* L	blinks		AE	W							+		
Chenopodium album gp	fat hen		ABFH	W	+								
Chenopodium spp	goosefoot etc		ABCDFH	W	++	++	+++	++	+	++	++	++	+
Atriplex spp	orache		ABFGH	W	++	++	+++	+	+	++	++	++	+
Linum usitatissimum L	cultivated flax		HI	W						+			
Vitis vinifera L	grape		FI	W	+			+		+		+	
Rubus fruticosus/idaeus	blackberry/raspberry		CFGH	W	I	+	+	+	+	+	++		
Aethusa cynapium L	fool's parsley		A	W			+						
Conium maculatum L	hemlock		CEG	W	+	+	+		+	+	+		
Apium sp			EFI	W									++
Torilis sp	hedge-parsley		ACD	W	+								
Apiaceae indet				W				+					+
Polygonum aviculare agg	knotgrass		ABG	W								+	
Polygonum sp			ABCDEFG	W					+				
Rumex acetosella agg	sheep's sorrel		AD	W			+						
Rumex spp	dock		ABCDEFG	W	+	+	+	++	+	+		+	
Urtica dioica L	stinging nettle		BCDEFGH	W	+			+	+	++	++		
Ficus carica L	fig		FI	W	+		+	+	+	++	++	+	
Betula sp	birch			W							+		
Corylus avellana L	hazel		CF	W				+					
Lithospermum arvense L	corn gromwell		A	W		+							
Hyoscyamus niger L	henbane		BDG	W					+	+		+	
Marrubium vulgare L	white horehound		BG	W	+		+		+	++	+		
Labiatae indet			ABCDEFI	W	++		+	+	+	++	++		
Sambucus nigra L	elder		BCFGH	W	+	+	+	+	+	+++	++	+	+
Eupatorium cannabinum L	hemp agrimony		E	W									+
Alisma spp	water plantain		E	W	++	+++	++	+		++++	+	+	++
Juncus spp	rush		ADEH	W	+++	+++	+++	+++	+++	+++	+++	++++	++++
Sparganium erectum L	branched bur-reed		E	W							+		
Eleocharis palustris/uniglumis	spike-rush		E	W	++	+	+			+	+		+
Schoenoplectus lacustris (L)Palla	bulrush		E	W						+			
Carex spp	sedge		CDEH	W	+++	+++	++++	+++	+++	+++	+++	++	+
Cyperaceae indet			ABCDEFI	W				++			+++	+++	
Poaceae indet	grass		ABCDEFHI	W	+								
Indeterminate				W	+	+	+	+	+	+	+	+	+
Indeterminate		WD		W					+			+	
Bryophyta indet	moss			W		+		+		++	++		

Table 37 The plant remains from site B, Open Area 14, periods 8 and 9

			Period		8	8	8	9	9	9	9	9	9
			Context		B[186]	B[160]	B[206]	B[150]	B[151]	B[221]	B[251]	B[166]	B[168]
			Sample		B{41}	B{42}	B{43}	B{33}	B{44}	B{45}	B{46}	B{38}	B{39}
Latin name	**English name**	**Plant part**	**Habitat/use**	**P**									
Triticum aestivum type	bread/club wheat		FI	C			3			1			
T cf *aestivum* type	bread/club wheat		FI	C	2		2				1		
Triticum spp	wheat		FI	C	2								
Triticum sp	wheat	R	FI	C			2	1	1				
Hordeum sativum L	barley		FI	C	1	1			1	1			1
cf *H sativum*	barley		FI	C				2	1				
Hordeum/Triticum sp	barley/wheat		FI	C				1			1		
Avena sp	oat		AFI	C		1	1		1				
cf *Avena* sp	oat		AFI	C	1								
Cerealia	indet cereal		FI	C			2	3	2		2		
Agrostemma githago L	corn cockle		AB	C							1		
Anthemis cotula L	stinking mayweed		ABGH	C		1							
Lolium spp	rye-grass		BDI	C							2		
Poaceae indet	grass		ABCDEFHI	C							1		
Indeterminate		WD		C	++++	+++	++++	++++	++++	+++	++++	+++	+++
Characeae			E	W					++				
Ranunculus acris/repens/bulbosus	buttercups		ABCDEG	W	+	+					+++		
R sceleratus L	celery-leaved crowfoot		E	W	+		+				+		
Ranunculus spp			ABCDEG	W					+		++		
Papaver somniferum L	opium poppy		BGHI	W	+		+			+		+	
P cf *somniferum*	opium poppy		BGHI	W							+		
Papaver spp	poppy		ABGHI	W					+				
Chelidonium majus L	greater celandine		BC	W	+	+			+	+		++	+
Fumaria sp	fumitory		ABC	W			+						
Brassica spp	wild cabbage/turnip/mustard		ABFI	W	+	+					+		
Brassica/Sinapis spp			ABFGHI	W	++		++	++	++	+	+++		+
Capsella bursa-pastoris (L) Medic	shepherd's purse		AB	W								+	
Reseda luteola L	weld/dyer's rocket		ABGHI	W	++	+	+	+	+	++	++		+
Viola spp	violet		ABCDG	W	++	++						++++	++
Hypericum sp	cat's ear		BD	W					+				
Silene spp	campion/catchfly		ABCDF	W	+	+	+	+	++	++	+++	+	
Lychnis flos-cuculi L	ragged robin		CDE	W	+		+	+	+	++	++	+	+
Agrostemma githago L	corn cockle		AB	W		+		+			+		
Stellaria media gp	chickweeds		ABCDE	W				+					
S graminea type	lesser stitchwort		CD	W	+		+				+		+
Caryophyllaceae indet				W						+	++		
Montia fontana ssp *chondrosperma* L	blinks		AE	W									++
Chenopodium hybridum L	maple-leaved goosefoot		AB	W		+							
Chenopodium spp	goosefoot etc		ABCDFH	W	++		++	++	++	++	++	+	+
Atriplex spp	orache		ABFGH	W	++	+	++	++	++	++	++	+	+
Malva sp	mallow		BCDF	W						+			
Vitis vinifera L	grape		FI	W	+		+				+		+
Rubus fruticosus/idaeus	blackberry/raspberry		CFGH	W	+	+	+	+	+	++	+		+
Potentilla spp	cinquefoil/tormentil		BCDEFGH	W		+		+			+		
cf *Prunus* sp			CFGI	W							+		
Aethusa cynapium L	fool's parsley		A	W	+						+		
Conium maculatum L	hemlock		CEG	W	+	++		+	+	+			
Apium sp			EFI	W			+			+			
Euphorbia helioscopia L	sun spurge		AGI	W	+				+			++	
E peplus L	petty spurge		AB	W								+++	+
Polygonum aviculare agg	knotgrass		ABG	W						+	+		+
P persicaria L	red shank		ABEH	W						+	+		
Fallopia convolvulus (L) A Love	black bindweed		ABF	W				+		+	+		
Rumex acetosella agg	sheep's sorrel		AD	W							+		
Rumex spp	dock		ABCDEFG	W	+		++	++	++	+	++		
Urtica dioica L	stinging nettle		BCDEFGH	W	++	+++	+		+	+	+		+
Cannabis sativa L	hemp		BGHI	W	+								
Ficus carica L	fig		FI	W	+++	++	++	+	+		++	++	+
Betula sp	birch		CDH	W	+							+	

Table 37 (cont)

Latin name	English name	Plant part	Habitat/use	P	8	8	8	9	9	9	9	9	9
			Context		B[186]	B[160]	B[206]	B[150]	B[151]	B[221]	B[251]	B[166]	B[168]
			Sample		B{41}	B{42}	B{43}	B{33}	B{44}	B{45}	B{46}	B{38}	B{39}
Corylus avellana L	hazel		CF	W				+			+		
Hyoscyamus niger L	henbane		BDG	W		+	+			+	+	++	+
Verbena officinalis L	vervain		BG	W	+	+							
Lamium sp	dead nettle		ABC	W								+	
Marrubium vulgare L	white horehound		BG	W	+	+			+	+			
Labiatae indet			ABCDEFI	W	+	++			++	++	+	+	+
Sambucus nigra L	elder		BCFGH	W	+	+	++	+	+++	++	+	+	+
Alisma spp	water plantain		E	W	+	+			++	+	+	+	
Juncus spp	rush		ADEH	W	+++	+++	+++	+++	+++	+++	+++	+	++
Lemna sp	duckweed		E	W				+					
Sparganium erectum L	branched bur-reed		E	W					+				
Eleocharis palustris/ uniglumis	spike-rush		E	W	+	+	+	++	+	+	++	+	+
Schoenoplectus lacustris (L) Palla	bulrush		E	W							+		
Carex spp	sedge		CDEH	W	+++	++	+++	++++	+++	++	+++	++	+
Cyperaceae indet			ABCDEFI	W	+	+		++			++		++
Indeterminate				W	+	+	+	+	+	+	+	+	+
Bryophyta indet	moss			W							++		

Table 38 The plant remains from site F

Latin name	English name	Plant part	Habitat/use	P	2	2	2	2	2	6	6	9	9
			Land use		OA1	OA1	OA1	OA1	OA1	OA1	OA1	B15	B15
			Context		F[88]	F[88]	F[88]	F[88]	F[88]	F[187/188]	F[6]	F[4]	F[97]
			Sample		F{3}	F{4}	F{5}	F{6}	F{7}	F{8}	F{3}	{F0}	F{9}
Indeterminate		WD		C	++			+		+	++	++++	++++
Characeae			E	W				+	+++				
Ranunculus acris/ repens/bulbosus	buttercups		ABCDEG	W		+	+			++++			+
R flammula L	lesser spearwort		EG	W						++			+
R subgen *Batrachium* (DC) A	crowfoots		E	W			+	+++	++++				
Papaver argemone L	long prickly-headed poppy		AB	W								+	
Hypericum sp	cat's ear		BD	W						+			
Stellaria media gp	chickweeds		ABCDE	W									+
S graminea type	lesser stitchwort		CD	W									++
Stellaria spp	chickweed/stitchwort		ABCDEG	W									++
Silene sp	campion/catchfly		ABCDF	W						+			
Chenopodium spp	goosefoot etc		ABCDFH	W	+		+			+		+	+
Linum sp	flax		ADHI	W									+
Rubus fruticosus/idaeus	blackberry/raspberry		CFGH	W			+		+	+	+		+
Potentilla spp	cinquefoil/tormentil		BCDEFGH	W							+		
Oenanthe aquatica (L) Poiret	fine-leaved watcrdropwort		E	W					+				
Apium spp			EFI	W						+			
Apiaceae				W						+			
Polygonum hydropiper/ mite	water pepper		E	W						+			
Polygonum sp			ABCDEFG	W		+				+			
Rumex acetosella agg	sheep's sorrel		AD	W									+++
Rumex sp	dock		ABCDEFG	W						+	+		
Urtica dioica L	stinging nettle		BCDEFGH	W		+	+	+	+	+	+		
Ficus carica L	fig		FI	W								+	+
Alnus glutinosa (L) Gaertner	alder		CE	W		+							
Solanum nigrum L	black nightshade		BF	W									+

Table 38 (cont)

			Period		2	2	2	2	2	6	6	9	9
			Land use		OA1	OA1	OA1	OA1	OA1	OA1	OA1	B15	B15
			Context		F[88]	F[88]	F[88]	F[88]	F[88]	F[187/188]	F[6]	F[4]	F[97]
			Sample		F{3}	F{4}	F{5}	F{6}	F{7}	F{8}	F{3}	F{0}	F{9}
Latin name	English name	Plant part	Habitat/use	P									
Mentha spp	mint		ABCEFGI	W					++	+	+		
Lycopus europaeus L	gipsy-wort		EH	W				+		+			+
Prunella vulgaris L	self-heal		BCDG	W									+
Sambucus nigra L	elder		BCFGH	W	+		+	+	+++	+	++		+
cf *Hypochaeris* sp	cat's ear		BD	W							+		
Alisma spp	water plantain		E	W				++	++				
Potamogeton sp	pondweed									+			
Juncus spp	rush		ADEH	W					+	++++	+++	+	
Iris pseudacorus L	yellow iris yellow flag		E	W				+					
Sparganium erectum L	branched bur-reed		E	W		+	+	+		++			
Eleocharis palustris/ uniglumis	spike-rush		E	W				+		++++			
Schoenoplectus lacustris (L) Palla	bulrush		E	W				+	++	+			
Carex spp	sedge		CDEH	W	+			++	+	++	+		+
Poaceae	grasses									+++			
Indeterminate				W		+	+	+	+	+	+	+	+
Indeterminate		ST		W	+		++	+++	++	++			
Indeterminate		WD		W	++	+++	++++	+++	++++	+++	++++		
Indeterminate		PT		W							+++		
Bryophyta indet	moss			W		+		+					

Table 39 The plant remains from site C, Building 13, period 7

			Context		C[187]	C[200]
			Sample		C{4}	C{3}
Latin name	English name	Plant part	Habitat/use	P		
Indeterminate		WD		C	+++	+++
Characeae			E	W		+
Ranunculus flammula L	lesser spearwort		EG	W	+	
R subgen *Batrachium* (DC) A	crowfoots		E	W		+
Ranunculus sp			ABCDEG	W	+	+
Stellaria sp	chickweed/stitchwort		ABCDEG	W	+	+
Aphanes arvensis agg	parsley piert		ABD	W	+	
Urtica dioica L	stinging nettle		BCDEFGH	W	+	
Sambucus nigra L	elder		BCFGH	W	+	
Alisma sp	water plantain		E	W		+
Juncus spp	rush		ADEH	W	+++	+
Indeterminate				W	+	+
Indeterminate		PT		W	+++	+++

Table 40 The plant remains from site D

			Period		5	6	7	7	11
			Land use		OA1	OA4	B6	OA4	OA4
			Context		D[69]	D[57]	D[54]	D[53]	D[2]
			Sample		D{6}	D{4}	D{2}	D{3}	D{1}
Latin name	English name	Plant part	Habitat/use	P					
Triticum aestivum type	bread/club wheat		FI	C		24		22	
T cf *aestivum* type	bread/club wheat		FI	C			1	3	
Triticum spp	wheat		FI	C		8		14	
Secale cereale L	rye		FI	C	3	1	1	4	
Triticum/Secale sp	wheat/rye		FI	C		1		1	
Hordeum sativum L	barley		FI	C		2			

Table 40 (cont)

			Period		5	6	7	7	11
			Land use		OA1	OA1	B6	OA1	OA1
			Context		D[69]	D[57]	D[54]	D[53]	D[2]
			Sample		D{6}	D{4}	D{2}	D{3}	D{1}
Latin name	English name	Plant part	Habitat/use	P					
Avena sp	oat		AFI	C		1			
cf *Avena* sp	oat		AFI	C		1		1	1
Cerealia	indet cereal		FI	C	1	5	3	16	
cf *Anthriscus* sp			BC	C				1	
Anthemis cotula L	stinking mayweed		ABGH	C		1		2	
Tripleurospermum inodorum (L) Schultz Bip	scentless mayweed		AB	C				4	
Lolium sp	rye-grass		BDI	C		1			
Poaceae indet	grass		ABCDEFHI	C				2	
Indeterminate		WD		C	++	++	++	++	+
Hordeum sativum L	barley		FI	M			+		
Avena sp	oat		AFI	M			+		
Apiaceae indet				M			+		
cf *Bromus* sp	bromes		ABD	M			+		
Indeterminate				M			+		
Indeterminate		ST		M			++++		
Indeterminate		WD		M			+++		
Cerealia	indet cereal	BN	FI	W			++++	++++	
Ranunculus acris/repens/bulbosus	buttercups		ABCDEG	W	+	++	++	++	
R sardous Crantz	hairy buttercup		ABE	W				+	
R flammula L	lesser spearwort		EG	W	+	+		+	
R sceleratus L	celery-leaved crowfoot		E	W	+	++++		+++	+
Ranunculus spp			ABCDEG	W	+	++			+
Papaver spp	poppy		ABGHI	W				++	
Fumaria sp	fumitory		ABC	W		+			
Brassica/Sinapis spp			ABFGHI	W			+	+	+
Raphanus raphanistrum L	wild radish/charlock		A	W		+			
Coronopus squamatus (Fskl) Ascherson	swine-cress		B	W		+		+	
Viola sp	violet		ABCDG	W				+	
Silene spp	campion/catchfly		ABCDF	W		++		+	
Lychnis flos-cuculi L	ragged robin		CDE	W				+	
Agrostemma githago L	corn cockle		AB	W			++++	+	
Stellaria media gp	chickweeds		ABCDE	W		+			
S graminea type	lesser stitchwort		CD	W		+		+	
Stellaria spp	chickweed/stitchwort		ABCDEG	W				+	
Silene/Stellaria sp	campion/stitchwort		ABCDEG	W			+		
Chenopodium album gp	fat hen		ABFH	W		+		+	
C murale L	nettle-leaved goosefoot		BD	W		++		++	
C rubrum L	red goosefoot		AB	W		++			
Chenopodium spp	goosefoot etc		ABCDFH	W	+	++	+	+++	+
Atriplex spp	orache		ABFGH	W	++	+++	+	+++	
Buxus sempervirens L	box leaves	LF	CI	W				+	
Vitis vinifera L	grape		FI	W		+	+++	+	
Rubus fruticosus/idaeus	blackberry/raspberry		CFGH	W	++	+++	+	++	
Potentilla spp	cinquefoil/tormentil		BCDEFGH	W			+++	+	
Fragaria vesca L	wild strawberry		CDF	W			+		
Potentilla/Fragaria spp			BCDEFGH	W			+		
Prunus spinosa L	sloe/blackthorn		CFG	W			+		
P domestica L	plum/bullace		CFI	W			++		
P avium type	cherry		CFGI	W		+	+++		
P avium/cerasus	sloe/cherry		CFGI	W	+				
Prunus spp			CFGI	W		+			
Malus domestica/sylvestris	apple/crab apple		CFHI	W			+++		
M domestica/sylvestris	apple/crab apple	EC	CFHI	W			++		
Pyrus/Malus sp	pear/apple		CFI	W				+	
Oenanthe aquatica/crocata	water dropwort		E	W			+		
Conium maculatum L	hemlock		CEG	W	+	+	+	++++	
Bupleurum rotundifolium L	hare's-ear		AG	W			+		
Apium graveolens/nodiflorum	wild celery/fool's watercress		E	W	+				
Torilis sp	hedge-parsley		ACD	W			+		

Table 40 (cont)

			Period		5	6	7	7	11
			Land use		OA1	OA4	B6	OA4	OA4
			Context		D[69]	D[57]	D[54]	D[53]	D[2]
			Sample		D{6}	D{4}	D{2}	D{3}	D{1}
Latin name	**English name**	**Plant part**	**Habitat/use**	**P**					
Apiaceae indet				W			+		
Polygonum aviculare agg	knotgrass		ABG	W	++	+++		++	
P persicaria L	red shank		ABEH	W	+	+++		++	
P lapathifolium L	pale persicaria		ABE	W	+	++			
P hydropiper/mite	water pepper		E	W		+			
Fallopia convolvulus (L) A Love	black bindweed		ABF	W			+	+	
Polygonum spp			ABCDEFG	W		+			
Rumex acetosella agg	sheep's sorrel		AD	W		+		+	
Rumex spp	dock		ABCDEFG	W		+	+	++	
Urtica urens L	small nettle		AB	W		+			
U dioica L	stinging nettle		BCDEFGH	W	++++	+++	++	+++	+
cf *Cannabis sativa*	hemp		BGHI	W				+	
Ficus carica L	fig		FI	W	+	+++	++++	+++	
Morus nigra L	mulberry		FHI	W			++++		
Corylus avellana L	hazel		CF	W	+++	++	+	+	
Hyoscyamus niger L	henbane		BDG	W				+	
Solanum nigrum L	black nightshade		BF	W	+	++++	+	++++	+
Verbena officinalis L	vervain		BG	W		++		+	
cf *Mentha* sp	mint		ABCEFGI	W				+	
Lycopus europaeus L	gipsy-wort		EH	W	+	++	+	+	
Prunella vulgaris L	self-heal		BCDG	W		+			
cf *Ballota nigra*	black horehound		CG	W				+	
Lamium purpurem L	red dead nettle		AB	W				+	
cf *Marrubium vulgare*	white horehound		BG	W		+		+	
Labiatae indet			ABCDEFI	W	+	+		++	
Sambucus nigra L	elder		BCFGH	W	++	+++	+	+++	
Anthemis cotula L	stinking mayweed		ABGH	W				+	
Chrysanthemum segetum L	corn marigold		AHI	W				+	
Carduus/Cirsium spp	thistles		ABDEG	W		+	+		
Lapsana communis L	nipplewort		BCF	W			++		
Leontodon sp	hawkbit		BDF	W		+			
Sonchus oleraceus L	milk- /sow-thistle		AB	W				+	
Sonchus asper (L) Hill	spiny milk- /sow-thistle		AB	W	+				
Alisma spp	water plantain		E	W				+	
Juncus spp	rush		ADEH	W	+	++	++	+++	+
Sparganium erectum L	branched bur-reed		E	W		+			
Eleocharis palustris/uniglumis	spike-rush		E	W		++	+	++	
Carex spp	sedge		CDEH	W	+	+++	++	+++	
Carex spp	sedge	UT	CDEH	W			++	+	
Poaceae indet	grass		ABCDEFHI	W	+			++	
Indeterminate				W	+		+	+	+
Indeterminate		LF		W	+			+	
Indeterminate		ST		W	++		++++	++++	
Indeterminate		TH		W				+	
Indeterminate		WD		W	++++	++++	+++	+++	+++
Bryophyta indet	moss			W			++	+	

Table 41 The plant remains from site E, *Open Area* 11, period 8

				Context	E[28]
				Sample	E{10}
Latin name	**English name**	**Plant part**	**Habitat/use**	**P**	
Triticum cf *aestivum* type	bread/club wheat		FI	C	1
Avena spp	oat		AFI	C	2
cf *Avena* sp	oat		AFI	C	3
Cerealia	indet cereal		FI	C	25
Anthemis cotula L	stinking mayweed		ABGH	C	2

Table 41 (cont)

Latin name	English name	Plant part	Habitat/use	Context Sample P	E[28] E{10}
Indeterminate		WD		C	+++
Ranunculus acris/ repens/bulbosus	buttercups		ABCDEG	W	+
R sceleratus L	celery-leaved crowfoot		E	W	+
Sambucus nigra L	elder		BCFGH	W	++
Indeterminate				W	+
Indeterminate		ST		W	++
Indeterminate		PT		W	++

Table 42 The plant remains from site G

			Period		1	6	7	7	7	7	7	7
			Land use		OA1	OA4	OA4	OA4	OA4	OA4	OA4	OA4
			Context		G[39]	G[33]	G[36]	G[19]	G[28]	G[30]	G[15]	G[26]
			Sample		G{5}	G{9}	G{7}	G{2}	G{3}	G{0}	G{1}	G{4}
Latin name	English name	Plant part	Habitat/use	P								
Triticum aestivum type	bread/club wheat		FI	C				1				
Triticum sp	wheat		FI	C					3			
Secale cereale L	rye		FI	C				4				
Triticum/Secale sp	wheat/rye		FI	C			1			1		
Hordeum sativum L	barley		FI	C					2	1		1
cf *H sativum*	barley		FI	C					6			
Hordeum/Triticum sp	barley/wheat		FI	C					1			
Avena sp	oat		AFI	C			1	2	36		1	17
Avena sp	oat	FL	AFI	C								1
cf *Avena* sp	oat		AFI	C					52		1	9
Cerealia	indet cereal		FI	C		1	2	9	234		7	57
Ranunculus acris/ repens/bulbosus	buttercups		ABCDEG	C								2
Agrostemma githago L	corn cockle		AB	C					5			
Chenopodium spp	goosefoot etc		ABCDFH	C					2			4
Vicia/Lathyrus/Pisum sp	vetch/tare/vetchling/pea		ABCDEFI	C					1			1
Polygonum aviculare agg	knotgrass		ABG	C								1
Rumex acetosella agg	sheep's sorrel		AD	C					1			
Rumex sp	dock		ABCDEFG	C					1			
Plantago major L	great plantain		ABC	C								1
Sambucus nigra L	elder		BCFGH	C								1
Anthemis cotula L	stinking mayweed		ABGH	C		1		3				
Anthemis sp	mayweed/chamomile		ABGH	C					1		1	1
Centaurea sp	knapweed/thistle		ABDGH	C					1			
Lapsana communis L	nipplewort		BCF	C					1			
Sparganium erectum L	branched bur-reed		E	C					1			2
Carex spp	sedge		CDEH	C								2
Lolium/Festuca spp	rye-grass/fescue		BCD	C					4			
Bromus spp	bromes		ABD	C				2	41	1		14
cf *Bromus* sp	bromes		ABD	C					13			12
Poaceae indet	grass		ABCDEFHI	C				1	31	1	2	3
Indeterminate				C				1	2		1	5
Indeterminate		WD		C	++	+++	++	+++	++++	+++	+	++++
Ranunculus acris/ repens/bulbosus	buttercups		ABCDEG	W			++					
R sceleratus L	celery-leaved crowfoot		E	W		++	+++	+		+		
R subgen *Batrachium* (DC) A	crowfoots		E	W			+					
Raphanus raphanistrum L	wild radish/charlock		A	W			+					
Silene spp	campion/catchfly		ABCDF	W			+					
Agrostemma githago L	corn cockle		AB	W			+					
Stellaria sp	chickweed/stitchwort		ABCDEG	W			+					
Chenopodium spp	goosefoot etc		ABCDFH	W		+	++	+	+			+
Atriplex spp	orache		ABEFGH	W			++	+		+		
Linum usitatissimum L	cultivated flax		HI	W			+					

Table 42 (cont)

Latin name	English name	Plant part	Habitat/use	P	1	6	7	7	7	7	7	7
			Period		1	6	7	7	7	7	7	7
			Land use		OA1	OA4	OA4	OA4	OA4	OA4	OA4	OA4
			Context		G[39]	G[33]	G[36]	G[19]	G[28]	G[30]	G[15]	G[26]
			Sample		G{5}	G{9}	G{7}	G{2}	G{3}	G{8}	G{1}	G{4}
Rubus fruticosus/idaeus	blackberry/raspberry		CFGH	W		+		+				
Potentilla spp	cinquefoil/tormentil		BCDEFGH	W			+					
Potentilla/Fragaria spp			BCDEFGH	W		+						
cf *Conium maculatum*	hemlock		CEG	W			+					
Euphorbia helioscopia L	sun spurge		AGI	W			+					
Polygonum aviculare agg	knotgrass		ABG	W			+					
P lapathifolium type	pale persicaria		ABE	W			+					
Fallopia convolvulus (L) A Love	black bindweed		ABF	W								+
Rumex acetosella agg	sheep's sorrel		AD	W						+		
Rumex spp	dock		ABCDEFG	W		+	+					
Urtica dioica L	stinging nettle		BCDEFGH	W	+	++	+++	++			+	
Ficus carica L	fig		FI	W								+
Corylus avellana L	hazel		CF	W						+		
Menyanthes trifoliata L	bogbean		EFG	W			++					
Lycopus europaeus L	gipsy-wort		EH	W			++					
Labiatae indet			ABCDEFI	W		+	+					
Sambucus nigra L	elder		BCFGH	W		+	+	+	+	+	+	+
Anthemis cotula L	stinking mayweed		ABGH	W			+					
Carduus/Cirsium spp	thistles		ABDEG	W							+	
Centaurea sp	knapweed/thistle		ABDGH	W			+					
Lapsana communis L	nipplewort		BCF	W			++					
Alisma spp	water plantain		E	W					+			+
Juncus spp	rush		ADEH	W	+++	++	+++	+++	+	+++	+	+++
Eleocharis palustris/uniglumis	spike-rush		E	W			+					
Carex spp	sedge		CDEH	W		+	++	++				
Poaceae indet	grass		ABCDEFHI	W			+					
Indeterminate				W		+	+			+		
Indeterminate		ST		W			++					
Indeterminate		WD		W		+	+++	+++		++		
Indeterminate		PT		W		+++	+++			+++		
Bryophyta indet	moss			W			++					

Table 43 The plant remains from site J

Latin name	English name	Plant part	Habitat/use	P	5	5	5	5	6	6	6	6	10
			Period		5	5	5	5	6	6	6	6	10
			Land use		OA3	OA3	OA3	OA3	OA4	OA4	OA4	OA4	OA4
			Context		J[90]	J[98]	J[88]	J[89]	J[25]	J[27]	J[22]	J[23]	J[2]
			Sample		J{7}	J{9}	J{6}	J{8}	J{4}	J{5}	J{2}	J{3}	J{1}
Triticum aestivum type	bread/club wheat		FI	C		1							
Triticum sp	wheat		FI	C						1			
cf *Secale cereale*	rye		FI	C			1						
Hordeum sativum L	barley		FI	C								1	
cf *H sativum*	barley		FI	C	1						1		
Avena sp	oat		AFI	C					1				
Cerealia	indet cereal		FI	C						1	1	1	
Indeterminate		WD		C	++	++	+	+	++	++	++	+	+
Chara sp	stoneworts		E	W	+			+	+	+	+	+	+
Ranunculus acris/repens/bulbosus	buttercups		ABCDEG	W	+	++					+	+	
R sceleratus L	celery-leaved crowfoot		E	W	+	++		+				++	+
R subgen *Batrachium* (DC) A	crowfoots		E	W	+							+	
Ranunculus spp			ABCDEG	W	+				+		+		
Brassica/Sinapis spp			ABFGHI	W								+	
Nasturtium officinale R.Rr	watercress		EFI	W							+		
Lychnis flos-cuculi L	ragged robin		CDE	W							+		

Table 43 (cont)

			Period		5	5	5	5	6	6	6	6	10
			Land use		OA3	OA3	OA3	OA3	OA4	OA4	OA4	OA4	OA4
			Context		J[90]	J[98]	J[88]	J[89]	J[25]	J[27]	J[22]	J[23]	J[2]
			Sample		J{7}	J{9}	J{6}	J{8}	J{4}	J{5}	J{2}	J{3}	J{1}
Latin name	**English name**	**Plant part**	**Habitat/use**	**P**									
Stellaria media gp	chickweeds		ABCDE	W		++						+	
Stellaria spp	chickweed/stitchwort		ABCDEG	W				+			+		+
Caryophyllaceae indet				W		+			+				+
Chenopodium album gp	fat hen		ABFH	W		+							
Chenopodium spp	goosefoot etc		ABCDFH	W	+	+++		+	+	+	++	+	+
Atriplex spp	orache		ABFGH	W		++			+		++		
Vitis vinifera L	grape		FI	W									+
Rubus fruticosus/idaeus	blackberry/raspberry		CFGH	W	+	++	+		+		+		+
Prunus avium type	cherry		CFGI	W									+
Prunus sp			CFGI	W							+		
Conium maculatum L	hemlock		CEG	W		+	+		+		+++	++	
Apium sp			EFI	W	+	+					+		
Apiaceae indet				W		+							
Polygonum aviculare agg	knotgrass		ABG	W	+	+			++	+	+	+	
Polygonum lapathifolium L	pale persicaria		ABE	W		+							
P hydropiper L	water pepper		E	W		++							
Polygonum spp			ABCDEFG	W		++					+		
Rumex acetosella agg	sheep's sorrel		AD	W		+							
Rumex spp	dock		ABCDEFG	W	+	+++					+	+	
Urtica urens L	small nettle		AB	W						+			
U dioica L	stinging nettle		BCDEFGH	W	+++	+++	+	++	+	+	+++	+++	++
cf *Humulus lupulus*	hop		CGHI	W		+							
Ficus carica L	fig		FI	W							+		+
Hyoscyamus niger L	henbane		BDG	W					+		+	+	
Solanum nigrum L	black nightshade		BF	W							+		
Lycopus europaeus L	gipsy-wort		EH	W		+		+			+	+	+
Lamium purpurem L	red dead nettle		AB	W		+							
Marrubium vulgare L	white horehound		BG	W		+							
Labiatae indet			ABCDEFI	W		+							
Sambucus nigra L	elder		BCFGH	W	++	++++	+++	++	++	++	++	+++	+
Chrysanthemum segetum L	corn marigold		AHI	W					+				
Carduus/Cirsium spp	thistles		ABDEG	W	+	++					+		
cf *Lapsana communis*	nipplewort		BCF	W	+								
Sonchus asper (L) Hill	spiny milk- /sow-thistle		AB	W	+	+							
Sonchus sp	milk- /sow-thistle		ABE	W		+							
Alisma spp	water plantain		E	W	+	++++	+	+	+		+	++	+
Potamogeton spp	pondweed		E	W		+++							
Juncus spp	rush		ADEH	W	++	+		+	+	+	+	++	
Eleocharis palustris/uniglumis	spike-rush		E	W			+						
Carex spp	sedge		CDEH	W		+			+	+	+	+	
Poaceae indet	grass		ABCDEFHI	W	+								
Indeterminate				W	+	+	+	+	+	+	+	+	+
Indeterminate		WD		W	++	+++		+		++	+++	+++	++
Indeterminate		PT		W	++								

Table 44 The plant remains from site L

			Period		2	2	2	6
			Land use		OA1	OA1	OA1	B4
			Context		L[57]	L[59]	L[61]	L[37]
			Sample		L{4}	L{2}	L{3}	L{1}
Latin name	**English name**	**Plant part**	**Habitat/use**	**P**				
Triticum sp	wheat	R	FI	C	1			
Indeterminate		WD		C	++	+	+	++
Ranunculus sceleratus L	celery-leaved crowfoot		E	W	+			
R subgen *Batrachium* (DC) A	crowfoots		F	W	+			

Table 44 (cont)

Latin name	English name	Plant part	Period	P	2	2	2	6
			Land use		OA1	OA1	OA1	B4
			Context		L[57]	L[59]	L[61]	L[37]
			Sample		L{4}	L{2}	L{3}	L{1}
			Habitat/use					
Stellaria media gp	chickweeds		ABCDE	W	+			
Chenopodium spp	goosefoot etc		ABCDFH	W	++		+	
Atriplex spp	orache		ABFGH	W	+			
Polygonum aviculare agg	knotgrass		ABG	W	+			
Urtica dioica L	stinging nettle		BCDEFGH	W	++			
Sambucus nigra L	elder		BCFGH	W				+
Alisma spp	water plantain		E	W	+			
Potamogeton spp	pondweed		E	W	+		+	
Eleocharis palustris/ uniglumis	spike-rush		E	W	+			
Carex spp	sedge		CDEH	W	+			
Indeterminate				W	+			
Indeterminate		WD		W		++	++	
Indeterminate		PT		W	+++			

General characteristics of the material

All nine sites produced variable amounts of plant remains, mainly preserved by waterlogging. There were smaller amounts of charred plant remains in most samples and mineralised remains in just one sample.

Sites B, D, F, G, H and J produced the richest plant assemblages with smaller quantities of botanical material from sites C, E and L. Seeds and fruits were the most common and easily identifiable remains although samples with good organic preservation also contained bran fragments and root/stem, moss, wood and occasional leaf fragments.

The waterlogged plant remains included a range of wild plants with a high frequency and species diversity of wetland (aquatic and bankside/marshland) plants, together with plants of disturbed (including cultivated) ground and waste places. Grassland and woodland/hedgerow plants were represented by smaller amounts of remains. Food plants preserved by waterlogging consisted mainly of fruits, with definite cultivars (eg, fig, grape, mulberry), cultivated/wild species (eg, apple, pear, plum/ bullace, cherry, sloe/blackthorn) and wild species (eg, blackberry/raspberry, elder, strawberry, hazel). Other potential economic plants included hop, flax, hemp and dyer's rocket.

Identifiable charred plant remains (with the exception of charcoal) consisted mainly of cereal grains plus very occasional pulses and weed seeds with the richest cereal assemblages being from site G (period 7). Charcoal fragments were present in virtually all the samples. Mineralised material was found in just one sample, from cesspit D[54] (period 7), consisting of a few cereals, stem and wood fragments.

The interpretation of the plant assemblages was carried out on a sample-by-sample basis taking account of habitat information for individual species and the potential uses of the different plants. Other biological and artefactual remains in the individual samples were also considered in the interpretation of the plant assemblages.

16.7 Animal bone

Kevin Rielly

Methods

Animal bones were recovered from seven out of the eight sites within this project. Particular areas within these seven sites were chosen for further study following a detailed assessment (Rielly 1997) and a thorough review of the stratigraphic and dating evidence. The selection process was principally dependent on the condition and size of individual assemblages, as well as their dating. Additional factors included the presence of hand-collected and sieved collections, plus the presence of unusual features referring to particular species and/or concentrations of particular skeletal parts. The chosen assemblages are described within the major text sections and the list of areas with bones are shown in Table 45. All seven sites with bones provided both hand-collected and sieved collections. The latter bones were

Table 45 Distribution of animal bone assemblages by site, period and land use

Period	5	6	7	8	9	10
Land use						
Building 6			D			
Building 13			C		C	
Building 15				F	F	
Structure 5		F				
Road 1			F			
Open Area 1	C, D	F, C				
Open Area 4		D	G, D			
Open Area 10			F			
Open Area 11				E	E	E
Open Area 13				C		
Open Area 14				F, B	B	

generally collected from samples with a minimum volume of 10 litres, these washed through a 1mm mesh using a Siraf tank. The resultant residue was then sorted by hand.

All the animal bones were recorded, on an individual basis, directly on to the MoLAS Environmental Archaeology Section ORACLE (version 7) database. Identifications of species and anatomy were aided by the use of the MoLSS Environmental Archaeology Section reference collections in conjunction with Schmid (1972) and Cohen and Serjeantson (1996). All available information for each bone was recorded, including: proportion present and zones represented (after D J Rackham 1986); age of the bone, this determined through the analysis of toothwear stages (after Grant 1982) and epiphysial fusion (after Schmid 1972); butchery, recording cut marks in terms of the tool used, the position of the cut and the direction of the blow; pathology, with a full description and notes taken concerning possible causes; other modifications such as gnawing and burning, in both cases noting the severity, and in the former case, the perpetrator; measurements, following von den Driesch (1976). Where it was impossible to determine exact identifications to species level, approximate classifications based on size were employed, for example, 'cattle-sized' and 'sheep-sized'.

Species representation: evidence for trends and status

An initial point to be discussed is the apparent paucity of bones recovered from the majority of these sites (see Tables 46, 48), in comparison to those from sites B and F (the Westminster Underground Station excavations), reflecting the greater size of the latter excavations. The majority of the bone-bearing deposits located within the smaller sites can be interpreted as resulting from the opportunistic dumping of waste materials, for example, backfills within a decommissioned drain or the use of waste for levelling purposes. In contrast, those found in site F, and especially in site B, clearly represent the organised dumping of waste within dug features constructed for that purpose. Obviously the major factor here is available space.

Overall, the bones found within all periods and locations invariably represent food waste (see Tables 47–9). A few non-food species were recovered, and these will be described later in this section. The great majority of the food waste, again throughout these sites, could be either identified as, or is likely to belong to, cattle, sheep/goat and pig. The cattle- and sheep-sized fragments are included in this statement (and see last section for descriptions/ use of size categories). It should be mentioned that the species amalgam 'sheep/goat' is very likely to be chiefly represented by sheep, as shown by the far larger quantity of identified sheep compared to goat bones (see Table 47).

Comparisons regarding the relative abundance of these three major domesticates must be limited to the larger bone collections, and in particular to site B (Table 46, with information taken from Table 47). Within this site, there would appear to be a similar level of use of all three species through the late medieval and early post-medieval occupation periods,

Table 46 Percentage representation of the major mammalian domesticates from site B, periods 8 and 9 (hand-collected data)

Period	Cattle %	Sheep/goat %	Pig %	N
8	48.8	34.9	16.3	381
9	47.2	36.9	15.9	233

N is the total number of cattle, sheep/goat and pig bones

with cattle dominant, followed by sheep/goat and then pig.

It is possible to make wider comparisons across the various temporal and spatial units regarding the representation of the other food species, referring here to the presence of game, of domestic birds, and also of fish. An additional and complementary comparison, stated within the relevant parts of this section, will refer to the presence of high-status food items.

The game species identified amongst these sites included deer (fallow and roe), hare, rabbit, ducks (including a wigeon-sized species and teal), partridge, heron, woodcock, wood pigeon, several passerines (thrush-sized and smaller) and swan. One or more of these species were found in most periods (except period 5) and within the majority of the sites. Clearly a large number of such species were potentially available as a minor food resource during these periods. A proportion of these can be classed as high-status items, including the deer, rabbit, heron and swan, essentially comprising the meats desired for feasting activities (see eg, Hammond 1995, 164). Various other species may also be included on this list, as woodcock and also thrushes and larks (the last may be present amongst the small passerines found at these sites), all of which were considered as the exclusive property of the lord of the manor (Hammond 1995, 76). The various deer species and rabbit are likely to have been imported from one or more of the deer parks situated within close proximity to the city (Grant 1988, 164; O Rackham 1986, 124). As well as an enclosed area for the hunting of game, a number of these parks also featured a specially constructed warren. The relative status of the rabbit, however, declined somewhat by the early post-medieval period (Cantor 1987, 37) with the establishment both of a far larger number of warrens and perhaps of this species outside the confines of these enclosures. As well as being a high-status food item, the heron can be indirectly linked to the practice of hawking, this being one of three especially sought-after prey items (the others being crane and curlew) captured by this method (Huff 1997, 8). The mute swan may represent a culled rather than a hunted bird. This species was brought into semi-domestication, coinciding with the onset of royal protection from the 13th century until the 18th century, during which time certain individuals and communities were granted licences to keep swans (Vesey-Fitzgerald 1946, 76).

There are at least four domestic bird species represented, including chicken, goose, duck, dove and peacock. All the goose and dove bones and the majority of those identified as duck, are actually within the size range of the wild progenitors, for

Table 47 Species representation – hand collection by period and site (total fragment count)

Period	5	6	6	7	7	8	8	8	8	9	9	9	9	10
Site	C	C	F	C	F	C	E	B	F	C	E	B	F	E
Cattle	3	1	2	1	16	1	6	186	5	0	6	110	0	5
Horse	0	0	0	0	0	0	1	0	0	0	0	0	0	0
Cattle-sized	1	2	10	1	48	3	11	329	9	0	21	170	23	13
Sheep/goat	6	0	0	5	8	0	0	89	7	0	1	57	10	0
Sheep	3	0	0	0	1	0	1	39	2	1	1	27	5	0
Goat	0	0	0	0	0	0	0	5	0	0	0	2	0	0
Pig	6	0	2	14	10	0	0	62	4	0	1	37	1	0
Sheep-sized	16	5	0	180	10	5	0	260	3	0	0	156	11	0
Fallow deer	0	0	0	0	1	0	0	1	0	0	0	0	0	0
Roe deer	0	0	0	0	1	0	0	0	0	0	1	0	0	0
Deer species	0	0	1	0	0	0	0	0	0	0	0	0	0	0
Hare	0	0	0	0	0	0	0	1	0	0	0	0	0	0
Rabbit	0	0	0	0	0	0	0	29	1	0	0	44	0	0
Dog	1	0	0	0	0	0	0	0	2	0	3	0	0	3
Cat	0	0	0	0	0	0	0	3	0	0	0	0	2	0
Small mammal	0	0	0	0	0	0	0	5	0	0	0	0	1	0
Rat-sized	0	0	0	0	0	0	0	1	0	0	0	6	1	0
Chicken	4	2	1	45	1	4	1	104	2	0	0	49	21	0
Chicken-sized	1	0	0	17	0	1	0	4	0	0	0	9	0	0
Goose	0	0	1	10	1	0	0	16	0	0	0	10	4	0
Goose-sized	0	0	0	2	0	0	0	0	1	0	0	1	0	0
Domestic duck	0	0	0	0	0	0	0	5	0	0	0	2	0	0
Domestic dove	0	0	0	0	0	0	0	6	0	0	0	4	18	0
Medium-sized duck	0	0	0	0	0	0	0	1	0	0	0	0	0	0
Teal	0	0	0	0	0	0	0	1	0	0	0	0	0	0
Swan	0	0	0	0	1	0	0	0	0	0	0	0	0	0
Heron	0	0	0	0	0	0	0	0	0	0	0	0	1	0
Partridge	0	0	0	0	0	0	0	2	0	0	0	3	0	0
Peacock	3	0	0	0	0	0	0	0	0	0	0	0	0	0
Cod	0	0	0	0	0	0	0	1	0	0	0	3	0	0
Conger eel	0	0	0	0	0	0	0	2	0	0	0	2	0	0
Haddock	0	0	0	0	1	0	0	0	0	0	0	0	0	0
Pike	0	0	0	0	0	0	0	1	0	0	0	0	0	0
Unidentified fish	0	0	0	0	0	0	0	0	1	0	0	0	0	0
Total	44	10	17	275	99	14	20	1153	37	1	34	692	98	21

example, greylag goose, rock dove and mallard respectively. This is fairly typical for the medieval and early post-medieval periods, signifying the absence of any noticeable size modifications within the domestic variants of these species. It is possible, however, that a few of these birds may represent game rather than domesticates. This is clearly not the case with the doves from period 9, Building 15, where the mix of ages strongly indicates the local presence of a dovecote. Chicken is by far the best represented of these species, especially within periods 7, 8 and 9. A particular concentration of chicken bones was found in period 7, Building 13, the abundance of which, in comparison to the dove bones described above from Building 15, may be related to the presence of a locally managed flock. Arguments concerning the keeping of doves and chickens are mentioned in the next section.

The peacock is the ultimate medieval ornamental and high-status feasting ingredient. This bird has a fairly strong flavour and would often accompany other similarly strong-tasting birds such as heron and swan (Hammond 1995, 130). One method of presenting this bird, and indeed other birds with a beautiful plumage, was to carefully skin and then roast the carcass. The skin would then be replaced and the bird positioned in such a way as to suggest that it was still alive. These would undoubtedly have provided 'spectacular table decorations, although the risk of infection from the uncooked skin would have been great' (Hammond 1995, 137–8). Thus the peacock recovered from the period 5 deposit can certainly be classed as a feast item.

A variety of fish species are represented, in particular within periods 7, 8 and 9 (Table 49). Here, the key species appear to be eel, gadids, herring, plaice/flounder and smelt. The gadids (the cod family) may be principally composed of cod and whiting, based on the identifiable fragments. A large proportion of the gadids were from relatively small fish, probably representing quite young individuals, weighing no more than about 2.0kg. It would appear, amongst these key species, that there is a noticeably larger proportion of eel and lesser proportion of gadids in the period 7 assemblage when compared to those from the two later periods.

A number of non-food species were recovered, including a few domesticates, small rodents and amphibians. The domesticates, horse, dog and cat, are all poorly represented, as would be expected within dumps largely composed of food waste. There are relatively large quantities of small rodent bones

Table 48 Mammal and bird representation – sieved collection by period and site (total fragment count)

Period	5	6	6	7	7	8	8	9	9
Site	D	D	F	D, G	C	E	B	B	F
Cattle	1	0	0	3	0	1	44	15	0
Horse	0	0	0	0	0	0	0	1	0
Cattle-sized	6	3	0	3	1	3	150	73	1
Sheep/goat	1	1	0	4	4	0	28	19	6
Sheep	0	0	0	1	0	0	1	3	0
Pig	0	3	2	5	12	0	31	13	1
Sheep-sized	18	12	0	88	208	20	356	134	3
Hare	0	0	0	0	0	0	1	3	0
Rabbit	0	0	0	0	0	0	44	12	3
Cat	0	0	0	0	0	0	0	1	6
Small mammal	3	0	0	5	2	0	39	19	1
Rat-sized	0	0	0	4	0	0	19	20	0
House mouse	0	0	0	1	0	0	1	0	5
Mouse-sized	0	0	0	15	0	0	0	5	39
Chicken	0	2	3	1	61	0	60	27	1
Chicken-sized	0	5	0	4	65	0	108	41	115
Goose	0	0	0	0	0	0	5	2	0
Goose-sized	0	0	0	1	1	0	3	1	0
Domestic duck	0	0	0	1	0	0	4	0	0
Domestic dove	0	0	0	0	0	0	1	1	66
Partridge	0	1	0	0	0	0	11	0	0
Woodcock	0	0	0	0	0	0	0	1	0
Wood pigeon	0	0	0	0	0	0	1	0	0
Large thrush	0	0	0	0	0	0	1	0	2
Small thrush	1	1	0	0	0	0	3	0	2
Thrush	0	0	0	0	0	0	1	3	0
Small passerine	0	0	0	0	0	0	7	4	5
Small mammal/unidentified bird	0	0	0	0	0	0	0	0	150
Total	30	28	5	136	354	24	919	398	406

Table 49 Fish and amphibian representation – sieved collection by period and site (total fragment count)

Period	5	6	7	7	7	8	8	9	9
Site	D	D	F	D, G	C	E	B	B	F
Chondrichthyes (probably Elasmobranchii)	0	0	0	0	0	0	11	0	0
Cod	0	1	0	1	2	0	38	9	0
Conger eel	0	0	0	0	4	0	9	0	0
Cyprinidae sp	0	1	0	0	1	0	1	0	0
cf Roach	0	0	0	2	0	0	0	0	0
Freshwater eel	0	0	0	0	139	0	54	30	10
Gadus (large)	0	1	0	0	0	0	19	12	0
Gadus (small)	0	10	0	5	29	0	260	51	0
Gadus (small) cf whiting	0	0	0	0	0	0	19	0	0
Gurnard sp	0	0	0	0	0	0	25	11	1
Herring	0	4	0	2	98	0	323	59	25
Mackerel	0	0	0	0	0	0	11	1	0
Pike	0	0	0	0	0	0	10	1	0
Plaice/flounder	0	2	0	0	34	0	41	7	5
Smelt	0	3	0	1	166	0	154	42	27
Spurdog	0	0	0	0	0	0	0	2	0
Thornback ray	0	1	0	0	0	0	6	0	0
Unidentified fish	67	23	1	182	35	43	55	55	35
Amphibian	0	0	0	5	0	0	8	2	0
Total	67	46	1	198	508	43	1044	282	103

(see Table 48) divided into rat-sized and mouse-sized, the former undoubtedly belonging to black rat, while the latter may be largely composed of house mice. Such bones were found throughout the periods 7, 8 and 9 samples, although it would appear that rats dominated the pit fill assemblages within site B (periods 8 and 9), while mice would appear to have been more prevalent within the palace yard (period 7) and Building 15 (period 9). This difference would coincide with the perceived view of rats as major exploiters of rubbish dumps, and of mice as preferring to live within houses with a ready supply of food. Whatever the truth of this statement, it would certainly appear that the Westminster settlement had a significant rodent problem throughout most of the medieval and early post-medieval periods.

Exploitation and organisation of animal products

Major domesticates

POST-MORTEM PRODUCTS

This section is essentially in two parts: first, the evidence for the method(s) of supply, namely the organisation behind the production of suitable animals for the meat markets; second, the evidence for a redistribution network from slaughter to consumer or craft workshop.

As well as external sources of supply (see below), the communities within this area would appear also to have been self-sufficient, at least to a limited extent, in all three major mammalian domesticates. This is shown by the presence of very young individuals (Tables 50–2), which can be interpreted as infant mortalities and therefore clear indicators of local production. There is a good collection of such individuals within the larger assemblages from sites B and F (periods 8 and 9). This is probably related to the continual problem within this analysis, that is, the likely link between available information and size of assemblage. Of some interest, therefore, is the relative abundance of such individuals within the period 7 deposits in Building 13 (Chapter 9.3). It may also be significant that the greatest density of youngsters amongst the two larger sites, represented by very juvenile lambs, was recovered from period 7 deposits in site F (OA10, R1). A case can perhaps be made for a decline in the use of local husbandry within the later medieval period in this general area.

Evidence for the organisation of the external supply of food animals to these communities can be ascertained from a review of the age evidence. Essentially this analysis aims to estimate whether the animals brought to the site had been specifically bred for their meat or for some secondary product.

The demand for a range of products forms part of the equation, in that the meats used will depend mainly on availability and preference. Each species will have an optimal meat weight, generally reached when the animal provides the

Table 50 Distribution of neonatal and infant bones (hand-collected and sieved data)

	Species	Cattle	Sheep/ goat	Pig	Chicken
Period	Land use				
7	Building 13	P	P	P	P
7	Open Area 10		P		
7	Road 1		P		
8	Open Area 11	P			
8	Open Area 14	P	P	P	P
9	Building 15		P		
9	Open Area 14	P	P		

Key
P = present

Table 51 Epiphysial fusion evidence for the major mammalian domesticates (hand-collected bones) from sites B and F

	Period	7	8		9	
Species	Age group	N	N	%F	N	%F
Cattle	FN		2		2	
	infant		5		6	
	early		30/2	93.7	18/4	81.8
	intermediate		4/2	66.6	8/1	88.9
	late		26/13	66.6	10/8	55.5
	vertebrae		10/14	41.7	4/4	50.0
Sheep/goat	FN		2			
	infant	6			1	
	early	1/0	45/0	100.0	24/3	88.9
	intermediate		10/0	100.0	11/1	91.6
	late	1/0	16/3	84.2	11/8	57.9
Pig	FN		1			
	infant					
	early	1/2	4/1	80.0	2/1	66.7
	intermediate	0/2	1/15	16.6	1/9	10.0
	late	0/3	1/9	10.0	1/3	25.0

Key
Period 7 data come from site F, OA10 and R1; period 8 and 9 data from sites B and F, OA14
N = number of fragments; with early through to vertebrae age groups = number of fused/unfused epiphyses
%F = percentage fused
FN = foetal/neonate
The epiphyses used in each age group are as follows: early = scapula P, humerus D, radius P, pelvis acetabulum, phalanges P; intermediate = tibia D, metacarpus and metatarsus D; late = humerus P, ulna P, radius D, femur P and D, tibia P and calcaneus P (where P = proximal and D =distal)

Table 52 Mandibular tooth eruption and wear data for the major mammalian domesticates (hand-collected bones) in periods 8 and 9 only; data from sites B and F, the former providing all but one of the ageable mandibles

	Cattle		Sheep		Pig	
Period	8	9	8	9	8	9
Age group						
1: dpm4w M1unw	1					1
2: M1w M2unw					1	1
3: M2w M3unw	1				2	1
4: M3w (< stage g)			3	1		
5: M3w (> = stage g)	2	1	2	3		

Key
Teeth: dpm4 = deciduous premolar 4; M1, 2 and 3 = adult molars 1, 2 and 3
Wear state: w = worn; unw = unworn
Wear stage: these follow Grant (1975) and (1982)

greatest return for the time spent in rearing and feeding. In addition there is a cut-off point in all three animals where the meat will have a markedly lower quality. The first of these two stages occurs before reaching adulthood, and is indicated here by the unfused intermediary epiphyses (Table 51) and by the mandibular age group 3 in Table 52, while the second stage cut-off is the fusion of the later epiphyses.

The age analysis is essentially limited to periods 8 and 9 (sites B and F), as only these assemblages provided suitably large datasets. Regarding cattle, the age profile shown by the epiphysial fusion evidence (Table 51) is clearly not one related to intensive meat production, since a very large proportion survived beyond the optimal age, here at approximately their second or third year. There is a slight difference in the proportions of fused intermediary epiphyses between the two periods, but this may just be a result of the relatively small quantities of ageable bones within this age group. A major cull prior to the fusion of the later epiphyses (this occurring in their fourth year), in both periods, may be indicative of a preference for older beef. Overall, the evidence does suggest that about half the animals represented were reared principally for their meat.

A very great proportion of the sheep, in both periods, survived into adulthood (intermediary epiphyses fusion at approximately 2 years of age). A large proportion of the animals in period 8 also survived beyond the late epiphyses fusion age of approximately 3.5 years, whereas those in period 9 suffered a major cull. While the evidence clearly points to a greater use of mutton within the later period, there is again a fairly large proportion of aged individuals older than young adults. In sharp contrast, the pigs are mainly represented by pre-adult individuals, a situation which reflects the essentially post-mortem uses of this animal. The obvious lack of adult animals may also indicate an intensive exploitation strategy in which animals were predominantly culled at their optimal meat weight.

Referring to the second part of this section (that is, the evidence for a redistribution network), the argument used is that concentrations of particular skeletal parts indicate the waste disposed of either by a butcher (generally the head and foot parts) or by the consumer (the remaining parts, this constituting the dressed carcass). There would appear to be a particular concentration of cattle-dressed carcass waste within the largest assemblages (ie, in site B, periods 8 and 9). The same pattern, though less pronounced, is also shown by the sheep bone collections from the same site and periods. These results, as well as suggesting the presence of the aforementioned redistribution network, are clearly indicative of waste from high-status households. It is noteworthy that the cattle bones are largely composed of upper limb parts, which would have carried the most and the best-quality meat. There is general evidence to show that poorer quality cuts of meat were also consumed in this area, which may represent the provision of such cuts or that animals were occasionally butchered and subsequently jointed within one or more of the nearby households. Of some interest is the clearly poor representation of cattle and sheep horn cores throughout the sites and periods. This offers further evidence for redistribution, with the horn cores perhaps being dispatched to the horn worker. It can be supposed that this either occurred locally or via the butcher(s) supplying this area with meat.

The butchery noticed amongst the bones is fairly typical of both the medieval and the post-medieval periods in London. When examining the larger assemblages, it can be seen that there is an extensive use of the cleaver, this instrument being used throughout the butchery process. Even though knife marks were more common on sheep and pig fragments, it would appear that even with these species the cleaver was the instrument of choice. There is a good representation of split vertebrae, especially cattle-sized, featuring all parts of the vertebral column. This is possibly related to the stage following the dressing of the carcass, that is, the production of halves. It has been suggested that the introduction of this method into the butcher's repertoire may have coincided with the 'cutting of the carcasses into more clearly prescribed separate joints' (Rixson 1989, 55). This, in turn, then relates to the establishment of professional butchers. Such butchery would appear to be absent from Late Saxon London, at least on the evidence from sites such as Bull Wharf (Rielly in prep), but is then much in evidence at various medieval sites from approximately the 12th century onwards. A noticeable feature, however, of these sites, as here, is that this division of the carcass was by no means consistently used. The presence of unsplit vertebrae could suggest either that a variety of methods was still available to the professional butcher, or that a portion of the meat was procured and butchered by the non-professional, possibly within the household. There are, however, remarkable consistencies regarding the production of the 'separate joints', as described above. Chops through or adjacent to the joint surfaces and through the shafts of the limb bones provided relatively small joints. There are also a number of rib and scapula fragments, in both periods 8 and 9 (within sites B and F), which have been chopped into smallish portions, that is, by two parallel transverse cuts. There is a marked under-representation of butchery marks that can be interpreted as being the result of meat-removal. While a skilled butcher need not necessarily leave any marks on the bone during this part of the butchery process, the poor representation of defleshing marks plus the size of the joints produced by the cleaver butchery may in fact suggest that meat was cooked on the bone.

Of some interest regarding a possible method of slaughter was the recovery of a sheep skull (from one of the period 9 site B pit fills) with a square puncture, measuring approximately 8mm to a side, through the left tempero-parietal suture, just above the mandibular joint. This was clearly the result of some implement being rammed through the skull from the right side of the head. Apart from supplying evidence for a rather unusual method of slaughter, it may also show that some of the animals brought to this general area during the early post-medieval period arrived on the hoof.

There is perhaps some slight evidence for local craft activities. A goat horn core from one of the site B pit fills dated to period 8 had been removed from the skull by chopping through the base. Unusually, the core also displayed a series of grazing chops around the base, a type of butchery which can perhaps be linked with the removal of the hornsheaf. The question then is whether this implies the presence of a local horn worker or whether this sheaf was removed, probably by the butcher, in order to be sent on to the craft workshop. Given the relatively poor representation of horn cores throughout the site (see above), it is perhaps more likely that horn working took place elsewhere, and that, occasionally, the horn was supplied to the workshops without the accompanying horn core. A similar conclusion was reached concerning a similar array of evidence at Roman and medieval Baltic Exchange (Rielly 2002, 96).

ANTE-MORTEM PRODUCTS

It is clear that a large proportion of the cattle and sheep within periods 8 and 9 survived beyond the ages of 4 years and 3.5 years respectively (the late-fusing age groups given in Table 51). In cattle, survival continued well beyond 7 to 9 years (the vertebral evidence), while a proportion of the sheep would appear to have been slaughtered between the ages of 4 and 6 years. This latter age range is taken from Payne, corresponding to stage G in his sequence of mandibular toothwear and eruption (Payne 1973, 293). The secondary usage of these animals can be ascertained with reference to the sex data. Such data, unfortunately, is generally too small to provide any valid conclusions. A number of sheep pelves from site B could be sexed from periods 8 and 9. These gave the following results: period 8, 9 male, 5 female; period 9, 3 male, 1 female. As the pelves acetabulum is one of the early fusing epiphyses, these results merely give the range of sexes of animals older than approximately 6 months. Obviously this information cannot readily be used to estimate the sex ratio of the adult animals. One possible indication of use, however, was supplied by the pelvis of an obviously aged cattle. The acetabulum (hip joint) showed severe eburnation (polishing) and peripheral boney growth, indicative of an advanced case of osteoarthritis. Such a condition may be linked with undue stress, suggesting that this animal had been used for work purposes. Another line of enquiry includes the presence of the very young calves, these found within several deposits (Tables 50–1). These may represent mortalities related to the use of cows for their milk.

Other species

A lesser, though significant, part of the meat diet in all periods was met by domestic birds, game and fish. It is certainly likely, considering the wealth of produce entering the town during the medieval period, that each of these species could represent a market purchase (see Hammond 1995, 40–1). The produce arriving at these markets, as suggested in the previous sections, may have derived from local as well as distant sources, here referring mainly to the major food animals, that is, cattle, sheep/goat and pig. Conversely, the game and fish species are more likely to represent, principally, the exploitation of local resources. Much of the game entering the town during the medieval period was essentially derived from the various estates, a large number of which were situated within the Home Counties (Grant 1988, 164; O Rackham 1986, 124). A point worth considering here, with respect to these estates, is the possibility that a proportion of the game found at these sites may in fact represent direct imports rather than purchases, being taken from properties connected either to the palace or to the abbey. It could also be assumed that the presence of certain fish species may be related more to their juxtaposition to sites of some affluence rather than to their availability at the town markets. Pike were commonly kept in estate ponds and eel traps were often associated with water mills. It can be conjectured that a number of water mills along the Thames were under either royal or church ownership; indeed, the abbey had one itself on the southern edge of Thorney Island and pike were kept in the Jewel Tower moat. Evidence of eels from water mills comes from references to ecclesiastical houses such as Evesham Abbey where the Domesday record mentions 2000 eels received from two mills on the River Avon (Hammond 1995, 23). Certainly this may explain the abundance of eels found within Building 13 in the northern precinct of the abbey.

The local supply of fish is suggested by the species represented as well as their size range (above, Species representation – evidence for trends and status). There is, however, very slight evidence for long-distance trade, as demonstrated by the haddock fragment found in a period 7 deposit. This species is essentially a northern North Sea fish (Wheeler 1979, 176–7). Any long-distance trade in foodstuffs poses a problem of preservation. It is significant, therefore, that the haddock bone, a cleithrum, was found to be butchered in such a way as to suggest that the head had been removed from the carcass. This type of butchery is a necessary prerequisite of a number of different methods of curing and/or preserving fish. Thus it can be conjectured that this bone represents the remains of a fish that had been caught and then preserved before being transported to the London fish market.

Amongst the bird domesticates, there would appear to have been a measure of local production, at least as far as chickens and doves were concerned. Evidence for this comes from the presence of very young birds, with noticeable concentrations of chicken in period 7, Building 13 (see Table 53), and of dove in period 9, Building 15. It can perhaps be assumed that chickens were kept within the abbey precinct during the later medieval period, while at least one of the former canons' houses, in the ownership of Ann Nelthorpe, is likely to have featured a dovecote. Of interest in this respect is the minimal representation of doves within the contemporary levels on site B (Tables 47–8), which perhaps demonstrates the very local maintenance and use of this species in relation to Building 15. These birds may have been kept partly for ornamental reasons and partly as a source of meat. It is interesting that relatively few young doves are represented in this assemblage, suggesting that they were clearly not subjected to an intensive meat exploitation strategy. Evidence in the shape of a pair of leg bones (tibias) containing medullary bone suggests that these birds were taken from a breeding flock. Such bone not only identifies the bird as female, but also shows that the bird was in lay (Driver 1982). Evidence was also found for a certain level of care and attention, as demonstrated by the presence of a bone (a tarsometatarsus, one of the lower hind limb parts) with a cleanly healed fracture.

Chickens were principally represented, in all periods, by adult birds (the fused bones in Table 53), perhaps signifying the importance of egg production. There is, however, a noticeably larger proportion of juvenile birds in periods 7 and 8 in comparison to period 9. A tentative inference can perhaps be drawn from the presence of very young birds within the earlier two periods and their absence in period 9. Given the above arguments for linking such birds with on-site breeding, it could be assumed that juvenile birds may have been more readily available on sites where chickens were locally produced. Egg production would favour the preferential culling of young males, with the majority of hens surviving to adulthood. There is no obvious indication that the juveniles are predominantly male (this based on the presence of spur scars, following West 1982), while the general mix of adult ages would suggest a less than intensive exploitation strategy for this commodity (Table 53).

The geese and ducks represented at this site were clearly all adults, with the notable exception of a few juvenile geese from Building 13 (period 7). This evidence does not necessarily show that geese as well as chickens were bred in the locality of this building, but it may show that its occupants had the wherewithal to procure such high-quality poultry for the table. Overall, however, the age of both the geese and the ducks suggests that they were principally bred for their eggs.

Finally, it can be assumed that each of the three non-food domesticates were used by the local occupants of these sites. There is the possibility that some of the dogs and cats were feral; otherwise, it can be conjectured that they may have been work animals or even pets. The size of the dogs, as well as of the horses, may be indicative of use, with the larger animals generally being used for hunting/guarding and riding respectively. No such animals were found at these sites, the dogs being rather small, while the horses can be described as large ponies (below, Animal size/type). It can perhaps be assumed that these animals were used for a variety of tasks, the dogs possibly as ratters or for small game, and the horses for carrying and pulling.

Animal size/type

The general size of cattle, sheep, dog and chicken are illustrated with reference to various selected measurements and, for the first three species, to their heights (as calculated using the factors described in von den Driesch and Boessneck 1974 and Harcourt 1974) (Tables 54–5). The evidence points to rather small and slender cattle and sheep, which is typical of animals recovered from medieval sites in London. Clearly such animals continued to be used well into the post-medieval period, although there was a notable increase in size amongst a small proportion of the cattle used from the 16th century onwards, as found for example at Finsbury Pavement (Rielly in prep). The chickens are similarly of a small medieval type, while the dogs are within the smaller half of the range of sizes known from this general period. They in fact resemble a small terrier, which may perhaps equate with a small hunting dog or 'ratter'. There was one measurement available for horse, this from a femur taken from a period 8 level from site E. Again, this is well within the range of sizes provided by numerous horses recovered from the late medieval period (Rackham 1995; Cowie and Pipe 1999).

There is some slight information concerning the 'type' of sheep represented at this site, as shown by the good representation of polled (hornless) skulls in site B. At this site, there were two polled and two horned skulls in period 8, and one polled against six horned in period 9. While the numbers are not large, the ratio of polled to horned may be significant, perhaps pointing to a 'type' where hornless ewes were being selected. Overall, the sheep are similar in build to the primitive Soay type, which generally has horned rams and about 50% horned ewes (Hall and Clutton-Brock 1995, 100).

Table 53 Chicken age and sex data

Period		7		8		9	
Collection		hand	sieved	hand	sieved	hand	sieved
Age							
epiphyses	fused/unfused	16/4	21/8	72/17	17/11	28/2	20/2
	infant	3	5	2			
	%fused	69.5	61.7	79.1	60.7	93.3	90.9
Sex							
Tarsometarsus	spurred/unspurred	0/1		6/6	0/2	1/2	0/2
Medullary bone: femur	presence/absence	0/4	1/7	0/10	0/2	1/4	0/2
tibiotarsus		0/2	0/2	1/8	0/3	2/6	0/1

Key
Period 7 data taken from site C, B13; periods 8 and 9 from site B, OA14 deposits
Infant = very young chicks
%fused = fused/fused + unfused + infant x 100
Sexing on adult bones only, ie fused epiphyses

Table 54 Distribution of shoulder heights for cattle, sheep and dog

Species	Period	Range (m)	Mean (m)	N
Cattle	8	1.04	1.040	1
Sheep	8	0.575–0.618	0.592	3
	9	0.553–0.631	0.595	5
Dog	10	0.303–0.331	0.317	2

Key
N = number of bones
Heights calculated following the methods described in von den Driesch and Boessneck (1974)

Table 55 Selected measurements of cattle, sheep, dog and chicken

Species	Period	Bone	Dimensions	Range (mm)	Mean (mm)	N
Cattle	8	mc	GL	169.2	169.2	1
	8	mt	Bd	50.2	50.2	1
	9	mt	Bd	51.3–62.6	55.5	4
	8	tibia	Bd	60.2–61.2	60.7	2
	9	tibia	Bd	62.2–62.3	62.2	3
Sheep	9	humerus	GL	140.6	140.6	1
	8	radius	GL	143.2–145.3	144.2	2
	9	radius	GL	146.2–157.0	151.1	3
	8	tibia	GL	205.4	205.4	1
	8	tibia	Bd	23.3–27.2	25.1	5
	9	tibia	Bd	24.2–27.0	25.5	5
	9	mc	GL	113.2	113.2	1
	8	mc	Bd	21.8–26.3	23.9	4
	9	mc	Bd	24.2–26.2	24.6	4
Dog	10	humerus	GL	96.2	96.2	1
	10	radius	GL	98.2	98.2	1
Chicken	8	ulna	GL	65.2–90.2	76.9	12
	9	ulna	GL	63.4–89.2	74.9	4
	8	t'm'tarsus	GL	65.2–97.1	78.3	8

Key
Bone: mc = metacarpus; mt = metatarsus; t'm'tarsus = tarsometatarsus
Dimensions: GL = greatest length; Bd = breadth at distal end
N = number of bones

16.8 Radiocarbon dating

Jane Sidell

Dating conventions used in the text and in Table 56 are detailed in Chapter 1.3, 'Dating conventions'.

Table 56 Radiocarbon dates obtained from the sites (calibration using curve of Stuiver et al (1998) using OxCal release 3.8 (Bronk Ramsey 2002))

Laboratory no.	Site	OD height	Material dated	^{14}C age radiocarbon years BP	d ^{13}C (l) measurements	2σ calibration calendar years BC/AD
Beta 88699 #	F[184]		wood	800 ± 60	-25*	AD 1040–1300
Beta 88700 #	F[185]		wood	890 ± 80	-25*	AD 1010–1280
Beta 119789 #	F (M1)	-0.73→-0.78m OD	organic sediment	3110 ± 60	-25*	1520–1210 BC
Beta 119790 #	F (M2)	-1.17→-1.22m OD	organic sediment	3570 ± 70	-25*	2140–1730 BC
Beta 122929 #*	F (M5)	-2.09→-2.12m OD	plant material	4300 ± 60	-25*	3100–2690 BC
Beta 127617 #	SGT94 (1)	-0.20→-0.24m OD	organic sediment	3300 ± 70	-25*	1740–1430 BC
Beta 127739~ #	SGT94 (2)	+0.08→+0.07m OD	organic sediment	2640 ± 40		900–760 BC
Beta 127616~ #	H	-1.23→-1.27m OD	organic sediment	3920 ± 40		2560–2280 BC
Beta 88701 #	B		organic sediment	2800 ± 70	-25*	1130–810 BC
Beta 88695 #	J[77]		wood	1080 ± 70	-25*	AD 770–1160
Beta 88696 #	J[80]		wood	970 ± 60	-25*	AD 970–1220
Beta 78163 #	G (1)		wood	740 ± 50	-25*	AD 1190–1390
Beta 78165 #	G (2)		wood	3350 ± 50	-25*	1750–1510 BC
HAR329 ‡	NPY74	0.84m from top pollen profile -0.10m OD	alder	2190 ± 60	-27.1	390–90 BC
HAR 330	NPY74	+1.00m OD	charcoal	960 ± 70	-26.9	AD 900–1240
HAR331 ‡	NPY74	0.14m from top pollen profile OD	wood	1520 ± 70	-26.2	AD 410–660
HAR332 ‡	NPY74	0.14m from top pollen profile +0.3m OD	unidentifiable wood	1400 ± 80	-25.3	AD 430–780
HAR1432	Jewel Tower ↔	none given	salvaged oak beam from roof	1310 ± 70	-26.0	AD 610–890 AD 497–520
HAR1433	Jewel Tower		elm pile	630 ± 80	-25.3	AD 1250–1440
HAR2765	Jewel Tower		oak	1630 ± 60	-26.1	AD 250–570 (AD 572–592)
HAR2766	Jewel Tower		oak	1540 ± 70	-25.7	AD 380–660 AD 547–572
HAR2692 ‡	WCG78	not given	oak heartwood	1350 ± 80	-28.8	AD 540–890
HAR2696 ‡	WCG78	not given	oak heartwood	1230 ± 80	-24.9	AD 660–980
HAR3423	WCG78		oak plank	1220 ± 80	-26.1	AD 660–980
HAR6393 ⊕	RCH80	c -1.40m OD	alder wood (worked)	2540 ± 70	-28.2	810–410 BC
HAR5741 ⊕	RCH80	c -2.00m OD	peat	8580 ± 110	-29.1	8000–7350 BC
HAR5742 ⊕	RCH80	c -0.50m OD	peat	4110 ± 80	-29.7	2880–2470 BC

Key
* estimated
~ AMS dating
\# JLEP dates
‡ from Greig (1992)
⊕ from Andrews and Merriman (1986)
↔ information here may have been transposed

FRENCH AND GERMAN SUMMARIES

Résumé

Des fouilles archéologiques furent exécutées à Westminster avant l'extension de la ligne de métro « Jubilee », entre 1992 et 1997. En outre, d'autres investigations furent conduites de 1992 à 1995 au sein du Palais de Westminster pour la Direction des Travaux Parlementaires. Westminster est l'un des sites majeurs du Royaume-Uni et représente l'un des dix sites anglais inscrits au Patrimoine mondial par l'UNESCO.

Cet ouvrage présente les résultats des fouilles entreprises par MoLAS dans les années 1990 mais prend aussi en compte les travaux antérieurs conduits depuis le XVIIIe siècle par des archéologues comme par des érudits. L'ensemble des données est présenté de manière synthétique pour permettre la meilleure compréhension possible du site. Les relevés ont établi avec précision l'emplacement des bâtiments subsistants ainsi que les zones d'intervention plus anciennes. Les importantes recherches paléoenvironnementales conduites à Westminster, déjà publiées ailleurs (Sidell et al 2000), sont ici résumées. L'un des principaux objectifs de ce projet était de fournir un cadre géologique, topographique et environnemental à Thorney Island, de définir l'emprise de l'île et des divers bras du fleuve et de comprendre leur évolution. Bien que certaines zones (en particulier la partie sud) et certaines périodes aient été moins bien couvertes que d'autres, l'objectif a été largement atteint et, pour l'essentiel, seuls des points de détail restent dans l'ombre. Notre compréhension de la nature, de la forme et de l'étendue de l'île depuis l'époque post-glaciaire jusqu'à aujourd'hui est solide ; de même sont désormais bien connus les variations du niveau du fleuve et ses effets sur les zones habitables tout comme les formes et la chronologie des tentatives de gains par les populations avoisinantes. Néanmoins, l'important hiatus existant dans les dépôts conservés sur le rivage entre l'Age du Fer et le XIIe siècle rend nos connaissances de l'environnement et des changements du régime fluvial de cette période plus fragiles.

L'activité la plus précoce remonte aux époques mésolithique et néolithique. Des ensembles de silex et deux phases de revêtement sont décrits ainsi qu'un certain nombre d'autres structures. Il existe aussi des signes d'activité au début de l'Age du Bronze.

Les traces d'occupation romaine demeurent ténues bien que des structures susceptibles d'appartenir à cette période et du mobilier suggèrent une certaine présence dans la zone. De même, les éléments d'époque anglo-saxonne sont maigres mais la découverte d'une structure en bois, peut-être un pont, associée à un fossé et à un revêtement en bois de la fin du Xe ou du début du XIe siècle, constitue un nouvel indice d'activité important et suggère une date d'occupation plus précoce que celle qui était jusqu'ici proposée pour le site du palais.

Au Moyen Age, les sites relèvent de trois ensembles distincts : le Palais de Westminster, l'abbaye et la ville.

Des fouilles limitées eurent lieu à l'intérieur de Westminster Hall, dont les fondations furent enregistrées. Au nord, se trouve un quai construit au XIIe siècle et adjacent à un bâtiment de pierre, peut-être une cuisine. Les portes en pierre de New

Palace Yard et de Green Yard ont été mises au jour ainsi que les bâtiments médiévaux en pierre qui les encadraient. Celui qui se trouvait dans l'enceinte extérieure a pu être une auberge (on y a fouillé une latrine contenant d'important objets en bois et en céramique), alors que les vestiges observés dans Green Yard ont pu appartenir à un bâtiment administratif. Les fouilles menées à proximité de Jewel Tower ont révélé la tranchée de construction du mur des douves et un tronçon du grand drain de l'abbaye. Les fondations de la chapelle Saint-Etienne ont aussi été observées et des archives des années 1940 montrent des niveaux de construction et de sols appartenant au cloître correspondant.

Un grand bâtiment du XIIIe siècle situé dans l'enclos de l'abbaye était associé à la foire d'Octobre. Dans son état d'origine, il présentait des murs couverts d'enduit peint et un passage central. Des transformations ultérieures virent l'insertion de cloisons en bois et de foyers.

L'occupation du rivage indique que les terrains situés au nord du palais furent progressivement conquis sur le fleuve et que presque toute la zone fouillée avait été gagnée au milieu du XIVe siècle, à l'exception du côté est qui ne le fut qu'au XVIe siècle. L'une des maisons canoniales de la chapelle Saint-Etienne fut découverte sur ces gains.

L'évolution post-médiévale inclut les transformations et finalement la reconstruction de la maison de l'enclos abbatial, l'édification d'une maison de qualité, en brique, sur l'ancien site de Woolstaple et celle de maisons construites au XVIIIe siècle, quand Westminster, devenu l'un des faubourgs de Londres, s'étendit.

Dans les sections récapitulatives qui concluent les chapitres 3 à 13, les découvertes récentes sont mises en contexte et les nombreuses investigations antérieures sont résumées pour fournir une vision générale du développement de Westminster. Les chapitres 14 et 15 fournissent un état des connaissances et énumère les lacunes les plus importantes.

Zusammenfassung

Vor Beginn der Verlängerungsarbeiten an der Jubilee Line der U-Bahn wurden zwischen 1992 und 1997 in Westminster Ausgrabungen durchgeführt. Zusätzlich fanden zwischen1992 und 1995 im Auftrag des parlamentarischen Arbeitsdirektorats Ausgrabungen im Westminster-Palast (das Parlamentsgebäude) statt. Westminster ist einer der bedeutendsten Orte im Vereinigten Königreich, dem von UNESCO der Status einer der ursprünglichen zehn Weltkulturerbe-Stätten Englands zuerkannt wurde.

Der vorliegende Bericht befaßt sich mit den archäologischen Untersuchungen, die vom Archäologischen Dienst des Museums von London (MoLAS) in den 90er Jahren durchgeführt wurden. Er berücksichtigt ebenfalls Ermittlungen archäologischer und altertumsforschender Art, wie sie im 18., 19. und 20. Jh. stattfanden, sowie Versuche, letztere in Zusammenhang zu setzen. Der Bericht ist in integrierter Form geschrieben, d.h. er verbindet die verschiedenen Handlungsfäden der Funde und Befunde, um ein besseres Verständnis der Ausgrabungsergebnisse zu ermöglichen. Vermessungsarbeiten bestimmen die Lage der noch stehenden Gebäude genau und lokalisieren auch präziser die Arbeiten früherer Archäologen und Altertumsforscher. Das anderweitig publizierte (Sidell et al 2000), bedeutsame paläo-umweltliche Projekt für Westminster wird zusammengefaßt. Eines der Hauptziele der hier behandelten Untersuchungen war, den geologischen, topographischen und umweltlichen Rahmen für Thorney Island zu erstellen, die Insel und ihre Flüsse zu definieren, um deren Entwicklung zu verstehen. Während einige Gegenden (insbesondere der Süden der Insel) und einige Zeiträume weniger gut erfaßt sind, wurde das Ziel im Großen und Ganzen erreicht, wobei der Rest das Niveau kleinerem Detail betrifft. Unser Verständnis für die Form, Gestalt und Größe der Insel von der postglazialen Zeit bis zur Gegenwart, für die wechselnden Flußniveaus und deren Auswirkungen auf die zum Bewohnen geeigneten Gebiete, sowie für die Art und die Datierung der Versuche, Land zu gewinnen, kann jetzt mit einem hohen Grad an Vertrauen angewandt werden. Die große Lücke von der Eisenzeit bis zum 12. Jh. hinsichtlich der Ablagerungen im Ufervorland des Flusses heißt jedoch, daß unsere Kenntnisse der Umwelt und der Wechsel im Flußsystem während dieses Zeitraums weniger verläßlich sind.

Die frühesten Aktivitäten datieren im Neolithikum. Feuersteinfunde aus dieser Zeit und zwei Phasen einer Uferbefestigung, sowie verschiedene andere Befunde werden beschrieben. Es gibt auch ein paar Nachweise für menschliche Präsenz in der älteren Bronzezeit.

Spuren römischer Tätigkeit bleiben schwach, obwohl einige Anzeichen möglicherweise aus römischer Zeit und einiges Fundmaterial weiterhin eine gewisse Präsenz in dieser Gegend nahelegen. Spuren angelsächsischer Aktivität sind ähnlich karg. Die Entdeckung einer Holzkonstruktion, vielleicht einer Brücke, und ein damit in Zusammenhang stehender Graben und eine Uferbefestigung aus dem späten 10. oder frühen 11. Jh. sind jedoch bedeutende Hinweise für Aktivität in der Gegend, und weisen auf ein früheres Datum als bisher angenommen für die Besiedlung des Palastareals hin.

Für das Mittelalter fallen die Fundstätten in drei Kategorien: solche innerhalb des königlichen Westminster-Palastes, solche innerhalb Westminster Abbey und solche in der Stadt.

Begrenzte Ausgrabungen fanden in der Westminster Hall statt, deren Fundamente aufgezeichnet wurden. Weiter nördlich lag neben einem Steingebäude, vielleicht einer Küche, ein im 12. Jh. gebautes Dock. Die steinernen Tore zum New Palace Yard und zum Green Yard mit mittelalterlichen Steingebäuden neben beiden wurden lokalisiert. Das Gebäude im äußeren Bezirk mag ein Gasthaus gewesen sein, in dessen Innerem eine Abtrittsgrube mit bedeutenden hölzernen und keramischen Fundgruppen lag. Das Gebäude am Green Yard war vielleicht ein Regierungsgebäude. Ausgrabungen beim Jewel Tower brachten den Konstruktionsschnitt für den Wassergraben und einen erhaltenen Abschnitt der großen Westminster Abbey-Drainage zutage. Die Fundamente der Stefanskapelle wurden aufgezeichnet und Unterlagen aus den 1940er Jahren zeigen Bautätigkeit und Fußböden des dazugehörigen Kreuzgangs.

Ein großes Gebäude aus dem 13. Jh. auf dem Gelände der Westminster Abbey stand mit der Oktobermarkt in Verbindung. In seiner ursprünglichen Form wies es bemalte Putzwände und einen Mittelgang auf. Spätere Änderungen brachten hölzerne Trennwände und Feuerstellen.

Landgewinnung im Ufervorland deutet darauf hin, daß die Areale nördlich des Palastes dem Fluß schrittweise abgerungen wurden, und daß fast das gesamte Ausgrabungsfläche um die Mitte des 14. Jhs, die Ostseite jedoch erst im 16 Jh., gewonnen war. Auf dem gewonnenen Land wurde ein Haus der Kanoniker der Stefanskapelle gefunden.

Die nachmittelalterliche Entwicklung umfaßt den Umbau und schließendlich den Wiederaufbau des Hauses auf dem Gelände der Westminster Abbey, den Bau eines hochwertigen Ziegelhauses auf dem Grund des früheren Woolstaple, sowie Häuser, die im 18. Jh. als Teil der Erweiterung Westminsters als Londoner Vorort gebaut wurden.

Beim jeweiligen Überblick am Ende der Kapitel 3–13 werden die jüngsten Ergebnisse in einen breiteren Zusammenhang gebracht und die vielen früheren Untersuchungen zusammengefaßt, um einen Gesamteindruck der Entwicklung in Westminster zu geben. In Kapitel 14 und 15 werden unseren gegenwärtigen Wissensstand dargelegt und die wichtigsten diesbezüglichen Lücken aufgezählt.

BIBLIOGRAPHY

Manuscript sources

British Library, London (BL)

Cotton MS Faustina A iii; B viii charters relating to Westminster Abbey

City of Westminster Archives, London (CWA)

10/272, 1039 17th- and 18th-century deeds relating to Westminster

Guildhall Library, City of London (GL)

Manuscripts Department, Christ's Hospital records

Historical Manuscripts Commission, London (HMC) (now part of The National Archives)

MSS of the Marquess of Bath at Longleat (catalogue)
Salisbury MSS (catalogue)

London Metropolitan Archives (formerly Greater London Record Office) (LMA)

BRA 437/09 bargain and sale of 26 March 1737 re property in Westminster

Museum of London

Hollar's view of New Palace Yard, 1647

Public Record Office, London (PRO) (now part of The National Archives)

Chancery: C 66 (patent rolls); C 135 (inquisitions *post mortem*); C 143 (inquisitions *ad quod damnum*)
Court of Common Pleas: CP 40 (plea rolls)
Exchequer: E 40 (Treasury of Receipt, Ancient deeds); E 179 (King's Remembrancer); E 315 (Court of Augmentations)
Probate: PROB 11 (wills proved in the Prerogative Court of Canterbury and other jurisdictions)
Office of Works: WORK 6

Society of Antiquaries of London

Copies by John Carter, 1790s, of murals in the king's chamber (or Painted Chamber)

Thynne Papers, Longleat, Wiltshire

(available on microfilm at Institute of Historical Research, University of London (IHR), and other repositories)
Vol 2 correspondence of Sir John Thynne senior (1542–57)
Vol 49 miscellaneous papers of the Thynne family (1561–76)
Vol 79 collection of inventories of household goods, plate etc at Longleat and other places belonging to the Thynnes (1546–1719)

Westminster Abbey Muniments, London (WAM)

17333, 17365, 17491, 18599 13th-century and later deeds

Printed and other secondary works

Abbott, W J Lewis, 1919 Implements from Cromer Forest Bed and the admiralty section, *Proc Prehist Soc E Anglia* 3, 110–14

Adkins, R, and Jackson, R, 1978 *Neolithic stone and flint axes from the River Thames*, Brit Mus Occas Pap 1, 137–9, London

Allen, P, and Vince, A, 1991 The archaeological context, in *Aspects of Saxo-Norman London: 2, Finds and environmental evidence* (ed A Vince), London Middlesex Archaeol Soc Spec Pap 12, 10–18, London

Andrews, D, and Merriman, N, 1986 A prehistoric timber structure at Richmond Terrace, Whitehall, *Trans London Middlesex Archaeol Soc* 37, 17–22

Armitage, P, Locker, A, and Straker, V, 1987 Environmental archaeology in London: a review, in *Environmental archaeology: a regional review* 2 (ed H C M Keeley), Engl Heritage Occas Pap 1, 252–331, London

Arthur, J R B, and Paradine, P J, nd *New Palace Yard, botanical remains*, Ancient Monuments Laboratory, London

Ayre, J, Wroe-Brown, R, and Malt, R, 1996 Aethelred's hythe to Queenhithe: the origin of a London dock, *Medieval Life* 5, 14–25

Ayre, J, and Wroe-Brown, R, with Malt, R, in prep *Queenhithe, excavations at Thames Court, City of London, 1989–97*, MoLAS Monogr, London

Barber, B, and Thomas, C, 2002 *The London Charterhouse*, MoLAS Monogr 10, London

Barratt, M, and Thomas, C, 1991 The London Charterhouse, *London Archaeol* 6, 283–91

Barrett, J, 1978 The prehistoric pottery from 106–114 Borough High Street, in Bird et al 1978, 197–9

Bayley, J, Freestone, I, Jenner, A, and Vince, A, 1991 Metallurgy, in *Aspects of Saxo-Norman London: 2, Finds and environmental evidence* (ed A Vince), London Middlesex Archaeol Soc Spec Pap 12, 389–405, London

Bedaux, J B, 1995 Profane en sacrale amuletten, in *Heilig en Profaan, laatmiddeleeuwse insignes in cultuurhistorisch perspectief* (eds A M Koldeweij and A Willemsen), 26–35, Amsterdam

de Beer, E S (ed), 1955 *Diary of John Evelyn*, Oxford

Beijerinck, W, 1947 *Zadenatlas der Nederlansche Flora I–II*, Wageningen

Berggren, G, 1981 *Atlas of seeds and small fruits of north-west European plant species: Part 3, Salicaceae-Cruciferae*, Stockholm

Betts, I M, 1990 Appendix 3: building materials, in Schofield et al 1990, 220–9

Betts, I M, 1992 Early pantiles in London, *Medieval Ceram* 16, 76

Betts, I M, 1996 New thoughts on bricks with sunken margins, *Brit Brick Soc Information* 68, 6–10

Betts, I M, 1997 Ceramic building material, in Milne 1997, 60–8

Betts, I M, 2002 *Medieval 'Westminster' floor tiles*, MoLAS Monogr 11, London

Binski, P 1986 *The Painted Chamber at Westminster*, London

Bird, J, Graham, A H, Sheldon, H L, and Townend, P, 1978 *Southwark excavations 1972–4*, London Middlesex Archaeol Soc and Surrey Archaeol Soc Joint Pub 1, London

Bishop, B J, 1996 Excavations at 47–67 Hopton Street, London SE1: the lithic material, unpub dissertation, Univ Leicester

Black, G, 1976 Excavations in the sub-vault of the *misericorde* of Westminster Abbey, February to May, 1975, *Trans London Middlesex Archaeol Soc* 27, 135–78

Blackmore, L, 1995 The middle Saxon pottery, in Mills 1995, 80

Bowsher, J, and Miller, P, in prep *The Rose and the Globe: playhouses of London*

Bradley, R, 2000 *An archaeology of natural places*, London

Brears, P, 1971 *The English country pottery: its history and techniques*, Newton Abbot

Bridgland, D R, 1994 *Quaternary of the Thames*, Geological Conservation Review Series, London

Brigham, T, 1990 The late Roman waterfront in London, *Britannia* 21, 99–185

Bronk Ramsey, C, 2002 *OxCal program 3.8*, Oxford

Brooke, C, and Keir, G, 1975 *London 800–1216: the shaping of a city*, London

Brown, A, 1997 *Alluvial geoarchaeology*, Cambridge

Brown, N R, 1985 Later Bronze Age and Early to Middle Iron Age pottery, in Wymer and Brown 1985, 77–88

Bulleid, A, and St George Gray, H, 1917 *The Glastonbury Lake Village: Vol II*, Glastonbury

Cal Chart R *Calendar of charter rolls*, 6 vols, 1903–27, London

Cal Close R Henry III *Calendar of close rolls: Henry III*, 14 vols, 1902–38, London

Cal Close R Richard II *Calendar of close rolls: Richard II*, 6 vols, 1914–27, London

Cal Lib R *Calendar of the Liberate rolls*, 6 vols, 1916–64, London

Cal Pat R *Calendar of the patent rolls*, 1894–1974, London

Cal S P Dom *Calendar of state papers, domestic: Edward VI, Mary, Elizabeth I and James I* (ed M Everett Green), 12 vols, 1856–72, London

Canham, R, 1978 Excavations at London (Heathrow) airport 1969, *Trans London Middlesex Archaeol Soc* 29, 1–44

Cantor, L, 1987 *The changing English countryside, 1400–1700*, London

Capon, W, 1824 *Views of Westminster*, London

Capon, W, 1923–4 *Views of Westminster: sketched 1801–15 and drawn in watercolours*, London

Chaplin, R E, 1971 *Report on animal bone from a Saxon occupation site, Whitehall, London*, London

Clapham, A, Tutin, T, and Moore, D, 1987 *Flora of the British Isles*, 3 edn, Cambridge

Clarke, S, 1883 The west side of Westminster Hall, *Archaeologia* 50, 9–16

Clay, P, 1981 The small finds – non-structural, in *The Austin Friars, Leicester* (eds J Mellor and T Pearce), CBA Res Rep 35, 130–45, London

Clifton-Taylor, A, 1987 *The pattern of English building*, 4 edn, London

Cohen, A, and Serjeantson, D, 1996 *A manual for the identification of bird bones from archaeological sites*, rev edn, London

Coles, J M, 1987 *Meare village east. The excavations of A Bulleid and H St George Gray 1932–56*, Somerset Levels Papers 13, Exeter

Collins, D, 1980 Flints, in Mills 1980, 27–8

Colvin, H M (ed), 1966 *Views of the Old Palace of Westminster*, Architect Hist 9, London

Colvin, H M, Allen-Brown, R, and Taylor, A J, 1963 *The history of the King's works*, I, London

Conheeney, J, 1995 Old Palace Yard: human bone, unpub MoLAS report

Cotton, J F, 1992 The struck flint, in Cowan 1992, 62–7

Cowan, C, 1992 A possible *mansio* in Roman Southwark: excavations at 15–23 Southwark Street, 1980–86, *Trans London Middlesex Archaeol Soc* 43, 3–191

Coward, B, 1983 *The Stanleys, Lords Stanley and Earls of Derby, 1385–1672*, Manchester

Cowie, R, 1988 A gazetteer of middle Saxon sites and finds in the Strand/Westminster area, *Trans London Middlesex Archaeol Soc* 39, 37–46

Cowie, R, and Blackmore, L, in prep *Early and Middle Saxon settlement in the London region*

Cowie, R, and Pipe, A, 1999 A late medieval and Tudor horse-burial ground: excavations at Elverton St, Westminter, *Archaeol J* 155, 226–51

Crook, D, 1980 Early rembrancers of the Exchequer, *Bull Inst Hist Res* 53, 21–2

Cunliffe, B, and Poole, C, 1991 *Danebury, an Iron Age hillfort in Hampshire: Vol 5, The excavations, 1979–88: The finds*, CBA Res Rep 73, London

Degnan, S, and Seeley, D, 1988 Medieval and later floor tiles in Lambeth Palace, *London Archaeol* 6, 11–18

Devoy, R J N, 1979 Flandrian sea-level changes and vegetational history of the lower Thames estuary, *Phil Trans Roy Soc, London Ser* B285, 355–410

Driver, J C, 1982 Medullary bone as an indicator of sex in bird remains from archaeological sites, in *Ageing and sexing animal bones from archaeological sites* (eds B Wilson, C Grigson and S Payne), BAR Brit Ser 109, 251–4, Oxford

Drury, P, 1993 Ceramic building materials, in Rodwell and Rodwell 1993, 7–13

Dugdale, W, 1817 *Monasticon Anglicanum: Vol I*, London

Dunning, G C, and Evison, V I, 1961 The Palace of Westminster sword, *Archaeologia* 98, 123–58

Dyer, C, 1989 *Standards of living in the later Middle Ages: social change in England* c *1200–1520*, Cambridge

Dyer, C, 2002 *Making a living in the Middle Ages: the people of Britain 850–1520*, New Haven and London

Eames, E S, 1980 *Catalogue of medieval lead-glazed earthenware. Tiles in the Department of Medieval and Later Antiquities, British Museum*, 2 vols, London

Edwards, R, 1974 *London potters circa 1570–1710*, J Ceram Hist 6, Stafford

Egan G, 1997 The non-ceramic finds, in Thomas et al 1997, 201–10

Egan, G, 1998 *The medieval household: daily living* c *1150–*c *1450*, Medieval Finds Excav London 6, London

Egan, G, and Pritchard, F, 1991 *Dress accessories* c *1150–*c *1450*, Medieval Finds Excav London 3, London

Ellis, B M A, 1995 Spurs and spur fittings, in *The medieval horse and its equipment*, c *1150–*c *1450* (ed J Clark), Medieval Finds Excav London 5, 124–50, London

Evans, J G, nd Land and freshwater molluscs, New Palace Yard, Westminster: London, unpub report, Ancient Monuments Laboratory, London

Field, D, and Woolley, A, 1984 Neolithic and Bronze Age ground stone implements from Surrey: morphology, petrology and distribution, *Surrey Archaeol Collect* 75, 85–109

Gibbard, P L, 1994 *Pleistocene history of the lower Thames valley*, Cambridge

Giorgi J, 1997 A summary of the assessment of plant remains from Jubilee sites, Westminster, unpub MoL report

Girling, M A, 1988, The bark beetle *Scolytus scolytus* (*Fabricius*) and the possible role of elm disease in the early Neolithic, in *Archaeology and the flora of the British Isles* (ed M Jones), 34–8, Oxford

Goffin, R A, 1991 A group of pottery from a medieval pit at 223–227 Borough High Street, Southwark, *London Archaeol* 6, 315–18

Goffin, R A, 1995 The accessioned finds, in Mills 1995, 87–90

Goffin, R, and Crowley, N, 1995 The building material, in Mills 1995, 97–102

Goodburn D, with Thomas, C, 1997, Reused medieval ship planks from Westminster, England, possibly derived from a vessel built in the cog style, *Int J Nautical Archaeol* 26 (1), 26–38

Grant, A, 1982 The use of toothwear as a guide to the age of domestic ungulates, in *Ageing and sexing animal bones from archaeological sites* (eds B Wilson, C Grigson and S Payne), BAR Brit Ser 109, 91–108, Oxford

Grant, A, 1988 Animal resources, in *The countryside of medieval England* (eds G Astill and A Grant), 149–87, Oxford

Green, H J M, 1976 Excavations of the palace defences and abbey precinct walls at Abingdon St, Westminster, 1963, *J Brit Archaeol Ass* 129, 59–76

Green, H J M, and Thurley, S J, 1987 Excavations on the west side of Whitehall: Part 1, From the building of the Tudor palace to the construction of the modern offices of state, *Trans London Middlesex Archaeol Soc* 38, 59–130

Green, H S, 1980 *The flint arrowheads of the British Isles*, BAR Brit Ser 75, Oxford

Greig, J R A, 1989, From lime forest to heathland – five thousand years of change at West Heath Spa, Hampstead, as shown by the plant remains, in *Excavations at the mesolithic site on West Heath, Hampstead 1976–81* (eds D Collins and D H Lorimer), BAR Brit Ser 217, 89–99, Oxford

Greig, J R A, 1992 The deforestation of London, *Rev Palaeobotany Palynology* 73, 71–86

Grew, F, 1984 Small finds, in Thompson et al 1984, 91–128

Griffiths, N, 1995 Harness pendants and associated fittings, in *The medieval horse and its equipment*, c *1150–*c *1450* (ed J Clark), Medieval Finds Excav London 5, 61–71, London

Hall, J G, and Clutton-Brock, J, 1995 *Two hundred years of British livestock*, London

Hammond, P W, 1995 *Food and feast in medieval England*, Gloucester

Harcourt, R A, 1974 The dog in prehistoric and early historic Britain, *J Archaeol Sci* 1, 151–75

Harvey, B, 1993 *Living and dying in England 1100–1540, the monastic experience*, Oxford

Harvey, J H, 1984 *English mediaeval architects: a biographical dictionary down to 1550*, rev edn, Gloucester

Hollestelle, J, 1976 *De steenbakkerij in de Nederlanden tot omstreeks 1560*, 2 edn, Arnhem

Honeybourne, M, 1932 The Sanctuary boundaries and environs of Westminster Abbey and the college of St Martin-le-Grand, *J Brit Archaeol Ass* 38, 316–33

Horsman, V, and Davison, B, 1989 New Palace Yard and its fountains: excavations in the Palace of Westminster, *Antiq J* 69, 279–97

Horwood, R, 1813 *Plans of the Cities of London and Westminster, the borough of Southwark*, 3 edn, reproduced in Margary, H, 1985 *The A-Z of Regency London*, Margary in assoc Guildhall Library, Kent

Huff, C, 1997 Falconers, fowlers and nobles: the sport of falconry in Anglo-Saxon England, *Medieval Life. The Magazine of the Middle Ages* 7, 7–9

Hurst, J G, 1960 A late medieval pit group at Westminster Abbey, *Antiq J* 40, 188–94

Keen, L, 1971 Medieval floor-tiles from Campsea Ash Priory, *Proc Suffolk Inst Archaeol* 32 (2), 140–51

Keily, J, 1998 The fabric of the medieval London house, in Egan 1998, 24–41

Keys, L, 1998 Wooden vessels, in Egan 1998, 196–217

Kingsford, C L, 1909 Sir Otho de Grandison, 1238?–1328, *Trans Roy Hist Soc* 3 series, iii, 125–95

Knowles, D, and Grimes, W F, 1954 *Charterhouse: the medieval foundation in the light of recent discoveries*, London

Knowles, D, and Hadcock, R N, 1971 *Religious houses of England and Wales*, 2 edn, London

Lacaille, L D, 1961 Mesolithic facies in Middlesex and London, *Trans London Middlesex Archaeol Soc* 20, 135

Lawrence, M J, and Brown, R W, 1973 *Mammals of Britain*, London

Lethaby, W R, 1906 The Palace of Westminster in the 11th and 12th centuries, *Archaeologia* 60, 131–48

Lewis, J, 1991 Excavation of a late Glacial and early Flandrian site at Three Ways Wharf, Uxbridge: interim report, in *The late Glacial in north-west Europe* (eds R N E Barton, A J Roberts and D A Roe), CBA Res Rep 77, London

Lewis, J, in prep *Three Ways Wharf, Uxbridge: a late Glacial and early Holocene hunter-gatherer site in the Colne valley*

Limbrey, S, nd New Palace Yard Westminster, stratigraphy and chronology of fluviatile deposits, unpub report

Lloyd, N, 1925 *A history of English brickwork*, London

Long, A J, Scaife, R G, and Edwards, R J, 2000 Stratigraphic architecture, relative sea-level and models of estuary development in southern England: new data from Southampton Water, in *Coastal and estuarine environments: sedimentology, geomorphology and geoarchaeology* (eds K Pye and J R L Allen), Geological Society Special Publication 175, 253–80, London

Longley, D, 1980 *Runnymede Bridge 1976: excavations on the site of a Late Bronze Age settlement*, Surrey Archaeol Soc Res Vol 6, Guildford

Malcolm, G, 1994 An archaeological evaluation of 18 Great Peter Street, unpub MoL report

Margeson, S, 1993 Dress fittings, in Margeson, S, *Norwich households: medieval and post-medieval finds from Norwich survey excavations 1971–8*, E Anglian Archaeol Rep 58, 4–44, Norwich

McIsaac, W, 1982 The small finds, in Mills 1982, 355–7

McKisack, M, 1959 *The fourteenth century*, Oxford

Meddens, F M, 1996 Sites from the Thames Estuary wetlands, England, and their Bronze Age use, *Antiquity* 70, 325–34

Merriman, N, 1987 A prehistory for central London?, *London Archaeol* 5 (12), 318–26

Merriman, N, 1990 *Prehistoric London*, London

Miller, P, and Stephenson, R, 1999 *A 14th-century pottery site in Kingston upon Thames, Surrey*, MoLAS Archaeol Stud Ser 1, London

Mills, P, 1980 Excavations at Cromwell Green in the Palace of Westminster, *Trans London Middlesex Archaeol Soc* 31, 18–29

Mills, P, 1982 Excavations at Broad Sanctuary, Westminster, *Trans London Middlesex Archaeol Soc* 33, 345–56

Mills, P, 1995 Excavations at the dorter undercroft, Westminster Abbey, *Trans London Middlesex Archaeol Soc* 46, 69–124

Milne, G, 1985 *The port of Roman London*, London

Milne, G, 1997 *St Bride's church, London: archaeological research 1952–60 and 1992–5*, Engl Heritage Archaeol Rep 11, London

Milne, G, and Milne, C, 1982 *Excavations at Trig Lane 1978*, London Middlesex Archaeol Soc Spec Pap 5, London

MoLAS, 2000 *The archaeology of Greater London: an assessment of archaeological evidence for human presence in the area now covered by Greater London*, MoLAS Monogr, London

Mook, W G, 1986 Business meeting: recommendations/ resolutions adopted by the twelfth international radiocarbon conference, *Radiocarbon* 28, 799

Moorhouse, S, 1980 Documentary evidence for medieval ceramic roofing materials and its archaeological implications: some thoughts, *Medieval Ceram* 12, 33–55

Morgan, W, 1682 '*London &c Actually Surveyed*', reproduced in Margary, H, 1977 '*London &c Actually Surveyed' by William Morgan, 1682*, Margary in assoc Guildhall Library, Kent

Moxon, J, 1700 *Mechanick exercises: or the doctrine of handy-works*, London

Murdoch T, 1991 *Treasures and trinkets*, London

Needham, S, 1987 The Bronze Age, in *The archaeology of Surrey to 1540* (eds J Bird and D G Bird), Surrey Archaeol Soc Spec Pap, 97–137, Guildford

Norman, P J, 1916, Recent discoveries of medieval remains in London, *Archaeologia* 67, 14–17

O'Connell, M, 1986 *Petters sports field, Egham: excavation of a Late Bronze Age/Early Iron Age site*, Surrey Archaeol Soc Res Vol 10, Guildford

Orton, C R, 1975 Quantitative pottery studies: some progress, problems and prospects, *Sci & Archaeol* 16, 30–35

Orton, C R, and Pearce, J E, 1984 The pottery, in Thompson et al 1984, 34–68

Payne, S, 1973 Kill-off patterns in sheep and goats: the mandibles from Asvan Kale, *Anatol Stud* 23, 281–303

Pearce, J E, and Vince, A G, 1988 *A dated type-series of London medieval pottery: Part 4, Surrey whitewares*, London Middlesex Archaeol Soc Spec Pap 10, London

Pearson, J L, 1884 *Report on Westminster Hall to the Select Committee on Westminster Hall (Restoration)*, London

Pipe, A, 1995 The animal bones, in Mills 1995, 104–11

Platts, E, 1976 The finds, in Black 1976, 158–70

Platts, E, 1980 The pottery, in Mills 1980, 26–7

Poole, C, 1991 Objects of baked clay, in Cunliffe and Poole 1991, 370–82

Poole, H, 1870 Some account of the discovery of the Roman coffin in the north green at Westminster Abbey, *Archaeol J* 27, 119–28

Power, E, 1941 *The wool trade in English medieval history*, London

Prehistoric Ceramic Research Group, 1995 *The study of later prehistoric pottery: general policies and guidelines for analysis and publication*, Oxford

Price, J E, 1870 Medieval kiln for burning encaustic tiles discovered near Farringdon Road, Clerkenwell, *Trans London Middlesex Archaeol Soc* 3, 31–6

Rackham, D J, 1986 Assessing the relative frequency of species by the application of a stochastic model to a zooarchaeological database, in *Database management and zooarchaeology* (ed L H van Wijngaarden-Bakker), *PACT* (*J European Study Grp Physical, Chemical, Biological Mathematical Techniques applied to Archaeology*) Res Vol 40, 185–92, Amsterdam

Rackham, D J, 1995 Appendix: skeletal evidence of medieval horses from London sites, in Clarke (ed) 1995, 169–174

Rackham, D J, and Sidell, E J, 2000 London's landscapes: the changing environment, in MoLAS 2000, 12–27

Rackham, O, 1986 *The history of the countryside*, London

Rayner, L J, 1997 Assessment of the prehistoric pottery from Royal Community Docks School, Newham, unpub MoL report

RCHME, 1924 Roy Comm Hist Monuments Engl, *Westminster Abbey*, London

RCHME, 1925 Roy Comm Hist Monuments Engl, *West London (excluding Westminster Abbey)*, London

Rich, E E, 1932–4 Mayors of the staples, *Camb Hist J* 4, 120–42

Ridgeway, V, 1999 Prehistoric finds at Hopton Street in Southwark, *London Archaeol* 9, 72–6

Rielly, K, 1997 The assessment of the animal bones from the Jubilee Line Extension sites (Southwark), unpub MoLAS report

Rielly, K, 2002 The animal bone, in Howe, E, *Roman defences and medieval industry*, MoLAS Monogr 7, 94–103

Rielly, K, in prep The animal bone, in Ayre, J, and Wroe-Brown, R, *Excavations at Bull Wharf and Upper Thames St*

Riley, H T (ed), 1859 *Munimenta Gildhallae Londiniensis...: Vol 1, Liber Albus*, London

Rixson, D, 1989 Butchery evidence on animal bones, *Circaea* 6(1), 49–62

Robinson, J A, 1910 The church of Edward the Confessor, *Archaeologia* 62, 81–100

Rocque, J, 1746 'Exact Survey of the City of London Westminster and Southwark and the Country 10 Miles Round', reproduced in Margary, H, 1971, *'Exact Survey of the City of London Westminster and Southwark and the Country 10 Miles Round' by John Rocque, 1746*, Margary in assoc Guildhall Library, Kent

Rodwell, W J, and Rodwell, K A, 1993 *Rivenhall: investigations of a villa, church and village 1950–77: Vol 2*, CBA Res Rep 80, London

Rogers, W, 1990 Mesolithic and Neolithic flint tool-manufacturing areas buried beneath Roman Watling Street in Southwark, *London Archaeol* 6(9), 227–31

Rosser, G, 1989 *Medieval Westminster 1200–1540*, Oxford

Ryan, P, 1996 *Brick in Essex from the Roman conquest to the Reformation*, Chelmsford

Salzman, L F, 1967 *Building in England down to 1540: a documentary history*, rev edn, Oxford

Samuel, M, 1994 Worked stone assessment from Parliament Square, unpub MoL report

Scaife, R G, 1988 The elm decline in the pollen record of south-east England and its relationship to early agriculture, in *Archaeology and the flora of the British Isles* (ed M Jones), 21–33, Oxford

Scaife, R G, Rackham, D J, and Perry, J, in prep *Palaeoenvironmental analysis of peat and the sedimentary sequence at Point Pleasant*, London

Schmid, E, 1972 *Atlas of animal bones for prehistorians, archaeologists, and Quaternary geologists*, Amsterdam

Schofield, J (ed), 1987 *The London surveys of Ralph Treswell*, London

Schofield, J, 1993 *The building of London from the Conquest to the Great Fire*, rev edn, London

Schofield, J, Allen, P, and Taylor, C, 1990 Medieval buildings and property development in the area of Cheapside, *Trans London Middlesex Archaeol Soc* 41, 39–237

Select Committee, 1885 *Rebuilding of the Houses of Parliament. Restoration of Westminster Hall*, London

Sidell, E J, 2003 Holocene sea level change and archaeology in the inner Thames estuary, London, UK, unpub PhD thesis, Department of Geography, University of Durham

Sidell, E J, Wilkinson, K N, Scaife, R G, and Cameron, N, 2000 *The Holocene evolution of the London Thames*, MoLAS Monogr 5, London

Sidell, E J, Cotton, J, Rayner, R, and Wheeler, L, 2002 *The prehistory and topography of Southwark and Lambeth*, MoLAS Monogr 14, London

Singleton, H R, 1973 *A chronology of cutlery*, Sheffield

Sloane, B, in prep *Excavations at the nunnery of St Mary de fonte clericorum, Clerkenwell, London*, MoLAS Monogr, London

Sloane, B, and Malcolm, G, in prep *Excavations at the priory of the Order of the Hospital of St John of Jerusalem, Clerkenwell, London*, MoLAS Monogr, London

Sloane, B, Swain, H, and Thomas, C, 1995 The Roman road and the river regime, *London Archaeol* 7(14), 359–70

Smirke, S, 1836 Remarks on the architectural history of Westminster Hall, *Archaeologia* 26, 406–21

Smirke, S, 1837 A further account of the original architecture of Westminster Hall, *Archaeologia* 27, 135–9

Smith, J T, 1807 *Antiquities of Westminster*, London

Smith, J, 1994 *7 Old Palace Yard*, RCHME Historic Buildings Report 7, London

Smith, T P, 1985 *The medieval brickmaking industry in England 1400–50*, BAR Brit Ser 138, Oxford

Smith, T P, 1997 Following the yellow brick road: the bricks from Whippingham, I o W, *Brit Brick Soc Information* 72, 12–15

Smith, T P, 1998–9 London's earliest medieval roofing tiles: a comparative study, *Medieval Ceram* 22–3, 66–71

Smith, T P, 2001 On 'small yellow . . . bricks from Holland', *Construction History* 17, 31–42

Smith, T P, 2002 The Flemish connection: cautions regarding some building materials terminology, *J Brit Archaeol Ass* 155, 272–7

Spencer, B, 1998 *Pilgrim souvenirs and secular badges:* c 1150–c 1450, Medieval Finds Excav London 7, London

Spurrell, F C J, 1885 Early sites and embankments on the margins of the Thames estuary, *Archaeol J* 42, 274

Stace, C, 1991 *New flora of the British Isles*, Cambridge

Steele, A, in prep *Excavations at the monastery of St Saviour Bermondsey, Southwark*, MoLAS Monogr, London

Stow, J, 1987 *The Survey of London*, London

Stuiver, M, and Kra, R S, 1986 Editorial comment, *Radiocarbon* 28, ii

Stuiver, M, and Polach, H J, 1977 Discussion; reporting of 14C data, *Radiocarbon* 19, 355–63

Stuiver, M, and Reimer, P J, 1986 A computer program for radiocarbon age calculation, *Radiocarbon* 28, 1022–30

Stuiver, M, Reimer, P J, Bard, E, Beck, J W, Burr, G S, Hughes, K A, Kromer, B, McCormac, F G, van der Plicht, J, and Spurk, M, 1998 INTCAL98 radiocarbon age calibration 24,000–0 cal BP, *Radiocarbon* 40, 1041–83

Stukeley, W M, 1790 The sanctuary at Westminster, *Archaeologia* 1, 43–8

Sullivan, D, 1994 *The Westminster corridor*, London

Swain, H, 1992 Prehistoric pottery, in Cowan 1992, 67–70

Swain, H, 1995 The prehistoric pottery, in Mills 1995, 69–124

Tait, H, 1960 Southwark delftware and the potter Christian Wilhelm, *Connoisseur* Part 1

Tanner, L E, and Clapham, A W, 1933 Recent discoveries in the nave of Westminster Abbey, *Archaeologia* 83, 227–36

Tatton-Brown, T, 1995, Westminster Abbey: archaeological recording at the west end of the church, *Antiq J* 75, 171–88

Taylor, A J, 1965, *The Jewel Tower, Westminster*, London

Taylor, H, 1996 Time and tide: a study of a site at Erith in the Thames estuary, unpub dissertation, Univ Sheffield

Thomas, C, and Cowie, R, 1998 Jubilee line – Westminster, a post-excavation assessment and updated project design for publication, unpub MoL report

Thomas, C, and Rackham, D J, 1996 Bramcote Green, Bermondsey: a Bronze Age trackway and palaeoenvironmental sequence, *Proc Prehist Soc* 61, 221–53

Thomas, C, Sloane, B, and Phillpotts, C, 1997 *Excavations at the priory and hospital of St Mary Spital, London*, MoLAS Monogr 1, London

Thompson, A, Grew, F, and Schofield, J, 1984 Excavations at Aldgate, 1974, *Post-medieval Archaeol* 18, 1–148

Thurley, S, 1999 *Whitehall Palace: an archaeological history of the royal lodgings 1230–1689*, London

Tout, T F, 1920–33, *Chapters in the administrative history of medieval England*, 6 vols, Manchester

van Beuningen, H J E, and Koldeweij, A M, 1993 *Heilig en Profaan, 1000 laatmiddeleeuwse insignes uit de collectie H J E van Beuningen*, Rotterdam Pap 8, Rotterdam

Vesey-Fitzgerald, B, 1946 *British game*, London

VCH, 1909 *The Victoria History of London: Vol 1*, London

Vince, A G, 1985, The Saxon and medieval pottery of London: a review, *Medieval Archaeol* 29, 25–93

von den Driesch, A, 1976 *A guide to the measurement of animal bones from archaeological sites*, Peabody Mus Bull 1, Cambridge, Mass

von den Driesch, A, and Boessneck, J A, 1974 *Kritische ammerkungen zur widerristhöhenberechnung aus langenmassen vor- und frühgeschichtlicher tierknochen*, Saugetierkundliche Mitteilungen 22, 325–48

Vulliamy, G, 1849 Proceedings of the Archaeological Institute, *Archaeol J* 6, 71

Ward Perkins, J B, 1940 *London Museum medieval catalogue*, London

Warren, S E, 1977 Excavation of a Neolithic site at Sefton Street, Putney, London, *Trans London Middlesex Archaeol Soc* 28, 1–13

Watson, B, Brigham, T, and Dyson, T, 2001 *London bridge: 2000 years of a river crossing*, MoLAS Monogr 8, London

Waugh, K, 1995 The Roman pottery, in Mills 1995, 80

Wessex Archaeology, 1994 *Storey's Gate, Westminster, London: archaeological on-site trial work (report no. W682)*, Salisbury

Westlake, H, 1923 *Westminster Abbey*, London

Wheeler, A, 1979 *The tidal Thames*, London

Whipp, D, and Platts, E, 1976 Westminster Hall excavation, *London Archaeol* 2(14), 351–5

Wilkinson, K N, Scaife, R G, and Sidell, E J, 2000 Environmental and sea level changes in London from 10,500 BP to the present: a case study from Silvertown, *Proc Geol Ass* 111, 41–54

Wilkinson, K N, Scaife, R G, and Sidell, E J, in prep Mesolithic environment and human activity in London: new evidence from Wandsworth, *J Envir Archaeol*

Williams, E, 1994 The treatment of a mysterious wooden object excavated at Parliament Square, London, unpub MoL report

Wilson, B, Grigson, C, and Payne, S, 1982 *Ageing and sexing animal bones from archaeological sites*, BAR Brit Ser 109, 91–108, Oxford

Wilson, C, 1990 *The Gothic cathedral*, London

Wilson, C, Gem, R, Tudor-Craig, P, and Physick, J, 1986 *Westminster Abbey*, London

Wragge, P, St Peter's Abbey, Westminster, in *VCH* 1909, 433–57

Wymer, J J, and Brown, N R, 1985 *Excavations at North Shoebury: settlement and economy in south-east Essex 1500 BC–AD 1500*, E Anglian Archaeol Rep 75, Norwich

INDEX

Compiled by Auriol Griffith-Jones

Page numbers in **bold** indicate illustrations, maps and tables
Streets and locations in London unless specified otherwise

Admiralty, Lords Commissioners of 128
agriculture 14, 71, 97
cereal cultivation 14–15, 35, 147
medieval 150
Roman/early Saxon 149
Ailnoth the engineer 63, 158
Almayne, house/inn 73, 151
antiquarian records and finds 6, 7
Roman sarcophagus 35
antler, worked 90
architectural fragments
Building 13 85, 86
pier base 107, 136
ard marks (possible) 15, 147
arrowheads, flint 22, **26–7**, 27, 172, 173, **174**
Austin Friars (Leicester) 78
axes, flint 15, **26–7**, 27, 172, 173

Baker, Abraham 129
Barry, Sir James 144
Bayeux Tapestry 47, **153**, 155
beads
bone 110, **110**
glass 110, **110**
belfry, Westminster Abbey 71, 73, 126, 153, 155
bell tower, Westminster Palace 99, 126, 159
Bermondsey 12
Bermondsey Abbey 125
Birdcage Walk 152
boat (timbers)
medieval (clinker-built 'cog') 75
Roman 35
bone, human, redeposited, period 10 136
bone objects, Late Saxon, needle 46
bones, animal 202–9, **202**, **203**, **204**, **205**, **206**, **210**
Late Neolithic/Early Bronze Age, horse 22
period 4 45
period 5 52
period 6 62, 65
period 7 79–80, 86, 89–90, 91, 92, 93
period 8 108, 109–10, 113
period 9 120, 123, 124, **203**
period 10 137
period 11 143
bones, bird 202–9, **202**, **204**, **205**, **209**, **210**
period 5 52
period 6 65
period 7 86, 91, 93
period 8 113
period 9 120, 124
bones, fish **202**, 203–6, **204**, **205**, 208–9
period 6 65
period 7 79, 80, 91, 92, 93
period 8 109, 110, 113
period 9 120, 124
period 11 143
boundaries
reused 62–3
stone-built 94
Bow Street 126
bowl, Roman 35, **37**
box (*Buxus sempervirens*) 91
Bramcote Grove 12
brick
Dutch 124
Dutch paving, post-medieval 178
'Flemish type' 177–8
red
late medieval/post-medieval 101–2, 120, 123, 130–1, 133, 136, 178
later post-medieval 137, 140, 142, 178
reused 137, 143
Roman 35, 38, 58, 85, 174, **174**, 175, 184
yellow, late medieval/post-medieval 178
bridge, conjectured, period 4 44, **44**, 155
Bridge Street 139, 143, 152
section **63**
see also site A; site N; Westminster Bridge
Bronze Age 147–8
dating evidence **25**, **31**
palaeoecology 14–15, 30, 31
ritual activity 147
see also Period 1; Period 2
bucket, period 11 140
Buckingham Palace 152
Building 1 (great hall) 3, 49, **50**, 51, 99, **100**
rebuilding ('repair') 99, 101, **101**, 113
Building 2 58, **58**, 75
Building 3 58, **59**, 66, 159
Building 4 58–61, **60**, **61**, 75
demolition, period 8 101
Building 5 (gatehouse to New Palace Yard) 75, **76**, **77**, 158
demolition, period 8 101, 126
Building 6 75–6, **76**, **77**, 78–80, **78**, **79**, 158
period 8 101–2, 107
period 9 118, **119**
period 10 (demolished) 129
see also site D
Building 7 **76**, 80
Building 8 (gatehouse to Green Yard) **76**, 80
period 10 129–30
Building 9 **76**, 80–1, 160
demolished 140
Building 10 (the Exchequer) 81–2
room A 81
room B 81–2, 104
Building 11 (St Stephen's chapel) 82–3, **82**, **83**
Building 12 85, **104**
Building 13 **76**, 85–7, **85**
period 8 102
period 9 118–19, **119**
Building 14 87, **87**, 102–3
Building 15 (canon's house)
period 8 103–4, **103**
period 9 120, **121**
period 10 (demolition) 130
Building 16 104
Building 17 (the Jewel Tower) 99, 104–5, **104**, **105**, 113, 130, 154, 156, 165
Building 18 105
Building 19 (St Stephen's cloister) 105–6, 113, 160
Building 20 (dwelling house for the Jewel Tower) 126, 130–1, **130**, **131**, 137
demolished, period 11 140, 142
Building 21 129, 131, **132**, 140
Building 22 130, 131–3, **132**, 137
pits 140
Building 23 133, 140
Building 24 133, **134**, **135**, 140
Building 25 133, **134**, 135, 140
Building 26 140
Building 27 140
Building 28 140
Building 29 140, 142, **142**
Building 30 (5 Old Palace Yard) 142
Building 31 (6–7 Old Palace Yard) 142
Building 32 143
Building 33 143
building materials 174–9
reused Roman 35–6, 38, 39, 58, 92, 174–5, **174**
see also brick; building stone; floors; tile
building stone
Caen 85, 86, 102
chalk 103, 131, 133
Kentish ragstone 35, 58, 59, 85–6, 133
Purbeck marble 101
Reigate 58, 59, 80, 136
Roman 35
Bull Wharf 158
Burghley, William Cecil, Lord 118
Burnell, Robert, archdeacon of York 74
butchery 113, 207–8
buttresses
Building 15 103
Westminster Hall 101

Canon Row 73, 89, 97–9, 140
buildings (east side) 116, 118, 126, 128
dean's house 98, 103
sale of houses (1547) 116
see also Building 15
Casteler, Richard 97, 116
cellar, period 11 140
cereals
barley (*Hordeum sativum*) 66, 79
oat (*Avena* spp) 66, 79, 91, 109, 143
rye (*Secale cereale*) 53, 71, 91
wheat (*Triticum* sp) (charred) 21, 66, 79, 91, 109
cesspit
Building 6, period 7 75, 79–80, 102
Building 23, period 10 133
Open Area 8, period 8 108
Open Area 11, period 10 137
Chamber, John, dean of college 98, 105
charcoal
Bronze Age 21
period 6 65
period 7 86, 91
period 8 108, 110
period 10 136
Charing Cross 71
Charterhouse 125, 154
cherry (*Prunus avium*) 68, 79
Christ's Hospital 73, 97, 116
cists, chalk-lined 153
clay, fired, Iron Age spindle whorl 30, 31, **32**
clay pipe, period 11 140
Clowson stream 71, 74, 106, 151
Clusebridge 74
Cnut, King 44, 155
coins
medieval 184, **184**, 188
Roman 35, **37**
Saxon 41, 45
Cooke, Allen, canon 118
copper-alloy objects
bell, period 7/8 109, **109**, 185, 188
buckle pin, medieval 112, 185
buckles, period 9 123, **123**, 124, 187
button 125, 187
clapper bell 123, 187
finger ring, medieval 124, 185
mount
for horse harness(?), period 7 94, **94**, 185–6, 188
medieval 122, 186
octofoil, medieval 102, 131, 185, 188
period 10/11 187
?necklace, period 8/9 110, **110**, 137, 187
pilgrim badge, period 8 112, **112**, 185, 188
pins, Saxon 45
slag/waste 137
vessel 187
medieval 137, 186
Covent Garden 49, 154
Cranmer, Thomas 98
Crispin, Abbot Gilbert 152
Cromwell Green 15, 23, **24**, **26**, 27
flints from **171**
see also site S
crucibles, ceramic, period 5 52, **53**, 112, 183, 184–5
Cumberland, Revd Dennison 116

Danebury hillfort (Hants) 31
daub, ?Roman 38, 179
David, Master, Henry III's surgeon 73, 74, 94
Dean's Yard, Nine Elms court 99
deer, remains 62, 90, 113, 123
Derby, Edward, earl of 118
Derby, William, earl of 118
Derby Court 128
Derby Gate 139
Derby House, Canon Row 118, 128, 140
Devensian Late Glacial period 10, 145
diatom evidence 29, 70, 147
Cocconeis placentula 96
Cyclotella striata 96
Cymatosira belgica 29
Nitzschia navicularis 13
Dissolution of the Monasteries (1540) 113, 115, 116, 125
ditches
boundary 73, 93, 157–8
drainage 93
period 6 64–5
period 8 108–9, **109**
reclamation, period 5 52, **52**, 53, **54**, 55
dock, Structure 5 **57**, 61–3, **62**, **63**, 158, 166
demolished 106
Domesday Survey 49
Dorset Court 140
Dorset House 118, 128, 140
dove, for food 120
Dover Castle (Kent) 158
drains
great, period 6 67–8, **68**
period 7 93
period 8 103, 104
period 9 118, 120
period 10 131, 136
Dunstan, St 2, 41, 44, 46, 152

Early Holocene period 10, 12, 145–6
Early–Middle Bronze Age (period 1) 14–15, **25**
Ebury Street 49
Edgar, King 41, 42, 46, 152
Edmund of Woodstock, earl of Kent, inn 74–5, 98, 99
Edward, the Black Prince 165
Edward the Confessor, King 2, 41, 42, 44, 47
coronation **162**
palace at Westminster 49, 151, 155
rebuilding of abbey 47–8, 49, 54
Edward I, King 156
Edward II, King 74
Edward III, King 156
and college of St Stephen 97–8, 113
and Jewel Tower 105, 156
Edward IV, King 99
Edward of Westminster, clerk of works 73, 74
Elizabeth I, Queen 118
Embankment 144
Enedehithe 73
Exchequer 56, 94, 156, 157, 159, 160
additions to 116, 125
Augmentation Office 160
thalamus secretorum 104, 159
see also Building 10

fairs
January 73
October (Great Fair of St Edward) 73, 92, 94, 99, 102, 113, 153
Farnham (Surrey) 99
feather-curling knife 132–3, **132**, 187, 188
Feckenham, Abbot of Westminster 116

fences, stake and wattle 88–9
Fennings Wharf barrow 147
field systems 149, 150
fig (*Ficus carica*) 53, 55, 66, 79, 91, 136
fish trap, period 7 89, 94
fishpond, Jewel Tower moat used as 105
flax (*Linum*) 115
Fleet, River 49
Fleet Street 71
flints and flint objects 1, **16–17**, 27–8
  assemblage 22, 25, **26**, 27, **27**
  axes 15, 27
  Bronze Age 18, 20–1, **20**, 23
  burnt unworked flint 174, **174**
  Mesolithic 15
  Neolithic 15, 27
  struck flint 170–4, **171**, **172**, **174**
floors
  brick and cobble 101
  brickearth 118
  clay 86, 102
  'humus' 87
  mortar 108, 133
  mortar and tile 87
  Purbeck marble 101
  red brick 130, 133
  Reigate stone 80–1, 118–19
  sand 86, 119
  sand and gravel 133
  stone chippings 86, 93, 102
food 109–10, 207–8
  venison 62
  see also bones, animal; bones, bird; bones, fish; butchery; plant remains
fountain, Westminster Palace 99, 158, 159
fruit 68, 79, 91, 136
  see also fig
Funge, Thomas 128

Gaimar, 12th-century writer 155
gardens 97, 98, 108, 124
  king's 99
  Old Palace Yard 137
  Whitehall Palace 118
Gaveston, Piers 156, 162
General Post Office site 31
geology 1, 9–12
  peat formation 30–1
  waterlaid deposits 20, **20**, **21**, 23
glass
  beaker, period 8 103, **103**, 120, 184
  blue, period 11 144, 187–8
  potash vessel, medieval 78, 184
  Roman 35
  vessel, medieval 112, 133, 184
  window, medieval 112, 133, 184
  wine, period 9/10 135, 187–8
Glastonbury and Meare lake village (Somerset) 31
goose 86
grape (*Vitis vinifera*) 68, 79, 91, 136
great hall (Building 1) 3, 49, **50**, 51, 99, **100**
  rebuilding ('repair') 99, 101, **101**, 113
  see also site S; site T; Westminster Hall
Great Peter Street, palaeoecology 30
Greater London Sites and Monuments Record (GLSMR) 6
Green Yard 157, 159–60
  boundary walls 159
  knights' chamber 159
  timber gate, period 6 67, 158, 159
  see also Open Area 5; site J
Grey, Katherine 118

Hanney, William 105
Hardgrey, Thomas, builder 105
Harold II, King 48
Hastings, Lady Dorothy 118
Hawksmoor, Nicholas 153
hazel (*Corylus avellana*) 14–15, 30, 53, 71, 79, 91
hearth
  brick
    period 8 101, 102
    period 10 131
  period 9 119
  see also ovens
hemp (*Cannabis* type) 71, 91, 115
Henry, earl of Cornwall 73
Henry I, King 3
Henry II, King 56, 68, 155
Henry III, King 2, 54, 155
  grants of land 73, 74
  and rebuilding of Westminster Abbey 71
Henry IV, King 151
Henry VII, King 3
Henry VIII, King 113, 115, 157
Herland, Master Hugh 99, 101
heron 120
Hertford, Edward Seymour, Lord 118
Hertford House, Canon Row 118
Higgins, Susanna 128
High Holborn (Watling Street) 49
Hollar, Wenceslaus, view of New Palace Yard **158**
Holmes, Benjamin 126, 128
Holy Way Tavern 102
horn core
  period 4 45
  period 5 52
  period 8 113
horn cores, worked 207–8
horse burial ground 151
horse ferry 151
Horsleydown 12
Horwood, R, map (*c* 1800) 139
House of Commons 156
  in St Stephen's chapel 115–16, 157
House of Lords 156–7
  period 10 126
houses
  on King Street 58, 68, 73, 123, **123**, 137
  periods 7 and 8 87, 102
  vicars' (St Stephen's cloister) 105, 106, 113, **160**
  see also Building 15; Canon Row; inns
Hunsdon, Lord 118
Husseborne, Walter de, keeper of Privy Palace 105
hypocaust, Roman 6, 35, 38, 39

inns 102
  of archbishops of York 74
  ?Building 6 80, 158
  earl of Cornwall's 73, 151
  earl of Kent's 73, 74–5, 98, 99
  Holy Way Tavern 102
  Saracen's Head 102, 110
  Sun 151
  White Horse alehouse 116
insect remains, Cladoceran *ephippia* 109, 136, 143
Iron Age (period 2) 29–32, **31**, **32–3**, 147–8
iron objects
  barrel hoop 131, 187
  bucket, period 11 140
  hinge 135, 187
  key, period 8 102, **102**, 185, 188
  knife, whittle tang, medieval 124, 185
  spur, period 7 93, **93**, 185
  staple 102, 187
  tool 94, 185
Isabella, Queen, widow of Edward II 74–5, 99
ivory objects, knife, period 10/11 132–3, **132**, 187, 188

jetton
  14th-century 184, **184**
  15th-century 124, 184, **184**
?jetty
  Structure 16, period 9 120, **121**
  Westminster Palace 158–9, 166
Jewel Tower
  moat 105, 108, 130
  see also Building 17
Jewel Tower garden 99
  1963 excavation 6
  precinct wall in 63, **64**
  see also Building 18; site R
John the cook, house of 74
John de Bedeford 97
John of Ockham, baron of the Exchequer 74
John Senche (Shenche), keeper of the palace 97
John of Upton, marshal 74
Jubilee Line Extension (JLE) 3, **4**, 5, **5**
Jumièges abbey (France) 47, 152

Kent, earl of *see* Edmund of Woodstock
kiln, period 11 142, **142**
kiln sites, Roman 35
King Street (former) 3, 49, 56, 113, 151
  demolished 139–40
  foreshore 65
  houses on 58, 68, 73, 123, **123**, 137
  and king's ditch 73, 97
  period 7 71, 94
  shops 74
king's garden 99
knife, ivory, period 10/11 132–3, **132**, 187, 188
Knight, Dr William, archdeacon of Richmond 116
Knuyff, Leonard, drawing 136–7

Labelye, Charles 139
Lambeth 144
land reclamation 3, 89, 96, 113, 122, 156, 166
  ditches, period 5 52, **52**, 53, **54**, 55
latrines 99
Lawrence, Richard 116
Le Quien, James 128
leather objects
  shoe, period 7 79, 186–7
  shoe ?sole 124
  with wooden strips 52, 187
Levelond family 74
Leyburn, Sir Roger de 74
Leyburn, William 74
lime (*Tilia*) 14, 30, 40, 71, 115, 147
Lincoln, Henry, earl of 128
Litlyngton, Abbot 2, 153
London Bridge 150, 158
London, city of 155
Long Ditch (Tyburn stream) 139
Long Woolstaple (road) 98, 103, 104, 116
Longditch 73
Lundenwic settlement 46, 155

Mall, The 152
Manchester Buildings, Canon Row 118, 120
Manchester, Edward, earl of 128
Manchester House 140
Manchester, Sir Henry Montague, earl of 128
Mansell, John 151
Mary I, Queen 3, 116
mayors, medieval 97
Mesolithic period (period 1) 10, 13, 14, 15, **25**, 146
mill 71, 154
moat, Jewel Tower 105, 108, 130
mollusc fauna
  Iron Age 29, 30
  period 3 34
  period 5 52
  period 6 66
  period 7 91, 93
  period 8 112
  period 10 136
monasteries
  French ducal 47
  precincts 154
Morgan, W, map of Westminster (1682) 126, **128**
Mortimer, Roger 75
mulberry (*Morus* sp) 79
mussel shell 119, 120

Nazard, Henry 87
?necklace, period 8/9 110, **110**, 137, 187
Nelthorpe, Ann 116
Neolithic period (period 1) 12, 13, 15, 22, **25**
  early population 146–7
  pottery 21, 23
Netherlands, imported bricks 177, 178
New Palace Yard 3, 56, 94, 102, 113, 157, 158–9, **159**
  bell tower 159
  boundary walls 158, 159
  fountain 99, 158, 159
  gates 80, 159
  great gatehouse *see* Building 5
  temporary buildings in 159
  see also Open Area 4; site D; site G
New Palace Yard site **5**
  period 2, ecology 30
  period 3, Roman 34
Newdigate, Francis 118
Nine Elms, foreshore 147
Norfolk, Thomas Howard, duke of 98
Norwich, bishops of 128
Norwich, William, bishop of 116

Odo, son of Edward of Westminster 74
Odo the goldsmith, keeper of works 74
Offa, King 41, 152
Old Palace Yard 157, 160–1, 169
  buildings **161**, 162–6
  fire (1512) 160
  gardens 137
  see also Open Area 6; site R
Open Area 1
  foreshore (east) 22–3, **22**, 30 1, 45, 122
  foreshore (north-east) 20–2, 44–5
  higher ground 23
  period 1 16, **19**, **25**
  period 3 (Roman) 35–6, 38
  period 5 (foreshore) 51–4
  period 6 (foreshore) 64–5
  River Thames 18, **19**, 20
    period 7 90–1
    period 8 106, 107
  see also site B; site P
Open Area 2, period 5 54
Open Area 3, period 5, flood layers 54
Open Area 4 (New Palace Yard)
  period 6 65–7
  period 7 91–2
  period 8 107–8
  period 10 136, **136**
  period 11 143
  plant assemblages 66, 136, 143
  see also Structure 10
Open Area 5 (Green Yard)
  period 6 67
  period 8 101
  see also Structure 10
Open Area 6 (Old Palace Yard) 157, 160–1
  period 6 67
  period 7 92
  period 8 108
  period 9 122
  period 10 136–7
Open Area 7
  period 6 67
  period 7 92
Open Area 8 (Westminster Abbey precinct, north) 154–5
  period 6, ditch 67
  period 7 92
  period 8 108
  period 10 133, 137
  period 11 143–4
  see also Building 2
Open Area 9 (Westminster Abbey precinct, south) 154
  great drain, period 6 67–8, **68**, **104**
  see also Building 18
Open Area 10 92–3, **111**
  Road 1 89, **90**
  robbed-out wall 108
  surfaces 122
Open Area 11
  period 7 93, **93**
  period 8 108–10
  period 9 123
  period 10 137
Open Area 12
  period 7 94
  period 8 110
  period 9 123

Open Area 13 111–12
- period 10 137
- well, period 8 106, 110, **111**, 112, **112**, 135
- *see also* Building 23; Structure 12

Open Area 14
- period 8 112–13
- period 9 123–5, **124**, 125
- period 11 144
- pit, period 10 137
- *see also* Building 15; site B; site H

Open Area 15, period 10 137
opus signinum 35, 38, 39, 179
- medieval 47
- reused 58

oratory, St Stephen's cloister 106
Ordinance of the Woolstaple (1353) 97
organic material
- ?leather or moss 52, 186
- composite 52, 187

Otho de Grandison 74, 75
Our Lady Alley 97
ovens (hearths), period 6 59, **60**, 61, **61**, 75
Oxford Street (Watling Street) 49
oyster shell
- period 5 52
- period 7 86, 91
- period 8 108, 110
- period 9 119, 124

Paget, William, Secretary of State 99
palaeochannels 18, 145
palaeoecology 1, 10, 12, 145–50
- period 1 14–15
- period 2 29–30, 31
- period 3 3, 34, 35
- period 4 40–1
- period 7 70–1
- period 8 96–7
- *see also* plant remains

Paris (France)
- Nôtre Dame 157
- Ste Chapelle (Ile de la Cité) 83, **84**, 157

Parliament, growing importance of 126, 137–8, 156–7, 169
Parliament House (Building 20) 126, 130–1, **130**, **131**, 137
- demolished, period 11 140, 142

Parliament Square *see* Building 6; site C(i); site D; site E; site J
Parliament Street 139–40, 152
- *see also* site U

Parliamentary Works Directorate 3
- sites **4**, **5**

partition, ?wooden
- Building 6, period 8 101, 102
- Building 13, periods 8 and 9 102, 118

peacock 52
Pearson, J L, report to House of Commons Select Committee (1884) 6
Pepys, Samuel 128
Period 1 (Mesolithic to Early–Middle Bronze Age, *c* 6000 BC–*c* 1500 BC) 10, **25**, 146
- archaeological plan **16–17**
- dating evidence **25**
- environmental background 13–15

Period 2 (Late Bronze Age and Iron Age, *c* 1500 BC–AD 43) 15, 29–32, 51, 147–8
- archaeological plan **32–3**
- dating evidence **31**

Period 3 (Roman, AD 43–410) 2, 34–9, 148–9, 168, 169
- archaeological plan **36–7**
- dating evidence **39**

Period 4 (Saxon, AD 410–*c* 1040) 2, 40–6, 149, 152, 155
- archaeological plan **42–3**
- dating evidence **46**

Period 5 (Saxo-Norman, *c* 1040–*c* 1150) 47–55, 151
- archaeological plan **48**
- dating evidence **55**

Period 6 (*c* 1150–*c* 1230)
- archaeological plan **57**
- dating evidence 63, **69**
- documentary background 56, 58

Period 7 (*c* 1230–*c* 1350)
- archaeological plan **72**
- dating evidence **95**
- documentary background 71, 73–5
- environmental background 70–1

Period 8 (*c* 1350–*c* 1540)
- archaeological plan **100**
- dating evidence **114**
- documentary background 97–9
- environmental background 96–7

Period 9 (*c* 1540–*c* 1600)
- archaeological plan **117**
- dating evidence **125**
- documentary background 115–16, 118
- environmental background 115

Period 10 (*c* 1600–*c* 1740)
- archaeological plan **127**
- dating evidence **138**
- documentary background 126, 128–9

Period 11 (*c* 1740–1834)
- archaeological plan **141**
- dating evidence **144**
- documentary background 139–40

Peter de Montfort 74
Petters Sports Field site (Surrey) 32
Phoenix Wharf, burnt mound 147
Pickleherring quay, Southwark, pottery 129
pins, copper-alloy 45
pipe, clay 140
pits 51–2, 66, 107–8, 109, 110, 131
- barrel-lined 131
- clay-lined, period 11 143–4
- rubbish 86, 108, 110, 112, 113, 123, 137
- *see also* cesspit

plague 153
plant remains 188–90, **189**, **190–202**, 202
- for animal feed and bedding 115
- aquatic species 14, 21, 30, 34, 40, 53, 66, 86, 91, 115, 136
- cereal 21, 35, 53, 66, 71, 79, 109, 143
  - bran 91
  - pollen 14, 15, 30, 147
- fen/bankside/marshland species 14, 16, 21, 22, 30, 40, 53, 66, 71, 79, 86, 91, 109, 115, 136, 143
- grasses (Poaceae) 70, 91, 115
- marine/estuary/salt-marsh species 29, 30, 70, 71
- Neolithic period 13, **190–1**
- period 1 13, 14–15, 21, 22, **189**, **190–1**, **199–200**
- period 2 30, 31, **189**, **190–1**, **195–6**, **200–1**
- period 3 34–5
- period 4 40–1
- period 5 53, **189**, **196–8**, **200–1**
- period 6 66, 68, **189**, **195–8**, **199–202**
- period 7 70–1, 79, 86, 91, 92, **189**, **191–2**, **196–8**, **199–200**
- period 8 109, 113, **189**, **191–3**, **194–5**, **198–9**
- period 9 115, **189**, **194–6**
- period 10 136, **189**, **200–1**
- period 11 143, **189**, **196–8**
- semi-woodland species 40, 53, 66, 79, 91, 109, 136
- from site B **190–5**
- from site C **196**
- from site D **196–8**
- from site E **198–9**
- from site F **195–6**
- from site G **199–200**
- from site H **190–1**
- from site J **200–1**
- from site L **201–2**
- tree root, Bronze Age 22
- wasteland species 21, 30, 40, 53, 66, 70, 79, 86, 91, 109, 115, 136, 143
- weeds, arable 66, 79, 91
- woodland species 14–15, 30, 40, 53, 70–1, 79, 91, 115, 147
- *see also* cereals; fruit; pollen; woodland

plants
- economic
  - period 8 113
  - period 9 115
- medicinal, period 7 91

Pleistocene period 12
pollen 146, 168
- Bronze Age 20
  - cereal 14, 15, 147
- Iron Age/Roman period 34
- period 8 96–7
- period 9 115
- Storey's Gate (diagram) **148–50**
- *see also* plant remains

population
- and ecological change 150–1
- Neolithic 146–7
- Roman/early Saxon 149

pottery, prehistoric **32–3**, 179–81, **179**
- Cromwell Green assemblage 180
- great hall (site T) assemblage 180
- Iron Age 30, 32, **32**
- Late Bronze Age, fineware 20, **20**, **22**, 179
- Late Neolithic/Early Bronze Age 21, 23, 25, 27, 30, 180
  - beaker 27, 180
- Middle Bronze Age, Deverel-Rimbury ware 22, **22**, 179–80
- from site F 179, **179**, 180
- from site G 179–80, **179**
- from site K 179, **179**, 180
- from Westminster Abbey dorter undercroft 180

pottery, Roman 35, 38
- Oxfordshire red colour-coated ware 35

pottery, Saxon 41, 45–6
pottery, medieval 35, 63, 103, 124, 181–3, **182**, **183**
- fabric and form codes **182**
- early medieval 92, 181, **183**
  - coarse London type (LCOAR) 181
  - early medieval coarse whiteware (EMCW) 52, **53**, 112, 183, 184–5
  - early medieval sand- and shell-tempered ware (EMSS) 181, **183**
  - early medieval shell-tempered ware (EMSH) 35, 181
  - early Surrey ware (ESUR) 181, 182, **183**
  - London area greyware (LOGR) 181, 182, **183**
  - shelly-sandy ware (SSW) 181
  - Stamford ware (STAM) 181, 182
  - Winchester ware 181
- imported
  - Andalusian lusterware (ANDA) 183
  - Dutch redware (DUTR) 183
  - Langerwehe stoneware (LANG) 183
  - Low Countries greyware (LCGR) 183
  - Rhineland, red-painted ware (REDP) 181, **183**
  - Saintonge wares (SAIG; SAIM; SAIN) 183
  - Siegburg (SIEG) 183
- later medieval
  - coarse border ware (CBW) 107
  - early Surrey-Hampshire border whiteware (EBORD) 124, **182**
  - Kingston-type ware (KING) 75–6, **77**, 78, **78**, **79**, 181, 182, **182**, **183**
  - south Hertfordshire-type greyware (SHER) 181
- London-type ware (LOND) 78, **78**, **79**, 93, **93**, 181, 182, **182**, **183**
- Mill Green ware (MG) 181, 182

pottery, post-medieval 107, 135, 181, **182**, 183, **183**
- fabric and form codes **182**
- early redware (PMRE) 124, **182**
- green glaze (PMSRG) 124, **182**
- imported
  - Beauvais green-glazed ware (BEAG) 183
  - Dutch redware (DUTR) 183
  - Dutch sgraffito-decorated ware (DUTSG) 183
  - Frechen stoneware 183
- redware (PMR) 183
- slipped redware (PMSR) 124, **182**
- tin-glazed ware (TGW) 129–30, **129**, 136, **136**, 181, 183, **183**

prehistoric activity 1–2, 168, 169
- *see also* Bronze Age; Iron Age; Mesolithic period; Neolithic period; Period 1; Period 2

Presteyk, William, canon 98

quay *see* dock
quernstone, Roman
- domestic 38, 184
- Mayen lava 38, 184

rabbit 113, 124
radiocarbon dating 13, 20, 31, **31**, 42, **46**, **69**, **210**
rats 79–80, 92, 120, 124
Richard, earl of Cornwall, inn 73, 151
Richard II, King 51, 108
Richmond Terrace
- Mesolithic site 14
- radiocarbon dates 31

ring, Roman 35, **37**
ritual activity 147, 169
river wall
- Structure 13, period 8 106, 135
- Structure 21, period 10 133, **134**, 135

Road 1 89, **90**, **103**, 107
Road 2 (St Stephen's Alley) 107
- (Canon Row), period 11 143

Road 3 (Bridge Street) 143
roads
- Open Area 10 89, **90**
- Roman alignments 35

Rocque, J, map (1746) 139
Roger de Heyton, surgeon to Edward III 97, 98, 99
Roman period (period 3) 2, 34–9, **36–7**, 148–9, 168, 169
- antiquarian finds 35
- dating evidence **39**

Round Woolstaple *see* Woolstaple Yard
royal churches, Saxo-Norman 47, 54
royal palaces 155–6
Runnymede Bridge site (Surrey) 32

Sadler, Sir Ralph 116
St Anne's almhouse 99
St Denis, church of 47
St Dunstan's chapel 56
St James's Hospital 151
St James's Park 151, 152
St John's, Clerkenwell 125, 154
St Katherine's infirmary hall and chapel 56, 99, 116, 154
St Margaret, parish and church of 155
St Margaret Street 80, 130, 140
St Martin in the Fields 151, 155
St Mary Bethlehem (Bedlam) 151
St Mary Clerkenwell 154
St Mary Graces 154
St Mary Rounceval, Hospital of 151
St Mary Spital 75, 78, 125, 154
St Peter, Westminster, College of 116
St Riquier (Picardy), church 47
St Stephen's Alley 98, 99
- Road 2, period 8 107

St Stephen's chapel 3, 56, 156, 157
- building phases 82–3, **82**, **83**, 113
- college of canons 97–9, 103–4, 113, 156, 160
- dissolution (1547) 115–16, 157
- earlier chapel 83
- *see also* Building 11; Canon Row; site P

St Stephen's cloister (Building 19) 105–6, 113, 160
- oratory 106

St Stephen's court 160, **160**
Sainte Chapelle (Ile de la Cité, Paris) 83, **84**, 157
Sanctuary Street 126
Saracen's Head tavern 102, 119
sarcophagus, Roman 35, 38, 39, 152, 153
Savoy palace (later Hospital) 151

Saxo-Norman period (period 5) 47–55, **48**
dating evidence **55**
town of Westminster 151
Saxon period (period 4) 2, 40–6, **42–3**, 149
dating evidence **46**
evidence for minster 152
evidence for palace 155
Scott, Sir George Gilbert 6, 38
sea levels 147
sedimentation 148
erosion and deposition 149–50
Shelley, Sir Richard 131
shoe, period 7 79, 124, 186–7
shops
King Street 74
New Palace Yard 102
Silvertown Urban Village, Newham 12
Simon de Montfort 156–7
site A (Bridge Street, St Margaret Street) **4**, **5**
see also Structure 13; Structure 14; Structure 24
site B (Westminster Station site 5) **4**, **5**, **19**
period 1 18, **19**, 20
period 2, Thames foreshore 30–1
period 5 51–4
ditches and pits 51–2
radiocarbon dates 31, **31**
see also Open Area 1; Open Area 14; Structure 15; Structures 17–20; Structure 23
site C(i) (Parliament Square) **4**, **5**
period 1 23, **25**
period 3 35–6, **37**, **38**
period 5 54
period 6 **59**
period 10 130
period 11 140
robbed-out wall 35–6, 38, **38**
see also Building 13; Building 22; Building 28; Open Area 8
site C(ii) (Parliament Street) **4**, **5**, **111**
period 4 44–5
see also Building 23; Building 26; Building 27; Open Area 1; Open Area 10; Open Area 13
site D (Parliament Square - Churchill Statue) **4**, **5**, 143
period 1 23, **25**
period 5, boundary ditch 52–3, **53**
period 6 **60**, 65
see also Building 5; Building 6; Building 21; Building 29
site E (Parliament Square - Canning Green) **4**, **5**
ditch, period 9 123, **123**
period 1, Bronze Age 14
period 7, palaeoecology 71
see also; Building 2; Open Area 11; Open Area 12
site F (Westminster Station sites 1, 2 and 6) **4**, **5**
ditch, period 9 125
period 1, Bronze Age 14–15, 20–1, **20**
period 4 45
period 6 64–5
period 7, palaeoecology 70–1
radiocarbon dates from 13
see also Building 15; Open Area 10; Open Area 14; site P; Structure 2; Structure 5; Structure 22
site G (New Palace Yard) **4**, **5**
period 1 22, **22**
flints 20, 22, **26**, 27–8
Roman quernstone 38, 184
see also Open Area 4
site H (Westminster Station site 4) **4**, **5**
period 1, Bronze Age 14
period 2 29
period 7 71, 91
period 8 96
radiocarbon dates from 13, 20
see also Open Area 14; Structure 16
site J (Parliament Square) **4**, **5**
period 6, pits and postholes 66
period 11 140
radiocarbon dates 42, **46**
see also Building 3; Building 7; Building 8; Building 9; Building 32; Building 33; Structure 4
site K (Canon Row vent shaft) **4**, **5**
period 1 21, **21**
period 5 53–4, **54**
period 7 91
see also Open Area 10
site L (Canon Row staircase 57) **4**, **5**
period 1 21
period 7 91
see also Building 4
site M (Parliament Street stairs and subway) **4**, **5**
site N (Bridge Street subway) **4**, **5**
see also Building 24; Building 25
site P (St Stephen's chapel)
period 1 **4**, **5**, 15, **16–17**
radiocarbon dates 20
see also Building 11; Open Area 1; site F; Structure 1; Structure 3
site Q (Chancellor's Court) **4**, **5**
period 1, Bronze Age waterlaid silts 20
site R (6–7 Old Palace Yard, Jewel Tower garden) **4**, **5**, 165
see also Building 12; Building 14; Building 20; Building 30; Building 31
site S (Westminster Hall, Cromwell Green) **4**, **5**, 104
period 1 23, **24**
period 8, flying buttresses 101
site T (Westminster Hall) **4**, **5**, 180
see also Building 10
site U (37–46 Parliament Street) **4**, 5, **5**
period 1 21–2
period 6 65
see also Open Area 10; Structure 7; Structure 8; Structure 9
slaughterhouses, Woolstaple Yard 129
Smirke, Robert, rebuilding works at Westminster Hall 49, 51
Smith Square 152
Smythe, Thomas 116
Somerset, Anne, duchess of 118
Somerset, Edward Seymour, duke of 118
Southwark islands, field systems 12
Southwell, Richard 116
Star Chamber 126, 156, 159
statue
conjectural, period 7 87
Roman 35, **37**
Storey's Gate site 5, **5**, 13–14
period 1, palaeoecology 14–15
period 2, palaeoecology 29, 30
period 7 70
period 8 96
pollen diagram **148**
Strand 151
Structure 1 (revetment) 15–16, **18**, 22–3
Structure 2 (postholes, ?fence) 15–16, **19**, 20–1, **25**
Structure 3 (revetment) 16, **18**, 23
Structure 4 (revetment) 41–2, 44, **44**, **45**, **46**, 51, 155
Structure 5 (dock) **57**, 61–3, **62**, **63**, 64, 88, 106, 158, 166
Structure 6 (precinct wall) 63–4, **64**, 71, 154
Structure 7 (stake and wattle fencing) **72**, 88–9, **88**, 106
Structure 8 (wall) 89
Structure 9 (stakes and wattle) **72**, 89, 106
Structure 10 (precinct wall) 89, **90**, 106
Structure 11 (precinct wall) 99, 106
Structure 12 (well) 106, 110, **111**, 112, **112**, 135
Structure 13 (river wall) 106, 135
Structure 14 (wall) 106–7, **111**
Structure 15 (timber waterfront) 107
Structure 16 (?jetty) 120, **121**
Structure 17 (stone foundations) 120, **121**
Structure 18 (wall foundations) 120, **121**, **122**
Structure 19 (wall foundations) 120, **121**
Structure 20 (slots) 120, **121**, 122, 143
Structure 21 (river wall) 133, **134**, 135
Structure 22 (wall foundations) **134**, 135–6
Structure 23 (brick wall) 143
Structure 24 (pier of Westminster Bridge) 143
Stukeley, William 7, 71, 73
stylus, Roman 35, **37**
Sulcard, monk 47
surfaces
cobbled yard, period 10 136
gravel, period 5 54
swan 93
swords, Saxon 41, 45

Thames, River 1, 3, 168
channel flows 70
embankment, 19th-century 144
flooding 40, 44, 45, 47, 53, 54–5, 150
navigability 146
palaeochannels 18, 29
palaeoecology 1, 10, 12, 14–15
period 1 13–14, 18, **19**, 20, 146
palaeoecology 14–15
period 2 29–30
palaeoecology 30
period 3 34, 35
period 4 44, 45, 47
palaeoecology 40–1
period 5 49
period 6 63, 68
period 7 70
period 8 96
possible site of ford 35
river levels 14, 15, 16, 25, 29–30, 31, 55, 65, 158
Roman crossing 35
tidal head 12, 14, 29, 40, 147, 148
tide levels 63, 70, 149
'Thames-Tilbury' model 12
Thieving Lane, period 7 71
Thirleby, Thomas, bishop of Westminster 116
Thomas of Houghton 82
Thomas of Westminster 74
Thorney Island **10–11**, 12, 167, 168
formation 146
geology 1, 9–10
and migration of tidal head 147
palaeoecology, period 1 14–15, 145
reclamation 3, 89, 96, 113, 122
Thorpe, John, artist 128
Thynne, Sir John 116, 118
Thynne, Sir Thomas 128
Thynne, Sir Thomas, 2nd Bt (Viscount Weymouth) 128
tile
floor
12th-century 'Westminster' type 61, 175
'Flemish' 124, 175–6
late medieval other English 175
medieval decorated 175, **175**
Penn type 175
post-medieval unglazed Netherlands 176
Roman 35, 36, 38, 39, 58, 92
flue 35, 39, **39**, 174
imbrex 35, 174
tegula 35, **39**, 174
roof
glazed peg, medieval 112, 124, 177
medieval 36, 103, 107, 176
pantile, 17th-century 112, 176, 177
peg 63, 85, 112, 124, 177
early modern 120
shouldered 176
slate, post-medieval 178
wall, 17th-century, tin-glazed 133, **135**, 176
timber
period 5
oak stakes 52
wattle 52
period 7, reused boat timbers 75
timber halls, Saxon 41
timber piles, Building 8, period 7 80
Tothill Fields 151
Tothill Street 3, 35, 49, 71, 73, 151, 152
abbey properties 154
gates into precincts 154
Treasury Green 15, 41
Treswell, Ralph, survey (1603–9) 108
Trevor family 116, 129
Tyburn, River 3, 9, 139, 145, 151
course to Thames 13–14, 146
period 8 96

Valerius Armandinus 35
Vaughan, John, canon 118
vault, brick barrel, period 10 133
vegetation
Early Holocene 145–6
elm loss, Mesolithic 146
introduced species 149
lime 147, 149
Mesolithic to Neolithic 146
see also woodland
Venour, Elizabeth, widow 97
vessel, Roman 35, **37**
vestibulum, interpretation of 47
vicars' hall, St Stephen's cloister 105, 106
vicars' houses, St Stephen's cloister 105, 106, 113, **160**
Victoria Tower, Saxon finds 41
vines 68
see also grape

wall plaster, painted, period 7 86, 102, 179
Wallinger, John 128
walnut (*Juglans*) 40, 71, 115, 149
Walter de Bedewynde, king's clerk 74
Walter de Wenlock, abbot of Westminster 87
water pipe, to Edward son of Odo's house 74
watercress 40, 149
waterfront, Structure 15, period 8 107
watering cans, post-medieval, ceramic 124, **124**
Watling Street (Herts, Middlesex) 35, 49
Watson, William 116
wattle fencing, period 7 88–9
well
medieval
brick 80
chalk and brick (Structure 12) 106, 110, **111**, 112, **112**, 135
early modern, barrel-lined 124, 125
period 10, brick 129, 137
Westbourne stream 151
Westminster **156**
archaeological and historical significance 1–2, 167–8
Bronze Age 15
further research questions 168–9
water gate 56, 158
Westminster Abbey 152–5, 168–9
abbot's house 99
almonry 151
almshouse (St Anne's) 99
antiquarian (Roman) finds 35, 38
in Bayeux Tapestry 47–8, **153**, 155
becomes cathedral 116
belfry 71, 73, 126, 153, 155
boundary walls 94
burial ground 153
cellarer's range 99, 154
choir 49, 153
cloister 154
dissolution (1540) 113, 115, 116, 157
fire (1298) 71, 99, 153
first foundation 2, 41, 42, 46, 152, 168–9
granary 99, 154
Henry VII's chapel 71, 154
infirmary cloister 99, 154
Lady chapel 113, 153
misericord 71
nave 48–9, 56, 99, 113, 153
outer court (Nine Elms) 99, 154
precincts 73, 86, 126, 153, 154–5
northern 154–5
southern 154

walls 63–4, **64**, 71, 89, **90**, 99, 106, 154
Pyx chapel 56, 154
rebuilding (Edward the Confessor) 44, 47–8, 49, 54, 152–3, **153**
refounded and rebuilt (11th–14th centuries) 2–3, 41, 42, 44, 71, 99, 153–4
restored as abbey under Mary I 116
sacristy 155
St Dunstan's chapel 56
Saxon timber building (minster) 41, 152
towers 48, 56, 153
undercroft 56
see also St Katherine's infirmary hall and chapel
Westminster Abbey site (misericord and undercroft) **5**, 41
boundary ditch 41–2, 44, 46
flood layers 54
period 2 31–2
period 3, Roman pottery 38
period 4 42, 44, 45–6
period 6 56, **57**, 58
Westminster Bridge 56
construction (1750) 139, 143, 144, 152
Neolithic axe 1, 15
possible pier 143
Saxon finds 41
Westminster Hall 4, 5, 49
see also Building 10; great hall; site S; site T; Westminster Palace
Westminster, manor of 49
Westminster Palace 3, 68, 155–66, 169
bell tower 99, 126, 159
cloisters 160–1, 164
documented buildings **161**
Edward the Confessor's 49
expansion 94
fire (1298) 71
fire (1512) 113, 115, 160
fire (1834) 144
fountain 99, 158, 159
king's ditch 73–4, 97, 157–8
layout and site 157
le Salcerie 98, 160
'lesser' or 'white' hall 56, 162, **162**
origins 155, 160
Painted Chamber 56, 156, 161, 162–3, **163**, **164**
period 8 99
period 10 126
precincts 73, 158
prince's palace 165
queen's chamber 156, 163, **164**, **165**
queen's chapel 163–4, **164**
river frontage and wall 166
walls and gates 99, 157–8
see also Green Yard; New Palace Yard; Old Palace Yard; St Stephen's chapel; Westminster Hall
Westminster, see of 116
Westminster, town of 49, 56, 58, 68
London wool staple at 97
medieval 71, 94, 151
period 9 125
urbanisation, periods 10 and 11 137, 144
Weymouth, Thomas, Viscount 128
Wharton House (later Dorset House), Canon Row 118, 128, 140
Wharton, Philip, Lord 118
Whitehall 144
Whitehall Palace 3, 56, 113, 115, 126, 152, 157
gardens 118
St John's chapel 56
Wilhelm, Christian, potter at Pickleherring quay 129–30
William the Conqueror 48, 54, 155
William de Sleford, canon 98
William II, King ('Rufus') 3, 49, 54
William III, King 126
William of Malmesbury 155
Winchester, Winifred, dowager marchioness of 116
wooden objects
attached to leather 52, 187
barrel bases, period 7 80, 186
stakes 52, 186
stirring stick, period 7 78, **79**, 186
vessel (bowl)
period 5 52, **52**, 186
period 7 78–9, **78**, **79**, 186, **186**
woodland 71, 145–6
alder carr 40, 65, 146, 149
Iron Age 30, 148
lime, Neolithic 14, 147, 149
oak/hazel, Bronze Age 14–15, 30, 146
Roman/early Saxon 40, 149
softwood plantation 70–1, 115, 150
Woolstaple (market) 3, 93, 97, 98, 156
Woolstaple Yard (Round Woolstaple) 73, 74, 97, 106, 110, **111**, 112, 116, 128–9, 138
buildings 112, 138
Wriothesley, Thomas, Lord, Lord Privy Seal 98

Yevele, Henry, and Jewel Tower 99, 105
York House 151
Young, Maurice, builder 105